T0321937

Research Anthology on Agile Software, Software Development, and Testing

Information Resources Management Association
USA

Volume III

Published in the United States of America by
    IGI Global
    Engineering Science Reference (an imprint of IGI Global)
    701 E. Chocolate Avenue
    Hershey PA, USA 17033
    Tel: 717-533-8845
    Fax: 717-533-8661
    E-mail: cust@igi-global.com
    Web site: http://www.igi-global.com

Library of Congress Cataloging-in-Publication Data

Names: Information Resources Management Association, editor.
Title: Research anthology on agile software, software development, and
  testing / Information Resources Management Association, editor.
Description: Hershey, PA : Engineering Science Reference, [2022] | Includes
  bibliographical references and index. | Summary: "This reference book
  covers emerging trends of software development and testing, discussing
  the newest developments in agile software and its usage spanning
  multiple industries, covering topics such as global software
  engineering, knowledge management, and product development"-- Provided
  by publisher.
Identifiers: LCCN 2021040441 (print) | LCCN 2021040442 (ebook) | ISBN
  9781668437025 (h/c) | ISBN 9781668437032 (eISBN)
Subjects: LCSH: Agile software development. | Computer programs--Testing.
Classification: LCC QA76.76.D47 R468 2022 (print) | LCC QA76.76.D47
  (ebook) | DDC 005.1/112--dc23/eng/20211021
LC record available at https://lccn.loc.gov/2021040441
LC ebook record available at https://lccn.loc.gov/2021040442

British Cataloguing in Publication Data
A Cataloguing in Publication record for this book is available from the British Library.

The views expressed in this book are those of the authors, but not necessarily of the publisher.

For electronic access to this publication, please contact: eresources@igi-global.com.

List of Contributors

Table of Contents

Section 2
Development and Design Methodologies

Volume II

Section 3
Tools and Technologies

Volume III

Section 4
Utilization and Applications

Volume IV

Section 5
Organizational and Social Implications

Section 6
Managerial Impact

Preface

As organizations grow to require new and innovative software programs to improve processes, there is a need for the science of software development to constantly evolve. Agile practices have shown great benefits for improving the effectiveness of software development and its maintenance due to their ability to adapt to change. It is essential for organizations to stay current with the developments in agile software and software testing to witness how it can improve business operations.

Staying informed of the most up-to-date research trends and findings is of the utmost importance. That is why IGI Global is pleased to offer this four-volume reference collection of reprinted IGI Global book chapters and journal articles that have been handpicked by senior editorial staff. This collection will shed light on critical issues related to the trends, techniques, and uses of various applications by providing both broad and detailed perspectives on cutting-edge theories and developments. This collection is designed to act as a single reference source on conceptual, methodological, technical, and managerial issues, as well as to provide insight into emerging trends and future opportunities within the field.

The *Research Anthology on Agile Software, Software Development, and Testing* is organized into seven distinct sections that provide comprehensive coverage of important topics. The sections are:

1. Fundamental Concepts and Theories;
2. Development and Design Methodologies;
3. Tools and Technologies;
4. Utilization and Applications;
5. Organizational and Social Implications;
6. Managerial Impact; and
7. Critical Issues and Challenges.

The following paragraphs provide a summary of what to expect from this invaluable reference tool.

Section 1, "Fundamental Concepts and Theories," serves as a foundation for this extensive reference tool by addressing crucial theories essential to understanding the concepts and uses of agile software, software development, and testing in multidisciplinary settings. The first chapter of this section, "Challenges and Trends of Agile," by Prof. Jorge Marx Gómez of Carl von Ossietzky Universität Oldenburg, Germany and Prof. Fayez Salma of Carl von Ossietzky Universität Oldenburg, Germany, studies agile methodologies and different challenges with suggested solutions generated from agile philosophy itself. The last chapter of this section, "A Historical and Bibliometric Analysis of the Development of Agile," by Profs. Sathiadev Mahesh, Kenneth R. Walsh, and Cherie C. Trumbach of University of New Orleans, USA, summarizes the traditional approaches and presents the conditions that led to agile approaches such as product complexity, shortened life cycle of the market, and eventually to the widespread acceptance of Scrum.

Section 2, "Development and Design Methodologies," presents in-depth coverage of the design and development of agile software for their use in different applications. The first chapter of this section, "Software Effort Estimation for Successful Software Application Development," by Prof. Syed Mohsin Saif of Islamic University of Science and Technology, India, explains different types of software applications, software estimation models, the importance of software effort estimation, and challenges faced in software effort estimation. The last chapter of this section, "A Simulation Model for Application Development in Data Warehouses," by Prof. Nayem Rahman of Portland State University, Portland, USA, presents a simulation model of a data warehouse to evaluate the feasibility of different software development controls and measures to better manage a software development lifecycle and improve the performance of the launched software.

Section 3, "Tools and Technologies," explores the various tools and technologies used in the implementation, development, and testing of agile software for various uses. The first chapter of this section, "Use of Qualitative Research to Generate a Function for Finding the Unit Cost of Software Test Cases," by Prof. Mark L. Gillenson of University of Memphis, Memphis, USA; Prof. Thomas F. Stafford of Louisiana Tech University, Ruston, USA; Prof. Yao Shi of University of Memphis, Memphis, USA; and Prof. Xihui "Paul" Zhang of University of North Alabama, Florence, USA, demonstrates a novel use of case research to generate an empirical function through qualitative generalization. This innovative technique applies interpretive case analysis to the problem of defining and generalizing an empirical cost function for test cases through qualitative interaction with an industry cohort of subject matter experts involved in software testing at leading technology companies. The last chapter of this section, "Metastructuring for Standards: How Organizations Respond to the Multiplicity of Standards," by Prof. Ronny Gey of Friedrich Schiller University Jena, Germany and Prof. Andrea Fried of Linköping University, Sweden, focusses on the appearance and implementation of process standards in software development organizations.

Section 4, "Utilization and Applications," describes how agile software is used and applied in diverse industries for various technologies and applications. The first chapter of this section, "Social Capital and Knowledge Networks of Software Developers: A Case Study," by Prof. VenuGopal Balijepally of Oakland University, Rochester, USA and Prof. Sridhar Nerur of University of Texas at Arlington, Arlington, USA, examines the structural and relational dimensions of developers' knowledge networks, identifies the specific actionable knowledge resources accessed from these networks, and explores how entry-level and more experienced developers differ along these dimensions. The findings from the qualitative analysis, backed by limited quantitative analysis of the case study data, underpin the discussion, implications for practice, and future research directions. The last chapter of this section, "A Game Theoretic Approach for Quality Assurance in Software Systems Using Antifragility-Based Learning Hooks," by Profs. Vimaladevi M. and Zayaraz G. of Pondicherry Engineering College, India, proposes an innovative approach which uses a fault injection methodology to perform the task of quality assurance.

Section 5, "Organizational and Social Implications," includes chapters discussing the impact of agile software on society and shows the ways in which software is developed in different industries and how this impacts business. The first chapter of this section, "Media Richness, Knowledge Sharing, and Computer Programming by Virtual Software Teams," by Profs. Idongesit Williams and Albert Gyamfi of Aalborg University, Denmark, concludes, based on the case being investigated, that rich media does not fit the task characteristics of a software programmer. It further concludes that media richness does affect knowledge sharing in these virtual teams. This is because the current lean media actually enables knowledge sharing as it fits the core characteristics of the software programming process. The last chapter of this section, "On the Rim Between Business Processes and Software Systems," by Profs. Ricardo J. Machado and Maribel Yasmina Santos of Universidade do Minho, Portugal and Prof. Maria Estrela Ferreira da Cruz of Polytechnic Institute of Viana do Castelo, Portugal, uses the information existing in business process models to derive software models specially focused in generating a data model.

Section 6, "Managerial Impact," presents the impact of agile software within an organizational setting. The first chapter of this section, "Boosting the Competitiveness of Organizations With the Use of Software Engineering," by Prof. Mirna Muñoz of CIMAT, A. C. Unidad Zacatecas, Mexico, provides a research work path focused on helping software development organizations to change to a continuous software improvement culture impacting both their software development process highlighting the human factor training needs. Results show that the implementation of best practices could be easily implemented if adequate support is provided. The last chapter of this section, "Measuring Developers' Software Security Skills, Usage, and Training Needs," by Prof. Daniela Soares Cruzes of SINTEF Digital, Norway; Prof. Tosin Daniel Oyetoyan of Western Norway University of Applied Sciences, Norway; and Prof. Martin Gilje Gilje Jaatun of SINTEF Digital, Norway, presents a survey instrument that can be used to investigate software security usage, competence, and training needs in agile organizations.

Section 7, "Critical Issues and Challenges," presents coverage of academic and research perspectives on challenges to using agile software in different methods, technologies, and techniques in varied industry applications. The first chapter of this section, "Towards a Security Competence of Software Developers: A Literature Review," by Prof. Nana Assyne of University of Jyväskylä, Finland, utilises a literature review to identify the security competences of software developers. Thirteen security competences of software developers were identified and mapped to the common body of knowledge for information security professional framework. The last chapter of this section, "Open Source Software Development Challenges: A Systematic Literature Review on GitHub," by Prof. Abdulkadir Seker of Sivas Cumhuriyet University, Turkey; Prof. Banu Diri of Yıldız Technical University, Turkey; Prof. Halil Arslan of Sivas Cumhuriyet University, Turkey; and Prof. Mehmet Fatih Amasyalı of Yıldız Technical University, Turkey, reviews the selected 172 studies according to some criteria that used the dataset as a data source.

Although the primary organization of the contents in this multi-volume work is based on its seven sections, offering a progression of coverage of the important concepts, methodologies, technologies, applications, social issues, and emerging trends, the reader can also identify specific contents by utilizing the extensive indexing system listed at the end of each volume. As a comprehensive collection of research on the latest findings related to agile software, the *Research Anthology on Agile Software, Software Development, and Testing* provides software developers, software engineers, computer engineers, IT directors, students, managers, faculty, researchers, and academicians with a complete understanding of the applications and impacts of agile software and its development and testing. Given the vast number of issues concerning usage, failure, success, strategies, and applications of agile software in modern technologies and processes, the *Research Anthology on Agile Software, Software Development, and Testing* encompasses the most pertinent research on the applications, impacts, uses, and development of agile software.

Chapter 54
MMT:
A Tool for Observing Metrics in Software Projects

Pekka Mäkiaho

University of Tampere, School of Information Sciences, Tampere, Finland

Katriina Vartiainen

University of Tampere, School of Information Sciences, Tampere, Finland

Timo Poranen

University of Tampere, School of Information Sciences, Tampere, Finland

ABSTRACT

This paper presents the Metrics Monitoring Tool (MMT) that was developed in university graduate and undergraduate courses on software project work in 2014-2016. The tool aims to support project members, project managers and upper management in reporting and monitoring software and project metrics for their easier and more effective utilization. The paper covers the development process of the tool, evaluation assessment, its current composition and features. The paradigm applied in this study is Design Science Research and the methods for evaluation include prototype, expert evaluation, case study and technical experiment. Data was collected from the tool users by two questionnaires. As a result, MMT was evaluated to ease the metrics handling, while several aspects related to the richness of functionalities and usability still require further development.

INTRODUCTION

This article extends the paper MMT – a Project Tool for Observing Metrics in Software Projects (Mäkiaho et al., 2016).

Project work and basic project management skills are essential to all computer science students (Computer Science Curricula 2013, 2013). In many universities, group work skills are learned as a part of different course assignments starting from the first year of studies. During the third or fourth year, when students have studied enough core courses, there can be a larger capstone project as a stand-alone course.

DOI: 10.4018/978-1-6684-3702-5.ch054

In addition to group work and communication skills required in the capstone project, students have a possibility to combine their knowledge from different courses, like programming, databases, software and user interface design, into practice when they implement a software product. The student teams need to find a suitable combination of software tools (Portillo-Rodríguez et al., 2012) to utilize in the project for programming, requirements management, communication, user interface design and other main software development activities.

When course staff organizes different capstone projects to a larger group of students, there are challenges in following and supervising many projects at the same time. The projects also generate many standard metrics: whether a specific deadline was met or not, whether a specific deliverable was returned on time, how many hours of work has been done so far by different students, etc. Then, depending on the field of study, there can be many other process and product related metrics. In software development projects, there can be metrics like the number of written code lines, number of planned features to be implemented, number of features under development at a given moment, number of implemented features so far, number of passed test cases, etc.

The motivation for developing the Metrics Monitoring Tool (MMT) originates from the University of Tampere Project Work (PW) and Software Project Management (SPM) courses. During the courses, undergraduate PW students act as software development team members, and graduate SPM students act as project managers for those teams. The overall objective of the teams is to design and implement a functioning piece of software for a real client during one semester.

Prior to implementing MMT there were several challenges related to collecting and monitoring student projects' metric data. The metric data was gathered by using weekly reports submitted by project managers via a text based email template. The main challenges in this conduct included the high amount of manual work of project managers in aggregating the metric data, inconsistencies in and varying formats of the submitted data, lack of visibility to projects' overall progression versus their goals, as well as limited visualization capabilities.

The authors wanted to create a tool to help students to report their progress and to see the state of their projects by using project metrics. The aim was also to help the course supervisors to more easily see the progression of multiple projects. Thus far, the authors have not found any existing tool to fill with the requirements mentioned above, which would not force the use of some particular project management tool, and which can be used web-based.

This paper presents the tool that was created as a solution to these issues; MMT is a software for observing and visualizing project metrics in software development projects. The tool helps project managers in reporting, team members to be more aware of the state of the project and the course staff to compare and follow how all projects are progressing. The requirements did not include the features of a typical software project management tool, like project planning and scheduling, resource allocation or change management. Thus, the MMT-tool cannot be called a project management tool and that is the reason, why the authors do not compare it to the common project management tools, like JIRA or Redmine. Based on the research needs, for example, the tool can be extended to collect new data in future. The authors present here the evolution process of the tool from the proof of concept version to the current version that is in production.

The rest of the paper is organized as follows. In the next section, a brief introduction to software project metrics is given. The Methods-section tells how the Design Science Research (DSR) -paradigm (Hevner et al., 2004) was applied to this research. Then, the development process and the implementation of MMT is described. After that the evaluation phases are introduced. The final section concludes the work.

SOFTWARE PROJECT METRICS

Software project management consists of five phases: initiating, planning, executing, monitoring and controlling, and closing (PMBOK, 2013). One of the most important reasons that a project fails is poor reporting of the project's status (Charette, 2005). Because of the poor reporting, the management does not know the state of the project and thus does not execute the right actions. So, projects often fail in the monitoring and controlling phases, as the management does not know the state of the project.

Software metrics can be used for measuring the characteristics of 1) a piece software, 2) a software development project, or 3) a software development process. According to Goodman (1993), utilizing software metrics entails "the continuous application of measurement-based techniques to the software development process and its products to supply meaningful and timely management information, together with the use of those techniques to improve that process and its products".

Moreover, software metrics focus either on controlling or predicting. The first relates to software development processes and the latter to software products (Sommerville, 2010). A controlling metric can for instance measure the average time used for fixing a bug whereas a predicting metric could focus on the total lines of code. Further, controlling metrics can be targeted at measuring the process or measuring the project (Fenton, 1991). Process metrics would support strategic decision making while project metrics lean towards supporting more tactical decisions (Fenton, 1991) on project progression, for example.

METHODS

The paradigm chosen for this research is Design Science Research. According to the design science principles (Hevner et al., 2004; Peffers et al., 2007) the researchers build an artefact to solve a problem and then evaluate how it succeeded. DSR usage in information systems development is defended by many researchers (Gregor & Jones, 2007; Hevner & Chatterjee, 2010; Hevner et al., 2004; March & Smith, 1995; Nunamaker et al., 1991; Peffers et al., 2007). In this research the researchers design, build and evaluate a software tool (MMT) that can be used for observing software project metrics. The research data can be divided into three classes: the data from observing the activities of the students in the Project Work courses, the documentation from the developing phases of the tool, and the data from the evaluation rounds of the software.

The activities of the students in the Project Work courses have been observed since the academic year 2011-2012. The researchers have collected metrics from the weekly reports, and on how deadlines have been kept. They have also set up Moodle questionnaires for finding out which software tools have been used in the projects, which metrics the students have observed, and what kind of processes they have followed. From the fixed-form weekly reports the researchers have read metrics on the statuses of requirements, the number of test cases, and the working hours done in the projects. In addition, Mäkiaho has acted as a supervisor in most of the projects and thus got data from the projects' progression in the formal project reviews.

The MMT software has been developed in the Project Work courses since the fall semester 2014. During each development iteration, a piece of working software, development documentation, testing documentation and the final report have been produced. Löytty participated in the Software Project Management course as a student during the fall semester 2015 and was a project manager of the team that implemented the first production pilot version of MMT (1.0). Mäkiaho and Poranen have acted as the client in these MMT projects and participated to the planning and testing phases.

In principle, the development process of MMT followed an iterative cycle where evaluation of early versions of the design fed into further developments of the solution (Hevner et al., 2004; Simon, 1996 cited in Hevner et al., 2004). According to the guidelines of DSR, design is a "search process" for finding a satisfactory solution to a problem, which "requires utilizing available means to reach desired ends while satisfying laws in the problem environment" (Hevner et al., 2004, p.83). The available means include "actions and resources" as well as knowledge of the application and solution domains. The desired ends mean the "goals and constraints" of the design. The laws consist of "uncontrollable forces" of the business environment. (Hevner et al., 2004, p.88)

THE DEVELOPMENT PROCESS AND FUNCTIONALITIES OF MMT

MMT has been developed iteratively in various phases by several teams as part of the PW, SPM, and PP (Programming Project) courses, where a preceding team generally hands the work over to the next team. The following paragraphs discuss the development, or Develop/Build–Justify/Evaluate (Hevner et al., 2004) cycle during which the tool has evolved from the initial proof-of-concept version 0.10 to the current version 3.0. Figure 1 provides a high-level illustration of this process incorporating the DSR aspects of means, ends and laws as well as the recurring steps of assessment and refinement (Hevner et al., 2004).

The first construct of the tool was initiated during the fall 2014 through the summer 2015. This early construct, a proof-of-concept version (versions 0.10-0.19), provided knowledge for upcoming work on desired features, deployable methods and anticipated pitfalls. Development of these versions faced some significant issues in project communication, requirements management, programming work and code quality. Also, some of the design decisions made during the proof-of-concept phase were deemed unsuitable after the client testing and evaluation.

Based on the evaluation results where the initial versions were judged to be of too low maturity for further development, the design was started afresh with revisited requirements, revised database design and a decision to go forward with a feasible model-view-controller (MVC) framework. This stage provided the basis (versions 0.2-0.9) for the first version (version 1.0) of the solution to go live with piloting use in the spring 2016. This version included the very basics of the required functions. Also, some usability issues and bugs remained unsolved in this version of the solution. However, the overall maturity level was perceived as high enough for initial production deployment and piloting.

Several bug fixes and usability improvements were implemented in the subsequent versions (versions 1.1-1.3) during the same spring, such as allowing users more flexibility in editing their working hours.

The version 2 has been implemented during the summer semester 2016 and the developing continues during the fall semester. Additional functional features have been introduced at this stage, like the possibility for giving feedback to project teams on their weekly reports. Further similar enhancements have continuously been implemented by students based on feedback collected from users. The current deployment version is 2.9, which is expected to be upgraded to version 3.0 by the end of the year 2016.

Currently MMT runs on a virtual server provided by the University of Tampere School of Information Sciences (School of Information Sciences, University of Tampere, 2016). It relies on an SQL database and is implemented in PHP. MMT utilizes CakePHP, an open source MVC framework for PHP, and Highcharts, a JavaScript library for presenting various kind of plots and charts.

Figure 1. Build-Evaluate process of MMT (adapted from Hevner et al., 2004; Simon 1996 cited in Hevner et al., 2004)

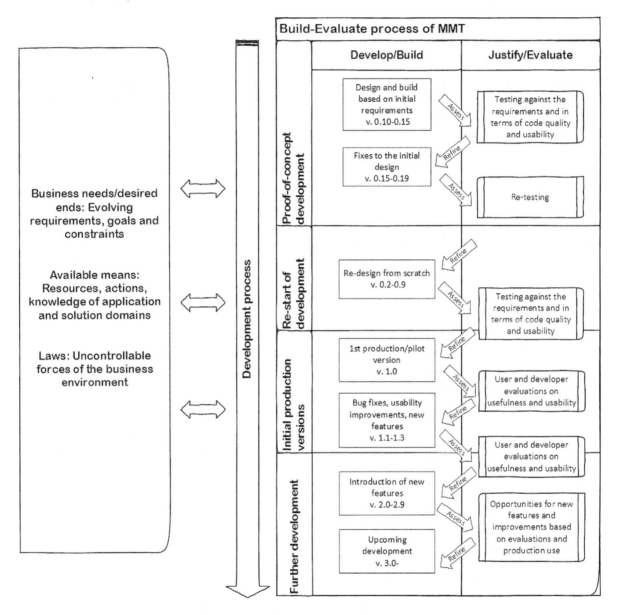

Figure 2 provides a high-level description of MMT's database and its relations: MMT contains users and projects. The users have inherent user roles, and additional project roles according to the members table. The projects have weekly reports and their related metrics stored in the respective tables. Similarly, the members have weekly and daily working hours. The tool presents projects' metrics, progression and status in graphs derived from data in the weeklyreports, metrics, workinghours and weeklyhours tables. Worktypes and metrictypes tables define the types of working hours and metrics that the tool uses. The notifications, newreports and comments tables are designed to allow for notifying of new reports and commenting functionalities.

Figure 2. Database diagram of the solution

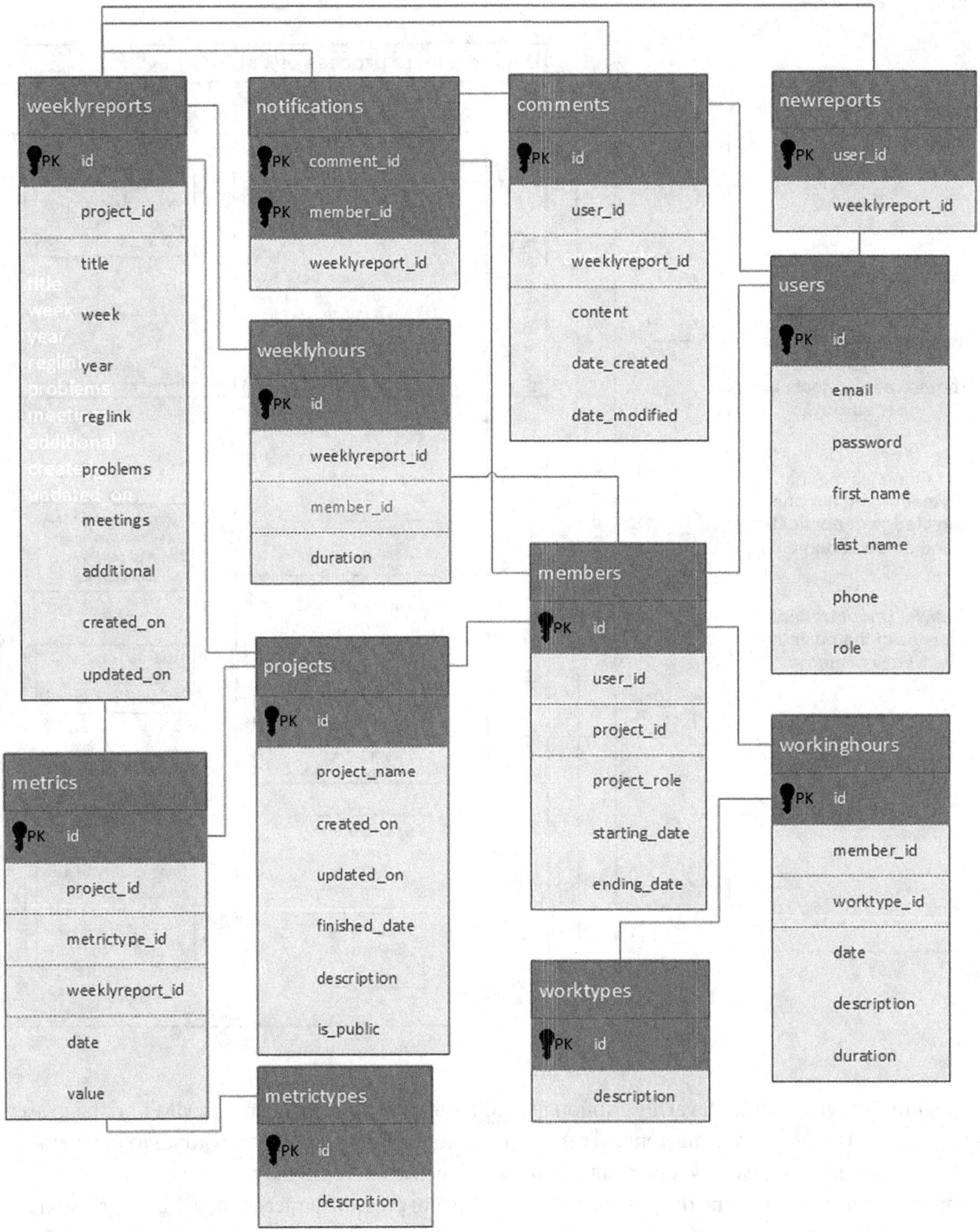

The current tool (version 2.9) includes the following features based on user and project roles: A public projects listing, public statistics and frequently asked questions (FAQs) are offered for all visitors of the MMT web site. Project developers can view reports and charts of their own and public projects as well as log and update their own daily working hours. Project managers can additionally compose weekly project reports, log hours on behalf of team members and assign and remove members of their projects. Project supervisors have similar rights as managers bar the hour logging functionality. Any project member and supervisors can comment on the weekly reports and give feedback about the tool to its developers. Additionally, the supervisor sees new, unread weekly reports on his or her page. In the near future, a notification function of unread comments on one's projects will also be introduced. Finally, a new user role, project client, is upon implementation. User and project basic data in the tool is maintained by admin users. The general look and feel of the tool is shown in Figure 3.

Figure 3. Layout and feel of MMT

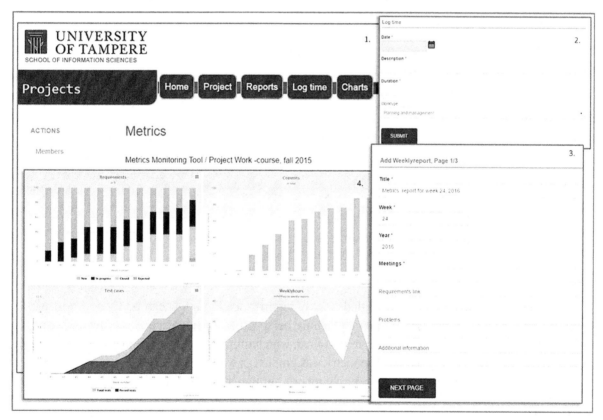

Figure 4 shows the supervisor's view of weekly report statistics, where "X" denotes a weekly report submitted on time, "L" a late delivery of a report, and "unread" a report that the supervisor has not read yet.

MMT generates the metric data from the weekly reports submitted by project managers. The current metrics include:

- The number of current sprints vs. planned sprints,

- The number of requirements in the statuses of New (i.e. unprocessed), In progress (i.e. currently being worked on), Closed (i.e. implemented) and Rejected (i.e. cancelled altogether),
- The cumulative number of code commits,
- The number of total test cases vs. passed test cases, and
- The number of working hours per person, team and work type

Figure 4. Supervisor's view of weekly report statistics

Public statistics

Weekly reports

	37	38	39	40	41	42	43	44	45	46	47	48	49	50	51	52
MMT2016	-	-	-	-	-	-	-	-	-	-	-	-	-	-	-	-
Applications for Public Transportation	X	L	X	L	L	X	X	X	X	X	X	X	X	X	X	X
Interactive photo displays	-	X	X	X	X	X	X	X	X	X	X	X	X	X	X	X
Free parking slots at the campus	-	L	X	L	X	X	X	X	X	X	X	X	X	X	X	-
NäeGofore	-	L	X	L	L	L	X	X	X	X	X	L	X	L	X	X
UtaSport	-	X	X	X	X	X	X	X	X	X	X	X	X	X	X	-
Penna	-	X	X	X	X	X	X	X	X	X	X	X	X	X	X	X

Additionally, the timeliness of submitted weekly reports (see Figure 4) can be used as a metric in monitoring the teams' performance from a teaching perspective. In future versions, derived metrics, such as traffic lights on project success, are designed, which utilize the data from the weekly reports in a more versatile way. MMT visualizes the metrics as graphs, as was portrayed in Figure 3. The user can also view the data in textual form in the weekly reports submitted by the project managers.

EVALUATION

Peffers et al. (2012) classified six artefact types that can be built in DSR: algorithm, construct, framework, instantiation, method, and model. MMT is an instantiation as it is a piece of software that will be put to real use in a real organization. They also classified the types of evaluation methods: logical argument, expert evaluation, technical experiment, subject-based experiment, action research, case study and illustrative scenario. Table 1 shows which evaluation methods were used for each version of MMT.

Table 1. Evaluation methods for each MMT-versions

Main version/ Evaluation Method	0	1	2
Prototype	Prototype versions 0.1 and 0.2.	-	
Expert evaluation	By supervisors/client.	By supervisors/ client and the developing team.	By supervisors/client and the developer.
Case study	-	Piloting in real environment.	Production use in real environment during fall semester 2016.
Technical experiment	Functional testing by the team. Experiments by the supervisors/ client.	Functional testing by the team. Experiments by the client/ supervisor.	Functional testing by the team. Acceptance testing by the supervisors/client.

Evaluation of the Version 0: Proof of Concept

The evaluation of the 0-versions (0.1-0.19) is based on the functional testing made by the developing team with the version 0.15. The client read the test report and according to him, there were too many defects to put the software to use. The team also proposed to correct bugs and some usability-issues before this could be put to (pilot) use.

The decision made in the spring 2015 was to continue the development. The versions 0.16-0.19 were implemented during the summer 2015. The client used the versions of software during the development and after getting the final version (0.19) of this phase. According to the experiments, some of the features worked ok but there were major usability issues and a lot of bugs. The test and final reports written by the developers further confirmed that this version could not be put to pilot use yet.

A new project team was formed among the Project Work course students in the fall 2015. One of the team's very first tasks was to evaluate the maturity of the current version including the source code and the documentation. After the evaluation, a decision was made, together with the client/supervisors, to start the building of the next version from scratch.

Evaluation of the Version 1: Piloting

Piloting the tool in production environment was started with the version 1.0 after the supervisor/client had accepted it based on the testing report and the recommendation by the project manager. After the piloting period, the solution was evaluated, which is covered in the following paragraphs.

The data was collected from the Software Project Management and Project Work courses at the School of Information Sciences, University of Tampere during the spring semester 2016. The projects started in January and ended in May. There were 4 project teams, 8 students (project managers) on the Software Project Management course and 15 students (developers) on the Project Work course, who used the pilot version of the tool.

Using MMT was mandatory to all teams for, at least, logging hours and weekly reporting. During the course, the teams had 5 reviews with the supervisor and the client and they also formed a final report at the end of the course. The supervisors observed the project teams by using MMT, participating in reviews and communicating in face-to-face -meetings and by email.

There were also two mandatory Moodle questionnaires for the students with questions on MMT and its usage. The first questionnaire was executed in the beginning of March, after the projects had started. The second questionnaire took place at the end of May, when all the projects had finished. The versions of MMT are related to the questionnaires so that the version 1.0 was in use before the first questionnaire. MMT was updated to the versions 1.1 and 1.2 before the second questionnaire. The version 1.3 was deployed just after the second questionnaire.

The four main features of the tool were logging hours, composing and viewing weekly reports and viewing the visual charts of the project metrics. Table 2 shows the average of the grades given by the students to each feature and MMT as a whole regarding usability, functionality and usefulness as well as the total grade. The scale was (1) poor, (2) fair, (3) good, (4) very good and (5) excellent.

Table 2. The average grade (1-5) given to each feature and to the feature's attributes

Feature/ Attribute	Logging hours	Viewing reports	Viewing charts	Composing reports	MMT-tool as a whole
Usability	4.5	4.3	4.75	4.3	3.2
Functionality	4.5	4.0	4.5	4.0	3.6
Usefulness	5.0	4.0	4.5	4.3	4.0
Overall	4.2	3.9	3.7	3.3	3.8

Logging Hours

Students were asked to use MMT for logging their working hours: whenever they worked for the project, they logged the date, the hours, the type of work, and the description in MMT. As this feature was mandatory to use for all students, it is not surprising that most of the comments related to this. When a weekly report was composed, the hours were copied to the weekly report's hours. Because of this, there were restrictions in editing the logged hours afterwards: In the version 1.0, a developer was not allowed to change the logged hours afterwards but had to ask his/her manager or supervisor to do it. In the questionnaire 1 this was complained about by two managers and two developers. This restriction was changed to version 1.1 so that also developers were allowed to edit the hours until the weekly report was sent. However, also this restriction was seen as a problem by one developer.

Overall, the logging hours -feature was seen as very useful: The managers said that it saved their time in comparison to a situation where they would have had to collect the hours manually or extract them from some other tool for the report. The developers reported that logging hours helped them to observe their own time usage.

Viewing Reports

The only reports one could get from MMT are the weekly reports composed by the managers. Viewing (weekly) reports was not seen very useful by the developers. However, there were comments on extending this feature: project managers from all teams, and also five developers, requested additional features for getting different kinds of reports from MMT, especially on working hours, by using various filters.

It was extremely useful for the supervisors to have all the reports from different weeks and different projects in one tool. Getting this information from one place reduced the time required for preparing to project meetings from 60-90 minutes to 15 minutes.

Viewing Charts

The charts show the state and the proceeding of the project in one view. One can see the current state and the history of the working hours, requirements, test cases and commits. For the supervisor, this feature is very important, as from the graphs one can not only see the history and the current state but also predict the project's progression and give some suggestions to the team.

The project members did not see the charts very useful now, but they would like to have additional charts on individual level, especially for seeing how the number of working hours has built up. The managers from all teams reported this feature to be very useful for seeing the status and proceeding. However, one team commented that viewing charts was not so useful from a project management point of view but it was interesting to compare their own project to other projects.

Composing Reports

Composing weekly reports is done by the project managers by the following Monday of each week. The managers reported the amount and states of test cases and requirements as well as the amounts of weekly hours per person, commits to the code repository, meetings and possible issues.

When creating a weekly report, each project member's working hours were automatically copied to the report as a template, and then the managers could modify these if needed. So, in the system there were reported weekly hours and working hours. This was seen very confusing. There were also some other usability issues. However, the feature was seen useful and it was reported to make reporting easier compared to writing and sending emails. In the previous semesters, the reports were sent by email and the average time for composing the report was 42 minutes. Now the average time was 16 minutes, varying from 2 to 30 minutes.

Evaluation of the Version 2: Production Use

Versions from 2.0 to 2.9 have been developed iteratively. At the end of the sprint the developers run the test cases in development environment. If the tests pass, the software is put to acceptance testing in the test server, which is identical with the production server. The acceptance test is done by the client and if the maturity of the software is good enough, the software is deployed to the production server.

The use of MMT is observed during the fall semester 2016, two Moodle questionnaires are set up for the students and the clients are interviewed. In the beginning of the year 2017, a similar analysis will be done as was done for the version 1.

To Be Developed

During the evaluation of the version 1, the researches asked in both questionnaires, which properties or features of the tool should be further developed. In several of the general comments, there were requested on using Bootstrap (Bootstrap) or a similar technology for increasing usability and support for mobile interface.

Restricting the editing of the logged hours afterwards was seen as a problem by both managers and developers. In the next versions, the restrictions could be removed.

The reports seen from the tool are limited only to the weekly reports composed by the managers. Also, the amount of different types of charts is quite limited. More flexible reports and charts could be available in the next versions.

Developing the tool into a real project management tool, like Redmine (Redmine), for not needing to use many different tools in the same project, was suggested by four managers. One manager asked for a feature that could predict the success of the project and to give tips to do the right actions. This feature has been in the product backlog from the very beginning and will certainly be implemented in the future.

CONCLUSION

Metrics Monitoring Tool benefits different user groups. Logging hours feature helps the project members to observe their own time usage. MMT reduces the time for creating weekly reports. Visualizing the metrics helps to monitor the projects. Especially from the supervisor's point of view: it is easy to catch, for example, if the amount of commits or working hours is not increasing fast enough, or if the requirements stay too long in certain states. When using MMT in teaching of software project work or in software development, there could be some material (lecture, video, online help) to introduce the tool for the users to help and to motivate them to use useful features.

Using the tool will be continued during the next semesters and new features will be developed on the base of this evaluation. It could also be worth researching further how the new features, like interactive commenting of weekly reports (implemented in version 1.3) or predicting the project's state (proposed to be developed) would help in teaching and software development.

REFERENCES

Bootstrap. *A framework for developing responsive, mobile first projects on the web.* Retrieved from http://getbootstrap.com/

Charette, R. N. (2005). Why Software Fails. *IEEE Spectrum.* Retrieved from http://spectrum.ieee.org/computing/software/why-software-fails

Computer Science Curricula 2013. (2013). *The joint task force on computing curricula.* Association for Computing Machinery (ACM) and IEEE Computer Society.

Fenton, N. (1991). *Software Metrics - A Rigorous Approach.* London, UK: Chapman & Hall.

Goodman, P. (1993). *Practical Implementation of Software Metrics.* London, UK: McGraw Hill.

Gregor, S., & Jones, D. (2007). The anatomy of a design theory. *Journal of the Association for Information Systems, 8*(2), 312–355.

Hevner, A., & Chatterjee, S. (2010). *Design research in information systems. Theory and practice*. New York: Springer Publishing. doi:10.1007/978-1-4419-5653-8

Hevner, A., March, S., Park, J., & Ram, S. (2004). Design Science in Information Systems Research. *Management Information Systems Quarterly*, *28*(1), 75–105.

Mäkiaho, P., Löytty, K., & Poranen, T. (2016). MMT – a Project Tool for Observing Metrics in Software Projects. *Proceedings of the International Conference on e-Learning – Proceedings from 2016 (e-Learning'16)* (pp. 80-85). Bratislava, Slovakia: ETN FETCH.

March, S. T., & Smith, G. F. (1995). Design and natural science research on information technology. *Decision Support Systems*, *15*(4), 251–266. doi:10.1016/0167-9236(94)00041-2

Nunamaker, J. R., Chen, M., & Purdin, T. (1991). Systems development in IS research. *Management Information Systems Quarterly*, *7*(3), 89–106. doi:10.1080/07421222.1990.11517898

Peffers, K., Rothenberger, M., Tuunanen, T., & Vaezi, R. (2012). Design Science Research Evaluation. In K. Peffers, M. Rothenberger, &, B. Kuechler (Eds.), DESRIST 2012, LNCS (Vol. 7286, pp. 398-410).

Peffers, K., Tuunanen, T., Rothenberger, M. A., & Chatterjee, S. (2007). A design science research methodology for information systems research. *Journal of Management Information Systems*, *24*(3), 45–77. doi:10.2753/MIS0742-1222240302

PMBOK. (2013). *A Guide to the Project Management Body of Knowledge* (5th ed.). Project Management Institute.

Portillo-Rodríguez, J., Vizcaíno, A., Piattini, M., & Beecham, S. (2012). Tools used in Global Software Engineering: A systematic mapping review. *Information and Software Technology*, *54*(7), 663–685. doi:10.1016/j.infsof.2012.02.006

Redmine. (n. d.). *Web-based project management and issue tracking tool*. Retrieved from http://www.redmine.org

School of Information Sciences, University of Tampere. (2016). *Metrics Monitoring Tool* [Software]. Retrieved from http://metricsmonitoring.sis.uta.fi/

Simon, H. A. (1996). *The Sciences of the Artificial* (3rd ed.). Cambridge, MA: MIT Press.

Sommerville, I. (2010). *Software Engineering* (9th ed.). Addison-Wesley.

This research was previously published in the International Journal of Human Capital and Information Technology Professionals (IJHCITP), 8(4); pages 27-37, copyright year 2017 by IGI Publishing (an imprint of IGI Global).

Chapter 55
Framework for Reusable Test Case Generation in Software Systems Testing

Kamalendu Pal

https://orcid.org/0000-0001-7158-6481

City, University of London, UK

ABSTRACT

Agile methodologies have become the preferred choice for modern software development. These methods focus on iterative and incremental development, where both requirements and solutions develop through collaboration among cross-functional software development teams. The success of a software system is based on the quality result of each stage of development with proper test practice. A software test ontology should represent the required software test knowledge in the context of the software tester. Reusing test cases is an effective way to improve the testing of software. The workload of a software tester for test-case generation can be improved, previous software testing experience can be shared, and test efficiency can be increased by automating software testing. In this chapter, the authors introduce a software testing framework (STF) that uses rule-based reasoning (RBR), case-based reasoning (CBR), and ontology-based semantic similarity assessment to retrieve the test cases from the case library. Finally, experimental results are used to illustrate some of the features of the framework.

INTRODUCTION

The strategic importance of software has long been understood by professionals and policymakers around the world (Dutta, Wassenhove & Kulandaiswamy, 1998). Software has become an indispensable part of every industry, from mobile phone manufacturers to the safe landing of spaceships. The advancement of software design and development is always an open topic for researchers to address complex systems with numerous domain-specific requirements. The success of a system is based on the quality result at every stage of development, and therefore, superior software development is an essential element of success. These quality-enhancing features become more important as the transition from hardware to software-

DOI: 10.4018/978-1-6684-3702-5.ch055

enabled products accelerates. Today's technological innovation in the software industry is similar to the early 1970s, when digital electronics began to replace the mechanical and analogue technologies that underpinned the products of attractive desktop calculators to black-and-white televisions.

The landscape of the top software dependent product and service companies is changing rapidly. The value is evolving fast as hardware features are mostly standardized and differentiate software between high and low end products. At the same time, more miniaturized computing power provides the value of embedded software in products is expected to continue its market demand. In fact, software enables an estimated *high percentage* of automotive product innovations, from entertainment to fatal accident avoidance systems (Charette, 2005; Charette, 2009). These new-generation, software-based touch-and-feel-sensitive systems are highly dependent on human-computer interactions. Computer interfaces are becoming more and more sensitive and demanding as the number of products increases, from biometrically detectable automotive unlocking systems to sophisticated automotive dashboards that design and use *intelligent software* displays. As software-based user interactions become the operational norm, software-driven automation of the design and development of these software systems promise a new degree of quality while reducing production costs. A company with consistently high-performing software has less downtime in operation and develops products with fewer disruptions that impact the end-user experience.

The automotive manufacturing industry is witnessing a new era of software-driven innovative products and processes. Particularly, using the Internet of Things (IoT) technologies and enhanced computing power in solving operational problems. For example, self-driven cars are slowly becoming a reality with high hope of commercialization for public transportation soon. The world would now have self-driven cars if the automotive industry could model very accurately the randomness of human-drivers and pedestrians on public roads. One solution to this problem would be restricted lanes for autonomous vehicles only. Self-driving cars can communicate and coordinate with each other that human drivers often fail to do. It should be noted that operational data analysis and error-free software systems are the main driving forces of these self-driven cars.

The road traffic and observation data of the self-driven car can reveal interesting patterns and correlations in the collected data set. The important mechanism for finding causal relationships is often guided by intelligent data analysis software controlled by artificial intelligent (AI) techniques. For example, algorithmic sorting, searching and data clustering are often used to analyze the observation data. In this way, the introduction of AI-based software applications improves human performance in using these automated systems.

Academics and practitioners (Holcombe, 2008) are pushing for innovations in software design and development based on artificial intelligence. At the same time, technological innovations and their applications are transforming information and communication technology (Prahalad & Mashelkar, 2010). The world of software design and development also focuses on technological innovation to enable efficient software design and development processes. True, innovative technologies and techniques are now shaping everything, from capturing software requirements to delivering software, and as new perspectives emerge, fully automated customer service in software development processes are on the horizon. The technologies that enable global software design and development, such as software development platforms and tremendous computing power, data storage, and innovative software testing techniques are rapidly advancing and becoming increasingly possible.

Software being developed in the industry requires careful operational planning and the coordination of required resources. The inception, design, implementation, testing and maintenance of a software product requires team effort and is organized and executed in such a way that the product customers are satisfied. Software lifecycle models distinguish between different phases or activities when creating software using feed-forward and feed-back loops according to the principle of separation of interests. This separation reduces the complexity of each phase or activity, but at the same time requires efficient and effective coordination.

Researchers (Shepperd & Schofield, 1997; Mair, Martincova & Shepperd, 2012) have also highlighted the critical importance of software testing and the appropriate use of relevant resources (e.g. time and cost) for the purpose of the software development are very important. Ultimately, the development costs for test cases are reduced and the quality of the implemented software systems improved (Nikolik, 2012). It is predicted that mathematically distorted information spent nearly sixty percent of the total software testing time designing test cases (Myers, Badgett & Sandler, 1997). As a result, the effective design and use of software test cases has become an attractive topic in software engineering research to automate software testing practice.

A case-based reasoning (CBR) is based on using information from previous situations to determine the results for new problems or cases (Pal, 1997) (Pal, 2017). This problem-solving strategy mimics human problem-solving activities to plan a decision based on past experience. A CBR system consists of a *case base*, which is the set of all cases known to the system. The case database can be considered as a particular kind of knowledge base containing only cases. When a new case is presented to the system, it will look at the case base in a *selection process* for similar cases that are most relevant to the present case. If a similar case is found, the system retrieves this case and tries to change it (if necessary) to find a potential solution to the new case. This process is called *adaptation*. The method of selecting and retrieving cases is referred to as "*similarity assessment.*" The similarity assessment is based on the best matching cases, ordered by some *similarity metrics* (Pal & Parmer, 2000). This case-similarity matching approach differs from a deductive rule-based approach in which problems are solved by chaining the inference rules (Pal & Campbell, 1997).

The knowledge intensive software test decision-making process, specialized software testers are often referred to as the "*previous test situation*". To aid this process, an automated software engineering CBR system should find cases that are most similar to a new test case and thus act as a base-case, and its solution can provide guidance for a new test case. However, this choice, which is cognitively a complex activity, is usually approximated by a simple metric scheme in case-based computing. Such a similarity assessment scheme for the present research will be described later in this chapter.

To deduce from past experience with software testing to interpret a new test case (as do software testers in the industry) or to find an equitable solution to a new problem (as the software test case generator does) is case-based analogical reasoning (or CBR) software testing. Often this test case generation is guided by RBR (Rule Based Reasoning). This hybrid knowledge-driven framework (i.e., CBR and RBR) is just right for reusable test case requirements. On the other hand, although there are many test cases that can be reused in the application of software tests, the testing process differs due to the different operating system, operating environment, hardware type, network conditions and end-user characteristics, and so on. This undoubtedly increases the complexity of the software test case, which determines the need to reuse test cases to account for various factors and to find the best solution based on the use of previous test cases. This makes CBR useful and highly appreciated.

This chapter examines three important aspects of software development, agile software development methods, the use of knowledge-based techniques, and software testing that benefit most from efficient software delivery. Customers are demanding rapidly developed software products, which is why software development companies are moving to agile methods to deliver high-quality applications in a short time. The programmers write and automate units of software systems and integration tests that provide good code coverage. They are disciplined in handling source code control and code integration. Qualified testers are involved from the beginning of the development cycle and given time and resources to adequately perform all required test forms. An automated software test suite that covers system functionality at a higher level is run and reviewed on a regular basis.

The rest of this chapter is structured as follows. Section 2 describes the background information of the software development and the agile methodologies. Section 3 provides an overview of the software unite testing deployment in the proposed framework. Section 4 deals with related research. Section 5 explains how to use the ontology in the software test case library. Section 6 contains information about retrieving and adaptation of test cases. Section 7 contains an experimental description of the reuse of test cases. Finally, section 8 gives a conclusion of research issues.

SOFTWARE DEVELOPMENT AND AGILE METHODOLOGY

Software is a series of instructions for the computer that perform a task, called a program. Simply software can be classified into two main categories: system software, and application software. The system software is made up of control programs. The application software is any program that processes data for the software system's user; and often it uses different mathematical models to automate the operational decision making (Pal, 2019).

Software development consists of transitions of system concept, requirements specification, analysis and design, implementation as well as testing and maintenance (Laplante, 2007). This abstraction applies both to the plan-driven process model (e.g. spiral (Boehm, 1988), the evolutionary model (Nauman & Jenkins, 1982), the unified process model (Kruchten, 2000), and, to a lesser extent, Agile models in which activities can be mixed, which completely eliminating transitions (e.g. in eXtreme Programming (Beck, 1999)).

About the V-Modell, which originates from the system technology (Forsberg & Mooz, 1991) and has been taken over into the software development (Pfleeger & Atlee, 2009), testing on a high level is often presented as quality assurance of the final product. As such, this link between software quality assurance and testing is an integral part of industry-specific problem analysis, solution design, and implementation. Many software companies have introduced agile development techniques to increase productivity. The main reason for adopting agile development methods throughout the project lifecycle is to produce higher-quality software in less time while reducing development costs.

In this way, the software industry has moved from traditional software development models to agile development to respond to ever-more-complex software and dynamic user demands. In contrast to traditional models, agile methodologies are characterized by shorter production times and intensive customer interaction. This customer-focused design and redesign practice accommodates the changes required by dynamic customer requirements. Although different software development methods use the same agile principles that are formulated in the *agile manifesto* (Beck et al., 2001), they differ in several parameters.

Agile software development became popular in the early years of this century when a group of developers met to discuss ways in which software development was considered a craft. After announcing the manifesto for agile software development, many different approaches, heuristics, tools, and techniques came to the fore. Excellent tests adapt to all these different contextual factors.

Agile development practice requires multi-functional teams that follow the principles of iterative and incremental development practice. The testing process should be well prepared for efficiency and testing should be done early and frequently. There must be a detailed agenda and specification of which test results should be available at the end of each iteration (or sprint).

The agile methodology, a conceptual framework for software development with face to face customer interaction, promotes the iterative development method throughout the project lifecycle. The agile software development team produces very few written documents compared to traditional software development models (e.g. Waterfall or V model). Agile methods focus on working software as a primary measure of progress. In addition, testing is always testing - the process of evaluating something by learning it through exploration and experimentation.

A BRIEF REVIEW OF SOFTWARE TESTING

Software companies are investing in quality assurance to reduce the cost of software development and maintenance and increase revenue and profit margins. To help increase net income, a quality assurance organization must consider the cost and value of the test-ware required for quality assurance of software artifacts such as requirements, specifications, designs, test case generation, and code.

In addition, modern software development is a knowledge-intensive activity. The number of resources available to modern software development is amazing. Process models, development methods, technologies, and development tools are part of the toolbox of the modern software designer, which includes several toolkits, configuration management tools, test suites, standards, and intelligent compilers with sophisticated debugging capabilities, just to name a few. The software engineer's vision of carefully crafting language statements into a work program is outdated and gives way to the use of a variety of tools and techniques that support the coordination of work and the creation of systems that conform to the complexity of the concept demanded by users of modern software, While it is unclear whether these tools had the impact expected from Computer Aided Software Engineering (CASE) providers, the burden on tool mastery (Brooks, 1987) for software developers has increased.

Much of the development cycle is spent on debugging, where the programmer performs a long, failure trace and tries to locate the problem in a few lines of source code to clarify the cause of the problem. In this way, testing among software quality assurance techniques is one of the most commonly used techniques in practice. Consequently, testing is also extensively studied in research. An important aspect of testing that is receiving a lot of attention in the issue of generating reusable test cases.

Software testing has been the most widely used software quality assurance technology for many decades. Due to its successful practical application, considerable research effort has been made to improve the effectiveness of tests and to scale the techniques for dealing with increasingly complex software systems. Therefore, automation of test activities is the key factor for improving test effectiveness. Automation involves four main activities: (i) generating tests, (ii) performing these tests on the system under test, (iii) evaluating the results of test procedures, and (iv) managing the results of test executions.

Comparison of Traditional and Agile Software Testing

It pays to understand the differences between traditional software testing and agile testing, as shown in Figure 1. Traditional software development uses a phased approach (e.g. requirement elicitation, specification, coding, testing, and release). Testing takes place at the end of the software development, shortly before the release. This is shown schematically in the upper part of Figure 1. The diagram is idealistic because it gives the impression that there is just as much time for testing as for coding. However, this is not the case with many software developments projects. Testing is 'squished' because coding takes longer than expected and the teams end up going through a code-and-fix cycle.

Figure 1. The difference between traditional software development model and agile model

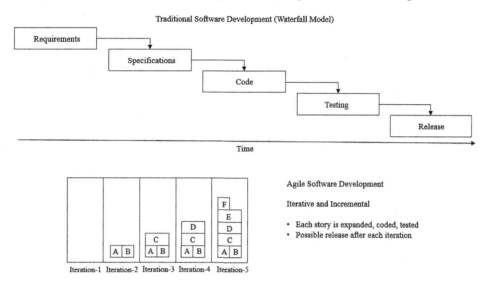

Agile is iterative and incremental. This means that the testers test each code increment as soon as it is complete. An iteration can only take a week or a month. The team builds and tests a bit of code to make sure it's working properly, and then proceeds to the next part that needs to be created. The agile software development is shown in the lower part of Figure 1.

The approaches to projects that agile teams pursue are diverse. A team can be dedicated to a single project or be part of another larger project. Every project, every team and sometimes every iteration is different. How a software development team solves problems depends on the problem, the people involved, and the software tools that the team will use.

The fact that knowledge in software development settings is both dynamic and situation-specific has led the research community to apply a CBR decision-support approach (Pal, 1999). The general CBR paradigm postulates that much of the human problem solving is to apply past experiences to analogously related situations. In this way, CBR-driven actions are based on past experience, and to the extent that one can remember the similarities and differences between current and past circumstances, successful, defective, and failed actions can be repeated, modified, or avoided. Early case-based systems focused on how this type of reasoning can be mimicked in artificial intelligence (AI) systems. Recent systems, however, have begun to examine how case-based technology can be used to support human decision-making by providing external memory for cases and effectively expanding one's own knowledge to incorporate the experiences of others (Kolodners, 1993; Goel & Diaz-Agudo, 2017; Pal & Palmer, 2000; Watson, 2003; Pal, 2017).

RELATED RESEARCH WORKS

In software testing, a program with well-designed input data is run to observe errors (Ipate & Holcombe, 1997; Mall, 2006; Jalote, 2006; Myers, 2004). In other words, software testing addresses the problem of effectively finding the difference between the expected behavior given by the system models and the observed behavior of the implemented system (Binder, 1999).

Software testing, on average, account for a large percentage of total development costs and would increase even further with the rapid growth in the size and complexity of software (Mall, 2008; Myers, 2004; Owterweil, 1996). As systems grow larger and more complex, testing time and effort is expected to increase. Therefore, the automation of software testing has become an urgent practical necessity to reduce test cost and time. In addition, the test case plays an important role in software testing, and the generation of test cases has generally been identified as an important research challenge. In recent years, a research group (Orso & Rothermel, 2014) presented the results of an informal survey in which researchers in testing were asked to comment on the most notable achievements of the research effort and the open challenges in the field. The most common keywords in the experts' answers are the word "generation", which, together with a few other terms such as "tools" and "practice". This observation confirms the importance of the topic of test generation approaches, which must be accompanied by good tool support to cover practical needs.

The recent survey (Anand et al., 2013) covers test-case and test data generation techniques that include various techniques like symbolic execution, model-based testing, combinatorial interaction testing, adaptive random testing, and search-based testing. Relevant work includes that of Mayrhauser's research project (Mayrhauser, 1994), which is a presumptive attempt to design a system that can use the idea of test case generation. In his work, he introduced a new method of test case generation to improve the reuse of test cases through domain analysis and domain modeling. After that, a lot of research was put into the reuse of the test case. It can mainly be divided into two aspects: the generation of reusable test-cases and the management of reusable test cases.

Xu and colleagues (Xu et al., 2003) advocated a theoretical model for generating and executing patterns, making the test cases independent of the software under test and achieving the goal of reusing tests. Wang has focused on a test-case generation approach based on ontology (Wang et al., 2007). To precisely and accurately describe the test case, Guo and his colleague (Guo et al., 2011) pointed to an ontology-based method widely used as the basis for the sharing and reuse of knowledge in information science. Researchers (Xiao-Li et al., 2006) developed a test case library and discussed the model of test case management. To aid effective reuse of tests, academics (Shao, Bai & Zhao, 2006) proposed a software test design model based on the analysis of reusable test assets and their relationships.

There are many outstanding researchers who focus on generating or managing test cases. However, there are only a few studies that focus on how reusable test cases can be efficiently retrieved from the test library. In recent years, CBR has been seen as an effective approach to improving this problem and the associated research is just beginning. As we know, CBR for test case generation involves the following steps: (1) retrieving relevant test cases from the test case library; (2) selecting a set of the most suitable test cases; (3) modify and evaluate the set of test cases in the test process; (4) storing the new test cases in the test case library as a valuable and reusable resource for future applications or systems. Throughout the process, it is a central issue to describe and retrieve the appropriate test cases. The biggest drawback of CBR is that the case is not easy to adapt and often requires artificial adjustment. However, if one uses ontology to describe the test case, the test case has a semantic capability that is easily modified. Therefore, the following section describes the ontology-based test case library and the retrieval of the reusable test case from this library by computing the semantic similarity between the test case and the test request.

USE OF ONTOLOGY IN SOFTWARE TEST CASE LIBRARY

Planning and running software tests require, among other things, specialized knowledge of testing techniques, criteria, artifacts, and tools (Ipate & Holcombe, 1997). This diversity of concepts and relationships makes it necessary to build a common understanding. Ontology is a technique for collecting domain knowledge and therefore offers great potential for the knowledge-rich testing process. Ontologies have acquired important roles in information systems, knowledge management and information exchange systems, and in the development of fields such as semantic technologies (Vasanthapriyan et al., 2017). When testing software, ontologies can provide a precise selection of terms for communication between testers, developers, managers, and users. Ontologies therefore reveal the hidden assumptions about this practice (Cai et al., 2009) and support the acquisition, organization, reuse, and exchange of knowledge in the domain.

Software test is a technique to obtain information about software systems quality. Performance test is a type of software test that aims at evaluating software performance at a given scenario, but it requires specialized knowledge about tools, activities and metrics of the domain. For example, in software engineering – the specification is described in natural language at first. The test requirements and the test cases are no exception. For the machine, there is no link between two different sentences with similar meaning which described by natural language. However, ontology can establish a semantic association between these two different sentences which can be understood by machine. There, this research project uses ontology to build the test-case library and model the test requirements.

Software testing is a technique for obtaining information about the quality of software systems. The performance test is a type of software test that aims to evaluate software performance in a given scenario. However, it requires specialized knowledge of domain tools, activities, and metrics. For example, in software engineering - the specification is first described in natural language. The test requirements and the test cases are no exception. For the machine, there is no connection between two different sets of similar meaning, which are described by the natural language. However, the ontology can produce a semantic association between these two different sets that can be understood by the machine. There, this research project uses the ontology to build the test case library and model the test requirements.

Ontology-Based Test Case Library

Ontology is a technique for representing and manipulating knowledge in a area of application (e.g., software testing). This chapter describes the definition of ontology-based test case and test case library as follows:

Definition 1. *An ontology is a structure*

$$O \cdot (C, \leqslant_C, R, \sigma, \leq_R)$$

consisting of (i) two disjoint sets C and R whose elements are called concept identifiers and relation identifiers respectively, (ii) a partial order $\leq_C$ on C, called concept hierarchy or taxonomy, (iii) a function σ: R→C+ called signature, and (iv) a partial order $\leq_R$ on R, called relation hierarchy, where $r_1 \leq_R r_2$ implies $|σ(r_1)|=|σ(r_2)|$ and $π_i(σ(r_1)) \leq_C π_i(σ(r_2))$, for each $1 \leq i \leq |σ(r1)|$.

Often researchers call concept identifiers and relation identifiers just concepts and relations, respectively for sake of simplicity.

Definition 2. *For a relation $r \in R$ with $|σ(r)|=2$, one can define its domain and its range by dom(r) $\Delta π_1(σ$
    (r)) and range(r) $\Delta π_2(σ (r))$.

If $c_1 \leq_C c_2$, for c_1, $c_2 \in C$, then c_1 is a subconcept of c_2, and c_2 is a subconcept of c_1. If $r_1 \leq_R r_2$, for r_1, r_2 $\in R$, then r_1 is a subrelation of r_2, and r_2 is a sub-relation of r_1.
If $c_1 \leq_C c_2$ and there is no $c_3 \in C$ with $c_1 <_C c_3 <_C c_2$, then c_1 is a direct subconcept of c_2, and c_2 is a direct super-concept of c_1. One can note this by $c_1 \prec c_2$. Direct superrelations, and direct subrelations are defined analogously.

Definition 3. *Let ⌊ be a logical language. A ⌊-axiom system for an ontology $\Delta \cdot (C, \leq_C, R, σ, \leq_R)$ is a pair*
    A:=(AI,α) where (i) AI is a set whose elements are called axiom identifiers and (ii) α: AI→Δ is a
    mapping. The elements of A:=α(AI) are called axioms.

An ontology with ⌊-axiom is a pair (Δ,A) where Δ is an ontology and A is a ⌊-axiom system for Δ.

Definition 4. *An ontology with ⌊-axiom is a pair (Δ,A) is consistent, if*

$$A \cup \{\forall x : x \in c_1 \rightarrow x \in c_2 \mid c_1 \leq c_2\} \cup \{\forall x : x \in r_1 \rightarrow x \in r_2 \mid r_1 \leq r_2\}$$

is consistent.

Definition 5. Test Case Ontology (TCO): *TCO consists of two sets – test case concepts (TCC) and relations (R), and these sets don't intersect with each other.*

For convenience, following basic relations of ontology are used in the rest of this chapter:

Theorem 1: P(x) relation. if the type of concept "C_1" is P, then it can be described as "$P(C_1)$". For example: has (C_1): means that C_1 is exist.

Theorem 2: R(x, y) relation. $\exists C_1, C_2 \in TCC$, if the type of relationship between concept "C_1" and "C_2" is "R" then the relation can be described as $R(C_1, C_2)$. For example: instance (C_1, C_2): describes the instance relationship between two concepts, it means that concept "C_1" is the instance of "C_2".

Definition 6. Test Case Library (TCL): TCL = {TCO, Rules}. Rules represent a set of inference rules, which is explained in detail below. Rule are used to modify the test case.

A test-case when testing software consists of a series of inputs, execution conditions, and expected results for a particular purpose. In the ontology-based test case library, the exact definition of terms can be represented by a set of description logic formulas. To clearly illustrate the process of reusing test cases, a test case is defined as a seven-tuple: {TID, TP, PR, TE, TI, TO, ER}, and the tuples are shown in Table 1.

Table 1. The properties of a test case

Property	Name of Property	Description
TID	Test Identification	Unique identifier of a test case
TP	Test Purpose	The indivisible purpose of the testing
PR	Precondition	The condition needs to meet before testing
TE	Test Environment	The environment needed in the testing
TI	Test Input	The input data
TO	Test Operation	The process of testing
ER	Expected Result	The expected result

Definition 7. Test Case Sequence (TCS): *The test case sequence is composed of the least one test case. And there is a certain sequence existed between the test cases. It can be defined as follows*:

$$TCS: \geq 1has\ (TOC) \wedge Pre\ (tco_i, tco_j) \wedge instance\ (tco_i, TCO) \wedge instance\ (tco_j, TCO)$$

For a better description, number restrictions and an R (x, y) relation are used in the formal expression of TCS.

- $\geq n\ R$: at least number restrictions, the number of relationship "R" is at least n.

- $\leq n\ R$: at most number restrictions, the number of relationship "R" is at most n.

- Pre (x, y): sequence relationship, it means that x is prior to y.

Ontology-Based Test Task

At the beginning of software testing, the testers must determine the test target. A test target can be represented as a set of test requirements. For example, for functional coverage testing, each function of the application or system awaiting a test corresponds to a test requirement. In addition, testers must also determine the test environment. Therefore, a test task can be defined as a 2-tuple (TT, TE) and TT refers to the test target while TE is the test environment. If TR represents the test requirement that cannot be subdivided into smaller requirements, TT can be defined as follows:

$$TT: \geq 1has\ (TR) \wedge Pre\ (tr_i, trj_j) \wedge instance\ (tr_i, TR) \wedge instance\ (tr_j, TR)$$

This definition is very similar to the definition of TCS. It also shows that at least one test case sequence is required to complete a test target.

Here is a simple example to illustrate the relationship between them. For example, suppose a test requirement set $R = \{tr_1, tr_2, tr_3, tr_4\}$, and there exists an order between them, such as $tr_1 \rightarrow tr_2 \rightarrow tr_3 \rightarrow tr_4$. One tries to find test case set $\{tc_{31}, tc_{32} \ldots tc_{3n}\}$ for tr_3, and test case set $\{tc_{41}, tc_{42} \ldots tc_{4n}\}$ for tr_4. In the actual testing, the number of test cases in each test case set for each test requirement is not equal. If the output of tc_{11} meets the precondition of tc_{22}, then one can add them into a same test case sequence. The rest can be done in the same way. Finally, the test case sequence for the specific test target can be found.

TEST CASE RETRIEVAL MECHANISM

If the test requirement (TR) is regarded as query case, and the test case library is viewed as case base, the reusable test case generation might be considered as searching the cases that has the highest degree of matching with query-case from case base. These analyze and rewrite the cases according to the actual conditions. This section will discuss these issues.

Figure 2. The proposed software framework

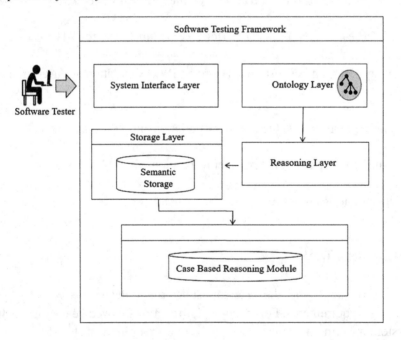

The software system framework shown in Figure 2 consists of three layers: system interface and ontology layer, storage and reasoning layer, and the last layer is a case-based reasoning layer. The process of the framework is summarized as follows. Via the interface for the sharing of experiences, software testers can comment on their testing knowledge with the aid of software testing variables. The semantic data is expressed in triplicate structures according to the concepts and relationships of the software testing ontology.

WordNet-Based Test Case Retrieval

The test case retrieval process consists of finding the test case whose TP matches the TR from the test case library. Since different people in software engineering have different expressions for the same requirement, the string comparison method, which only judges if all strings are the same, is not applicable here. In this chapter, the ontology similarity calculation method is used to obtain a test set of cases in which the TPs of each test case semantically match the TR to varying degrees. The calculation of the ontology similarity is based on the WordNet, a large lexical database for English. Nouns, verbs, adjectives, and adverbs are grouped into groups of cognitive synonyms (synsets), each of which expresses a particular concept. Synsets are interlinked by conceptual-semantic and lexical relationships (Miller, 1995; Fellbaum, 1998). The approach of this chapter distinguishes the part of the language to which the word belongs. Different parts of speech have different weights in the calculation. As mentioned above, TP refers to the indivisible purpose of the test. Each test case can be modeled as a node in the ontology diagram. TP, which should contain a verb and multiple nouns, is a property of the node.

There are many methods to measure the semantic similarity of ontology based on WordNet (Budanitsky & Hirst, 2001). In general, these methods can be divided into the following categories: (1) based on the path length of the concept; (2) based on information; (3) based on features; (4) other comprehensive calculation method. Because one has to find as many test cases as possible to account for in the retrieval phase for reusable test cases, when calculating the similarity of two concepts, only two basic factors are considered: the concept path length (h_w) and the coincide path length (h); and they are defined as follows:

Definition 8. Concept Path Length (h_w): The path length from concept to the root.
Definition 9. Coincide Path Length (h): The length of the overlap path from two concept to the root.

This path calculation technique is used to retrieve a similar test case from the test case library. Suppose that there are two concepts W_i and W_j. The concept path length of W_i is h_{wi}, and the concept path length of W_j is h_{wj}. The length of coincide path between them is h. The definition of contact ratio (cr) is as follows:

$$cr = \begin{cases} \dfrac{h}{(h_{wi} + h_{wj})/2} & h_{wi} \neq h_{wf} \\[2em] \dfrac{h}{h_{wi}} & h_{wi} = h_{wf} \end{cases}$$

Then the similarity between W_i and W_j can be calculated as follows:

$$sim\left(w_i, w_j\right) = \frac{e^{cr} - e^{-cr}}{e^{cr} + e^{-cr}}$$

And the similarity between TP and TR can be obtained by the following formula:

$$sim(TP, TR) = \alpha.sim(verb_{TP} + verb_{TR}) + \beta._{ij}^{Maxsim(noun_{TP}+noun_{TR})}$$

In the above formula, α and β are the factor parameters whose value ranges in (0, 1), and $\alpha + \beta = 1$; $\alpha \geq \beta$.

For the two concepts W_1 and W_2, their location relation in WordNet can be classified into two categories: (1) the coincide path length is 0 (h = 0); (2) the coincide path length is greater than 0 (h > 0). According to information theory, in the first case there is almost no similarity between W_1 and W_2. In the second case, the greater the ratio of the coincide path length in the concept path length, the less the similarity between W_1 and W_2.

Take for example, {mammal, bird, dog, cat} to prove the validity of the formula suggested in this chapter above. Figure 3 shows the part of the hierarchical semantic structure in WordNet that contains the four nouns. The results of the similarity calculation are shown in Table 2.

Figure 3. The part of the hierarchical semantic structure in WordNet

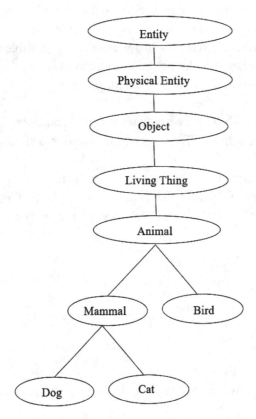

The results show that the similarity between mammal and dog is greater than in mammal and bird. And the similarity between dog and bird is the lowest in the results. This not only corresponds to the facts, but also to information theory. Therefore, the formula can be used to retrieve similar test cases from the test case library.

Rule-Based Test Case Adaptation

In this framework, rule-based techniques are used to adopt the previous test-cases for the present case. There are three types of situations in this framework: rewriting, modifying the script execution command, and changing environment variables.

In different test environments, the execution command of the test case and the environment variables of the test case are different. However, the system has a robust function implementation and business logic that does not change with the environment. Therefore, the system must change the related information of test cases retrieved from the test case library according to the test environment specified in the test task using the case selection algorithm.

The operating system is an important element in the test environment. For example, the following rewrite rules for test cases apply to Windows and Unix:

(1) Rewrite the operating system running the test case if the operating system information of the test case differs from that of the test task.

testTask(?tt) ^ hasOS(?x, ?tt) ^ testcase(?c) ^ hasOS(?y, ?tc)^ different(?x, ?y) -> transoms(?x, ?c)

(2) Modify the script execution command.

Is-OS(?x, Windows) ^ script(?file) -> execute("cmd" + ?systemDrive + ?file) Is-OS(?x, Linux) ^ script(?file) -> execute("./" + ?file)

Other changes caused by changing the test environment can be written to similar rule types.

TEST CASE REUSE EXPERIMENT

The implemented system uses a test case library consisting of 155 test cases and 16 rules. The system uses OWL to describe the test case and SWRL to describe the rewrite rules. In one experiment, the test task was broken down into six test requirements. The experimental results are shown in Table 3.

Table 2. The similarity calculation results of the four nouns

(W_1, W_2)	h	h_{w1}	h_{w2}	cr	Sim (w_1, w_2)
(mammal, bird)	4	5	5	4/5	0.6640
(mammal, dog)	5	5	7	5/6	0.6823
(dog, cat)	5	7	7	5/7	0.6134
(dog, bird)	4	7	5	4/7	0.5164

Table 3. Results of the experiment

No	Test Cases	Sim (TP, TR) ≥ 0.6	Percentage	Time
01	16	10	0.625	4.01
02	14	8	0.571	3.87
03	10	7	0.7	3.73
04	10	6	0.6	3.73
05	15	9	0.6	3.88
06	23	11	0.478	4.13

CONCLUSION

This chapter describes how to generate reusable test cases from a test library based on the ontology. Here, the knowledge base is the case library, which depicts what can be learned from a test case and defines the rules that were used to adapt the retrieved test case. In addition, it was argued that each test case in the case library differs from the others, but the semantic similarity between the test cases can be calculated using a particular calculation approach. The results of the presented experimental calculation show that the approach proposed in this chapter can significantly reduce the time required to generate reusable test cases and reduce the workload of the software testing process.

The chapter also suggested an approach to calculate the ontological semantic similarity between test case and test request based on the specific algorithm. However, this approach is too crude at this time and more appropriate approaches need to be identified in future research. Moreover, the presented approach did not consider coverage of the generated test case sequence, and the test case sequence generation process still requires manual intervention. It also fails to create a fully machine-generated test case. In the future, more test cases would be used for experimental exercises, and research plans to validate the proposed technique in practice.

REFERENCES

Anand, S., Burke, E. K., Chen, T. Y., Clark, J. A., Cohen, M. B., Grieskamp, W., ... McMinn, P. (2013). An orchestrated survey of methodologies for automated software test case generation. *Journal of Systems and Software, 86*(8), 1978–2001. doi:10.1016/j.jss.2013.02.061

Beck, K. (1999). Embracing change with extreme programming. *Computer, 32*(10), 70–77. doi:10.1109/2.796139

Beck, K., Beedle, M., Bennekum, A. V., Cockburn, A., & Cunningham, W. (2001). *The Agile Manifesto.* Software Development.

Binder, R. V., Legeard, B., & Kramer, A. (2015). Model-based testing: Where does it stand? *Communications of the ACM, 58*(2), 52–56. doi:10.1145/2697399

Boehm, B. W. (1988). A spiral model of software development and enhancement. *Computer, 21*(5), 61–72. doi:10.1109/2.59

Brooks, F. P. (1987). No Silver Bullet: Essence and Accidents of Software Engineering. *Computer*, *20*(4), 10–19. doi:10.1109/MC.1987.1663532

Budanitsky, A., & Hirst, G. (2001). Semantic Distance in WordNet: An Experimental Application-Oriented Evaluation of Five Measure. *Proceeding Workshop WordNet and Other Lexical Resources, Second Meeting of the North American Chapter of the Association for Computational Linguistics*.

Cai, L., Rensing, C., Li, X., & Wang, G. (2009). Novel gene clusters involved in arsenite oxidation and resistance in two arsenite oxidizers: Achromobacter sp. SY8 and Pseudomonas sp. TS44. *Applied Microbiology and Biotechnology*, *83*(4), 715–725. doi:10.100700253-009-1929-4 PMID:19283378

Charette, R. N. (2005). Why Software Fails. *IEEE Spectrum*, *2*.

Charette, R. N. (2009). This Car Runs on Code. *IEEE Spectrum*, *1*.

Dutta, S., Wassenhove, L. N. V., & Kulandaiswamy, S. (1998). Benchmarking European Software Management Practices. *Communications of the ACM*, *41*(6), 77–86. doi:10.1145/276609.276623

Fellbaum, C. (1998). *WordNet: An Electronic Lexical Database*. Cambridge, MA: MIT Press. doi:10.7551/mitpress/7287.001.0001

Forsberg, K., & Mooz, H. (1991). The relationship of system engineering to the project cycle. In *Proceedings of Annual Conference of the National Council on System Engineering*. National Council on Systems Engineering. 10.1002/j.2334-5837.1991.tb01484.x

Goel, A. K., & Diaz-Agudo, B. (2017). *What's hot in case-based reasoning?* AAAI.

Guo, S., Tong, W., Zhang, J., & Liu, Z. (2011). An Application of Ontology to Test Case Reuse. *International Conference on Mechatronic Science, Electrical Engineering and Computer*, Jilin, China.

Holcombe, M. (2008). *Running an Agile Software Development Project*. Hoboken, NJ: John Wiley & Sons; doi:10.1109/MEC.2011.6025579.

Ipate, F., & Holcombe, M. (1997). An integration testing method that is proved to find all faults. *International Journal of Computer Mathematics*, *63*(3-4), 159–178. doi:10.1080/00207169708804559

Jalote, P., & Jain, G. (2006). Assigning tasks in a 24-h software development model. *Journal of Systems and Software*, *79*(7), 904–911. doi:10.1016/j.jss.2005.06.040

Kolodner, J. (1993). *Case Based Reasoning*. Morgan Kaufmann. doi:10.1016/B978-1-55860-237-3.50005-4

Kruchten, P. (2000). *The Rational Unified Process: An Introduction* (2nd ed.). Boston, MA: Addision Wesley Longman Publishing.

Laplante, P. A. (2007). *What Every Engineer Should Know about Software Engineering* (1st ed.). CRC Press. doi:10.1201/9781420006742

Mair, C., Martincova, M., & Shepperd, M. (2012). An Empirical Study of Software Project Managers Using a Case-Based Reasoner. In *Proceedings of 45th Hawaii International Conference on System Science*, (pp. 1030-1039). IEEE Computer Society. 10.1109/HICSS.2012.96

Mall, R. (2006). *Fundamentals of Software Engineering* (2nd ed.). Prentice Hall.

Mayrhauser, A. v., Walls, J., & Mraz, R. (1994). Sleuth: A Domain Based Testing Toll. In *IEEE International Test Conference* (pp. 840-849). 10.1109/TEST.1994.528031

Miller, G. A. (1995). WordNet: A Lexical Database for English. *Communications of the ACM, 38*(11), 39–41. doi:10.1145/219717.219748

Myers, G. J. (2004). *The Art of Software Testing* (2nd ed.). Hoboken, NJ: John Wiley & Sons.

Nauman, J. D., & Jenkins, A. M. (1982). Prototyping: The New Paradigm for System Development. *Management Information Systems Quarterly, 6*(3), 29–44. doi:10.2307/248654

Nikolik, B. (2012). Software quality assurance economics. *Information and Software Technology, 54*(11), 1229–1238. doi:10.1016/j.infsof.2012.06.003

Orso, A., & Rothermel, G. (2014). Software testing: a research travelogue (2000–2014). *Proceedings of the on Future of Software Engineering*, 117-132.

Owterweil, L. (1996). Strategic directions in software quality. *ACM Computing Surveys, 28*(4).

Pal, K. (1999). An approach to legal reasoning based on a hybrids decision-support system. *Expert Systems with Applications, 1*(1), 1–12. doi:10.1016/S0957-4174(99)00015-9

Pal, K. (2017). Supply Chain Coordination Based on web Service. In H. K. Chan, N. Subramanian, & M. D. Abdulrahman (Eds.), *Supply Chain Management in Big Data Era* (pp. 137–170). Hershey, PA: IGI Publication. doi:10.4018/978-1-5225-0956-1.ch009

Pal, K. (2019). Markov Decision Theory-Based Crowdsourcing Software Process Model. In V. Gupta (Ed.), *Crowdsourcing and Probabilistic Decision-Making in Software Engineering: Emerging Research and Opportunities* (pp. 1–22). Hershey, PA: IGI Global Publishing.

Pal, K. & Campbell, J.A. (1997). An application of rule-based and case-based reasoning within a single legal knowledge-based system. *ACM SIGMIS Database: the DATABASE for Advances in Information Systems, 28*(4), 48-63.

Pal, K., & Palmer, O. (2000). A decision-support system for business acquisition. *Decision Support Systems, 27*(4), 411–429. doi:10.1016/S0167-9236(99)00083-4

Pfleeger, S. L., & Atlee, J. M. (2006). *Software Engineering: Theory and Practice*. London, UK: Pearson.

Prahalad, C. K., & Mashelkar, R. A. (2010). Innovation's Holy Grail. *Harvard Business Review, 88*(7/8), 132–141.

Shao, Z. L., Bai, X, Y., & Zhao, C.C. (2006). Research and implementation of a reuse-oriented test design model. *Journal of Mini-Micro Systems, 27*, 2150-2155.

Shepperd, M., & Schofield, C. (1997). Estimating software project effort using analogies. *IEEE Transactions on Software Engineering, 23*(11), 736–743. doi:10.1109/32.637387

Vasanthapriyan, S., Tan, J., Zhao, D., Xiong, S., & Xiang, J. (2017). An Ontology-based Knowledge Sharing Portal for Software Testing. *IEEE International Conference on Software Quality, Reliability and Security*, 472-479. 10.1109/QRS-C.2017.82

Wang, H., Xing, J., Yang, Q., Song, W., & Zhang, X. (2016). Generating effective test cases based on satisfiability modulo theory solvers for service-oriented workflow applications. *Software Testing, Verification & Reliability*, *26*(2), 149–169. doi:10.1002tvr.1592

Watson, I. (2003). *Applying Knowledge Management: techniques for building corporate memories*. San Francisco, CA: Morgan Kaufmann Publishers.

Xiao-Li, L., Wei, G., Xin-Li, C., & Ke-Gang, H. (2006). Designing a test case library system of supporting sharing and reusing. *Journal of Computational Science*, *33*, 290–291.

Xu, R., Chen, B., & Chen, B., Wu, M., & Xiong Z. (2003). Investigation on the pattern for Construction of Reusable Test Cases in Object-oriented Software. *Journal of Wuhan University*, *49*(5), 592–596.

KEY TERMS AND DEFINITIONS

Case-Based Reasoning: The main idea of case-based reasoning (CBR) is to adapt solutions that were used to solve previous problems and use them for solving latest problems (cases). A CBR system consists of a case base (which is the set of all cases that are known to the system) and an inferencing mechanism to drive a solution from the stored cases.

Critical Software Systems: Software whose failure would impact safety or cause large financial or social losses.

Ontology: Information sharing among business partners using information system is an important enabler for business operations management. There are different types of data to be shared across business operations, namely – order, demand, inventory, shipment, and customer service. Consequently, information about these issues needs to be shared in order to achieve efficiency and effectiveness. In this way, information-sharing activities require that human and/or machine agents agree on common and explicit business related concepts (the shared conceptualizations among hardware/software agents, customers, and service providers) are known as explicit ontologies; and these help to exchange data and derived knowledge out of the data to achieve collaborative goals of business operations.

Rule-Based Reasoning: In conventional rule-based reasoning, both common sense knowledge and domain specific domain expertise (i.e. software testing) are represented in the forms of plausible rules (e.g. IF <precondition(s)> THEN <conclusion(s)>. For example, an instance of a rule in common law: IF {(Jo has a driving license) AND (Jo is drunk) AND (Jo is stopped by police)} THEN {(Jo's driving license will be revoked by the transport authority)}. Moreover, rule-based reasoning requires an exact match on the precondition(s) to predict the conclusion(s). This is very restrictive, as real-world situations are often fuzzy and do not match exactly with rule preconditions. Thus, there are some extensions to the basic approach that can accommodate partial degrees of matching in rule preconditions.

Software Life Cycle Processes: It provides a framework for the sequence of activities to be performed for software projects.

Software Process Standards: It presents fundamental standards that describe activities performed as part of the software life cycle. In some cases, these standards also describe documents, but these represent plans for conducting activities.

Software Quality: Software engineering standards, if sufficiently comprehensive and if properly enforced, establish a *quality system*, a systematic approach to ensuring software quality, which is defined as (1) the degree to which a system, component, or process meets specified requirements and (2) the degree to which a system, component, or process meets customer or user needs or expectations.

Software Quality Assurance: Software quality assurance is defined as follows (1) a planned and systematic pattern of all actions necessary to provide adequate confidence that an item or product conforms to established technical requirements and (2) a set of activities designed to evaluate the process by which products are developed or manufactured.

Software Testing: Software testing provides the mechanism for verifying that the requirements identified during the initial phases of the project were properly implemented and that the system performs as expected. The test scenarios developed through these competitions ensures that the requirements are met end-to-end.

Verification and Validation: The process of determining whether the requirements for a system or component are complete and correct, the products of each development phase fulfill the requirements or conditions imposed by the previous phase, and the final system or component complies with specified requirements.

This research was previously published in Software Engineering for Agile Application Development; pages 212-229, copyright year 2020 by Engineering Science Reference (an imprint of IGI Global).

Chapter 56
An Effective Approach to Test Suite Reduction and Fault Detection Using Data Mining Techniques

B. Subashini

K.L.N College of Engineering, Madurai, India

D. Jeya Mala

Department of Computer Applications, Thiagarajar College of Engineering, Madurai, India

ABSTRACT

Software testing is used to find bugs in the software to provide a quality product to the end users. Test suites are used to detect failures in software but it may be redundant and it takes a lot of time for the execution of software. In this article, an enormous number of test cases are created using combinatorial test design algorithms. Attribute reduction is an important preprocessing task in data mining. Attributes are selected by removing all weak and irrelevant attributes to reduce complexity in data mining. After preprocessing, it is not necessary to test the software with every combination of test cases, since the test cases are large and redundant, the healthier test cases are identified using a data mining techniques algorithm. This is healthier and the final test suite will identify the defects in the software, it will provide better coverage analysis and reduces execution time on the software.

1. INTRODUCTION

Software testing is a process of executing a program or application with the intent of finding errors in the software. A test case is an identity which is associated with a program. The primary purpose of a test case is to find bugs. A potential drawback in testing is the creation of a large number of test cases, a test suite. Test cases should be created with high probability to uncover bugs. Testing the software or application with test suite takes an enormous amount of time in execution and it also increases the

DOI: 10.4018/978-1-6684-3702-5.ch056

computational effort of running the entire test suite. Complete software testing means every statement in the program and every possible path combination with every possible combination of data must be executed. In this paper, the combinations of test cases are created using IPOG_D algorithm with the help of parameters and constraints for the specific system (Lei, Kacker, Kuhn et al., 2008). Lot of test cases are generated using this IPOG_D algorithm and it may be redundant. It is necessary to identify irrelevant and redundant test cases and reduce it. For the reduction of test case, the feature selection is the first step for eliminating irrelevant attributes in the data set. Then classification technique is applied to find the accuracy of the testing application. Secondly, the test data is checked with the training data for the fault detection. The resultant and reduced test data is used to test the program and check the program for coverage analysis and execution time. By this usage of reduced test suite, the time, cost and effort for execution of the program may be reduced as because of the removal of redundant test cases by the mining technique. It may improve the effectiveness of software testing by the selection of effective test cases.

2. MATERIALS AND METHODS

2.1. Background

Software testing is an action to confirm the actual outcomes with the expected outcomes and assure that the product framework is without defect. Test Case is a cluster of activities executed to check a specific aspect or effectiveness of programming application. The objective of any product venture is to formulate test cases which meet client prerequisite. In this article, huge records of the test case are automatically generated by using the combinatorial testing method, it may be redundant and it is required to eliminate repeated test cases. Test suites are minimized and the faults are forecasted by using the classification technique. Reduction in test suite will minimize the time of execution, effort and it will provide better coverage analysis.

2.2. Combinatorial Testing

Pairwise testing is a combinatorial method of test cases in software testing, the input parameters for the system is tested with all possible discrete combinations of the values of parameters. The combinatorial testing focuses on t-way test data generation, where each test t contains a set of values for parameters. When the combinations of input parameters increase the testing will be effective with all possible combinations of values (Lei et al., 2008). Since, the effort of testing is based upon the input parameters, each and every parameter much contribute to a fault and the faults are caused by the interaction between the inputs, these possible combinations of test cases are produced with high-quality testing of coverage in the system.

Each and every program or a system contains a distinct series of behaviors; first, the input parameters for the system must be fully identified. The input values pass for the parameters is identified as second. Thus, the possible input values for each and every parameter for the system are identified and the values are passed. The values passed to the input parameter may be passed upon boundary value analysis, equivalence partitioning method or random value testing method. Each and every value for the parameter contains both the valid as well as invalid data.

The lists of values for each parameter are combined using IPO algorithm. The values for each parameter are combined using t-way data generation to generate combinatorial test suites.

The overview of the algorithm IPO is given as, with any t parameters for testing the system, every combination of values of these parameters should be covered in the system by at least one of the combinations of the test. The parameters in this IPO algorithm are extended by horizontal growth. The number of values which is not covered by the system is extended by vertical growth (Lei et al., 2008).

2.2.1. The framework of the IPOG

For building a system with t-way parameter, the first t-way is the first parameter, the t-way parameter can be extended till the strategy includes all parameter for the system. The addition of parameters consists of two steps 1) horizontal growth 2) vertical growth.

The horizontal growth extends the new parameter till the system reaches the goal. The vertical growth extends the test values for the parameters if the coverage of the system is not tested. The IPOG algorithm utilizes local optimums to provide a bound of accuracy for worst case scenarios. The Fire Eye tool implements the IPOG algorithm to generate combinatorial test suites for users. The test cases are automatically generated by this tool for some case studies. These test cases are treated as an original test suite or training test set. Since the test cases generated by this tool for the system are large and redundant. The main goal of test suite reduction is to reduce the number of test cases by eliminating irrelevant and infeasible test cases. It results in saving of software resources, cost and time devoid of executing the complete test suite. Test suite reduction techniques must also ensure that the reduced test suite ought to achieve the same coverage as the original test suite.

2.3. Test Suite Minimization

In Software Development Life Cycle, a test suite which is commonly known as validation suite is a collection of test cases. The test cases are intended to be used to test a software program for the success. The test cases generated for a miniature program is much greater. When testing the program with this set of test cases subsequently it takes much time. In order to stay away from this strategy test suite minimization plays a vital role in testing the program with minimum test cases and with minimum time consumption (Raamesh et al., 2009, 2010).

In this proposed work, data mining technique is applied for the reduction of test suites which result in better coverage like original test suite and for detecting faults in the test cases. The flow diagram of the proposed framework is given as Figure 1.

2.3.1 Proposed Framework

2.3.1.1. Test Case Generation

As enormous values of experiments are generated automatically by the combinatorial examination design method, all the experiments are not necessary for testing the program. It is basic for limiting test suite. Since significant numbers of attributes are given for a period of the test suite, yet simply the required numbers of properties are required for the time of yield.

Figure 1. Proposed Framework

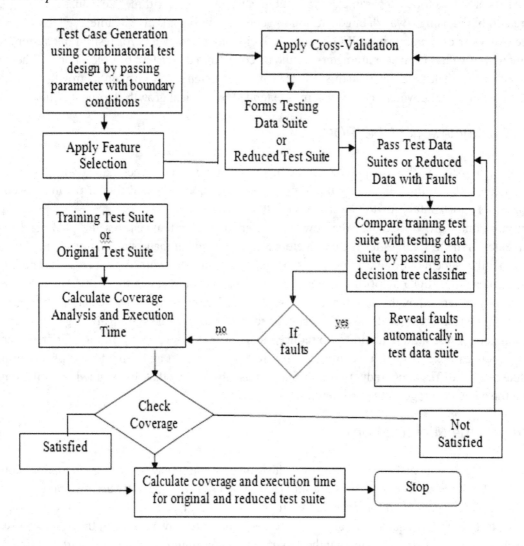

Data Mining likewise is prevalently known as Knowledge Discovery in Databases (KDD) (Gupta et al., 2015). It is a semi-robotized procedure of discovering designs in the information. There are various data mining techniques available for mining different kinds of data, including association rule, classification, and clustering (Raamesh et al., 2009; Williams et al., 2005).

2.3.1.2. Feature Selection

Feature subset in mining is the way toward recognizing and expelling however many unimportant and repetitive data as could be expected. This lessens the length of data and enables learning calculations to work quicker and all the more successfully.

Feature creation is a route toward choosing the subset of pertinent features. The Correlation Feature Selection measure assesses subsets of highlights on the idea of the accompanying speculation: "Great element subsets contain includes very associated with the grouping, nevertheless uncorrelated to every other". The accompanying condition gives the value of a component subset S comprising of k highlights:

$$Merit_{S_k} \quad \frac{k\overline{r_{cf}}}{\sqrt{k + k(k-1)\overline{r_{ff}}}}$$

In this paper, after removing the irrelevant information, the concluding data set of the test suite is considered as a training test suite. This training test set acted as an original test experiment and it is passed as a commitment to the application program. The time of execution and coverage analysis for the program is prepared.

2.3.1.3. Cross-Validation

Since the preparation test suites are vast it is significant to make smaller the test suite. The test suites are reduced with the aid of the cross-validation method. The randomized values of testing data suite are selected from the training data suite using the cross-approvals of 10 value which uses k-fold cross-justification.

In this work, the subsample of test experiment is taken as consideration for testing data set. As the testing data set are reduced, the effort is reduced for testing the application program with the condensed test suite. It is also a need to make confident that the coverage analysis should be better or same as that of the unique test suite. The carrying out time is also calculated with the reduced test suite.

2.3.1.4. Fault Prediction

Faults in programming frameworks keep on being a remarkable issue. Numbers of various strategies were utilized for programming fault prediction like genetic programming, decision trees, Naïve Bayes approaches, neural network, artificial immune system and fuzzy logic algorithms (Golnoush Abaei et al., 2013).

In this work, the condensed experiments are considered as a testing data set. The condensed test suite is incorporated with some faults. The trying data suite has been practiced by using the preparation data suite; it is mandatory to check the model by making predictions against the test data suite.

The subsamples of test informational index contain the known esteems for the quality, it is significant to foresee the deficiencies against the test informational collection. The forecasts of deficiencies for the test suites are done naturally utilizing decision tree based classifier algorithm.

Choice Trees calculation makes the collection of conceivable information esteems. The informational index is isolated into a preparation set and testing set, a large portion of the information is utilized for preparing, and a littler segment of the information is employed for testing. Here, the preparation data set operates as original test suite and testing data set take actions as a testing test suite. The prediction of faults in the reduced test suites are automatically detected and automatically changed using the decision tree algorithm. The fault prediction margin value is calculated with the help of training test suite and testing test suite.

The illustration of the trial experiment suite contains both fault and non-fault prone test suites. The procedure is repetitive until fault prone test suite is converted into non-fault prone test suite using the classifier algorithm.

Subsequent to foreseeing the deficiencies in the testing test suite and it is fault free, the testing test suite is finalized as the lessened test suite. Exactness for both original or unique test experiment and diminished test experiment is computed.

2.3.1.5. Coverage Analysis

Measure of testing performed by an arrangement of experiments is called Test Coverage. Test scope measures the measure of testing carry out by an arrangement of test. It will incorporate gathering data about which parts of a program are really executed when running the test experiment and outline out which branches of contingent justifications have been taken. The basic coverage is exercised by using

$$Coverage = \frac{Number\ of\ Coverage\ items\ exercised}{Total\ number\ of\ coverage\ items} \times 100$$

In this paper, the preparation test suite and testing test suite are considered as a unique and lessened test suite. It is essential to check code scope for both the first or unique and diminished test suite.

The unique test suite gives good coverage and it takes more time to execute since the test experiments are large. The code scope is recognized by using the lessened test suite, it will likewise give great scope with less execution time.

If the code scope of the diminished suite is not good, then the process will be repeated to take better test experiment to achieve better code scope as like first test suite. After all the process is over with test suites the completing time and code scope for either the first or original and the lessened test suite are calculated. From this analysis, the diminished test suite will be enough for testing the program quite than using first test suite. It spares time, exertion, cost and better scope.

2.3.1.6. Algorithm

Generate test cases (t1, t2 …tm) using automated tools and it is treated as an original test suite.

1. Apply feature selection for selecting the required attributes to be output.
2. This original test suite act as a training test suite (t1, t2 …tn).
3. Pass the original test suites to software application code.
4. Detect the execution time of test cases, coverage analysis.
5. Apply cross validation method in the training data set.
6. The randomized test suite forms the reduced test suite or testing data suite. This forms the sub-samples of training data suite and it is considered as a testing data suite (t1, t3, t5, …tn)
7. Add faults into testing data suite.
8. Apply decision tree classifier algorithm.
9. Compare training data suite with the testing data suite and the faults should be automatically re-vealed using decision tree classifier algorithm.
10. If fault occurred reveal the fault repeatedly
11. If no faults occurred pass the reduced test suite to the application code.
12. Check the coverage analysis of the program
13. If the coverage analysis of the reduced test suite is satisfied as like the original test suite.
14. Calculate the execution time and coverage analysis of the reduced test suite.
15. Compare step 4 and step 14
16. If not good coverage repeat step 5.

3. EVALUATION AND RESULT ANALYSIS

3.1. Test Case Generation

In this paper, large numbers of test cases are generated using combinatorial test design algorithm.

3.1.1. Combinatorial Test Suite Generation

Consider the first case study, from Table 1, the placement selection which has nine parameters: Each of these parameters can take on one of five possible options. The tool generates a combinatorial test suite for the given input. The user enters the list of parameters and the possible values which are required for their system to be tested either it may be a nominal value, boundary value or categorical value. The possible value depends upon the requirements specification of the system. The tool then automatically generates t-way test suite based on the IPOG_D algorithm with the strength of parameters for the coverage of test data, which the user needs (Lei et al., 2007). If the strength of test suite is 2 then it creates less number of test suites, if the strength becomes higher than the test suite created by the tool is large which covers all the test data for the system and the coverage of testing will be good, but care should be taken that the strength must be always less than the number of parameters list.

Sample combinations of test suite created for the system of case study 1: the biggest among three numbers (Figure 2).

The combinations of the 3 numbers, a, b, c, are combined with strength = 3 and the resultant combinations are given as (Figure 3),

The combinations of the attributes for student placement selection are combined and the resultant combinations are given as Figure 4,

The number of test suites created for case study: 1 checking biggest among three numbers, the sample test suites created for this system is 144 having strength = 3.

The number of test suites created for case study: 2 student placement selection, the number of test suite generated for the parameters with the strength 5 is 3750 test suite (Table 2).

The sample test suites are given below as,

Here, in Table 3, the number of test suite created for case study of some programs are given as,

3.2. Feature Selection

In this paper, various attribute selection evaluator and the methods are evaluated for selecting the relevant attributes. The Subset evaluator with Search method is used for selecting and ranking the attributes. Correlation Feature selection measure evaluates the subsets of features on the basis of

$$\text{Merit } S_k = \frac{k\overline{r_{cf}}}{\sqrt{k + k(k-1)\overline{r_{ff}}}} \qquad (1)$$

Here rcf is the average value of all the feature-classification correlations, and rff is the average value of all the feature-feature correlations.

Figure 2. Boundary value for biggest among three numbers

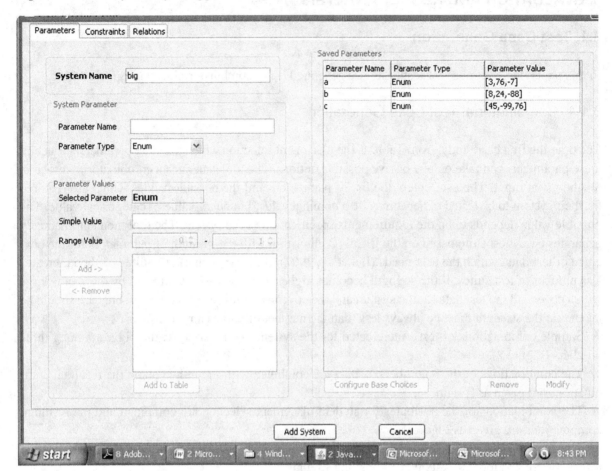

Information gain can be evaluated for ranking the attributes using

$$Gain(A) = Info(D) - Info_A(D) \qquad (2)$$

In the above case study: 1 of biggest among three numbers the input variables are taken as a, b and c (Table 4). These input variables are all needed for the program so all the variables are taken into consideration and test inputs are passed to the program.

In the above case study: 2 of placement selection the input variables used name, roll no, sex, communication, board, 10th mark, 12th mark, UG percentage, PG percentage, Number of PG arrears. Depending on this data the eligibility criteria for the student to attend an interview with the company to be selected. Since the required or relevant attributes for this case study are rollno, 10th mark, 12th mark, UG percentage, PG percentage, and Number of PG arrears. So, the selection of relevant attributes is preferred.

Since the test cases created by the combinatorial test cases are larger and it is not able to store the output of the program manually the test cases are given as input to the testing program and the output of the program is stored automatically.

Figure 3. Combinations of test cases for biggest among three numbers

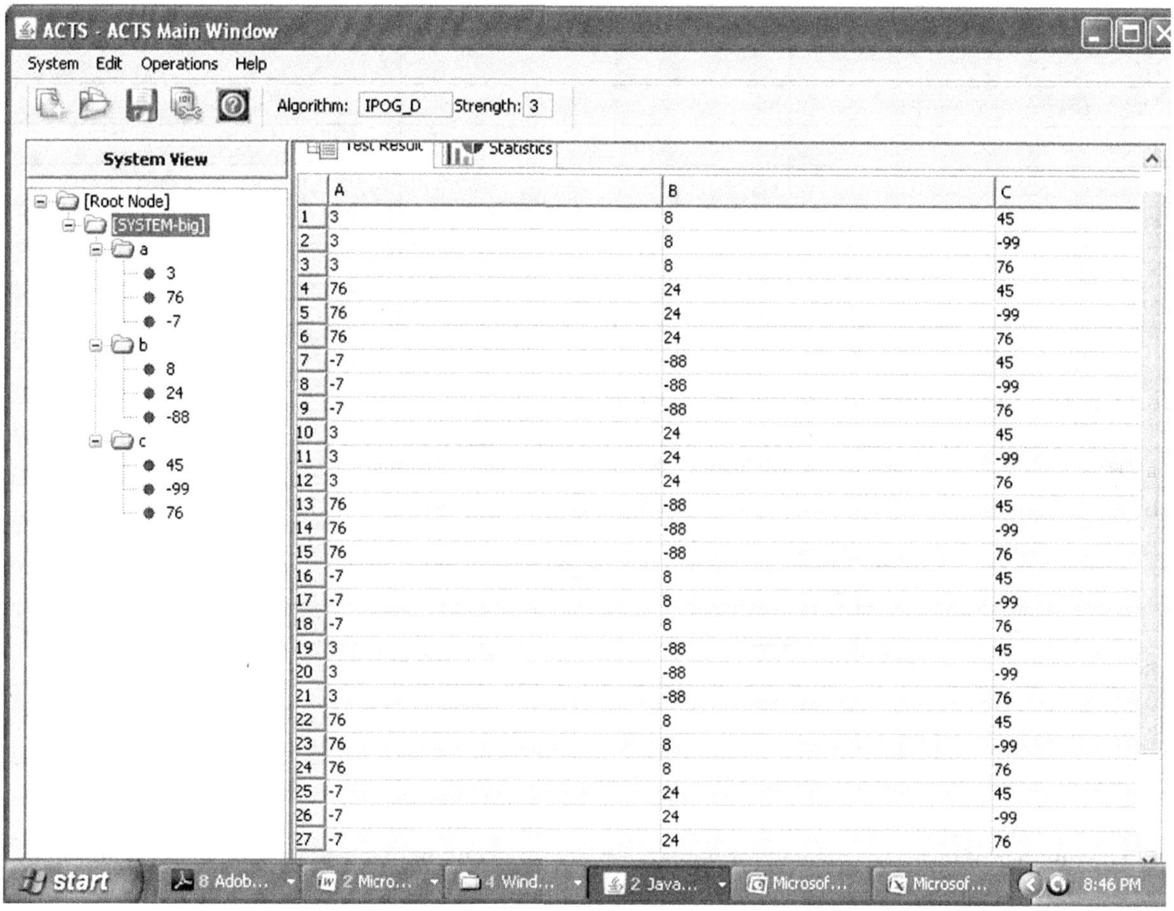

ACTS - ACTS Main Window

System   Edit   Operations   Help

Algorithm: IPOG_D   Strength: 3

System View — Test Result / Statistics

[Root Node]
- [SYSTEM-big]
  - a
    - 3
    - 76
    - -7
  - b
    - 8
    - 24
    - -88
  - c
    - 45
    - -99
    - 76

	A	B	C
1	3	8	45
2	3	8	-99
3	3	8	76
4	76	24	45
5	76	24	-99
6	76	24	76
7	-7	-88	45
8	-7	-88	-99
9	-7	-88	76
10	3	24	45
11	3	24	-99
12	3	24	76
13	76	-88	45
14	76	-88	-99
15	76	-88	76
16	-7	8	45
17	-7	8	-99
18	-7	8	76
19	3	-88	45
20	3	-88	-99
21	3	-88	76
22	76	8	45
23	76	8	-99
24	76	8	76
25	-7	24	45
26	-7	24	-99
27	-7	24	76

start   8 Adob...   2 Micro...   4 Wind...   2 Java...   Microsof...   Microsof...   8:46 PM

Figure 4. Combination of test cases for placement selection

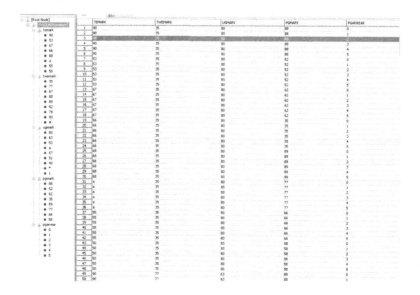

Table 1. Test suite created for biggest among three numbers

a	b	c
111	a	45
222	50	45
333	60	78
444	65	64
555	56	58
666	56	56
777	53	35

Table 2. Test suite created for Placement Selection

RollNo	Name	Sex	Communication	Board	10th mark	12th mark	UG %	PG %	Pg Arrear
111	Aaa	M	Good	Cbse	a	45	67	67	0
222	Bbb	F	Average	State	50	45	67	67	1
333	Ccc	F	Good	State	60	78	77	75	0
444	Ddd	F	Average	Cbse	65	64	66	64	1
555	Eee	M	Average	Cbse	56	58	57	57	4
666	Fff	M	Good	State	56	56	57	58	0
777	Ggg	M	Average	State	53	35	)	67	3

The number of test cases created for biggest among three numbers is 144 the output is set automatically and the sample test cases are given as below in Table 5,

The number of test cases created for placement selection is 3750 the output is set automatically based upon conditions. If the person has no arrear and all marks >=60, the person is eligible for company=tcs, If the person has arrear>=0 and arrear<=3 and all marks >=55, the person is eligible for company=Wipro., If the person has arrear>3 and arrear<=5 and all marks >=55, the person is an eligible for company=other company. If the person has scored any of the mark <55 then the person is eligible for company=not eligible. If the data for marks is entered as wrong input then the class label is given for eligible for company=not valid. The sample test cases for placement selection are given as below in Table 6,

Next process is testing the program with test cases. The repository contains the test cases. JUNIT is applied for testing the program with the test suites, which contains in the repository. Testing the program or software with both positive and negative way and with both the valid and invalid inputs identifies the behavior of the program (Mei, Hao, Zhang et al., 2012). This is an effective part of testing.

A good test case is designed in such a way that it is a high probability of finding an error. The given input data is passed to the program and check the expected output. If the output shaped by the program and the expected output is very similar then the test case is said to be a pass (passed test case) otherwise it is said to fail (failed test case). The numbers of passed and failed test cases are calculated and the execution time for these test cases is also calculated.

Table 3. Creation of Test Suites

Program	No Of Parameters	Strength for the parameters	Total No. of Test Suites (t-way combinations of parameters)
Biggest among 3 numbers	3	2	49
		3	144
Placement Selection	10	2	145
		5	3750
Login form (Username, Password)	2	2	36
Quadratic Equation	3	2	56
		3	144
Bank loan dataset	14	-	4522
Student Mark Analysis	21	-	108
Employee Increment details	14	2	13347
		3	22281
Eligibility for voting	8	3	120
		4	240
Iris Dataset	4	2	66
		3	216
Weather dataset	5	2	70
		3	210
Types of triangle	3	3	144

Number of Passed and failed test cases and its execution time is calculated as

$$Timeexec = EndTimeexec - StartTimeexec \qquad (3)$$

Execution trace is based on effective testing to adequately cover program logic, all conditions and statements which are executed by a test and trace are gathered. Execution trace of the test is using the test inputs to exercise each test run is passed or failed and checks the coverage information of the program.

Now, the Table for case study 1: is changed to the format, the class label used for the classification technique is pass or fail, if the given test input and the expected output of the program are identical then the class label is set as pass otherwise the class label is set as fail. Table 7 shows the class label set for the biggest among three numbers.

The test suites are given as input and the status of each and every test cases (pass or fail) are identified and stored in the repository. While executing all these test cases, the execution time of these test suites is calculated, the execution time calculated for biggest among three numbers are given as Figure 5.

Now, the Table for case study 2(Placement Selection): is changed to the format, the class label used for the classification technique is pass or fail, if the given test input and the expected output of the program are identical then the class label is set as pass otherwise the class label is set as fail and it is stored in the repository. The sample test cases are given below in Table 8 as,

Table 4. Attribute Selection

Case studies	Evaluator	Search Method	Selected Attributes
Biggest among numbers	CorrelationAttributeEval	Ranker	3
	InfoGainAttributeEval		
	GainRatioAttributeEval		
Placement Selection	CfsSubsetEval	BestFirst	6
	CorrelationAttributeEval	Ranker	9
	InfoGainAttributeEval		
	GainRatioAttributeEval		
Quadratic Equation	CorrelationAttributeEval	Ranker	3
	InfoGainAttributeEval		
	GainRatioAttributeEval		
Bank loan dataset	CfsSubsetEval (job,loan,net_salary)	BestFirst	3
	CorrelationAttributeEval	Ranker	14
	InfoGainAttributeEval		
	GainRatioAttributeEval		
Student Mark Analysis	InfoGainAttributeEval	Ranker	13
	GainRatioAttributeEval		
Employee Increment details	InfoGainAttributeEval	Ranker	13
	GainRatioAttributeEval		
Eligibility for voting	InfoGainAttributeEval	Ranker	8
	GainRatioAttributeEval		
Iris Dataset	InfoGainAttributeEval	Ranker	4
	GainRatioAttributeEval		
Weather dataset	CfsSubsetEval	BestFirst	2
	CorrelationAttributeEval	Ranker	4
	InfoGainAttributeEval		
	GainRatioAttributeEval		
Types of triangle	CorrelationAttributeEval	Ranker	3
	InfoGainAttributeEval		
	GainRatioAttributeEval		

While executing all these test cases, the execution time of these test suites is calculated, the execution time calculated for Placement selection is given as Figure 6.

Likewise, for all the case studies, the test cases are passed using JUnit and the class label for each input is identified, the execution time is calculated for test suites and the corresponding output for each case study is given below in Table 9,

Table 5. Sample output set for biggest among three numbers

a	b	c	result
92	90	6	a
g	9	100	not_valid
92	-1	100	c
(	112	6	not_valid
-102	112	6	b

Table 6. Sample output set for placement selection

Roll No	10th mark	12th mark	UG %	PG %	Pg Arrear	Eligibility company
1	a	45	67	67	0	not_valid
2	56	56	57	58	0	Wipro
3	60	78	77	75	0	tcs
4	50	45	67	67	1	not_eligible
5	57	58	56	57	5	other
6	67	45	67	67	0	tcs

Table 7. Class label set for biggest among three numbers

a	b	c	result	Class label(Cl)
92	90	6	a	Pass
g	9	100	not_valid	Fail
102	90	45	a	Pass
92	-1	6	b	Fail
92	-1	100	c	Pass
14	9	100	c	Pass
g	0	6	not_valid	Fail
(	112	6	not_valid	Fail
-102	112	6	b	Pass
14	90	6	b	Pass
14	-1	6	a	Pass
92	9	11	a	Pass
92	9	45	c	Fail
14	0	6	a	Pass
14	0	100	c	Pass
14	0	11	a	Pass
14	0	45	c	Pass
102	90	6	a	Pass

Figure 5. Running test suite, identifying the status of test cases and calculation of execution time

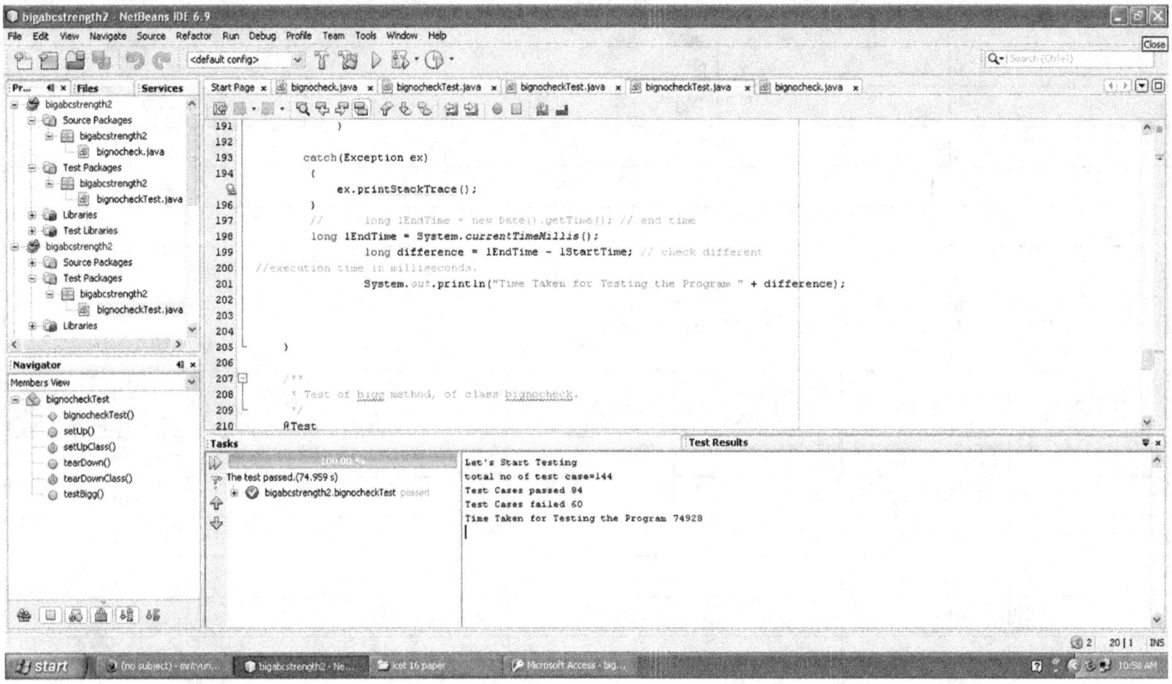

The relationship between the code coverage and number of test cases described by the following expression is given by

$$C(x) = 1 - e^{(-p/N)*x} \tag{4}$$

When testing the program or software with the test suites, coverage analysis will be confirmed for the concern program or software. Some test case may cover all the lines in the program; some may uncover some lines in the program. So, coverage analysis plays a role to check whether all the statements, conditions, paths are covered by the test suite (Figures 7 and 8).

Table 8. Class label set for biggest among three numbers

Roll No	10th mark	12th mark	UG %	PG %	Pg Arrear	Eligibility company	Class label(Cl)
1	a	45	67	67	0	not_valid	Pass
2	56	56	57	58	0	Wipro	Pass
3	60	78	77	75	0	tcs	Pass
4	50	45	67	67	1	not_eligible	Pass
5	57	58	56	57	5	other	Pass
6	67	45	67	67	0	tcs	Fail

Figure 6. Execution time calculated for Placement selection

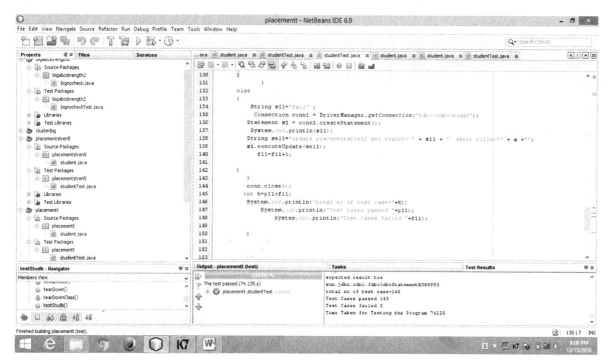

Table 9. Calculation of execution time for training set

Program	Reduced Parameters	Strength for the parameters	Time taken for Execution
Biggest among 3 numbers	3	2	28281
		3	74928
Placement Selection	6	2	71282
		5	420926
Login form	2	2	1650
Quadratic Equation	3	2	25281
		3	80811
Bank loan dataset	14	-	186647
Student Mark Analysis	13	-	174926
Employee Increment details	14	2	256826
Eligibility for voting	8	4	67568
Iris Dataset	4	3	63246
Weather dataset	4	3	71256
Types of triangle	3	3	62579

The coverage of the program is given as

Figure 7. Coverage analysis with test suite

Since it takes more time for executing the test cases, this paper aims to reduce the size of the test suite and remains the same coverage as the original test suite. Data mining technique, classification is applied for the reduction in the test suite and it predicts the behavior of the data.

Classification is a data mining and machine learning approach, useful in software bug prediction. The algorithm processes a training set containing a set of attributes and the respective outcome, called goal or prediction attribute. The testing data set tries to discover the relationship between the attributes that would make it possible to predict the outcome which possess fault prediction in software testing before testing the application.

The objects in the dataset of Placement Selection which contains roll no, tenth mark, 12th mark, UG Percentage, PG Percentage, No of arrears in PG and the resultant value of the eligible company of each person. The class values for the data set are given as pass or fail. This dataset contains 10 attributes, since these attributes of 10 are reduced to 6 attributes by using correlation-based feature selection.

Figure 8. Coverage result after the execution of test suites

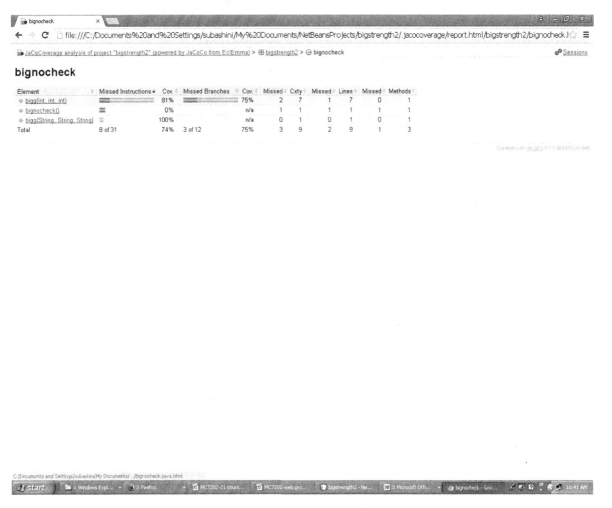

With these 6 attributes values and the resultant value of Eligibility Company and the resultant test case with pass or fail, the program is treated as a training data set. The model derived from that classification, the testing data set can then predict if a data given for eligibility for placement selection according to attributes of training data. The training datasets need to be in arff format. The testing datasets need to be in arff format. The sample training and testing

The objects in this dataset of biggest among three numbers which contain a, b, c and resultant value. The class values are given as pass or fail. The dataset contains 4 attributes a,b,c, result value, with this information classification model is used to find whether the test case is pass or fail for the program. The model derived from that classification, the testing data can then predict if a data is given for finding biggest among three numbers according to attributes of training data. The training datasets need to be in arff format. The testing datasets need to be in arff format. The sample training and testing data set are,

Training data Set for Placement Selection

@relation placement

@attribute name string
@attribute rollno numeric
@attribute board{cbse,state}
@attribute commu{good,bad}
@attribute temark numeric
@attribute tweemark numeric
@attribute ugmark numeric
@attribute pgmark numeric
@attribute pgarrear numeric
@attribute classlabel {tcs,wipro,not_eligible,other}
@attribute result {fail,pass}
@data
aaa, 1, cbse, good, 67, 45, 67, 67, 0, tcs, fail
bbb, 2, state, bad, 50, 45, 67, 67, 1, not_eligible, pass
ccc, 3, state, good, 60, 78, 77, 75, 0, tcs, pass
ddd, 4, state, good, 65, 67, 67, 68, 1, wipro, pass
eee, 5, cbse, good, 67, 88, 88, 66, 2, wipro, pass
fff, 6, cbse, bad, 56, 56, 57, 58, 0, wipro, pass
ggg, 7, cbse, good, 78, 77, 64, 64, 3, wipro, pass
hhh, 8, cbse, good, 56, 56, 57, 57, 4, other, pass
iii, 9, state, good, 57, 58, 56, 57, 5, other, pass
jjj, 10, state, good, 66, 66, 66, 66, 3, wipro, pass
kkk, 11, state, good, 65, 64, 66, 65, 1, wipro, pass
lll, 12, cbse, good, 66, 65, 65, 64, 4, other, pass
mmm, 13, cbse, good, 65, 62, 66, 66, 2, wipro, pass
nnn, 14, state, average, 50, 45, 51, 52, 3, not_eligible, pass
ooo, 15, state, average, 50, 45, 51, 52, 5, tcs, fail
ppp, 16, cbse, average, 50, 45, 40, 62, 0, not_eligible, pass
qqq, 17, cbse, good, 50, 45, 77, 62, 1, not_eligible, pass
rrr, 18, state, good, 50, 45, 40, 62, 2, not_eligible, pass
sss, 19, cbse, good, 56, 57, 58, 59, 0, wipro, pass
ttt, 20, state, good, 65, 66, 63, 65, 4, other, pass
uuu, 21, cbse, good, 50, 45, 53, 35, 0, not_eligible, pass
vvv, 22, state, good, 50, 45, 53, 35, 1, not_eligible, pass
www, 23, cbse, bad, 50, 45, 53, 35, 2, not_eligible, pass
xxx, 24, state, good, 56, 58, 59, 59, 2, wipro, pass
yyy, 25, state, good, 56, 57, 56, 58, 1, wipro, pass
zzz, 26, state, good, 45, 67, 67, 67, 0, not_eligible, pass
a, 27, state, good, 45, 67, 67, 67, 1, not_eligible, pass
b, 28, state, good, 45, 67, 67, 67, 2, not_eligible, pass
c, 29, state, average, 45, 67, 67, 67, 3, not_eligible, pass
d, 30, state, good, 45, 67, 67, 67, 5, not_eligible, pass
e, 31, state, average, 55, 58, 56, 59, 5, other, pass
f, 32, state, good, 45, 67, 57, 89, 1, not_eligible, pass
g, 33, state, bad, 89, 90, 88, 87, 0, tcs, pass
h, 34, state, good, 55, 58, 59, 59, 2, wipro, pass
i, 35, cbse, good, 45, 67, 57, 89, 5, not_eligible, pass
k, 36, cbse, bad, 45, 67, 51, 52, 0, not_eligible, pass

The testing data set for Placement Selection
(with faults)

@relation placement

@attribute name string
@attribute rollno numeric
@attribute board{cbse,state}
@attribute commu{good,bad}
@attribute temark numeric
@attribute tweemark numeric
@attribute ugmark numeric
@attribute pgmark numeric
@attribute pgarrear numeric
@attribute classlabel {tcs,wipro,not_eligible,other}
@attribute result {fail,pass}
@data
aaa, 1, cbse, good, 67, 45, 67, 67, 0, tcs, pass

(but the result is fail)

bbb, 2, state, bad, 50, 45, 67, 67, 1, not_eligible, pass
ccc, 3, state, good, 60, 78, 77, 75, 0, tcs, pass
ddd, 4, state, good, 65, 67, 67, 68, 1, wipro, pass
eee, 5, cbse, good, 67, 88, 88, 66, 2, wipro, pass
fff, 6, cbse, bad, 56, 56, 57, 58, 0, wipro, fail

(but the result is pass)

ooo, 15, state, average, 50, 45, 51, 52, 5, tcs, fail
ppp, 16, cbse, average, 50, 45, 40, 62, 0, not_eligible, pass
hhh, 8, cbse, good, 56, 56, 57, 57, 4, other, pass
iii, 9, state, good, 57, 58, 56, 57, 5, other, pass
rrr, 18, state, good, 50, 45, 40, 62, 2, not_eligible, fail

(but the result is pass)

sss, 19, cbse, good, 56, 57, 58, 59, 0, tcs, pass

(but the result is fail)

ttt, 20, state, good, 65, 66, 63, 65, 4, other, pass
uuu, 21, cbse, good, 50, 45, 53, 35, 0, not_eligible, pass

Decision tree induction is the learning of a decision tree from class-labeled training tuples to find the accuracy of the data set. When the training and testing data are passed as an input for decision tree algorithm, then the possible splits are made between attributes for the training dataset as

<u>Training data Set for biggest among three numbers</u>

@relation bigstren3

@attribute a {92,14,g,(,102}
@attribute b {90,-1,9,0,112,56,1}
@attribute c {6,100,11,45}
@attribute classlabel {a,b,c,not_valid}
@attribute result {fail,pass}

@data
92,90,6,a,pass
g,9,100,not_valid,fail
102,90,45,a,pass
92,-1,6,a,pass
92,-1,100,c,pass
92,-1,11,a,pass
92,-1,45,a,pass
14,9,6,a,pass
14,9,100,c,pass
14,9,11,a,pass
14,9,45,c,pass
g,0,6,not_valid,fail
g,9,11,not_valid,fail
g,0,100,not_valid,fail
102,56,6,a,pass
102,56,100,a,pass
102,56,11,a,pass
g,9,45,not valid,fail
102,56,45,a,pass
92,90,6,a,pass
92,90,100,c,pass
92,90,11,a,pass
92,90,45,a,pass
14,-1,6,a,pass
14,-1,100,c,pass
14,-1,11,a,pass
14,-1,45,c,pass
G,9,6,not valid,fail
(,0,6,not valid,fail
102,112,6,b,pass

<u>The testing data set for biggest among three numbers</u>
(with faults)

@relation testbigstren3

@attribute a {92,14,g,(,102,*}
@attribute b {90,-1,9,0,112,56,1}
@attribute c {6,100,11,45}
@attribute classlabel {a,b,c,not_valid}
@attribute result {fail,pass}

@data
102,-1, 45, a, fail   (but the result is pass)
92, 90, 11, a, pass
102, 112, 6, b, pass
102, 112, 6, b, fail   (but the result is pass)
14,-1,100,c,pass
92,9,100,c,fail   (but the result is pass)
g,0,6,not_valid,pass   (but the result is fail)
(,112,11,not_valid,pass   (but the result is fail)
(, 90, 45, not_valid, fail
102,56, 6, a, fail   (but the result is pass)
102,9,100,a,fail   (but the result is pass)
102,90,100, a,pass
g,56,11,not_valid,pass   (but the result is fail)
102,90,11,a,pass
92, 9, 11, a, pass
102, 90,100, a, fail   (but the result is pass)
92,9,12,a,pass
92,56,11,a,pass
14,9, 11, a,pass
14,90, 100, c,fail   (but the result is pass)

$$\text{Info}_A(D) = -\sum_{j=1}^{v} \frac{|D_j|}{|D|} \times \text{Info}(D_j) \qquad (5)$$

The expected information needed to classify for the dataset is given by

$$\text{Info(D)} = -\sum_{i=1}^{n} P_i \log_2 P_i \tag{6}$$

Info(D) is also known as the entropy of D. Information gain is defined as the difference between the original information requirement and the new requirement. The information gain for the given dataset is calculated as

$$\text{Gain(A)} = \text{Info(D)} - \text{Info}_A(D) \tag{7}$$

The algorithm uses a percentage split and cross-validation of 10 folds (Table 10). With percentage split, the data set is divided into a training set and a test set. For the training set, 70% of the instances is used for the training date set, the test set as remaining part. Cross-validation is especially used when the amount of data is limited. Cross-validation repeats the training and testing process several times with different random samples. The standard for this is 10-fold cross-validation. The data is divided randomly into 10 parts in which the classes are represented in approximately the same proportions as in the full dataset. Each part is held out in turn and the algorithm is trained on the nine remaining parts; then its error rate is calculated on the holdout set. The accuracy value is calculated.

training data: 1 11 21 31 41 51 61 71 81 91 101 111 121 131 141 2 12 22 32 42 52 62 72 82 92 102 112 122 132 142 3 13 23 33 43 53 63 73 83 93 103 113 123 133 143 4 14 24 34 44 54 64 74 84 94 104 114 124 134 5 15 25 35 45 55 65 75 85 95 105 115 125 135 6 16 26 36 46 56 66 76 86 96 106 116 126 136 7 17 27 37 47 57 67 77 87 97 107 117 127 137 8 18 28 38 48 58 68 78 88 98 108 118 128 138 9 19 29 39 49 59 69 79 89 99 109 119 129 139
test data: 0 10 20 30 40 50 60 70 80 90 100 110 120 130 140

After accuracy value is calculated, fault revealing is also automatically done in the program using classification technique. The testing data set contain some faults in the result. The testing data set is compared with the training data set and the faults in test cases are identified and the faults in the particular test cases are revealed and the resultant value is changed and it is given below in Table 11 as,

The testing with a wrong class label can be changed to a correct class label when the testing data is compared with the training data. By using test data set for testing the program reduces execution time and coverage when compared with training data set.

The evaluation of the training data set, training dataset with 10 fold cross-validation, split 70% training data with 30% test data, user supplied test data before and after revealing data set is given in Table 12 as

The graph of the above data is given as Figure 9.

The accuracy percentage of the data set is calculated and it is given in Table 13 as

The accuracy value for the i) faulty data set is calculated, ii) after fault revealing the data set is considered to be fault revealed data set and it is given as input as the testing data set and the accuracy value is calculated, iii) the training data set alone is given without the testing data set with a 10 fold cross validation and the accuracy value is calculated iv) split of training data set is done, with 70% training data set and 30% as testing data set and the accuracy value is calculated and it is given below in Table 14,

The Confusion Matrix for various data set is given in Table 15 as,

Table 10. Accuracy calculation using training and test data with the fold. Cross-validation 10. The table shows for group 0

a	b	c	Class label	result	classification
92	90	6	a	pass	pass
14	9	45	c	pass	pass
102	56	6	a	pass	pass
14	1	100	c	pass	pass
(	0	11	not_valid	fail	fail
92	56	45	a	pass	pass
(	56	11	not_valid	fail	fail
g	1	45	not_valid	fail	fail
92	112	6	b	pass	pass
g	90	100	not_valid	fail	fail
14	1	100	c	pass	pass
g	56	6	not_valid	fail	fail
102	1	100	a	pass	pass
14	0	11	a	pass	pass
(	56	45	not_valid	fail	fail

correct: 15 wrong: 0 accuracy: 1.0

cross validation on group: 0

average accuracy of cross validation is 1.0

Table 11. Fault revealing in testing data

a	b	c	Class label	result
102	-1	45	a	Pass(Fault revealed)
92	90	11	a	Pass
102	112	6	b	Pass
102	112	6	b	Pass(Fault revealed)
14	-1	100	c	Pass
92	9	100	c	Pass(Fault revealed)
g	0	6	not_valid	Fail(Fault revealed)
(	112	11	not_valid	Fail(Fault revealed)
(	90	45	not_valid	Fail
102	56	6	a	Pass(Fault revealed)
102	9	100	a	Pass(Fault revealed)
102	90	100	a	Pass
g	56	11	not_valid	Fail(Fault revealed)
102	90	11	a	Pass
92	9	11	a	Pass
102	90	100	a	Pass(Fault revealed)
92	9	12	a	Pass
92	56	11	a	Pass
14	9	11	a	Pass
14	90	100	c	Pass(Fault revealed)
14	9	6	a	Pass
14	9	6	a	Pass(Fault revealed)
14	9	100	c	Pass

Table 12. Evaluation of data set

Data Set	user-supplied test set (before fault reveal)	user-supplied test set (after fault reveal)	Training data set	Training data set with 10-fold cross-validation	Evaluation of split 70.0% train, remainder test
Correctly Classified Instances	12	23	144	144	43
Incorrectly Classified Instances	11	0	0	0	0

Then the testing data set alone is taken into consideration. The testing data sets are passed as an input for the program to test the program using JUnit tool, (Mei, Hao, Zhang et al., 2012). The test data is passed and the execution time of the program is calculated and the coverage analysis yields the same result as that of the original test suite. Thus, the test suite is reduced with the help of the data mining technique and the resultant execution time is given as Figure 10.

Figure 9. Correctly and Incorrectly classified instances

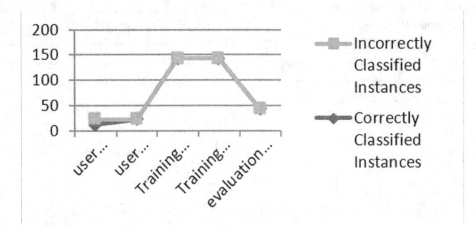

Table 13. Correctly and incorrectly classified instances in percentage

	User-Supplied test set% (before fault reveal)	user-supplied test set% (after fault reveal)	Training data set %	Training data set with 10-fold cross-validation %	Evaluation on split 70.0% train, remainder test %
Correctly Classified Instances	52.1739%	100%	100%	100%	100%
Incorrectly Classified Instances	47.8261%	0%	0%	0%	0%

The testing data set, test the program with the test suites and the coverage analysis of the program is given as Figure 11,

The coverage percentage of the program is calculated using test suites passed to the program. The coverage statistics of the program is given as Figure 12,

The specific criteria for each case study with its original and reduced test suite, coverage analysis of original and reduced test suite, execution time of original and reduced test suite is given in Table 16 as

The specification criteria of the original test suite and the reduced test suite are given by the graph. When executing the program with original test suite it takes much-added execution time to perform the program. When the reduced test suite is used, its execution time becomes very less and the effort of human in testing the program is decreased. The graph is specified as follows in Figure 13.

Coverage of program can be tested with both original test suite and reduced test suite and it is given as Figure 14,

The execution time is much more condensed with reduced test suite when compare with the original test suite and it is given as Figure 15,

Table 14. Accuracy of training and testing data set

Detailed Accuracy By Class: for user-supplied test set (Before fault reveal)								
TP Rate	FP Rate	Precision	Recall	F-Measure	MCC	**ROC Area**	PRC Area	Class
0.111	0.214	0.250	0.111	0.154	-0.133	**0.448**	0.376	fail
0.786	0.889	0.579	0.786	0.667	-0.133	**0.448**	0.585	pass
Weighted Average								
0.522	0.625	0.450	0.522	0.466	-0.133	**0.448**	0.503	
Detailed Accuracy By Class: for user-supplied test set (After fault reveal)								
TP Rate	FP Rate	Precision	Recall	F-Measure	MCC	**ROC Area**	PRC Area	Class
1.000	1.000	1.000	1.000	1.000	1.000	**1.000**	1.000	fail
1.000	1.000	1.000	1.000	1.000	1.000	**1.000**	1.000	pass
Weighted Average								
1.000	1.000	1.000	1.000	1.000	1.000	**1.000**	1.000	
Detailed Accuracy By Class: evaluate on training data & 10-fold cross-validation								
TP Rate	FP Rate	Precision	Recall	F-Measure	MCC	**ROC Area**	PRC Area	Class
1.000	1.000	1.000	1.000	1.000	1.000	**1.000**	1.000	fail
1.000	1.000	1.000	1.000	1.000	1.000	**1.000**	1.000	pass
Weighted Avg.								
1.000	1.000	1.000	1.000	1.000	1.000	**1.000**	1.000	
Detailed Accuracy By Class: split 70.0% train, remainder test								
TP Rate	FP Rate	Precision	Recall	F-Measure	MCC	**ROC Area**	PRC Area	Class
1.000	1.000	1.000	1.000	1.000	1.000	**1.000**	1.000	fail
1.000	1.000	1.000	1.000	1.000	1.000	**1.000**	1.000	pass
Weighted Avg.								
1.000	1.000	1.000	1.000	1.000	1.000	**1.000**	1.000	

Table 15. Confusion matrix for the dataset

	User-Supplied test set % (before fault reveal)		user-supplied test set % (after fault reveal)		evaluate on training data & 10-fold cross-validation		split 70.0% train, remainder test		classified as
	a	b	a	b	a	b	a	b	
a	1	8	4	0	60	0	19	0	a=fail
b	3	11	0	19	0	84	0	24	b=pass

Figure 10. Test program using reduced Testing data set and Execution time calculation

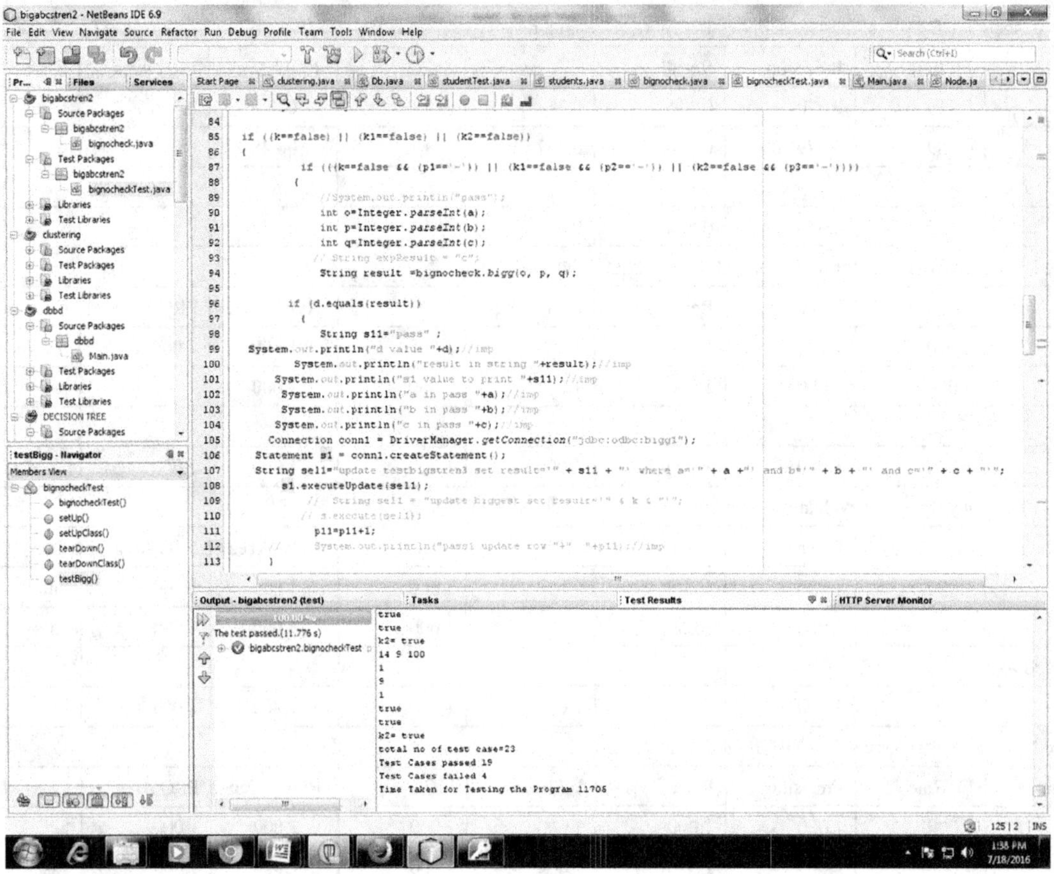

Figure 11. Coverage analysis of testing data set in the program

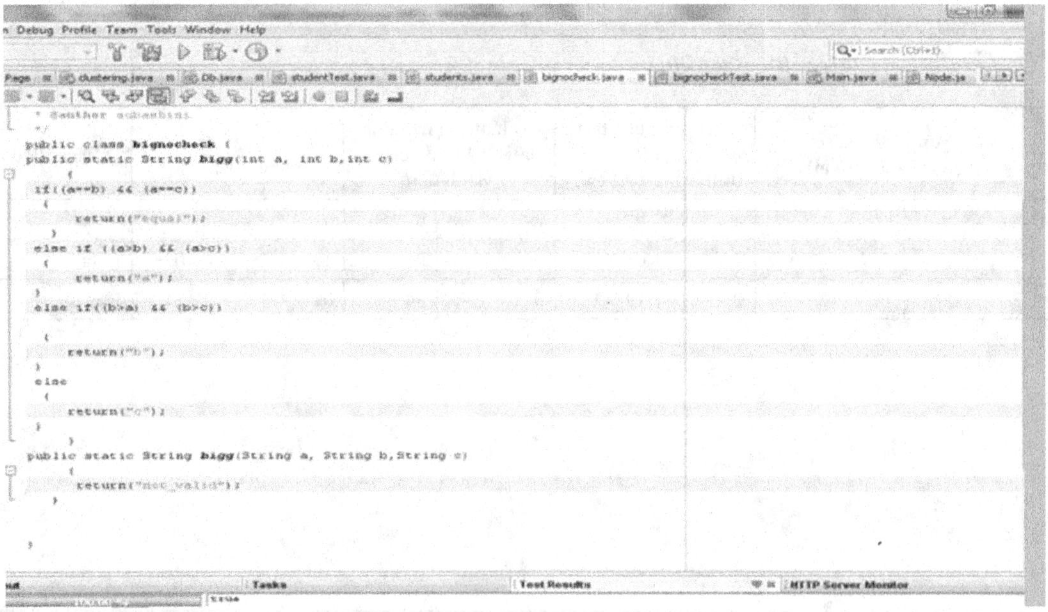

Figure 12. The coverage statistics

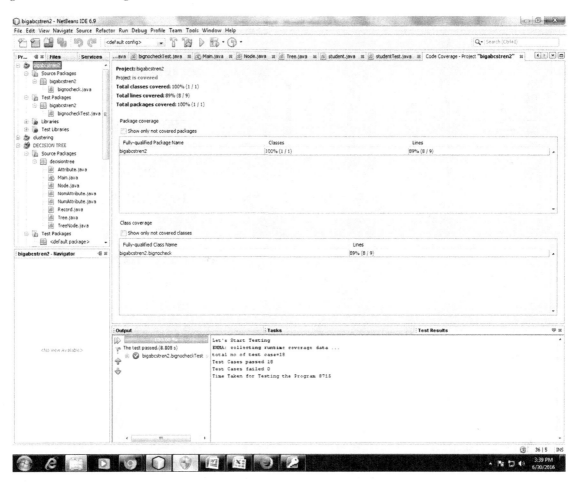

Figure 13. Comparing Original and Reduced Test Suite

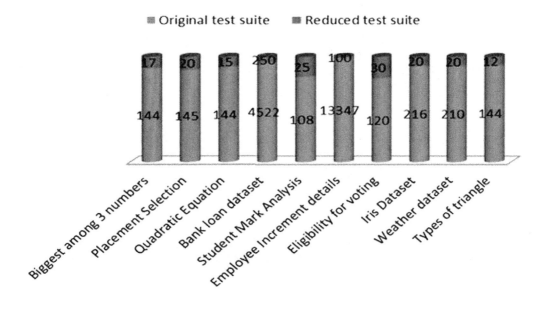

Figure 14. Coverage analysis of original with reduced test suite

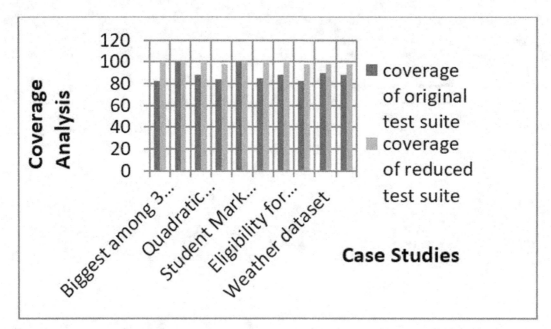

Figure 15. Execution time for original and reduced test suite

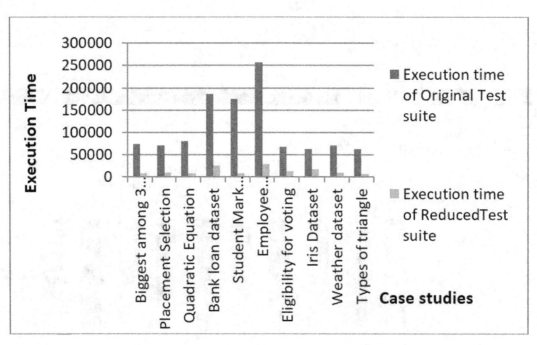

Table 16. Specification of dataset with size, execution time and coverage

	Specification	Initial number of the test suite	Reduced test suite
Biggest among 3 numbers	Size of test suite	144	23
	Coverage	82%	100%
	Execution time	74928	11708
Placement Selection	Size of test suite	145	20
	Coverage	100%	100%
	Execution time	71282	9257
Quadratic Equation	Size of test suite	144	15
	Coverage	88%	100%
	Execution time	80811	8324
Bank loan dataset	Size of test suite	4522	250
	Coverage	84%	98%
	Execution time	186647	25645
Student Mark Analysis	Size of test suite	108	25
	Coverage	100%	100%
	Execution time	174926	8236
Employee Increment details	Size of test suite	13347	100
	Coverage	85%	100%
	Execution time	256826	29465
Eligibility for voting	Size of test suite	120	30
	Coverage	88%	100%
	Execution time	67568	12784
Iris Dataset	Size of test suite	216	20
	Coverage	82%	98%
	Execution time	63246	18325
Weather dataset	Size of test suite	210	20
	Coverage	90%	98%
	Execution time	71256	9346
Types of triangle	Size of test suite	144	12
	Coverage	88%	98%
	Execution time	62759	6524

4. CONCLUSION

Data mining has the potential in the software testing in reducing the test suite. Classification technique is used in this paper for the selection of limited attributes using feature selection technique. This is treated as a training data set. Random testing data set can be taken from the training data set, inject faults in data set and apply classification algorithm. The algorithm predicts the faults in the data set and automatically reveals the fault in the dataset. The coverage and execution time analysis is calculated for both the training and the testing data set. If the coverage in program is satisfied with the testing data set then stop testing the application otherwise the testing data set will be again chosen until it satisfies the coverage criteria. Hence, fault prediction will result in good accuracy using classification algorithm and reduced test suites will yield a good result with maximum coverage, less effort and with reduced execution time in testing the application. In future, various classification algorithm will be used in revealing faults in the test suites, and in calculating the accuracy value for the test suites for the real world problems.

REFERENCES

Harris, P., & Raju, N. (2015). A Greedy Approach for Coverage-Based Test Suite Reduction. *The International Arab Journal of Information Technology*, *12*(1).

Abaei, G., & Selamat, A. (2014, May). A survey on software fault detection based on different prediction approaches. *Vietnam Journal of Computer Science*, *1*(2), 79–95. doi:10.100740595-013-0008-z

Raamesh, L., & Uma, G. V. (2010). An Efficient Reduction Method for Test Cases. *International Journal of Engineering Science and Technology*, *2*(11).

Bokil, P., Krishnan, P., & Venkatesh, R. (2015). Achieving Effective Test Suites for Reactive Systems using Specification Mining and Test Suite Reduction Techniques. *Software Engineering Notes*, *40*(1).

Chauhan, R., Batra, P., & Chaudhary, S. (2014). An efficient approach for test suite reduction using density based clustering technique. *International Journal of Computers and Applications*, *97*(11).

Coutinho, A. E. V. B., Cartaxo, E. G., & de Lima Machado, P. D. (2016). Analysis of distance functions for similarity-based test suite reduction in the context of model-based testing. *Software Quality Journal*, *24*(2), 407–445.

Dallmeier, V., Knopp, N., Mallon, C., Fraser, G., Hack, S., & Zeller, A. (2012). Automatically generating test cases for specification mining. *IEEE Transactions on Software Engineering*, *38*(2), 243–257.

Gayatri, N., Nickolas, S., Reddy, A. V., Reddy, S., & Nickolas, A. V. (2010). Feature Selection Using Decision Tree Induction in Class Level Metrics Dataset for Software Defect Predictions. In *Proceedings of World Congress on Engineering and Computer Science (Vol. 1)*.

Gupta, R., Gawhade, S., & Vishwamitra, L. K. (2015). Performance Analysis of Software Quality using Data Mining Techniques. *International Journal of Master of Engineering Research and Technology*, *2*(1).

Ilkhani, A., & Abaee, G. (2011). Extracting Test Cases by using Data Mining; Reducing the Cost of Testing. *International Journal of Computer Information System and Industrial Management Applications*, *3*, 730-737.

Jyoti, B., & Sharma, A. K. (2014). Test Case Suite Reduction of High Dimensional Data by Automatic Subspace Clustering. *International Journal of Soft Computing and Engineering*, *4*(1).

Khan, S. U. R., peck Lee, S., Parizi, R. M., & Elahi, M. (2013). An analysis of the code coverage-based greedy algorithms for test suite reduction. In The Second International Conference on Informatics Engineering & Information Science (ICIEIS2013) (pp. 370-377). The Society of Digital Information and Wireless Communication.

Raamesh, L., & Uma, G. V. (2009). Knowledge Mining of Test Case System. *International Journal on Computer Science and Engineering, 2*(1), 69–73.

Kumar, G., & Bhatia, P. K. (2013). *Software testing optimization through test suite reduction using fuzzy clustering.* CSIT.

Kumari, A. C., Srinivas, K., & Gupta, M. P. (2013). RegressAid-A CASE Tool for Minimization of Test Suite for Regression Testing. *International Journal of Computers and Applications, 71*(18).

Last, M., Friedman, M., & Kandel, A. (2003). The Data Mining Approach to Automated Software Testing. *Communications of the ACM.*

Last, M., Friedman, M., & Kandel, A. (2004). Using data mining for automated software testing. *International Journal of Software Engineering and Knowledge Engineering, 14*(04), 369–393. doi:10.1142/S0218194004001737

Lei, Y., Kacker, R., Kuhn, D. R., Okun, V., & Lawrence, J. (2008). IPOG/IPOG-D: Efficient test generation for multi-way combinatorial testing. *Software Testing, Verification & Reliability, 18*(3), 125–148. doi:10.1002tvr.381

Lessmann, S., Baesens, B., Mues, C., & Pietsch, S. (2008). Benchmarking Classification Models for Software Defect Prediction: A Proposed Framework and Novel Findings. *IEEE Transactions on Software Engineering, 34*(4), 485–496. doi:10.1109/TSE.2008.35

Lin, J.-W., & Huang, C.-Y. (2009). Analysis of Test Suite reduction with enhanced tie-breaking techniques. *Information and Software Technology, 51*(4), 679–690. doi:10.1016/j.infsof.2008.11.004

Lin, Y.-D., Chou, C.-H., Lai, Y.-C., Huang, T.-Y., Chung, S., Hung, J.-T., & Lin, F. C. (2012). Test Coverage Optimization for large code problems. *Journal of Systems and Software, 85*(1), 16–27. doi:10.1016/j.jss.2011.05.021

Mei, H., Hao, D., Zhang, L., Zhang, L., Zhou, J., & Rothermel, G. (2012). A static approach to prioritizing junit test cases. IEEE Transactions on Software Engineering, 38(6), 1258-1275.

Muthyala, K., & Naidu, R. P. (2011). The Novel Approach to Test Suite Reduction using Data Mining. *Indian Journal of Computer Science and Technology, 2*(3).

Raamesh, L., & Uma, G. V. (2010). Reliable Mining of Automatically Generated Test Cases from Software Requirements Specification (SRS). *IJCSI International Journal of Computer Science Issues, 7*(1).

Raamesh, L., & Uma, G. V. (2010). Method to Improve the Efficiency of the Software by the Efficient Selection of the Test Cases from Test Suite using Data Mining Techniques. *International Journal of Computer Science Issues, 7*(1).

Raamesh, L., & Uma, G. V. (2009) UML Generated Test Case Mining Using ISA. In *International Conference on Machine Learning and Computing* (pp. 188-192). Singapore: IACSIT Press.

Raamesh, L., & Uma, G. V. (2011). Data Mining based Optimization of Test Cases to Enhance the Reliability of the Testing. In Advances in Computing and Information Technology, CCIS (Vol. 198, pp. 89-98). Springer.

Riquelme, J. C., Ruiz, R., Rodriguez, D., & Ruiz, J. J. S. A. (2009). Finding Defective Software Modules by Means of Data Mining Techniques. *IEEE Latin America Transactions*, 7(3), 377–382.

Rout, J. P., Mishra, R., & Malu, R. (2013). An effective test suite reduction using priority cost technique. *International Journal of Computer Science & Engineering Technology*, 4(4), 372-376.

Shen, Y. & Liu, J. (2009). Research on the Application of Data Mining in Software Testing and Defect Analysis. In *IEEE Second International Conference On Intelligent Computation Technology and Automation*. 10.1109/ICICTA.2009.384

Tallam, S., & Gupta, N. (2006). A concept analysis inspired greedy algorithm for test suite minimization. *Software Engineering Notes*, 31(1), 35–42.

Vegas, S., Juristo, N., & Basili, V. R. (2009). Maturing Software Engineering Knowledge through Classifications: A case study on Unit Testing Techniques. *IEEE Transactions on Software Engineering*, 35(4), 551–565. doi:10.1109/TSE.2009.13

Williams, C. C., & Hollingsworth, J. K. (2005). Automatic mining of source code repositories to improve bug finding techniques. IEEE Transactions on Software Engineering, 31(6), 466-480.

Zeng, F., Li, L., Li, J., & Wang, X. (2009, June). Research on test suite reduction using attribute relevance analysis. In *Eighth IEEE/ACIS International Conference on Computer and Information Science ICIS 2009* (pp. 961-966). 10.1109/ICIS.2009.139

This research was previously published in the International Journal of Open Source Software and Processes (IJOSSP), 8(4); pages 1-31, copyright year 2017 by IGI Publishing (an imprint of IGI Global).

Chapter 57
SERIES:
A Software Risk Estimator Tool Support for Requirement Risk Assessment

Chetna Gupta

Jaypee Institute of Information Technology, India

Priyanka Chandani

Jaypee Institute of Information Technology, India

ABSTRACT

Requirement defects are one of the major sources of failure in any software development process, and the main objective of this chapter is to make requirement analysis phase exhaustive by estimating risk at requirement level by analyzing requirement defect and requirement inter-relationships as early as possible to using domain modeling to inhibit them from being incorporated in design and implementation. To achieve this objective, this chapter proposes a tool to assist software developers in assessing risk at requirement level. The proposed tool, software risk estimator, SERIES in short, helps in early identification of potential risk where preventive actions can be undertaken to mitigate risk and corrective actions to avoid project failure in collaborative manner. The entire process has been supported by a software case study. The results of the proposed work are promising and will help software engineers in ensuring that all business requirements are captured correctly with clear vision and scope.

INTRODUCTION

Every software system exhibit uniqueness and contains significant numbers of uncertainties in terms of key objectives, specific features, preferences and user expectations. This makes software structurally complex and versatile which progressively evolves over time to accommodate changing customer requirements, latest market demand, new sophisticated technologies, imprecise estimation of budget, schedules, product deployment and maintenance (Mens, 2012). These factors have strong impact on software development and strongly support the need of proactive assessment measures to control these

DOI: 10.4018/978-1-6684-3702-5.ch057

uncertainties. If failing to do so, it raises the possibility of potential risk throughout the project lifecycle ranging from delays to economic losses to customer dissatisfaction. According to PMBOK reports (2017), the global software market which is at US$333 billion in 2016 estimated to grow by 7.2% and global software projects (US and Europe) success in 2015 is 29% only (CHAOS, 2015) while 71% of projects have failed, due to diverse reasons and risks (Vahidnia, Tanriöver&Askerzade, 2016). Therefore, it is desirable to follow software risk analysis and management practices to understand, identify, and manage underlying risks to prevent the loss further in expenditure (Samantra, Datta, Mahapatra, &Debata, 2016). In software engineering domain, risk is considered as a potential problem or unwanted outcome that might have positive or negative consequences on a project PMBOK (2017). However, according to to(Hijazi, Alqrainy, Muaidi, &Khdour, 2014) risks in software development do appear due to items (usually called software risk factors) that present a threat to software project success. According to (Chen & Huang, 2009) problems in requirement are considered as one of the major sources of project failure constituting nearly 32.65%. These problems include analyzing imperfection that compromises requirement correctness, completeness, stability and meeting the objectives/ project goals and such imperfections are categorized as defects within requirements. These requirement defects are most expensive problems that persist throughout the software life cycle (Hamill & Katerina, 2009) and can be generated from different perspectives of users, practitioners, project execution or knowledge. The cost to fix a defect varies according to how far along you are in the software life cycle. The cost of fixing requirements defects is 3 times higher in the course of design, 10 times higher during development, 50 times higher at the time of testing and up to 100 times higher after the release (Boehm &Basili, 2001; Pressman, 2014). Hence, it is desirable to include risk management practices in every software project as early as possible, in particular, within Requirements Engineering (RE) phase. A project without risk management admits severe problems such as reworks of project artifacts and cost/schedule overrun.

In the past, literature has explored various issues concerning risk factors in software projects (Hijazi, Alqrainy, Muaidi, &Khdour, 2014; Islam &Houmb, 2010; Christiansen, Wuttidittachotti, Prakancharoen, &Vallipakorn, 2015) but the research is general in nature, not concentrating on perspectives including risk assessment and estimation practices in requirement engineering phase itself, uncovering requirement defects. Risk management is one such influential approaches acknowledged by all the project management and software engineering guidebooks (PMBOK, 2017; Pressman, 2014, CMMI, 2010; Thayer &Dorfman, 2013; SWEBOK, 2014). Risk can arise in any phase of the software development lifecycle and can be detrimental to the project causing huge losses. In the study conducted by (Hijazi, Alqrainy, Muaidi, &Khdour, 2014), key risk factors that threaten each phase of Software Development Life Cycle (SDLC) are presented which according their study claimed that every phase of SDLC is vulnerable to several types of risks. Many such risk factors are discussed that are common to most software development projects. With a successful risk management practices employed particularly in RE phase and by identification/analysis of risk factors related to requirements, a project manager can prevent potential risks and deter project failures. However, a comprehensive risk management plan is not possible due to paucity of resources and more onus is on saving time and budget and due to that the benefit of risk management practices cannot be reaped.

This paper proposes a tool to assist software developers in assessing risk at requirement level. The proposed tool, **S**oftwar**ERi**sk**Es**timator, SERIES in short, helps in early identification of potential risk where preventive actions can be undertaken to mitigate risk and corrective actions to avoid project failure in collaborative manner. The business objective to mitigate risk is fulfilled through the proposed tool, though it is separated from the technology implementation alike the MDA (model driven architecture) approach(Rhazali et al., 2020; Rhazali, Hadi&Mouloudi, 2016). Here, the requirements are listed down and analyzed further, the stakeholder and developer viewpoint is ascertained to deepen the understanding on the business models (CIM) created. The interaction diagram and uses cases are created based on the clear understanding from business models.The risk identification and mitigation at the forefront eases the stages of Platform Independent Model (PIM) and Platform Specific Model (PSM)of the application development when MDA approach is followed.

RELATED WORK

This section discusses literature on various techniques and approaches presented in the past related to requirements defects, defect classification, risk assessment and management and its impact on success of any software project. Requirements defects have an impact throughout the project lifecycle, detecting and correcting those defects is the most expensive activities in software development (Kumaresh, Ramachandran, 2012).It is essential to identify and analyze various requirement defects before a decision of inclusion of a requirement is taken in software development. These defect identification and analysis techniques or models are essential in order to be sure that all the requirements are captured correctly which focus on delivering value to the customer and are selected by taking right decision using risk estimation. Many software development organizations have successfully applied various defect analysis and prevention techniques showing significant reductions in errors (Mays, 1990; Suma &Gopalakrishnan, 2008; Kumaresh&Baskaran, 2010). Using a proper defects classification and taxonomy for requirements is essential to analyze the problems and their root causes which further reduce the risks associated with requirements. Some of the popular approaches for defect classification are Beizer taxonomy (Beizer, 1990), Orthogonal Defect Classification (ODC) approach (Chillarege et al., 1992), HP approach (Grady, 1992), IEEE taxonomies (1998), Margarido (Margarido, Faria, Vidal & Vieira, 2011), Walia (Walia& Carver, 2009) and Huffman Hayes (Hayes, 2003).

Risks in software projects can occur in any of phase of software development life cycle (SDLC) and should be handled there and then using strategies planned for individual phases of SDLC. Risk assessment and management is recognized as an essential practice which helps in identifying, analyzing, and mitigating risks and risk factors before they materialize into problems (PMBOK, 2017; Pressman, 2014; SWEBOK, 2014).Various approaches in the past have focused on assessing risks in all phases of software life cycle, by integrating risk management practices at every phase. However, several attempts have been made to integrate risk analysis in the initial phases of the software lifecycle process, which contribute towards increasing the software project success by fixing risk at the earliest (Vahidnia, Özgür&Askerzade, 2017; Bhukya&Pabboju, 2018; Cornford, Feather, Heron & Jenkins, 2006).

In the past, a few studies have ascertained systematic models of risk assessment using Analytic Hierarchy Process, Bayesian belief network, machine learning, risk metrics, fuzzy entropy, goal-oriented methodologies, decision trees, UML etc. (Hsieh, Hsu & Lin, 2016; Ghane, 2017; Meng, 2017; Zhi, Zhang, Liu &Shen, 2017; Kamila &Sutikno, 2016; Cailliau&Lamsweerde, 2015; Sipayung&Sembiring, 2015; Anthony, Noraini, Nor &Jusoh, 2015; Asnar, Giorgini&Mylopoulos, 2011; Amber, Shawoo& Begum, 2012; Li, & Liu,2009; Kumar &Yadav, 2015), they cumulatively conclude that assessment of risk can effectively give consistent software quality by reducing the exposure to software risk.Additionally, some research work(Amber, Shawoo& Begum, 2012; Lobato et al., 2012; Gallardo, 2012) also deals with specific cases like risk management in requirement engineering, risk-based testing, project risk dependencies, etc. The existing models of risk management have minimal focus towards considering software risks in early stage of SDLC. Adoption of early risk discovery and the corresponding mitigation strategy helps in minimizing the loss in software project.

SERIES: PROPOSED SOFTWARE RISK ESTIMATOR TOOL

The analysis in the risk assessment approach is often an interactive and iterative procedure, which requires elaborate discussions within/with the project teams and stakeholders. The calculations are monotonic and it is essential for the researchers and project teams to concentrate on the data with the stakeholders. Based on the quantative data it is easier for taking the decision on the validity of a risk. This paper aims to develop a risk management tool to identify, access and manage risk in requirements engineering and reduce chances of failure and disagreement between the project teams and stakeholders along with varied other business or technical challenges to develop a quality product. An attempt is made to keep the overhead specific to risk estimation activity as low as possible and developed tool to support labor-intensive aspects of the process to reduce the effort and time. This tool is built using VBA macros on Microsoft Excel 2017. The implementation of software tool supports the execution of the risk estimation process, as well as the capturing of the information inferred during this process. Final risk values are computed using viewpoints of both stakeholder and developer for enhancing effective communication between both the parties.

Elicitation of Stakeholder's Value (S_v)

The process starts with capturing the stakeholder's value (preference) for each requirement based on three main parameters namely, urgency, necessity, and business importance/value. These preferences are captured using interactive GUI provided by SERIES tool. Stakeholder's can select one out of five categories. Table 1 presents the description of each category and its corresponding value.

Table 1. Requirement Categorization

Type	Remarks	Weight
Mandatory	Essential to have with primary importance	5
Major	Good to Have with secondary importance	4
Moderate	OK to Have with tertiary importance	3
Minor	Can Have but can do without	2
Malformed	Should not Have, good to be without	1

Figure 1 provides a snapshot of initial preferences provided by stakeholder's for an example set of 12 requirements selected from a sub module of an example project, which assists clients to provide bays for customer parking through mobile application on android and IOS platforms is selected to carry out results analysis. The project has 12 high-level requirements (refer Table 2) consisting of 20 sub-modules with 112 sub- requirements in total. A high level architecture is shown in Figure 2 and its corresponding interaction diagram detailing out the high level of abstraction and flow of control between the objects and messagesis shown in Figure 3. It shows the behavior of the system and helps in identifying the events which define the execution flow in the application. The interaction diagram shows the main modules which are login, location management, rate management system, profiling, notifications and commission. The rate management system module encloses the audit log, rate tester and publishing as well. The execution flow of all the possible paths corresponding to all the requirements can be defined and analyzed from the diagram.

Elicitation of Developer's Value (D_v)

Developers follow a twofold process in which first of all requirements are analyzed for presence of any defects and later a relationships among requirements (dependency) are studied using domain modeling to understand the potential impact of requirements on one another. Requirement defects refer to analysis conducted on each independent requirement to check whether it meets intended purpose and satisfies business value to the stakeholder. Requirements defects have a considerable impact on whole software lifecycle and specific defects classification is essential for root cause analysis of the problems, in order to understand risks associated with requirements problems. Using this approach, developers will be able to gain key information to support risk estimation using defects and dependency analysis.

Table 2. Requirement Set of industrial project data

Requirement Number	Requirements Details
R1	**User Management**: The super admin's, admin's (suppliers) and their employee's should be able to login to Self Service Portal to manage the units, suppliers and their existing rates
R2	**Recurring Rate Management**: The Supplier should be able to view (week and day) the recurring rates through a concerned week. The rates can be edited, deleted or created, the rates shall be flat or incremental, draft rates can be created
R3	**Event Rate Management**: The Supplier should be able to view (week and day) the event rates through a concerned week. The rates can be edited, deleted or created, the rates shall be flat or incremental, draft rates cannot be created
R4	**Audit Log**: The events or behaviors by the user can be Audit checked. The whole length of check has to be 90 days
R5	**Rate Tester**: The rates (recurring and event) can be modified by the supplier, there should be a rate tester component which can metric the rate on filtered clauses for the supplier to view
R6	**Rate Publishing Service**: the published rates should have an option to become live to the market based upon the desire of the supplier
R7	**Types**: The application should take care of On Demand and Reservation rates for super admin users
R8	**Profiling**: The supplier admin can modify the profile assigned. The admin should have a privilege to create, delete sub users, it should work on Siri and Google Assistant, the super admin can create users
R9	**Notification Service**: Upon Configuration of an Email Address, the supplier should get notifications for all behaviors
R10	**Locations Management**: The locations viewed to a supplier should be geo located. The MAPs should be visible to view the exact location with address. The supplier should on view it's company locations, the super admins can view/ update all locations
R11	**Commission Service**: The admin's should have a functionality to modify the commission earned by XXX company from Suppliers, the commission service should sent weekly emails (configurable) to BOD only if good total commission is earned
R12	**Access Management**: The super admin user can revoke rights of normal user

Figure 1. Snapshot of Elicitation of stakeholder's preference (S_v)

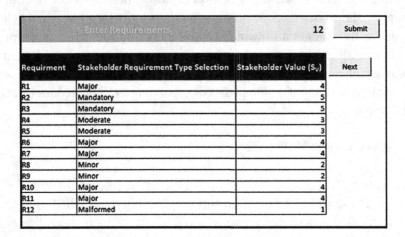

Figure 2. High Level Architecture

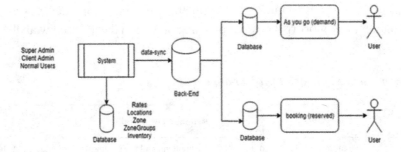

Defect Analysis

Having a specific defects classification for requirements is important to analyze the root causes of problems to access risk associated with it. Literature lists following defect taxonomies which are available for classifying the defects namely, Orthogonal Defect Classification (ODC) approach (Chillarege et al., 1992), HP approach (Grady, 1992),Beizertaxonomy (Beizer, 1990), IEEE taxonomies (1998) and Huffman Hayes (Hayes, 2003). For this work, Hayes (Hayes, 2003) taxonomy is used because it is most relevant to this research as their approach emphasized on requirements rather than on design and code to classify defects and is summarized in Table 3.

Each requirement is validated with respect to (w.r.t.) presence of type of defect(s) listed in Table 2. This mapping will help in addressing defects related to requirements enabling project managers to visualize and access potential benefit or risk between the needs and expectations of stakeholders for both individual and as well as set of requirements depicting whole project.

After mapping of requirement with each defect type, percentage score of each defect type is computed. This score is defined as the percentage of total number of requirements in a particular defect category with the total number of requirements as calculated using equation (1)

Percentage of defect by category= Rd/Rt (1)

where,

Rd = Number of requirements in a particular defect category

Rt = Total number of requirements

Table 3. Defect Types

Type of Defect	Remarks
Incomplete	Fails to fully describe all the requirements of a function
Missing	Fails to specify lower level of abstraction of higher level or specification of missing value in a requirement
In-Correct	Fails to fully describe system with respect to input or output value or specification of incorrect value in requirement
Ambiguous	Difficult to understand or having lack of clarity
Infeasible	Impossible or not feasible to implement with respect to factors like speed, cost
Inconsistent	Incompatible having internal or external conflicts
Over Specification	Having excessive detail for operational need leading to additional system cost
Non-Traceable	Requirement which cannot be traced to other phases
Unachievable	Requirement which is specified but not achievable in the product lifetime
Non verifiable	Failure to verify and validate the requirement by any testing method
Misplaced	Information that is marked in different segment of requirement document
Intentional Deviation	Specified at the higher level but deviated from the purpose at the lower level from specifications
Redundant	Requirement already specified elsewhere in the specification

(Hayes, 2003)

For instance, if two requirements are mapped to defect category "missing" and there are 8 total requirements then the score value for percentage of defect category will be 2/8 = 25%. These defect categories are assigned weights w.r.t. to the score value computed in equation (1). These values are relative to specific project at hand and is purely based on results and mapping of requirement defects.

Next, weights are assigned to define the level of risk by considering the score of defect category. This will help project managers to visualize risk and its root cause to assist management decision making. Table 4 presents various levels of this classification, its description and corresponding weight. These weights are represented as a set of values from 0 to 5 representing very low, low, moderate, high, very high and extreme values respectively.

Table 4. Level classification of percentage of defect score

Percentage of Defects by Category Score	Description	Weight
> 25%	Extreme high chances of defect	5
20-25%	Very high chances of defect	4
15-20%	High chances of defect	3
10-15%	Nominal chances of defect	2
5-10%	Low chances of defect	1
< 5%	Very Low chances of defect	0

Figure 3. Interaction Diagram

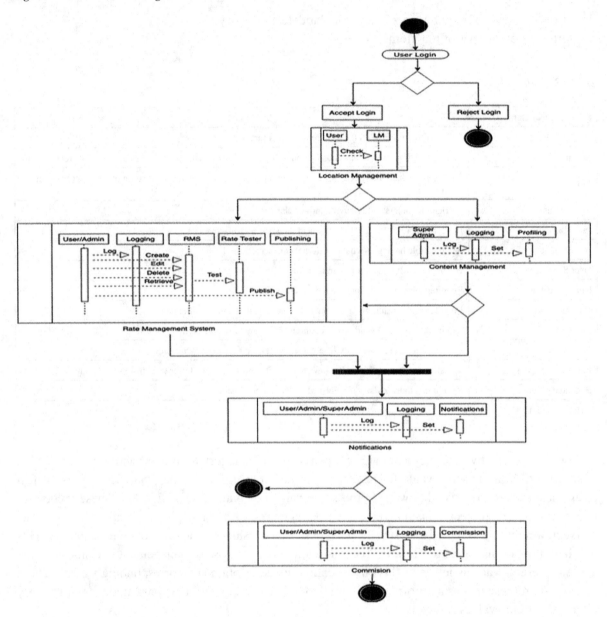

Lastly, a defect score of each individual requirement will be computed to access risk and its consequences throughout the whole project. This requirement defect weight score is defined as summation of weights corresponding to each defect category computed in Table 4, w.r.t. of each requirement belonging to different defect categories and is summarized in equation (2). For instance, if a requirement has two defects namely, ambiguous and incomplete then the requirement defect weight (Dw) will be summation of defect weight of ambiguous and defect weight of incomplete category computed in Table4.

$$Requirement\ defect\ value\left(Dw\right) = \sum_{i=1}^{n}\left(Rdwi\right) \tag{2}$$

Rdwi – weight of each defect category in a requirement

Finally, defect density is computed for each requirement and is defined as percentage of requirement defect weight with summation of all defect weights equation 3.

$$Defect\ Density\ D_d\left(\%\right) = \frac{D_w}{D_{size}} \tag{3}$$

where, D_w is the defect weight of the requirement and D_{size} is summation of all defect weights

Figure 4. Snapshot of Computation of Defect Analysis

Requirment	Defect Type	Requirement Defect Weight	Defect Density (D_d)	Next
R1	Incomplete, Ambiguous	5	9.6	
R2	Over Specification	2	3.8	
R3	Over Specification	2	3.8	
R4	Incomplete	3	5.8	
R5	Missing	4	7.7	
R6	Missing, Non-Traceable	5	9.6	
R7	Incomplete, Ambiguous	5	9.6	
R8	In-Correct, Infeasible	5	9.6	
R9	Missing	4	7.7	
R10	Missing, In-Correct	8	15.4	
R11	In-Correct, Inconsistent	5	9.6	
R12	In-Correct	4	7.7	

Dependency Analysis

Each requirement is assigned a weight score according to influence of a node connection in a dependency graph. In a dependence flow graph, nodes represent requirements which are dependent on other requirements and edges represent dependence among them. Often dependency is represented over time and it indicates that a latter requirement cannot be processed until its dependencies are fulfilled. The purpose of using dependency graphs is to capture interactions among requirements which help developers to (i) analyze requirements for counting in-stream (incoming edges) and out-stream (outgoing edges) dependencies for a given node (ii) find an implementation order such that the dependencies are satisfied by the time we get there (iii) draw inferences among indirect dependent (transitive) requirements (iv) highlight and expedite non linear branching situations while prioritization. Non linear branching refers to situations when at a given point there are more than one requirement available for implementation and the decision of assigning higher rank is based on the fact that, their dependencies are satisfied.

For this purpose we use the concept of Eigen centrality measure (Eigenvector) to analyze nodes of a dependency graph to identify the influence of node connection in a graph. Given the adjacency matrix in the form of dependency graph, an automated procedure selects the values corresponding to requirements to compute eigenvector score for each node in a dependency graph. For the example project discussed in section 3, Eigen centrality measure score are as follows:

A high score measure depicts more importance as it is less dependent in terms of inter -connections with other nodes. Now the relative dependency score value for each requirement will be computed by summing up the eigenvector score of each dependent requirement as shown in Figure 6.

Figure 5. Adjacency matrix, Eigenvector values

Requirements	Eigen score
R1	3.3663
R2	1.3348
R3	1.3348
R4	0.6355
R5	0.6355
R6	1.2443
R7	0.00059
R8	1
R9	0.576
R10	0.576
R11	1.2348
R12	0.435

Figure 6. Snapshot of Dependency Score calculation

Requirment	Depedent On	Dependency Score (Dep$_r$)	
R1	R5 - R8	4.3663	Next
R2	R1 - R9	3.9423	
R3	R1 - R4	4.0018	
R4	R1 - R5 - R8	5.0018	
R5	R1 - R2 - R9 - R10	5.8531	
R6	R1 - R3 - R4	5.3366	
R7	R1 - R2 - R3 - R4 - R5 - R6 - R9 - R10	9.7032	
R8	R1 - R2 - R3 - R4 - R5 - R6 - R7 - R9 - R10	9.70379	
R9	R2 - R6 - R10	3.1551	
R10	R1 - R5 - R9	4.5778	
R11	R5 - R8	1.6355	
R12	R1 - R9	3.9423	

RELATIVE RISK SCORE

Finally, relative risk score value is computed which is defined as the multiplicative factor of stakeholder's value (Sv) and developer's analysis of summation of defect density score and dependency score for each requirement and given in equation 4:

$$Relative\ Risk = S_v \times D_v \tag{4}$$

where, D_v is summation of defect density and dependency score

Figure 7. Snapshot of Final Risk Score Computation

Requirment	Stakeholder Value (Sv)	Developers Value (Dv)	Relative Risk Score
R1	4	14.0	55.9
R2	5	7.7	38.7
R3	5	7.8	39.0
R4	3	10.8	32.4
R5	3	13.6	40.7
R6	4	14.9	59.7
R7	4	19.3	77.2
R8	2	19.3	38.6
R9	2	10.9	21.7
R10	4	20.0	79.9
R11	4	11.2	44.9
R12	1	11.6	11.6

Relative risk score for example scenario taken as case study is given in Figure 7.

A high score measure depicts more risk which implies the relative impact and urgency of a risk as compared to another one in that project. It can vary between different kind of projects and portfolio the company is aligned with. The comparison helps in fixing the risk with the highest relative score affecting the overall success of the project.

VALIDATION

A survey through a series of meetings with the project practitioners was done to understand their general experience of including such tool particularly in requirement engineering phase. The brainstorming sessions were included before the risk estimation tool was presented and later their view was taken on effectiveness of approach in risk management and was formally done with the people involved. The results of feedback in general conclude that risk estimation indeed has a positive effect on the software project when integrated with the early phase. It is effective in terms of finding requirements which have high risk based on the understanding of the defects and the interactions among the requirements. The actual project estimation on real project data was compared with the estimation results of risk estimation approach and concluded that the proposed tool lead to saving of considerable project time. This process helps in reduction of system testing time period desired by the testers and stakeholders. As per the feedback from the survey participants, it was also found out that the activities of the approach did not incur any extra burden to requirement engineering.

CONCLUSION

This chapter presents a software risk assessment model which computes risk of implementing requirements at the very first stage of software development life cycle. Through this work, it is shown that how categorization of requirements and their defects as well as requirement dependency can be used to understand the requirements and know the risk level. Requirement understanding and classification helps in identifying specific information on defects which can improve the validation process. The viewpoints of both stakeholder and developer help in computing the final risk values using both defect score and dependency score. Through the computed risk values, the tool identifies risky requirements which are communicated further to the stakeholders to fix the defects in them by explaining the modalities of the process. It will help in decreasing the chances of failure, risk, and conflicts between stakeholder and developer and other challenges involved to develop the project.

REFERENCES

Amber, S., Shawoo, N., & Begum, S. (2012). Determination of Risk During Requirement Engineering Process. *International Journal of Emerging Trends in Computing and Information Sciences, 3*(3), 358–364.

Anthony, B., Noraini, C. P., Nor, R. N. H., & Jusoh, Y. Y. (2015). A risk assessment model for collaborative support in software management. *9th Malaysian Software Engineering Conference (MySEC)*, 217-223. 10.1109/MySEC.2015.7475224

Asnar, Y., Giorgini, P., & Mylopoulos, J. (2011). Goal-driven risk assessment in requirements engineering. *Requirements Engineering Journal, 16*(2), 101–116. doi:10.100700766-010-0112-x

Beizer, B. (1990). Software testing techniques (2nd ed.). New York, NY: Van Nostrand Reinhold.

Bhukya, S. N., & Pabboju, S. (2018). Software engineering: Risk features in requirement engineering. *Cluster Computing*, 1–13.

Boehm, B., & Basili, V. (2001). Software Defect Reduction Top 10 List. *IEEE Computer, 34*(1), 135–137. doi:10.1109/2.962984

Cailliau, A., & Lamsweerde, A. (2015). Handling knowledge uncertainty in risk-based requirements engineering. *IEEE 23rd International Requirements Engineering Conference (RE)*.

Chen, J. C., & Huang, S. J. (2009). An empirical analysis of the impact of software development problem factors on software maintainability. *Journal of Systems and Software, 82*(6), 981–992. doi:10.1016/j. jss.2008.12.036

Chillarege, R., Bhandari, I. S., Chaar, J. K., Halliday, M. J., Moebus, D. S., Ray, B. K., & Wong, M. Y. (1992). Orthogonal Defect Classification-A Concept for In-Process Measurements. *IEEE Transactions on Software Engineering, 18*(11), 943–956. doi:10.1109/32.177364

Christiansen, T., Wuttidittachotti, P., Prakancharoen, S., & Vallipakorn, S. (2015). Prediction of Risk Factors of Software Development Project by using Multiple Logistic Regression. *Journal of Engineering and Applied Sciences (Asian Research Publishing Network), 10*(3).

Cornford, S. L., Feather, M. S., Heron, V. A., & Jenkins, J. S. (2006). Fusing quantitative requirements analysis with model-based systems engineering. *Proceedings of the 14th IEEE international requirements engineering conference,* 279–284. https://en.wikipedia.org/wiki/Eigenvector_centrality

Gallardo, E. (2012). Using Configuration Management and Product Line Software Paradigms to Support the Experimentation Process in Software Engineering. *Proceedings of International Conference on Research Challenges in Information Science RCIS-2012*, 1-6. 10.1109/RCIS.2012.6240454

Ghane, K. (2017). *Quantitative planning and risk management of Agile Software Development. In IEEE Technology & Engineering Management Conference.* TEMSCON.

Grady, R. B. (1992). *Practical Software Metrics for Project Management and Process Improvement.* Prentice-Hall.

Hamill, M., & Katerina, G. P. (2009). Common Trends in Software Fault and Failure Data. *IEEE Transactions on Software Engineering*, *35*(4), 484–496. doi:10.1109/TSE.2009.3

Hayes, J. H. (2003). Building a Requirement Fault Taxonomy: Experiences from a NASA Verification and Validation Research Project. In *Proceedings of the 14thInternational Symposium on Software Reliability Engineering (ISSRE'03).* Denver, CO: IEEE Computer Society. 10.1109/ISSRE.2003.1251030

Hijazi, H., Alqrainy, S., Muaidi, H., & Khdour, T. (2014). A Framework for Integrating Risk Management into the Software Development Process. *Research Journal of Applied Sciences, Engineering and Technology*, *8*(8), 919–928. doi:10.19026/rjaset.8.1054

Hsieh, M. Y., Hsu, Y. C., & Lin, C. T. (2016). Risk assessment in new software development projects at the front end: A fuzzy logic approach. *Journal of Ambient Intelligence and Humanized Computing*, *9*(2), 295–305. doi:10.100712652-016-0372-5

IEEE. (1998). *IEEE Standard for Software Reviews.* IEEE Std 1028– 1997, 1–37.

IEEE Computer Society Professional Practices Committee. (2014). *Guide to the Software Engineering Body of Knowledge (SWEBOK® Guide), Version 3.0.* IEEE.

Islam, S., & Houmb, S. H. (2010). Integrating Risk Management Activities into Requirements Engineering. *2010 Fourth International Conference on Research Challenges in Information Science RCIS-2010*, 299-310. 10.1109/RCIS.2010.5507389

Kamila, A. R., & Sutikno, S. (2016). Analysis of cause and effect relationship risk using fishbone diagram in SDLC SPASI *v. 4.0* business process. *International Conference on Information Technology Systems and Innovation (ICITSI)*, 1-5.

Kumar, C., & Yadav, D. (2015). A Probabilistic Software Risk Assessment and Estimation Model for Software Projects. *Procedia Computer Science*, *54*, 353–361. doi:10.1016/j.procs.2015.06.041

Kumaresh, S., & Baskaran, R. (2010). Defect Analysis and Prevention for Software Process Quality Improvement. *International Journal of Computers and Applications*, *8*(7), 42–47. doi:10.5120/1218-1759

Kumaresh, S., & Ramachandran, B. (2012). Defect Prevention based on 5 dimensions of Defect Origin. *International Journal of Software Engineering and Its Applications*, *3*(4).

Li, X., & Liu, Q. (2009). Requirement Risk Assessment Focused-on Stakeholder Risk Analysis. *Proceedings of 33rd Annual IEEE International Computer Software and Applications Conference, COMPSAC '09, 1*, 640-641. 10.1109/COMPSAC.2009.199

Lobato, L. L. (2012). Risk Management in Software Product Lines: An Industrial Case Study. *Proceedings of International Conference on Software and System Process ICSSP*, 180-189. 10.1109/ICSSP.2012.6225963

Margarido, I. L., Faria, J. P., Vidal, R. M., & Vieira, M. (2011).*Classification of defect types in requirements specifications: Literature review, proposal and assessment.* Paper Presented at *6th Iberian Conference on Information Systems and Technologies (CISTI)*, Chaves, Portugal.

Mays, R. G. (1990). Applications of Defect Prevention in Software Development. *IEEE Journal on Selected Areas in Communications, 8*(2), 164–168. doi:10.1109/49.46867

Meng, Y. (2017). Study on software project risk assessment based on fuzzy analytic hierarchy process. *IEEE 3rd Information Technology and Mechatronics Engineering Conference (ITOEC)*, 853-857.

Mens, T. (2012). On the complexity of software systems. *IEEE Computer, 45*(8), 79–81. doi:10.1109/MC.2012.273

Pressman, R. S. (2014). Software Engineering: A Practitioner's Approach (8th ed.). Academic Press.

Project Management Institute. (2017). A guide to the project management body of knowledge (PMBOK ® guide), Sixth Edition. PMI.

Rhazali, Y., Hachimi, A., Chana, I., & Lahmer, M. (2020). *Automate Model Transformation From CIM to PIM up to PSM in Model-Driven Architecture. In Modern Principles, Practices, and Algorithms for Cloud Security.* IGI-Global.

Rhazali, Y., Hadi, Y., & Mouloudi, A. (2016). CIM to PIM Transformation in MDA: From Service-Oriented Business Models to Web-Based Design Models. *International Journal of Software Engineering and Its Applications, 10*(4), 125–142. doi:10.14257/ijseia.2016.10.4.13

Samantra, C., Datta, S., Mahapatra, S., & Debata, B. (2016). Interpretive structural modelling of critical risk factors in software engineering project. *Benchmarking, 23*(1), 2–24. doi:10.1108/BIJ-07-2013-0071

Sipayung, J. J. P., & Sembiring, J. (2015). Risk assessment model of application development using Bayesian Network and Boehm's Software Risk Principles. *International Conference on Information Technology Systems and Innovation (ICITSI)*, 1-5. 10.1109/ICITSI.2015.7437722

Software Engineering Institute. (2010). CMMI for Systems Engineering/Software Engineering/Integrated Product and Process Development, V1.3. Pittsburgh, PA: Author.

Suma, V., & Gopalakrishnan Nair, T. R. G. (2008). Effective Defect Prevention Approach in Software Process for Achieving Better Quality Levels. Proceedings of World Academy of Science, Engineering and Technology, 32.

Thayer, R. H., & Dorfman, M. (2013). Software Engineering Essentials: Vol. 3. *The Engineering Fundamentals* (4th ed.). Software Management Training Press Carmichael.

Vahidnia, S., Özgür, Ö., & Askerzade, I. (2017). An Early Phase Software Project Risk Assessment Support Method for Emergent Software Organizations. *International Journal of Advanced Computer Science and Applications*, 8(5), 2017. doi:10.14569/IJACSA.2017.080514

Vahidnia, S., Tanriöver, O., & Askerzade, I. (2016). An Evaluation Study of General Software Project Risk Based on Software Practitioners Experiences. *International Journal of Computer Science and Information Technology*, 8(6), 01–13. doi:10.5121/ijcsit.2016.8601

Walia, G. S., & Carver, J. C. (2009). A systematic literature review to identify and classify software requirement errors. *Information and Software Technology*, 51(7), 1087–1109. doi:10.1016/j.infsof.2009.01.004

Zhi, H., Zhang, G., Liu, Y., & Shen, Y. (2017). A novel risk assessment model on software system combining modified fuzzy entropy-weight and AHP. *IEEE 8th Conference on Software Engineering and Service Science*, 451-454.

Chapter 58
Auditing an Agile Development Operations Ecosystem

Aishwarya Subramanian
University at Buffalo, SUNY, Buffalo, USA

Priyadarsini Kannan Krishnamachariar
University at Buffalo, SUNY, Buffalo, USA

Manish Gupta
University at Buffalo, SUNY, Buffalo, USA

Raj Sharman
University at Buffalo, SUNY, Buffalo, USA

ABSTRACT

In an enterprise software development, DevOps is a practice of integrating development and operations to deliver cost-efficient, improved quality solutions to the customer by automating the existing processes to achieve "continuous delivery." In the current dynamic IT Ecosystem where there is a rising need to prove a competitive edge to maximize profitability, it is pivotal to drive business value with profound emphasis on quality. Agile enables us to take calculated risks during development whereas its affinity to adopting DevOps will promote continuous delivery with reduced friction to improve business efficiency. As this approach requires a change in people, process, technology, culture, usage of right tools and techniques, the early involvement of IT Auditors during the process of transformation could aid to build effective Risk Management strategies to handle organizational challenges. This article aims to present a risk-based audit approach to effectively use audit tools and techniques in an Agile-DevOps transformation environment to achieve maximum business value.

DOI: 10.4018/978-1-6684-3702-5.ch058

1. INTRODUCTION

In today's dynamic business environment where there is a critical need to be on par with changing business requirements, organizations are moving towards agility. An Agile approach enables organizations to respond faster to changes, gain a competitive advantage in the market by providing customer value-driven outcomes (Mitch et al., 2017). In the current software development arena, Agile is the mainstay of every organization that intends to respond quickly to the business requirements. As agility has engulfed the software development in the recent times, DevOps has been the engine to drive the mindset and bring about organizational transformation. DevOps is the integration of Software Development and Operations in the early stage of the Software Development Life Cycle to enable cross-functional teams to collaborate and deliver faster, quality technical solutions to address the business problems.

The traditional waterfall methodology works in a linear fashion, which requires clear, concise requirements before the beginning of the development phase. Each phase works iteratively and is dependent on the completion or outcome of the previous phase. Unlike Waterfall methodologies, Agile projects deliver a shippable product in frequent iterations (sprints), which reap benefits at an earlier stage and is adaptive to the customer feedback. DevOps being cross-functional has the ability to drive the Application Life Cycle in an agile environment. DevOps can integrate operation teams into agile development teams focusing on the quality of deliverables and continuous integration of the deliverables to maximize the efficiency of the agile chasm. Agile methodology typically reduces the development timeframe for new processes by simultaneously increasing the flexibility for existing processes, when additional requirements are to be modified. This, in turn, allows the product owners to satisfy client demands in less time, gaining more clients with low adaptation costs and finally increased revenue with continuous delivery, continuous integration, continuous testing, continuous monitoring and continuous feedback. (Virmani, 2015). The maturity of DevOps framework that we use in an agile environment will contribute to the success factor of the transformation.

Agile organizations respond to the changes quickly and encourages to be flexible. But to be successful, an agile organization must also know the art of balancing between structure and flexibility. If the requirements are changing continuously in a certain period of time, then it will be challenging for agile teams to accommodate the change requests. To address this challenge of agile' s flexible nature without affecting the productivity, DevOps could come into play which will enable continuous integration until deployment and continuous monitoring after release. It is important for agile organizations or projects to understand that balancing the edge between order and chaos determines success. This clearly depicts that an agile process can be disadvantageous if the agility factor is not regulated properly, and the level of agility needs constant monitoring in a project implementation scenario. A recent survey (Tech Beacon, 2018) states that 84% of enterprises have adopted some aspects of DevOps principles in their environment. This is a very significant metric that portrays how DevOps has pre-occupied the recent enterprise space. The ability to deliver software projects with speed and stability is evident from the facts that enterprises adopt DevOps into their delivery strategies. The evolving trend of DevOps has been quite notable since 2017 as the world is moving towards automation. In a 2017 survey (Tech Beacon, 2017), most organizations have moved towards agile and 27% of teams have adopted DevOps transformation in their organization. In fact, two-thirds described their company as either "pure agile" or "leaning towards agile," A hybrid approach is used by 24 percent of respondents, which shows that they are practicing at least some agile principles in their implementation and management of their software development projects. Only nine percent responded that they are using "pure waterfall" or "leaning towards waterfall". It is believed that good management can amplify the effects of integrating agile and DevOps transformation in an enterprise ensuring faster time to market.

Having known the nature of the agile approach, the importance of agility and its contribution to the growth and success of an organization creates an inevitable need to ensure if the agile processes are essentially serving the organization's objectives and to evaluate the agile software developments' ability to respond to changes to deliver consistent business value. The auditing methods of agile software development in a DevOps integrated environment is instrumental in assuring the effectiveness of the transformation. Auditing of agile development cannot be laid out as a single standard process containing several procedures; rather, it requires the understanding of the project, organizational context and the evaluation of risks to define clear audit scope and procedures. The Agile-DevOps ecosystem creates challenges for IT Auditors regarding ensuring their objectivity without effecting their independence to provide reasonable assurance to the management of the system of operations.

This paper proposes a risk-driven audit model for auditing agile software development in a DevOps integrated environment, highlighting the roles of IS auditors in the auditing process across the phases of development. This paper also identifies the different ways of using agile processes followed in the project and gear them as an aid for audit, without changing any existing processes. The motivation for this paper is to help auditors acquire an agile attitude and adapt their audit approach to be able to audit an agile project operating with DevOps principles. Our model is designed from an agile perspective, considering the pace of the project implementation.

The rest of the paper is structured as follows. In the next (second) section, an overview of research on agile approach in software development and the importance of IT Auditing is presented. In the third section, the publications and citations related to the agile development and DevOps Transformations, the challenges and risks in auditing agile software development process in a DevOps integrated environment to set forth the researches in this field. Subsequently, prior research on agile and the audit techniques/ issues auditing agile development, followed by a brief account of the contributions made by the papers in this special issue. In the fourth section, we talk about the proposed model for risk-driven audit process of agile software development and the role of IT auditors. This also includes the effective use of agile techniques in continuous auditing. Also, the auditing process check points are defined, which aids an auditor to perform verification on the process front. In the fifth section, Agile-DevOps risks are discussed, and the sixth section describes the auditing of agile implementation in a DevOps integrated agile environment. Finally, the conclusions, key findings and directions for future research are discussed.

2. BACKGROUND AND PRELIMINARIES

'Agile is a software development approach that helps teams respond unpredictability through incremental, iterative work cadences and empirical feedback' (Agile, 2016). The concept of agile started emerging in the early 1990s, as personal computing began to grow rapidly in the enterprise leading to a problem called "the application development crisis," or "application delivery lag." This estimation showed that it took about an average of three years to develop and deploy a qualified application, even after identifying the exact business problem to be solved. This time span was very high as the business needs to be evolved over the specified period which has eventually led to projects scrap ups after its beginning. This issue that revolved around traditional software development methodology was the reason behind the birth of agile principles and methods (Varhol, 2016). As agile started intruding the organizations, it was considered as the greatest challenge to the traditional waterfall methodologies. Agile also requires requirements gathering and requirement analysis in the initial stages of the project, like waterfall methodologies but the project releases are agile and delivered in sprints for continuous user acceptance.

2.1. Study of a Proven Agile-DevOps Development Practice

In Agile software development, work is confined to a regular, repeatable work cycle, known as a sprint or iteration. Agile (Scrum) sprints is usually a two-week span or a month long in different projects. Every sprint produces a usable tested software product, in the order of business priorities set. Testing occurs at the end of each sprint, and issues are fixed accordingly, rather than fixing the bugs at the end of the development cycle, which reduces the cost of defect fixing and prevents the transport of defects along the phases. The agile development is within a fixed time box, with short-term goals defined which prevent project overruns. A DevOps transformed organization will have an operations team working in sync with the development team to monitor the continuous improvement and integration. It fuels quality through cross-functional collaboration in an agile environment. For effective customer service, the affinity of Agile and DevOps could optimize customer satisfaction. In an Agile methodology, The Agile Product owner is the one who prioritizes the features to be delivered for a release from the backlog of user stories, and this helps the team in delivering a tangible output for each sprint/release to the customer. The process is iterative and incremental. A release may require multiple sprints, each iteration of work is built on the previous iterations or sprints, adding to or modifying some of the previous work to produce the next iteration. And agile teams are self-organizing, traditional project manager for coordination activities are not required, and collaborating with each other and getting things done is the norm. DevOps uses processes and tools to bring in the culture of development and operations team working together to make concrete progress.

In agile practices, A Scrum Master is a servant leader helping the team be accountable to themselves for the commitments they make (Hartman, 2009). This means that the agile team works together and builds the ability to manage themselves, their work and the scrum master helps the team in getting this attitude. He helps in removing the impediments faced by the team that affects the progress of sprint deliveries and team performance. These are basic entities for an effective agile implementation. Each Product is associated with a Product Owner who owns the product. He creates Product Backlog items and orders them based on the business value. The scrum master drives the vision of the Product Owner in achieving the goal. The success of agile approach has many reasons (Miller, 2001), few of the characteristics that attracted the organizations and the benefits that brought are given below:

- Delivering the tested working software iterations at regular intervals – Ability to refine the backlog items and changes as required
- Fixing time-box for every iteration – Implementing only the necessary, valuable features in the initial sprints
- Adapting the process and project activities in case of new risks - Ensures goals are met
- Favoring individuals and interactions over process and technology - Optimum utilization of talent
- Creating a Collaborative environment - Effective project delivery integrating the sprint deliverables

2.2. Why IT Auditing?

Organizations spend a lot of money on Information Technology(IT) to gain benefits that technology can bring to their business operations and services. In a practical scenario, IT can introduce risks to the organizations using weaknesses and vulnerabilities in the IT systems and business processes. This requires a professional, such as an IT auditor, to identify and assess the inherent risks associated with implementing IT systems operating in any organization. Those risk factors include systems-related issues, such as systems development, change management, and vulnerabilities, and other technology specific-factors (Singleton,2014).

The IT auditor's role has evolved to reasonably assure that adequate and appropriate controls are in place for the effective functioning of the systems. The primary role of an audit function, except in areas of advisory services, is to provide reasonable assurance as to whether competent and reliable internal controls are set up and are working as expected in an efficient and effective manner (Senft et al., 2012). Hence, IT audit functions are important for an effective IT and project functioning, and when auditing a DevOps integrated Agile environment, careful diligence is required from an auditor as the Agile and DevOps audit procedures and tests should check if the implementation is by compliance and organizational goals. An IT auditor has to possess an open mindset to understand the nature of processes followed and also requires deliberation in verifying the controls, processes, and metrics as the improper implementation of agile, due to lack of in-depth understanding of process by the management or team which can potentially cause serious problems impacting the success of the project.

3. LITERATURE REVIEW

The literature review consisted of reviewing agile software development approach, DevOps transformation and its impact in an agile environment along with analyzing the challenges and exploring the ways of auditing agile software development and processes. The articles reviewed met the criteria for analysis by containing some information regarding project management, agile development, DevOps principles, risks, barriers and challenges of agile development and the benefits of auditing and its capabilities for agile auditing implementation in a DevOps integrated environment. In today's business setup, organizations are facing more pressure than ever, to respond to market's dynamic demands with speed and precision by delivering new business value as quickly as possible to gain a competitive edge with a continuous focus to quality. Adding to the unpredictable nature of business needs- the multifaceted nature of organizations and the interest for project initiatives execute new business ideas; also the need for implementation that take advantage of the recent technical innovations seeks attention ("Oracle Primavera," 2011).

Balancing stakeholders in an agile and DevOps environment is crucial to the success of project management. (Bierwolf et al., 2017). This paper discusses DevOps as a change in culture in the project environment which adopts an agile mindset in its approach. The traditional approaches are compared with the recent agile approaches, and various risk mitigation factors are discussed. The description of hard and soft controls in place are discussed and concludes that DevOps integrates soft controls in place and transformation requires a change in the attitude of the organization.

As more organizations move towards DevOps transformations and adopting agile methodologies, the internal audit teams are facing challenges in their approach and interactions with the agile teams (Tilk, 2016). To overcome the challenges faced by auditors who are tuned to the traditional methodologies, the author suggests the internal auditors get involved early in the process when the team defines its risk management approach and strategy. Auditors have to effectively spend a lot of time in understanding the context of the Agile processes used in the specific projects owing to the rise of agile variants existing in the industry. Once the process is thoroughly established and understood by the auditors, it is important to establish controls in place. For example, documentations such as user stories, product backlogs, test cases and results have to emphasize in the agile teams for effective functioning. The risk profile of the project has to be established based on the inbuilt internal controls. In a DevOps adopted agile environment where cross-functional collaboration of teams co-exists, it is significant to lay stringent segregation of duties which shouldn't involve developer to get into the production environment. This could affect the security of the systems, and the controls have to be carefully examined by the auditors. Agile methodologies' risk of evolving project requirements should also be carefully managed independently by establishing controls in place from the beginning. The right expertise at the right juncture is highly for the auditors to carefully evaluate and report the agile processes to provide a reasonable assurance of the project. There has been a growing trend in software development through the agile approach, and so, the study of risks in such environments becomes imperative (Shrivastava & Rathod, 2015). This paper talks about the Evaluating the Industrial Practice of Integrating Risk Management with Software Development and the following criteria are considered: Organizational levels, Integration aspects, Integration problems, Importance of process integration, Applicability of risk management in agile context.

The paper by Holler (2010) explains the basic need for organizations to adopt agile implementations. As the most of the software organizations are working under stringent time constraints and the development environment is highly volatile, which introduces frequent changes and unpredictability in the system requirements, there is the need for transformation of the development approach from traditional heavyweight processes to lightweight incremental and iterative methods like Agile. Hence, many organizations are adopting an agile methodology for software development, which helps them to accelerate delivery schedules, adapt to the changing business needs, align business and technology goals and generate competitive advantage (Holler, 2010).

The setting up an agile implementation not only requires the project to be an ideal candidate for agile but also requires self-managing teams among developers and management. This transition takes time and resources, but should not be neglected (Moe et al., 2010). The paper discussed that the software producers are expected to be nimble enough to mirror the fast-paced changes in their customer's needs and environment changes, which paves the way for agile methodology. The author explored the major factors of agile methods that improve the success of agile and concluded that the benefits of using agile methods range from 10% to 100% for increased cost-effectiveness, productivity, quality, cycle-time reduction, and customer satisfaction. (Rico, 2008)

In the paper titled "Organizational Theories: Some Criteria for Evaluation," the author had discussed on a set of ground rules for the management practices and the organization standards. All the theories are developed over time based on falsifiability and utility. (Bacharach, 1989) The theories have to be constructed in a way that an empirical refutation is possible and it should be utilized by the systems. Every theory should have an ability to prove as right or wrong. As we adopt agile methodologies and techniques, it is imperative that the set of tools are evaluated based on a certain criterion to prove them successful in the organization. The conceptual understanding of the case studies and analyzing large data sets of successful transformations are critical in framing theories and methodologies to prove them to be successful.

The tools and techniques using Stakeholder theory have been discussed in the paper 'The Conceptual Model for Agile Tools and Techniques' (Haines et al., 2017). This paper meticulously analyzes the importance of carefully selecting an agile technique by analyzing the pros and cons of all the techniques such as Team Involvement, Continuous Customer Feedback, Pair Programming, Automated Acceptance Testing, Refactoring Code, User Acceptance Testing, and Meetings. The importance of selecting a proper agile technique that suits the organizations and the specific project is very pivotal to the success of methodologies.

In relevant to the discussion of the agile tools and techniques, The paper titled "Comparative analysis of Two Popular Agile process Models Extreme Programming and Scrum" discuss on the pros and cons of choosing Extreme Programming or Scrum practices in an agile environment (Anwer, F. et al., 2017). The core values of XP and Scrum models are distinguished and infer that XP has a set of defined principles whereas Scrum is a very open framework that allows the Development team to make changes as and when required focusing on a simple design to be delivered to the customer at every sprint. This reveals that agile techniques have evolved over a period and the adaption depends on the organization. With DevOps into the agile environment, it is rather more challenging to select the right agile technique and implement it for the success of the project.

The paper titled " IT software development and IT operations strategic alignment: An agile DevOps model"(Hart, M. 2017) explains the importance of DevOps in an agile environment. The empirical study made by the author proved that DevOps fosters cross-functional collaboration between the teams to enable faster delivery to the market with agile principles. It is also interesting to note that DevOps principles and philosophies are linked to Social Capital theory which states that the resources which are actively involved in social relations facilitate much faster, collective action. Indeed, this proves that adopting DevOps in an agile method will foster social relations for successful actions.

As we discuss more on Agile and DevOps integrated environments, researchers have studied intensive, collaborative, knowledge sharing processes through which the birth of software emerges. (Ghobadi S et al., 2015) Several obstacles are certain in a demanding knowledge sharing environment in today's diverse work culture where social differences, cultural differences, cross-functional collaborations could exist as a barrier to impact the transformation. As Agile-DevOps is an organizational mindset and change of culture, it is inevitably associated with risks and challenges. The risks have to identify at an early stage, understood by the drivers of the transformation, and develop strategies to mitigate the risks.

In an Agile environment, the technical debt could be a significant risk factor as it can accumulate owing to the needs of the significantly reduced development time by adhering to strict time boxing, and constantly deliver functional requirements for business use. (Amany E et al., 2015) To identify and asses various risk factors that could be associated with Agile- DevOps transformation approach, and to establish risk mitigation strategies, an IT Auditor's contribution to the organization is highly significant. An IT Auditor is expected to understand and adopt the fundamental philosophies of Agile and DevOps before auditing the Information systems and providing a reasonable assurance to determine the success of the transformation. The extensive literature review has contributed to understanding the fundamental theories of the agile methodologies and the organization's necessity to adopt DevOps transformation in their march towards delivering high business value.

4. PROCESS FOR AUDITING AGILE

An auditor auditing agile development must be receptive to the information, and the best way to learn the subject before auditing an agile project is by listening, observing and understanding the project context and the maturity of agile implementation in the project. The auditor should be diligent of the associated risks with the Agile-DevOps transformation environment. In their auditing journey, there are some significant challenges for auditors and project teams in ensuring an efficient audit, as it requires them to work together in harmony. A successful audit requires the project team and auditor to share the same objective of developing a product with low risk, yet effective and efficient controls in place. Auditing agile development is a team effort combining both the auditor and the auditee which requires the build of trust and understanding, right from the early stages of the audit. Hence, the first step is to involve the internal IT auditors early in the product life cycle right from project kick-off meetings to share and make him understand the product vision.

To be successful in auditing Agile projects in a DevOps integrated environment, the auditor must know the Agile Framework and DevOps Principles. Auditors are also in a state where their technical skill sets have to be honed to understand the architecture of the system to devise effective audit approaches with the aid of technology, automation and explore different types of audit tests to respond to new business processes and systems. Technology experts are an asset to be a part of audit engagement teams to drive the auditing process by providing valuable suggestions on the technical front.

4.1. Role of IS Auditor in an Implementation Based on Agile-DevOps Approach

The IS audit function helps to identify, review, and provide suggestions for the key controls associated with the project and assures that the system will support effective business processes and enforce business controls on an ongoing basis.

- The internal auditor's participation is essential across all the critical phases of the project implementation and aids for successful implementation and deployment.
- In an implementation project, an internal auditor plays a key role in identifying the project risks, can be involved in Sprint planning, review and retrospective meetings to identify and analyze the risks which can be addressed in the life cycle leading to low cost and quality deliverables at the end of each sprint. This could be possible only in a medium to large sized projects where there is a scope of accommodating an internal auditor in the project lifecycle. Practically, an IT Auditor can be involved in the sprint meetings to address if there are any specific issues or risks identified in the project life cycle and provide advisories to mitigate the risks.
- Figure 1 shows the process of auditing agile based implementation where the roles of IS Auditor is explained when it goes through the phases.

4.2. Pre-Audit Assessment

A prior understanding of the business process and the technical framework is pivotal to an Auditor before the beginning of the audit process. The Auditor can choose to probe structured interviewed questions to the Product Owner and Scrum Master to understand the importance of the Product and its business value. The Auditor is expected the understanding of the Scrum Framework and DevOps principles before the audit assessment. A successful audit depends on the prior preparation by both the Audit team and the Auditee, before the onsite audit. Auditing agile is dependent on the project context and implementation, not a standard procedure that applies to any agile project, for a flexible, agile implementation, the following techniques can be used by an auditor to help kick-start an audit: Pre-Audit survey is a tool for audit team to learn more about the auditee's organization, includes a set of questionnaires to gather necessary information prior to performing an onsite audit, this survey covers assets, organization structure, important aspects of the auditee's systems/project to be audited. The lack of a pre-audit phase reduces the effect of an audit, leads to delays and poor time management on-site and in the worst case, prevents an audit from being completed. Information checklists specifies the list of documents required for an effective audit, which aids project team to be well prepared for an audit.

Figure 1. Process of Auditing Implementation based on Agile approach

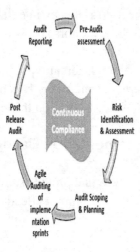

4.3. Pre-Audit Survey Execution Steps

The following steps are recommended for Pre-Audit survey execution:

- The auditors have to establish contact with the senior manager/s, Product Owners, Scrum Masters, and other senior executives like CIO and CEO, to get an idea about the items that will be reviewed during the audit.
- The auditors will be involved in requesting the documentation including Product Backlogs, Refinements, Sprint Backlogs, business processes documents, system design and business requirement documents and the history of audit papers.
- The organization normally nominates one or more individuals from the team to assist auditors to move freely in the organization and help find the people, information, etc. necessary to perform audit who act as management liaison points.

The primary output of this phase is an Audit Engagement Letter, the contact lists and other preliminary documents for the audit process. The documentation is given by the auditee and the information gathered in pre-audit, greatly helps in drafting the audit plan.

4.4. Risk Identification and Risk Assessment

An Agile implementation methodology will greatly reduce the risk of an enterprise software implementation project not being running overtime or beyond the defined scope and budget. Performing system development in an agile approach requires more emphasis on risk analysis, and the assessor should be cognizant of the risks involved in the current environment. When integrating DevOps, the challenges are high on the bar, and it requires meticulous risk management practices and experienced practitioners to be involved in the process to drive the success of the transformation.

Figure 2 shows the risk management framework to be adopted for an effective agile based implementation:

Figure 2. Exemplary Risk Process Management Framework

4.4.1. Identifying Risks-Developing Risk Profile

Compiling a comprehensive list of internal operational challenges and risks is vital to developing a risk profile. Risk profile is an organization-wide risk registry that must be updated throughout the project as risks are identified, including the unanticipated risks caused by new investments. Proactive, consultative engagement is required for risk profile to be effective. Identify and prioritize all the related risks and perform cause analysis to understand the effect of those risks, if left unattended, may cause higher levels of risks. In Agile environments, the development project team shares the responsibility for identifying risks that might impact a sprint, project or the course of development. The following agile processes aid in identifying risks in an agile development project:

- **Daily Scrum:** Strong forum for identifying risks when performing daily tasks

- **Requirements Workshop:** The team and the project manager discuss new ideas to adjust or correct the requirements so that it minimizes the risk
- **Sprint Planning:** Planning poker used to estimate the relative size of a user story, gives the opportunity to reduce the risk associated or break down the stories.
- **Sprint Review:** Gives opportunity to identify, access and respond to risk
- **Sprint Retrospective Meeting:** Identify the problems that were hurdles/risks for the implementation

4.4.2. Classify and Quantify Risks

Risk assessment requires adopting a suitable framework that enables the prioritization of risks and the ability to classify risks as real risks or opportunities. The risk appetite of an organization decides the risk assessment methods and the risk treatment that can be performed on the identified risks. It requires to have a prior plan on what data or metrics needs to be collected and managed, to enable effective risk management as well as for agile process implementation, periodically measuring the risks. The following risk analysis and management process can be adopted for the agile development scenario:

1. What are the uncertainties that exist in the organization?
2. What is the impact of risks to the organization?
3. What is the expected frequency of risk occurrence?
4. What are the steps for Risk Mitigation?
5. What are the costs of setting up countermeasures to predict uncertainties and are these justifiable regarding monetary returns, feasibility, and relevancy? (Dennis, et al., 2015)

The risk factors identified/to be identified by the auditor can be classified into four categories: Operational, Financial, Technological and Miscellaneous. Considering the implementation of the system, the following areas or risk factors may be considered: Product risk, Customer Relationships, Production-Network & Hardware availability, Human Resources- Personnel issues and Quality Assurance- Maintenance issues. The suggestion of the risk assessment procedures for an agile based implementation is to use a mix of qualitative and quantitative risk approaches. Quantitative risk analysis to be employed for situations where the risk can be anticipated numerically based on a data set and quantitative risk analysis to be used to weigh and rank the risks based on relative comparison to the risk appetite and exposure of the organization.

The basic flow in assessing the risks identified:

- Assemble the identified risks across the sprints
- Identify the occurrence and impact of the risks identified in the project implementation and its processes
- Categorize the risks by using the categories defined across the organization or by the project, depending on the purpose of the project
- Prioritize the risk events and update the findings in risk register along with the risk-event matrix

4.4.3. Risk Treatment

Risk treatment is the crucial step in risk management, where we decide about what action to be taken on the risks that are identified, ranked and assessed. The general options available are Avoidance, Mitigation, Transference, Acceptance. This decision to be taken based on the occurrence of the risk and its impact on the business and its processes. Risks in the agile implementation in a DevOps environment are to be managed by associating user stories with themes and ensuring that risks are identified in the project sprints. The target of each sprint should include 'minimizing risk in the project.' A risk-adjusted backlog is efficient in controlling and managing risks in an agile environment. A risk-adjusted backlog takes into consideration the amount of risk a feature or a story places on the project. The need to have a risk-adjusted backlog is to make sure the agile implementation delivers artifacts that are of business value and the risk reduction items, which inherently maximizes the value. Risk adjustment enables us to identify and mitigate critical risks in the initial sprints development (Canty,2015).

4.4.4. Review and Retrospection

This phase is about Tracking, Monitoring and Auditing the identified risks. The Sprint retrospective meetings enable the review of risks faced during the project and help in continuous risk assessments throughout the implementation. The risk register is reviewed to see if the high severity risks are treated and the cause analysis report updated if any. The retrospective methods are employed to analyses the weaknesses or deficiencies and to prevent their recurrence. Possible Risk areas to be reviewed continuously when auditing an agile based development project include cost (Hardware, Software, licenses, updates, maintenance), extensive training for faculty and staff; and productivity across sprint deliveries.

4.5. Audit Scoping and Planning

In this phase, the auditors determine the main areas of focus and areas that are explicit to be tagged as out of scope. This decision drives the audit process, and the audit planning also involves the important tasks such as interviewing the product owner and Scrum Master to determine their "success criteria" for this agile project audit. This will help auditors to check if the success criteria reflect the needs and how it is measured. When defining the Audit Scope for implementation on agile approach, the following are to be considered:

- Understanding the organizational setup, culture, policies and security implications
- Understanding the project context and technical complications
- Getting access to the release plan and the sprint plan, including the planned components that are to be delivered
- Looking if there are plans for automated integration of the developed components with any existing systems
- Analyze to identify the existing IT controls, process controls, and other security controls.

Audit requirements have to be identified and finalized in audit planning phase, and the following will be included for analysis:

- Organizational requirements about system implementation
- Customer's expectations
- Regulatory requirements
- Security requirements

4.6. Agile Auditing of Implementation Sprints

The main purpose of implementation audit is to ensure if the sprint is working towards delivering the incremental and iterative development of business objectives planned. Also, focuses on the verifying the design and Implementation of controls for new systems, considering project risk and capability assessment. Figure 3 shows the areas that are predominantly covered for Implementation audit of the sprints.

Figure 3. Areas for Agile Audit Implementation

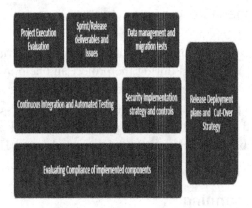

4.6.1. Project Execution Evaluation

For the status of activities or tasks of current sprint, Sprint dashboard can be reviewed. Also, as part of the evaluation, ensuring if the user stories that are of higher priority based on the risk assessment procedures and ensured if they meet the completion criteria for project schedule can be done. Release backlog can be verified to evaluate if the implementation goes as per business priorities. Also, evaluating the way, the project tasks were divided across sprints -Work breakdown structures would be useful. Lastly, another way is through reviewing of user stories about estimation procedure which drives the project schedule.

4.6.2. Sprint/Release Deliverables and Issues

Some of deliverables and issues could be known through the following:

- Reviewing User stories and Requirement engineering processes of the system
- Reviewing plans for user training and project team training plans on the implementation
- Evaluating how the issues raised in scrum meetings are handled
- Accountability for the completed user stories by the user story owner

- Verify if user stories are closed only based on completion of agreed "done" criteria

4.6.3. Data Management and Migration Tests

As we are working on auditing a new implementation, the business data and other transactions performed prior may have to be migrated to the new environment. Audit procedures must include procedures to validate the data conversion and must review the data migration strategies and appropriate approval cycles involved.

4.6.4. Continuous Integration and Testing

Continuous integration is an ongoing activity in the agile development process adopted for our implementation. For successful integration of components implemented in sprints, it is suggested that an auditor must ensure if the following are performed: 1) Configuration management tool is updated with the modules implemented in every sprint, 2) Automated integration tests are triggered for the components that are tagged as completed as part of a sprint and 3) Test results are reviewed and appropriate actions are taken by the team.

4.6.5. Security Implementation Strategy and Controls

Security issues need to be discussed when developing requirements for the system because it should be intertwined along with the system to be effective.

An auditor evaluating system implementation on agile methodology should perform the following:

- Review the Security Implementation strategy approval procedure and review if it aligns with organization's security policies
- Review the data classification scheme and the guidelines for access controls
- Review the release plan to verify for sprints involving security controls deployment and testing
- Verify if the implemented existing access controls, process controls are working as designed

4.6.6. Evaluating Compliance with Implemented Components

The components can be evaluated with the following steps:

- Reviewing implemented components using appropriate sampling techniques to confirm that it is performing as planned, or was appropriately adjusted.
- Compliance tests are to be done to ensure if the controls in place are performing as per control objectives defined. The general and technical Controls are evaluated for its compliance and verified if the controls are implemented based on the results of cost-benefit analysis.
- Substantive tests are to be performed by an auditor on suspected and critical transactions among modules, which need further analysis to ensure its correctness and integrity.
- The audit function can help to identify, review, and provide suggestions for key controls associated with the project and can assure that the system will support business processes

4.6.7. Release Deployment Plans and Cut-Over Strategy

The auditor has to verify the following in the release management:

- Release deployment plans mentioning the timelines and the sprints included in the release need to be laid down and approved by management
- Verify if the cut-over strategy is chosen considering the factors, less on-going risks, Cost-Effective, enhance the business process, should include roll back strategy as well.
- Verify if the cutover plan document is owned by a manager or key stakeholder, and managed very tightly.

4.7. Audit Reporting

Post completion of the audit, the auditor summarizes the audit result, conclude the findings and identifies the control weaknesses. For the agile implementation of any system, Auditor's report should include results specific to the processes audited, and the system and its tested interaction, inconsistencies in the agile development processes followed in project, impact of the identified weaknesses on the completeness, validity, and functioning of system, audit evidence based on the right sample set chosen from the population, to perform the audit procedure and weaknesses should be associated with appropriate action plans to be implemented. The auditor and the auditee are engaged in discussion and have to mutually accept on the findings, and the follow-up plans are discussed.

4.8. Post Implementation Audit

Post Implementation audit is an important audit function, which verifies if the user requirements and the purpose of the project are met. In an agile based implementation, retrospection meeting is a post-implementation activity, which will happen after every release or for every sprint, by the project team, where auditors might be passively involved to understand how the project release went through. The retrospective is a collaborative process among the scrum team, the product owner, and the Scrum Master and other members involved in the project. The following are the key elements of retrospective meetings:

- Ways for process improvements at the end of every sprint
- All team members identify what went well and what could be improved
- The scrum team members provide suggestions for process improvement

   The Product Owner is responsible for organizing the review and accountable for the results. The post-implementation strategy should be in place to execute, as soon as acceptance tests are run, but mostly executed after few months of deployment. The auditor needs to ensure if the if 'DONE' definitions set for sprints or release based on the completion of user stories, component delivery is completed. This is a measure of agile implementation's success. Benefit realization will be performed by the auditor by verifying the user stories for its completion and the verification of completed stories in release backlog to see if they are prioritized based on the business needs. The following questions may be asked to assess benefits realization 1) Did the implementation meet the business need? 2) Did it achieve the estimated ROI? And 3) Did it capture the market needs; did it meet the client needs?

4.9. Compliance Monitoring and Enforcement

Continuous Monitoring is essential to verify that business activity is performed as intended without compromising on the regulations. It is required to include monitoring controls in the processes which assist the auditors to perform an independent, objective audit. In an agile implementation, the work is based on the prioritization of the tasks by the team based on the business value, which are the user stories for each release. The sprints are time-boxed, usually two weeks and run within a fixed budget and the project scope can be altered by the team to finish a sprint and deliver it on time. This shows that the main controls to be established are on the project team and activities, which are not easy to measure and affect the project's progress. Thus, continuous monitoring is the most important in agile development scenario with DevOps integration.

The monitoring controls adopted by the auditor can be,

- Checking Sprint release Minutes of meetings
- Reviewing Sprint planning document
- Monitoring Agile dashboard showing the schedule, the progress of activities
- Reviewing technical controls like logs
- Reviewing the user story estimation and prioritization procedures
- Attending project initiation meetings

An auditor can choose to continuous monitor the environment at his discretion in concurrence with the Senior Management.

4.9.1. Auditing Process Checkpoints

The auditor must ensure that the following agile processes have been performed through proper approval, within timelines at different phases of the project, Figure 4 shows the documents and checkpoints to be verified by an auditor:

Figure 4. Auditing guidelines

PROJECT PHASES	AGILE PRACTICES/PROCESSES
Requirements Engineering	User stories log & prioritization, Product backlog and sprint backlog maintenance
Project Planning	Sprint Planning document, Release planning document
Project Management and Monitoring	Agile/SCRUM stand-up meetings, Burn down charts, Sprint review meetings, minutes of meetings
Software Quality Assurance	Automated user acceptance tests, Automated unit tests, System tests results
Risk Identification and Monitoring	Retrospective meetings, Root cause analysis of risks

5. AGILE-DEVOPS RISK ANALYSIS

5.1. Agile-DevOps Business Capabilities and Risks

DevOps can be defined as, "The practice of operations and development engineers participating together in the entire service life cycle, from design through development to production support" (Agile Admin). DevOps is an organization level mindset and change to the organization culture rather than a method/ system to adopt. The organizations typically undergo DevOps transformations on an enterprise level to implement in every product delivery. As it is large level enterprise-wide transformation, it is highly essential for the management to analyze the existing challenges and the potential risks as an introduction to the transformation. It is a culture change as a whole in an enterprise, and it could not be easier done as said. The collaboration between the application developers and the delivery teams is highly essential to bring the transformation. People, Process, and Technology are the three key elements of a successful organization. Managing human resources and bringing in a mindset change to every individual is one of the biggest challenges in adopting transformations. The three elements should co-exist with each other for a smooth, seamless transformation. Having mentioned that, the philosophies of DevOps not just confined to the application development life cycle but contributes to the success of the continuous improvement in product delivery. The focus is mainly on how effectively the members adopt to the change, interact and collaborate with one another in delivering a successful product. The DevOps principle is to satisfy the customer by ensuring continuous quality deliverables with a focus on continuous improvement.

When the business needs are carefully evaluated and analyzed, the projects are decided if its best suited for DevOps using "Pace Layering" method. The organization should identify the intend of optimization. In today's business environment, the capacity and agility to respond to the changing customer needs, business competitions, and being cognizant of the potential threats are considered a critical business capability (Prahalad, 2009). This need of the business can be fulfilled by the agility nature of our implementation and by identifying and managing the risks in the system to be implemented. The major step towards attaining business capability can be done by investigating the system and its environment for the existing risks and finding out the chances of emerging risks which can be a threat to the system/ organization. The applications have to be carefully evaluated based on the rate at which the system is required to be changed.

Let us discuss the various risks associated with DevOps transformation in an organization level in the following lines.

5.1.1. Business Risks

The organizations adopt DevOps transformation to prove a competitive advantage over the competitors with shorter time to market. Is it always possible to realize the competitive edge? Is it always possible for the companies to be at the shorter time to market? These are some of the important aspects to be considered during adoption. If the organization fails to successfully transform and adopt to transformations, the market will be potentially captured by someone who is at an even pace with the traditional technologies. The recent data proves that even Fortune 500 companies fail during DevOps transformation with its incapability to survive in the transformation. The business needs have to be carefully analyzed and the need for transformation should be considered before beginning the actual process. The definition of DevOps should be defined as per the needs of the specific organization and analyze its impact on the actual transformation.

5.1.2. Security Risks

Cloud computing is a game changer in the modern way of development where adopting DevOps principles in its environment could be a challenge by managing associated risks and challenges. (Michele et al., 2015). As cloud technologies rule the industry, DevOps Implementation is also on the rise in a cloud-based environment like AWS, Netflix where the need for continuous integration is typically high. The cloud environments are equally prone to security threats and vulnerabilities due to the rise of cyber security crime rates in the recent times. Considering this aspect, DevSecOps is the trend of the moment where the need to integrate security into development and operations is the key to the success of the DevOps transformation. In a recent data, it is stated that AWS deploys new code in its environment every 11.7 seconds (Tech Beacon, 2017) As the deployment is highly agile quantitatively, it demands test automation in the environment to make sure that fast-paced deliverables don't affect the quality of the code. These concepts are equally tricky as the industry has to revolutionize the whole system with automation, cloud in a DevOps integrated Agile environment.

5.1.3. Governance Risks

Resistance is natural to any change, and it is a herculean task to bring about any change in an organization. The governance impact is high to drive the changes in the mindset of the people. The change could adversely affect the existing productivity if resisted by the human resource in the organization. It is also challenging to convince all the stakeholders to accept DevOps mindset and drive transparency throughout the process. To understand and analyze the impact, It is vital to measure the existing performance of the processes using various statistics and data models to conclude on the impact of DevOps adoption in the organization. The adoption should comply with the existing regulations and should not violate the compliance policies at any stage. It is the responsibility of the IT Auditors and Risk Management group to jump early in the lifecycle to drive the process in the right direction following COBIT Framework.

5.1.4. Quality Assurance Risks

In an agile environment where speed is the essence, quality should not be compromised. As the teams focus more on the deadlines of the deliverables, quality should also be a priority as any product will fail without meeting the quality standards. DevOps will not be successful when quality is compromised as the need for introducing DevOps in an agile environment is to keep a check on the quality of the product. While DevOps must be aligned with organization goals, objectives and customer demands, it should also ensure high-quality performance on a continuous basis. Quality Assurance is the key driver to maintain DevOps integrated agile environment in any ecosystem, and it is the top concern.

5.2. Agile-DevOps and Auditing

To maximize the probability of success, the risks associated with a task must be minimized (Barki, 1993; Jiang & Klein, 1999). And, audit firms minimize the risk of audit failure through the identification of inherent, control, detection risks and provides reasonable assurance that material risks are within the limit and an acceptable audit risk level (Alvin et al., 1997). As Agile-DevOps unison is a great challenge in itself, identifying the risks associated, mitigating the risks, preventing the risks could be achieved by placing appropriate controls in place. To ensure the success of the transformation, the impact has to be effectively audited and measured quantitatively with statistical models based on the audit reports provided by the internal and external auditors to conclude on the success of the transformation. The need for internal auditors will be on the rise as they are typically the part of the lifecycle since the beginning to ensure that the controls are in place. As Agile-DevOps are prone to security attacks, auditing could keep a check on integrating Security aspects into the framework which will assure the quality of the product delivered. By all means, it is evident that auditing is the key to the success of the implementation.

6. AUDITING AN AGILE-DEVOPS IMPLEMENTATION

Auditing a DevOps integrated Agile model is one of the biggest challenges of the recent times in an auditing arena. As companies embrace DevOps transformations to achieve increased agility and reduced costs, there is an increase in the need for auditing the controls to provide a reasonable assurance of the transformation. To provide reasonable assurance of the transformation, DevOps practitioners are also impacted by a lot of challenges in the evolving trends to go about the Audit process (Moyle, 2015).

6.1. Security Controls

To start with auditing process, the first step would be to analyze the business needs of adopting DevOps in their environment and testing the security controls in place. Security is a critical aspect in which most of the DevOps environment considerably fail to prove their worth. The system has to automatically update patches in the adopted environment to ensure continuous integration and continuous improvement. As the patches are updated automatically, the auditors have to test the patch timestamps and releases to ensure the correctness and accuracy of the production environment. To ensure uninterrupted delivery in a DevOps environment, there should be remediation to the existing security systems which could help in case of failures. The firewalls have to carefully designed and implemented and should have backups in case of failure to effectively manage the unforeseen risks that could impact the system. Compromises of security controls are prone to threats and vulnerabilities to the system which could have a potential impact directly on the production environments thereby causing a serious business impact. In large businesses, if these controls are not properly audited by the auditors, the damages could be huge and unrecoverable.

6.2. Automation Controls

As DevOps becomes an integral part of an agile ecosystem, the need for automation is highly essential. It is the responsibility of Quality Assurance engineers to work in coherence with internal auditors during their journey of automation. During an automation journey, various tools and techniques are effectively implemented across all the platforms. The configuration of the systems is modified on driving the automation journey. During this process, the engineers have to ensure that the existing functionalities are not adversely impacted. As automation engulfs the business systems, Auditors shoulder great responsibility in assessing the risks of the automated environment focusing on continuous delivery and performance.

Internal Auditors have to play the key role from the beginning of the automation lifecycle, analyze the automated areas and establish the controls in place during the process. The external auditors have to ensure the accuracy of the log files in an automated environment and probe for substantial analysis of the logs with the automation engineer to ensure the effectiveness of the system in a production environment. The auditors have to ensure the integrity of the system is maintained in an automated environment.

6.3. Inventory Management Controls

Inventory and supply chain logistics is a huge arena that could operate in an Agile environment. In an accelerated DevOps model, maintaining the assets, analyzing the business needs of the assets and procuring the required assets could be the greatest challenge. There should be an automated asset management that records all the assets of the organization and controls their supply chain pattern for effective maintenance. At a given pint of time, the auditors have to verify the asset management using various tools to ensure the correctness of the data provided.

6.4. Training Controls

The need for training and documenting policies & procedures cannot be understated in a newly adopted Agile-DevOps integrated environment. As agile works on sprints and each sprint is very fast paced, the documentation is not usually elaborate in an agile environment. In fact, this is one of the setbacks that agile environment is working on in the recent times to accommodate detailed documentation procedures without compromising speed. When DevOps also come into the picture, the documentation of policies and procedures have to explain to the developers and engineers to understand the methodology. It is imperative for all the stakeholders to understand the framework before being the part of the actual execution. The internal auditors have to effectively contribute in defining the policies and procedures by the industry standards while the external auditors will review the policy documents to ensure their complete coverage of the process.

The auditors have to ensure if frequent training programs are conducted with various training personnel to bring the mindset to the people to embrace the change leading to a successful transformation.

7. CONCLUSION

Organizations are moving towards a collaborative agile development approach by embracing DevOps transformation in their processes. DevOps is not a process transformation but rather a culture transformation in the mindset of the people. As the digital era progresses towards clasping Automation and Artificial Intelligence techniques, there is a huge demand for increased agility and reduced costs to showcase a competitive edge in the business. To realize the organization goals effectively, there is a need for customizing the audit practices which are originally developed for auditing the traditional development methodologies. As rightly stated, "Change is the only constant" in this world. The research methodology suggested in this paper provides strategies for an IT auditor to define, establish and audit the controls by being an integral part of the DevOps Lifecycle in an agile ecosystem. When enterprises march from legacy systems towards adopting novel tools and techniques in an agile environment striving for continuous performance and delivery, it is pivotal to ensure security and provide quality assurance of the system.

The paper has proposed primarily a conceptual framework for auditing an Agile-DevOps environment, considering the implications and nature of agile and discussed the role of IT auditor across all the phases of the transformation. The paper also depicts the risk management steps and methods to ensure successful implementation of DevOps in an agile world. The emphasis here is placed on the necessity of understanding of the Agile-DevOps transformation and ensuring the need for auditors to understand and effectively manage the risks associated with the success of the transformation. Needless to state, as everything march towards agility, the auditors also have to march towards agility by protecting the regulations of the framework.

REFERENCES

Agile Methodology. (2016). Agile Methodology- The Agile Movement. Retrieved from http://agile-methodology.org/

Anwer, F., Aftab, S., Shah, S. S. M., & Waheed, U. (2017). Comparative Analysis of Two Popular Agile Process Models: Extreme Programming and Scrum. Retrieved from https://www.researchgate.net/profile/Shabib_Aftab/publication/316845761_Comparative_Analysis_of_Two_Popular_Agile_Process_Models_Extreme_Programming_and_Scrum/links/5913588fa6fdcc963e7ee052/Comparative-Analysis-of-Two-Popular-Agile-Process-Models-Extreme-Programming-and-Scrum.pdf

Arens, A.A. & Loebbecke, J.K. (1997). Auditing, an integrated approach (7th ed.). Prentice Hall.

Bacharach, S. B. (1989). Organizational theories: Some criteria for evaluation. *Academy of Management Review*, *14*, 496–515.

Barki, H., Rivard, S., & Talbot, J. (1993). Toward an Assessment of Software Development Risk. *Journal of Management Information Systems*, *10*(2), 203–225. doi:10.1080/07421222.1993.11518006

Beaumont, M., Ben Thuriaux-Alemán, P. P., & Hatton, C. (2017). Using Agile approaches for breakthrough product innovation. *Strategy and Leadership*, *45*(6), 19–25. doi:10.1108/SL-08-2017-0076

Bierwolf, R., Frijns, P., & van Kemenade, P. (2017). Project management in a dynamic environment: Balancing stakeholders. doi:10.1109/E-TEMS.2017.8244226

Canty, D. (2015). *Agile for Project Managers*. CRC Press. Retrieved from https://dl.acm.org/citation.cfm?id=2800357

Donmez, D., & Grote, G. (2015). Two sides on the same coin – how agile software development approach uncertainty as threats and opportunities?

Elbanna, A., & Sarkar, S. (2016). The Risks of Agile Software Development: Learning from Developers. *IEEE Software*, *33*(5), 72–79. doi:10.1109/MS.2015.150

Ghobadi, S., & Lars, M. (2017). Risks to effective knowledge sharing in Agile Software Teams: A model for assessing and mitigating risks. Retrieved from https://onlinelibrary-wiley-com.gate.lib.buffalo.edu/doi/epdf/10.1111/isj.12117

Guerriero, M., Ciavotta, M., Gibilisco, G. P., & Ardagna, D. (2015). SPACE4Cloud: a DevOps environment for multi-cloud applications. doi:10.1145/2804371.2804378

Haines, T., Idemudia, C. E., & Mahesh, S. R. (2017). The conceptual model for agile tools and techniques. *American Journal of Management*, *17*(3). Retrieved from http://www.na-businesspress.com/AJM/HainesT_17_3_.pdf

Hart, M. (2017). IT software development and IT operations strategic alignment: An agile DevOps model. Retrieved from https://search.proquest.com/docview/1881835724?accountid=14169

Hartman, B. (2009). New to Agile? What Does the ScrumMaster Do Anyway? *Agileforall*. Retrieved from http://agileforall.com/new-to-agile-what-does-the-scrummaster-do-anyway/

Holler, R. (2010). Five Myths of Agile Development. *Versionone*. Retrieved from http://www.versionone.com/pdf/AgileMyths_BetterSoftware.pdf

IBM. (n.d.). Adopting the IBM DevOps approach for continuous software delivery. Retrieved from http://www.ibm.com/developerworks/libraryld-adoption-paths/

Jiang, J. J., & Klein, G. (1999). Risks to different aspects of system success. *Information & Management*, *36*(5), 263–272. doi:10.1016/S0378-7206(99)00024-5

Miller, G. (2001). *The Characteristics of Agile Software Processes*. IEEE Computer Society.

Moe, N. B., Dingsøyr, T., & Dybå, T. (2010). A teamwork model for understanding an agile team: A case study of a Scrum project. *Information and Software Technology*, *52*(5), 480–491. doi:10.1016/j.infsof.2009.11.004

Moyle, E. (2015). Devops Practioner Considerations. In *ISACA Conference 2015*. Retrieved from http://informationsecurity.report/Resources/Whitepapers/edbb342e-447a-427d-a7b2-83c4bcbacdb9_DevOps-Practitioner-Considerations_whp_Eng_0815.pdf

Prahalad, C. K. (2009). In volatile times, agility rules. *Business Week*, *80*(September), 21.

Oracle Primavera. (2011). The Yin and Yang of Enterprise Project Portfolio Management and Agile Software Development: Combining Creativity and Governance.

Rico, D. F. (2008). What is the Return on Investment (ROI) of agile methods? *Methods*.

Senft, S., Gallegos, F., & Davis, A. (2012). *Information technology control and audit*. Auerbach Publications.

Shrivastava, S., & Rathod, U. (2015). Categorization of risk factors for distributed agile projects. *Information and Software Technology*, *58*(February), 373–387. doi:10.1016/j.infsof.2014.07.007

Singleton, T. (2014). The Core of IT Auditing. *ISACA Journal*, *6*. Retrieved from https://www.isaca.org/Journal/archives/2014/Volume-6/Pages/The-Core-of-IT-Auditing.aspx

TechBeacon. (2017). Retrieved from https://techbeacon.com/survey-agile-new-norm

TechBeacon. (2018). Retrieved from https://techbeacon.com/8-devops-trends-watch-2018

Tilk, D. (2016). 5 Steps to agile project success: the dynamic, fast-paced nature of Agile software development requires auditors to think differently about internal controls. *AcademicOneFile*. Retrieved from http://link.galegroup.com/apps/doc/A450695664/AONE?u=sunybuff_main&sid=AONE&xid=d44691ee

Varhol, P. (2016, November 21). The complete history of agile software development. *TechBeacon*. Retrieved from https://techbeacon.com/agility-beyond-history%E2%80%94-legacy%E2%80%94-agile-development

Virmani, M. (2015). Understanding DevOps and bridging the gap from continuous integration to continuous delivery. doi:10.1109/INTECH.2015.7173368

This research was previously published in the International Journal of Risk and Contingency Management (IJRCM), 7(4); pages 90-110, copyright year 2018 by IGI Publishing (an imprint of IGI Global).

Chapter 59
Weaving Security into DevOps Practices in Highly Regulated Environments

Jose Andre Morales

Software Engineering Institute, Carnegie Mellon University, Pittsburgh, USA

Hasan Yasar

Software Engineering Institute, Carnegie Mellon University, Pittsburgh, USA

Aaron Volkmann

Software Engineering Institute, Carnegie Mellon University, Pittsburgh, USA

ABSTRACT

In this article, the authors discuss enhancing a DevOps implementation in a highly regulated environment (HRE) with security principles. DevOps has become a standard option for entities seeking to streamline and increase participation by all stakeholders in their Software Development Lifecycle (SDLC). For a large portion of industry, academia, and government, applying DevOps is a straight forward process. There is, however, a subset of entities in these three sectors where applying DevOps can be very challenging. These are entities mandated by security policies to conduct all, or a portion, of their SDLC activities in an HRE. Often, the reason for an HRE is protection of intellectual property and proprietary tools, methods, and techniques. Even if an entity is functioning in a highly regulated environment, its SDLC can still benefit from implementing DevOps as long as the implementation conforms to all imposed policies. A benefit of an HRE is the existence of security policies that belong in a secure DevOps implementation. Layering an existing DevOps implementation with security will benefit the HRE as a whole. This work is based on the authors extensive experience in assessing and implementing DevOps across a diverse set of HREs. First, they extensively discuss the process of performing a DevOps assessment and implementation in an HRE. They follow this with a discussion of the needed security principles a DevOps enhanced SDLC should include. For each security principle, the authors discuss their importance to the SDLC and their appropriate placement within a DevOps implementation. They refer to a security enhanced DevOps implementation in an HRE as HRE-DevSecOps.

DOI: 10.4018/978-1-6684-3702-5.ch059

1. INTRODUCTION

A highly regulated environment (Hrebiniak & Joyce, 1985; Edwards, 1977; Blau et al., 2000; Rasmussen et al., 2009) (HRE) is typically characterized by the following: air-gapped physical spaces and computer systems with heightened security and access controls, segregation of duties, inability of personnel to discuss certain topics outside of specific areas, and the inability to take certain artifacts off premises. An HRE is put to use when secrecy and controlled access is required for proprietary tools, methods, techniques, and intellectual property. DevOps, with and without a security component, has been proven to increase effectiveness and, most importantly, efficiency of an SDLC. As a result of this, several entities that utilize HREs such as the US Department of Defense (LaPlante & Wisnieff, 2018; Dioguino, 2016) are implementing DevOps into their SDLC. Currently, there is minimal literature on implementing DevOps in an HRE explaining the mechanics, expectations, challenges, realities, and paths to success in comparison to currently used non-DevOps models (Bruza, 2018; Farroha & Farroha, 2014). In this paper, our leverage our experiences with DevOps and security to address these issues. There is no known data set of metrics for DevOps in an HRE and an approach based on the scientific method is not possible at this time. This work seeks to enhance current literature with an experience-based approach to Secure DevOps. For the purpose of this work, the term air-gapped is meant describe physical spaces, personnel, computer systems, and other technologies that are isolated from all entities that are external to the HRE. We have mentioned only some of the characteristics of an HRE as the list changes on a case by case basis. An HRE can be referred to as a closed area, classified space, controlled access area, or Sensitive Compartmented Information Facility (SCIF). The definition of an HRE used in this paper is not the same as government regulation. Those policies are focused on how to conduct business, financial responsibilities, and disclosure filing, just to name a few. Regulatory policies are required for various sectors of industry and overseen by federal agencies such as the U.S. Securities & Exchange Commission (SEC), the U.S. Food and Drug Administration (FDA), and the Federal Communications Commission (FCC).

Each of the previously mentioned obstacles characterizing an HRE can impose several barriers impeding the full incorporation of DevOps (Hüttermann, 2012; Bass, Weber, & Zhu, 2015) practices into a Software Development Lifecycle (SDLC) (Yasar, & Kontostathis, 2016). In this paper, we follow the core DevOps definition of uniting software development and IT operations into one singular process. We focus on implementing the following DevOps principles in an HRE:

1.   Open communication between all stakeholders
2.   Infrastructure as Code (IaC)
3.   Environment parity
4.   Centralized documentation
5.   Continuous completion and deployment of small tasks
6.   Performance monitoring
7.   Accurate production environment replication
8.   End user feedback loop
9.   Automation
10. Software artifact versioning

We consider Secure DevOps (DevSecOps) to be the implementation of diverse security principles to an existing DevOps implementation (Mohan, & Othman, 2016; Myrbakken, & Colomo-Palacios, 2017). The key purpose of DevSecOps is to decrease the possibility of deploying vulnerable code and systems. We focus on the following security principles for DevOps in an HRE:

1. Security requirements
2. Secure coding
3. Testing for vulnerabilities
4. Testing for unexpected behaviors
5. Misuse cases

Based on the security requirements of organizations we have worked with regarding DevOps, we determined these principles should be present in any DevOps implementation and an appropriate focus of this work. In general, HREs tend to exist in isolation with gaps between personnel and projects. Isolation is in direct contrast to DevOps, where the main goal is to establish open communication between all members and stakeholders of a project. In order to implement DevOps practices in an HRE, the current state of the SDLC process must be clearly understood. This can be accomplished as part of a DevOps assessment (Forsgren, et al., 2017). Once the assessment is completed, obstacles impeding the current SDLC process should be identified and analyzed one by one to determine if DevOps practices can overcome the barrier. A list of recommendations should be submitted to relevant project stakeholders who must verify which recommendations are implementable within all the boundaries of applicable policies (Cois, Yankel, & Connell, 2014). In some cases, it is acceptable for a recommendation to fall outside the scope of DevOps. These recommendations should still be submitted since they are part of the reality of customizing traditional DevOps practices into tailored versions benefiting a specific HRE situation. We refer to the process of assessing, implementing and customizing DevOps practices for the SDLC of an HRE as HRE-DevOps and when security principles are included, IIRE-DevSecOps. In the contributions of this paper, we:

1. Detail the process of conducting a DevOps assessment for a highly regulated environment (HRE).
2. Describe enhancing a DevOps implementation with security principles.
3. Present typical HRE characteristics that are obstacles to a DevOps implementation.
4. Explain realities of these assessments which fall outside of preconceived notions.
5. Provide several approaches to resolve or minimize obstacles typically present in an HRE.
6. Give a process to document and present identified obstacles.

The remainder of this paper discusses each of the steps in the process of assessing and implementing DevOps practices and the enhancement of those practices with security principles in an HRE. The remaining sections are as follows: Section 2 is HRE Assessment, Section 3 is Analyzing SDLC obstacles, Section 4 is DevOps and non-DevOps Recommendations, Section 5 is Implementing recommendations, Section 6 is Assessing the DevOps posture of an HRE, Section 7 is General HRE strategies, Section 8 is HRE secure DevOps, and Section 9 is Conclusions and future work.

2. HRE ASSESSMENT

Before commencing an assessment, expectations should be set with HRE personnel. From the beginning, HRE personnel should know that DevOps practices will likely not solve all issues faced in their SDLC. The assessment of an HRE will typically include recommendations that may not be part of DevOps practices but is essential to improving the SDLC. The overall assessment goals should be:

1. Identify the root causes of bottlenecks and pain points that occur within the HRE when executing the SDLC.
2. Recommend DevOps solutions as broadly as possible.
3. Recommend non-DevOps solutions when improvements cannot be achieved with DevOps approaches.
4. Establish the HRE's DevOps posture (Forsgren, et al., 2017) and identify SDLC components needing improvement in order to consider implementing DevOps practices.

At the commencement of an assessment it is critical to clearly detail what will be assessed in regards to personnel, systems, and processes. Clearly state that the focus of the assessment is to improve the SDLC in an HRE including: current software lifecycle, technology being used in that process, and professional interactions of personnel regarding the process. The culture of the SDLC creates an environment which can include assumptions, beliefs, default decision making, group discussions, teamwork, and reliance between individuals. It is non-trivial to understand the culture of a group of people when implementing the SDLC, especially in an HRE (Harvey, et al., 2002). One way to gather understanding, besides interviews, is to observe the personnel in performing daily work tasks on an actual project, asking questions to clarify doubts, and documenting every step of one member for each project role type.

When assessing an HRE, a substantial amount of time should be spent in interviewing personnel, primarily developers and engineers, to understand how the SDLC process is currently implemented (Rong, Zhang, & Shao, 2016). Keep in mind the SDLC can be implemented very differently for each HRE, and for different development groups within one HRE. The assessors must understand every HRE's process and obstacles in detail including imposed policies affecting the SDLC in some way. It is critical to understand the policies that dictate that certain components of the SDLC must be carried out in a specific way. When assessing a software development group in an HRE, consider the following questions:

1. How is stakeholder communication accomplished, how often, by what means?
2. Do all requirements come at the beginning of a project or are some added after work has begun?
3. How is artifact delivery carried out?
4. How are HRE external stakeholders given access to artifact documents and project progress?
5. Is there a feedback loop between stakeholders, especially developers, and end users in the production environment?
6. Are staging environments used always, never, or only when the production environment is inaccessible?
7. Can changes be made to an artifact during and after initial deployment?
8. What is the project authorization process?
9. What other bottlenecks, not covered here, are causing delays to project commencement and completion?
10. What is the hardware acquisition process?
11. Are there any non-HRE development activities contributing to the project and how are they managed?

The process of carrying out an assessment should include several on-site visits, shadowing of daily work and conference calls. Assessor-led meetings with HRE personnel should occur to discuss:

Assessor observations of the SDLC process. When presenting an assessor's observations to HRE personnel, it is best to divide the observations by the components of the SDLC. The assessor should first describe their understanding of the process for the specific component and validate its correctness with HRE personnel. For each component, the assessor should point out observations considered standard SDLC practices, non-standard practices, and expected standard practices not observed. Standard SDLC practices greatly facilitate implementing DevOps since those practices function the same as they would in a non-HRE entity. When a non-standard SDLC practice is observed, HRE personnel should explain in detail why it is in use, the unique conditions that led to its use, and more importantly, if it is the result of imposed policies or other measures unique to the HRE. Identifying standard and non-standard practices is based on the assessor's knowledge of observing SDLC implementations in non-HRE environments. The assessor should attempt to establish if a non-standard practice is in use because it provides a benefit to the SDLC. If yes, then consider if replacing it with a DevOps approach can achieve the same or improved benefits.

Obstacles stated by HRE personnel. As discussions about the current SDLC implementation progress, an assessor can expect HRE personnel, in most cases, to quickly reveal the pain points and bottlenecks making their job harder. In some cases, the personnel are eager to discuss these in search of a solution and should be given high priority. Pain points and bottlenecks are typically symptoms of a root cause. The assessor must discuss in depth with HRE personnel and review documentation to find the root cause(s) leading to these symptoms. An obstacle can be created for each root cause. The assessor needs to craft a precise statement that describes the obstacle and validate its correctness with personnel. It must be mutually agreed if a stated obstacle is out of scope of the SDLC. Depending on the scenario, these particular obstacles may not get addressed, and this should be made clear to the HRE personnel. Out of scope items should be documented and included in the final assessment report. For each obstacle, the assessor must determine if it exists due to conditions stemming from imposed policies or operational concerns. Unless informed otherwise by HRE personnel, an assessor should assume these reasons are non-negotiable and removing or ignoring them is not an option.

Inferred obstacles observed by the assessor. It is possible that an HRE can have obstacles that personnel do not recognize. In observing the day to day operations of the HRE, an assessor can discover a process negatively affecting the SDLC. The HRE personnel may not be aware of this and not consider it an obstacle. It is important, in these cases, to point out the observed obstacle and its negative impact. The assessor must make clear to personnel why this is an obstacle. The assessor should detail its negative impact on the SDLC process along with potential benefits from its removal or modification, assuming its existence is not the result of a mandatory imposition. Only if the HRE personnel agrees that this is an obstacle which they have overlooked can it be addressed. If there is disagreement, the inferred obstacle should be listed in the final report.

An effective assessment occurs when HRE personnel feel comfortable in open conversation with assessors inside an HRE. This implies no negative impact or retaliation can occur for expressing their concerns and frustrations. Achieving this can be done in negotiations with HRE management. The most effective people to engage are the actual developers performing the day to day tasks of the SDLC for various projects. These people are closest to the work and they are most aware of the obstacles impeding their productivity. Assessments will benefit from the availability of diagrams, manuals, and any other documentation detailing the SDLC process. Reviewing the HRE's software development plan (SDP) provides the basis for the SDLC (Darling, 1993; Boehm & Ross, 1989; Cagle, Rice, & Kristan, 2015). Desk instructions for developers can also give great insight on their current SDLC process and if the day-to-day developer activities actually follow the instructions and SDP. Walking through an actual completed or ongoing project facilitates the discovery and detailing of obstacles in the SDLC. Any discovered differences between daily work routines and documented processes should be included in an assessment if it impacts the SDLC in a negative way.

3. ANALYZING SDLC OBSTACLES

As previously stated, bottlenecks and pain points are typically symptoms of an existing problem. Discovering the root cause of these problems serves to describe an obstacle that should be addressed. An obstacle can be described as a composition of the following four parts:

1. Description of the obstacle.
2. Reason for the obstacle's imposition.
3. Method in which the obstacle is imposed.
4. Reason why it is an obstacle.

A method can be characterized as a series of actions that when followed enforces the obstacle. The method and reason are critical when determining which obstacles can and cannot be addressed with assessor recommendations. If the reason for an obstacle is policy imposition or obligatory conditions within the HRE, the obstacle cannot be removed. If any other reason is given for an obstacle, it can be considered for removal or modification. Often, actions can be streamlined while still enforcing the obstacle. This does not hold true in specific cases where a single or series of actions are imposed by policy or HRE conditions. Here are some examples of obstacles:

3.1. Obstacle 1 Description

Code development details cannot be shared with operators. Reason: Security concerns over proprietary tactics. Method: Implement air gapped environments for the physical locations and computer networks of the development and IT operations teams. Actions: 1. Place each team in physically separate buildings 2. Isolate the developer and operator networks by using different IP ranges with internal-only access 3. Provide individual email servers filtering out communication between members of different teams 4. Developer software licensing must not be shared between teams. Reason why it's an obstacle: Developers cannot discuss during code development if the approaches they are using will be effective in production operations. This increases the potential for defects or unexpected side effects that could be avoided if discussions were allowed.

3.2. Obstacle 2 Description

All physical software artifacts related to a project must be stored in a single isolated and secure location. Reason: Facilitates retrieval of physically secured archived projects for the development team. Method: Designate a multi-shelf archive closet in an isolated area with pre-approved badge access. Actions: 1.

Identify an isolated room with badge access 2. Clearly mark Development Team Archive Closet 3. Provide access during 9am-5pm to developers on an as needed basis. Reason why it's an obstacle: Developers work well into the night and cannot access artifacts after 5pm. This holds back project progress and/or completion.

3.3. Obstacle 3 Description

Projects must be approved by a member of the senior leadership prior to commencement. Reason: Administrative management policy. Method: Member of senior leadership is given project description for approval with signature. Actions: 1. Stakeholder will provide needs to development team 2. Team formalizes needs into mutually agreed project document containing description and requirements 3. Document officially sent to senior leadership for approval 4. Work commences upon approval receipt. Reason why it's an obstacle: A project's approval could have very long delays. Project completion is due within a specified time and there is no compensatory time added for delayed approval. This drastically cuts into the time left to complete a project. Developers may rush to meet the timeline producing, in some cases, an inferior final result.

3.4. Obstacle 4 Description

The operational testing environment is air gapped from the development team. Reason: The operational testing environment is highly secure due to imposed requirements. Method: Approved software changes are hand carried into the operational testing environment on portable media by security personnel. Actions: 1. Software development team member submits a software change request 2. The software change is packaged by a configuration management team 3. The software change is vetted by the security team to determine its security posture 4. The configuration management team copies the software change onto portable media 5. The physical security team transports the portable media into the operational testing environment Reason why it's an obstacle: A software change workflow that involves multiple teams performing manual processes can add many more hours or days to a continuous integration/continuous deployment cycle (Virmani, 2015; Hilton et al., 2016) in the SDLC.

The above summarizes some sample obstacles following our definition of an obstacle's components. Obstacle 1 is in place to protect personally identifiable information (Schwartz, & Solove, 2011) (PII). It is not stated to be a policy, so it may be modifiable or removable. Closely reading the actions, it becomes clear that some of these, such as separate work locations and IP ranges, cannot be removed due to HRE conditions. In this case, the actions taken to implement air-gapped environments are governed by their own set of imposed policies likely not removable or modifiable. Obstacle 2 is imposed by the development team's desire to easily access artifacts that are physically secured. This is not an imposed policy and actions can be modified to overcome the obstacle. The reason for obstacle 3 is imposed policy. The actions used to enforce are not themselves imposed policy or part of an HRE. There may be ways to modify the actions to better deal with this obstacle and ensure adherence to the policy, but these will need to be discussed and agreed to by HRE personnel. Obstacle 4 is isolating highly secure systems and operators. It is enforced by the HRE and the actions are likely mandated by policy. There may be few possible modifications in this obstacle, the assessment team will have to analyze closely with HRE personnel. This small sampling of obstacles illustrates the importance of understanding the reasons for an obstacle's existence and the actions enforcing it. In all four cases the stated reasons are the critical component to decide if the obstacle can be addressed in some way or not at all.

When interviews and on-site visits are completed, a list of agreed upon obstacles is presented. For each obstacle in the list, the assessment team must decide if a DevOps approach can be put in place to address it or if some other non-DevOps solution can be used. Here is a list of some obstacles that can be expected to exist in an HRE:

1. Air-gapped environment.
2. Slow project approval.
3. Slow hardware and software acquisition.
4. No software version control.
5. No centralized document repository.
6. No communication with stakeholders.
7. Loss of project work time.
8. Partial or no production environment access.
9. New requirements late in SDLC.
10. No centralized software installation.
11. High attrition of contract personnel.
12. Slow fulfillment of IT requests.

The above list generalizes, from our real-world experience, the obstacles that could be present in an HRE. It is not exhaustive and each of the development groups within an HRE will have specific circumstances leading to unique obstacles. Once each obstacle has been reviewed and documented, the next step is to make recommendations.

4. DEVOPS AND NON-DEVOPS RECOMMENDATIONS

The goal of an assessment is to remove or alleviate the obstacles that HRE personnel face when executing the SDLC. In some cases, DevOps can help reach that goal. In other cases, non-DevOps approaches are appropriate. This mix of approaches is prevalent in HREs. The assessment team should focus on applying DevOps followed by non-DevOps recommendations. It should not be the policy of an assessor to not address obstacles if a DevOps approach cannot be applied. Below we discuss possible recommendations for the previously presented generalized obstacle list.

4.1. Air-Gapped Environment

A key component of all HREs is areas that are isolated or air-gapped (Byres, 2013; NEI; Allcorn, Diamond, & Stien, 2002; Storms, 2015). These silos separate personnel and technology from other groups of the same entity and outsiders. These environments are in direct contrast to cooperation and inclusion of all stakeholders throughout the SDLC process, which is a cornerstone of DevOps principles. Due to imposed policies regarding security, it will be difficult to include all stakeholders throughout the SDLC. One approach is inclusion of persons allowed to be in the HRE representing a stakeholder that is not allowed. This person can create reports for the stakeholder with HRE security and management approval for external distribution. A typical HRE's security focus is on the outflow of information and less on the inflow. This can allow stakeholders to openly contact HRE personnel, via email or phone, with questions and requests. Personnel can reply within the bounds of security policies. Assessors should ask the details of what is allowed and not allowed in both physical and digital silos. It may be the case that a stakeholder is not allowed physically in a silo but is allowed to view materials online that are stored in a silo. In the case where a stakeholder is disallowed in both physical and digital spaces, a representative may be needed. If that is not possible, arrangements can be made for reoccurring meetings in a non-HRE to provide HRE-approved updates and status.

4.2. Slow Project Approval

In an HRE, most projects must be submitted via a formal process up a management chain to a senior leadership member who provides approval. This can be a very time-consuming process that absorbs work cycles from developers. Time is further consumed when multiple senior members claim authority and debate who should rightfully approve a project. Typically, time is not added on to a project schedule when this occurs, and developers are rushing to complete the work. This breaks several DevOps principles, primarily the ability to deploy multiple versions of a software during development for testing and feedback. One approach to overcome this is designating a middle management member as a proxy approver for projects. This person is physically located with the developers and can quickly provide authorization following guidelines provided by senior leadership. The project is simultaneously sent via the normal approval route while work commences in a timely manner. Since the proxy approves projects based on predetermined guidance by senior leadership, chances of a rejection are low. Another approach is to empower the stakeholder requesting the project to approve work commencement. This is possible in scenarios where the stakeholder is authorized to use a source of funding for these projects and is approved to task the development team.

4.3. Slow Hardware and Software Acquisition

HREs may have to deal with hardware and software acquisition processes which are burdened with several approvals and processing steps. These typically occur at the beginning of a project, but could happen at any point, and can cause significant delays or time consumption. In general, acquisition is not related to DevOps. Solutions to improving the internal acquisition process would be non-DevOps. Dealing with the obstacle can, on the other hand, be eased with DevOps concepts. At the requirements stage of the SDLC, a review of needed software and hardware should be conducted between all parties. Based on the agreed upon needs, extra time can be budgeted to allow for acquisition thus not affecting the development time. A good DevOps environment, even in an HRE, is equipped with modern development technologies. Being DevOps proactive requires developers to explore new commercial tools and techniques as they come to market. Adding new tools and techniques can narrow the need for software and hardware acquisition to cases where very specific items are required.

4.4. No Software Version Control

Maintaining software and its dependencies in a version control system (VCS) is critical to a successful DevOps implementation (Fischer, Pinzger, & Gall, 2003; Cois, Yankel, & Connell, 2014; Fuggetta, & Di

Nitto, 2014). In some cases, the developers may deliver multiple versions of the same product to different entities. Due to project urgency or imposed policy, those products may lack clearly marked version numbers. This can create a scenario where various groups are testing different versions of the software resulting in mixed feedback causing delays to project completion. A solution is based on how project artifacts are delivered: if via a repository where others download from, then that repository should, at a minimum, have version control on the developer side and assure users can only download the latest version. This should be accompanied with alerts and updates either in the repository, email, or other communication channels to users informing they may have an older version and should consider updating. Depending on the reason for this obstacle, these actions can be less restrictive to the point of labeling new version numbers into the filenames directly. If delivery is made via a physical medium such as a USB drive, CD, or DVD, ideally it should be marked with a version number. If that is not possible, the developers should assure the items on the device are the expected version. An alternative is to generate numeric sequences for software versions. The generation method should assure unique sequences every time. Recipients will still know if two products are different versions based on the numeric sequence. These devices need to be version marked in some way to avoid confusion if several are stored in one place. An end user should not have to insert a device to discover the version number. In ideal cases, implementing the complete DevOps concept, all stakeholders have access to a centralized repository storing downloadable historical versioned archives of project artifacts.

4.5. No Centralized Document Repository

During the SDLC, project stakeholders will create notes, updates, requests, instructions, guidance, and many other types of documents. These documents are often stored in various locations. This results in stakeholders, primarily end users, accessing obsolete documentation on the project that do not include the latest updates, features, installations and usage instructions. In a DevOps process, centralized document repositories are critical to provide visibility to all stakeholders. One approach is to provide HRE external stakeholders with documentation possessing appropriate distribution approvals. Another option is to electronically expose the repository's documentation to specific external stakeholders via secure networks having appropriate security access controls. Stakeholders will have access only to what they need to read. Requests can be made for other documentation that can be made available with appropriate approvals.

4.6. No Communication with Stakeholders

Some stakeholders do not have a direct line of communication with the personnel developing their product in an HRE. This breaks the fundamental DevOps principle of involving all stakeholders in each step of the SDLC. The problem is critical in relation to project requesters and end users. An absent requester can lead to vague or unverified project requirements. An absent end user can result in no or minimal project feedback which is imperative to testing and development in the DevOps process. It must be established at project commencement who the stakeholders are and verify available communication channels. Each stakeholder should have one or more representatives available to participate if they are unavailable. This way, full stakeholder participation throughout the SDLC can be achieved.

4.7. Loss of Project Work Time

For several reasons, some of which we have already discussed, budgeted project schedule time can be reduced to levels that risk successful project execution. In an HRE, there could be many cases where a project may require start to finish completion in hours or days. The approval processes for software and hardware acquisitions, software change requests, and others can place project completion at risk. Unfortunately, hardware and software acquisition are likely beyond the control of project developers. In these cases, project time extensions must be requested, or requirements reduced to a set that is achievable in the remaining time allotment. A DevOps approach to minimize lost project time is being proactive in developer, industry, government, and consumer technology communities. Part of this approach is to acquire, investigate, and create new tools and techniques for both common and specialized applications. In cases where project approval is delaying work start, one approach would be assigning a senior member of the development team such as an immediate manager that is physically located with the team to give immediate approval to all projects with completion times below some threshold. That threshold could be hours, days, or weeks. The project approval request should simultaneously be submitted into the usual process of approval with an additional marking of "expedited approval due to project schedule pressure."

4.8. Partial or No Production Environment Access

For projects developed in an HRE, scenarios will likely arise where the production environment is not available to the development team to create a replica as a staging environment for testing. Testing in a non-accurate staging environment is full of risks. This breaks two critical DevOps concepts. First, the ability to complete small tasks of a project and release it as a version to the end user for testing and feedback, referred to as continuous integration/continuous deployment (CI/CD) (Virmani, 2015; Hilton et al., 2016). This is a critical DevOps component because it enables the rapid build, testing, and deployment of small incremental code changes minimizing expenditure of time and money. Second, without testing on an accurately replicated staging environment, no real-world feedback can be provided on quality and performance. One approach would be to elicit as much detail as possible about the production environment from all accessible sources and replicate as accurately as possible within the development team's work space as a staging environment. This form of internal testing would provide all stakeholders, especially the developers, some confidence the final product will work as expected in the production environment. Ideally, testing occurs in an accurately replicated production environment with end user feedback. In absence of that scenario, testing in a staging environment which is an accurate as possible replication of the production environment could be the next best choice.

4.9. New Requirements Late in SDLC

Following the DevOps process, requirements for software development are acquired at the requirements stage of the SDLC with all stakeholders involved. In the dynamic nature of HREs, requirements can arise in the later stages of the SDLC process. Accepting a new requirement at later SDLC stages can have broad impacts on the entire project consuming significant time for design, development, and testing. Ideally it is best that no requirements arise in late SDLC stages. If a new late stage requirement must be considered, here is some guidance to help decide if the requirement should be accepted or not. First, identify who is giving the requirement. It should only be the original requester, an internal developer, or an operator or end user in response to unexpected production environment changes. The original requester can create new requirements for essential functions to the original project. Adding non-essential features or enhancements should not be accepted and instead placed on an optional project backlog. An internal developer can provide new requirements based on unique technical domain knowledge of hardware or software. A developer may be aware of fine grained system details that need specific treatment to avoid unexpected outcomes. In this case, the requirement must be approved by the original requester. Production environments are dynamic in nature and can change at any moment. When one of these changes impacts the execution of software being developed for that environment, the end user or operator must inform the developers in order to address appropriately. If a requirement meets one of the above criteria, the development team, and all other stakeholders, should assess and assure the time needed to implement and test the requirement is within current time budgets. If needed time goes beyond current time budgets, either a request for additional time is approved or the new requirement is placed on an optional project backlog or rejected. Another option is to swap the new requirement with another requirement that is deemed non-essential and relabeled optional. In order to deal with "late stage" requirements better, developers should follow the DevOps concept of progressing a project through the entire SDLC process one small task at a time. Ideally, a "late stage" requirement will only impact one or a few completed tasks. A small task contains a small amount of source code in a single unit such as a function or class. This simplifies the task of modifying and testing code that addresses last stage requirements.

4.10. No Centralized Software Installation

Some HREs may lack a centralized software artifact repository that stores released versions software artifacts. This can enable irregular software deployments, resulting in different versions of the same software being deployed throughout an environment, leading to several problems. Not having a centralized software deployment process violates the DevOps principle of environment parity (Hoffman, 2016). This principle dictates that all machines used in the same group or for the same purpose are setup and configured identically. For developers, this is critical. As an example, building code using two versions of the same library can produce significantly different outcomes. In the case of production environments, developers should deliver software for testing contained within the staging environments that are used for their own internal testing. The staging environment, as previously discussed, should either be an exact copy or accurate as possible replica of the expected production environment. Fortunately, there are several system container and virtual machine technologies available to easily establish environment parity. Developers should deploy one virtual machine image for all developer workstations at the start of each new project. This assures all developers are working on identical systems. The virtual machine should be archived and marked as designated for this project. Internal testing in a staging environment can occur using a virtual machine replicating the production environment. Virtual machines containing new project versions can be placed in a container and sent to external stakeholders for testing. This assures external testing is done in the exact same environment as internal developer testing. Environment parity provides several advantages, the most critical being the elimination of system differences as a source of reported problems when testing or running a project's software. A development team can create a centralized automated service to provision and deploy systems and software. This is the DevOps principle of Infrastructure as Code (IaC) (Artac et al., 2017; Hummer et al., 2013). This principle supports environment parity by deploying pre-configured systems, networks, and environments as needed by developers, operators, and testers. At the start of a project all stakeholders should agree on the systems and environments needed to build and test a project. These are built prior to project commencement and can be deployed automatically when needed. The service should track all personnel's deployments and launch automatic updates when changes to the base system occur ensuring environment parity throughout the project's life cycle.

4.11. High Attrition of Contract Personnel

In an HRE, not all personnel are full time employees. It may be the case where some personnel are third-party contractors. These contractors work for variable periods of time, from days to years. An environment of contractors working on a project for short periods of time does not establish a long-lasting culture of DevOps within an HRE. Once a person understands the DevOps process being carried out at an HRE, it becomes part of daily work life. When all, or most, members of a group think the same way about DevOps, they are more likely to work seamlessly together as one cohesive unit. Regularly bringing new contract personnel up to speed on the team's DevOps process can delay, sometimes significantly, a project's completion. Ideally, contractors should persist until project completion or for several years with the same group to sustain a long-lasting DevOps culture. If it is unavoidable to retain contractors beyond short periods, a DevOps training should be a pre-requisite for a new contractor, or any team member, to join a group. This training indoctrinates a person in the DevOps process of a specific group. The training should consist of a lecture and sample project where the trainee carries out the project using the learned DevOps process. Once completed, the trainee should shadow an established group member with same job type to observe firsthand the DevOps implementation. The group members collectively test the trainee's DevOps understanding and approve the contractor's entry to the group. The time spent training is variable and dictated by the group's suitability assessment. The training should always be performed in the same manner for each new group member and carried out by the same instructor. This person should be a full-time employee whose only job function is to provide training for specific HRE groups. Instructor training should be dictated and managed by HRE personnel.

4.12. Slow IT Request Fulfillments

All HREs will submit IT requests for a diverse set of needs. In cases where a request holds back project progress, the developers should not be held accountable for internal IT delays. Much like hardware and software acquisition, there may be little that can be done, from a DevOps perspective, to change the internal IT process of fulfilling requests. One approach to alleviate slow requests is to implement the DevOps principle of IaC as previously discussed. Another approach to minimize IT requests is to assess required access, authorizations, systems, configurations, accounts, and other similar needs as part of the requirements gathering stage and fulfilled before any development starts. This can minimize IT requests to only unexpected occurrences. A proactive approach is to routinely assure developers have all they need for daily work. This is easily achievable with an IaC service. In accordance with the DevOps principle of environment parity, establishing a core set of tools and techniques that are available via IaC facilitates the assurance of access to all group members. Under these scenarios, only unique cases where specialization is required would an IT request be submitted.

We have addressed only general obstacles that one should expect in an HRE. There can be several more for specific circumstances in an HRE. The solutions may not always be rooted in DevOps principles. Overall, the goal is to create a more cohesive and inclusive group of stakeholders for a project which is a critical component of any successful DevOps implementation. At this point in the assessment, an internal write up of recommendations for each obstacle is in place. This list should be reviewed by HRE personnel. A list of recommendations, mutually agreed upon between the assessment team and HRE personnel, is submitted in the final report.

5. IMPLEMENTING RECOMMENDATIONS

Once recommendations are finalized, the next step is for HRE personnel to implement them. The role of the assessor in this stage can be to assist in the implementation or end the engagement. Ideally, the assessment team, which possess DevOps domain knowledge, should assist HRE personnel in implementing recommendations. The best approach is to implement one recommendation at a time. Assessors and HRE personnel should work closely together to identify the processes and systems that will be modified by the implementation and the affected team members. In some cases, modifying existing or acquiring new hardware and software may be required. Given our previous discussion of hardware and software acquisition and IT requests, completing an implementation may take longer than expected. Each implementation may require significant time and effort to place within imposed policies and HRE constraints while others are simple and straightforward. It should be expected that some recommendations may need modifications resulting from discoveries while attempting to implement. HRE personnel should be made aware of this possibility beforehand. As an implementation is completed, a test period with one or more projects should be observed to assure the expected outcome has been achieved. Documenting observations and interviewing HRE personnel for feedback is critical to assure the implementation worked and the personnel using it are satisfied. If this is not the case, assessors and HRE personnel should identify what is not working, the reason for it and attempt a fix. This may not always be achievable and thus some recommendations may only be partially implemented. Once all recommendations have been addressed, assessors should observe their use in a project. The assessors and HRE personnel should decide how many recommendations to fully implement before observing the newly enhanced SDLC process in one or more projects. It is critical to conduct satisfaction surveys and solicit feedback from HRE personnel and stakeholders to assure that overall, the assessment and resulting recommendations have improved the SDLC of the HRE entity.

Based on our discussion of overcoming general obstacles and our experience in this area, we can state that the following practices can be implemented in several HREs within imposed policies:

1. Communication with all stakeholders can be conducted on a regular basis (Fuggetta & Di Nitto, 2014).
2. Developers can use current technology to assure all project development environments are configured in exactly the same way establishing environment parity. These technologies can be applied to internal testing and production environment replication.
3. All written artifacts can be centrally stored and made available to stakeholders.

These practices are generalized and can be applied to many HRE entities. Achieving these practices will greatly enhance the DevOps posture for any HRE entity.

6. ASSESSING DEVOPS POSTURE OF AN HRE

A critical component in a DevOps assessment is the ability to measure, or at a minimum demonstrate, how far or near the SDLC DevOps implementation of a group in an HRE is in comparison to a fully implemented ideal DevOps SDLC process before and after an assessment. This measurement will likely be subjective as each group may have their own view on the ideal DevOps SDLC process. The HRE personnel should explain what their ideal DevOps SDLC looks like with guidance from the assessors. In order to acquire the pre-assessment posture, an assessor should survey HRE personnel about the following general desirable properties in their current SDLC:

1. **Length of Project Life:** This is the amount of time from start to finish of a project. Is it within budgeted time or is additional time regularly required?

2. **Source Code Commits Per Day:** This is a reflection of code development tasks. If a task is too large, it may not be completed and committed in one day. Multiple smaller tasks may be easier to complete and commit in a single day. Is the group satisfied with the commits per day? Does it support scheduled project completion?

3. **Stakeholder Communication:** How well and often does this occur? Is the group capable to speak with a stakeholder as often as needed or desired?

4. **New Employee Spin Up Time:** How much time is needed to indoctrinate a new employee in the group's SDLC process?

5. **Consistent Development Environment:** This relates to environment parity. Is the various environments being used by developers and other HRE personnel kept consistent and up to date with tools, updates, features, etc.?

6. **Tooling Usage:** This refers to development team tools such as chat services, version control systems, testing and development infrastructures, automated IT request fulfillments, and other similar tools. Are these tools available to developers and do they function effectively? Are there multiple tool sets for the same purpose? Can the current tool set be reduced to exclude those not favored by developers?

7. **Consistent Appropriate Staff:** Does the HRE provide long term, well-qualified personnel that are assigned to specific job functions such as: IT infrastructure, software deployment, programmers for specific languages, unit testers, system integration, etc.?

8. **Production Deployment:** How often is code pushed to production for end user feedback? Is it hourly, daily, weekly, longer? Is deployment performed by one person or a group? Is deployment a consistent, repeatable process or is it a unique effort each time? Is approval required? How long is the wait for approval? Does it negatively affect the deployment process?

For each desirable property listed above, a measure of 1 to 5 can be assigned. A measure of 1 is the worst case possible and a measure of 5 is the ideal case. For example, consider Commits per day, a 1 could mean the group has very large tasks that cannot be completed and committed in one working day. A 5 would indicate multiple small incremental tasks are being completed and committed on a daily basis. A group is free to add their own desirable properties to this list. The assessor should assure additional properties pertain to DevOps and do not overlap with listed properties. The ideal DevOps SDLC expressed by the group in pre-assessment will serve as the threshold to reach with recommendations. After observing all recommendations in action for one or more projects, conduct a post-assessment survey to re-assess how near to the ideal DevOps SDLC the group has reached. This will serve as a measure of how effective the assessment and recommendation implementation has been. For those properties in which the group feels they are still lacking, discuss the reasons why and recommend what can be done to improve.

At three to six months after completing an assessment, the assessors should return to repeat the post-assessment survey to assure satisfaction has sustained or improved. HRE personnel should be asked if new obstacles have arisen resulting from the assessment. If possible, assessors should observe one or more projects to validate the SDLC is being implemented as recommended. Deviations should be pointed out and remedied if possible and deemed necessary. Negative survey results and new obstacles can be the focus of a new assessment specific for these issues. HRE personnel should be informed that DevOps implementation, especially in an HRE, may involve multiple assessments with each refining the SDLC process to a point where personnel is satisfied and no new issues have arisen.

7. GENERAL HRE DEVOPS STRATEGIES

The following are, based on our experience, some general DevOps strategies that can be implemented in an HRE. These strategies address some of the large-scale issues that can arise in these environments with potential approaches to addressing them.

7.1. Implementing SDLC in Air-Gapped Environments

One of the biggest obstacles to DevOps in an HRE is air-gapped spaces and systems. This disallows several DevOps principles such as stakeholder collaboration, frequent production environment deployment and end user feedback. One general approach to alleviating this obstacle is to sustain an open environment outside the HRE for development and testing. It is important to realize development itself is typically not a security or proprietary concern. The specific techniques and data that are sometimes in use typically are security or proprietary concerns. It is best to perform as much development as possible in an open environment outside of the HRE. This would allow a straight application of DevOps to the SDLC. Development in the HRE should be restricted to scenarios of security or proprietary concerns. In most HREs, all development is performed in air-gapped environments due to imposed policies or consolidation of work. When carrying out a project in an air-gapped space, consider using a staging environment which replicates the production environment within the air-gapped space. Assuming all the other SDLC components are in one space, adding the staging environment provides the needed infrastructure for the SDLC. This facilitates implementing traditional DevOps within an air-gapped space while assuring no imposed policy or HRE requirement breaches occur. This is assuming there are no imposed policies disallowing full SDLC development to occur within one air-gapped space. The staging environment should exist in its own network and hardware so deployments from developers occur as usual but internally. Personnel should be assigned the roles of end users. They should not have insight of the production environment outside of requirements. They should interact with the staging environment and provide feedback leading to code improvement as an end-user feedback loop.

7.2. Fast Track DevOps for Short Project Times

It may be the case where a project needs to be completed in hours or days. In these cases, the development team may be unable to perform the entire DevOps SDLC process as desired. To deal with short completion times, consider reducing the DevOps of the SDLC to the following critical components:

1. Accurate production replication and staging environment testing
2. End user feedback
3. Regular stakeholder updates

Ideally, the full DevOps process should be carried out regardless of budgeted time. In practice, this is likely very difficult in cases of severe time constraints. Keeping the stakeholder informed and assuring the product will work in the expected manner in the production environment are the key goals. Note that no late stage requirements should be allowed in time constrained projects.

7.3. Common Simulation Environments

As we have previously discussed, it can be a challenge, in some cases, to access and accurately replicate actual production environments. One approach that the HRE DevOps community can take is to ask manufactures of various production environment systems to create a simulated version of their systems. When commencing a project, all stakeholders can come to agreement that a manufacturer's simulation system is suitably equivalent to the actual production environment of a project, meaning the simulation system performs all needed tasks to fulfill the project. Under this agreement, developers can conduct all internal testing using the simulation system as the staging environment and report results to stakeholders. By agreeing on a simulation system provided by the manufacturer, environment parity of the staging environment with the production environment and an effective end user feedback loop are assured, thus fulfilling these two core DevOps principles.

8. HRE SECURE DEVOPS

The term "Secure DevOps" indicates security is given high priority throughout the SDLC (Dullmann, Paule, & Hoorn, 2018; Farroha, & Farroha, 2014). General software development security practices are implemented at each stage of the cycle (Yasar, & Kontostathis, 2016; O'Neill, 2017; Storms, 2015). The ultimate goal of Secure DevOps is assuring security is a standard part of the SDLC. When addressing this in an HRE, it is important to identify secure DevOps practices that are already in place due to imposed policies or HRE constraints. It is possible that practices already present may be applied to all or specific projects. Attempt to understand why some practices are only for specific projects and, if appropriate, suggest that these practices should be applied to all projects. It may be the case, in some HREs, that secure DevOps is routinely practiced and referred to by a different name. In these cases, the assessor should review these practices and suggest modifications if beneficial. It is also important to have a group of security experts as stakeholders. The main security components for DevOps in an HRE are:

1. Security requirements at the requirements gathering stage.

2. Secure coding practices at the development stage.
3. Testing for vulnerabilities and unexpected behaviors.
4. Creation of misuse cases addressing security concerns such as breaches and attacks.

It is likely the case that many security principles can be crafted and enumerated as components for implementation in DevOps. The components listed here cover broad areas of finer grained security concerns that will be addressed. As a whole, this set of components address a very diverse landscape of proactive and reactive security concerns. Ideally, security should be included in the initial DevOps implementation. Weaving in security to an existing DevOps implementation is harder to fulfill. The difficulties occur primarily in redesigning processes and tools belonging to a DevOps model that itself may still not be fully embraced by the HRE personnel. The following is a discussion for each of the aforementioned security components along with their implementation in the SDLC.

8.1. Security Requirements

For any software development project, security considerations should always start at the requirements gathering stage of the SDLC. Addressing security issues at this stage are the easiest and least costly. The requirements gathering process should be enhanced in two fundamental ways with respect to security:

1. For each requirement, the security implications should be considered.
2. A separate set of security requirements should be crafted and included.

It is imperative to have one or more designated security experts as members of the requirements gathering team. It will be the role of the designee to lead the creation of security related requirements. For each requirement, any potential threat that can arise must be considered. This can be accomplished with misuse cases, discussed later in this section. A requirement having security concerns can be redefined to eliminate the threat while still fulfilling the original intent. In some cases, the requirement has to include a security policy identifying what must be implemented to ensure the mitigation of one or more identified threats. It is important to document when a policy is modified for security reasons. The documentation should include:

1. Originally stated requirement.
2. Identified security concerns.
3. Impacts of the concerns on a system.
4. Recommended modifications.
5. Restated requirement.

A potential addition could be an explanation of how the restated requirement eliminates the security concerns. It is clear that restated requirements should not introduce further security concerns. If, for some reason, a restated requirement introduces new security concerns, then the requirement should be considered for a complete redesign and reconsideration.

An additional set of security requirements should be part of the complete requirements set for any software project. These requirements state specific security controls that a system should implement to achieve a desired or required level of security. First, the security engineer must understand the top security concerns of a client and create requirements addressing those. Second, the engineer must analyze the proposed system based on the requirements and enhance with appropriate security controls such as authentication, restricted access, encryption, and user privileges. Identifying which security controls should be in place needs to be discussed and approved by all stakeholders. A review of HRE imposed security policies is needed to assure no overlap occurs for a proposed security control.

8.2. Secure Coding

In the code development stage, secure coding practices should be a default implementation for developers. There is a well-established corpus of materials detailing how to write secure source code for a variety of programming languages. Typically, secure coding aims at avoiding the unintended introduction of vulnerabilities and unauthorized access to data. Typically, at the source code level, a vulnerability can arise from logic flaws, mishandled memory, and unbounded variables amongst others. Daily code reviews by development teams is critical to identifying these defects. In an HRE, the focus can be on the protection of sensitive data, leakage of personally identifiable information (PII), or unintended disclosure of the inner workings of tools, techniques, and methods. Before development commences, the developers along with stakeholders should agree on which security concerns are of high priority. Code reviews should be conducted with a focus on these concerns. A security code audit should also be conducted. The audit reviews source code to verify that all the security requirements:

1. Are present.
2. Have been correctly implemented.
3. Work as intended.
4. Occur at the appropriate points in execution.
5. Do not introduce new security concerns.

There are diverse automated tools to review source code and discover vulnerabilities. These tools should be part of the DevOps security process in an HRE. As part of improving a development team's secure coding abilities, meetings should occur to detail discovered faulty code. A secure code writing expert should state and explain to the team members the reasons why a piece of code introduces a vulnerability, how to fix the code by removing and replacing the faulty segment, and the impact of the modification on code block execution. To further sharpen the skill set of the developer's exercises should be given which focus on code review, identifying faulty code, and rewriting code which removes the faulty segment while still achieving the intent of the original code. Vulnerability Testing. A long and well-established practice exists and is commonly used for vulnerability discovery. In general discovery occurs in two forms: static and runtime analysis. There are several techniques in use today including:

Static code analysis. Specific inputs purposely crafted and simulated in source code tracing with the goal of gaining unauthorized access to a system or data.

Fuzz testing. This automates submission of various inputs (both crafted and random) in executing code in order to assure exception handling is functioning properly and no unexpected behaviors occur (Godefroid, Levin, & Molnar, 2008; Godefroid, 2007) Known vulnerability and malware scan. Both source and executable code are scanned with third party software to identify publicly known threats. This can be extended to open source third-party libraries.

A unique characteristic of an HRE is the environments in which vulnerability testing occurs. In a non-HRE with DevOps implemented, environment parity amongst development, staging, and production environments is assured by provisioning them with the same automated IaC scripts. By using continuous delivery and continuous integration, new code versions can be deployed to both staging and production environments for testing which includes vulnerability discovery on a regular basis which can occur multiple times a day. In an HRE, there is the potential lack of parity between staging and production environments and limited or no access to the actual production environment. This creates a scenario where testing results may not be completely relied upon. Since staging may not have parity with production, the vulnerability discovery results from staging are not guaranteed to be reproducible in production thus leading to rework. The lack of access to the actual production environment makes it more difficult to validate test results discovered in the staging environment. It also makes it impossible to discover new vulnerabilities existing only in production. Even a minor difference between staging and production environments can lead to the deployment of undiscovered vulnerabilities. It may be the case, in an HRE, that deployment to production occurs with the assumption that some vulnerabilities may exist undiscovered due to the inability of establishing full parity between production and staging environments.

One potential approach to deal with this issue is assuming a basic production environment configuration which we call the minimum technology set approach (MTS). Developers can assess, along with stakeholders, the MTS needed for a piece of software to run correctly. A staging environment can be built based on this MTS and vulnerability discovery performed. The assumption is, if no vulnerabilities are found and the software runs correctly, then in production it should also function as expected. This includes a further assumption that any technology present in production and not in staging will have no negative effect on proper software execution. In order to establish high confidence in the MTS, developers should implement a piece of software using the most basic technologies possible. This minimizes interactions with the actual production environment and reduces the chance of conflicts with unexpected technologies that could hinder or halt proper execution.

Another potential approach to dealing with sub-optimal production environment parity is assuming the presence of several conflicting technologies that can hinder or halt execution. We call this approach a conflictive production environment (CPE). Using CPE, developers purposely create a staging environment with an exhaustive mix of technologies, both hardware and software, that can realistically disrupt proper execution of deployed code possibly by invoking undiscovered vulnerabilities. The code then needs to be hardened to disallow these conflicting technologies to interfere with its execution. One approach is to avoid process or service interaction, a second approach is strong exception handling, a third approach is alternate paths to completion if a conflicting technology succeeds in hindering or halting execution. The software produced using the CPE approach will be resistant to conflicting technologies and is highly likely to run correctly in production. A limitation to this approach is the extent of introduced conflicting technologies in the staging environment. In practicality, it is likely not possible to guarantee all conflicting technologies have been tested in staging. It can also be the case that two technologies running alone do not pose a conflict but running together will hinder or halt the deployed software. The exhaustiveness of enumerating conflictive technologies and the various ways disruption can occur either by running alone or in concert with others may limited by the domain knowledge of the developers. Security engineers should be included to leverage their domain knowledge in the selection of technologies to produce disruptive environments.

A third approach to dealing with sub-optimal parity is validating a production environment to be appropriate for the software. We call this approach production environment validation (PEV). When using PEV, developers embed a list of conditions that an environment must satisfy. If all conditions are satisfied, the software will run. If a condition is not satisfied the software will never execute and, when appropriate, log an alert documenting this action. The number of conditions that must be satisfied can be as broad and diverse as the developers deem necessary. The goal of PEV is to assure the production environment is identical or highly similar to the staging environment. The more similarity exists, the less likely a vulnerability will be discovered and a software will be disrupted. By establishing parity using PEV, the developers can control the software's exposure to potential conflicts and discovery of unexpected vulnerabilities.

Third party libraries are in common use across HREs due to their strong community support and free availability. It is sometimes not clear how exhaustive the vulnerability scanning is of third-party libraries. When an HRE decides to incorporate third party libraries into a project they run the risk of introducing unknown vulnerabilities. The best case is for an HRE not to use third party libraries or any open source code. In cases when the decision is made to move forward with using third party libraries, HRE personnel should consider using libraries whose source code is available. This will ensure all vulnerability testing can be performed. The scope of usage of third-party libraries should be limited to non-critical aspects of the code that run in a separate execution thread. The reasoning is if the library is compromised and the software crashes, the critical components may be able to continue executing.

Using containers to overcome sub-optimal production environment parity is a popular choice and appropriate for an HRE. Containers enable functional and security testing of code all within in the same environment upon which it will be executed when deployed to a production environment. The key point to consider is that the parity issues between staging and production previously discussed here apply equally. In cases where containers are used, HRE personnel should attempt to achieve parity between staging and production for the host environment where mounting and execution will occur.

8.3. Misuse Cases

A misuse case specifies a scenario in which a malicious actor interacts with a system in a non-expected manner with the intent of gaining illicit access (Sindre, & Opdahl, 2005; Alexander, 2003). Misuse cases express scenarios that should not happen. These cases expose potential threats which lead to the creation of new security requirements for the software. Misuse cases are normally part of the requirements gathering phase and act as a negative form of use cases, which specify what should happen in a software system. An effective misuse case leads to the identification of one or more threats which are addressed with new security requirements. The entity invoking the misuse case could be intentional or accidental. The creation of misuse cases must be bound within a realistic scope. In other words, the software is realistically capable of facilitating the occurrence of a defined misuse case. A security requirements engineer should be designated to help design misuse cases. The cases should be shared with all stakeholders for mutual agreement that there exists a realistic probability the case can occur.

Implementing security principles into existing DevOps of an HRE can be a challenging task. Some of the requirements are satisfied by HRE imposed security policies. In general, these security principles are well known in the software development world and their use is understood and regularly practiced. The biggest hurdles, just like implementing DevOps in general, are the HRE environment and culture. All security principles weaved into an existing DevOps implementation must be assured not to violate

HRE-imposed policies and to not overlap or repeat any of those policies. This requires an understanding the HRE-imposed security policies. The most difficult tasks are fully integrating security into an existing HRE SDLC and achieving adoption by HRE personnel.

9. CONCLUSION

In this paper, we have discussed HRE-DevSecOps which is the enhancement of a DevOps implementation in highly regulated environments (HREs) with security principles. We first detailed the process of assessing and implementing DevOps practices in HREs. The restrictions imposed in an HRE disallow the direct implementation of traditional DevOps in an SDLC process but may satisfy some of the required security principles. We have described how to perform a DevOps assessment in an HRE and how to identify bottlenecks and pain points. A process is given to document these problems as obstacles. Several general obstacles that are likely present in an HRE is described along with approaches to overcome or alleviate each one. Some recommendations are likely not part of DevOps but will improve the SDLC in some way. Innovation enters the process by assessors thinking outside the box in finding unique ways to overcome obstacles in implementing DevOps in an HRE. We presented the security details that should be woven into an already existing DevOps implementation. We discussed unique HRE obstacles that increase the difficulty in implementing tasks and provide approaches to overcome these obstacles. The ultimate goal is to place an HRE's DevOps posture as close to an ideal scenario as possible. A method to establish this posture in pre and post assessment is given. In achieving an improved DevOps posture, the underlying SDLC will benefit from both DevOps and non-DevOps enhancements. The resulting DevOps SDLC will be a process that started as a traditional DevOps process that is molded and customized to an HRE group's specific environment and needs, enhanced with security. We refer to this process as HRE-DevSecOps. Once implemented, this customized version will further bring an HRE development team closer to their ideal DevSecOps SDLC scenario. Future work will focus on a scientific approach to assess the effectiveness of HRE-DevSecOps in an HRE using performance metrics collected in real time.

ACKNOWLEDGMENT

This material is based upon work funded and supported by the Department of Defense under Contract No. FA8702-15-D-0002 with Carnegie Mellon University for the operation of the Software Engineering Institute, a federally funded research and development center. (DISTRIBUTION STATEMENT A) This material has been approved for public release and unlimited distribution. Please see Copyright notice for non-US Government use and distribution. Carnegie Mellon and CERT are registered in the U.S. Patent and Trademark Office by Carnegie Mellon University. DM18-0273

REFERENCES

Alexander, I. (2003). Misuse cases: Use cases with hostile intent. *IEEE Software*, 20(1), 58–66. doi:10.1109/MS.2003.1159030

Allcorn, S., Diamond, M. A., & Stien, H. F. (2002). Organizational silos: Horizontal organizational fragmentation. *Psychoanalysis, Culture & Society*, 280–296.

Artac, M. (2017). DevOps: Introducing Infrastructure-as-Code. In *IEEE/ACM 39th International Conference on Software Engineering (ICSE-C)* (pp. 497–498).

Bass, L., Weber, I., & Zhu, L. (2015). *DevOps: A Software Architect's Perspective*. Addison-Wesley Professional.

Blau, G., Mehta, B., Bose, S., Pekny, J., Sinclair, G., Keunker, K., & Bunch, P. (2000). Risk management in the development of new products in highly regulated industries. *Computers & Chemical Engineering*, *24*(2-7), 659–664. doi:10.1016/S0098-1354(00)00388-4

Boehm, B. W., & Ross, R. (1989). Theory-W software project management principles and examples. *IEEE Transactions on Software Engineering*, *15*(7), 902–916. doi:10.1109/32.29489

Bruza, M. R. (2018). An Analysis of Multi-Domain Command and Control and the Development of Software Solutions through DevOps Toolsets and Practices. *Air Force Institute of Technology Wright-Patterson AFB OH*. Retrieved from http://www.dtic.mil/dtic/tr/fulltext/u2/1055982.pdf

Byres, E. (2013). The Air Gap: SCADA's Enduring Security Myth. *Communications of the ACM*, *56*(8), 29–31. doi:10.1145/2492007.2492018

Cagle, R., Rice, T., & Kristan, M. (2015). DevOps for Federal Acquisition. In *IEEE Software Technology Conference*.

Cois, C. A., Yankel, J., & Connell, A. (2014). Modern DevOps: Optimizing software development through effective system interactions. In *2014 IEEE International Professional Communication Conference*, (pp. 1–7). 10.1109/IPCC.2014.7020388

Dioguino, T. (2016). DevOps: Transforming Military Application Delivery Lifecycles. *Hewlett Packard Enterprises*. Retrieved from http://www.fedinsider.com

Dullmann, T. F., Paule, C., & Hoorn, A. V. (2018). Exploiting DevOps Practices for Dependable and Secure Continuous Delivery Pipelines. In *IEEE/ACM 4th International Workshop on Rapid Continuous Software Engineering* (pp. 27–30).

Edwards, F. R. (1977). Managerial Objectives in Regulated Industries: Expense-Preference Behavior in Banking. *Journal of Political Economy*, *85*(1), 147–162. doi:10.1086/260549

Farroha, B. S., & Farroha, D. L. (2014). A Framework for Managing Mission Needs, Compliance, and Trust in the DevOps Environment. In *IEEE Military Communications Conference* (pp. 288–293). 10.1109/MILCOM.2014.54

United States Federal Communications Commission (FCC). (n.d.). Retrieved from **Error! Hyperlink reference not valid.**https://www.fcc.gov/

United States Food and Drug Administration (FDA). (n.d.). Retrieved from **Error! Hyperlink reference not valid.**https://www.fda.gov/

Fischer, M., Pinzger, M., & Gall, H. (2003). Populating a Release History Database from version control and bug tracking systems. In *International Conference on Software Maintenance* (pp. 23–32). 10.1109/ICSM.2003.1235403

Forsgren, N., Tremblay, A., Chiarini, M., VanderMeer, D., Humble, J., Maedche, A., ... Hevner, A. (2017). *DORA Platform: DevOps Assessment and Benchmarking* (pp. 436–440). Designing the Digital Transformation.

Fuggetta, A., & Di Nitto, E. (2014). Software Process. In *Proceedings of the on Future of Software Engineering* (pp. 1–12).

Godefroid, P. (2007). Random Testing for Security: Blackbox vs. Whitebox Fuzzing. In *Proceedings of the 2nd International Workshop on Random Testing*. 10.1145/1292414.1292416

Godefroid, P., Levin, M. Y., & Molnar, D. (2008). Automated whitebox fuzz testing. In *Proceedings of the Network and Distributed Systems Security Symposium*.

Harvey, J., Erdos, G., Bolam, H., Cox, M. A. A., Kennedy, J. N. P., & Gregory, D. T. (2002). An analysis of safety culture attitudes in a highly regulated environment. *Work and Stress*, *16*(1), 18–36. doi:10.1080/02678370110113226

Hilton, M. (2016). Usage, Costs, and Benefits of Continuous Integration in Open-source Projects. In *Proceedings of the 31st IEEE/ACM International Conference on Automated Software Engineering* (pp. 426–437). 10.1145/2970276.2970358

Hoffman, K. (2016). *Environment Parity*. O'Reilly Media.

Hrebiniak, L. G., & Joyce, W. F. (1985). Organizational Adaptation: Strategic Choice and Environmental Determinism. *Administrative Science Quarterly*, *30*(3), 336–349. doi:10.2307/2392666

Hüttermann, M. (2012). *DevOps for Developers*. Apress. doi:10.1007/978-1-4302-4570-4

Hummer, W. (2013). *Testing Idempotence for Infrastructure as Code*. Middleware.

LaPlante, W., & Wisnieff, R. (2018). *Design and Acquisition of Software for Defense Systems*. Department of Defense, Defense Science Board.

Mohan, V., & Othman, L. B. (2016). Secdevops: Is it a marketing buzzword? In *Second International Workshop on Agile Secure Software Development*.

Myrbakken, H., & Colomo-Palacios, R. (2017). *DevSecOps: A Multivocal Literature Review. In Software Process Improvement and Capability Determination* (pp. 17–29). Springer International Publishing. doi:10.1007/978-3-319-67383-7_2

Nuclear Energy Institute (NEI). (n.d.). Nuclear Power Plant Security and Access Control. Retrieved from https://www.nei.org/Nuclear-Power-Plant-Security-and-Access-Control

O'Neill, D. (2017). Secure DevOps Foundations for Large-Scale Software Systems. *Crosstalk*, 24–27.

Rasmussen, R. (2009). Adopting Agile in an FDA Regulated Environment. In *Proceedings of the 2009 Agile Conference* (pp. 151–155). 10.1109/AGILE.2009.50

Rong, G., Zhang, H., & Shao, D. (2016). CMMI Guided Process Improvement for DevOps Projects: An Exploratory Case Study. In *Proceedings of the International Conference on Software and Systems Process* (pp. 76–85). 10.1145/2904354.2904372

Schwartz, P. M., & Solove, D. J. (2011). The PII problem: Privacy and a new concept of personally identifiable information. *NYUL rev., 86*, 1814.

United States Securities and Exchange Commission. (n.d.). Retrieved from https://www.sec.gov/

Sindre, G., & Opdahl, A. L. (2005). Eliciting security requirements with misuse cases. *Requirements Engineering, 10*(1), 34–44. doi:10.100700766-004-0194-4

Storms, A. (2015). How Security can be the Next Force Multiplier in DevOps. In *RSA Conference*.

Virmani, M. (2015). Understanding DevOps and bridging the gap from continuous integration to continuous delivery. In *Fifth International Conference on the Innovative Computing Technology* (pp. 78–82). 10.1109/INTECH.2015.7173368

Yasar, H., & Kontostathis, K. (2016). Where to Integrate Security Practices on DevOps Platform. *International Journal of Secure Software Engineering, 7*(4), 39–50. doi:10.4018/IJSSE.2016100103

This research was previously published in the International Journal of Systems and Software Security and Protection (IJSSSP), 9(1); pages 18-46, copyright year 2018 by IGI Publishing (an imprint of IGI Global).

Chapter 60
Tools and Platforms for Developing IoT Systems

Görkem Giray

https://orcid.org/0000-0002-7023-9469

Independent Researcher, Turkey

ABSTRACT

The internet of things (IoT) transforms the world in many ways. It combines many types of hardware and software with a variety of communication technologies to enable the development of innovative applications. A typical IoT system consists of IoT device, IoT gateway, IoT platform, and IoT application. Developing these elements and delivering an IoT system for fulfilling business requirements encompasses many activities to be executed and is not straightforward. To expedite these activities, some major vendors provide software development kits (SDK), integrated development environments (IDE), and utility tools for developing software to be executed on IoT devices/gateways. Moreover, these vendors utilize their cloud platforms to provide fundamental services, such as data storage, analytics, stream processing, for developing IoT systems. These vendors also developed IoT specific cloud-based services, such as connectivity and device management, to support IoT system development. This chapter presents an overview of tools and platforms provided by five major vendors.

INTRODUCTION

The Internet of Things (IoT) has attracted considerable interest in many various domains, including smart cities, retail, logistics, manufacturing, agriculture, and health. In line with this interest, designing and developing IoT systems have become mainstream. In theory, it is possible to develop an IoT system using many types of hardware, developing software with many tools and programming languages and even designing a special communication protocol for data exchange. On the other hand, using standard hardware and communication protocols, reusing software libraries and platforms have many advantages, including: (1) decrease in development time and hence time-to-market; (2) decrease in cost due to economies of scale; (3) interoperability with other systems via standards. This chapter attempts to provide an

DOI: 10.4018/978-1-6684-3702-5.ch060

overview of some tools and platforms that can be used for developing software for the IoT. These tools encompass Software Development Kits (SDK), Integrated Development Environments (IDEs), utility tools for developers, and IoT platforms that provide some common basic functionalities for IoT systems.

Section 2 begins with an overview of the foundational concepts underlying the IoT and then presents the brief descriptions of the elements making up a typical IoT system. Section 3 summarizes the tools and platforms offered by major vendors (Amazon, Bosch, Google, IBM, and Microsoft) to develop IoT systems. Section 4 discusses the current state of software development for IoT devices, the fundamental services delivered by IoT platforms and capabilities offered by IoT platforms for handling IoT big data. Finally, Section 5 concludes the chapter.

BACKGROUND

The "IoT" concept and IoT systems make use of many concepts that are available in various disciplines, including software engineering, software architecture, and cloud computing. The following subsection titled "foundational concepts" summarizes these concepts and the relationships among them. The second subsection presents the main components of a typical IoT system.

Foundational Concepts

IoT systems are made up of many distributed components interacting via a network. To cope with the complexity of such a system, *abstraction* and *encapsulation* are key concepts. A group of functionality can be encapsulated and provided as services; which is the approach of *Service Oriented Architecture (SOA)*. *Cloud computing* extends the scope of these services to infrastructures, platforms, even applications. The remainder of this section briefly describes these concepts and clarifies the relationships among these concepts.

Abstraction is one of the fundamental cognitive activity associated with problem-solving. Abstraction is a technique for coping with complexity. Abstraction means preserving essential and eliminating unessential information about an entity from a specific perspective for an objective. This helps to focus on the big picture and thus cope with the complexity. Encapsulation complements abstraction by hiding the internal functioning of an entity and providing an interface to exhibit the behavior of the entity. In short, an entity is known by its interface presenting its services to outside world and its internals is hidden from the outside world. The examples of such an entity vary in size and can be a procedure, a class, a layer, a library, even a platform. For instance, encapsulation in object-orientation is the packaging of attributes representing state and operations into a class and provide an interface to access the services provided by that class (Page-Jones, 1999). Figure 1 illustrates how an IoT device can be abstracted and represented as a class. Data and implementation details are encapsulated in the class; the operations of sending data and resetting are provided to the outside world.

Abstraction and encapsulation can be done at any level, at a micro level, such as a class, at a higher level, such as establishing layers while designing the architecture of a system. An architecture encompasses the major components and their interrelationships at a certain level of detail in line with the objective in drawing that architecture. Figure 2 illustrates how the components of an IoT system can be organized as layers to cope with complexity (Köksal & Tekinerdogan, 2017). Each layer has a group of cohesive responsibilities, such as security layer providing the security functionality for the system. Each layer encapsulates the implementation details necessary for fulfilling its responsibilities and communicates with the other layers through interfaces.

Figure 1. A sample abstraction of an IoT device

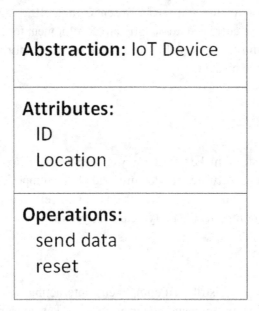

Figure 2. A sample layered architecture for an IoT system
(adapted from (Köksal & Tekinerdogan, 2017))

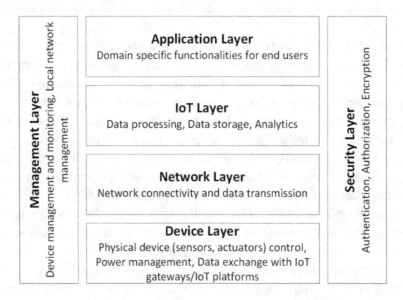

A *layered architecture* is a type of architectural style that partitions the concerns of a system into stacked layers (Meier, 2009). Architectural styles provide an abstract framework and a set of principles for a family of systems for shaping the architecture of a system (Meier, 2009). They promote design reuse and help architects in avoiding reinventing the wheel. SOA is another architectural style where complex and monolithic systems are decomposed into distributed components that provide and/or consume services (Bass et al., 2012). Service provider and consumer components can be developed using different programming languages and deployed on different platforms (Bass et al., 2012). These components can be deployed independently and can be part of different systems or even belong to different organizations (Bass et al., 2012). Their interfaces describe the services they provide (Bass et al., 2012). Two basic types of method to access web services are SOAP and REST. SOAP stands for "Simple Object Access Protocol" and specifies a communication protocol, which enables XML-based message exchange. REST (Representation State Transfer) is an architectural style rather than a protocol itself. It applies a few constraints to clarify communication and resource management.

With the advent of the Internet as a communication infrastructure and the design approach to provide functionality through services (SOA), many varieties of services have been made available to be used by both systems and end users worldwide. These services are designed to be consumed at different levels, as infrastructure, platform, and software. The umbrella term for this approach is *cloud computing*, which enables ubiquitous, convenient, on-demand access to a shared pool of configurable resources (e.g., servers, networking, databases, software, and more) (Mell & Grance, 2011). It provides five essential characteristics: namely on-demand self-service, broad network access, rapid flexibility on scalability, measured service, and resource pooling (Mell & Grance, 2011). Computing resources are pooled to serve multiple consumers using a multi-tenant model (Mell & Grance, 2011). Multi-tenancy is an approach to share a computing resource between multiple consumers by providing every consumer a dedicated share of the resource, which is isolated from other shares regarding performance and data privacy (Krebs et al., 2012).

Cloud computing services are mainly offered in three main types of models: *Infrastructure as a Service (IaaS)*, *Platform as a Service (PaaS)*, and *Software as a Service (SaaS)*. These service models determine the types of computing resources offered to consumers. A simplified view of three service models of cloud computing is displayed in Figure 3 and explained as follows.

- *IaaS* provides some fundamental computing resources, mostly computation, storage, and network. Consumers (generally engineers dealing with system and network) have significant control over operating systems, storage, and applications to be deployed; however, do not have control over the underlying hardware infrastructure (Mell & Grance, 2011). Some examples of IaaS include Amazon Web Services, Google Cloud Platform, and Microsoft Azure. IaaS provides an infrastructure to process (computing), store (storage), and exchange (network) a huge amount of data sensed by IoT devices, which is generally the case for IoT systems.

- *PaaS* provides some programming languages, libraries, services, and tools to develop and deploy applications on a cloud infrastructure for software developers (Mell & Grance, 2011). Developers have control over the applications to be developed and deployed as well as some configuration settings for the hosting environment; however, does not have any control over the infrastructure (Mell & Grance, 2011). Some examples of PaaS include Amazon Relational Database Service and Google App Engine. Generally, PaaS also provides some general purpose services, such as storage management, analytics, to be used by software developers. For instance, a storage management service (such as Amazon Relational Database Service) can use the storage services provided by an IaaS to physically store data and provide a number of services for developers to operate a database in the cloud. Briefly, common functionalities related to data storage are encapsulated as storage management services and provided to developers through APIs. Such common functionalities can be used by developers to store and analyze the huge amount of data produced and consumed by IoT systems. Moreover, some vendors (such as Amazon, Google, Microsoft) also provide some services at PaaS level specific to the IoT. Such services include device registry and device management.

- *SaaS* provides applications to be used through a web browser, mobile application, or a programming interface (Mell & Grance, 2011). Consumers (generally end users) do not have any control on the platform and infrastructure services; they can only control some application settings that can be changed through a user interface or programming interface. Some examples of SaaS include Gmail by Google and Office 365 by Microsoft.

Figure 3. Three service models of cloud computing

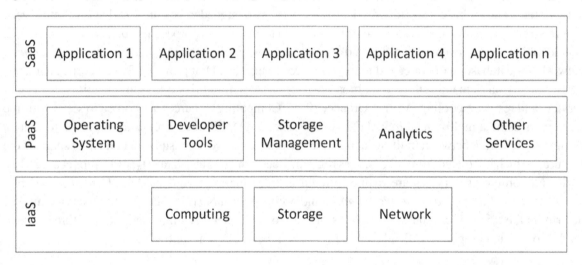

This chapter focuses on PaaS model of cloud computing since it can provide important benefits to software developers in developing IoT systems. Developers can abstract away the configuration details of the application server, operating system, storage, etc. and focus on the specific functionalities of the IoT system they work on. Moreover, reusing services brings time and cost savings.

An Overview of IoT Systems

IoT refers to the global network of IoT devices, which enables these devices to send and receive data. IoT utilizes the current Internet infrastructure, standards, and technologies to interconnect these IoT devices. Even though there are many ways of visualizing IoT systems, Figure 4 displays a simplified view of an IoT system.

IoT devices sense data from the real world, send them to an IoT platform directly or via an IoT gateway. Data may be processed, stored by an IoT platform and served to an IoT application for further processing to meet the specific needs of a domain.

Figure 4. A simplified view of an IoT system

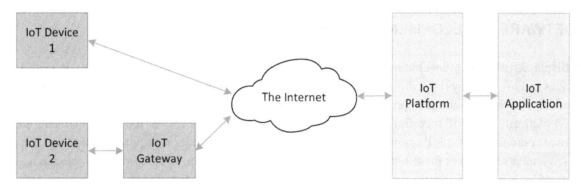

The main elements of an IoT system, namely IoT device, IoT gateway, IoT platform, and IoT application are described briefly as below:

- **IoT device:** IoT devices (also called things, connected devices, smart devices, smart objects, etc.) are capable of sensing data from the real world and communicating these data electronically to an IoT gateway and/or to an IoT platform/application over a connection. Generally, IoT devices gather data through their sensors (e.g. temperature) and some of them take actions through their actuators (e.g. turn on air condition remotely). The capabilities of IoT devices differ, some of them can only sense some data whereas some others can process these data and send it through the Internet using a secure and Internet ready protocol.
- **IoT gateway:** IoT gateways play an intermediary role between IoT devices and IoT platforms. IoT gateways receive data from IoT devices, may translate, filter, aggregate, cleanse data and direct these data to IoT platforms. IoT gateways may translate data since IoT devices are not supporting an Internet ready protocol, such as AMQP, MQTT, and HTTPS. IoT gateways may filter, aggregate, and cleanse data to optimize bandwidth usage. The responsibilities of a gateway can be fulfilled using field and/or cloud gateways ("Microsoft Azure IoT Reference Architecture," 2018). As the name implies, field gateways are usually collocated with IoT devices and do some local processing before sending data to an IoT platform. Cloud gateways are software components managing communication with IoT devices/gateways and hosted in the cloud as a part of an IoT platform. The use of field and cloud gateways depends on the requirements and available resources in a specific project.
- **IoT platform:** IoT platform refers to a combination of some basic functionalities common to most IoT systems. These functionalities are generally delivered as PaaS and encompass computation, storage, analytics, device management, etc.
- **IoT application:** An IoT application is specific to a domain and implements the requirements of a specific business model. It utilizes IoT platform for common basic functionalities.

- **IoT system:** An IoT system (or IoT solution) is a composition of the elements explained above and fulfills some specific requirements. For instance, in an IoT system for waste management, sensors in containers (IoT devices) can sense data to detect rubbish levels in containers. These sensors can send these data to an IoT platform (possibly via IoT gateways) to have the trash collection routes optimized. An IoT application can visualize optimized routes for end users.

SOFTWARE DEVELOPMENT FOR THE IoT

As displayed in Figure 4, developing IoT systems involves the integration of various elements. Various IoT devices and IoT gateways have different computing, storage, and networking capabilities. These capabilities designate the limitations imposed on the software components that will run on these devices. Many cloud platforms (not IoT specific) provide various capabilities, which can be reused when developing software components for IoT systems. A particular array of competencies is required to develop each of these elements and bring these together to have a complete IoT system. Various vendors provide many types of tools and ready to use services in order to develop IoT systems much faster with a reasonable cost. It is reported that more than 450 vendors provide IoT platforms as well as some tools for developing software for IoT systems (Williams, 2017). This section provides the tools and capabilities offered by major vendors, namely Amazon, Bosch, Google, IBM, and Microsoft.

Amazon Web Services IoT Platform

Amazon Web Services (AWS) IoT platform enables IoT devices to connect to AWS platform services and IoT applications to interact with IoT devices. Figure 5 shows a simplified view of an IoT system using the tools/services provided by Amazon.

Figure 5. An IoT system architecture based on Amazon tools/services
(adapted from ("AWS IoT," 2018))

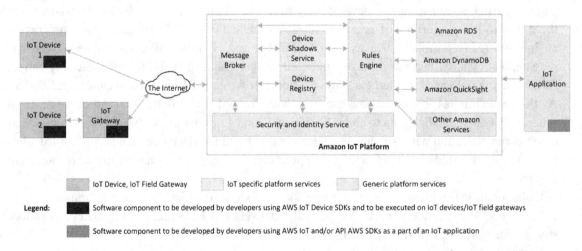

The *AWS IoT Device SDKs* ("AWS IoT Device SDK," n.d.) include some open-source libraries and a developer guide that enable IoT devices to connect, authenticate, and exchange data with AWS IoT platform using the MQTT, HTTP, or WebSockets protocols. The SDK supports Embedded C, JavaScript, Arduino Yun, Java, and Python. Developers can use one of these SDKs to develop software IoT device/gateway client software.

Message broker provides a secure mechanism for IoT devices, Amazon IoT platform, and IoT applications to exchange data. It supports MQTT and MQTT over WebSocket and provides an HTTP REST API for data exchange.

Rules engine processes (such as augment, filter) data and sends them to other services, such as to be stored by Amazon RDS, to be analyzed by Amazon QuickSight.

Device shadows service stores current and desired states of IoT devices in the AWS cloud. IoT devices can send their state data to device shadow service through the message broker to be used by other IoT devices, AWS services, and/or an IoT application. Similarly, AWS services and/or an IoT application can update the desired state of an IoT device using device shadow service. This desired state is sent to the corresponding IoT device immediately or when the device comes online if it is not connected to a network/the Internet at all time.

Device registry keeps track of the metadata of IoT devices. It establishes an identity for devices and manages devices' attributes and capabilities (such as a capability of reporting temperature and its unit of measure).

Security and identity service provides controlled access to services and resources. The message broker and rules engine use this service to exchange data securely with IoT devices and other services.

Message broker, rule engine, device shadows, device registry service, and security and identity service are platform services especially provided for IoT systems. These services can be combined with the rest of the AWS platform services, such as Amazon RDS and DynamoDB to store data, Amazon QuickSight to analyze data. Amazon provides AWS IoT API ("AWS Documentation," n.d.) and AWS SDKs ("Tools for Amazon Web Services," n.d.) to integrate IoT applications with AWS platform services. AWS IoT API enables developers to programmatically create and manage IoT devices, certificates, rules, and policies using HTTP or HTTPS requests. AWS SDKs include language-specific APIs and currently have support for programming languages such as Java, Node.js, Python, Ruby, Go, C++. A developer can use Eclipse IDE along with AWS SDK for Java ("AWS SDK for Java," n.d.) and AWS Toolkit for Eclipse ("AWS Toolkit for Eclipse," n.d.) to develop an IoT application interacting with AWS platform services. AWS Toolkit for Eclipse is an open source plug-in for the Eclipse Java IDE and aims to increase developer productivity by facilitating development, debugging, and deployment of Java applications.

Bosch IoT Suite

The Bosch IoT Suite ("Bosch IoT Suite," n.d.) is an IoT platform, which provides some basic capabilities needed to build IoT applications. These capabilities encompass management of IoT devices and gateways, secure access management, and data analysis. Bosch IoT Suite services provide its capabilities under six titles as displayed in Figure 6.

IoT Hub supports connectivity and messaging between IoT devices and platform.

IoT Things keeps track of the data on IoT devices. These data are able to manage life cycle of devices, to keep track of relationships among devices, and to make search on device data. The service provides a RESTful API and Java client for access and integration.

IoT Rollouts is a service for rolling out software updates to IoT devices and gateways. This service is compatible with Eclipse hawkBit's APIs ("Eclipse hawkBit," n.d.). hawkBit is a domain independent back-end framework for rolling out software updates to IoT devices and gateways. It aims to provide a base to develop services/applications for software updates independent from particular application domains and hence IoT applications.

IoT Remote Manager provides device management and monitoring capabilities for IoT gateways and IoT devices. It mainly offers remote management of applications (remote install, uninstall, update, configure), firmware and file update, remote configuration and provisioning, remote monitoring and diagnostics, and remote security administration.

IoT Analytics provides common analysis capabilities for processing device generated data to gain insights.

IoT Permissions enables the management of users, groups, roles, and applications including authorization and authentication. The service provides a RESTful HTTP API and Java client libraries to be used by IoT applications. An IoT application can register users, groups, roles, and applications at IoT Permissions along with the permissions granted. Afterwards, the IoT application can use this service to authenticate and authorize the incoming requests.

Figure 6. An IoT system architecture based on Bosch tools/services

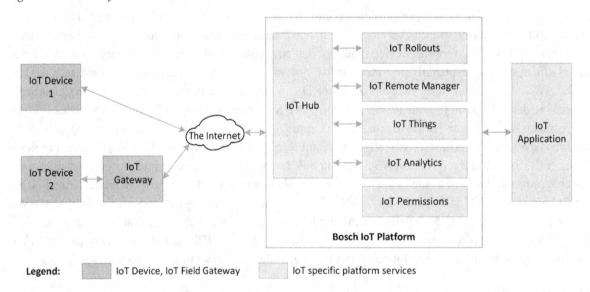

Google IoT Platform

Google utilizes its Cloud Platform to provide an IoT platform for IoT systems. Most of the components of this platform are independent of the IoT, such as storage and analytics; some of the components are offered for the IoT, such as Cloud IoT Core. Google Cloud Platform provides the following capabilities related to the IoT ("Overview of Internet of Things," 2018; "Cloud IoT Core," n.d.) (as displayed in Figure 7):

Figure 7. An IoT system architecture based on Google tools/services

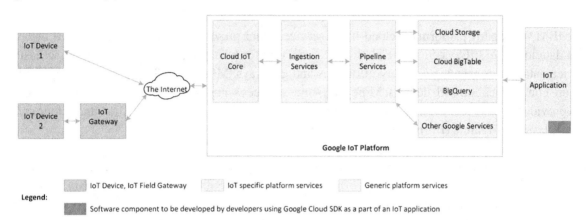

Cloud IoT Core provides services to manage IoT devices and process data being generated by those devices. Cloud IoT Core is composed of a device manager and a protocol bridge. The device manager is able to register IoT devices either manually through a console or programmatically. It establishes an identity for each device, provides a mechanism for authentication and maintains a configuration for each device. The protocol bridge enables the communication between IoT devices/gateways and Google Cloud Platform. It supports secure connection over MQTT. It passes telemetry to ingestion services for further processing.

Ingestion services classify and direct telemetry to other services. The other platform services and IoT applications can subscribe to specific streams of telemetry and ingestion services can direct corresponding streams to these services/applications. Moreover, these services can buffer telemetry to handle data spikes. These services can be used through HTTPS REST APIs and gRPC ("GRPC," n.d.), an open source remote procedure call framework.

Pipeline services provide some capabilities to process data such as transformation, aggregation, and enrichment. For instance, captured data can be transformed to another unit of measure; can be aggregated with data received from other devices; can be enriched with other data about the device.

Storage services offer a variety of storage solutions ranging from storage for unstructured blobs of data (such as video or image) to key-value and relational databases.

Analytics services provide capabilities for analyzing accumulated data to look at trends and gain insight.

Google Cloud SDK ("Google Cloud SDK," n.d.) encompasses a set of tools, which enables management of services hosted on Google Cloud Platform.

Developers can use cloud platform services by making direct HTTP requests to Google Cloud APIs. These APIs expose a JSON REST interface. As an alternative, Google provides a client library ("API Client Libraries," n.d.) for all of its Cloud APIs that enables access for those using programming languages available. Currently, Java, .NET languages, Python, JavaScript, and Objective C are supported. More programming languages, including Go, Ruby, Node.js will be supported in the future.

IBM Watson IoT Platform

The IBM Watson IoT platform is a cloud-based service, which provides application access to IoT devices and data to create IoT systems. The platform can be used for managing devices, storing and accessing device data and connecting a variety of devices and gateways. MQTT and TLS protocols are used for secure communication with devices. Moreover, some services regarding analytics and data visualization are provided on this platform. The services provided by the platform can be classified under four areas as displayed in Figure 8 (Börnert et al., 2016):

- *Connection* service is concerned with connecting and managing IoT devices. Device management capabilities include device reboot, firmware update, device diagnostics and metadata gathering, bulk device addition, and removal.
- *Information management* services are about data storage and transformation. These services provide access to real-time and historical data gathered from IoT devices.
- *Analytics* services provide some capabilities for processing and visualizing data.
- *Risk management* services are concerned with security, authentication, and prevention of fraud.

Figure 8. An IoT System Architecture based on IBM tools/services

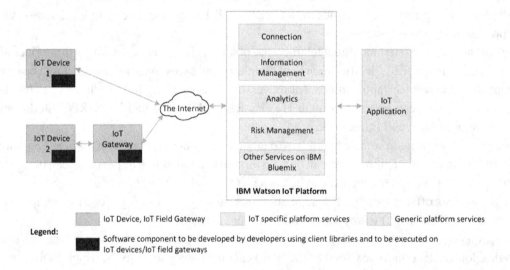

The Watson IoT Platform provides an HTTP REST API that provides access for IoT applications to: (1) manage (create, delete, update, list, view details) IoT devices; (2) diagnose IoT devices (retrieve and clear logs/device error codes); (3) determine connection problems (retrieve device connection logs); (4) view the last event for a specific device; (5) track usage by retrieving total amount of data used; (6) query service status.

Client libraries ("IBM Watson IoT – GitHub," n.d.) provide reusable code for developing software that runs on IoT devices and gateways to interact with Watson IoT Platform. The libraries are provided for different programming languages, namely C++, C#, embedded C, Java, mBed C++, Mode.js,

Python. Although there are some differences among the features provided by the libraries for different programming languages, there are some main features provided, which can be summarized as follows:

- Connecting IoT devices/gateways with Watson IoT Platform
- Sending data using MQTT/HTTP
- Performing client side certificate based authentication
- Connecting IoT devices/gateways to Watson IoT Platform device management service
- Enabling devices/gateways to automatically reconnect to Watson IoT Platform while they are in a disconnected state

Microsoft Azure IoT Platform

Azure IoT device SDK is a set of libraries for developing software for IoT devices. The aim of the SDK is to facilitate sending messages to and receiving messages from the Azure IoT Hub service via a secure connection. The SDKs are open source and hosted on GitHub ("Microsoft Azure – GitHub," n.d.). The different variations of the SDK support different operating systems such as Windows, Linux, real-time operating systems (RTOS); a variety of programming languages, namely C, C#, Java, JavaScript, and Python; diverse data exchange protocols, such as AMQP, MQTT, HTTP/REST.

Azure IoT gateway SDK is a set of libraries, which enables the software development for IoT gateways. It is open source, based on standards, and runs on many types of hardware.

Azure IoT Gateway SDK creates a module pipeline for implementing the specific requirements of an IoT system. While existing modules decrease development and maintenance costs, customized modules also can be implemented. Figure 9 shows an example scenario. IoT device 1 and 2 can communicate via protocol 1 and 2 respectively. Both of these protocols are not Internet-ready and hence translated to an Internet ready protocol using a module (translate module). Afterwards, data are aggregated to optimize bandwidth usage (aggregate module) and sent to the Internet (send module) to an IoT platform.

Azure IoT Services ("Microsoft Azure IoT Reference Architecture," 2018), displayed in Figure 10, refers to the IoT platform developed and maintained by Microsoft and offers some common services, such as storage, analytics, etc., for IoT applications.

Figure 9. An example scenario for IoT gateway implemented using modules

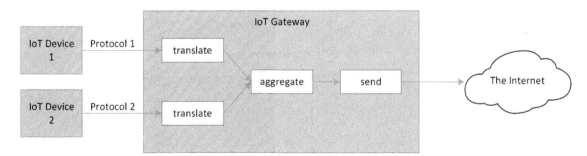

Azure IoT Hub allows secure bidirectional communication between IoT devices and gateways. IoT Hub manages connections at transport protocol level, protects the communication path, authenticates and authorizes devices toward the system.

Provisioning API handles the device life cycle that enables to add and remove devices to an IoT system. This API implements the external interface to enable changes on device identity store and device registry.

Device identity, registry, and state store provide storage services for device data. Identity store provides security credentials for registered IoT devices. Registry stores descriptive information about devices along with some indexing capabilities for fast lookups. State store is for storing incoming data from devices to be used for the operations related to state data.

Stream processors facilitate data flow either by moving or routing data without any transformation or by performing complex event processing. For instance, a stream processor may listen only to special types of events; whereas another processor can perform complex event processing tasks such as data aggregation or analytics tasks such as detecting anomalies and generating alerts.

Analytics services offer processing capabilities for data streams. Moreover, machine learning algorithms are provided for predictive scenarios such as error detection.

Storage services encompass many types of databases, e.g., relational, big data, key-value, document, as well as blob storage for unstructured data for text or binary data at massive scale.

UX services provide some tools for visualizing data; for instance, Power BI to create dashboards and Bing Maps to display data on a map.

Business integration services are responsible for the integration of IoT platform with specific IoT applications.

Figure 10. An IoT System Architecture based on Microsoft tools/services

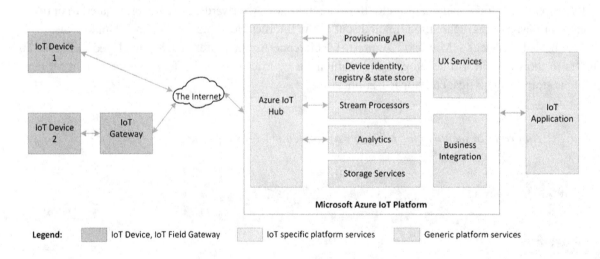

DISCUSSION

While IoT system development may seem similar to web or mobile development, in practice it requires a broad spectrum of tools, technologies, and skills (Taivalsaari & Mikkonen, 2018). This broad spectrum should cover many aspects of embedded, web, and mobile software development. Moreover, the distributed nature of IoT devices might complicate software development, deployment, and maintenance. In some cases IoT devices may consist of various hardware platforms with different capabilities and development environments. Managing this heterogeneity through appropriate level of abstraction is another challenge. Huge volume of data collected via many IoT devices is another issue to be tackled. Cloud-based IoT platforms are important enablers of IoT system development. Such platforms provide many infrastructural services (Such as storing and processing big data) encapsulated in separate components with well-defined interfaces. Such components not only streamline IoT system development, but also reduce entry barriers by offering economic and scalable back-end services.

Software Development for IoT Devices

IoT devices are hardware platforms that provide limited programming and execution capabilities. Therefore, there are many challenges associated with programming, deploying, and maintaining software for IoT devices. Software development for IoT devices generally follows the approach of embedded programming in which the application developed is tightly coupled with the hardware platform. There are efforts to decouple applications from hardware platform by providing programming languages that enable higher levels of abstraction and virtual machines to isolate application from the underlying hardware platform (Ahmadighohandizi & Systä, 2016; Sivieri et al., 2016). Such efforts are also closely related to a recent trend called edge computing (Shi et al., 2016). Edge computing proposes to move the computing from IoT platforms to IoT devices and gateways whenever feasible. Such an approach requires the development of more complex software for IoT devices and gateways. To achieve this, developers need more capable tools and programming languages that provide higher level of abstraction. Kiuas is an effort towards providing a programming environment for IoT devices (Selonen & Taivalsaari, 2016). This cloud-based environment provides a visual and textual development environment in which developers develop code regarding IoT device management, sensor data collection and visualization, device actuation etc.

Deployment for IoT devices and gateways are another pain point which should be addressed. In-place deployment for a huge number of IoT devices with a big bang approach might be risky for many IoT systems. A possible problem with the production environment might cause serious damages. For IoT devices which can host and execute two separate versions of an application, old and new versions can co-exist for a period of time (blue-green deployment pattern (Fowler, 2010)). During this period, if a problem arises, the system can switch to the old version. The challenge of blue-green deployment pattern might be ensuring the synchronization of persistent data for old and new versions (Ahmadighohandizi & Systä, 2016).

Maintainability of software residing on IoT devices and gateways is another potential problem area. Various kinds of hardware platforms, protocols, architectures, programming languages make IoT systems complex and therefore difficult to understand, even for experienced developers (Corno et al., 2018). To address this challenge there are efforts to provide documentation techniques (such as code recipes in (Corno et al., 2018)) independent from programming languages and run-time environments. Enriching code with such documentation techniques can help developers to understand existing code and make software maintenance easier.

Building general purpose applications for IoT devices and making them available through an application store is another challenge for software development on IoT devices. Apart from specific applications running on IoT pre-defined devices, such applications should be much more flexible in handling heterogeneous hardware platforms and communication protocols. (Kubitza, 2016) proposes an IDE providing abstraction mechanisms for handling hardware heterogeneity to build general purpose applications for IoT devices.

IoT Platforms

IoT platforms are treated as important enablers and backbones for realizing IoT business cases and developing IoT systems ("IoT Analytics," 2015). Such IoT platforms offer some common fundamental services, which are abstracted as and encapsulated in components. Components provide access to their services by following the SOA approach and generally using REST architectural style. Such components in IoT domain provide services regarding connectivity, device management, security, and data storage.

A connectivity layer that is handling communication over different protocols is the gate of IoT platforms to IoT devices. Amazon's Message Broker, Bosch IoT Hub, Google Cloud IoT Core, IBM Connection service, and Azure IoT Hub provide secure mechanisms for data exchange between IoT devices/gateways and IoT platforms. Device management ensures IoT devices/gateways are running properly with up-to-date software installed on them ("IoT Analytics," 2015).

Device management capabilities encompass some common tasks such as device provisioning, remote configuration, management of software updates, and troubleshooting ("IoT Analytics," 2015). Such services are critical for the operation of an IoT system with thousands or even millions IoT devices/gateways. Amazon recently announced AWS Device Management component, which makes it easy to onboard, organize, monitor, and remotely manage IoT devices ("AWS IoT Device Management Overview," n.d.). Bosch IoT Rollouts service takes care of deploying software to IoT devices/gateways. IoT Remote Manager provides device management and monitoring capabilities for IoT devices/gateways. Google does not provide an explicit component dealing with device management. IBM Connection service and Microsoft Azure IoT Hub provide device management capabilities besides connectivity. Closely related with device management, IoT platforms involve some components for persisting IoT device/gateway metadata and state data. Amazon device registry keeps track of the metadata of IoT devices. Amazon device shadow service stores the current and desired states of IoT device and enables to update states of IoT devices through message broker. Bosch IoT platform keeps track of device metadata through IoT Things component. Google IoT platform manages device metadata through device manager component present in Cloud IoT Core. Connection service in IBM Watson IoT platform includes some functionality regarding device metadata gathering. Microsoft Azure IoT platform handles device life cycle through Provisioning API and stores device metadata in device identity, registry, and state store.

Security, which is a cross-cutting concern for such platforms, is handled by various components. Amazon IoT platform has a separate security and identity service for controlling access to services and resources. Bosch IoT Permissions enables the management of users, groups, roles, and applications including authorization and authentication. Google Cloud IoT Core includes a mechanism for authentication. IBM Risk management services are concerned with security, authentication, and prevention of fraud. Microsoft Azure IoT Hub provides protection of communication path, device authentication and authorization.

Data storage is one of the pivotal requirements of an IoT platform. Generally, IoT platforms utilize existing storage solutions present on cloud platforms for storing IoT data. Bosch IoT platform is a platform specifically developed for IoT systems. This platform can run other general purpose cloud platforms, such as Amazon Web Services, and uses the storage services of these platforms, such as Amazon RDS and Amazon DynamoDB.

Many IoT systems have various analytics functionalities for processing IoT data and enabling informed actions. Such functionality is within the scope of big data analytics and discussed in the next subsection.

Handling IoT Big Data

As more and more data are digitized, the term "big data" is becoming more important for many domains as well as IoT. A growing number of IoT devices and related systems generate massive amounts of data. Relational databases do not meet all the requirements for the IoT, especially scalability requirements. Consequently there is a need for alternative approaches for processing and storing big data produced by IoT systems. As the IoT spreads over, distributed computing models and non-relational data storage approaches started to provide part of the solution. Having these on integrated cloud environments addresses the need for scalability required by IoT systems.

Amazon provides Amazon RDB for storing structured data and Amazon DynamoDB for unstructured data. Amazon QuickSight provide some functionalities for analyzing data. As mentioned earlier, Bosch IoT platform can be hosted on a general purpose cloud platform, such as Amazon Web Services, and use the storage and analytics capabilities of that platform. Moreover, Bosch IoT platform includes IoT Analytics component, which provides common analysis capabilities for processing device generated data to gain insights. Google, IBM, and Microsoft utilize general purpose storage and analytics components to store and analyze IoT big data. Some platforms also has some services to process streams of IoT data, such as stream processors of Microsoft Azure.

CONCLUSION

With more and more connected devices to be in use in forthcoming years, IoT is an active focus area for industry. In line with this trend, IoT systems meeting business requirements with reasonable cost have to be developed within an acceptable timeframe. The development of IoT systems is not straightforward and must be supported with a variety of tools and platforms. Cloud platform providers utilize their existing cloud services to form IoT specific platforms. Such platforms include IoT specific services, especially connectivity and device management. Big data storage and processing services are key for obtaining benefits from IoT data. As stated by (Wortmann, 2015), "the support of the latest and continuously evolving standards as well as the integration of adequate end-to-end tool chains even in the embedded software domain to enhance developer productivity represent further important challenges in the development of IoT platforms".

REFERENCES

Ahmadighohandizi, F., & Systä, K. (2016, September). Application development and deployment for IoT devices. In *European Conference on Service-Oriented and Cloud Computing* (pp. 74-85). Springer.

API Client Libraries | Google Developers. (n.d.). Retrieved from https://developers.google.com/api-client-library/

AWS Documentation - AWS IoT - API Reference. (n.d.). Retrieved from http://docs.aws.amazon.com/iot/latest/apireference/API_Operations.html

AWS IoT Developer Guide. (2018). Retrieved from https://docs.aws.amazon.com/iot/latest/developer-guide/iot-dg.pdf

AWS IoT Device Management Overview - Amazon Web Services. (n.d.). Retrieved from https://aws.amazon.com/tr/iot-device-management/

AWS IoT Device SDK. (n.d.). Retrieved from https://aws.amazon.com/iot-platform/sdk/

AWS SDK for Java. (n.d.). Retrieved from https://aws.amazon.com/sdk-for-java/

AWS Toolkit for Eclipse. (n.d.). Retrieved from https://aws.amazon.com/eclipse/

Bass, L., Clements, P., & Kazman, R. (2012). *Software Architecture in Practice* (3rd ed.). Addison-Wesley Professional.

Börnert, C., Clark, K., Daya, S., Debeaux, M., Diederichs, G., Gucer, V., ... Thole, J. (2016). *An Architectural and Practical Guide to IBM Hybrid Integration Platform*. IBM Redbooks.

Bosch IoT Suite. (n.d.). Retrieved from https://www.bosch-iot-suite.com/

Cloud IoT Core. (n.d.). Retrieved from https://cloud.google.com/iot-core/

Corno, F., De Russis, L., & Sáenz, J. P. (2018, May). Easing IoT development for novice programmers through code recipes. In *Proceedings of the 40th International Conference on Software Engineering: Software Engineering Education and Training* (pp. 13-16). ACM. 10.1145/3183377.3183385

Eclipse hawkBit. (n.d.). Retrieved from https://www.eclipse.org/hawkbit/

FowlerM. (2010). *BlueGreenDeployment*. Retrieved from https://martinfowler.com/bliki/BlueGreenDeployment.html

Google CloudS. D. K. (n.d.). Retrieved from https://cloud.google.com/sdk/

GRPC. (n.d.). Retrieved from https://grpc.io/

IBM Watson IoT - GitHub. (n.d.). Retrieved from https://github.com/ibm-watson-iot/

IoT Analytics. (2015). *IoT Platforms - The central backbone for the Internet of Things*. Retrieved from https://iot-analytics.com/product/iot-platforms-white-paper/

Köksal, Ö., & Tekinerdogan, B. (2017). Feature-Driven Domain Analysis of Session Layer Protocols of Internet of Things. In *IEEE International Congress on Internet of Things (ICIOT)* (pp. 105-112). IEEE.

Krebs, R., Momm, C., & Kounev, S. (2012). Architectural Concerns in Multi-tenant SaaS Applications. *Closer*, *12*, 426–431.

Kubitza, T. (2016, November). Apps for Environments: Running Interoperable Apps in Smart Environments with the meSchup IoT Platform. In *International Workshop on Interoperability and Open-Source Solutions* (pp. 158-172). Springer.

Meier, J. D., Hill, D., Homer, A., Jason, T., Bansode, P., Wall, L., ... Bogawat, A. (2009). *Microsoft application architecture guide*. Microsoft Corporation.

Mell, P., & Grance, T. (2011). *The NIST definition of cloud computing*. NIST.

Microsoft Azure – GitHub. (n.d.). Retrieved from https://github.com/azure/

Microsoft Azure IoT Reference Architecture. Version 2.0. (2018). Retrieved from https://aka.ms/iotrefarchitecture

Overview of Internet of Things. (n.d.). Retrieved from https://cloud.google.com/solutions/iot-overview

Page-Jones, M. (1999). *Fundamentals of Object-Oriented Design in UML* (1st ed.). Addison-Wesley Professional.

Selonen, P., & Taivalsaari, A. (2016, August). Kiuas – IoT cloud environment for enabling the programmable world. In *Software Engineering and Advanced Applications (SEAA), 2016 42th Euromicro Conference on* (pp. 250-257). IEEE.

Shi, W., Cao, J., Zhang, Q., Li, Y., & Xu, L. (2016). Edge computing: Vision and challenges. *IEEE Internet of Things Journal*, *3*(5), 637–646. doi:10.1109/JIOT.2016.2579198

Sivieri, A., Mottola, L., & Cugola, G. (2016). Building internet of things software with eliot. *Computer Communications*, *89*, 141–153. doi:10.1016/j.comcom.2016.02.004

Taivalsaari, A., & Mikkonen, T. (2018, April). On the development of IoT systems. In *Fog and Mobile Edge Computing (FMEC), 2018 Third International Conference on* (pp. 13-19). IEEE. 10.1109/FMEC.2018.8364039

Tools for Amazon Web Services. (n.d.). Retrieved from https://aws.amazon.com/tools/?nc1=f_ls

Williams, Z. D. (2017). *IoT Platform Comparison: How the 450 providers stack up* [White paper]. Retrieved July 19, 2018, from https://iot-analytics.com/iot-platform-comparison-how-providers-stack-up/

Wortmann, F., & Flüchter, K. (2015). Internet of things. *Business & Information Systems Engineering*, *57*(3), 221–224. doi:10.100712599-015-0383-3

ADDITIONAL READING

Botta, A., De Donato, W., Persico, V., & Pescapé, A. (2016). Integration of cloud computing and internet of things: A survey. *Future Generation Computer Systems*, *56*, 684–700. doi:10.1016/j.future.2015.09.021

Giray, G., Tekinerdogan, B., & Tüzün, E. (2017). Adopting the Essence Framework to Derive a Practice Library for the Development of IoT Systems. In Z. Mahmood (Ed.), *Connected Environments for the Internet of Things* (pp. 151–168). Cham: Springer. doi:10.1007/978-3-319-70102-8_8

Giray, G., Tekinerdogan, B., & Tüzün, E. (2018). IoT System Development Methods. In Q. F. Hassan, A. R. Khan, & S. A. Madani (Eds.), *Internet of Things: Challenges, Advances and Applications* (pp. 141–159). Chapman & Hall/CRC Press.

Gorton, I., & Klein, J. (2015). Distribution, data, deployment: Software architecture convergence in big data systems. *IEEE Software*, *32*(3), 78–85. doi:10.1109/MS.2014.51

Grover, M., Malaska, T., Seidman, J., & Shapira, G. (2015). *Hadoop Application Architectures: Designing Real-World Big Data Applications*. O'Reilly Media, Inc.

Big data and cloud computing:Hashem, I. A. T., Yaqoob, I., Anuar, N. B., Mokhtar, S., Gani, A., & Khan, S. U. (2015). The rise of "big data" on cloud computing: Review and open research issues. *Information Systems*, *47*, 98–115. doi:10.1016/j.is.2014.07.006

Mistrík, I., Bahsoon, R., Ali, N., Heisel, M., & Maxim, B. (Eds.). (2017). *Software Architecture for Big Data and the Cloud*. Morgan Kaufmann.

Riggins, F. J., & Wamba, S. F. (2015, January). Research directions on the adoption, usage, and impact of the internet of things through the use of big data analytics. In *System Sciences (HICSS), 2015 48th Hawaii International Conference on* (pp. 1531-1540). IEEE. 10.1109/HICSS.2015.186

Software development for IoT:Taivalsaari, A., & Mikkonen, T. (2017). A roadmap to the programmable world: Software challenges in the IoT era. *IEEE Software*, *34*(1), 72–80. doi:10.1109/MS.2017.26

KEY TERMS AND DEFINITIONS

Communication Protocol: Communication protocols are formal descriptions of formats and rules for producing digital messages for electronic data exchange.

Device Management: Device management is the application of a set of methods, techniques, tools to manage IoT devices throughout their lifecycle. The fundamental activities of device management are provisioning and authentication, configuration and control, monitoring and diagnostics, and software updates and maintenance.

Integrated Development Environment (IDE): An IDE is an application, which provides some facilities (such as source editor, configuration management, builders, runtime, testing, debugger, etc.) to developers for software development.

IoT Application: An IoT application is specific to a domain and implements the requirements of a specific business model. It utilizes IoT platform for common basic functionalities.

IoT Device: IoT devices (also called as things, connected devices, smart devices, smart objects, etc.) are capable of sensing data from the real world and communicating these data electronically to an IoT gateway and/or to an IoT platform/application over a connection.

IoT Gateway: IoT gateways play an intermediary role between IoT devices and IoT platforms. IoT gateways receive data from IoT devices, may translate, filter, aggregate, cleanse data and direct these data to IoT platforms.

IoT Platform: IoT platform refers to a combination of some basic functionalities common to most IoT systems. These functionalities encompass computation, storage, analytics, device management, etc.

IoT System: An IoT system (or IoT solution) is a composition of the elements, namely IoT device, gateway, platform, application, and fulfill some specific requirements. For instance, an IoT system for waste management can detect rubbish levels in containers to optimize the trash collection routes.

Software Development Kit (SDK): An SDK supports developers for software development by providing some functionality in the form of a set of libraries and hence foster software reuse.

This research was previously published in the Handbook of Research on Big Data and the IoT; pages 223-241, copyright year 2019 by Engineering Science Reference (an imprint of IGI Global).

Chapter 61
Coverage Criteria for State–Based Testing:
A Systematic Review

Sonali Pradhan

Siksha 'O' Anusandhan University, Bhubaneswar, India

Mitrabinda Ray

Department of Computer Science and Engineering, Siksha 'O' Anusandhan University, Bhubaneswar, India

Srikanta Patnaik

ⓘ https://orcid.org/0000-0001-8297-0614

Siksha 'O' Anusandhan University, Bhubaneswar, India

ABSTRACT

State-based testing (SBT) is known as deriving test cases from state machines and examining the dynamic behaviour of the system. It helps to identify various types of state-based faults within a system under test (SUT). For SBT, test cases are generated from state chart diagrams based on various coverage criteria such as All Transition, Round Trip Path, All Transition Pair, All Transition Pair with length 2, All Transition Pair with length 3, All Transition Pair of length 4 and Full Predicate. This article discusses a number of coverage criteria at the design level to find out various types of state-based faults in SBT. First, the intermediate graph is generated from a state chart diagram using an XML parser. The graph is traversed based on the given coverage criteria to generate a sequence of test cases. Then, mutation testing and sneak-path testing are applied on the generated test cases to check the effectiveness of the generated test suite. These two are common methods for checking the effectiveness of test cases. Mutation testing helps in the number of seeded errors covered whereas sneak-path testing basically helps to examine the unspecified behavior of the system. In round trip path (RTP), it is not possible to cover all paths. All transition is not an adequate level of fault detection with more execution time compared to all transition pair (ATP) with length 4 (LN4). In the discussion, ATP with LN4 is the best among all coverage criteria. SBT can able to detect various state-based faults-incorrect transition, missing transi-

DOI: 10.4018/978-1-6684-3702-5.ch061

tion, missing or incorrect event, missing or incorrect action, extra missing or corrupt state, which are difficult to detect in code-based testing. Most of these state-based faults can be avoided, if the testing is conducted at the early phase of design.

INTRODUCTION

Testing at the early phase of software development life cycle can able to find the ambiguities and inconsistencies in the design and hence, design should be enhanced before the program is written (Antonio et al., 2002; Sundararajan et al., 2017). Research is going on state-based testing (SBT) to find effective test cases and to minimize cost of the test suite (Agrawal et al., 1989; Holt et al., 2014). For this, Unified Modeling Language (UML) diagrams are used to generate test cases. Initially testers were going for traditional testing, which is also known as code coverage testing. But, state-based coverage cannot be achieved in code-based testing (Binder, 2000). To achieve this, tester generates test scenarios from the state chart diagrams and then test cases are generated from these scenarios. Test cases are generated at design level and coverage analysis is performed from the source code. The diagrams are generated at the design stage of development life cycle. Generating test cases based on UML diagrams come under Model Based Testing (MBT). It is a better testing approach than code-based testing as it detects the error at the early phase which requires less cost to fix it (Chen & Wang, 2014; Dias Neto et al., 2007). MBT are conducted for the following reasons:

- To get an abstract model of the system;
- Validate the model;
- Generate and execute test cases;
- Assigning pass/fail verdict;
- Analyzing the execution result;
- When it is not required to model the full system;
- To prevent fault;
- To reduce cost with updating test cases.

Early testing activities make early fault detection (Binder, 2000; Broy et al., 2005) and more and more articles are referred to as MBT using state-based testing. In a very recent article, we find in MBT, where it elaborates several findings from MBT users in industry, security testing and various MBT challenges (Utting et al., 2016). Utting and Legeard (Briand & Labiche, 2001) have proposed a SBT technique to design black box testing. State-based testing is primarily considered as a black box testing to generate test cases (Briand & Labiche, 2001).

A test case is a document, which has a set of test data, expected results with preconditions and post conditions. Test case is a particular test scenario in order to verify action against a specific requirement. There are different types of software faults that can be found in different ways (y Hernández & Marsden, 2017). A set of test cases is called a test suite. To examine the effectiveness of the test suit, tester goes for the mutation testing and sneak-path testing. Mutation testing technique is applied on the generated test suite to measure its efficiency. In mutation testing, a faulty version of a software system is generated by introducing some mutant in the software, which is known as mutant operators (Chen & Wang, 2014).

Some mutants still undetected after conformance testing. So, another way of testing where remaining mutants are killed is known as sneak-path testing (Chen & Wang, 2014; Utting et al., 2016). Conformance testing is seeking to test specified behavior of the model and also it is equally important to test unspecified behavior of the model through sneak-path testing (Chen & Wang, 2014). Complete testing is not cost-effective as it takes longer time to investigate the software. The complete software testing is also known as exhaustive testing (Ostrand & Balcer, 1988). Therefore, testing must be performed on selected subsets, but not the whole domain of testing, which makes effective software testing. In a very recent approach, a non-deterministic action system model is used for generating a number of mutants (Aichernig, 2016). In the paper (Aichernig, 2016), original model is executed and tested for conformance after the mutants are generated, so that conformance check is done efficiently, and the complete testing is not possible. Test cases help us in retrieval of important information. Different types of tests are more effective for different classes in the model (Jacky et al., 2007). Enabling graphical interfaces MBT is a novel technique for graphical user interfaces (GUI) testing (Belli & Beyazıt, 2017; Reed & Angolia, 2018). In this survey paper, first, we discuss the SBT by generating test cases based on various types of state-based coverage criteria. Next, mutation testing and sneak-path testing are discussed and applied on the generated test cases to measure the efficiency.

In conformance testing, sometimes the tester skips to know the effect of some coverage criteria which are very useful in testing. In the paper (Durelli et al., 2018), an experimental comparison of edge, edge-pair, and prime path criteria are used. To find a very accurate idea of fault finding ability and cost of several criteria, three structural coverage criteria are used in that paper. They are edge coverage, edge-pair coverage and prime path coverage and they find prime path coverage is detecting more faults with higher cost (Durelli et al., 2018). The main objective of testing is to detect faults in the program and to provide more assurance on the quality of the software. For the high-quality software, the researchers are more concerned about the test cases. To achieve these objectives, different state machines are used. The paper discusses state-of-the-art of state-based testing with several coverage criteria. This paper guides the tester to set the coverage criteria of state-based testing within the available test resources. The main objective here is to review the current state coverage criteria for UML state chart diagram and presents a suitable coverage criterion to achieve the highest coverage.

The remainder of this paper is divided into four sections. Section 2 contains the Materials and Methods which describe the background study, related work and the details of the methods used. Section 3 presents the result and discussion of the study and finally, Section 4 describes the conclusion and future scope.

MATERIALS AND METHODS

In this section, first, we give the preliminary idea of the state based machine, where various elements of the state chart diagram are discussed with an example. Then, we discuss the existing work on SBT. Finally, we discuss on generation of test cases based on different coverage criteria from two state chart diagrams. We consider the state chart diagrams of two familiar case studies, Bank Account processing & ATM Card processing. We examine the efficiency of the test cases using mutation testing and sneak-path testing.

Background Study

We present a state chart diagram of Stack operation as an example. The growth of black box tesing gradually tends to MBT (El-Far et al., 2001; Dias Neto et al., 2007; Koopman et al., 2013). MBT is a state-based testing, in general term, test case generation and test result evaluation are done on the model of the system under test. SBT is done to derive test cases and to examine the dynamic behaviour of the system (Antoniol et al., 2002; Agrawal et al., 1989; Chen & Wang, 2014). States are explained by their property, a constraint that must always be true when the SUT is in that state. State-based testing thus validates the states that are achieved, adaptable and the transitions that are evoked according to the requirement. State transition testing is used, in a finite state machine having finite number of different states and the transitions are from one state to another state. The system and the tests are based on the model. A finite state machine can handle the dynamic behaviour of the system where you get a different output for the same input. The advantage of the state transition technique is that according to the tester's need, the model can be abstract or can be detailed. A part of the system is more important, if it requires more testing and a greater depth of detail can be modelled. The system is less important that requires less testing, the model can use a single state otherwise system goes for series of different states. State- based testing is a technique to validate software systems by generating test cases from models. A test suite can be generated according to defined coverage criteria (Boberg, 2008; Chow, 1978). State-based test automation is sometimes considered to be the fourth generation in test automation (Briandet al., 2004). These advantages of state transition technique come under at very little extra cost. When an event occurs, an action is taken, and a transition occurs to a new state from a current state. The state of a state chart will be represented by a state variable and by discrete data type. Set of possible states in the state chart is always fixed. When it is in a particular state, the properties and behaviour of the state chart are same. An abstraction of the values and links of an object is a state. Its assets exceed its liabilities depending on either solvent or insolvent. A state is represented sometimes in round shape or a rectangle with rounded corner. A state has different compartments such as Name compartment, which holds the name in string form as a state and it is optional. State activities are the internal actions hold in the state machine. To enter or exit from a state, internal transition occurs. From this entering and exiting, the status of the state is known. Elements in state chart diagram are initial state, final state, activity state, event, and action and guard condition. Initial state is represented as a filled black rounded circle. The state chart diagram has only one initial state. A final state shows the end of an object existence in the state diagram. When an object is destroyed and stops responding to events, we know that it reached the final state. This is shown as an arrow, which is pointing to a filled circle nested inside another circle representing the object's final state. A state chart may have more than one final state but have only one initial state. An activity state is initiated by the event during which some internal processing of the object is performed. Only one activity is done for an event. An event is the input to a state chart and in action a state chart makes a transition to a new state. In some state chart diagrams, some events will cause associated transitions to new states, while other events do not cause transitions. An action is an output activity of an object that is initiated by an event. Guard conditions affect the behavior of a state machine by enabling actions or transitions only to evaluate TRUE or FALSE according to the conditions given.

State machine diagrams are similar to activity diagrams with little changes in its notations and usage. It describes the behavior of objects that act differently according to state with their state of moment. Basic states and actions are shown below in the state chart diagram. Figure 1 illustrates a state machine diagram of stack operation. State coverage, event coverage and transition coverage can be tested from the state chart diagram shown in Figure 1. There are five states. They are Initial, Empty, Holding, Full and Final. The events covered are create (), add (PUSH), delete (POP) and destroy. The test case that covers a transition T: is create, push, push, push, [Full], that shows transition moves from the Initial state to Full state.

Test cases are derived from state machines in the state-based testing that checks the expected system behavior. State-based testing validates the transitions and the states reached in the SUT. Using the generated tests cases, the tester checks whether the test cases are sufficiently cover the requirements or not. This can be verified through mutation testing. Mutation testing is also known as mutation analysis (Jia & Harman, 2011).

Figure 1. State chart diagram of Stack operation (Source: http://www.chegg.com/homework-help/ questions-and-answers/intra-class-testing-using-state-machine-diagram-20points-create-project-call-stack-first-w-q25561374)

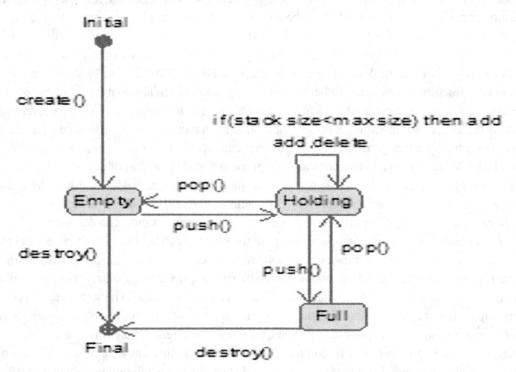

Related Work

In this section, we discuss the related works, which are divided into three categories: (i) model-based testing, (ii) state-based testing, (iii) cost-effectiveness testing. The complexity in code-based testing is that it can achieve 100 percent code coverage but it does not say about the behaviour of the system under test as it may not fulfil the state based coverage (Binder, 2000). In MBT, abstractions are applied when modelling, fault is prevented and cost can be reduced with updating test cases (Antoniol et al., 2002; Binder, 2000). But some complexities are there in MBT. The main complexity that the tester finds from MBT is that the number of paths in the model can be very large, which difficult to cover and a time is taking process (Binder, 2000). The behaviour of the system is needed to be checked as the system behaves differently to the same inputs in different states. This MBT works, if the mathematical model is deterministic (resulting behaviour depends upon initial state and input) or can be transformed into a deterministic one. MBT is a better testing approach than code-based testing (Binder, 2000). MBT approaches are divided into two parts i.e. quantitative analysis and qualitative analysis. In quantitative analysis, the information is about the application of MBT in the testing level of software engineering. The main three approaches of MBT are graphical test modelling approach, environment approach, and system model driven test generation. Looking at these three important criteria, MBT tool is selected. We provide a list of tools supported by MBT approaches, in Table 1. The blank references in Table 1 represents open source for that particular Tool.

Every year some new MBT tools are going to be published. It is not possible to get information about all the tools. A systematic mapping of MBT tools is given in the paper, published in the year 2010 (Shafique & Labiche, 2010), which helps academic researchers a lot. In the qualitative analysis, cost, effort, limitations, complexity, input and pre-requirements are considered. In this part, quality of output generated from MBT is discussed. Qualitative analysis is divided into three parts (i) Coverage criteria for testing (ii) Limitations of Behavior model (iii) Cost and complexity of MBT. In the testing coverage criteria, control-flow or a data-flow strategy is used. Control-flow coverage criteria is used until 1999 (Dalal et al., 1999) and data-flow analysis has been more common after 1999 (Dias Neto et al., 2007). Full system will be evaluated with small modules which made the control-flow a better approach with increasing complexity and size of the system. Model should be corrected to generate test cases. With the MBT approaches, model checking strategies are used to ensure accuracy (Dias Neto et al., 2007). The level of complexity is defined with following points:

- **High:** No supporting tool, manual steps, requirement of translation between models, incomplete output and instrumentation of the code;
- **Intermediate:** Intermediate model, complex model notation and using appropriate tool;
- **Low:** UML and FSM model are used, tools available, completely automated and empirical evaluation.

Here, we are giving the emphasis on state-based testing and state-based testing is a kind of MBT (El-Far et al., 2001). In state-based testing, tester observes the state change in the SUT. In state-based testing, tester also observes for state coverage, transition coverage and action coverage. Chow's (1978) strategy which deals with the verification of control structures at the design level is called automata theoretic testing. That automata theoretic testing could find operation errors, extra states, missing states, and transition errors in a finite state machine. But, this method can only be used when the control structures are represented by finite state machine. Again W-method is presented by Chow (1978). Chow generated test sequences from a spanning tree of the finite state machine to the behavior of the SUT (1978). The same method is modified by Binder (2000) and that is used in Round Trip Path (RTP) as a coverage criteria of UML context. Combining W-method and Binder's proposed method, traversing the transition tree to cover all paths. If the state is repeated, which is already in the path is the stopping state. Opposing Chow's method, Binder denotes the RTP strategy. It says that covering should be done for all transitions in sequence that begin and end with the same state and simple paths are covered from initial to final state. Only necessity taken to Binder's approach is machine flattening and removing the concurrency of the machine. Turner (1993) proposed state-based testing and investigates some new coverage criteria. Most studied coverage criteria are Full Predicate (FP), Round Trip Path (RTP), and All Transitions (AT), All Transition Pairs (ATP), ATP paths of length 2 (LN2), ATP paths of length 3 (LN3), and ATP paths of length 4 (LN4) (Chen & Wang, 2014; Utting et al., 2016; Chow, 1978). These different criteria are described with examples in Section 2.3 (Coverage Criteria). The FP criterion tends to obtain when model has guard conditions and FP has higher or similar mutation score as ATP, although at a higher cost (Chen & Wang, 2014; Jun Pang et al., 2013). From the experimental results (Oftedal, 2011), it is shown that the coverage criteria AT, RTP, ATP, and LN4 generate high quality test suites and they are sufficient powerful to detect the seeded faults that is the mutation testing.

Table 1. MBT supporting tools

Tool	Modified Year	References	Input Format	Type	Description
Test	2016	(Hoisl & Sobernig, 2014)	Custom (Gherkin based)	Commercial	Gherkin is a language which is used as a syntax for generating test cases from textual models
BPM-Xchange	2014		BPMN, UML	Commercial	Based on different criteria test cases are generated by BPM-Xchange from business process models and it provides leading technology for continuous process management
Conformal Creator	2016	(Li &Yan, 2016)	Activity Diagrams, DSL	Commercial	This is based on a graphical domain specific action language and activity diagram and it ensures that timing constraints are correct and complete.
Conformal Designer	2014	(Huima, 2007)	UML, State machines, QML (QT Modelling Language). It is an interface specification and programming language	Commercial	Models can be created as Qutronic modeling language (QML), QML is used to design user interface centric applications and tool is also useful for UML state chart machines
DTM (Dialogues testing method)	2013		Custom activity model	Commercial	Structural coverage is selected by DTM (Dialogues testing method), it is an interface for drawing functional test models for MBT.
freeMBT	2014		Custom (ALL)	Open source	Test cases are automatically generates by Free Model-Based Testing (fMBT). It is capable for off-line and on-line MBT
JSXM	2014		EFSM (called Stream X-machines)	Academic	It generates test cases and takes model animation as its input
JtorX	2014	(Belinfante,2010)	Labelled Transition Systems (A LTS format)	Open source	JtorX is a reimplementation of TorX implemented in Java with additional features
MaTeLo	2013	(Dulz et al., 2003)	Markov chains	Commercial	Markov Test Logic is an automatically generated test suites and commercial product to generate function test cases, it uses all transition coverage strategy and random generation oriented by profiles
MBT suite	2016		UML or BPMN	Commercial	This tool can generate test cases from UML diagrams for example state chart diagram using path coverage, state coverage, action coverage, etc.
Model Unit	2014	(Utting, 2012)	EFSM	Open source	This tool is used to write Java classes for simple finite state machine or extended finite state machine and test cases are generated using various coverage criteria testing with models
PyModel	2013	(Jacky, 2011)	Python source	Open source	This tool is used for on-the-fly testing and offline testing
RT-Tester	2014	(Peleska, 2013)	UML/SysML, Matlab	Commercial	RT-Tester is used for UML/SysML or Matlab models, and generate test cases from various coverage criteria
Smart testing certify	2014	(Bouquet et al., 2008)	UML+OCL	Commercial	This tool uses UML models, OCL constraints and various coverage criteria of the model
TestCast	2014	(Ernits et al., 2006)	UML state machines	Commercial	It generates TTCN (Tree and Tabular Combine Notation) test cases from UML state machines. It is a language testing reactive system based on requirement and model structure coverage
T-VEC	2013	(Pasareanu& Schumann, 2009)	Simulink	Commercial	Its generate test cases for syatem supporting model translation, test vector generation and model checker and it also supports Math Works Simulink models based on different coverage criteria

It is observed that AT does not provide a sufficient level of fault detection (Belli et al., 2016). With the exception of results reported in (Offutt & Abdurazik, 1999), where only 54 percent of mutants were killed, ATP has shown to be a rather strong coverage criterion as compared to AT and RTP, although at a higher cost. Comparing AT and ATP, RTP is shown to be more cost-effective (Belli et al., 2016). It is observed that, some faults remain undetected and RTP testing is not enough in some situations. For the weaker form of RTP this is true. Then again RTP is compared to random testing in (Muller, 2002).

RTP strategy makes some fault undetected but RTP strategy is somehow effective in detecting faults. There in comparison 90 percent of the faults are detected by RTP and 70 percent faults are detected from random testing and from the results it is known that some sort of faults are undetected in RTP. By combining RTP with Category-Partition (CP) method, the tester can enhance the fault detection, but with increased cost. Tester can easily modify the test specification when required, and the complexity is controlled by CP method (Tiwari & Goel, 2013). RTP is combined with white box testing, it provides better fault detection capability. Mutation testing and sneak-path testing are used for evaluation of test generation methods (Chen & Wang, 2014). In that paper, research has evaluated state-based coverage criteria, the focus is directed towards fault detection effectiveness based on artificial seeded faults (e.g., with mutation operators). Artificial seeded fault is the mutation analysis. It is a very common approach in cost-effectiveness of SBT. Using mutation testing test suite can be made more capable to detect the faults. The number of mutants killed by specific test suite divided by total number of mutants is the mutant score, which measures the cost-effectiveness of the test suite.

The final facet of SBT is sneak-path testing. A series of controlled experiments is done to investigate the impact of RTP for cost and fault detection, compared with structural testing (Tiwari & Goel, 2013; Petriu & Rouquette, 2010). Experiments are extended to more test, the sneak-path testing (Jun Pang et al., 2013). All the test above discussed are about conformance testing, where specified behavior of the test model is taken, but the unspecified behavior should be tested because to make the test suite more efficient. Sneak-path testing is done to verify the nonappearance of unspecified behavior in the SUT. So the tester aims at sneak-path testing. Unintentional sneak-path is taken as the unspecified behavior of the test model. Sneak-path testing is a very important test in SBT strategy and it is strongly recommended in the SBT testing process (Tiwari & Goel, 2013; Petriu & Rouquette, 2010). Using mutation testing and sneak-path testing, the efficiency of the test suite is measured. Looking at this context, coverage criteria with AT, RTP, and ATP with mutation testing and sneak-path testing are discussed below.

Test Case Generation Criteria From State Chart Diagrams

This section introduces some common transition-based coverage criteria used in test case generation for state models. In code-based testing, test case generation criteria are- statement coverage, branch coverage and condition coverage. Similarly, at design level, the test cases are generated from design diagrams with various coverage criteria. We discuss various coverage criteria at design level from state chart diagram. These are- All States coverage, All Transitions coverage, Round Trip Paths coverage, All Transition Pairs with LN2, LN3, LN4, Full Predicate coverage, All-Paths coverage. We have taken two state models as our case studies. A state chart diagram of Bank Account processing is shown in Figure 2 and a state chart diagram of ATM Card processing is shown in Figure 3. To create the state models, we have used Umbrello UML Modeller. Umbrello UML Modeller is used to create diagrams for designing and documenting the systems. For example, in Bank Account processing, the object Bank Account class has different states like Empty, Created, Debited and the transitions between them are created by the tool as a complete state model. EclEmma, which is a free Java code coverage tool for Eclipse. The EclEmma brings code coverage analysis directly into Eclipse workbench. EclEmma supports Junit test to cover the codes.

All state coverage visits every model state at least once. This criterion covers all states in every state chart diagram for basic test generation (Utting & Legeard, 2010). All Transition criteria says, without any specific order every transition is exercised at least once in the state machine covering all states, events and actions (Holt et al., 2012). AT criteria is the minimum amount of coverage achieved by the tester when testing the software, but tester cannot avoid AT testing strategy. A state chart diagram of Bank Account processing is shown in the case study of Figure 2. In Figure 2, it has 3 states. They are Empty, Credited and Debited. It has two events, amount-deposit and amount-withdraw. Finally, the transition coverage are Empty to Credited and Credited to Empty and so on. Figure 2 shows the sequences of transitions represented from the example model of Bank Account processing and t_i represents states of transitions. AT: T1=(t1, t2, t6); T2= (t1, t2, t3, t4); T3= (t1, t2, t3, t5); T4= (t1, t2, t8); T5= (t1, t7). Test suite 1 [T (I)] =5 (5 number of test cases are generated for AT).

In RTP technique, all paths in the state machine is covered that begin and end with the same state. The RTP technique will find missing states, incorrect or missing transition, actions and outputs and it can also detect existence of the undesirable states (Holt et al., 2012). The test tree that covers the RTP criteria is called a transition tree. If the same node is existing anywhere in the transition tree, is the final state in the state machine. In RTP strategy, it covers all simple paths as well as all round-trip paths that begin with the initial state to the final state. By traversing all paths in the transition tree, the total transitions are covered. The RTP criteria generating test cases for the state chart diagram shown in Figure 2 is as follows:

RTP: T(II) = (t1, t2[amount>balance],t6); (t1, t2, t3[amount<balance],t5; (t1, t2, t3,t4);(t1, t2, t6,t7);(t1,t2,t8), Test suite 2 [T(II)]=5 (5 number of test cases are generated for RTP).

All Transition Pair criteria covers all pairs of adjacent transitions of the state machine. Each adjacent paired transitions covers from state S_a to S_b and from state S_b to S_c in the state machine. In the ATP strategy, test suite contains ATP paths of length 2 (LN2), ATP paths of length 3 (LN3), ATP paths of length 4 (LN4) tests, covering the pairs of transitions in sequence. ATP: T(III) = (t1,t2,t6,t2); (t1,t2,t6,t7); (t1,t2,t3,t4); (t1,t2,t3,t5) Test suite 4 [T (III)] =4 (4 number of test cases are generated for ATP). ATP with LN2: T (III) = (t1, t2, t6); (t1, t2, t3) ;(t1, t2, t8) Test suite 3 [T (III)] = 3 (3 number of test cases are generated for ATP with LN2). ATP with LN3: T (IV) = (t1, t2, t3, t4); (t1, t2, t3, t5); (t1, t2, t6, t7), Test suite 5 [T (IV)] = 3 (3 number of test cases are generated for LN3). ATP with LN4: T (V) = (t1, t2, t3, t4) ;(t1, t2, t6, t2, t3); (t1, t2, t6, t2, t8); (t1, t2, t3, t5, t2); (t1, t2, t3, t5, t7), Test suite 6 [T (V)] = 5 (5 number of test cases are generated for LN4).

In the Full Predicate (FP) coverage strategy, each predicate on guarded transitions of the state machine is tested independently. Full Predicate (FP) is given by the test suite that each item in each predicate transitions with guarded conditions is tested separately (Holt et al., 2012). FP: (t1,t2,t6); (t1,t2,t3);(t1,t2,t3,t5).

All-Paths coverage specifies that each executable path should be followed at least once when executing the abstract test case. It is generally impractical as some models typically contain an infinite number of paths due to loops (Utting & Legeard, 2010), for that the tester does not prefer this criterion.

Figure 2. State chart diagram of class Bank Account, in case study Bank Account processing

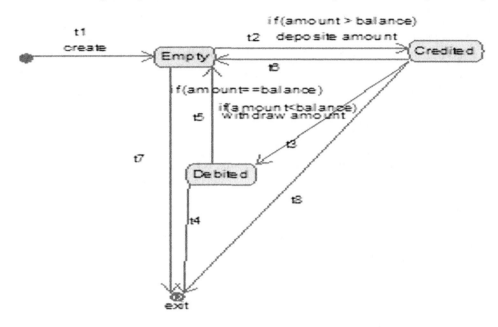

Figure 3. State chart diagram of class ATM Card, in case study ATM Card processing (Source:https://www.google.co.in/search?biw=1280&bih=694&tbm=isch&sa=1&ei=FjFLWqbmCMeDmQHvgZn AAQ&q=%28locked%2C+accepting%2C+unlocked%29+state+chart+diagram+for+atm+card&oq =%28locked%2C+accepting%2C+unlocked%29+state+chart+diagram+for+atm+card&gs_l=psy-ab.3...43807.48665.0.49093.13.13.0.0.0.0.393.3103.3-)

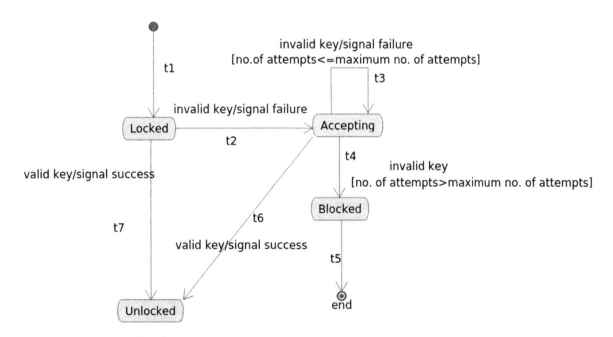

Figure 3 shows the sequence of transitions represented from the example model of ATM Card processing. In Figure 3, it has state coverage, event coverage and transition coverage. Figure 3 has four states. They are Locked, Unlocked, Accepting and Blocked. It has two event coverage as valid-key and invalid-key. It has transition coverage from one state to another state. For example, some valid transitions are Locked to Unlocked, Locked to Accepting, and Accepting to Accepting and so on.The transitions in Figure 3 are as follows:

AT:T(I) = (t1,t2,t3,t4,t5);(t1,t2,t3,t6);(t1,t7)

Test suite [T (I)] = 3 (3 number of test cases are generated for AT)

RTP: No RTP execution here for the state machines

We had taken the same ATP, ATP with LN2, ATP with LN3 and ATP with LN4 in another state machine for finding the test suites:

ATP: T (II) = (t1, t2, t3, t4) ;(t1, t2, t3, t6)

Test suite [T (II)] = 2 (2 number of test cases are generated for ATP)

ATP with LN2: T(III) = (t1,t2,t3);(t1,t2,t4);(t1,t2,t6)

Test suite [T (III)] =3 (3 number of test cases are generated for LN2)

ATP with LN3: T(IV) = (t1,t2,t3,t4);(t1,t2,t3,t6);(t1,t2,t3,t3);(t1,t2,t4,t5)

Test suite [T (IV)] = 4 (4 number of test cases are generated for LN3)

ATP with LN4: T(V) = (t1,t2,t3,t4,t5);(t1,t2,t3,t3,t6);(t1,t2,t3,t3,t4) Test suite [T(V)]=3 (3 number of test cases are generated for LN4)

Mutation Testing

The efficiency of the test cases are measured from the source code at the code level. The objective here is to measure the fault detection capabilities of the generated test cases using mutation testing. Giving mutants (seeded faults) in the code program, mutation testing is done using the test cases already generated. When a test suite detects the seeded fault, it is known that the mutant is killed by the test suite. The number of mutants killed by a particular test suite divided by the total number of mutants, is calculated as mutation score. The mutation score is the measurement of an effective test suite to detect faults. Some equivalent mutants are not countable in the mutation analysis as they are equivalent to the correct software. Same procedure is followed in our study. Different types of mutants are given to test the effectiveness of the test cases. Some mutation testing are 1- Type-1 mutation testing 2- Type-2 mutation testing 3- Second order mutation testing, etc. In Type-1 mutation testing random part of the code is changed, making "+" to "-" or "-" to "+". This type of mutants is called code mutant. Then, the generated test suite is run to check whether the test suite is able to detect the mutant or not. Type-2 mutation testing is very much similar to Type-1 but, in Type-2 the difference is that it starts with an input, if that works "ok", then goes for random testing and checks with existing test suite. But a small change in input can have a large effect on the output. Type-2 mutation testing is known as Fuzzy testing also. Mutation testing strategies are either in first order form or in the second order form. In the first order, 10 percent to 20 percent random selection of a portion of the generated mutant is taken and tested to measure cost-effectiveness. In the Second order mutation testing two mutants are combined together to get one component to test, depending on how the mutants are chosen from the code. These combined mutants are called "Random mix mutants". Those mutants that are not giving errors that should be discarded from the set of mutants. The paper (Belli et al., 2016), introduces the concept of model-based mutation testing (MBMT). Model-based mutation testing (MBMT) approach is used to generate mutants based on the model of the system under consideration (SUC), there they inject faults in the model rather than the implementation. Without the source code, MBMT not only enables the application of mutation testing but also evaluates the fault detection ability (Belli et al., 2016).

MBT is very much useful when code is not available to the tester. Code based testing used some larger set of operators in the program where, MBT used smaller operators to generate mutants. Mutants generated in MBT are classified into more categories than code-based mutants. So, mutation testing in MBT enhances fault detection ability of the test suite. Mutants given to demonstrate the feasibility of the mutation testing in SBT are as follows: 1- Wrong-start-state: starting state will be wrong instead of taking correct starting state (default state), so that it generates mutant. 2- State-missing: any state is missing from the model, generates mutant and the change is observed in the other states. 3- State-extra: extra state is given to generate mutants. 4- Event-missing: some event is missing to generate mutants and investigation occurs whether existing test suite is enough to debug it. 5- Event-extra: extra event is given with existing events and mutant is generated. 6- Event-exchanged: swapping of events from one state to another state to generate mutants (Turner & Robson,1993). These mutants are called automatic generated "Model mutants", by which test cases are examined. We have used different kinds of state-based mutants. Such as incorrect transition, missing transition, missing or incorrect event, missing or incorrect action, extra missing or corrupt state, which are seeded in the code and mutation testing is conducted.

Sneak-Path Testing

We have taken another method to measure the efficiency using sneak-path testing. A sneak-path is a bug that allows an illegal transition. In other way, a sneak-path is created, if there is an unspecified transition occurred. Sneak-path testing aims to verify the absence of sneak-paths and to show how the SUT handles them in a correct way. The unspecified transitions occur in various ways. The faults in the source code reflected the modelling errors in the case studies by seeding some sneak-paths. In the case studies, the seeding faults types for sneak-path testing are: 1- Additional unspecified transitions 2- Missing guarded transitions 3- Giving incorrect guard on transitions 4-Unspecified event given A couple of faults are seeded in the source code to check the effectiveness of the generated test cases at the design level.

For the case study, Bank Account processing, the fault type, Additional unspecified transitions are: Adding some unspecified transitions in the model which is erroneous. The transition erroneously added from state Empty to state Debited in Figure 4.

2- Missing guarded transition: Guard Condition is missing from state Credited to state Debited in Figure 5.

3- Giving incorrect guard on transitions: Incorrect guard condition from state Credited to state Debited shown in Figure 6.

Figure 4. Part of the state chart diagram of Bank Account class, in Bank Account processing case study, showing unspecified transition from state Empty to Debited

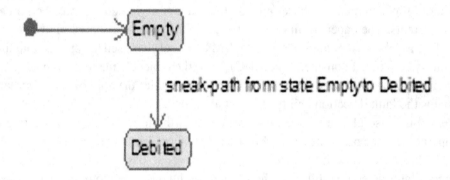

Figure 5. Another part of the state chart diagram of Bank Account class, in Bank Account processing case study, showing missing guarded transition as (amount < balance = withdraw amount) from the state Credited to Debited

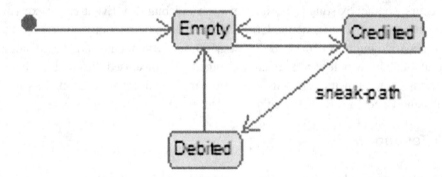

Applying sneak-path testing for the case study second (ATM Card processing), some specific seeded faults are as follows:

1. **Additional unspecified transitions:** Adding some unspecified transitions in the model which is erroneous. The transition is erroneously added from state Unlocked to Blocked;

2. **Missing guarded transitions:** An expected guarded transition is missing from state Accepting to state Blocked showing the sneak-path in Figure 9;

3. **Giving incorrect guard on transitions:** when a guard condition is seeded as false, it creates a fault. That is shown in Figure 10.

Figure 6. Another part of the state chart diagram of Bank Account class, in Bank Account processing case study, showing guard condition (amount< balance = false) from the state Credited to Debited

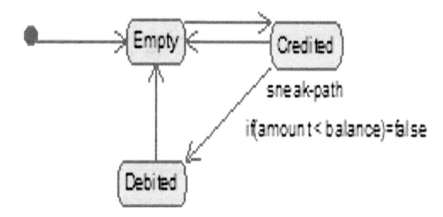

Figure 7. Part of the state chart diagram of Bank Account class, in Bank Account processing case study, showing incorrect event as If (amount<balance then deposit amount) from the state Credited to Debited

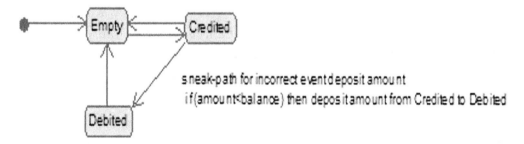

Figure 8. Part of the state chart diagram of ATM Card class, in ATM Card processing, showing an unspecified transition from the state Unlocked to Blocked

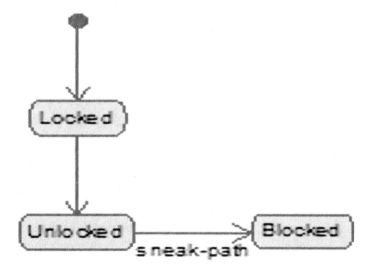

Figure 9. Another part of the state chart diagram of ATM Card class, in ATM Card processing, showing a missing guarded transition as (no. of attempts>maximum no. of attempts) from the state Accepting to Blocked

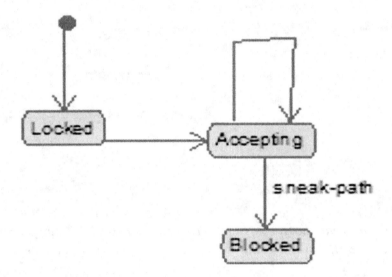

Figure 10. Another part of the state chart diagram of ATM Card class, in ATM Card processing, showing a guard condition as false from the state Accepting to Blocked

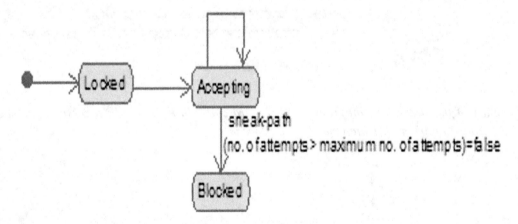

RESULT AND DISCUSSION

Conformance testing is not sufficient to detect various types of faults. Apart from mutation testing, sneak-path testing is required to check the unspecified behavior of the system. Complementing conformance testing with sneak-path testing, killing the rest of the mutants is the additional work with reasonable cost in preparation and execution time. Sneak-paths are tested in both the case studies with various unspecified behavior such as additional unspecified transitions, missing guarded transitions, giving incorrect guard on transitions, unspecified event given to the transitions etc. The coverage criteria, All Transition, has been found not to be an adequate level of fault detection with more execution time compared to other coverage criteria and with larger test suite. RTP makes some path uncovered and in some cases, RTP is not occurring. All Transition Pair with LN4 is the best among all coverage criteria with covering all transitions and all states with minimizing the test suite.

We tried to find the efficiency of state-based testing using different coverage criteria. In the first case study (Bank Account processing), we found that All Transition Pair with LN4 is the best for having more genuine test cases covering all the required transitions. In the execution of the transitions t5 and t7 are uncovered in LN2. Total number of test cases we found is 6 covering all important transitions in LN2 and LN3. In All Transition Pair of length 4 the state coverage ratio is more compares to AT, RTP, ATP with LN2 and ATP with LN3. Some transitions are uncovered by RTP coverage criteria. So, ATP with LN4 in the first case study (Bank Account processing) has better fault detection capability than Round Trip Path (Holt et al., 2012).

In the second case study (ATM Card processing), we found All Transition Pair with LN4 is the best state coverage criteria. In All Transition Pair the test cases can be reduced. In Figure 3, Round Trip Path is not applicable as there is no round-trip path occurring with traversing the transitions. Though AT covers all transitions and all the states but, it generates larger test suite. So, All Transition is a tedious and time taking process as compared to ATP with LN3 and LN4. We observed, All Transition Pair with LN4 coverage criteria has proper fault detection capability in our cases. ATP with LN4 is taken as the better one in both the case studies having more state coverage. For sneak-path testing, seeded sneak-paths are shown in Figure 4 to Figure 10 for the two case studies. In sneak-path testing, tester looks for illegal transitions and evading guard conditions and also needs to check each state's illegal events. We assess the cost-effectiveness of our test cases in both the case studies. Test scenarios of our work are described in Table 2 and Table 3. Each Table has four columns that are Test Identification (Test ID), Coverage criteria, Test suite identification and state coverage ratio in percentage. Table 4 describes the overall scenarios of our two case studies. The state coverage ratio we calculated as:

Number of states covered/total number of states * 100

Table 2. State coverage ratio of various state-based coverage criteria of class Bank Account, in Bank Account processing

Test ID	Coverage Criteria	Test Suites	State Coverage Ratio in Percentage
I	All Transition	T(I)	73
II	Round Trip Path	T(II)	81
III	All Transition Pair	T(III)	90
IV	ATP with LN2	T(IV)	77
V	ATP with LN3	T(V)	83
VI	ATP with LN4	T(VI)	93

Table 3. State coverage ratio of various state-based coverage criteria of class ATM Card, in ATM Card processing

Test ID	Coverage Criteria	Test Suits	State Coverage Ratio in Percentage
I	All Transition	T(I)	50
II	All Transition Pair	T(I)	70
III	ATP with LN2	T(II)	50
IV	ATP with LN3	T(III)	73
V	ATP with LN4	T(IV)	75

Table 4. Ratio of various state coverage criteria in two case studies

Test ID	Coverage Criteria	State Coverage Ratio in Case Study-1	State Coverage Ratio in Case Study-2
I	All Transitions	73	50
II	Round Trip Path	81	-
III	All Transition Pair	90	70
IV	ATP with LN2	77	50
V	ATP with LN3	83	73
VI	ATP with LN4	93	75

Looking at the reported results for fault detection ability shown in Table 2, Table 3 and Table 4, we found that ATP killed more mutants (100%) compared to other coverage criteria (Offutt et al., 1999; Offutt et al., 2003; Paradkar, 2004). In the paper (Holt et al., 2014), the result is the combination of coverage criteria, test oracle and test model. They found that sneak-path test suite is equal to the number states in the system under test. In our paper, we tried to take some sneak-paths with missing guarded transitions, unspecified transitions, showing guarded transitions false instead of true etc., those are evaluated in finding out the effectiveness of our test cases. The implementations of the test cases are shown below in Figure 11 to Figure 14.

CONCLUSION

Although, MBT is not a new area of research, evaluating state-based testing approach is a challenging area in software testing. For SBT, the emphasis is to ensure efficient state-based fault detection within limited testing time. State-based testing is a framework for model testing and without knowing the internal structure, tester can test the behaviour of the system. Taking such advantages of state-based testing, we observed that ATP with LN4 is the best among all coverage criteria. It executes every satisfiable path as well as detects missing transitions. The sneak-paths are undetected by conformance testing. Hence, to evaluate the test suites generated by various coverage criteria, sneak-path testing is a necessary step as it helps to prepare the test suite more effectively for detecting unspecified behaviour of the system under test. To identify differences in fault detection ability, different test oracles can be taken, to extend our investigation.

Figure 11. Program implementation of test cases with Junit tool for case study Bank Account processing

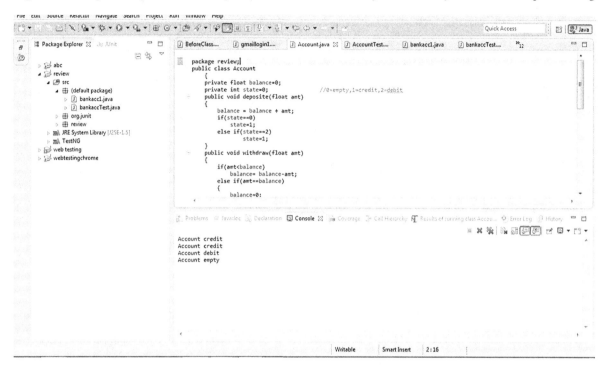

Figure 12. Assert method for the class Bank Account showing test cases pass

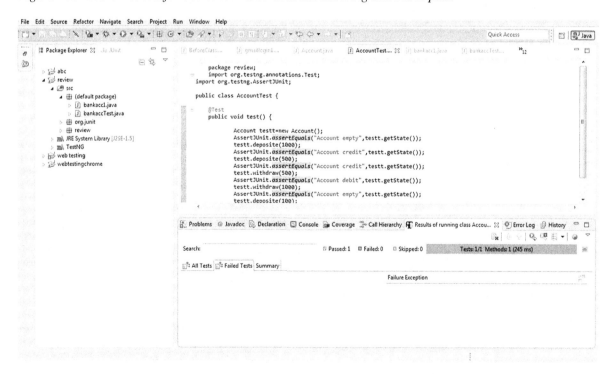

Figure 13. Program implementation of test cases with Junit tool for case study ATM Card processing

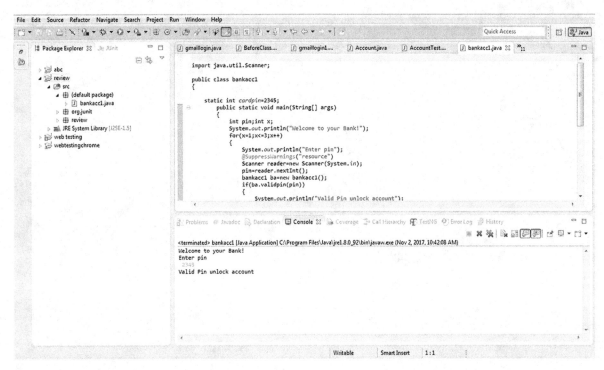

Figure 14. Assert method for the class ATM Card processing showing test cases pass

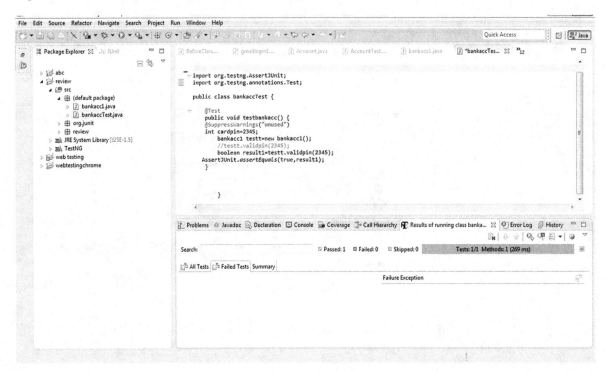

REFERENCES

Agrawal, H., DeMillo, R., Hathaway, R., & Hsu, W., Krauser, E., & Spafford, E. (1989). Design of mutant operators for the C programming language. *Technical Report SERC-TR-41-P, Software Engineering Research Center*, Department of Computer Science, Purdue University, Indiana.

Aicherning, B. K., & Tappler, M. (2016). Symbolic input-output conformance checking for model-based mutation testing. *Electronic Notes in Theoretical Computer Science*, *320*, 3–19. doi:10.1016/j.entcs.2016.01.002

Antoniol, G., Briand, L. C., Di Penta, M., & Labiche, Y. (2002). A case study using the round-trip strategy for state-based class testing. In *Proceedings of the13th International Symposium on Software Reliability Engineering* (pp. 269-279). 10.1109/ISSRE.2002.1173268

Belinfante, A. (2010). JTorX: A tool for on-line model-driven test derivation and execution. In *International Conference on Tools and Algorithms for the Construction and Analysis of Systems* (pp. 266-270). Berlin: Springer. 10.1007/978-3-642-12002-2_21

Belli, F., Beyazıt, M., Budnik, C. J., & Tuglular, T. (2017). Advances in model-based testing of graphical user interfaces. *Advances in Computers*, *107*, 219–280. doi:10.1016/bs.adcom.2017.06.004

Belli, F., Budnik, C. J., Hollmann, A., Tuglular, T., & Wong, W. E. (2016). Model-based mutation testing approach and case studies. *Science of Computer Programming*, *120*, 25–48. doi:10.1016/j.scico.2016.01.003

Binder, R. V. (2000). *Testing object-oriented systems: models, patterns, and tools*. Addison-Wesley Professional.

Boberg, J. (2008). Early fault detection with model-based testing. In *Proceedings of the 7th ACM SIGPLAN workshop on ERLANG* (pp. 9-20). 10.1145/1411273.1411276

Bouquet, F., Grandpierre, C., Legeard, B., & Peureux, F. (2008). A test generation solution to automate software testing. In *Proceedings of the 3rd international workshop on Automation of software test* (pp. 45-48). ACM. 10.1145/1370042.1370052

Briand, L., & Labiche, Y. (2001). A UML-based approach to system testing. In *International Conference on the Unified Modeling Language* (pp. 194-208). Berlin: Springer.

Briand, L. C., Labiche, Y., & Wang, Y. (2004). Using simulation to empirically investigate test coverage criteria based on statechart. In *Proceedings of the 26th International Conference on In Software Engineering ICSE* (pp. 86-95). *IEEE*. 10.1109/ICSE.2004.1317431

Broy, M., Jonsson, B., Katoen, J. P., Leucker, M., & Pretschner, A. (2005). *Model-based testing of reactive systems. Advanced Lectures: Outcome of a research seminar*. Springer Verlag. doi:10.1007/b137241

Chen, G. Y. H., & Wang, P. Q. (2014). Test case prioritization in a specification-based testing environment. *Journal of Software*, *9*(8), 1–9.

Chow, T. S. (1978). Testing software design modeled by finite-state machines. *IEEE Transactions on Software Engineering*, *SE-4*(3), 178–187. doi:10.1109/TSE.1978.231496

Dalal, S. R., Jain, A., Karunanithi, N., Leaton, J. M., Lott, C. M., Patton, G. C., & Horowitz, B. M. (1999). Model-based testing in practice. In *Proceedings of the 21st international conference on Software engineering* (pp. 285-294). ACM.

Dias Neto, A. C., Subramanyan, R., Vieira, M., & Travassos, G. H. (2007). A survey on model-based testing approaches: A systematic review. In *Proceedings of the 1st ACM international workshop on Empirical assessment of software engineering languages and technologies: held in conjunction with the 22nd IEEE/ACM International Conference on Automated Software Engineering (ASE)* (pp. 31-36). 10.1145/1353673.1353681

Dulz, W., & Zhen, F. (2003). Matelo-statistical usage testing by annotated sequence diagrams, Markov chains and ttcn-3. In *Proceedings of the Third International Conference In Quality Software* (pp. 336-342). 10.1109/QSIC.2003.1319119

Durelli, V. H., Delamaro, M. E., & Offutt, J. (2018). An experimental comparison of edge, edge-pair, and prime path criteria. *Science of Computer Programming, 152*, 99–115. doi:10.1016/j.scico.2017.10.003

El-Far, I. K., & Whittaker, J. A. (2001). Model-based software testing. Encyclopedia of Software Engineering.

Ernits, J. P., Kull, A., Raiend, K., & Vain, J. (2006). *Generating tests from EFSM models using guided model checking and iterated search refinement. Formal Approaches to Software Testing and Runtime Verification* (pp. 85–99). Berlin: Springer.

Hernández, Y. (2017). Offshore software testing in the automotive industry: A case study. *International Journal of Information Technology Project Management, 8*(4), 1–16. doi:10.4018/IJITPM.2017100101

Hoisl, B., Sobernig, S., & Strembeck, M. (2014). Comparing three notations for defining scenario-based model tests: A controlled experiment. In *9th International Conference on IEEE In Quality of Information and Communications Technology (QUATIC)* (pp. 180-189).

Holt, N. E., Briand, L. C., & Torkar, R. (2014). Empirical evaluations on the cost-effectiveness of state-based testing: An industrial case study. *Information and Software Technology, 56*(8), 890–910. doi:10.1016/j.infsof.2014.02.011

Holt, N. E., Torkar, R., Briand, L., & Hansen, K. (2012, November). State-based testing: Industrial evaluation of the cost-effectiveness of round-trip path and sneak-path strategies. In *23rd International Symposium on IEEE Software Reliability Engineering (ISSRE)* (pp. 321-330). 10.1109/ISSRE.2012.17

Huima, A. (2007). *Implementing conformiq qtronic. Testing of Software and Communicating Systems* (pp. 1–12). Berlin: Springer.

Jacky, J. (2011). PyModel: Model-based testing in Python. In *Proceedings of the Python for Scientific Computing Conference*.

Jacky, J., Veanes, M., Campbell, C., & Schulte, W. (2007). *Model-based software testing and analysis with C*. Cambridge University Press. doi:10.1017/CBO9780511619540

Jia, Y., & Harman, M. (2011). An analysis and survey of the development of mutation testing. *IEEE Transactions on Software Engineering, 37*(5), 649–678. doi:10.1109/TSE.2010.62

Koopman, P., Achten, P., & Plasmeijer, R. (2013). Model-based shrinking for state-based testing. In *International Symposium on Trends in Functional Programming* (pp. 107-124). Springer.

Li, Y., Yan, K., Lee, H. W., Lu, Z., Liu, N., & Cui, Y. (2016). Growth of conformal graphene cages on micrometre-sized silicon particles as stable battery anodes. *Nature Energy*, *1*(2), 15029. doi:10.1038/nenergy.2015.29

Müller, P. (2002). *Modular specification and verification of object-oriented programs*. Springer-Verlag. doi:10.1007/3-540-45651-1

Offutt, J., & Abdurazik, A. (1999). Generating tests from UML specifications. In *International Conference on the Unified Modeling Language* (pp. 416-429). Springer. 10.1007/3-540-46852-8_30

Offutt, J., Liu, S., Abdurazik, A., & Ammann, P. (2003). Generating test data from state-based specifications. *Software Testing, Verification & Reliability*, *13*(1), 25–53. doi:10.1002tvr.264

Oftedal, K. (2011). Random Testing versus Partition Testing [Master's thesis]. *Institute for datateknikk og informasjonsvitenskap*.

Ostrand, T. J., & Balcer, M. J. (1988). The category-partition method for specifying and generating fuctional tests. *Communications of the ACM*, *31*(6), 676–686. doi:10.1145/62959.62964

Pang, J., Liu, Y., & Mauw, S. (2013). *Algorithm for basic compliance problems*. ICSTW.

Paradkar, A. (2004). Plannable test selection criteria for FSMs extracted from operational specifications. In *15th International Symposium on IEEE Software Reliability Engineering ISSRE* (pp. 173-184). 10.1109/ISSRE.2004.28

Pasareanu, C. S., Schumann, J., Mehlitz, P., Lowry, M., Karsai, G., Nine, H., & Neema, S. (2009). Model-based analysis and test generation for flight software. In *Third International Conference on IEEE In Space Mission Challenges for Information Technology SMC-IT 2009* (pp. 83-90). 10.1109/SMC-IT.2009.18

Peleska, J. (2013). Industrial-strength model-based testing-state of the art and current challenges. arXiv:1303.1006

Petriu, D. C., Rouquette, N., & Haugen, O. (2010). Model driven engineering languages and systems.

Reed, A. H., & Angolia, M. (2018). Risk management usage and impact on information systems project success. *International Journal of Information Technology Project Management*, *9*(2), 1–19. doi:10.4018/IJITPM.2018040101

Shafique, M., & Labiche, Y. (2010). A systematic review of model based testing tool support (Technical Report SCE-10-04). Carleton University, Canada.

Sundararajan, S., Bhasi, M., & Pramod, K. V. (2017). Managing software risks in maintenance projects, from a vendor perspective: A case study in global software development. *International Journal of Information Technology Project Management*, *8*(1), 35–54. doi:10.4018/IJITPM.2017010103

Tiwari, R., & Goel, N. (2013). Reuse: Reducing test effort. *Software Engineering Notes*, *38*(2), 1–11. doi:10.1145/2439976.2439982

Turner, C. D., & Robson, D. J. (1993). The state-based testing of object-oriented programs. In *Proceedings Software Maintenance CSM-93 conference on IEEE* (pp. 302-310).

Utting, M. (2012). How to design extended finite state machine test models in Java. In *Model-Based Testing for Embedded Systems* (pp. 147–169). CRC Press.

Utting, M., & Legeard, B. (2010). *Practical model-based testing: A tool approach*. Morgan Kaufmann.

Utting, M., Legeard, B., Bouquet, F., Fourneret, E., Peureux, F., & Vernotte, A. (2016). Recent advances in model-based testing. *Advances in Computers*, *101*, 53–120. doi:10.1016/bs.adcom.2015.11.004

This research was previously published in the International Journal of Information Technology Project Management (IJITPM), 10(1); pages 1-20, copyright year 2019 by IGI Publishing (an imprint of IGI Global).

Chapter 62
Techniques and Trends Towards Various Dimensions of Robust Security Testing in Global Software Engineering

Muhammad Sulleman Memon
QUEST, Pakistan

Manzoor Ahmed Hashmani
University Technology PETRONAS, Malaysia

Mairaj Nabi Bhatti
Shaheed Benazir Bhutto University, Pakistan

Muhammad Shafique Malik
QUEST, Pakistan

Naveed Murad Dahri
WAPDA College, Pakistan

ABSTRACT

With the growth of software vulnerabilities, the demand for security integration is increasingly necessary to more effectively achieve the goal of secure software development globally. Different practices are used to keep the software intact. These practices should also be examined to obtain better results depending on the level of security. The security of a software program device is a characteristic that permeates the whole system. To resolve safety issues in a software program security solutions have to be implemented continually throughout each web page. The motive of this study is to offer a complete analysis of safety, wherein protection testing strategies and equipment can be categorized into: technical evaluation strategies and non-technical assessment strategies. This study presents high-level ideas in an easy form that would help professionals and researchers solve software security testing problems around the world. One way to achieve these goals is to separate security issues from other enforcement issues so that they can be resolved independently and applied globally.

DOI: 10.4018/978-1-6684-3702-5.ch062

INTRODUCTION

The internet revolutionized our society, affected the software program industry, and the change of statistics and expertise became a principal part of software development, promoting the globalization of the software program industry (Banerjee & Pandey, 2009). this variation in information flow removes the constraints of conventional initiatives and promotes the free go with the flow of statistics, sources, and information between tasks. Software industry globalization includes several aspects, such as part of the external and collective externalization development process, extensive use of a collaborative environment to facilitate the introduction of an entire new software development model, such as resource exchange and open source (Sodiya, Onashoga, & Ajayĩ, 2006) Resources for sharing knowledge are more than just promoting reuse and teamwork. They also bring new challenges to the software engineering community (SE) knowledge and resources are no longer managed by a single project or organization, but are now distributed across multiple projects, organizations and even in the global software ecosystem (Porru, Pinna, Marchesi, & Tonelli, 2017). One of the challenges arising from this exchange of knowledge is Information Security (IS). This is becoming a major threat to the software development community. In essence, it promotes the notion that IS should take into account different security concepts (safe coding practices, knowledge of software security vulnerabilities in the development process and the importance of IS to the analytical software community are reflected in the fact that it is an integral part of the current SE best practices (Papadakis et al., 2019). Software checking out is a very useful manner to run an application looking for errors. It is identified that 40% to 50% of total growth spending is consumed on software testing. Some of the significant software testing techniques classified by purpose are precision tests, performance tests, safety tests and reliability tests. The software test can be called the software quality measurement process that is being developed and the detection of errors in a program. In addition, it is also a system to determine the consistency of the security characteristics of the software application with the design (Dhir & Kumar, 2019). the security requirements of the blanketed software program are: confidentiality, authentication, availability, authorization, integrity and non-repudiation. other requirements are the protection of private access control, protection management, auditing, and so on. software protection is the protection of software towards attacks. the priority for safety tests increases day by day (Villani, Pontes, Coracini, & Ambrósio, 2019). Software security testing is also categorized as revision techniques, objective identity and evaluation, and goal analysis of vulnerability. security checking out equipment have additionally been evolved for supply code analysis, code evaluate, packet analysis, binary code penetration takes a look at, wireless detector, static analysis tool, check gear, source code protection evaluation, static code evaluation, vulnerability analysis tools and vulnerability assessment. evaluation software program (Villani et al., 2019). The tools are important for collaboration amongst team participants as they facilitate, automate and manage the complete improvement system. Adequate software program assist is especially needed in global software engineering because distance exacerbates coordination and manipulate issues, at once or not directly, because of its poor results on conversation .

The unit test is carried out by the developers and the software is divided into smaller and more convenient units, which has the advantage of detecting functional and software warranty problems at the beginning of the life cycle. The regression test is essential if the code has changed. this could be used to calculate the relative assault surface from one model to any other and use it to see if the security status of the software program is enhancing or deteriorating. The distinction among software program safety and software program security is the existence of intelligent attackers who attempt to damage the system. software program excellent, reliability and safety belong to this family. Intruders can make the most this software to open protection holes. With the development of the internet, software safety issues are getting less applicable. Many critical software applications and offerings require complete security features in opposition to malicious attacks. The desires of protection testing on those systems encompass the identification and removal of software program flaws that could cause security breaches and security protection validation. Vulnerability tools are packages that perform the stages of vulnerability analysis and assessment evaluation. Vulnerability analysis defines, identifies, and categorizes security holes. Weaknesses in computer systems include networks, servers, or communication channels. similarly, vulnerability evaluation can predict the effectiveness of the proposed measures and examine how well they work after the use of them. These tools are based on a database containing system and port service security holes, package compilation anomalies, and all the information needed to validate potential routes to exploitable programs. Security controls used to determine whether these security controls work properly and security assessments that validate the presence of penetration tests are common security testing techniques (Braz & Robert, 2006).

GLOBAL SOFTWARE SECURITY TESTING

Global security software quality checking is the key factor of software engineering. The software is completely secure when it behaves certified in the existence of malicious attacks (Dhir & Kumar, 2019). To ensure the security of the software, the security check manner is implemented. software protection assessments are a chain of procedures designed to ensure that the computer code fulfills its function. The principle of the software check is to confirm the best, estimation the consistency of the software or confirm and validate it (Villani et al., 2019). Security tests are achieved to affirm statistics loss in the strict feel by encrypting the application or by the usage of an extensive variety of software and hardware, firewalls, and so on. After implementation, this will create troubles for quit users. the correct framework for developing protection during the design section is related to the quality and security of the software program (Arkin, Stender, & McGraw, 2005).

SOFTWARE SECURITY RULES

Banerjee and Pandey actually have 21 security rules that guarantee that there is space to create a safe and reliable software development when applied from the beginning of SDLC, that is, from the rules of the requirements analysis phase avoid the introduction of vulnerabilities in the software system (Banerjee & Pandey, 2009). The rules are the following:

1. Knowledge rules: These rules continually learn new information about security aspects and update existing knowledge for software development teams including software developers, software evaluators and software architecture (Sodiya et al., 2006).
2. Rules of prevention: You should avoid all types of threats from within but not from outside and synchronize the security of the software to solve it later.
3. Rules of responsibility: The rules of responsibility monitor all tasks / activities / acts performed during operations / events and achieve the prevention of violations of the security policy and com-

pliance with the specific responsibility for those acts. Suggest that you need to maintain (Porru et al., 2017).

4. Confidentiality rule: This rule implies that confidentiality should be maintained by preventing unauthorized persons from accessing information (Papadakis et al., 2019).

5. Integrity rules: Integrity wishes to be maintained by ensuring that the data is not modified by unauthorized people and no longer detected with the aid of authorized users.

6. Availability rules: These rules define the need to maintain a balanced approach between security and availability. This always provides a highly secure and highly available system (Dhir & Kumar, 2019).

7. Rules of non-repudiation: The cause of non-repudiation is to ensure that the transaction by means of any of the parties that can be used by a relied on third birthday celebration is not desired (Dhir & Kumar, 2019).

8. Access control rules: This rule requires that get entry to to resources and services must be primarily based on permissions, and if allowed, users must be allowed and denied access to the resources and services. indicates get admission to to services accessed by those eligible users (Papadakis et al., 2019).

9. Identification and authentication rules: This rule mean that an identification and authentication process need to be implemented to determine which users can log in to the system and its legal context.

10. Precision rules: these rules propose that software development teams must carry out diverse moves, activities, techniques, approaches and tasks with accuracy and precision every time (Sodiya et al., 2006).

11. Integrity rules: these policies imply that the diverse necessities, protocols, requirements or guidelines designed to certify a software program system should anyhow be consistent.

12. Authorization rules: The guidelines suggest that an approval method wishes to be implemented to decide what an entity can do within the system.

13. Privacy regulations: guarantee that a person has the right to manipulate how, how it's far used, what it's miles used for and what it intends to apply personal data about personal information (Dhir & Kumar, 2019).

14. Evaluation rules: This rule evaluates all processes regardless of size and recommends that software developers be evaluated after they have been created (Sodiya et al., 2006).

15. Better rules: This rule implies that safety is a subset of quality and that control and variability of safety functions depend on quality (Sodiya et al., 2006).

16. Flexibility rules: these rules should not be strict security requirements, but should be viable and flexible (Sodiya et al., 2006).

17. Reinforcement rules (protection): This rule means that the various processes used in the security engineering process must be protected by their individuality and integrity (Sodiya et al., 2006).

18. Ambiguity rules: This rule means that the relevant details should be clear and concise in order to easily implement software security (Sodiya et al., 2006).

19. Error classification rules: These rules require that errors be classified according to a scheme that includes a series of security rules to better understand issues that may affect software security (Arkin et al., 2005; Braz & Robert, 2006).

20. Auditing rules: These rules should be implemented to determine responsibility for software security and to help redesign complete testing security policies and procedures for implementing secure software systems.
21. Interoperability rules: This rule means that if there is extra software program that interacts or communicates with each other, all software program involved in that interaction or communication desires to be protected.

LITERATURE REVIEW

Complete background details of software security appeared. In the black box, test tools were introduced. Information systems have been protected by a modeling language, where security is an essential measure of software engineering (Banerjee & Pandey, 2009). The ease of use and approval of user security systems have developed a main problem in efficiency research (Sodiya et al., 2006). The definition was discussed, as well as the category of software security tests and the methods and tools for software security testing were examined(Braz & Robert, 2006). Safety measures are developed with the arrival of security tools and techniques (Dias Neto, Subramanyan, Vieira, & Travassos, 2007). The main problem was the protection of data against unauthorized access and corruption of data resulting from malicious acts (Mistrík, Grundy, Van der Hoek, & Whitehead, 2010). The different security test methods proposed so far have been discussed here. Safety tests are considered a continuous process throughout the SDLC to involve security tests in the software development life cycle. The secure software development life cycle (SSDL) and SDLC security contact points are proposed for the same purpose. Software security tests can be updated using security attributes, tools, templates and, most importantly, the test cases used in the tests(Kumar, Khan, & Khan, 2014) . The security test consists of identifying the behavior of its attributes in front of an attack that can damage all the software. During each security test, it is verified that all security factors work correctly or not. If the factors work correctly, the software is safe. This is a set of activities that includes the preparation of the test plan and related activities. The safety assessments are part of the evaluation of the safety properties and their factors; the ones are as compared to the useful specification document and the pinnacle design of the development system (M. E. Khan, 2010). Security testing with a dependent technique throughout the lifecycle helps to understand the quality of the software and its protection against known threats and risks. To maintain the quality of the software, it's far needed to test the security of the software in a possible way. The final goals of the safety checks are to validate the robustness and to save you any security breach from stepping into the software (Kumar et al., 2014). Each software program is integrated into many modules, which has several protection attributes. Consequently, to gain the specific ways wherein a system needs to be modified, in which the safety attributes are within the center. From this system, we will decide, before the software program tests, what number of assessments have to be achieved. Safety tests can be supplemented in different ways and safety tests have different meanings or methods (Tian-yang, Yin-Sheng, & You-yuan, 2010). Research on human factors in software security is lacking and that developers are often considered the "weakest link". Developers have more technical experience than typical end-users, but should not be confused as security experts (Bayuk, 2013). Handling security tasks with developer-friendly security tools or programming languages to avoid security errors (Gupta, Verma, & Sangal, 2013) needs help. For this understand security concepts and developer knowledge, explore the utility of available security development tools, and propose tools and methodologies to help developers create secure applications.

RESEARCH BACKGROUND

How security is linked to software tests identify the quality of the software under development and find errors. The determination of the software program check may be shown with the following Figure 1 and Table 1.

Figure 1. Detail of software testing

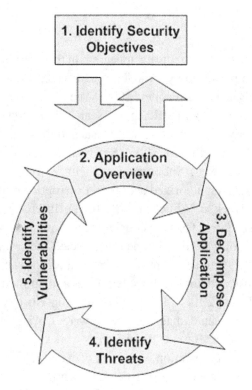

Table 1. Detail of software testing

Software Testing	Detail
Quality assurance	Observe the software engineering methods and techniques used to ensure quality
Verification/validation	Take a look at if the software program meets the specs and fulfills its feature
Correctness	It determines whether the software thus developed meets the requirements of the user or not
Reliability Estimation	This is the estimation of the reliability of our software, that is, it is free of defects

However, the software test refers to a process for looking for errors when running the program. Software tests could be divided into proofs of reliability, security tests and performance tests. The correction test could be divided into white zone, black area and gray zone. The black box is then divided with the participation of the user and without user participation and other methods. Robustness tests are subject to reliability tests. The security tests can be subdivided into techniques of objective analysis, identification, analysis and vulnerability. The following diagram shows some of the most important software testing techniques, classified according to their purpose (Bayuk, 2013). The correction test determines whether the software meets the requirement or not. The tests of white boxes, black boxes or gray boxes are not limited to precision tests. The goal of performance testing is to support low latency, high performance, and low performance on a web site. "Reliability tests" identify all faults in a system and eliminate them before system implementation. "Security tests" guarantee authorized access. The security tests have to do with the identification of the weaknesses and weaknesses of a system(Takanen, Demott, Miller, & Kettunen, 2018).

SECURITY REQUIREMENT ELICITATION

Requirements engineering is a key component of any software. The SDLC requirements collection phase is considered the most important and serious phase. This phase is for managing clients directly. The security requirements depend on the purpose of the construction of the system. Traditionally, security requirements have been viewed as "non-functional" or "quality" needs such as reliability, scalability and robustness. Security requirements are generally created once the product and sales are complete, which causes vulnerabilities in the software. The acquisition of requirements involves interactions with customers to find, verify, detail and analyze the requirements. This level is the key source for the remaining phases of SDLC, and when it becomes the most solid base, other phases can be firmly built to produce high quality products (Gupta et al., 2013). The software security requirements are:

- Verifiable (practical safety requirements are verifiable, however non-practical protection necessities are not verifiable)
- Clear, concise and clear.
- Software engineers can implement them without knowledge of security.
- Proper use for development can prevent recent software vulnerabilities(Bayuk, 2013) .

Categories of Security Requirements

Functional safety requirements are safety precautions that are incorporated into each functional requirement. It is often said that this will never happen again. This requirement artifact can, as an instance, be derived from misuse instances. Non-practical safety necessities list properties which can be architectural requirements associated with security, such as robustness and minimal overall performance and scalability. those forms of requirements are usually derived from architectural concepts and good exercise standards. Derived security requirements are derived from functional and non-functional protection requirements (M. E. Khan, 2010).

- Functional safety requirements
- Non-useful security requirements
- Derived protection requirements
- Software used in software development in case of abuse

Steps for Security Requirement Elicitation

It provides a requirement engineering process that includes the following activities took eight steps to get the following security requirements (Tian-yang et al., 2010).

1. Identify the asset
2. Functional Requirements
3. Security Requirements
4. Threat and Attack Tree
5. Assess Risk
6. In vivo and in vitro determination
7. Nonfunctional Requirements

Iteration: Claims that 1 to 7 may be repeated until it's far identified that each one security requirements have been met.

Kinds of Security Requirements

Security audit requirements, privacy requirements survival requirements, security system maintenance requirements and physical protection requirements (Bayuk, 2013).

Threat Modeling for Security Requirement Elicitation

threat modeling may be used as a basis to identify safety requirements. chance modeling entails knowledge and identifying diverse threats to the system. for the duration of the editing and evaluation of protection necessities, those threats were analyzed and it turned into decided to mitigate or accept the risks related to the threats (Gupta et al., 2013). The modeling of threats and the identity of safety necessities can provide the premise for the final levels of a security system. threat modeling system that begins with the identity of system belongings and capacity threats to those assets. If entry factors result in access to assets, there is a threat attacks to achieve that threat may be described using a variety of diagrams For instance, the system can save passwords which might be an asset to the adversary, and the risk is that the adversary steals those passwords (Takanen et al., 2018).

Modeling Security Requirements With Abuse Cases

In the case of misuse or abuse, it may be used to quickly obtain safety requirements. Business analysts need to research the business, discover important assets and safety services, become aware of vulnerabilities, analyze make the most instances, and endorse mechanisms for protection requirements (Devanbu & Stubblebine, 2000). An example of abuse is a use case in which the result of the interaction is detrimental to the system, one of the actors or one of the interested parties in the system. Interactions can be harmful if the system is compromised (sensitivity, integrity or availability). A method to achieve the objectives of a Distributed Aircraft Maintenance Environment (DAME) system by effectively combining the functional requirements with the safety requirements and the required iterations and interactions between the functional requirements processes and the requirements processes. The requirements process should focus on:

- Considering the system as a "black box"
- Consider the concerns of the assets
- That they are not system functions

Difficulties in Security Requirements Gathering

- Security is constantly changing.
- Software security requirements tone positive.
- Software security requirements should be language and platform independent.
- The security requirements of the software are verifiable and the development process can be verified to work.
- All you need for your project is security software requirements.

SOFTWARE TESTING TOOLS AND TECHNIQUES

in recent times, we will gain many software checking out tools within the market. the choice of equipment is primarily based totally on the requirements of the mission and the economic tools (Proprietary / commercial) or the unfastened gear (Open supply equipment) that interest free trial tools may additionally have some obstacles within the listing of product functions, consequently, it is far based totally entirely on what you are searching out and your necessities are met in the loose version or you pick a fee software with take a look at tools. The tools are divided into unique classes as follows: check control equipment is useful check equipment, load the test tools, Open source equipment and Proprietary / commercial tools (Tian-yang et al., 2010). In this study, many articles on safety testing techniques were reviewed. Software Engineering Basics.

- Code review
- Automatic static analysis
- Binary code analysis
- Fuzz test
- Fault injection risk analysis of source code and binary code
- Vulnerability scan

- Penetration test

1. **Risk Analysis:** Hazard analysis is accomplished in the course of the design segment of the improvement to identify security necessities and identify protection risks. danger modeling is a systematic system used to identify software threats and vulnerabilities. It enables you examine and bear in mind the safety threats that device designers may also face. consequently, risk modeling is executed as a risk evaluation of software improvement. In fact, designers can mitigate ability vulnerabilities and attention on restrained resources to awareness at the maximum vital parts of the gadget. it is

advocated to create and file threat models for all programs. risk models must be created in SDLC as quickly as possible. moreover, as programs evolve and evolve, they must be reviewed. To create a threat model, comply with a simple technique according to NIST 800-30 [7] for threat evaluation. This technique means the following:

a. Decomposition of the application: Over the manual inspection procedure, understand how the function, its assets, features and connectivity.

b. Asset definition and classification: Classify assets into tangible assets and intangible assets and classify them rendering to commercial status.

c. Investigate possible vulnerabilities (technical, operational or management).

d. Investigate possible risks: Use threat scenarios or attack trees to create realistic views of possible attack methods from an attacker's point of view.

e. Create mitigation strategies: develop mitigations for each threat that you consider realistic.

2. **Code Review:** Source code changes are made by fixed study. Procedure of manual verification of source code to detect security vulnerabilities. Many critical security flaws cannot be detected by other test and analysis procedures. according to the safety community, there's no substitute for certainly inspecting the code to hit upon subtle vulnerabilities. not like private third-party software testing, along with running systems, while trying out a software, you need to make the source code available for testing. Source code analysis is the best method for technical testing, as many unintended but important security issues are very difficult to find in other forms of analysis penetration testing. The advantages of code review are integrity, efficiency and accuracy. In large code bases, this shortcoming is not realistic. To detect run-time errors, you need a highly qualified, cumbersome and non-workable reviewer. Using source code, testers can determine exactly what is happening and eliminate black-box testing guessing. Source code reviews include concurrency issues, cryptographic weaknesses and even backdoors, trojans and other malicious code. These problems are often considered as the most damaging vulnerabilities of websites. The analysis of the source code is very effective in finding implementation problems, such as sections of code that have not been validated for entry procedures or open failure control. The source code that is being implemented may not be the same as the one being analyzed, so operational procedures must also be reviewed. Code review is a time-consuming task, but when a reviewer with the right level of experience runs the review, the most complete and accurate results are obtained at the beginning of the analysis procedure, before the reviewer becomes tired. It is common for reviewers to first check each line of code very carefully and then, gradually, skip most of the code. Determine the actual software landscape. It is important to note that it is not possible to perform a complete manual review as the base code size grows. Code revisions can also help detect signs of the presence of malicious code.

3. **Automatic Static Analysis:** Computerized static evaluation is an evaluation that performs inspections without running software program and makes use of static evaluation equipment. In maximum cases this indicates analyzing the supply code of this system, but there are several tools for statically analyzing binary executables. because static evaluation does not require a fully integrated or installed model of the software program, it can be performed iteratively at some stage in the software implementation. automatic static analysis does not require test instances, and the code does not know what to do(Kumar et al., 2014). The primary purpose of static evaluation is to find security flaws and discover answers. The results of the static analysis tool provide sufficient detail about potential software failure points so that software vulnerabilities can be classified and

prioritized according to the level of risk presented to the system by the developer. it's far viable in the existence cycle. The simplest tests are executed in small code devices (individual modules or functional processing units) that can be corrected tremendously without problems and quickly before being introduced to a big code base. by repeating the evaluate and checking out before the complete device code is fixed, you may ensure that the smallest flaws are addressed. Static evaluation tools are effective in detecting violations of language policies, including buffer overflows, library misuse, type checking, and other flaws. Static analysis equipment can scan very big code bases in a quite short time compared to other techniques. The reviewer's work is restrained to the execution of the tool and the interpretation of its results. Static analysis tools aren't efficient sufficient to come across anomalies that human reviewers can judge. This device can provide additional benefits by permitting developers to perform scans as they increase and cope with capacity safety vulnerabilities at the beginning of the method. in addition, the extent of revel in required for automatic critiques is lower than that required for manual evaluations. in many instances, this device gives certain statistics about the observed vulnerabilities, inclusive of recommended mitigations.

4. **Error Injection of Binary Code and Source Code:** Error injection of source code is a testing method designed by the software security community. Binary fault injection is intended to support security penetration testing. The injection of faults in the source code causes stress in the software, causes problems of interoperability between components, simulates a failure in the execution environment and, therefore, a security threat that is not revealed by traditional testing techniques. To reveal. Injection of safety failures extends the injection of standard faults by adding error injection. This allows the evaluator to analyze the security of the movement and the state changes that occur when the software is exposed to any change in the environmental data. The software program interacts with the execution environment through calls to the operating system, calls to remote processes, software application interfaces, man-machine interfaces and the like. Binary fault injection approach monitoring the execution of the fault injection software at runtime. as an instance, while monitoring a device name hint, the tester identifies the machine name call and the decision code / return value (offers access strive success or failure. In case of binary failure is injected into environment resources) Environmental faults around the program are particularly useful due to the fact they are probably to reflect real assault eventualities. A tester that fully understands the safety of the software system's safe operation, conditions and properties under all possible operating conditions as completely as possible.

5. Fuzz Testing: Fuzzing is a generation that reveals extreme safety flaws in any software at a fraction of the cost and time. Fuzz testing randomly selects invalid information in the software under test, through its surroundings or different software additives. Fuzzing refers to a random character generator to test an software by inserting random data into the interface. In other words, it means injecting noise into the program's interface. Fuzzy assessments are applied via a application or script that sends a combination of inputs to the software to reveal the software program response. The concept is to look for exciting application behavior due to noise injection. this may indicate the presence of vulnerabilities consisting of HTTP entries and different software program failures. Their cost is their specificity because they often display protection vulnerabilities that cannot be recognized via commonplace testing tools such as vulnerability scanners and fault injectors. Fuzzing may be considered as the venture of blind fishing with the intention of discovering completely surprising problems in the software. as an instance, a tester intercepts data examines from a file by a software and replaces that data with random bytes. As a result, if the application fails,

the application may not have performed the necessary checks on the data in the file, and the file can be considered to be in the correct format. The missing control can be exploited by an attacker who replaces the read file and replaces the file to exploit the race condition, or an attacker who has already destroyed the application that created the file. the principle purpose of fuzzing is to evaluate the protection of the capabilities. because fuzzing is basically a functional check, it can be accomplished in numerous steps throughout the development and testing manner.

6. **Binary Code Analyses:** Binary code analysis uses reverse engineering techniques and binary analysis. It is implemented as a decompiler, disassembly of binary code, and a scanner. This reflects the degree of reverse engineering that can be done in the binary. The most annoying way is the binary scan. Analyze the machine code to model independent representations of the binary scanner language, program behavior, data flow and control, call trees and external function calls. Such models can be traversed by automatic vulnerability scanners to find common coding errors and vulnerabilities caused by simple backdoors. Source code editors can use this model to generate a readable program behavior for the user. This allows you to manually review security weaknesses at the design level and subtle backdoors that automatic scanners cannot find. The most annoying reverse engineering method is decompilation. The binary code is designed in reverse of the source code in all modes and they can acquire the equal security code assessment strategies as the original source code and other white box tests. However, be aware that decompilation is technologically problematic. The best of the supply code generated by the decompilation is frequently very poor. This code is not as easy to navigate and understand as the original supply code and might not appropriately reflect the original source code. this is especially true if the binary is obfuscated or if an optimization compiler is used to generate the binary. In fact, it isn't realistic to generate essential supply code in this manner. anyways, analyzing the decompiled source code is a great deal more difficult and slower than reviewing the original source code. due to this, decompilation for protection analysis makes feel only for the most crucial and highly effective components. The second exit is disassembly. In this assembly, binary code is designed for the language of intermediate assemblers (Porru et al., 2017). The disadvantage of disassembling is that the resulting assembler code only makes sense by experts who are familiar with its particular assembler language and are good at detecting safety-related components in the assembler code. It is something that can be analyzed in a certain way.

7. **Vulnerability Scanning:** Application vulnerability scanners are a totally critical software program safety testing technology. those tools scan the software's going for walks software to detect I / O styles related to recognized vulnerabilities. application-level software uses computerized vulnerability scanning. it is also used for web servers, database management systems, and some operating systems. These vulnerability patterns, or "signatures", are essentially an automatic comparison of tool patterns, as they match the signatures required by antivirus and the "dangerous code configuration" required by automatic source code scanners. Automated vulnerability scanners can find simple patterns related to vulnerabilities, but identify the risks associated with aggregating vulnerabilities, or identify vulnerabilities that result from unpredictable combos of enter and output patterns it can't be identified. similarly, to signature-based totally scanning, a few web software vulnerability scanners run "automatically assessing state applications" using vulnerability attack patterns based on simulated attack patterns and fuzz testing techniques and are based on vulnerability signatures Similar to analysis, full-state assessment analysis can only detect known types of attacks and vulnerabilities (Mistrík et al., 2010). Most vulnerability scanners attempt to offer a mechanism to feature

vulnerability styles. The current technology of scanners can carry out unsophisticated evaluation of the risks related to vulnerability aggregation. in many cases, particularly for industrial vulnerability scanners (COTS), this tool additionally affords information and steering on the way to mitigate detected vulnerabilities. common application vulnerability scanners can most effective recognize a number of the kinds of vulnerabilities found in large applications. In fact, it solves what patches can alleviate. recognition on the vulnerabilities that need to be done. As with different signature-based scanning tools, application vulnerability scanners can report fake positives except the tester recalibrates them. The evaluator interprets the scanner's results significantly to avoid identifying what is really a benign problem as a vulnerability and not to ignore the real vulnerability in question Detect detection It was ignored by the tool. For this reason, it is important to combine different test methods to verify the vulnerabilities of the software in different ways. While none of these methods alone is appropriate, they can be combined to greatly increase the likelihood of finding a vulnerability (Braz & Robert, 2006). Because automatic vulnerability scanners are based on signatures, such as antivirus, they must be updated frequently with new vendor signatures.

8. **Penetration Testing:** An alternative name for penetration testing is ethical piracy. Testing network security is a very common practice. even as penetration testing has established to be effective for network protection, this approach does no longer certainly translate into applications. Penetration analysis is the "art" of testing applications that work with your "live" execution environment to find security vulnerabilities for the purpose of this guide. Penetration testing examines whether the system resists an attack well, and what to do if it cannot withstand it. Penetration evaluators also try to exploit the vulnerabilities they have detected and those found in previous reviews (Sodiya et al., 2006). Penetration test types include black box, white box and gray box. The penetration tests of the black box do not give knowledge to the application of the testers (Dias Neto et al., 2007). The intrusion of the white box is the opposite of the black box, since it provides the tester with complete information about the application. The most commonly used gray box penetration test is a test that gives the examiner the same authority as a regular user to simulate a malicious prisoner. It became found via other tests achieved out of doors of the actual manufacturing environment. Intrusion assessors need to expose the device to sophisticated multi-pattern attacks designed to trigger a complex series of actions on all components of the machine, along with nonadjacent components. Those are kinds of conduct that cannot be imposed or discovered by another check technique. Because penetration tests are this type of vulnerability that is often overlooked in other test methods, it is used to find security issues that can be attributed to software architecture and design.

SECURITY TESTING

Software security might be expressed in capacity. The software security tests have been configured as a compliance verification process. The security tests are divided into functional tests and vulnerability tests. The security test software validates the functional safety requirements. To preserve the property of that software, it is vital to check the safety of the software in manageable manner. The viable objectives of the safety tests are to authorize the robustness and avoid the penetration of security flaws inside the software program. A tribulation procedure is vital to ensure that the entire system can be included against diverse malicious assaults and vulnerabilities due to the situation. To reap it, here is a projected in Figure 2 framework that complements in that of the security assessments. here are the steps on this existence cycle of safety assessments (Gupta et al., 2013).

Figure 2. Security testing finalized life cycle
source: Gupta et al., 2013

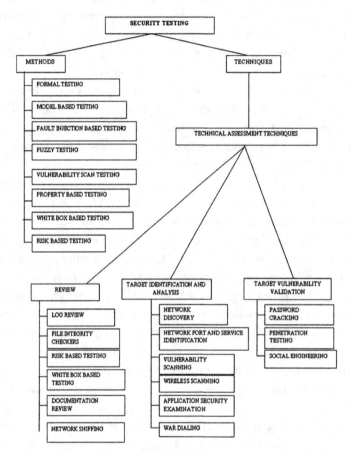

Finalize the Security Test Plan

An adequate test strategy ought to be ready for a higher implementation of the protection tests that encompass those phases.

Finalize Security Test Types

The security tests embody one or more tests primarily based mostly on the preliminary targets of the security software program, defined at a few degrees in the interview with the mission. The reason for this project is to pick the safety assessments of the software program to be performed and no longer to put affect them. Ultimately, software program safety tests that may be automatic with security trying out tools ought to be completed (Mead & Stehney, 2005).

Finalize Security Test Schedule

The software protection test application ought cloud be finalized. It includes the test phases, the beginning of the intention, the cease dates of the aim and many obligations. It also describes how it is going to be studied, followed and tested.

Organize Security Test Team

With all kinds of safety tests, the software check has to be prepared. The software program finding out the crew is chargeable for the design and execution of the assessments and the assessment of the results. While the improvement corrects the defects, the software program finding out institution retests the defects to affirm the correction.

Establish Software Security Test Environment

On this requirement, software protection test environments are finalized. The goal of the security check environment is to offer a physical framework for protection test actions. Key additives of security environments consist of the capability to carry out physical assessments, gear, and technology. software technology has to be configured. This consists of putting in test software and dealing with carriers.

Install Security Test Tool

Security techniques and tools should guide users through the test task. The fact that security tests are used to prevent smart opponents from reaching their goal is probably a useful tool to help human evaluators instead of trying to replace them. The test tools should be tested to see if they are ready for the test.

Software Security Design Test Case

The security strategy for designing software program security take a look at scenarios is to focus on the subsequent four protection additives: control, illegal activities are immaterial and material resources of an entity. The evaluation method to enumerate what needs to be included, which include the amount of software, is the fee, use and traits. Threats are the occasion which could cause damage to software loss or feasible damage to software program safety. security controls are measures of protection against loss or damage. it is crucial to evaluate the performance of the software's protection mechanisms, in addition to the capabilities themselves. beneath you may find a few questions and issues related to the security performance of the software program.

Availability

How long is the software program or manage available to perform vital safety responsibilities. Software security assessments generally require greater availability than different parts of the software program software.

Survival

How could be the software recognize the failures principle and assaults or normal failures? This consists of guide for emergency operations within the occasion of a failure, backup operations and then returning to the regular function.

Accuracy

How correct is the safety check of the software program? The accuracy of the measurement covers the quantity, regularity and implication of errors.

Response Time

Desirable reaction time or not? A sluggish response time can cause customers to pass software program protection controls. The reaction time can also be critical for manipulate management.

Through-Put

The safety verification of the software is like minded with the required usability. The potential consists of the average package and the user load of software program security and service requests.

Review \ Approve Software Security Tests

On this phase of the cycle, the test instances and gear are prepared and the security situations are authorized for execution inside the subsequent section. Includes the following steps.

Schedule \ Conduct Security Review

The software protection check plan have to be planned and reviewed in advance. The evaluators have to attain the ultimate copy of the examination. The proper motive of this project is for the improvement and development organization or the sponsor to accept and be given the revised plan. as with any revision or revision, the insured objects must be present. the primary is the definition of what is going to be mentioned approximately protection trying out (Gupta et al., 2013). the second one deals with important info related to this. The third is the synthesis of assessments and protection equipment. The last detail is precision.

Obtain Validation

Validation is essential in a test attempt as it improves test and development resource. The excellent technique is to set up a proper approval procedure for a software program application safety check plan. In this situation, use the control approval paperwork. in the connected record, the today's software protection check plan and suggests that everyone feedback to your remarks were blanketed. The software program protection check plan will evolve with each new release, but it will be protected within the change.

Execute Software Security Tests

This section executes all organized and accepted check instances the use of the tools and strategies defined within the ultimate section. This section consists of the following steps.

Regression Test the Software Security Fixes

The cause of this project is to retry protection checks that have detected screw ups throughout the preceding protection test cycle for that segment. The regression takes a look at method is used for this mission. The regression check is a software protection approach that detects errors that others purpose. specific check situations are prepared for this challenge in comparison to a checklist organized to hit upon mistakes. A reassessment matrix hyperlinks the test instances to the functions.

Execute New Software Security Test

The purpose of this mission is to carry out the brand-new software program application protection tests organized sooner or later of the preceding existence cycle of the safety exams. Inside the previous section, the check team had up to date the features, the software fragment and the popularity tests for the current phase.

Document Software Security Defects of Overall Result

At the same time as acting the software program safety take a look at, the outcomes ought to be recorded and recorded within the malicious program monitoring database. These software program protection flaws are classically associated with individual tests. A file is ready for this mistake record. The motive of this venture is to file the ones security flaws correctly with their lifestyles and the practice of a whole report of failures (Păsăreanu & Visser, 2009)

DESIGN LEVEL SECURITY

Here, designers, developers and designers conduct in-depth research on the specification of requirements and model the elements of secure design, software architecture, safe design revisions and threats according to specific requirements. The design phase is generally for functionality and is performed in accordance with the specifications provided by the client. Designers create very technical design specifications that focus on the way to implement the machine. purposeful and non-functional necessities are required to describe the security capabilities of the system.

Security Design Principles

There are numerous protection design principles that provide recommendations on the way to design a secure machine. safety layout suggestions want to be acknowledged earlier and may be integrated into SDLC in advance. Principles of security layout(Agrawal, Khan, & Chandra, 2008).

1. The principle of minimum privilege: the subject must have the necessary privileges to complete his task, and his rights must be destroyed after use.
2. Fail-safe default value principle: This principle way that the default value is the lack of access permission. A safety scheme identifies the conditions below which access can be granted. If a movement fails, the device is as secure as when the action became initiated.
3. The economic principles of the mechanism: keep the design mechanism called the KISS principle as simple as possible.
4. Complete Intermediary Principle: If access to privileges is authorized, all access must be verified and protected.
5. Principles of open design: Design must not be a secret, safety mechanisms should be unrelated to the lack of knowledge of capacity attackers, but should be unrelated to the presence of specific attackers which are more easily protected using passwords and other protection implementations.
6. Principle of privilege separation: It requires multiple conditions and presents privileges that do not depend on single situations.
7. Principle of the less common multiple mechanism: insist that the mechanisms should not be shared. When sharing, all exchange mechanisms represent the possibility of information routes between users, so they must be designed with great care so that security is not involuntarily compromised.
8. The principle of psychological acceptability: The addition of security mechanisms, especially in human interfaces, should not introduce further complexity to the system, and the proper protection mechanisms should be carried out automatically (Agrawal et al., 2008) .

Threat Modeling for Design Level Security

threat modeling is an iterative technique for modeling security threats, identifies design flaws that may be exploited by these threats, designs systems safely, and mitigates them You can take measures for add threat modeling at all stages of SDLC, but is basically considered at the design stage. At the time of design, the system allows the designer to verify and discover if the design meets the acceptable level of risk. Design flaws can be exposed, and information collected in this approach is used to enhance the satisfactory of design protection before imposing the system. Designers, software managers and designers can participate in threat modeling. The main benefits of risk modeling at design level security include identification of security issues, investigation of threats and potential vulnerabilities, planning of security tests in response to identified threats, and vulnerability in design and development. There is a design, identify and reduce software support costs. As when the product goes into production, protection flaws can be reduced extensively (M. E. Khan, 2010).

Systematic Approach to Create a Threat Model

The five main steps to modeling a threat are: It is an iterative approach that can be used to discover more about design throughout the development life cycle. Figure 3 Figure 3 illustrates the iterative threat modeling process.

The five steps in threat modeling are:

Step 1: Clarification of security objectives by clearly identifying security objectives and focusing on threat modeling activities, you can analyze the amount of work required in the next step.

Step 2: Create a general description of the application. This step helps to list the key features of the application that help identify the relevant threat used in step 4.

Step 3: Disassembly of applications A detailed investigation of the application and an understanding of the mechanism of the application facilitate the search of detailed threats.

Step 4: Threat Identification Use the details in steps 2 and 3 to identify the application context and the threats associated with that context.

Step 5: Identify vulnerabilities and identify application layers that identify vulnerabilities associated with threats. Use the vulnerability categories to focus on areas where errors occur most frequently.

Figure 3. The iterative threat modeling process
source: S. A. Khan & Khan, 2013

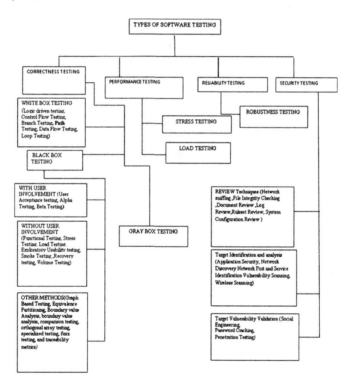

Security Patterns for Design Phase

The first to adapt design patterns to information security. It is easy to document what the system should do, and difficult to identify to list what the system should not do. They proposed a safety design pattern for information security (M. E. Khan, 2010). The security pattern is as follows:

1. Single access point: provides a security module and a way to log in to the system. This pattern suggests that there is only one way to enter the system.
2. Management point: Security management organizations and their certification and impact approval are two basic elements of this pattern.

3.   Role: Organize users with similar security privileges.

4.   Session: The location of global information in a multi-user environment.

5.   Full view with errors: Shows exceptions as necessary, show full view to the user

6.   Restricted view: Users can only see what they have access to.

7.   Secure access layer: application security integration and low-level security

8.   Privilege Summary: Added support by other privileged users.

9.   Journaling: keep a complete record of the use of resources.

10. Get out with grace: Design systems to fail safely.

at the end of the design, the attack surface is analyzed. If the place of the attack surface is large, the above method is repeated until the attack surface reaches the minimum degree. At each stage of software development, we proposed safety patterns from the point of view of the concept of security. In addition, the results of the research on the use of the proposed security standards are presented, such as the requirements phase, the design phase and the pattern of the implementation phase and the methodology to develop the software system (Vemulapati, Mehrotra, & Dangwal, 2011).

Design Review

The project manager oversees regular revisions of system features system performance, performance requirements, security requirements, and platform characteristics. At the end of the design phase, a system / subsystem design review is conducted to resolve any open issues related to one or more architectural designs and design decisions for the entire system or subsystem.

CATEGORY OF SECURITY TESTING

Protection exams may be classified as safety test techniques and protection test techniques Figure 4 indicates its classification.

Figure 4. Classification of Security Testing

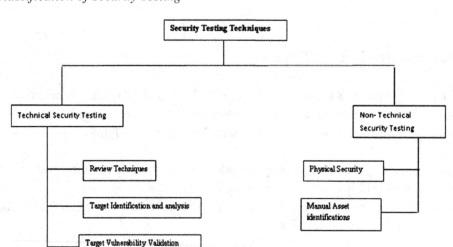

Methods Security Testing

Formal Security Tests

The formal approach of safety testing is to build a mathematical model of the software program. It additionally presents a form specification that is compatible with some formal specification languages. The formal security test methods are essentially methods of model verification and verification of theorems. There are some limitations of the formal security test method. With regard to the proof of theorems, it is difficult to realize automatically, it is necessary that the members of good quality analyze it. Therefore, check the design instead of the current code. When, as in the verification method of the model, states of practical implementation are needed, they are less useful (Kumar et al., 2014).

Model Based Security Testing

This type of test creates a software behavior version and a structure model that analyzes its behavior and dimensions by using exploring situations from some UML models, which includes activity diagrams, software program structures (Kumar et al., 2014).

Safety Tests Based on Fault Injection

This method makes a specialty of the interaction points of the software and the surroundings, consisting of the user enter, the record system, the environment variable, and the network interface. This technique facilitates the software to reach this state, which is not possible with other strategies(Kumar et al., 2014).

Fuzzy Testing

Diffuse tests focus on detecting vulnerabilities related to security objectives. The purpose of the blur test is to test the program by injecting it with random data to see if it can function normally with unclear inputs. Fuzzy tests simply create coded data and detect flaws in the tested software that are very difficult to implement with other logical test techniques (Kumar et al., 2014).

Vulnerability Scanning Testing

The susceptibility analysis recognizes the risks and security vulnerabilities of the software during the analysis (Kumar et al., 2014).

Property Based Testing

Transfer the security property of the software to the specification. It is focus on specific safety properties that can meet the classification and priority requirements(Kumar et al., 2014).

White Box Based Security Testing

It is a static test technique that aims to directly view the information directly from the source code. You may encounter security errors, such as a buffer overflow. Advanced technologies for the integrated investigation of data flow analysis, limit analysis and assumption (Kumar et al., 2014).

Risk Based Security Testing

Gary McGraw investigated on safety tests and risk analysis of risks. Security tests combined with the life cycle of software development are combined, before, with risky security vulnerabilities (Kumar et al., 2014).

Classification of Security Testing Techniques

protection checking out strategies may be classified into technical protection assessments and non-technical protection exams. Technical security tests are divided into strategies to review, identify and analyze goals and validate vulnerabilities. Non-technical safety checking out may be divided into bodily safety and guide asset identification. there are numerous securities trying out strategies to assess the level of security of systems and software, grouped together in the review techniques, identification techniques and objective analysis and validation of vulnerabilities.

Review Techniques

those strategies are used to evaluate systems and software to locate vulnerabilities. these strategies are generally executed manually. View documentation, records, rule sets, system configuration, network and files.

Analysis Techniques and Target Identification

The technical procedures to find and analyze the objectives are to find active devices and their ports and associated facilities, and analyze them to detect possible vulnerabilities. These techniques are: network detection, vulnerability scan, wireless scan, passive wireless scan, active wireless scan, wireless device detection and Bluetooth scanning.

Validation Techniques and Target Vulnerability

The test techniques identify the presence of vulnerabilities according to the specific technique used. These techniques are: decryption of passwords, intrusion tests and social engineering.

ANALYSIS OF CURRENT TRENDS

RQ.1: What is the link between security testing and software testing? but, software program checking out is a technique of identifying capacity errors within the device so that it can be debugged quickly. Software tests are separated into several subcategories, such as test tests, performance tests, reliability tests and safety tests. The corrective evidence is divided into a black area, a white area and a gray area, while the black zone is divided with the user's participation and without user participation or other methods. Performance tests could be separated into stress tests and load tests. Robustness tests are subject to reliability tests. Security tests can be subdivided into techniques to review, identify and analyze objectives and validate the vulnerability of the destination. Figure 5 illustrates the software testing techniques.

Figure 5. Types of Software Testing

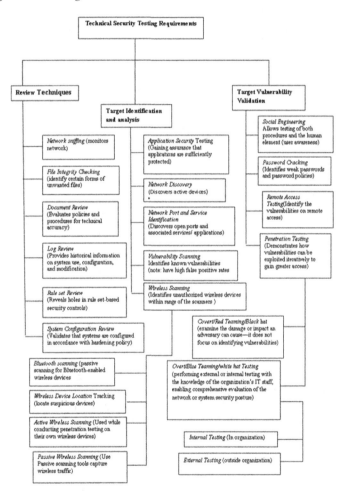

RQ.2 How security tests can be labeled in distinct strategies. safety trying out strategies may be labeled as technical safety exams and non-technical protection assessments. The technical protection takes a look at is divided into strategies to study, discover and analyze goals and validate their vulnerabilities. Non-technical protection checks may be divided into physical security and manual identification of assets. This can be seen in Figure 6.

Figure 6. Represents specific software testing techniques

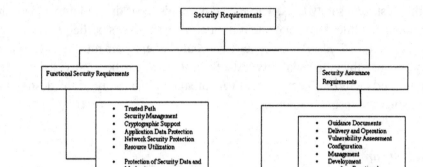

There are many protection testing techniques (shown in Figure 6) for evaluating the security measures of any system or community. The different software security testing techniques are as follows:

RQ.3: How to classify protection checks in exclusive methods? security trying out methods can be categorized into: property checks, vulnerability tests, blur exams, version-based totally safety tests, security checks, formal protection assessments, security testing based on test failures (monolithic functional) with white box test (based on functional synthesis).

Figure 7. Represent different technical security testing techniques

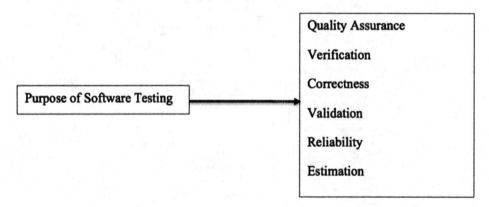

RQ.4: How to classify the different security requirements? The requirements for protection checking out may be labeled into three classes: safety and safety characteristic. The useful protection necessities can be labeled in Figure 8 .

Figure 8. Different security requirements

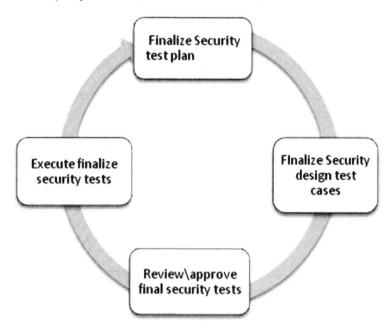

CONCLUSION AND FUTURE WORK

It analyzes the definition, type, principal methods, tools and techniques of software security and also introduces a software program protection life cycle. the principle strategies used in the protection checks are in brief defined. This record will help evaluators and beginners plan a security development lifecycle. This work is done to enhance the reliability and safety of the software. in-depth research into safety checking out strategies and techniques. Conclude that an objective vulnerability evaluation can assist the developer to find out vulnerabilities and solve them greater efficaciously. techniques and strategies of security tests. further, these strategies can be carried out in internet vulnerability detection tools to affirm the respective vulnerability so one can produce a better scanner in the destiny. We have completed our pleasant to symbolize the challenge very well and successfully. The future goal of this work will be to identify the factors and develop a security framework using security features to improve security and make the software more reliable.

REFERENCES

Agrawal, A., Khan, R., & Chandra, S. (2008). Software Security Process–Development Life Cycle Perspective. *CSI Communications*, *32*(5), 39–42.

Arkin, B., Stender, S., & McGraw, G. (2005). Software penetration testing. *IEEE Security and Privacy*, *3*(1), 84–87. doi:10.1109/MSP.2005.23

Banerjee, C., & Pandey, S. (2009). *Software security rules, SDLC perspective.* arXiv preprint arXiv:0911.0494

Bayuk, J. L. (2013). Security as a theoretical attribute construct. *Computers & Security, 37*, 155–175. doi:10.1016/j.cose.2013.03.006

Braz, C., & Robert, J.-M. (2006). *Security and usability: the case of the user authentication methods.* Paper presented at the IHM. 10.1145/1132736.1132768

Devanbu, P. T., & Stubblebine, S. (2000). Software engineering for security: a roadmap. *Proceedings of the Conference on the Future of Software Engineering.*

Dhir, S., & Kumar, D. (2019). Automation Software Testing on Web-Based Application. In Software Engineering (pp. 691–698). Singapore: Springer. doi:10.1007/978-981-10-8848-3_67

Dias Neto, A. C., Subramanyan, R., Vieira, M., & Travassos, G. H. (2007). A survey on model-based testing approaches: a systematic review. *Proceedings of the 1st ACM international workshop on Empirical assessment of software engineering languages and technologies: held in conjunction with the 22nd IEEE/ACM International Conference on Automated Software Engineering (ASE) 2007.* 10.1145/1353673.1353681

Gupta, S., Verma, H. K., & Sangal, A. L. (2013). Security attacks & prerequisite for wireless sensor networks. *Intl Journal of Engineering and Advanced Technology, 2*(5), 558-566.

Khan, M. E. (2010). Different forms of software testing techniques for finding errors. *International Journal of Computer Science Issues, 7*(3), 24.

Khan, S. A., & Khan, R. A. (2013). *Software security testing process: phased approach.* Paper presented at the International Conference on Intelligent Interactive Technologies and Multimedia. 10.1007/978-3-642-37463-0_19

Kumar, R., Khan, S. A., & Khan, R. A. (2014). Software Security Testing A Pertinent Framework. *Journal of Global Research in Computer Science, 4*(3).

Mead, N. R., & Stehney, T. (2005). Security quality requirements engineering (SQUARE) methodology (Vol. 30). New York, NY: ACM. doi:10.21236/ADA443493

Mistrík, I., Grundy, J., Van der Hoek, A., & Whitehead, J. (2010). Collaborative software engineering: challenges and prospects. In Collaborative Software Engineering (pp. 389–403). Berlin, Germany: Springer. doi:10.1007/978-3-642-10294-3_19

Papadakis, M., Kintis, M., Zhang, J., & et al, . (2019). Mutation testing advances: An analysis and survey. *Advances in Computers, 112*, 275–378. doi:10.1016/bs.adcom.2018.03.015

Păsăreanu, C. S., & Visser, W. (2009). A survey of new trends in symbolic execution for software testing and analysis. *International Journal of Software Tools for Technology Transfer, 11*(4), 339–353. doi:10.100710009-009-0118-1

Porru, S., Pinna, A., Marchesi, M., & Tonelli, R. (2017). *Blockchain-oriented software engineering: challenges and new directions.* Paper presented at the 2017 IEEE/ACM 39th International Conference on Software Engineering Companion (ICSE-C). 10.1109/ICSE-C.2017.142

Sodiya, A. S., Onashoga, S. A., & Ajayĩ, O. (2006). Towards Building Secure Software Systems. *Issues in Informing Science & Information Technology, 3.*

Takanen, A., Demott, J. D., Miller, C., & Kettunen, A. (2018). *Fuzzing for software security testing and quality assurance*. Artech House.

Tian-yang, G., Yin-Sheng, S., & You-yuan, F. (2010). Research on software security testing. *World Academy of Science, Engineering and Technology, 69*, 647–651.

Vemulapati, J., Mehrotra, N., & Dangwal, N. (2011). *SaaS security testing: Guidelines and evaluation framework*. Paper presented at the 11th Annual International Software Testing Conference.

Villani, E., Pontes, R. P., Coracini, G. K., & Ambrósio, A. M. (2019). Integrating model checking and model-based testing for industrial software development. *Computers in Industry, 104*, 88–102. doi:10.1016/j.compind.2018.08.003

This research was previously published in Human Factors in Global Software Engineering; pages 219-251, copyright year 2019 by Engineering Science Reference (an imprint of IGI Global).

Chapter 63
Metastructuring for Standards:
How Organizations Respond to the Multiplicity of Standards

Ronny Gey
Friedrich Schiller University Jena, Germany

Andrea Fried
Linköping University, Sweden

ABSTRACT

This chapter focusses on the appearance and implementation of process standards in software development organizations. The authors are interested in the way organizations handle the plurality of process standards. Organizations respond by metastructuring to the increasing demand for standardizing their development processes. Standards metastructuring summarizes all organizational mechanisms for facilitating the ongoing adaption of global standards to the organizational context. Based on an in-depth single case study of a software developing organization in the automotive technology sector, the authors found four areas of metastructuring, four roles for standard mediation, and four types of metastructuring activities. With the case study, they encourage further research that proves standards in use and how organizations respond to the challenges of standardization.

INTRODUCTION

The multiplicity and plurality of standards is one of the challenging issues for modern working organizations. In the light of the recent economic developments and the imposed dependency of economic decisions on standards it is important to elaborate on these challenges, changes and risks which confront organizations within an audit society of organized uncertainty (Power, 1997). In this context, we will contribute to the question of how organizations respond to and cope with the consequences evolving from the multiplicity and plurality of process standards. We chose an exploratory study on the micro level within a single software development organization.

DOI: 10.4018/978-1-6684-3702-5.ch063

Research on standards has many facets. On the one hand, we distinguish research on standards focusing on the design mode and, on the other hand, the use mode of standards (following Orlikowski, 1992). This distinction emphasizes the occurrence of social construction, both, before and after a standard is enacted in an organization. It refers to processes of setting and following standards. The *design* mode describes the process of standardization on the standard setting bodies' and/ or the related stakeholder's side. Hereby, researchers have inquired how standards emerge, how standard setting bodies are organized and how these bodies determine the content of standards, as well as, how they convince potential stakeholders to certify their organizations (Blind and Mangelsdorf, 2016; Brunswicker et al., 2015; DongBack, 2013; Egyedi, 2008; Furusten, 2000; Marimon et al., 2009; Tamm Hallström, 2004, Wiegmann et al., 2017).

For this paper, the *use* mode of standards is of special interest. The use mode literature on process standards is chiefly shaped by the research on the ISO 9000s and ISO 14000s process quality norms, culminating in the following two topics in the early 2000s. Firstly, there is an extensive amount of literature about the motivation and barriers of the implementation of standards (Boiral, 2003; Niazi et al., 2005; Zeng et al., 2007). This literature focuses on the influence of the implementation of process standards on product quality, on the organizational performance and the obstacles and limitations while putting a standard into effect. Secondly, there is a discussion around process standards that reflects on the requirements for a 'good' organization. This can be measured through customer satisfaction, defined responsibilities, the reduction of production and management mistakes, quality assurance, documentation of all processes, decisions and related audits (Lawrence and Phillips, 1998). Finally, little research has been done on the social construction of standards, in particular, on standards as a form of regulation or as a code of corporate governance and on the functioning of these code regimes (Jakobs, 2006; Power, 1997; Seidl, 2007; Wieland, 2005). Thereby, code regimes are specific types of standards which regulate corporate behavior based on a 'comply-or-explain rule'. Seidl (2007) investigates code regimes in view of parameters that influence the effectiveness of a code regime. Important for our understanding of standards is here the conclusion that the de-facto content of a standard is determined to a significant extent by standard followers and not by standardization bodies.

Besides these studies, we can resume that the social construction of standards by organizations plays a minor role on the use mode of standards in the existing research. Thus, we deem it as important to elaborate on this subject since we do not sufficiently know how organizations themselves adopt multiple standards in reaction to a number of institutional pressures. With this contribution we intent to provide empirical insights on a micro level addressing organizational issues of standard multiplicity and plurality.

The contribution of this article is threefold. Firstly, we elaborate on the institutional answers how organizations deal internally with the plurality and multiplicity of standards. In contrast to standardization *by* organizations and standardization *as* organization, we are dealing with the standardization of organizations. Standardization of organizations relates to the question of "how standards are adopted, diffused, implemented, avoided, and altered in the course of their implementations" (Brunsson et al., 2012, p. 614).

Secondly, we focus on the empirical phenomenon of standard-use mediators and their metastructuring activities (Orlikowski et al., 1995). In consequence of the development of a so-called "standard bible" by the software organizations, standard-use mediators occur in organizations as a response to a multi-facet standardization pressure from the institutional environment of organizations. We believe that the way organizations meta-structure multiple process standards has an enormous influence e.g. on the innovating activities of an organization (Fried, 2010; Fried et al., 2013).

Finally, while referring to metastructuring we base our argumentation on structuration theory (Giddens, 1984). Local organizational structures depend on the institutional environment which is propagated by professionals and associations to promote collective goods as standards. Likewise, mutual interferences between the local organizational actions and structures and the institutional environment can be observed. We suppose that, in order to function, process standards are structured and swayed by internal mediators. The structuration of standards is influenced by the mediators' interpretation of their working environment, their access to resources and the normative rules they are confronted with (Barley, 1986; DeSanctis and Poole, 1994; Weick, 1990).

For exploring the phenomenon of standard-use mediators and their metastructuring activities in detail, the chapter is structured as follows. The subsequent section will provide the theoretical background on metastructuring and standard-use mediation. Starting from the theory on structuration by Giddens (1984), we will present metastructuring as a phenomenon which Orlikowski et al. (1995) first introduced in the area of technology research. Section 3 describes the research design of our case study. We chose an exploratory approach within a single software development organization. In particular, process standards will be introduced as the empirical object of interest. The findings of our case study *A-Suppliers* are presented in section four. The empirical investigations will highlight the use mode perspective on standards. We intend to attract the readers' attention to how A-Suppliers has decided to address plurality and multiplicity of process standards. In the discussion, we provide insights into metastructuring as a powerful mechanism in dealing with multiple and plural process standard requirements in organizations. Standard-use mediators are explored and investigated regarding the metastructuring *process*, metastructuring *areas* as well as the different *activity types* of metastructuring connected to these areas. The conclusion section provides supplementary notes on future research and limitations of standard metastructuring.

METASTRUCTURING OF STANDARDS IN THE CONTEXT OF USE

In general, standards can be understood as rules. Rules sanction social conduct and constitute meaning (Giddens, 1984). Standards focus on something "to be reached, be it in terms of quality or quantity, extent or intensity, precision or value, technique or morality"(Ortmann, 2010, p. 204). Process standards are the center of interest in our empirical investigations. They represent "how organizational processes should be designed and controlled" (Brunsson and Jacobsson, 2000b, p. 4).

From our point of view, standards are solely those rules (a) which are purposefully set, which are (b) strongly formalized and written down (for instance by standardization bodies) and, finally, which (c) cover and adapt generalized, comparable occasions among organizations (e.g. processes, technical or social requirements, performance). Thus, standards are only those rules "which tend to be [...] developed and adopted through explicit procedures that historians can trace" (Timmermans and Epstein, 2010, p. 71). Moreover, standards are rules which are often connected to a certification by an organization-external party (certification body). Thereby, certification is an evaluation process of the compliance with predefined requirements. It results in a document (certificate) that is trusted to be evidence of requirement compliance, assuming a comparability among certified organizations. Alternatively for certification the terms *appraisal* (e.g. for the CMMI[1] standard) or *assessment* (e.g. for the ISO/IEC 15504 standard) are used for the external evaluation by a certification body and its assessors.

By choosing a structuration theory viewpoint, we also need to address the relation between the design and the use of standards. This relation is to be seen as "recursive, i.e. that the formulation of rules (possibly) constitutes their application and vice versa" (Ortmann, 2010, p. 205). People are knowledgeable agents who can construct alternative meanings of once designed standards. They are able to redefine and modify standards in an emancipatory way and shape the meaning, purpose and ways of standard usage. Standards do not exist without human activity; they are enacted by actions (Fried et al. 2013).

In the scope of this paper, we report on a specific type of structuring activity around process standards within organizations. We focus on a process Orlikowski et al. (1995) called *metastructuring*. Metastructuring was primarily used in the context of technology research. Yates et al. (1999) observed that "a few members of the project group explicitly engaged in activities that facilitated both early and ongoing use of the new technology by the rest of the project group" (Yates et al., 1999; for technology structuring see also Okamura et al., 1994 and Orlikowski et al., 1995). These activities included (1) guidelines for the use of a new (conference) technology, (2) provision of qualification and follow-ups in using the technology as well as (3) modification of the technology according to contextual, project-specific requirements. Orlikowski et al. (1995) summarized metastructuring "as an organizational mechanism for facilitating the ongoing adaptation of technologies, their use, and organizational contexts to each other and to changing conditions" (Orlikowski et al., 1995, p. 441).

Four types of metastructuring were classified in technology research: establishment, reinforcement, adjustment and episodic change (Orlikowski et al., 1995). During *establishment,* the mediators come into play and enact their roles in the organization. Mediators are a group of individuals who intervene significantly to modify and to adapt new material artifacts to the organization in an appropriate manner. They pre-shape the material artifact before the actual users apply it. Therefore this activity is called metastructuring. Moreover, in addition to other actors like promoters or trainers, mediators do not only intervene reactively in the initial stages of establishment. Mediators act pro-actively. They are institutionally recognized and play an ongoing role. Internal technology consultants or the employees of the IT department can be considered as mediators. Of course, they set up the infrastructure and implement the new material artifact. They also need to promote and to support it, write user-guides and especially convince managers or key personnel in the organization to adopt the new technology. When it comes to *reinforcement*, mediators maintain their operations and reinforce its vision. An ongoing training on the new material artifact is offered. Moreover, they ease the use of the system, collect user feedback and, as a consequence, try to intensify the usage. During *adjustment,* they react on the given feedback and usage tendencies. This includes smaller and less radical modifications of the artifact in use. The most dramatic changes are considered during the *episodic change* period. Significant improvements and corrections to the functionality or the technical core of the system are accomplished.

What started in the context of technology use gained further influence especially in socio-technical studies on electronic communication or collaboration. Henriksen et al. (2002) explored web-based group ware, Bansler and Havn (2004) a virtual workspace and Janneck and Finck (2006) researched online communities. Clear and MacDonell (2011) analyzed email data of global virtual teams. Metastructuring is also very prominent in studies on medical technology. Novak et al. (2012; 2012a), Davidson and Chiasson (2005) and Davidson and Chismar (2007) all studied the implementation of medical IT systems. The study by Rodon et al. (2011) portrayed the post-implementation phase of inter-organizational information systems and especially focused on managerial interventions and users' appropriation. They reported that metastructuring might have an important impact on the structuring processes of other users while applying the different types of metastructuring activities. Overall, these authors characterized the process as very complex and rather complicated to understand. Thus, they call for additional research on different technologies (Bansler and Havn, 2004) and raise the question of other potential sources of mediation (Rodon et al., 2011).

In the metastructuring discourse, the scope of technology is restricted to material artifacts of various hardware and software configurations (Orlikowski, 1992). It is emphasized that there is a distinction between the material nature of technologies and the human activities designing and using these artifacts. Similarly, for standards as artifacts and their rule-like character, the need to be enacted in order to be effective in organizational life is evident. On this basis, we ask whether the implementation of other artifacts than technologies - like standards - also trigger such metastructuring activities in organizations. Standards are powerful rules in a globalized world. The way organizations deal with facing a plurality and multiplicity of standards is an urgent matter that needs clarification. Accordingly, our interest is to observe whether similar powerful mechanisms can be found within the 'world of standards' (Brunsson and Jacobsson, 2000c) and which influence metastructuring can have on the effectiveness of software development processes.

CASE STUDY DESIGN

We use a case study approach to investigate contemporary phenomena in their real-life context (Yin, 2003). As typical for qualitative studies, the personal realm of experience of each interviewee lies in the center of our analysis. We chose interviews as the main data gathering technique. The result is a single exploratory case study. We analyzed the interview data with a qualitative content analysis to explore qualified hypotheses (Krippendorff, 2004; Kohlbacher, 2006). It enables the researcher to include textual information and to identify its properties systematically.

Eight interviews were conducted in October 2010. Each of them lasted between 80 and 100 minutes. Later on, two additional interviews were necessary to clarify some data and to gain some more fine-grained information. With an emphasis on the Capability Maturity Model Integration (CMMI) as the process standard all interviews were part of a larger, multi-case study undertaking (Fried et al., 2013) exploring the relationship between standardization and innovation in software development organizations. CMMI is a standard for software process improvement (Humphrey, 1992). Since 2002, it has been the successor to CMM. When we speak about CMMI in this study, we refer to either CMMI (since 2002) or to CMM (before 2002). The interviews involved strategic planners, managers responsible for the implementation of process management standards, team leaders and software engineers of one working context (see Table 1). They were semi-structured to allow flexibility and to ensure that we focus on interesting phenomena. Further, a narrative interview style was chosen to stimulate reports about a variety of expressions and experiences in terms of process standards.

The subjects of the interviewees' narrations and requests by the interviewer were centered on the history of the organization, the history, implementation and usage of process management standards, the procedure of certification audits as well as the individual and organizational experiences with process management standards. The interviewees were asked to reflect on changes in the course of time.

The recorded interviews were transcribed and afterwards coded and analyzed with *Atlas.ti* (Muhr, 1991), a software for qualitative data analysis. The anonymized publication of our findings was requested by the organization. Where necessary, sensitive data was paraphrased and marked by square brackets. The analysis of the case is based on a code-name schema. The initial code-names and their mutual relations are depicted in Figure 1.

Table 1. Data of Interviewees

Name	Position	Experience	
		CMMI	**A-Suppliers**
A1	Process Coach (PC)	10 years	>15 years
A2	Head of QM	5 years	>15 years
A3	Former CIO, now Board Member	5 years	>15 years
A4	SW Developer, Project Leader	5 years	>15 years
A5	Process Coach (PC)	5 years	12 years
A6	SW Developer, SW Architect	5 years	8 years
A7/A9/A10	Head of a Process Group (PG) unit	12 years	5 years
A8	Former Head of Process Group (PG)	5 years	13 years

Figure 1. Code-names for Content Analysis

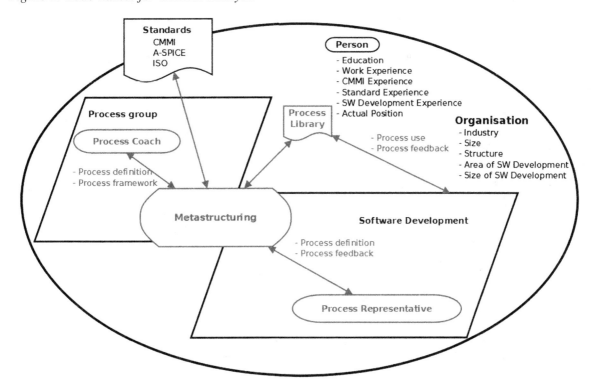

Among the team members, we agreed on the initial code-name schema in advance. However, it was constantly extended during the analysis. In the end we coded additional relational information and thus extended the code-name schema during the analysis. We ended up with 31 different code names.

Moreover, to achieve an adequate level of validity we used multiple sources of evidence. Most of the data was gathered from the transcriptions of the interviews. Additionally, we participated in a guided tour through the production area as well as the software development office where the interviews were subsequently conducted. After each interview and during the lunch and coffee breaks we prepared protocols of the past interviews. We focused not only on context information but also on the emotional setting of the interview situation. The next section provides our findings on metastructuring at A-Suppliers.

FINDINGS ON METASTRUCTURING AT A-SUPPLIERS

Findings

The investigated organization *A-Suppliers* acts in the automotive technology sector and produces electronic control units which includes systems for ABS, ESP, exhaust and engine controls. They employ about 5,000 system developers, of which about 3,000 are directly involved in software development. The employees who worked in the department at that time mostly had an electrical engineering background. As an automotive supplier they have to consider several industry-related standards (e.g. ISO 26262, A-Spice, ISO 16949). Automotive SPICE (A-SPICE) is thereby the most important standard for the automotive industry. A-Suppliers has long-term experience in process management.

In 1999, the head of software development came up with the idea of continuous process improvement: "*[...] he always had this state of the art development with a process improvement infrastructure in mind.*" *(A1:069)*. The first trigger for CMMI came from inside the company but was also motivated by external customers starting to demand CMMI certification: "*[the customer] finally required it from [A-Suppliers]. So the pressure from outside of [A-Suppliers] came in, from the customer.*" *(A1:069)*.

In the software development unit, they set up a pilot project to accomplish a CMMI certification. We regard it as first *establishment* step since they implemented a new standard, CMMI, and they established their own roles as process coaches (PC):

And the project leader [...] had to build up a project team and he took some of the specialists out of various departments. And I was one of them, especially for the whole quality management stuff and subcontract management at that time. So it was three of us, so-called coaches [...] trying to establish some processes. (A1:17)

After more than three years, in 2002, they successfully got CMMI level 3 certification. Directly after their certification, they turned the pilot project into an own department:

There have been some people assigned but it was more or less a project. And then [...] it was established as a department. So there was a budget allocated, there have been head count allocated, there was work space and everything allocated. (A8:021)

Taking this step to bring together the process experts under one organizational unit was considered highly important. Now they could handle all relevant standardization topics in one specialized organizational unit. As a significant correction of the standard-use at A-Suppliers in terms of CMMI, we assess this step as an *episodic change*. After a certain time, the organization again expanded its competences since they had to deal not only with CMMI, but also with other standards:

CMMI is one of them. There is still A-SPICE and all the other models and standards, which are handled within the process group. (A1:045)

And also we have to implement some ISO topics, for Safety management, ISO 26262 and 16949. (A7:39)

As a result, the process experts could now focus entirely on standardization and process-related tasks - a significant and *episodic change*. They gained more expertise in the area while collaborating closely in the new department. Therefore, the time necessary to achieve a new certification was reduced by more than a year:

And this makes it much easier, because if you do something you do it for all projects. It makes it much easier [...] So we reached CMM level 3 in 2002 and level 3 CMMI in 2004. (A1:101)

Whereas formerly only standards from the domain of software development were part of its work items, in 2006 the process group (PG) took over the responsibility for all the process standards, organization-wide (*episodic change*). Again, we regard it as a reaction to the increased attention and importance of standardization at A-Suppliers and their environment. Since CMMI continuously gained influence in the automotive industry, the suppliers consequently had to suit these needs. Since then, the PG has consequently acted as a standard-use mediator for the whole organization. In fact, the engineers were faced with several standards which made their work more complex and difficult to handle. In some cases, it led to a decreased productivity: "*[...] if you use the wrong interpretation for the requirements or for the standard and then you end up with a lower productivity.*" *(A2:067)*. Thus, reducing complexity by mediating between user and standards was the main idea of a distinct PG:

[...] we are reducing complexity for the engineer. Because otherwise, we would challenge our experts for hardware or software to interpret the standard in the right way and this is absolutely not necessary. (A2:087)

Instead, the process experts now deal with the multiplicity of standards. It necessarily means that all standards "*[...] are inputs to the process development. So now you have to find a process design which jointly or comparably fulfills these requirements.*" *(A2:079)*. Interviewee [A9] described this process in detail as follows:

So, we have a process library where all processes for our product development can be found. And we mapped all artifacts, all work products with CMMI or A-Spice. This means, we have the models and the best practices in the database [....] We have the models in the process library and we have the processes of the different products in the library. And then, we link the artifacts or work products with the requirements of the models or standards. With that, we know about our evidences, what we cover and where we still have gaps which need to be closed. With this way, we ensure that if you follow the process library then you fulfill the standards or models. (A9:61)

The PCs interpret each single standard; there are several experts for each. The interpretation of standards can be seen as *establishment* as well as *adjustment*. While interpreting a new standard for the first time, they establish the standard in the company, whereas minor *adjustments* in the interpretation happen on a regular basis. Furthermore, they compare the standards among each other to find overlapping parts and keep the process descriptions as lean and therefore as user-friendly as possible - a sign for *reinforce-*

ment. Creation (*establishment*) and maintenance (*reinforcement*) of the standard script are an immense effort, which is mutually accomplished by the PG in collaboration with the process representatives (PR).

The process library is based on a web-based technology, where all the mappings between the different standards and the product processes only need to be done once. Subsequently, it can be consistently displayed. A-Suppliers even reviews the standard conformity of the process library by internal or external assessments:

[...] after we mapped A-Spice we had an A-Spice assessment by an external A-Spice principal. He reviewed how far the mapping is correct. [...] And we do it for CMMI as soon as we renew the mappings for our appraisal. [...] So, either we review or we get assessed externally. (A9:73)

For ISO 26262, we had a [technical assessment organization] doing the assessment, also for our process library. [...] and for ISO 16949 we actually had our quality surgeon in the organization. He did an ISO 16949 audit for the mapping. (A9:81)

Once the mapping is done, the different standards are not explicitly specified to the user. It reduces complexity since now they only have to interact with the process library instead of all the different standards itself:

[...] this is a documentation of all the processes and you will never find a position inside all these processes, where CMMI or A-Spice is mentioned in reference to. So we hide all these frameworks, all the requirements from our engineers. They only have to follow our internal processes, process descriptions. (A2:083)

Regarding the standard script or the production process, all organizationally relevant information is collected in the process library. As a result, the process library is a highly valuable and critical tool in the organization:

If you look in our process system, you see the processes and the tasks. You see the roles and linked to the roles are the requirements, the capabilities and also the trainings to achieve the know-how. (A2:211)

The interviewees confirmed that the process library dramatically eases the training on-the-job period for new employees or for the achievement of further job qualifications since: *"they start to work and they can be sure if they follow the process library it will be okay." (A7:315)*. The process coaches now accomplish a part of the corporate training, the one regarding all process issues (reinforcement). All interviewees demonstrated an exclusively positive attitude towards the process library (PL). Some actually expressed being proud of what they achieved with this tool:

We built up this tool and now we are in the version 3.3 of the process library [...] So it took nearly 3 years to set up the whole system because it is, you can imagine, it is a rather complex and consistent system. So an auditor, whatever kind he is, has no chance to detect gaps or weaknesses. He can do internal checking and so on. So at least the instruction side is complete. And the auditors give up [...] (A2:295)

In this system, the so-called process representatives that work in the relevant operational departments define the operational processes. This happens when the technology is established, as well as when *adjustments* to the relevant processes are required. The PR is linked to the PG and cooperates in all respective process tasks - an integrated and participative approach between the PG and the operational departments:

We have some process representatives [in the operational departments]. And there, we make the process definition. So the process representative is responsible for the process definition. He gets support from my side or from other people from the PG. And the developers were included in discussions in certain groups. Not all, but certain from different departments to get different opinions and different needs. So normally, we had teams, the project leader was the process representative. And there was a PG coach in the process team. And there were different representatives for the different departments in the project team for this certain process group. (A5:113)

The user participation continues once the processes are defined and implemented. Literally everybody in the organization can provide feedback on the processes, either reporting it to the PRs: "*We get indirect feedback via the process representatives.*" *(A2:115)* or by using the process library: "*There is a feedback button for each process. And they can give feedback, change requests.*" *(A2:095)*. In this way, an organized feedback system for the users of the processes was established in order to interact about the process landscape. The PR has the responsibility for handling the feedback requests and, as a main user of the process itself, he also actively produces feedback (*reinforcement*).

Due to the organization-wide interaction with it, the process library is the central technology in the standard mediation process at A-Suppliers. Design and maintenance receives a high attention, especially from the PG. Reflecting the size of the organization and the amount of standards which need to be served, they decided to dedicate a single full-time position to the editorial maintenance of the PL, the script editor (SE):

It is absolutely necessary, it won't work otherwise. So, the PRs describe, they are responsible for the content. But, you need somebody who is doing the formal review of the content. If everybody writes what he wants, everybody has an own style of writing. And it has to be used, it has to be understood. (A9:141)

Above all, this continuous development required support and motivation from the very top of the organization:

And PQ is the successor organization of the original PG. So it is also sustainable in the organization. But without [A3] as strong mentor on the higher management level, this wouldn't have had happened. And we had a second mentor in the board here in [A-Suppliers], which is [the CMMI board member]. He was also convinced that it will help. So also [A3] had a backup on [the executive management level]. (A8:041)

With the support of the higher management, the implementation of a PG at A-Suppliers became a broad change management success. A further significant proportion of it can be ascribed to the slow implementation of CMMI and the whole process landscape at A-Suppliers:

And it depends on how you communicate it and how you work with the people. If you just send an email: 'Here is the process library, you have to use it.' It will not work. You will have to do shit work [continuous motivation, explanation and convincing]. And to communicate it, change management is the best way to describe it. (A7:339)

As highlighted before, the role of the PRs and the established feedback procedures stand for the participative and integrated approach. This is a crucial factor in the standardization process at A-Suppliers highlighted by interviewee A2, the head of the quality management department:

Because we want to have the experts for the products also writing proper processes for them. And we, we supply the model competence let me say. We do some coaching for the process representatives, to bring in the model competence for ISO 26262 and so on. So this is the corporation model and I think, if you want, you can call it decentralized process organization. This is distributed responsibility. (A2:115)

The PG is now a fully established actor in the organization of A-Suppliers. As such, they have concrete tasks, roles dedicated to these tasks and well-defined processes for their actions. Further, they recently showed signs of confidence towards their own role and its importance to the company. They reported on a study about *"process modeling for the process library of the future"* (A9:209). In this way, they emphasized their pro-active role in the company towards processes:

[…] we as process group, we feel ourselves appointed to look ahead. We don't want to stand still. With the new product generation, we are also looking at process development and how we can achieve it in the future. (A9:213)

As the interviewee mentions, the A-Suppliers' PG intends to predict how the standard and process handling within the organization can be enhanced. Further, they are likewise engaged directly or indirectly on the side of the standard-setting bodies in the creation and maintenance of the standards they use. They not only translate and use the different standards while creating and maintaining their process library; they also give feedback and help with designing the standards they use as members of the standardization bodies. Whether it be the ISO standards, A-Spice or CMMI, for each an own standardization and/or certification body promotes and supervises the standard implementation. The PG of A-Suppliers participates in these activities:

[…] we are sitting in the standard committees of A-Spice and ISO 26262. We also have people working directly with the SEI. We have these people. These are central positions at A-Suppliers. And we do communicate directly with them. So, when someone sits in the committee of A-Spice and they discuss the next version […] no matter which subject, then it always ends up on my desk. Then, I do check whether I have comments from my point of view. Does it fit or not for my requirements. (A9:249)

Summary of Findings

We present the summary of our findings along three different aspects of the metastructuring approach. First, we outline the process of metastructuring and its evolution over time. Then, we describe the areas in which metastructuring activities appear. Finally, we highlight different types of metastructuring activities that we found in the A-Suppliers case.

The Process of Metastructuring

A-Suppliers developed step-by-step an entire department as standard-use mediators (see Figure 2). They reacted to the increasing amount of process standards they are confronted with (CMMI, A-SPICE, ISO26262, ISO16949). Since 2000, A-Suppliers has been dealing with an increased standard complexity due to the advent of standards like CMMI or A-Spice. First, they gathered initial experiences within a pilot project to learn about CMMI implementation requirements (cf. Figure 2 - step 1). Then, the number of required standards increased and the software-related standard script is developed to integrate different standard requirements (cf. Figure 2 - step 2).

After this step, the appearance of metastructuring results in a new department, the process group (PG) (cf. Figure 2 - step 3), which then handles requirements of process standards organization-wide. The project group's task is the fulfillment of the standard requirements for the whole organization. The group manages the process library which was developed to ease maintenance and enhancement of the standard script. Within the PG, the relevant positions executing these tasks are the process coaches (PC). They are supported by the PRs. In the end, a new department and its roles as well as new artifacts, the standard script and the process library, emerge.

Figure 2. Process of Metastructuring at A-Suppliers

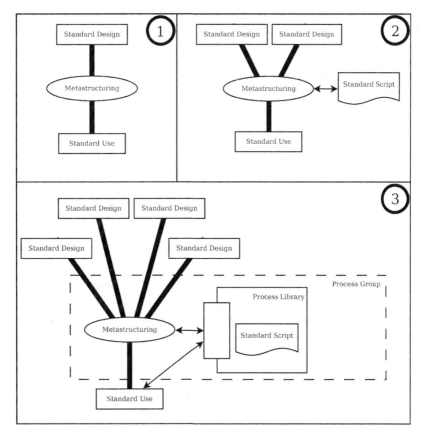

The Areas of Metastructuring

At A-Suppliers there are four areas of metastructuring: (A) managing the standard script, (B) managing the process library, (C) handling internal/corporate standards and (D) coping with external/international standards (Figure 3).

Figure 3. Areas of Metastructuring at A-Suppliers

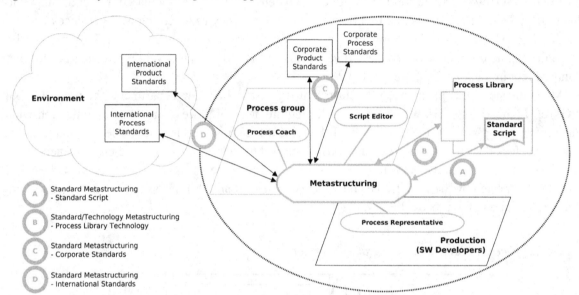

To start with (D), the PG takes external standards, interprets and applies them as input for the design of the corporate standard script embodied in the process library (cf. Figure 3 (D)). This is mainly the task of the PCs. Little involvement of the PRs is needed. Feedback for the creators of standards (e.g. standardization bodies) is sometimes provided. For most of the applied standards, A-Suppliers is represented with at least one person in the standardization body. This could also be verified by the authors by researching the internet regarding the relevant committees. However, influence on the design process of CMMI is reduced to feedback via change requests (Software Engineering Institute, 2012).

As a second metastructuring area, the PG has to take into consideration corporate standards (cf. Figure 3 (C)): directives towards process, products or even corporate identity. The corporate standards change the design of the standard script but the process itself was not described explicitly throughout the interviews. A-Suppliers has full control over design and usage of their own corporate standards. The interviewees described this process as integrated and participative and we assume that this metastructuring area is a full and open structuring process. This task is primarily accomplished by the PCs of the process group, although the nature of an internal standard allows a broader participation of the PRs in the structuring of these standards.

Thirdly, the standard script is designed by the PG in close collaboration with the PRs of the operational departments (cf. Figure 3 (A)). In (software development) organizations, standard scripts are internally often called 'standard bible' or 'process management policy' which contain an aggregated version of several different standards – often overlapping, sometimes conflicting. A-Suppliers' tasks are separated; the PRs are responsible for defining the processes in the standard script, for the training on these processes and also for feedback and improvement of the process while the PC defines the broader process framework for the whole organization and further consults the PRs in their tasks. The standard script is then used by the software engineers (cf. Figure 3 (A)). Different feedback loops, either by using the process tool or via the PRs, were reported. Thus, the creation and use of a standard script embodied into the process library can be regarded as a vital structuring process. The standard script is the result of a translation process of several external and internal standards into a single internal one (cf. Figure 3 (C) and (D) as input for (A)).

Finally, we found another metastructuring area in the design, usage and maintenance of the (web-based) technology on which the process library is based (cf. Figure 3 (B)). A service provider developed the underlying technology of the process library as a customer development. As such, A-Suppliers had and still have full control over the implemented functionality. On the one hand, they considered standard specific requirements for the design of the technology. On the other hand, the technological restrictions influenced the representation of the standard script within the process library.

The Types of Metastructuring Activities

At A-Suppliers, the PG accomplishes the metastructuring activities to cope with the multiplicity and plurality of standards. Nevertheless, the process of metastructuring itself is not fully separated from the activities of the software engineers. A-Suppliers set up an integrated and participative environment where structuring in respect of the different standards is executed by different roles, both in the PG as well as in the software development department. Whereas a process coach (PC) works in the PG, the process representatives (PR) are based directly in the operational department, acting as standard-use mediators.

In Table 2 we summarized the different mediation activities related to four different roles - *process representative, process coach, script editor and process library consultant* – categorized along the four types of metastructuring activities: *establishment, reinforcement, adjustment* and *episodic change* (Orlikowski et al., 1995). At A-Suppliers, a significant part of the responsibility over standard structuring still remains with the operational departments. Furthermore, the *script editor* can be seen as a proof for this approach: the recently installed role fulfills the tasks of a standard script mediator. She/he streamlines the process descriptions of the different authors. Literally everybody at A-Suppliers can describe, maintain or give feedback on the processes. Hence, the process library is considered as a mass media within A-Suppliers which needs to be read and understood by every employee. The script editor can be regarded as a consequence of the integrative approach towards processes. Everybody participates but the uncontrolled growth needs to be harmonized professionally afterwards. The script editor is another example for the step-by-step development of an entire mediator department that reflects the complexity of the standard environment of A-Suppliers.

DISCUSSION

Our findings show that the powerful mechanism of metastructuring, originally described in technology research, exists for software development and process standards in the same way. A-Suppliers is an example for the contextualization of standards in use and provides insights in dealing with multiple and plural standard requirements in organizations. We term this specific type of metastructuring *standard metastructuring* since it structures users of standards "by influencing their interpretations and interactions, by changing their institutional context of use and by modifying the [standard] itself" (Orlikowski et al., 1995, p. 425). We verified that standard metastructuring is an explicit, to a large degree conscious and ongoing set of activities and a powerful mechanism in dynamic environments of software development organizations.

Table 2. Metastructuring Activities of the Different Mediatior Roles along the Phases of the Metastructuring Process

	Process Coach (PC)	Process Representative (PR)	Script Editor (SE)	Process Library Consultant (PLC)
Establishment	• set up standard pilot project (e.g. CMMI) • defining their own role as PC • set up process infrastructure • interpretation of each standard • creation of the standard script • creation of the process library	• creation of the standard script • defining the operational processes		creation of the process library
Reinforcement	• lean and user- friendly process descriptions • maintenance of the standard script • maintenance of the process library • training for standard- related tasks	• maintenance of the standard script • collect, produce and treat user feedback • process training for owned processes	• lean and user-friendly process descriptions • maintenance of the standard script	maintenance of the process library
Adjustment	• changing the interpretation of each standard • smaller changes to the process library	changing the operational processes		smaller changes to the process library
Episodic Change	• expanding responsibilities (more standards & sub-units to serve) • significant changes to the process library			significant changes to the process library

Roles and Organizational Sub-Units in Standard Metastructuring

Looking at the process, areas and activity types, metastructuring of the standard script is considered as a very complex task for which standard mediators as experts have to be appointed and trained. The process group (PG), process consultants (PCs), process representatives (PRs) and the script editor (SE) act as standard mediators, or what Adler (2005, p. 417) calls shepherds. On this, we agree with Brunsson (2000a) and Tamm Hallström (2000) that "many of the actors in the area of quality are so-called intermediaries; they pass the standard on to users" (Tamm Hallström, 2000, p. 91). However, some of these intermediaries can be users as well: the PRs. The standard mediators now solve tasks which were formerly in the hands of each software engineer: assessment of new or changed standards, interpretation of standards, definition of processes, training on processes, preparation and execution of standard appraisals or handling the feedback for each standard. The role of the standard mediator is comparable to the role of the technology mediator since they serve as (1) an organizational mechanism (2) to facilitate the adaptation of technologies/the interpretation of standards (3) and the organizational context (4) ongoing and to changing conditions (Orlikowski, 1995).

When Orlikowski et al. (1995) first presented their theory on metastructuring; they made general propositions about the specific characteristics of mediators towards the mediation process. Therefore, she called for further research on characteristics and differentiations of mediators. With our study, we show first evidence regarding the differentiation of specific metastructuring roles. In our case, the organization differentiated a rather user-centered role, the PR, a standard-driven role, the PC, a standard and technology-driven role, the SE and a technology-driven role, the PLC. The differentiation of roles depends on the scope and complexity of the mediation task. We analyzed two bifurcations: firstly, when more and more standards come into play complexity increases and the organization differentiates between user- and standard-centered roles; secondly, when the organization starts to develop a standard script based on a technology infrastructure, enhancement and maintenance of the script and technology become crucial for the enactment of standards. The organization appoints specific roles for these tasks, for instance a SE or specific technology consultants, the PLCs. The role of the script editor is designed to streamline the process descriptions of the different authors for the standard script. Several distinct employees right up to everybody can participate in describing, maintaining or at least in giving feedback on the standard script. However, it needs to be read and understood by every employee and the uncontrolled growth needs to be harmonized professionally afterwards.

In standard metastructuring, the user-centered role of the process representative (PR) needs further explanations. As stated by Fleck (1994), the configuration of technology is highly important for a successful implementation and use of the technology and thus demands substantial inclusion of the user. This counts for process standards likewise. Processes and their contexts are very much organization-specific and demand a sensible handling in situations of organizational change. This leads to the conclusion that user-centered metastructuring in the process standard context is of high importance and highly relevant for organizations. This renders the role of PRs as central for a standard metastructuring that respects the use-mode of standards.

While looking at standard mediators and the differentiation in roles and organizational sub-units, researchers of technology-use can also draw conclusions from the alignment research stream. Here, "the question of stability and change in role relationships" is investigated and therefore "the use of a technology might alter or confirm an existing social order" (Leonardi and Barley, 2010, p. 25). Alignment to new standards leads to the creation of new roles and new organizational sub-units. First there were experienced users who enacted an implicit structuring process. The transition from implicit to explicit structuring was accomplished when these users were selected to exercise the new role as standard-mediators. This argumentation is supported by the findings of Yates et al. (1999) on implicit and explicit structuring of mediators for an electronic communication media.

The Process of Standard Metastructuring

Technology mediators "create policies, procedures, guidelines, templates, access mechanisms, applications, and physical configurations which alter the technology itself" (Orlikowski et al., 1995, p. 437). In the context of standard metastructuring, the same mediating activities exist. During *Establishment,* standard mediators set up the process infrastructure and define the operational processes. They define their own role and they start interpreting each applicable standard. At this point, the mediators could also create the standard script and the process library. However, these two tasks could also be accomplished at a later stage of metastructuring as an *Episodic Change*. In *Reinforcement,* mediators improve process descriptions and maintain the standard script and the process library. They set up and undertake standard and process training and they collect and treat user feedback. The user feedback and smaller changes to the interpretation of standards and the process library lead to changes of these items during the *adjustment* phase. During the *episodic change,* mediators make significant changes to the standard script or the process library and they expand their responsibilities. They incorporate either new standards to structure or new organizational sub-units which would then start using their standard metastructuring service.

Differences between standard and technology metastructuring tasks originate from the very differences between the artifacts to structure and the practices that appear around these artifacts: between standards and information systems as the somewhat classical artifacts of technology structuring. In organizational practice, organizations often have to consider several standards (Djelic and den Hond, 2014). For various reasons, some of these standards and its requirements overlap each other, yet they are to be considered likewise in the standard script. In technology structuring, there is no such thing as a standard script. Further, organizations avoid enacting several technologies for the same task. Hence, chances are rare to integrate several technologies into a single, central one. Consequently, the differences between standard and technology metastructuring concern the tasks around the creation and maintenance of the standard script and, during e*pisodic change,* the task of expanding responsibilities to incorporate more standards in the metastructuring activities.

Orlikowski et al. (1995, p. 437ff) described the process of metastructuring after the *establishment* phase as periodic changes from *reinforcement* and *adjustment* to *episodic change.* In standard metastructuring, we find the same steps of periodic changes. Orlikowski (1996) and Leonardi (2007) described these steps as "a phased sequence of emergent and cumulative changes" (Leonardi and Barley, 2010, p. 28). Standard metastructuring develops from implicit structuring, to explicit structuring with ongoing and further differentiating roles and own organizational structures like differentiated groups or departments.

Standard Script and Process Library

For the process of standard metastructuring, the artifacts of standard script and process library play a significant role. With the standard script, we emphasize that standards have to be encoded in the organizational practices to be effective. Following Barley and Tolbert (1997) and Gioia and Poole (1984) on scripts we can describe standard scripts as 'realized standards' that are and have to be encoded and enacted in the organization's stock of knowledge and practices. In the case of multiple standards, organizations enact a single standard script that fits all the standards that are to be followed by the organization. The more standards the organization follows, the more complex the enactment of the standard script becomes. In that situation, organizations revert to sophisticated tools that organize the different standards requirements and its references in the standard script. We call these tools a process library. Once a process library is implemented, the organizational members access the documentation of the standard script only through the process library interface. For them, the process library represents the standard script and the both are irrevocably entangled.

When looking deeper into the practices that emerge around the process library and the standard script, researchers could draw further insights from research on *boundary objects* (Carlile, 2002; Levina and Vaast, 2005; Star and Griesemer, 1989; Star, 2010). We consider the process library or the standard script as a boundary object that resides between social worlds (e.g. standard world, engineering world, world of HR), where the tool has different meanings (standard world: to integrate different standards and to design the standard script; engineering world: to create and derive engineering processes, world of HR: to plan and execute professional training) (Star and Griesemer, 1989). The standard mediators could be analyzed as boundary-spanners-in-practice (Levina and Vaast, 2005) whose task is to process and transform knowledge (Carlile, 2002).

Standard Metastructuring and Standardization Research

Brunsson (2000a), Tamm Hallström (2000) as well as Timmermans and Epstein (2010) argued about the relation between *designer* and *user* of a standard. They concluded that there is a sharp distinction between both: "Standards are presumed to be in the public interest, but the public to whom standards apply is usually not directly represented in standard creation" (Timmermans and Epstein, 2010, p. 77). Whereas this might be true for specific types of standards, we have to differentiate in the case of process or product standards that apply to organizations. In our study, the organization engages in the process of standard setting via participation in standard setting bodies. Further, the organizational users of the standard engage in the internal standard setting process via feedback options and via different roles that structure the internal use of standard by setting the organizational standard script. "The trick in standardization appears to be to find a balance between flexibility and rigidity and to trust users with the right amount of agency to keep a standard sufficiently uniform for the task at hand" (Timmermans and Epstein, 2010, p. 81). This raises the question of how much "distance in time and space" (Brunsson, 2000a, p. 27) we actually speak when it comes to design and use of a standard, especially when dealing with procedural standards (Timmermans and Epstein, 2010, p. 72). In the area of technology structuring, Orlikowski (1992, p. 407) speaks about the interpretive flexibility of technology. This flexibility refers to the engagement of users of a technology in its constitution. With an increasing distance in time and space, "the likelihood that the technology will be interpreted and used with little flexibility [...]" (Orlikowski, 1992, p. 421) also increases. This phenomenon occurs for technology as well as for standards.

With our research on the micro level of standardization, we start to counter the fact that "studies of standardization have neglected the crucial role of technical experts on the receiving end of standards" (Sandholtz, 2012, p. 670). Sandholtz (2012) described two different cases of decoupling (malignant and benign) while implementing the ISO 9000 standard. Further, Fried et al. (2013) analyzed organizations that temporarily loosely couple or decouple their innovating activities from the reigning standard script to avoid disturbing their innovating activities. As highlighted in this research, organizations could refer to standard metastructuring to avoid disturbances at the receiving end of standards. We regard process consultants, process representatives, script editors and process library consultants as the "group of internal experts to standardize their own work processes in a manner consistent with external certification demands" (Sandholtz, 2012, p. 676).

However, whether a standard is experienced as coercive or enabling by its users depends not only on decoupling approaches or standard metastructuring. Various contextual factors should be taken into account: management commitment (Adler et al., 2005a; Boiral, 2003), staff participation (Adler et al., 2005a; Allison and Merali, 2005; Boiral, 2003; Lavellée and Robillard, 2012; Sandholtz, 2012), culture (Braa and Hedberg, 2002; Müller et al., 2010; Ngwenyama and Nielsen, 2003) or the appropriation of standards (Gey, 2011). For the latter, standardization research could benefit tremendously from contemporary technology studies on appropriation (Leonardi et al., 2016, Quinones et al., 2013, You et al., 2015).

CONCLUSION

In this contribution, we examined how software development organizations deal with the multiplicity and plurality of standards. We used a social constructivist viewpoint of technology use in organizations and focused on the use-mode of standards (Orlikowski, 1992). We found that metastructuring is an important mechanism for organizations to handle complexity arising from the use of multiple process standards. Relating to Orlikowski et al. (1995) on technologies, we called it *standard* metastructuring since it has a considerable influence on how users perceive, interpret and apply these standards. We used the concept of technology structuring and applied it to standards as the artifacts to structure. The results show that the structuring of standards has a lot in common with the structuring of technologies, even though they are not technologies themselves. Additionally, because of the increased number of standards to handle, the organization developed a process library. This software solution consists of all standards embodied in the standard script as well as options to access information, to define processes and to give feedback on processes.

We understand this exploratory study as a starting point for a more systematic examination on standard metastructuring and the process of metastructuring. We tried to adopt the metastructuring concept from the technology world for the world of standards. Therefore, it was necessary to discuss the differences between standards and technology as well as the resulting differences for the metastructuring concept. We further enhanced the metastructuring concept by a proposition towards different types of metastructuring activities. We assume that the more complex the standard landscape an organization is confronted with, the more likely is the differentiation in several mediator roles.

The scope of this study is limited and calls for further research. For instance, more in-depth research is needed regarding the specific activities of standard metastructuring. We suggest further investigation of different types of metastructuring and their coercive and enabling character. This might involve ambiguities of the different standards while asking how these ambiguities are resolved during the metastructuring process. Empirical studies could also show to what extent standard-use mediation varies with the type of standard and individuals involved.

Most prominently, there is the question of how much "*distance in time and space*" (Brunsson, 2000a, p. 27) should be taken into consideration when it comes to the design and use of a standard. Prospective studies could explore the mentioned distance in time, space and other categories, e.g. social distance. Researchers in the area of standardization should always keep in mind that "*differences between presentation and practice, between formal structures and actual operations, and between what people say and what they do*" (Brunsson and Jacobsson, 2000b, p. 130) can be encountered.

In summary, a well-managed process of standard metastructuring represents a relevant factor for organizations introducing and using new process standards as a response to changing market requirements or to an increased focus on process quality and process maturity of organizations. However, the process does not automatically result in a successful outcome, which calls for a comprehensive and careful implementation and continuous adaption to a changing environment.

REFERENCES

Adler, P. (2005). The evolving object of software development. *Organization, 12*(3), 401–435. doi:10.1177/1350508405051277

Adler, P. S., McGarry, F. E., Irion-Talbot, W. B., & Binney, D. J. (2005a). Enabling process discipline: Lessons from the journey to CMM Level 5. *MIS Quarterly Executive, 4*(1), 215–227.

Allison, I., & Merali, Y. (2007). Software process improvement as emergent change: A structurational analysis. *Information and Software Technology, 49*(6), 668–681. doi:10.1016/j.infsof.2007.02.003

Bansler, J., & Havn, E. (2004). Technology-use mediation. Making sense of electronic communication in an organizational context. *Scandinavian Journal of Information Systems, 16*, 57–84.

Barley, S. (1986). Technology as an occasion for structuring: Evidence from observations of ct scanners and the social order of radiology departments. *Administrative Science Quarterly, 31*(1), 78–108. doi:10.2307/2392767 PMID:10281188

Barley, S., & Tolbert, P. (1997). Institutionalization and structuration: Studying the links between action and institution. *Organization Studies, 18*(1), 93–117. doi:10.1177/017084069701800106

Blind, K., & Mangelsdorf, A. (2016). Motives to standardize: Empirical evidence from Germany. *Technovation, 48-49*(1), 13–24. doi:10.1016/j.technovation.2016.01.001

Boiral, O. (2003). ISO 9000: Outside the iron cage. *Organization Science, 14*(6), 720–737. doi:10.1287/orsc.14.6.720.24873

Braa, J., & Hedberg, C. (2002). The Struggle for District-Based Health Information Systems in South Africa. *The Information Society, 18*(2), 113–127. doi:10.1080/01972240290075048

Brunsson, N. (2000a). Organizations, Markets, and Standardization. In N. Brunsson & B. Jacobsson (Eds.), *A World of Standards* (pp. 21–40). Oxford, UK: Oxford University Press.

Brunsson, N. (2000b). Standardization and uniformity. In N. Brunsson & B. Jacobsson (Eds.), *A World of Standards* (pp. 138–151). Oxford, UK: Oxford University Press.

Brunsson, N., & Jacobsson, B. (2000c). The contemporary expansion of standardization. In N. Brunsson & B. Jacobsson (Eds.), *A World of Standards* (pp. 1–19). Oxford, UK: Oxford University Press.

Brunsson, N., & Jacobsson, B. (2000c). *A World of Standards*. Oxford, UK: Oxford University Press.

Brunsson, N., & Jacobsson, B. (2000d). Following standards. In N. Brunsson & B. Jacobsson (Eds.), *A World of Standards* (pp. 127–138). Oxford, UK: Oxford University Press.

Brunsson, N., Rasche, A., & Seidl, D. (2012). The dynamics of standardization: Three perspectives on standards in organization studies. *Organization Studies, 33*(5-6), 613–632. doi:10.1177/0170840612450120

Brunswicker, S.; Rodriguez, J. A. & Wareham, J. D. (2015). Governing Standardization through Formal and Informal Standard Development Organizations. *Academy of Management Proceedings 2015*.

Carlile, P. R. (2002). A Pragmatic View of Knowledge and Boundaries: Boundary Objects in New Product Development. *Organization Science, 13*(4), 442–455. doi:10.1287/orsc.13.4.442.2953

Clear, T., & MacDonell, S. G. (2011). Understanding technology use in global virtual teams: Research methodologies and methods. *Information and Software Technology, 53*(9), 994–1011. doi:10.1016/j.infsof.2011.01.011

Davidson, E., & Chiasson, M. (2005). Contextual influences on technology use mediation: A comparative analysis of electronic medical record systems. *European Journal of Information Systems, 14*(1), 6–18. doi:10.1057/palgrave.ejis.3000518

Davidson, E., & Chismar, W. (2007). The interaction of institutionally triggered and technology-triggered social structure change: An investigation of computerized physician order entry. *Management Information Systems Quarterly, 31*(4), 739–758.

DeSanctis, G., & Poole, M. S. (1994). Capturing the complexity in advanced technology use: Adaptive structuration theory. *Organization Science, 5*(2), 121–147. doi:10.1287/orsc.5.2.121

Djelic, M. L., & den Hond, F. (2014). Introduction: Multiplicity and plurality in the world of standards. *Business and Politics, 16*(1), 67–77. doi:10.1515/bap-2013-0034

Egyedi, T. M. (2008). An implementation perspective on sources of incompatibility and standards' dynamics. In T. M. Egyedi & K. Blind (Eds.), *The Dynamics of Standards* (pp. 28–43). Cheltenham, UK: Edward Elgar.

Fleck, J. (1994). Learning by trying: The implementation of configurational technology. *Research Policy, 23*(6), 637–652. doi:10.1016/0048-7333(94)90014-0

Fried, A. (2010). Performance measurement systems and their relation to strategic learning: A case study in a software-developing organization. *Critical Perspectives on Accounting, 21*(2), 118–133. doi:10.1016/j.cpa.2009.08.007

Fried, A., Gey, R., Pretorius, A., & Günther, L. (2013). Decoupling from standards - process management and technical innovation in software development organisations. *International Journal of Innovation Management, 17*(4), 1–34. doi:10.1142/S1363919613500126

Furusten, S. (2000). The knowledge base of standards. In N. Brunsson & B. Jacobsson (Eds.), *A World of Standards* (pp. 71–85). Oxford, UK: Oxford University Press.

Gey, R. (2011). Appropriation of Software Process Improvement Standards: An Empirical Study in Software Development Organizations. *Proceedings of the 8th International Conference on Intellectual Capital, Knowledge Management & Organisational Learning*, 182–189.

Giddens, A. (1984). *The constitution of society: Outline of the theory of structuration*. Cambridge, UK: Polity Press.

Gioia, D., & Poole, P. (1984). Scripts in organizational behavior. *Academy of Management Review, 9*(3), 449–459.

Henriksen, D., Nicolajsen, H., & Pors, J. (2002). Towards variation or uniformity? Comparing technology-use mediations of web-based groupware. *Proceedings of the European Conference on Information Systems 2002*, 1174–1184.

Humphrey, W. (1992). Introduction to software process improvement. Technical report, Software Engineering Institute, Carnegie-Mellon University.

Jakobs, K. (2006). Shaping user-side innovation through standardisation: The example of ICT. *Technological Forecasting and Social Change, 73*(1), 27–40. doi:10.1016/j.techfore.2005.06.007

Janneck, M., & Finck, M. (2006). Appropriation and mediation of technology use in stable self-organised online communities. *Web Based Communities, Proceedings of IADIS International Conference*, 149–156.

Kohlbacher, F. (2006). The use of qualitative content analysis in case study research. *Forum Qualitative Social Research*, *7*(1).

Krippendorff, K. (2004). *Content analysis: An introduction to its methodology*. Thousand Oaks, CA: Sage Publications.

Lavallée, M., & Robillard, P. N. (2012). The impacts of software process improvement on developers: a systematic review. *Proceedings of the 2012 International Conference on Software Engineering*, 113-122. 10.1109/ICSE.2012.6227201

Lawrence, T., & Phillips, N. (1998). Commentary: Separating play and critique. *Journal of Management Inquiry*, *7*(2), 154–160. doi:10.1177/105649269872010

Leonardi, P. (2007). Activating the informational capabilities of information technology for organizational change. *Organization Science*, *18*(5), 813–831. doi:10.1287/orsc.1070.0284

Leonardi, P., & Barley, S. (2010). What's under construction here? Social action, materiality, and power in constructivist studies of technology and organizing. *The Academy of Management Annals*, *4*(1), 1–51. doi:10.1080/19416521003654160

Leonardi, P. M., Bailey, D. E., Diniz, E. H., Sholler, D., & Nardi, B. (2016). Multiplex Appropriation in Complex Systems Implementation: The Case of Brazil's Correspondent Banking System. *Management Information Systems Quarterly*, *40*(2), 461–473. doi:10.25300/MISQ/2016/40.2.10

Levina, N., & Vaast, E. (2005). The Emergence of Boundary Spanning Competence in Practice: Implications for Implementation and Use of Information Systems. *Management Information Systems Quarterly*, *29*(2), 335–363.

Marimon, F., Heras, I., & Casadesús, M. (2009). ISO 9000 and ISO 14000 standards: A projection model for the decline phase. *Total Quality Management*, *20*(1), 1–21. doi:10.1080/14783360802614257

Muhr, T. (1991). Atlas/ti - a prototype for the support of text interpretation. *Qualitative Sociology*, *14*(4), 349–371. doi:10.1007/BF00989645

Müller, S. D., Mathiassen, L., & Balshøj, H. H. (2010). Software Process Improvement as organizational change: A metaphorical analysis of the literature. *Journal of Systems and Software*, *83*(11), 2128–2146. doi:10.1016/j.jss.2010.06.017

Ngwenyama, O., & Nielsen, P. A. (2003). Competing values in software process improvement: An assumption analysis of CMM from an organizational culture perspective. *IEEE Transactions on Engineering Management*, *50*(1), 100–112. doi:10.1109/TEM.2002.808267

Niazi, M., Wilson, D., & Zowghi, D. (2005). A maturity model for the implementation of software process improvement: An empirical study. *Journal of Systems and Software*, *74*(2), 155–172. doi:10.1016/j.jss.2003.10.017

Novak, L., Brooks, J., Gadd, C., Anders, S., & Lorenzi, N. (2012a). Mediating the intersections of organizational routines during the introduction of a health IT system. *European Journal of Information Systems*, *21*(5), 552–569. doi:10.1057/ejis.2012.2 PMID:24357898

Novak, L. L., Anders, S., Gadd, C. S., & Lorenzi, N. M. (2012). Mediation of adoption and use: A key strategy for mitigating unintended consequences of health IT implementation. *Journal of the American Medical Informatics Association*, *19*(6), 1043–1049. doi:10.1136/amiajnl-2011-000575 PMID:22634157

Okamura, K., Orlikowski, W., Fujimoto, M., & Yates, J. (1994). Helping CSCW applications succeed: the role of mediators in the context of use. *Proceedings of the 1994 ACM conference on computer supported cooperative work*, 55-65. 10.1145/192844.192871

Orlikowski, W. (1992). The duality of technology: Rethinking the concept of technology in organizations. *Organization Science*, *3*(3), 398–427. doi:10.1287/orsc.3.3.398

Orlikowski, W. (1996). Improvising organizational transformation over time: A situated change perspective. *Information Systems Research*, *7*(1), 63–92. doi:10.1287/isre.7.1.63

Orlikowski, W., Yates, J., Okamura, K., & Fujimoto, M. (1995). Shaping electronic communication: The metastructuring of technology in the context of use. *Organization Science*, *6*(4), 423–444. doi:10.1287/orsc.6.4.423

Ortmann, G. (2010). On drifting rules and standards. *Scandinavian Journal of Management*, *26*(2), 204–214. doi:10.1016/j.scaman.2010.02.004

Power, M. (1997). *The audit society: rituals of verification*. Oxford, UK: Oxford University Press.

Quinones, P.-A., Teasley, S. D., & Lonn, S. (2013). Appropriation by unanticipated users: looking beyond design intent and expected use. *Proceedings of the 2013 conference on computer supported cooperative work*, 1515-1526. 10.1145/2441776.2441949

Rodon, J., Sese, F., & Christiaanse, E. (2011). Exploring users' appropriation and post-implementation managerial intervention in the context of industry IOIS. *Information Systems Journal*, *21*(3), 223–248. doi:10.1111/j.1365-2575.2009.00339.x

Sandholtz, K. W. (2012). Making standards stick: A theory of coupled vs. decoupled compliance. *Organization Studies*, *33*(5-6), 655–679. doi:10.1177/0170840612443623

Seidl, D. (2007). Standard setting and following in corporate governance: An observation-theoretical study of the effectiveness of governance codes. *Organization*, *14*(5), 705–727. doi:10.1177/1350508407080316

Seo, D. B.DongBack. (2013). Analysis of Various Structures of Standards Setting Organizations (SSOs) that Impact Tension among Members. *International Journal of IT Standards and Standardization Research*, *11*(2), 46–60. doi:10.4018/jitsr.2013070104

Software Engineering Institute (SEI). (2012). *Change Requests*. Retrieved January 15, 2017 from http://www.sei.cmu.edu/cmmi/solutions/crs/index.cfm

Star, S. L. (2010). This is not a boundary object: Reflections on the origin of a concept. *Science, Technology & Human Values*, *35*(5), 601–617. doi:10.1177/0162243910377624

Star, S. L., & Griesemer, J. R. (1989). Institutional Ecology, 'Translations' and Boundary Objects: Amateurs and Professionals in Berkeley's Museum of Vertebrate Zoology. *Social Studies of Science, 19*(3), 387–420. doi:10.1177/030631289019003001

Tamm Hallström, K. (2000). Organizing the process of standardization. In N. Brunsson & B. Jacobsson (Eds.), *A World of Standards* (pp. 85–100). Oxford, UK: Oxford University Press.

Tamm Hallström, K. (2004). *Organizing international standardization. ISO and the IASC in quest of authority*. Cheltenham, UK: Edward Elgar.

Timmermans, S., & Epstein, S. (2010). A World of Standards but not a Standard World: Toward a Sociology of Standards and Standardization. *Annual Review of Sociology, 36*(1), 69–89. doi:10.1146/annurev.soc.012809.102629

Weick, K. (1990). Technology as equivoque: sensemaking in new technologies. In P. S. Goodman & L. S. Sproull (Eds.), *Technology and Organizations* (pp. 1–44). San Francisco, CA: Jossey-Bass.

Weick, K. E. (1976). Educational organizations as loosely coupled systems. *Administrative Science Quarterly, 21*(1), 1–19. doi:10.2307/2391875

Wiegmann, P. M., de Vries, H. J., & Blind, K. (2017). Multi-mode standardisation: A critical review and a research agenda. *Research Policy, 46*(8), 1370–1386. doi:10.1016/j.respol.2017.06.002

Wieland, J. (2005). Corporate governance, values management and standards: A European perspective. *Business & Society, 44*(1), 74–93. doi:10.1177/0007650305274852

Yates, J., Orlikowski, W., & Okamura, K. (1999). Explicit and implicit structuring of genres in electronic communication: Reinforcement and change of social interaction. *Organization Science, 10*(1), 83–103. doi:10.1287/orsc.10.1.83

Yin, R. K. (2003). *Case Study Research*. Thousand Oaks, CA: Sage Publications.

You, S., Robert, L. P. Jr, & Rieh, S. Y. (2015). The Appropriation Paradox: Benefits and Burdens of Appropriating Collaboration Technologies. *Proceedings of the 33rd Annual ACM Conference Extended Abstracts on Human Factors in Computing Systems*, 1741-1746. 10.1145/2702613.2732919

Zeng, S., Shi, J., & Lou, G. (2007). A synergetic model for implementing an integrated management system: An empirical study in China. *Journal of Cleaner Production, 15*(18), 1760–1767. doi:10.1016/j.jclepro.2006.03.007

ENDNOTE

[1]   For a collection of reference models for process improvement, see Humphrey (1992).

Section 4
Utilization and Applications

Chapter 64
Social Capital and Knowledge Networks of Software Developers:
A Case Study

VenuGopal Balijepally
Oakland University, Rochester, USA

Sridhar Nerur
University of Texas at Arlington, Arlington, USA

ABSTRACT

Software development is a problem-solving activity, where ideas are combined in complex ways to create a software product that embodies new knowledge. In this endeavor, software developers constantly look for actionable knowledge to help solve the problem at hand. While knowledge management efforts in the software development domain traditionally involved technical initiatives such as knowledge repositories, experience factories, and lessons-to-learn databases, there is a growing appreciation in the software community of the role of developers' personal knowledge networks in software development. However, research is scarce on the nature of these networks, the knowledge resources accessed from these networks, and the differences, if any, between developers of different experience levels. This research seeks to fill this void. Based on a case study in a software development organization, this research explores the nature of knowledge networks of developers from a social capital perspective. Specifically, it examines the structural and relational dimensions of developers' knowledge networks, identifies the specific actionable knowledge resources accessed from these networks, and explores how entry-level and more experienced developers differ along these dimensions. The findings from the qualitative analysis, backed by limited quantitative analysis of the case study data underpin the discussion, implications for practice and future research directions.

DOI: 10.4018/978-1-6684-3702-5.ch064

INTRODUCTION

The software development field has experienced unprecedented growth in the last over a decade. The imperative for business agility as well as rapid advances in technology have shortened product lifecycle times across organizations (Baskerville & Pries-Heje, 2004). Software development, once believed to be the exclusive preserve of computer programmers, who worked in relative isolation, is increasingly becoming a socio-technical endeavor (Doherty & King, 2005; Luna-Reyes et al., 2005), characterized by extensive collaboration and knowledge sharing. This is particularly manifest in agile development methodologies that emphasize collaborative development through self-organizing teams (Beck & Andres, 2005; Boehm & Turner, 2005; Cockburn, 2000; Batra et al., 2011; Erickson et al., 2005). Members of such teams have to be versatile, capable of working on all aspects of software development and playing roles outside their functional expertise. As Ambler (2004) points out, agile developers have to be "generalizing specialists". The perceptible shift towards lean principles (i.e., eliminating waste, building quality into the process, creating knowledge, quickly delivering value, etc.), as articulated by Poppendieck and Poppendieck (2006), increasingly requires developers to have an expanded skill-set that balances soft and hard skills (Gallagher et al., 2010). In short, the imperative to deliver value in ever-decreasing cycle times compels developers to actively seek information and actionable knowledge during the software development process.

Software development is an inherently complex process that is fraught with uncertainties, both in terms of volatile requirements and technological intricacies (Assimakopoulos & Yan, 2006; Nerur & Balijepally, 2007). Knowledge plays a critical role in mitigating the ambiguity of this process and arriving at an acceptable solution. In this knowledge creation endeavor (Aurum et al., 2003; Bjørnson & Dingsøyr, 2008), software developers are constantly looking for help, in terms of actionable knowledge, to wrap their heads around the problem at hand. It is not uncommon for software developers to scour the Internet—blogs, technical forums and list serves, among others—to acquire problem-specific knowledge (Assimakopoulos & Yan, 2006). Knowledge management (KM) systems, where available, could serve as valuable sources of information relating to business processes, or the technology domain. Appreciating the criticality of knowledge exchange in software development, organizations have been undertaking KM initiatives (e.g., Basili et al., 1994; Desouza et al., 2006; Dingsøyr, 2005; Komi-Sirvio et al., 2002; Rus & Lindvall, 2002).

Despite the proliferation of KM systems and knowledge depositories in IT organizations, there is evidence to suggest that software developers rely to a greater extent on their personal contacts for actionable knowledge and tips (Newell, 2004). For most problems, especially those that embody tacit knowledge, interacting with peers at a personal level appears to be a viable option because it entails less personal cost to developers, relative to other avenues (Desouza, 2003a). Therefore, software developers do look beyond impersonal sources such as the Internet or knowledge repositories for help. Clearly, this is not consistent with the stereotypical perception of software developers as nerds who relish and excel on their one-on-one dealings with computers, rather than being adept at social interactions with people (Fitz-Enz, 1978). In this regard, there is some evidence of research interest in the knowledge networks of software developers (e.g. (Assimakopoulos & Yan, 2006; Aurum et al., 2008; Desouza, 2003; Méndez-Durón & García, 2009). Also, there is some research to understand the differences in the knowledge seeking behaviors of developers of varying experience levels (e.g. Desouza et al., 2006; Walz et al., 1993). However, IS research on the knowledge networks of software developers is still in its infancy.

Some of the findings in management literature relating to the actionable knowledge afforded by social capital to individuals in organizations is based on study of knowledge workers in consulting teams (Cross & Sproull, 2004). We believe, unlike other types of knowledge workers, software developers may need to access actionable knowledge much more expeditiously, due to some unique characteristics of software development task. For instance, developers in agile teams are expected to analyze requirements, code and release working software regularly which requires collaborating on a continuous basis with the end users/product owners (Batra et al., 2011). Practices such as daily stand-up meetings, developer role rotation, quick prototyping all require that developers are able to access any actionable knowledge that they need at any stage of their daily work expeditiously to stay productive. So, developers certainly have a great incentive to seek such actionable knowledge in a highly efficient manner so as not to get bogged down. Knowledge ambiguity in software development tasks, that results from the specificity, complexity and tacitness of knowledge, could certainly be high due to the diverse forms of knowledge involved (e.g., domain knowledge, technical knowledge, project scheduling knowledge, etc.). Empirical research suggests that knowledge ambiguity adversely affects knowledge transfer (Simonin, 1999; Van Wijk et al., 2008). So, it is reasonable to expect some differences in knowledge seeking behaviors between software developers and other knowledge workers in organizations based on the nature of their work.

There is, as yet, no clear understanding of the personal networks of developers. Neither do we fathom the differences, if any, between the networks of developers of different experience levels. Some recent research suggests that developers rank personal experience as the most important source for their judgments concerning various aspects of software development. Peers, mentors/managers, trade journals and research papers are other sources they rely on in the decreasing order of their importance (Devanbu et al., 2018). With experience, it is reasonable to expect developers to accumulate topic knowledge (i.e., knowledge relating to the meaning of words or definitions from textbooks or dictionaries) and episodic knowledge (i.e., knowledge acquired from the previous use of or experiences with topic knowledge) (Robillard, 1999) that could help them better navigate novel situations in their daily activities. Therefore, it is reasonable to expect knowledge seeking behaviors of developers to change over time with experience. Comprehending the differences in the nature of personal networks and knowledge seeking behaviors of developers of different experience levels should help broaden our understanding of the knowledge requirements of different developer groups. Also, it may indirectly throw some light on how experience may shape developers' knowledge seeking behaviors. Such an understanding should help IT organizations to formulate more holistic KM initiatives that are better aligned with the knowledge needs of different developer groups, with positive implications for developer productivity and performance. Given the current hiatus in our understanding of this phenomenon, this research seeks to explore: A. the nature of knowledge relationships among software developers, and B. the actionable knowledge accruing from these relationships during software development. Specifically, we examine the following research questions:

1. What are the types of information contacts utilized by software developers during software development?
2. What is the nature of relationships between software developers and these information contacts?
3. What actionable knowledge do software developers seek from their information contacts?
4. How do entry-level and more experienced developers differ in terms of knowledge relationships and actionable knowledge sought from their information contacts?

To this end, we use structural and relational dimensions of social capital articulated by Nahapiet and Ghoshal (1998) to analyze the personal knowledge networks of software developers. In terms of theoretical contributions, this research extends the social capital theory to a new context (i.e., software development). Also, this research adapts Cross and Sproull's (2004) actionable knowledge dimensions to the software development domain and identifies the specific actionable knowledge dimensions relevant to developers in their daily work. In addition, this research extends the original framework by identifying additional actionable knowledge dimensions—affective resources (i.e., emotional support) and arbitration—valued by software developers. Finally, this research highlights developers' experience as an important explanatory factor in comprehending the differences in personal networks and knowledge seeking behaviors of software developers.

The rest of the paper is organized as follows. First, a brief description of the background literature is provided to highlight the gaps in extant research. Next, the research methodology is explained, along with the dimensions of social capital and actionable knowledge. Subsequently, findings of the study are presented, followed by discussion of implications, future research directions and conclusions. The next section provides a brief summary of extant literature on KM in software development.

KNOWLEDGE MANAGEMENT IN SOFTWARE DEVELOPMENT

Software development is a knowledge intensive activity involving "progressive crystallization of knowledge into a form that can be read and executed by a computer" (Robillard, 1999). Adding to the challenge, such knowledge is typically distributed across several dimensions—spatial (knowledge residing among people distributed across geographic locations), temporal (developers having to comprehend and complete jobs started earlier by others, especially in large products with high developer turnover), technological (developers needing to listen to the 'talk back' from the system, especially when using various tools during system development), and social (knowledge pooled from several people from multiple domains) (Ye et al., 2004).

Highlighting the centrality of knowledge in software development, Wohlin, Šmite, and Moe (2015) proposed a theory of software engineering that focuses on the intellectual capital (Subramaniam & Youndt, 2005) available to a software team. Intellectual capital of an organizational entity is an aggregation of its human capital (skills, capabilities, and knowledge embedded in humans), social capital (resources embedded within and accessed through network of relationships) and organizational capital (the institutionalized knowledge and experience embedded in software code, software documentation and documented work processes (Wohlin et al., 2015). According to Wohlin et al. (2015), when developing software, performance is a result of mobilizing and balancing the various intellectual capital components to help solve the software task at hand in line with an organizational objective (e.g., how well or how fast to be done). The performance outcome of the software development task is compared with the objective(s) to judge the level of its success.

Based on Polanyi (1966), knowledge involved in software development is both tacit (knowledge which cannot be easily articulated and is situated in practice) and explicit (knowledge that could be articulated and documented in books, manuals, databases, design documents etc.). Research, however, suggests that knowledge involved in software development is, to a great extent, tacit (Robillard, 1999). Implicit knowledge is another knowledge dimension articulated in the literature—knowledge that is believed to be tacit, but could be articulated and made explicit (Aurum et al., 2008). Another distinction made in the context of software development is between topic knowledge and episodic knowledge—topic knowledge (also called semantic knowledge) refers to the meaning of words or definitions from textbooks or dictionaries, while episodic knowledge is what one acquires from the previous use of or experiences with topic knowledge (Robillard, 1999). Results from a meta-analysis suggest that ambiguity of knowledge negatively affects its acquisition and transfer (VanWijk et al., 2008)—i.e., higher the tacitness, specificity and complexity of knowledge the more difficult it is to transfer. Also, size of the organization and its absorptive capacity are found to be positively associated with knowledge transfer within the organization, while age of the organization or the extent of its decentralized structure had no effect on knowledge transfer.

The concept of tacit knowledge has been extended to the group level with group (or team) tacit knowledge considered to be socially constructed through social interactions (i.e., socialization) (Erden et al., 2008). It is rooted in the complex web of individual relationships and activities and in the group culture, norms and routines. Ryan and O'Connor (2009) define team tacit knowledge as the aggregate of the tacit knowledge within the team that is articulable, with different members possessing different aspects of it. Erden et al. (2008) argue that group tacit knowledge is synergistic and greater than the aggregate of individual abilities giving the group the ability to deal with ongoing complexity, generate consensus around the best course of action for achieving desired outcomes and find the means for achieving them. Team tacit knowledge, which is acquired and shared through quality social interactions within the team, along with team transactive memory is known to be a predictor of the effectiveness of a software team (Ryan & O'Connor, 2009, 2013).

Hansen et al. (1999) suggest codification and personalization as two KM strategies for organizations. While codification entails capturing, storing and sharing knowledge with organizational members in a systematic manner, personalization strategy, also sometimes referred to as skills management (Dingsøyr & Røyrvik, 2001), involves storing the lists of knowledge resources and competencies in organization, as in "yellow pages". This is consistent with the notion that expertise coordination, which entails knowing where expertise is located, and bringing it to bear where it is needed, is a critical success factor for project team performance (Faraj & Sproull, 2000; Oshri et al., 2008).

Findings from a meta-analysis (VanWijk et al., 2008) in management domain suggest that the extent of knowledge transfer is positively associated with performance and innovation in organizations. Also, the level of similarity in the vision and systems between organizational units or organizations is found to facilitate knowledge transfer while cultural distance between them inhibited knowledge transfer. Extant research in software development domain suggests that receiving knowledge from other software developers in the organization provides performance benefits to software developers. The performance benefits are enhanced in the presence of high task autonomy and high-quality social exchanges between developers and their supervisors (Ozer & Vogel, 2015).

Realizing the importance of knowledge exchange and combination in software development, organizations have been undertaking KM initiatives, such as knowledge repositories (Rus & Lindvall, 2002), experience factories (Basili et al., 1994; Dingsøyr, 2005), lessons-to-learn databases, data transfer days (Komi-Sirvio et al., 2002), postmortem reviews (Birk et al., 2002; Dingsøyr, 2005), postmortem reports, and postmortem stories (Desouza et al., 2006). Use of conversational technologies such as discussion forums, weblogs and wikis are another option explored in organizations (Wagner & Bolloju, 2005). Petter et al. (2007) provide a useful comparison of ten knowledge tools used in software development based on five fundamental questions relating to knowledge sharing. Extent of IT use in software teams is known to affect knowledge exchange and knowledge combination (Mehta et al., 2014). In the software testing domain, facilitating reuse of knowledge embedded in test cases through automated support helps expedite software development and delivery (de Souza et al., 2015). More broadly, removing obstacles and facilitating project level knowledge flows is known to improve software development processes (Mitchell & Seaman, 2016). Software community is increasingly realizing that KM efforts should not just focus on explicit knowledge, but on tacit knowledge as well (Bjørnson & Dingsøyr, 2008).

Prior literature alludes to five different approaches to knowledge management in software development—system school (focuses on technological solutions to store knowledge as in knowledge repositories), cartographic school (focuses on locating knowledge sources through creating knowledge maps and knowledge directories), engineering school (focuses on knowledge flows and knowledge sharing processes in organizations—e.g., mentoring programs, project retrospectives, etc.), organizational school (focuses on instituting organizational networks for knowledge sharing as in communities of practice), and spatial school (focuses on workspace designs for enabling knowledge sharing as in open office plans, public taskboards and whiteboards that highlight current project status, etc.) (Earl, 2001).

Globally distributed software development projects might pose certain unique challenges to knowledge sharing due to temporal distances, geographical distances and socio-cultural distances (Ågerfalk & Fitzgerald, 2006). Dingsøyr and Smite (2014) evaluate the effectiveness of different knowledge management schools for globally distributed software teams. Based on their research, system school is considered to be quite effective in overcoming temporal and geographic distances involved in globally distributed teams and is not affected by socio-cultural distances involved therein. One challenge with system school is that knowledge repositories could become information graveyards with knowledge only stored without being retrieved unless data search is easy and user friendly. Also, it could be problematic for new projects due to the absence of prior collaboration history (Dingsøyr & Smite, 2014). Cartographic school is not quite popular in globally distributed teams due to the inherent difficulty involved in identifying and mapping knowledge resources. Intrinsic challenges in implementing standard processes and practices across locations makes engineering school a difficult option for globally distributed teams. Building communities of practice for sharing knowledge (organizational school) also becomes challenging in global teams as face-to-face interreactions become difficult due to the differences in time zones. While use of taskboards to communicate project status (spatial school) is quite popular among collocated software teams, this again would be quite challenging for global teams to adopt and implement (Dingsøyr & Smite, 2014).

Despite the proliferation of KM initiatives, literature suggests that there is a general lack of confidence among software development organizations concerning knowledge sharing and KM activities (Aurum et al., 2008; Ruggles, 1998). Interestingly, many case studies in organizations found only modest benefits to KM implementation initiatives, such as improvement in the work situation for software professionals, rather than more substantive benefits such as lower production costs or enhanced quality of software produced (Dingsøyr & Conradi, 2002). On an encouraging note, one study suggests that software developers start using knowledge repositories several years after their initial introduction (Dingsøyr, Bjørnson, & Shull, 2009).

There is a growing perception that technology-centered solutions may not be the primary approach to KM in software development (Kautz & Thaysen, 2001; Komi-Sirvio et al., 2002), as software developers turn more to informal relationships for knowledge sharing than to knowledge repositories (Newell, 2004). This is consistent with evidence from other knowledge domains. For instance, Robinson (2010) found that design engineers spent less time locating the human information sources and once found getting information from them than when searching from non-human sources. For consultants in IT services organizations, knowledge codifiability (i.e., the extent to which the knowledge could be encoded and documented) was found to have no effect on the choice of consultant's information seeking from either digital source or the human source. However, knowledge complexity negatively affected seeking information from digital sources but not from human sources. Also, when seeking information from human sources the consultants' behavior was driven by the expertise and accessibility of the sources. However, when seeking information from non-human sources (e.g., digital knowledge repositories) they were motivated by the amount of information available in the repository and whether other team members with whom they had close ties were using those digital sources (Su & Contractor, 2011). Thus, there may be efficiencies to be gained for knowledge workers when tapping human sources over non-human sources for information.

This signals a transition from first generation KM, where knowledge was considered a possession to be codified and disseminated through technological tools, to second generation KM, where knowledge is recognized as socially embedded in the communities of practice, to be harnessed through organic support structures (Buono & Poulfelt, 2005). As against a knowledge repository, which is a people-to-document initiative, a knowledge network involves a people-to-people effort (Bush & Tiwana, 2005). For software team members, awarareness of expertise location is critical to knowledge exchange. For instance, evidence suggests that awareness of expertise location mediates the relationship between team characteristics such as relationship commitment and relationship norms and knowledge contribution within the team (Chang et al., 2013).

Incidentally, there is a possibility for interaction between knowledge codification and. knowledge network approaches pursued in organizations. For instance, with increases in codification, knowledge sharing networks could experience some damage. Individuals may try to protect their networks by hoarding knowledge even in the presence of some non-trivial incentives available for codification (Liu et al., 2010). However, empirical evidence suggests that in settings where future knowledge sharing potential is considered high, pursuing a combination of the two approaches together is superior to pursuing either approach alone as the loss of some network ties (some of which could be mitigated with appropriate rewards) could be more than offset by increased benefits from codification. On the contrary, in settings where future knowledge sharing potential is considered low, increases in codification could impair existing knowledge sharing networks (Liu et al., 2010).

Informal networks serve as valuable sources of information for innovation in organizations (Assimako-poulos & Yan, 2006; Johannisson, 1998; Powell, 1998; Swan, et al., 1999). Informal communiction helps in the transmission of knowledge that is either tacit or is too 'contextually embedded' for transmission by other means (Patnayakuni et al., 2007). It helps in exchange of tacit knowledge without converting to explicit knowledge, through deep open-ended conversations (Alavi & Leidner, 2001), which Nonaka (1994) refers to as the socialization process of knowledge conversion. Though, building a good personal network may take some time and effort, it could still be an efficient option for developers when seeking information (Kautz & Kjærgaard, 2007). Research suggests that software developers' individual network building is positively influenced by project team's perception of its criticality for project success and the overall knowledge sharing climate in the organization (Hoegl et al., 2003; Méndez-Durón & García, 2009). In software projects, developers' having direct links with customers was found to positively correlate to project success, while indirect links through intermediaries or customer surrogates was found to be less desirable, due to information filtering and possible information distortion involved therein (Keil & Carmel, 1995).

Trust inherent in the relationships is an important factor that shapes the knowledge sharing intentions and behaviors in teams (Yang & Farn, 2009). For instance, Yuan, Zhang, Chen, Vogel, and Chu (2009) empirically demonstrate that in software developer dyads mutual trust mediates the positive effect of project commitment on knowledge sharing (both explicit and implicit knowledge), which in turn positively affects coordination effectiveness within the dyad. A distinction is sometimes made between two types of trust inherent in relationships, cognition-based trust vs. affect-based trust. Cognition-based trust results from individuals making a reasoned and informed choice on who to trust based on evidence of trustworthiness (Lewis & Weigert, 1985), while affect-based trust is based on emotional connections such as friendship, care or love (Lewis & Weigert, 1985; McAllister, 1995). Yang and Farn (2009) empirically demonstrate that affect-based trust in teams fosters knowledge sharing intentions while external behavior control (i.e., conditions external to the person that facilitate knowledge sharing behaviors) positively moderates the relationship between knowledge sharing intention and knowledge sharing behavior.

Xu, Kim, and Kankanhalli (2010) studied employee motivations for dyadic information seeking in organizations relating to two types of information - task information (i.e., technical problem solving information related to job task) and social information (i.e., relating to interpersonal relationships and social environment in the organization) and found that perceived information relevance was a significant antecedent of source preference for information seeking related to both task and social information, while perceived relational benefit (i.e., closer personal and work relationship expected with a source by way of information seeking) had a greater effect on source preference for social information seeking than on task information seeking.

One catergorization of knowledge sharing in teams is based on whether such knowledge sharing is driven by job requirements tied to organizational rewards (i.e., in-role) or goes beyond job requirements to be deemed proactive citizenship behavior (i.e., extra-role) (Organ, 1988). Some prior research explored how the personality characteristics of developers affected their knowledge sharing behvairos, both in-role and extra-role. Cui (2017) report that Openness to Experience of developers has a significant effect on their extra-role knowledge sharing but not on their in-role knowledge sharing. Also, Agreeableness of developers was found to have a significant effect on both in-role and extra-role knowledge sharing, while Extraversion was found to affect neither of them.

In general, face-to-face meetings are considered the best way to share knowledge, as software developers typically trust people in their vicinity over any experts or databases (Komi-Sirvio et al., 2002). For instance, informal settings (e.g., game rooms, where developers could play and interact) and emergent structures were found to be quite effective in fostering exchange of tacit knowledge (Desouza, 2003b). There is also an increasing realization that for effective knowledge sharing, the KM systems should not just point to the resources, but also facilitate dialog between individuals (Desouza, 2003a). Therefore, organizations are urged to consider facilitating both formal and informal mechanisms for knowledge sharing (Aurum et al., 2008).

Some research evidence suggests that the choice of team members seeking information sources internal to the team versus external to the team is dependent on team characteristics such as psychological safety (a shared belief within team members that the team is safe for interpersonal risk-taking (Edmondson, 1999)—i.e., team members in high psychological safety settings preferring internal sources while team members in low psychological safety settings preferring external sources (Safdar et al., 2017). The relationship between psychological safety and preference for internal information sources is positively moderated by team diversity—i.e., members in high psychological safety settings have a higher preference for internal information sources when team diversity is high than when it is low (Safdar et al., 2017).

Knowledge sharing involved in open source software (OSS) projects is another interesting area explored in prior IS research. For instance, in OSS projects knowledge received through inbound ties of its members and contributors is known to enhance project success, as also having members who actively contribute knowledge to other projects (Méndez-Durón & García, 2009). Based on social network analysis of communication patterns of Source Forge projects data, Long and Siau (2007) report that OSS projects evolve from a single hub (comprising core developers) at the beginning to a core-periphery structure where the core consists of a densely connected group of developers surrounded by a sparsely connected group of developers at the periphery. This implies that communication patterns and resultant network structures evolve over time in OSS projects as developers get a sense of the project complexities and the competencies and motivation/commitment of the members involved. In a related study involving Source Forge project data, Long and Siau (2008) found that network structure (e.g., degree of centralization) in OSS teams is signficantly associated with quantity of knowledge sharing but not with the quality of knowledge sharing.

In terms of KM behaviors, important differences have been reported between developers of different experience levels. Experienced developers understand that the initial system requirements are fuzzy as the users themselves do not understand the requirements all too well in the initial stages of systems development (Walz et al., 1993). In their problem-solving activities, they prefer seeking private knowledge (knowledge drawn from own personal experiences and events) over public knowledge (knowledge drawn from external sources and artifacts), mainly on efficiency considerations. They also prefer to create own solutions, when unable to find information from their private knowledge domain (Desouza et al., 2006). Rookie developers, on the other hand, expect clearer and more detailed system specifications from users (Walz et al., 1993). They are also more likely to dip into public knowledge sources, as they afford legitimation and reduce the risk of being questioned. This also mitigates their chance of missing any interdependencies of systems and procedures that are not directly apparent. On the downside, they risk getting overwhelmed by the information overload and, thereby, fail to pick the right information, or use it appropriately (Desouza et al., 2006).

The above summary of literature suggests that there is a growing appreciation of the importance of software developers' personal knowledge networks in software development. However, there is as yet no clear understanding of the nature of these networks, the kind of actionable knowledge sought from them by the developers, and the differences, if any, between networks of developers of different experience levels. The social capital perspective, which we discuss next, provides the framework to analyze the developers' knowledge networks and the actionable knowledge exchanged through these networks.

SOCIAL CAPITAL AND ACTIONABLE KNOWLEDGE

Social capital is "the sum of the actual and potential resources embedded within, available through, and derived from the network of relationships possessed by an individual or social unit" (Nahapiet & Ghoshal, 1998). Social capital theory conceives networks of relationships as another form of capital that could bestow important benefits to the individual or the group in social interactions. While human capital rests in the individuals, social capital is rooted in the network of contacts and relationships of the social entity—individual, group or organization (Bourdieu, 1986; Coleman, 1988; Putnam, 1993). The social capital construct captures both the network structure and the nature of resources available through the network (Seibert et al., 2001), which enhances its appeal.

Social capital may be viewed in terms of its three distinct dimensions identified in the literature: structural, relational and cognitive (Nahapiet & Ghoshal, 1998). Structural dimension refers to the pattern of connections between the various network contacts, while cognitive dimension refers to the resources that shape common interpretations and shared representations among people involved (e.g., rational arguments or even metaphors and myths). Relational dimension refers to the personal relationships such as friendship, respect and admiration developed over long periods of interaction, that help realize social objectives such as prestige, approval or sociability (Nahapiet & Ghoshal, 1998). Structural and cognitive dimensions of social capital could stimulate higher relational capital (e.g., trust and trustworthiness) over time (Tsai & Ghoshal, 1998). Paralleling these dimensions, Ye (2005) articulate structural, relational and cognitive proximities as the dimensions of knowledge collaboration in software development.

There are several benefits to social capital articulated in literature such as: access to broader sources of information; improved quality, relevance and timeliness of information accessed; enhanced power, influence, control and status for the individuals (Adler & Kwon, 2002); enhanced scope for entrepreneurship and innovation (Ibarra, 1993; Yli-Renko et al., 2001; Young et al., 2001) with positive externalities from individuals to the broader aggregate and vice-versa (Adler & Kwon, 2002); increased solidarity among the network actors to foster collective action (Leana & Van Buren, 1999); reduced need for formal controls due to strong norms and beliefs (Coleman, 1988); reduced opportunism and transaction costs due to enhanced trust (Putnam, 1993); and higher possibility for flexible work organization (Leana & Van Buren, 1999).

According to Baker and Dutton (2006), social capital is positive if it helps individuals to learn, grow and realize their goals in organizations in better and innovative ways. Such positive social capital results from adopting means that build generative capacity (ability to renew, expand and strengthen capabilities that help combine or configure resources in innovative ways) for the entities involved. They articulate two forms of positive social capital that are mutually reinforcing—high quality connections (HQC) and reciprocity. HQCs are dyadic connections (a connection could be short term in nature, unlike a relationship that has long term connotation) characterized by mutuality, vitality and positive regard (Dutton & Heaphy, 2003). HQCs are marked by higher emotional capacity, tensility (resilience to withstand setbacks and stress in the relationship), and higher capacity for connectivity (Baker & Dutton, 2006). HQCs facilitate heightened engagement (Kahn, 1990), attachment and commitment (Labianca et al., 2000), coordination (Gittell, 2003), positive emotions and learning (Fredrickson, 1998), growth (Baker & Dutton, 2006) and performance (Baker & Faulkner, 2004). Reciprocity, on the other hand, entails providing something of value to others without expecting anything in return immediately. Thus, some level of altruism, at least in the short term, is involved, though it may serve long term self-interest of the individual (Taylor, 1982).

While there are numerous benefits to social capital articulated in literature, a potential downside to social capital, particularly in closed networks, could stem from close ties promoting conformity and collective blindness, thereby stifling creativity and innovation (Coleman, 1988). There are also costs to maintaining the social capital networks in terms of time and effort expended. This calls for weighing the information benefits against maintenance costs to strike the right balance (Adler & Kwon, 2002; Leana & Van Buren, 1999).

In terms of actionable information resources tapped by knowledge works from network contacts, Berends (2005) and Cross and Sproull (2004) offer two useful frameworks for categorizing them. Based on two field studies in industrial research organizations Berends (2005) proposed a taxonomy of knowledge sharing moves in organizations and the effects of knowledge sharing. The proposed taxonomy of knowledge sharing moves includes five categories—descriptions, suggestions, evaluations, questions, and actions—while the taxonomy of effects of these knowledge sharing moves include three direct effects—contribution to a solution, change in the problem (i.e., problem reformulation) and activating individuals—and two indirect effects—development of background knowledge and development of knowledge about others. Based on a qualitative study in a Big Five Accounting firm, Cross and Sproull (2004) proposed a framework comprising of five types of actionable knowledge sought by knowledge workers in organizations from their information contacts—problem solutions, referrals, problem reformulation, validation and legitimation. In this study we draw on the social capital theory to explore the information relationships of developers and adapt Cross and Sproull's actionable knowledge framework, which we believe to be quite novel and insightful, to the software development domain to classify the knowledge resources sought by developers from their information relationships.

RESEARCH METHOD

This research employs a case study approach as case studies help study a phenomenon along with the contextual conditions surrounding it. They also afford the opportunity to undertake both qualitative and quantitative analysis of the phenomenon and the situational factors (Yin, 2001). Therefore, as a research strategy, case study approach helps understand the dynamics involved within single settings (Eisenhardt, 1989). A case study is well suited to our objective of exploring theoretical insights into the knowledge networks of software developers for the following reasons: First, our research questions are exploratory in nature and consist of both 'how' and 'what' questions. Second, even the 'what' questions are quite broad and fall into the exploratory category suggested by Yin (2001). Finally, we seek to generate theoretical insights for future hypotheses testing which plays into the strengths of case study approach. We use multiple-case design to collect and analyze qualitative data from interviews with developers. To supplement our qualitative analysis, we also conduct limited quantitative analysis (Bourgeois & Eisenhardt, 1988; Eisenhardt, 1989). For this, we collected some quantitative data from a survey questionnaire as well as coded some interview data into quantitative form.

Site selection

This research uses a single-site "multiple-case" design. The single-site design helps control for the impact of organizational factors, such as size, structure, and culture, as well as factors extraneous to the organization, such as competitive positioning and market forces. The study also involved two levels of analysis (Yin, 2001)—at the level of a software developer of a given experience level (entry-level/experienced) and at the level of a general software developer. XYZ Corp., a midsize full-service IT solutions provider based in the North-East United States, offered a practical setting to explore our research questions. XYZ Corp offers custom software solutions, IT infrastructure services, IT staffing services and call center/business process outsourcing (BPO) services to Fortune500 corporations, state government agencies and local non-profit organizations. As is typical for IT solutions providers in the United States, XYZ Corp, also has two offshore units based in India: an offshore development center to develop software and a BPO/call center to provide BPO services to its US based clients. This twenty-five-plus year old company is ISO 9001 certified in domestic and offshore software development and call-center services. We chose this organization to explore our research questions for multiple reasons. First, as a full-service IT solutions provider, it has a software development unit that develops software products for both internal and external customers. As is emblematic of software development organizations, it has an offshore development center (in India) that supports its US unit. Next, its software development unit was not only ISO 9001 certified and quite mature with twenty plus years of experience in delivering software services to organizations in varied industries, but also had a good mix of developers of different experience levels to complement our research effort. Last, but not the least, its management was quite willing to offer support for our research effort.

Case selection

We adopt a theoretical replication strategy to select our cases for the two conditions of interest in our study—entry level and more experienced developers. However, within each condition, we adopt a literal replication strategy when choosing multiple cases. The case organization provided us an initial list of ten developers who could participate in the study. To select subjects appropriate for our research questions, we conducted a survey of these developers, eliciting their personal demographic details, such as their experience, designation, role etc., and the details of a project they were currently working on or had worked-on in the recent past. The developers were requested to provide names and details of the top five contacts they relied on for informational help, when working on this current/recent project. The details for each information contact collected through the questionnaire included some relational characteristics elaborated further in a later section. Based on the initial details provided by these subjects and consistent with the theoretical and literal sampling criteria suggested by Yin (2001) for multiple case design, we selected three developers with less than three years overall experience and three developers with more than three years overall experience, to represent the entry-level developers and the more experienced developers, respectively. The choice of less than three years of experience for defining less experienced developer group is consistent with what was used in some of the previous studies (e.g., Björklund, 2013). Also, another study found developer fluency (i.e., ability to quickly and accurately complete software project tasks irrespective of their importance or complexity) to continue to improve for at least three years into their project tenures, the time period involved in that study (Zhou & Mockus, 2010). Thus, we deem three years of experience to be a reasonable threshold to categorize developers into the two experience categories. Having some data collected through a questionnaire ahead of telephone interviews helped us to understand the profile of each developer and his/her personal/work context ahead so that the telephone interview time could be more efficiently used to probe the developer's knowledge seeking behaviors. Table 1 summarizes profiles of the study subjects.

Table 1. Profiles of software developers interviewed for the case study

	Overall Experience	**Experience with the current organization**	**Gender**	**Place of Work**
Subject 1	1.2	1.2	Female	India
Subject 2	2.5	2.5	Male	India
Subject 3	1.9	1.9	Female	India
Subject 4	9	2	Male	USA
Subject 5	3.3	1.7	Male	India
Subject 6	5.5	3.5	Male	India

All the developers were of Indian-nationality with five developers based in XYZ Corp's offshore facility at India and one developer based in their USA office. The average IT experience of the entry-level (subjects 1, 2 and 3 in Table 1) and the more experienced developers (subjects 4, 5, and 6 in Table 1) were 1.9 and 5.9 years, respectively. Telephone interviews were conducted with these 6 developers exploring the nature of relationship of each developer with his/her top 5 informational contacts and the actionable knowledge received from each contact. The interviews were conducted by one of the authors, with each interview lasting approximately 50 minutes. The interviews were recorded with the consent of the participants and transcribed to enable data analysis. The data collection was done at two levels: at the level of a developer and at the level of his/her relationship with an information contact, when working on a software project. In all, 30 information relationships were explored for the six developers (6 x 5), 15 each for the two developer categories—entry-level and experienced.

In multiple case designs, the number of cases sampled is highly discretionary and is subject to researchers' judgment (Yin, 2001). One criterion suggested for judging adequacy is to look for theoretical saturation—i.e., when information is repeating across cases and new incremental learning is minimal (Eisenhardt, 1989; Paré, 2004; Yin, 2001). Guest, Bunce, and Johnson (2006) suggest that in studies with high levels of homogeneity of study populations, a sample of six interviews are generally sufficient to draw common themes and meaningful interpretations. Based on post-hoc analysis of their data set comprising 60 interviews to understand the minimum number of interviews at which data saturation set in, they found that most overarching coding themes that they identified in the study were discovered after the first six interviews. As our case study involved one software development organization where the developer population is relatively homogenous. sampling three cases (with 15 embedded information relationships) each at the level of the developer groups (i.e., developers of two experience levels) and six embedded cases (with thirty embedded information relationships) at the developer level was deemed satisfactory based on theoretical saturation observed from interview responses. In addition, based on Guest et al. (2006) we believe the six cases (i.e., developer subjects) that we sampled for this study is an adequate sample size for drawing meaningful themes and interpretations that we showcased in this study.

Protocol Development and Data Collection

Consistent with the procedures suggested by Yin (2001), we developed a framework to guide our data collection efforts, that is based on social capital theory. We posit that software development projects benefit from not just the human capital, but also from the social capital of its developers. Software developers bring not just their abilities and experience to solve the software problem at hand, but also seek and mobilize informational resources from their information contacts. While, it is reasonable to expect these contacts to predominantly come from within the same organization, they may also, to a lesser extent, come from beyond the organizational domain. As the social capital construct captures both the network of relationships of individuals and the resources rooted in those relationships, we seek to capture the former through the social capital dimensions identified by Nahapiet and Ghoshal (1998), and the latter through the actionable knowledge dimensions articulated by Cross and Sproull (2004).

Social Capital Dimensions

In this research, we first seek to examine the structural and relational social capital dimensions of software developers and the differences between the entry-level developers and the more experienced developers, on these dimensions.

Structural Dimension

This dimension refers to the overall pattern of connections between actors. This parallels the concept of structural embeddedness articulated by Granovetter (1985), which at the individual level refers to the overall network of relationships of individuals that influences their economic behaviors and outcomes. The structural dimensions examined here include organizational proximity (whether the contacts are from within the same organization or from outside the organization), physical proximity (whether the contacts are from the same office as the developers or from outside the office), functional proximity (whether the contacts are from the same functional domain as the software developers or from other functional domains) and hierarchical proximity (whether the contacts are higher in hierarchy, same level or lower in hierarchy than the developers) (Levin & Cross, 2004).

Relational Dimensions

This dimension refers to the personal relationships such as friendship, respect and admiration developed over long periods of interaction that help realize social objectives such as prestige, approval or sociability (Nahapiet & Ghoshal, 1998). The relational dimensions examined here include tie-strength (closeness of working relationship between the developer and a contact), friendship (the level of personal acquaintance between the developer and a contact outside of work-related areas), availability (the level of accessibility of a contact to the developer, when needed) and reciprocity (level of mutual help inherent in the relationship) (Levin & Cross, 2004). Figure 1 summarizes the social capital dimensions of software developers examined in this research.

Figure 1. Social capital dimensions of software developers

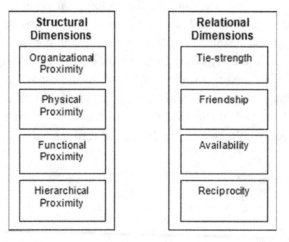

Actionable Knowledge

Actionable knowledge is the knowledge useful to make headway on a current task or assignment (Cross & Sproull, 2004). Based on a qualitative study in a business consulting environment, Cross & Sproull (2004) identified five types of actionable knowledge received by consultants: solutions (both declarative and procedural knowledge), referrals (pointers to other people with relevant knowledge or capabilities or to specific information in databases, electronic resources or manuals), problem reformulation (help in defining or reframing problem dimensions), validation (help in enhancing confidence in one's solution or problem-solving approach) and legitimation (help from an influential person to bolster one's proposal). We adapt these actionable knowledge dimensions to the software development context. In addition, we found two additional resources valued by software developers when analyzing interview data—arbitration (help from an influential authority to resolve differences between parties) and emotional support ("expression of concern, compassion, sympathy and esteem" (Hill, 1991). These social capital resources sought by the developers are summarized in Figure 2.

Figure 2. Social capital resources accessed by software developers

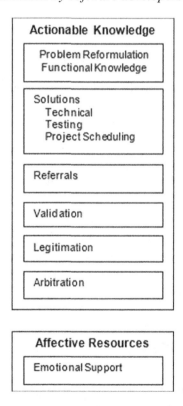

As alluded to earlier, we used a survey questionnaire to elicit the following details from each subject ahead of the interviews: subject's demographic background, details of a current or recent project engaged in, subject's top five information contacts in this project and the relational (i.e., tie strength, friendship and availability) characteristics of subject's relationship with each contact. For these relational dimensions of social capital, which we specified a-priori, we used measures adapted from extant literature. As a-priori specification of constructs, when possible, and use of validated measures, help improve the empirical grounding of the case study findings (Eisenhardt, 1989), the measure for tie-strength was adapted from Hansen (1999) and Levin and Cross (2004), while the measures for friendship and availability were adapted from Levin and Cross (2004). These measures based on a Likert scale from 1 to 7 are listed in the Appendix. In the interest of parsimony and consistency of analysis across constructs, the data for these constructs was then coded as low (<=2), medium (>2 to <=5) or high (>5).

Further, for other social capital dimensions (structural dimensions—organizational proximity, physical proximity, functional proximity and hierarchical proximity; relational dimension—reciprocity), as also the actionable knowledge sought from each information contact, we gleaned the details from interviews and later coded into quantitative term as follows:

- Organizational (locational) proximity of the contact: 1. in the same function in the same office; 2. in the same function in a different office; 3. in a different function but in the same office; 4. in a different function and in a different office; 5. outside the company.
- Hierarchical level of the contact: 1. two or more levels below the subject; 2. one level below the subject; 3. equal level as the subject; 4. one level above the subject; 5. two or more levels above the subject; 6. does not apply.
- Physical proximity of the contact to the subject: 1. worked immediately next to the subject; 2. same floor and same hallway as the subject; 3. same floor but different hallway; 4. different floor; 5. different building; 6. different city; 7. different country.
- Functional proximity of the contact to the subject: 1. from the same functional domain as the subject: 2. from a different functional domain.
- Reciprocity - Whether the subject received more help from the information contact than the help he/she provided to the contact in return is elicited in the interviews and coded as: 1. Received less help than provided in return (negatively skewed) 2. Even levels of help received and help provided (Even); 3. Received more help than provided in return (positively skewed).

Therefore, the qualitative data from the interviews, not only supported our qualitative analysis, but also helped us to undertake limited quantitative analysis. We believe, the strategy of combining qualitative and quantitative evidence from interviews and survey questionnaire data (Bourgeois & Eisenhardt, 1988; Eisenhardt, 1989), has been quite fruitful in providing a more coherent understanding of developers' personal networks and their knowledge seeking behaviors.

DATA ANALYSIS AND FINDINGS

We first discuss developers' structural and relational dimensions followed by the actionable knowledge provided by their information contacts. We used within-case analysis and cross-case pattern matching strategies (Eisenhardt, 1989) to draw findings at the two levels of analysis—a general developer level and at the level of a developer of given experience level (entry-level/experienced).

Structural Dimensions of Developers' Social Capital

The overall patterns of connections of software developers' networks constitute the structural dimension of their social capital. Structural social capital enables conduits for collective action through the established roles, procedures and the physical setting. Depending upon their experience levels, developers' informational contacts could span across organizational boundaries, physical proximity barriers or organizational hierarchical levels.

Organizational Proximity

For software developers, information contacts from within the organization could be an efficient option for actionable knowledge due to lower access costs involved. Organizational contacts such as team members, hierarchical superiors, functional and technical experts, all may have some stake in the project, direct or indirect, that increases the likelihood of better response. Here is an illustrative comment of a developer about one of his organizational contacts: "yes, he was heading our project, right? So he's the first person to know about product delays, so we need to contact him." As another developer reflects about a contact, "yeah, because the web pages I developed and he developed were very (much) related, so I would talk to him regarding business requirements". As shared context and common understanding of organizational procedures among the organizational communities of practice (Brown & Duguid, 1991; Wenger & Snyder, 2000) increases the odds of receiving more relevant information from internal rather than external sources, this could certainly be another important motivating factor to look for intra-organizational contacts.

Entry-level developers, who, owing to their inexperience, undergo a steeper learning curve in their daily work than their more senior colleagues, may have higher incentive to reduce their access costs by looking for readily available sources in their vicinity. They may efficiently tap into these internal sources on a broad range of issues as one developer alludes, "I go to him for core technical and business process issues… While working, when I get deeper into the work I get some doubts regarding the business process. I go and ask him and he clarifies the doubt and if necessary he makes changes (in specifications)". Where information is needed from the client or any other external sources, they could still rely on their organizational contacts to get it for them. As one developer remarked, "anything is beyond my level, I go to him and ask him… because he was not involved in getting the project requirements initially, so he had to go back to clients sometimes (to get clarifications)."

On the other hand, more experienced developers are likely to deal directly with external clients for requirements collection, and thus cultivate external relationships spanning organizational boundaries. As one experienced developer remarked about his external customer contact, "he was our client. Initially he was interacting with our team manager and later on I was directly interacting with him. Especially in the later part of the project he started directly interacting with me… when our team manager went for a one month leave ... (from) then on he interacted with both of us. If there was any design issue he would talk to my team manager and if it is functional aspect and new modules are to be done or other integration aspect, bugs (etc.), he used to talk to me directly."

The findings from the limited quantitative analysis also are in line with the qualitative findings—i.e., the subject developers in the case organization overwhelmingly relied on their intra-organizational contacts (93% of contacts). Interestingly, entry-level developers seem to rely exclusively on intra-organizational informants, while more experienced developers try reaching out, to a limited extent, to contacts from outside the organization (13%).

Physical Proximity

For developers it may also be quite efficient to tap into information contacts from within the same office as office setting affords multiple opportunities for interaction such as telephone conversations, personal meetings and even informal conversations over lunch. As one developer remarked about a valuable internal contact for him and his team, "whenever we have any doubt we just call him, and then on the phone itself he will clarify many things. If it is still not clear, we will ask him whether we could come and see him. Nine out of ten times he'll respond very quickly and positively and ask us to come immediately. When he is really busy … will say, let us meet at lunch."

Quantitative analysis also suggests that software developers at this organization do seem to rely overwhelmingly on information contacts from within the same office (87% of contacts). In fact, entry-level developers' had contacts exclusively from within the same office, while experienced developers had some contacts from outside their respective offices (27%). No wonder developers trust people available in the vicinity more than any experts or knowledge repositories (Komi-Sirvio et al., 2002)

Functional Proximity

Developers in the case organization appear to rely heavily on contacts from within the same IT function. One developer describes the relationship with his internal IT contact as follows: "he has worked (previously) on the scheduler functionality. We had (recently) ported from version 2 to version 3. Version 2 functionality was also retained. So, we did in a certain fashion so that it is considered as an add-on application…The scheduler functionality he wrote was very old. I had to find out exactly where which functions …and which components he used in order to debug it. Because scheduler was not working due to some unknown reasons, so, I had to get to him to understand it speedily. You also get the context behind those decisions at that time." Thus, accessing expertise relating to the technologies or the system requirements appears to be one reason for reaching out to these internal IT contacts.

Developers also seem to reach out to contacts from other functional domains to a limited extent, particularly for eliciting systems requirements. As one developer explains, "whenever any requirement comes from the HR Department, if it is a lower level one then we approach her (i.e., a functional contact)… (For instance) they wanted a birthday alarm (feature). That is, when there is birthday of an employee falling in the current month, they want to display birthday greetings on the pay slip itself…. and at that time we approached her (for seeking clarifications)."

Typically, networks that span functional boundaries help tap unique information, not ordinarily available within the functional silos of organizations, with potentially high knowledge payoffs. For entry-level developers there appears to be greater need to reach out to functional contacts as one entry-level developer puts it, "technically, everybody can do the coding at the same level; everyone is ok with the technology. So, only thing was we had to understand the HR policies, finance policies etc." Here is another illustrative comment of this developer about a functional contact: "he was just like consultant for us. For every requirement we need him—PF calculations… income tax calculations… etc. He used to provide reference of web sites, provide the printouts of materials, … pay structures of different employees and used to ask us to test out the income tax calculations for those structures and … after every module he used to verify the data. Virtually for every requirement, we needed him." Thus, for entry-level developers the need to tap into contacts from other functional areas appears to stem mainly from their inadequate understanding of the functional aspects of the system.

The quantitative analysis also suggests that developers in the case organization seem to rely heavily on contacts from within the same IT function (two-thirds of contacts). However, developers seem to reach out to contacts from other functional domains to a limited extent (one-third contacts). In addition, entry-level developers appear to have a higher proportion (47%) of their knowledge relationships from other functional areas compared to experienced developers (20%).

Hierarchical Proximity

For developers, hierarchical superiors could serve as valuable contacts. Here is an illustrative comment of a developer about his top information contact who was his hierarchical superior: "for knowledge transfer for our team members, he has provided all the resources for helping them out. Because of his immense help, we were able to finish the testing in four months." In general, turning towards hierarchical superiors for help appears to be quite logical as they are expected to have greater access to project-specific knowledge.

For entry-level developers, looking up to their hierarchical superiors appears to be the primary option. Here is an illustrative comment from an entry-level developer: "as this is my first project ... I wouldn't approach the project lead for many of the things because he was the senior most (person). I would approach my senior team colleagues for doubts relating to the business processes." Not surprisingly, entry-level developers, being the junior-most employees in the organization, have to primarily rely upon their immediate hierarchical superiors for help, as their horizontal peers, who are equally new to their jobs, may not have the information they need.

For experienced developers the priorities appear to be quite different as this developer explains, "As the team lead I have to train them and I should have the information first ... and I have to assign individual tasks to individual members in my team. So I don't need to depend on my team members for information. But in some cases, actually in some work aspects, I have to take some help, but not that much. As I mentioned earlier they are all new to this project. So, each and every task I had to train them". Thus, not surprisingly, experienced developers generally appear to have much less need to turn to their subordinates for help, particularly the new bees. But, in some cases they did look lower down for help. . For instance, an experienced developer had this to say about his contact who was his hierarchical subordinate, "he is ... expert in income tax calculations... All my three team members are new to this product... So he used to help us and my team members with those income tax calculations. For my work also he helped a lot, by clarifying those formulas." Thus a person lower in hierarchy could be a valuable knowledge contact, particularly if this person happens to be expert on a topic or had previously worked on a related project.

The quantitative analysis also suggests that developers seem to rely on their hierarchical superiors (64%) to a greater extent than on their peers (32%) for actionable knowledge. For entry-level developers, reliance on hierarchical superiors as information contacts appears to be more pronounced (80% with superiors vs. 20% with peers). Experienced developers were more even in terms of having hierarchical superiors (46%) or hierarchical peers (46%) as their information contacts, but not as many subordinates (only 8%).

Summary

Evidence relating to the structural dimensions of developers' social capital suggests that developers' information contacts overwhelmingly came from within the same organization and even the same offices. Also, these contacts were predominantly from within the IT function and tended to be hierarchical superiors. While entry-level developers had only intra-organizational contacts, all from within the same offices, more experienced developers did have some top information contacts from outside their offices and even from outside the organization, mainly from external clients. Also, entry-level developers predominantly relied on their hierarchical superiors for information while more experienced developers depended evenly on their hierarchical superiors and organizational peers.

Relational Dimensions of Developers' Social Capital

Relational social capital refers to the dyadic resources embedded in relationships such as friendship, feeling of closeness or interpersonal solidarity and trust (Moran, 2005; Nahapiet & Ghoshal, 1998). This relates to the relational embeddedness (Granovetter, 1992) concept that refers to the personal relationships between individuals developed over long periods of interactions that influence human behavior. The knowledge relationships of developers of different experience levels could differ in terms of their levels of tie-strength, friendship, availability and reciprocity.

Tie-Strength

In general, developers appear to have high tie strengths with many of their information contacts. As these knowledge contacts represented the top information sources of the developers, not surprisingly, developers rated a majority of these relationships as high in tie-strength. As one entry-level developer remarked about one of his high tie-strength contacts, "he is very helpful in gathering requirements … he actually guides us. He conducts regular meetings. If any problems come up, he helps us. He comes daily to our desk to say hi to us… He maintains that kind of rapport with the team members." Here is an illustrative comment of a developer about a high tie strength internal contact: "generally as a colleague we discuss what should we do next… if we are having any issues how should we resolve, etc. When we are sitting in the cafeteria also we will be discussing sometime, what is the issue?… how should we work? As we are all colleagues we'll be free with each other, generally we discuss and resolve them. Sometimes when we're discussing (some difficult issues) he might say - don't worry, I will be coming to your seat and we will check out what is the problem." Thus, developers appear to value information contacts that maintained close personal rapport and provided some kind of mentoring, and rated those relationships as high in tie-strength.

While entry-level developers did not report any low tie-strength contacts, experienced developers did have some. As one experienced remarked about his internal information contact of low tie-strength, "she was only associated for about couple of months. She then left. She was colleague to me, same level as mine. We used to discuss about the functionality as it was new to all of us … and then share the work". This is another illustrative comment relating to an external contact of low tie-strength, "He was our client… Basically if I had a doubt in the requirements, I used to call him … to get more clarifications before I start to work." Thus, such low tie-strength contacts typically tended to be either organizational contacts with whom the developers had brief, yet significant working relationships or external client contacts.

The quantitative analysis also suggests that developers, irrespective of their levels of experience, had high tie strength with a majority of their information contacts (60%). Developers had a third of their contacts of medium tie-strength (33%), and only a small proportion of contacts of low tie strength (7%). There were, however, minor differences between developers of different levels of experience in this regard. While entry-level developers had no low tie-strength contacts, more experienced developers did have some (13%).

Friendship

Although developers had high tie-strength relationships with a majority of their contacts, only a few seem to qualify as high in friendship. An entry-level developer had this to say about her friendly contact: "this is the first project for both of us... I would ask her sometimes, if she knew she would tell me, otherwise we would approach somebody else... if I'm stuck with something she sits beside me and sometimes provide the solution." Thus, entry-level developers appear to tap into other newbies and develop friendship networks. Here is another illustrative comment from a developer about his contact who happened to be his college buddy: "He is my college friend, one of my close friends. He has worked for nearly 2 to 3 years in a customer care center... I asked him about the functional requirements (of the application and) how people do various things on the application." Thus, developers sometimes tapped into their close buddies, especially if they had expertise, or some previous experience, in the area of interest to the developers.

Many developers' appear to maintain moderate levels of friendship with their information contacts, but with some it was definitely low. A developer has this to say about the relationship with his top information contact that was low on friendship: "he is the project manager of the complete payroll product. Not only this project, he takes care of other projects also. He has joined us at the beginning of this customization part for this new client about five months back. As he is the project lead, we are not that close. Only project related issues we used to discuss." Low friendship relationships with information contacts are understandable as many working relationships may not have personal friendship components in them. Professionalism, and not friendship, may drive many relationships, particularly with hierarchical superiors,

The quantitative analysis also affirmed the qualitative findings on the friendship networks. Although developers had high tie-strength relationships with a majority (60%) of their contacts, they were not high on friendship levels. In fact, developers across experience levels had only a few relationships (7%) that were high on friendship. Developers, however, rated a majority of their information relationships (60%) as moderate in friendship, with one-third of the relationships rated as low in friendship. No meaningful differences were evident between the entry-level and the more experienced developers in this regard.

Availability

For an information source to be valuable to a developer, he/she should be available and easily accessible, when needed. The physical proximity of most of the contacts to the developers definitely enhances their availability. In some cases, when the contact was busy, they could always get back quickly enough. As one developer remarked, "Sometimes, in some rare cases, he may be busy and in the next hour, or the next day, he'll come back to us to check if it has been sorted out."

Quantitative analysis also suggests that the availability of information sources was rated high in a majority of developers' relationships (60%). There were minor differences among developers, with experienced developers having higher proportion of high availability contacts (60%) compared to the entry-level developers (50%). This is not surprising, as their relative seniority would help them command the attention and availability of their contacts.

Reciprocity

Developers, in general, appear to have received more help than they had provided in turn from many of their information contacts, while entry-level developers appear to engage in reciprocal relationships, particularly with their hierarchical equals, on a more even keel. One entry-level developer remarked thus, "Both of us are at the same level regarding technical or business requirements. I would approach her and she would also approach me for help… (on) business related issues." Another entry-level developer had this to say about his functional contact, "she will always be asking for help from us, like support … so when she gets (into) any difficulty in using it (i.e., the application), she calls us and we'll help her." Thus, for some entry-level developers reciprocity entailed returning favors to their functional contacts by providing technical support.

For experienced developers reciprocity certainly was more even as one experienced developer remarked, "mostly I used to contact him for letting him know the status and if there are any issues … He involved me in various other projects (to share my expertise)… where we used to have some design problems and some technical issues." Here is another illustrative comment from an experienced developer about a more even reciprocal relationship: "If it all if there is any issue in Java application that he's working on, he used to ask me for help. Then we used to work together. It was vice versa. I used to contact him in case of any issues related to databases or design issues. He used to contact me if there are any issues in the design solutions to problems." Thus, for experienced developers, reciprocity with their hierarchical superiors involved returning favors through sharing of their expertise.

The quantitative analysis also suggested that, developers received more help than they had provided in return from more than half their contacts (55%), while it was more even with more than a third of their contacts (38%). Entry-level developers had more skewed relationships in terms of reciprocity compared to their more experienced peers. Specifically, entry level developers had marginally higher proportion of relationships (60%) where they received more help than they had provided, than did more experienced developers (50%). Interestingly, entry-level developers reported providing more help than they had received in a few relationships (7%), while more experienced developers had no such relationships.

Summary

Evidence concerning relational factors of social capital suggests that developers' strength of ties with majority of their contacts were high, their friendship levels moderate and the reciprocity of ties low, with developers receiving more help than they had provided in return. The availability of these contacts when needed was also moderate to high. While entry-level developers had either high or moderate tie-strengths with their information contacts, experienced developers did have some top information contacts of low tie-strength. While entry-level developers had more positively-skewed relationships in terms of reciprocity and received more help than they had provided to their contacts, experienced developers had more even relationships in terms of reciprocity. Entry-level developers sometimes returned favors to their functional contacts with technical support, while experienced developers reciprocated by sharing their expertise. Entry-level developers did have a few negatively-skewed relationships, where they provided more help than they had received, but more experienced developers reported no such relationships. Table 2 summarizes the findings relating to developers' social capital dimensions. The next section explores the actionable knowledge received by developers from their contacts.

Table 2. Summary of findings relating to social capital dimensions of software developers

S.No.	Social Capital Dimensions	Entry-level Developers	Experienced Developers
I	Structural		
	Organizational Proximity	All information contacts from the same organization	Majority (87%) of information contacts from the same organization and the rest from outside the organization
	Physical Proximity	All information contacts from the same office	Majority (73%) of information contacts from the same office and the rest from outside the office
	Hierarchical Proximity	Majority (80%) of information contacts are hierarchical superiors and the rest (20%) are hierarchical peers	Information contacts evenly distributed from among hierarchical superiors and peers (46% each), with the rest being hierarchical subordinates
	Functional Proximity	More even distribution of information contacts from within the same IT function (53%) and from without (47%)	Majority (80%) of information contacts from the same IT function
II	Relational		
	Tie-strength	High tie-strength with majority (60%) of information contacts and moderate tie-strength with the rest. No information contacts of low tie-strength	High tie-strength with majority (60%) of information contacts and moderate tie-strength with approx. a quarter (27%) of contacts and low tie-strength with the rest
	Friendship	Moderate friendship with majority (60%) of information contacts, low friendship with a third (33%) of contacts and high friendship with the rest	Similar profile as the entry-level developers
	Availability	Availability of approx. half (53%) of the information contacts is high, for 40% it is moderate and for the rest it is low	Availability of two-third (67%) of the information contacts is high, for approx. a quarter of them (27%) availability is moderate and for the rest it is low
	Reciprocity	In majority (60%) of relationships, reciprocity is positively skewed with more help received than provided; approx. quarter (27%) of relationships are even with the rest (13%) negatively skewed with more help provided than received	Half the relationships positively skewed with more help received than provided and the rest being even. No negatively skewed relationships

Actionable Knowledge

Actionable knowledge is the knowledge useful to make headway on a current task or assignment. Adapting the actionable knowledge dimensions identified by Cross and Sproull (2004) to the software development domain, we found that developers sought actionable knowledge from their contacts in terms of problem reformulation (requirements knowledge), solutions (technical solutions, testing solutions, project scheduling solutions), referrals, validation, and legitimation. In addition, we found developers receiving two additional resources from their contacts—emotional support, an affective resource and arbitration help.

Problem Reformulation

Software developers value information sources that can help define or reframe the problem dimensions so that new clarity emerges concerning the problem. Typically, clarifications concerning functional requirements of system being developed would help developers to recast and refine the problem, so that, they are able to come up with the solution. As one developer remarked, "coding is pretty much the same, but coming to policies, they are different and we are not very equipped with that and we do not have previous knowledge about that." Thus, developers considered help on functional requirements to be more important than help on technical matters. Functional requirements become an important concern for developers because the initial requirements may be incomplete. As one developer remarked about a contact, "he was the team lead before me. He is the person who explained (to) me the whole HRMS flow when I came into the team for the first time. He explained to me everything like how we should be handling the client? What kind of work we should do while payroll verification is going on at the end of the month? How we should work with the accounts department? What kind of information we should be gathering?" Apparently, for help on functional matters, developers typically turned to contacts who were originally involved in the business requirements gathering, or had worked on earlier versions of the product.

The quantitative analysis on the data coded from interviews also suggests that software developers looked for information on functional requirements in a vast majority (93%) of their knowledge relationships. This has been consistent across developers of different experience levels.

Solutions

Software developers did value actionable knowledge from their contacts that lead to solutions for problems at hand. Solutions involve both declarative and procedural knowledge for solving a problem at hand (Cross & Sproull, 2004). For developers, such solutions ranged from technical or testing matters to project scheduling issues.

Technical Knowledge

When faced with novel technologies, developers typically go through some learning curve. Learning together with a team member was a useful option for some developers as illustrated by this developer comment: "we were working on Cold Fusion and that was new to both of us, so we were learning it and doing at the same time". Another developer echoed similar thoughts: "during the first month of our project, I would approach her for technical help. As we both were new to the Dot Net framework, so we would approach each other to get our problems solved… if I'm stuck with something, she sits beside me and sometimes provide the solution". The technical help received ranged from architectural design to database design to troubleshooting issues. Here is another illustrative comment from an entry-level developer: "it was initial first few months of the project. Everything seemed correct, but it (the program) was giving errors. Then I approached him and we debugged it together. We found that someone had changed the database table column structure." The quantitative analysis of the interview data suggests that developers received technical help from less than half of their contacts (40%). Interestingly, entry-level developers reported receiving technical help from more contacts (53%) than did more experienced developers (43%).

Testing Knowledge

Developers report receiving testing help from some of their contacts. This is an illustrative comment from an entry-level developer about a contact providing such help: "when we have any problems in testing, he will be there with us in the meetings and tell us if it is valid or not, how to go about that." The quantitative analysis of the interview data also suggests that developers reported receiving testing related help from a third of their information contacts. The trend was roughly consistent across developers of different experience levels.

Project Scheduling

Developers report receiving help on project scheduling issues from some of their contacts when needed. Here is an illustrative developer comment: "every week we used to have status meeting … (to) let him know what is the timeline that we have …We have a plan for releasing some of the e-mail features in between and chat features after that. So we used to keep track of the work to be done at a particular point of time and he used to help… We used to be very open to the client, if it all if there is any issue … we used to let him know… So being a part of the (same) organization he used to help us with the issues that we had." As project management is a higher level function, not surprisingly, developers received such help from contacts who were their hierarchical superiors, as illustrated by a developer's comment: "as a project manager (he) used to take care of the schedule… (when) anything was needed he used to help." The quantitative analysis of the interview coded data also confirmed this with developers' reportedly receiving project scheduling related help from many of their information contacts (41%). More experienced developers report receiving such help from a higher proportion of their information contacts (51%) compared to entry-level developers (33%).

Referrals

Developers report receiving referrals to information sources in a few instances when their contacts could not themselves offer any direct help. Here is an entry-level developer's illustrative comment on the subject: "for provident fund rules, once he had taken me to a manufacturing firm, as we were developing the product for manufacturing organizations, to get an understanding of how they follow these provident fund rules and how statutory forms will be filled in." The quantitative analysis also suggested that software developers received referrals from some of their contacts (23%). Entry-level developers report receiving received referrals from marginally greater number of their contacts (27%) than did their experienced counterparts 20%).

Validation

Validation may typically involve a supervisor or somebody higher in hierarchy as one developer elaborates: "yes, after doing what he tells, I just tell him what I had done, because he only understands business process completely". Validation is also sometimes sought from team members or peers, as alluded to by a developer: "because we both worked on the same thing together, we were validating each other when working". Based on the quantitative analysis also software developers sought validation for their work from about half of their information contacts (52%). Interestingly, entry-level developers sought validation from more of their sources (72%), compared to their more experienced counterparts (29%).

Legitimation

Legitimation entails seeking approval and support of an influential person to the approach being followed. Here is an illustrative comment of an experienced developer about an influential organizational contact who provided such help: "He's the senior most and technically very strong... He has given the requirements and solutions as to how to do that also. And after that we have done a prototype of the application and have shown him a demo. After the demo he used to give suggestions and his feedback and... if he wants any changes in the existing prototype ... Once the prototype was approved by him, we start developing the actual ... application." One developer who was directly dealing with an influential customer contact explains his interactions thus: "he gave all the requirements... Yes, sometimes the requirements are really vague and ... I used to do the user interface and then call him back and show him what it is and then discuss it". Quantitative analysis of the interview data also confirms that developers sought legitimation from about a quarter of their sources (24%), with entry-level developers seeking such help from more sources (27%) than did their more experienced counterparts (21%).

Arbitration

Arbitration involves seeking help from an influential authority to resolve differences between parties. We found one instance of an experienced developer seeking arbitrating help from an information contact stacked higher up in hierarchy: "in testing if we find any issues, we used to post into the defect tracking tool and inform him ... sometimes the development guys don't agree with them. At that time he used to sit with us and he used to take up with the development guys and tell them to fix the problem." We did not find any instances of entry-level developers seeking such help from their contacts.

Emotional Support

In addition to actionable knowledge resources, software developers also reported receiving emotional support, an affective resource, from their contacts. Emotional support is the "expression of concern, compassion, sympathy and esteem" (Hill, 1991). As one developer recalled receiving such help from his contact, "if we are not in a good mood or if we are not able to finish the task, ... he will give us time or provide motivation... Yes, when we were stressed out, he will ask us to go to some parties, and he also arranges parties for us." Specifically, developers report receiving emotional support from about a third of their contacts (31%), which was roughly the case across developers of different experience levels.

Summary

Evidence suggests that developers in the case organization overwhelmingly sought actionable knowledge on functional requirements from their contacts. Functional knowledge helped developers in reformulating the problem in new ways, thereby helping generate a better solution. Next in the order of importance of actionable knowledge resources was validation help, followed by solutions for technical, project scheduling and testing related issues; legitimation and referrals were the least important resources sought. In addition to actionable knowledge resources, developers also received emotional support from a third of their contacts. Entry-level developers sought solutions more on technical matters and less on project scheduling matters from their contacts, compared to their experienced counterparts. Entry-level developers sought validation from their contacts to a great extent, which was far less important to experienced developers. Legitimation was also sought to a marginally greater extent by the entry-level developers compared to the experienced ones. Table 3 summarizes the findings relating to the actionable knowledge and affective resources received by software developers.

Table 3. Summary of findings relating to actionable knowledge received by software developers

S.No.	Actionable Knowledge/ Affective Resources	Entry-level Developers	Experienced Developers
I	Problem Reformulation		
	Functional Knowledge	Received help on functional requirements from an overwhelming majority (93%) of information contacts	Similar profile as the entry-level developers
II	Solutions		
	Technical	Received technical solutions from about half (53%) of information contacts	Received technical solutions from less than half (43%) of information contacts
	Testing	Received testing solutions from a third (33%) of information contacts	Received testing solutions from little over a third (36%) of information contacts
	Project Scheduling	Received project scheduling solutions from a third (33%) of information contacts	Received project scheduling solutions from half (50%) of the information contacts
III	Referrals	Received referrals from about a quarter (27%) of information contacts	Received referrals from less than a quarter (20%) of information contacts
IV	Validation	Received validation help from approx. three-fourth (73%) of information contacts	Received validation help from just less than a third (29%) of information contacts
V	Legitimation	Received legitimating help from approx. a quarter (27%) of information contacts	Received legitimating help from less than a quarter (21%) of information contacts
VI	Arbitration	Not received	Received arbitration help from less than a tenth (7%) of information contacts
VII	Affective Resources		
	Emotional Support	Received emotional support from approx. a quarter (27%) of information contacts	Received emotional support from more than a third (36%) of information contacts

DISCUSSION AND IMPLICATIONS FOR PRACTICE AND RESEARCH

As alluded to in the methods section, this research used multiple case design involving multiple levels of analysis (Yin, 2001). As the research insights are based primarily on qualitative findings from a single organizational setting, we are mindful that they ought to be deemed as 'untested hypotheses', generalizable only to the case organization (Lee & Baskerville, 2003) or to similar organizations, at best. Hence, we interpret the findings accordingly. Also, the study findings are based on questionnaire responses and detailed interviews conducted with six developers from the case organization, which could be considered a limitation. We are also mindful that interviewing a larger number of developers could have revealed some additional insights or empirical realities. However, as alluded in an earlier section, based on Guest et al. (2006) and based on theoretical saturation that we observed from the interview responses, we believe this is an acceptable sample size for drawing meaningful themes and interpretations showcased in this study. To our knowledge there is no prior research in management or other domains that explored differences in the structural and relational dimensions of social capital of knowledge workers of different experience levels and the differences in the types of actionable knowledge accessed from personal networks by these workers. So, we allude to somewhat relevant research findings from other business domains when discussing our findings.

It has been long suggested that people prefer to turn to others for information, rather than search through documents (Allen, 1977; Mintzberg, 1973; Pelz & Andrews, 1966). Long before the advent of the Internet, Allen (1977) found that scientists and engineers were five times more likely to tap people over file cabinets or databases for information. Our findings suggest that even in the current Internet age, software developers still rely overwhelmingly on their information contacts for actionable knowledge in their daily work. Personal networks help developers to get a feel for what is important and whom to approach to prioritize resources and tasks (Kautz & Kjærgaard, 2007). This is consistent with empirical evidence in software development field (Newell, 2004) and in related business domains (Cross & Sproull, 2004; Robinson, 2010). For instance, one study reported that 95% of the consultants sampled for the study from a Big Five accounting firm obtained all the actionable knowledge that they needed during the course of their daily work from their information contacts (Cross & Sproull, 2004). Another study found that design engineers in engineering organizations are able to locate and access information more quickly from a human information source compared to a non-human source (e.g., a report) (Robinson, 2010). So, our finding is in line with the current economic thought that views organizational networks as the 'plumbing' that support the 'project ecologies' created around project teams, organizational users, external customers and other stakeholders during the duration of a project (Grabher & Ibert, 2006). The qualitative findings of our study highlight important differences in the profiles of entry level and more experienced developers, in terms of the characteristics of their knowledge networks and the resources sought. This should contribute to theory building relating to knowledge networks of software developers.

Structural Characteristics of Developer Networks

One important research finding is that developers predominantly relied on intra-organizational contacts for actionable knowledge in their daily work--entry level developers relied exclusively on intra-organizational contacts, while experienced developers reached out, to a limited extent, to contacts from beyond organizational boundaries. Findings from a meta-analytic study suggest that the choice of internal vs. external sources for expertise seeking in organizations by knowledge workers is dependent upon several contextual factors including accessibility of the source (Hertzum, 2014). Organizations, as knowledge creating entities (Spender, 1996), are privy to a wealth of knowledge embedded in its people, processes and products that is of value to its own people, including its software developers. Extant research in software development suggests that receiving knowledge from other developers in the organization positively impacts the performance of software developers (Ozer & Vogel, 2015). Also, the performance benefits are expected to be higher when the task autonomy for developers and the quality of social exchanges of developers with their supervisors are high than when they are low (Ozer & Vogel, 2015).

Another insight of the study is that developers overwhelmingly relied on information contacts from within the same office—the entry level developers exclusively relied on developers from the same office while the more experienced developers had a quarter of their network contacts from outside their offices. The propinquity effect in network relationships is quite understandable as face to face interactions between actors working in close physical proximity help create ties and enhance the cooperation and solidarity among actors (Kwon & Adler, 2014). For instance, in R&D lab settings, while proximity enhanced interactions and innovation output among R&D professionals, the frequency of interactions suffered when their offices were more than 15.2 meters apart (Allen, 1977). Among teachers it was found that if they had classrooms in close proximity or took breaks at around the same time they communicated more with each other and felt connected and close (Reagans, 2011).

Extant research evidence suggests that developers tap into their supervisors' expertise to a greater extent than other sources (Xu et al., 2010). Consistent with this finding, the entry level developers in the case organization relied predominantly on their hierarchical superiors. Empirical evidence from management research suggests that there are positive externalities to an individual's brokerage position in terms of second order benefits to other actors in the individual's network. For instance, if a focal actor is connected to a broker who is senior or hierarchical superior, then the focal actor is able to draw second order benefits and add value to others in his/her network (Galunic et al., 2012).Thus, in addition to direct benefits related to information and expertise, software developers could benefit from the positive externalities stemming from the brokerage positions of their hierarchical superiors, which makes such relationships logical and compelling. Unlike entry level developers, the more experienced developers in the case organization had more even information relationships with hierarchical superiors/peers and hierarchical subordinates. This is understandable since developers with more seniority do need to rely on their subordinates for specific competencies.

Research evidence in HRM suggests that employees typically seek feedback from within the same department as they perceive such feedback received from colleagues and managers/coaches to be useful, while managers seek much less feedback from colleagues within the same department than from other external sources (van der Rijt et al., 2013). In contrast to this, entry level developers in the case organization had even relationships with contacts from within IT and from other functional areas, while more senior developers had a majority of their contacts from within the IT domain. One possible reason could be that unlike HRM domain, in software development developers constantly need functional information concerning the business processes being implemented in the software, which requires them to be in touch with the users in other functional areas. Entry level developers need help relating to both technical and functional issues, while more senior developers have to rely on their subordinates within IT domain for their technical skills and expertise.

Relational Characteristics of Developer Networks

The developers in the case organization, both entry level and the more experienced ones, had high tie strength with a majority of their contacts. This is generally consistent with extant research evidence— i.e., job interdependence between source and the developers in project teams contributes to personal relationships as also perception of quality of the source (Xu, et al., 2010). Thus, it is reasonable to expect strength of such ties to be high.

One insight of this study is that developers report moderate to high friendship levels with their top information contacts. As friendships help developers overcome barriers, both interpersonal and informational, cultivating a friendly atmosphere within project teams and the organization should be a positive enabler for knowledge sharing in software teams. This is consistent with a previous research finding that highlights the positive value of developer-customer ties evolved outside of the development environment to project outcomes (Keil & Carmel, 1995).

Quality (i.e., reliability and relevance) of information shared and accessibility of source are definitely important factors when people seek expertise and help from others in organizations (Hertzum, 2014; Su & Contractor, 2011). Consistent with prior research findings, developers in the case organization relied on information sources whose availability was high, with experienced developers reporting higher proportion of high availability sources than entry-level developers. This is logical as senior developers would be able to command higher attention and accessibility of their sources owing to their longer tenures and higher standing in the organizational hierarchy.

Entry-level developers in the case organization received more help than they provided to their contacts than experienced developers, who had more even reciprocity in their relationships. In fact, experienced developers did not have any relationships where they received less help than they had provided. This is understandable as entry level developers may not have the knowledge and expertise to be of significant help to their information contacts. However, this is unlike research evidence that we found concerning other knowledge workers where no significant differences were reported between senior vs. junior design engineers in terms of whether they spent more time asking questions or answering questions from others. That is, reciprocity levels were not dissimilar between design engineers of different experience levels (Robinson, 2010). This may need further exploration to see if these differences in findings stem from the differences in the task domains or owing to other factors relating to research designs or organizational settings.

Resources Accessed from Developer Networks

An important study finding is that help on functional requirements of the system is the top knowledge resource sought from information contacts by developers across experience levels. As system requirements collection in software projects rarely ends with full understanding of the requirements, but is typically "shut down" based on project scheduling requirements (Walz et al., 1993), developers constantly look for help on business/functional issues. Prior IS research underscored the criticality of effective communication between developers and users/functional experts to project success (Gallivan & Keil, 2003).

Entry-level developers sought technical help and validation help to a greater extent compared to their experienced counterparts, while experienced developers sought help on project scheduling matters to a greater extent than their entry level counterparts. This is to be expected as developers' needs tend to evolve with experience from technical to more project scheduling needs. Actionable information concerning referrals and legitimation were sought more evenly by both groups of developers. Also, arbitration help was sought to a limited extent by more experienced developers while entry level developers did not demonstrate a need for it in the case organization. As arbitration involves some resolution of disputes this may squarely falls in the need set of experienced developers as entry-level developers cannot afford to engage in disputes in the first place.

Another key insight of this study relates to the emotional support received by developers in their daily work—developers across experience levels sought not only information resources from their contacts, but also affective resources. According to Person-Environment fit theory in the management domain, an employee experiences positive outcomes when there is a fit between his/her needs (i.e., desires/preferences for the availability of certain resources or characteristics in the work setting) and the supplies (i.e., the extent to which the resource or the characteristic is perceived to be existing) in the work setting (Kahn, 2007). As relationships are at the core of organizational life, employees experiencing a "relational-needs fit" in work environments (i.e., when their personal needs are perceived to be met in their work relationships) demonstrate higher psychological commitment to others at work and perceive overall positive outcomes from these relationships (Ehrhardt & Ragins, 2019). Thus, when developers in need of emotional support receive such support in their work setting, this could help enhance their psychological commitment to the team and its members with positive outcomes for both developers and software teams.

Theoretical Contribution

This study makes the following theoretical contributions to the research on the knowledge networks of software developers. First, it adapts the structural and relational dimensions of social capital enunciated by Nahapiet and Ghoshal (1998) and the actionable knowledge framework of Cross and Sproull (2004) to explore the knowledge networks of software developers. Second, it introduces developers' experience as a defining grouping factor to further disassemble and explore differences in the knowledge networks and the actionable knowledge needs of developers at different experience levels. This study also makes some modest theoretical contributions to the research on social capital and information networks of knowledge workers in organizations. First, by conceptualizing experience as an important grouping factor that enhances our understanding of the knowledge networks and information needs of software developers, it highlights the possibility of exploring experience as a grouping variable for probing the information networks and information needs of other knowledge workers in organizations. However, some of the structural and relational dimensions of social capital and the actionable knowledge resources sought by knowledge workers are domain specific and need to be contextualized for the specific domains of the knowledge workers. Second, this research conceptualizes affective resource as another valuable resource afforded by knowledge networks to knowledge workers in organizations in general and software developers in particular. Thus, affective resource (e.g., emotional support) could be a valuable addition to the other actionable knowledge resources sourced from knowledge networks that were identified in prior management literature. Together, they provide a more comprehensive picture of resources afforded by knowledge networks to individuals in organizations.

Contribution to Software Practice

The findings of this research have important implications for practitioners, particularly in small and medium software organizations, similar in profile to that of the case organization. An important finding of this research relates to functional requirements of the system being the top knowledge resource sought by developers across experience levels. As the success of any systems development effort relies heavily on how well functional requirements of the system are elicited and coded into the system, making functional expertise readily accessible to developers, either through collocation or, better still, through embedding representatives from functional domains in the software teams, when feasible, are sound options to explore. Instituting formal knowledge transfer initiatives, particularly with regard to functional knowledge from resident experts, is another option worth considering. This may also involve creating and nurturing communities of practice that could potentially yield benefits at multiple levels—individuals, community and the organization (Millen et al., 2002; Thompson, 2005).

One insight of this study is that developers report moderate to high friendship and high tie strength with a majority of their information contacts with some reciprocity inherent in those relationships. In this research we focused on the basic reciprocity between pairs of individuals. However, reciprocity also exists in other forms such as generalized reciprocity, also called third-party reciprocity. Generalized reciprocity, a hallmark of larger systems such as communities of practice, involves a general belief that contributing to the community benefits all. Thus people are motivated to contribute to the community with the implicit trust that others would pitch in to help when they are in need. Generalized reciprocity expands the capacity for resource exchange by increasing the speed, scope and efficiency of exchanges and increases the probability that right resource reaches the right need (Baker & Dutton, 2006). Some argue that reciprocity comes naturally to humans as they are ''hard wired' for reciprocity, based on evolution (Gouldner, 1960). Creating a friendly workplace and providing opportunities for developers to meet outside the workplace through company sponsored picnics and retreats could help foster developer networks high in tie strength, reciprocity and friendship levels.

As pressures due to impending deadlines and technological complexities are the norm in software projects, software organizations should institute mentoring programs (Bjørnson & Dingsøyr, 2005), preferably with developers being able to choose their mentors. These formal mentors should not only focus on grooming and professional development activities, but also strive to act as emotional buffers, 'lending their shoulders' when developers are in distress, while sharing their joys and emotions. Any such efforts should be need-based as emotional support could sometimes be 'too much of a good thing' if employees receive more support than they need making them feel that their privacy boundary has been violated which could make them withdraw from relationships (Ehrhardt & Ragins, 2019).

Recent research in the management domain suggests that individuals not only engage in vicarious learning (i.e., learning from another person's experience through observation and imitation) (Bandura, 1969), but also engage in coactive vicarious learning with other individuals (say, a team member) by intentionally sharing and jointly processing the team member's experiences in their mutual interactions. Thus, coactive vicarious learning helps the individual to co-create an emergent, situated understanding of the other member's experiences (Myers, 2018). Efforts to foster a knowledge sharing climate (Chase, 1997; Davenport et al., 1998; Demarest, 1997; Gold et al., 2001; Lee & Choi, 2003), improving the access and availability of functional experts to developers when needed, creating informal settings (e.g., game rooms (Desouza, 2003b), social events etc.) for fostering personal bonds and strengthening ties between software developers and functional experts, are some approaches to consider for stimulating knowledge sharing in software development teams. The objective should be to provide multiple contact points and chances for personal interactions among developers and with other stakeholders of software projects.

Regarding differences between developers of different experience levels, one insight of this study is that entry-level developers tend to overwhelmingly rely upon intra-organizational contacts, who typically are their hierarchical superiors, for actionable knowledge in their daily work. IT leadership, project managers, and senior developers should be cognizant of this and be accessible and available to them to maximize the contributions of these rookie developers to the project outcomes. As role models, who demonstrate desired knowledge sharing behaviors, are critical to foster a knowledge sharing climate (Desouza, 2003b), the functional contacts and experienced developers in the team should be encouraged towards that end and also be evaluated on their knowledge sharing behaviors. Some recent research suggests that for software managers to be effective, soft skills and abilities such as growing talent, inspiring team, driving the alignment, clearing path for execution, guiding the team and building team culture are more important than having strong technical skills (Kalliamvakou et al., 2019). Thus, team leads and project managers should be motivated and rewarded for fostering knowledge sharing cultures within their project teams.

In terms of actionable knowledge accessed from information contacts, entry-level developers in the case organization sought technical help and validation help to a greater extent compared to their experienced counterparts. Although entry-level developers tend to have theoretical understanding of the latest technologies, they do need guidance and 'hand-holding' when implementing such technologies in software projects. The onus will be on technical leads and project managers to provide such guidance and validation support, not just when sought, but also to proactively organize technical trainings and knowledge transfer workshops, for grooming and leveraging the talents of these developers.

Enablers of positive social capital work through providing either higher motivation or greater opportunities, or both. One such enabling practice is "huddles" that originated from Xerox Corp (Baker & Dutton, 2006; Podolny, 1992). In this practice, any employee needing assistance from others could request for a short duration huddle (typically about 15 minutes). The employees called for help are expected to drop their work and participate in the huddle with the knowledge that they too could call one in the future when in need. "Peer assists" or "personnel transfers" (Baker & Dutton, 2006; Pfeffer & Sutton, 2000) is another reciprocity enabling practice developed by folks at British Petroleum that could be of value for software teams. This involves managers loaning their talented individuals to other departments or projects on request. Thus, managers willingly forego the contributions of these employees for the duration of the loan with the knowledge that they could similarly call on other managers in the future when in need. This certainly is another useful practice to consider for software organizations.

Another key difference found between entry-level and experienced developers is that while entry level developers relied exclusively on intra-organizational contacts, experienced developers reached out, to a limited extent, to contacts from beyond organizational boundaries for information in their daily work. Such boundary-spanning activities make them privy to non-redundant information, which enhances their value to software teams and the organization. For instance, research findings in software outsourcing suggest that boundary spanning positively moderates the effectiveness of formal controls on project outcomes (Gopal & Gosain, 2010). Needless to say, such behaviors should be encouraged and suitably rewarded.

Future Research

The role of networks and members' network ties in fostering an environment conducive to the creation and exchange of knowledge has attracted the attention of researchers in other disciplines, such as management. The social capital that inevitably accrues to actors in a network has also been subjected to close scrutiny in the academic community. However, there has been less research on these issues in the context of software development. This is rather surprising, given that the creation, dissemination and management of knowledge is an integral and vital part of software development. Our study is a preliminary step in gaining some insights into how networks influence knowledge seeking and sharing behaviors among developers of varying experience levels.

This exploratory case study helps in drawing theoretical insights relating to the social capital of software developers and the actionable knowledge resources developers draw from their information contacts. Future studies should do empirical testing of these qualitative findings and explore the effect of software developers' social capital on project outcomes. Specifically, they should focus on understanding which characteristics of developers' networks and what actionable knowledge components sought from these networks contribute to valued outcomes for the developers and the software teams. It is also of interest to see how developers' experience and project characteristics affect these relationships. As Ghobadi and D'Andra (2012) suggest, there are cooperative and competitive dynamics inherent in cross-functional software development teams. Understanding how the social capital of developers affects such dynamics in producing positive systems development outcomes should be of great value to both academics and practitioners. The developers in this study were all Indian nationals. Future research should examine if there are differences in the knowledge networks and knowledge seeking behaviors of developers of other nationalities.

CONCLUSION

As software development is an intensive knowledge creation activity, software developers constantly look for actionable information from various sources to help solve the task at hand, whether involving requirements analysis, system design, coding or bug-fixing. Based on a case study in a software development organization, this research explores the personal knowledge networks of software developers in terms of their structural and relational characteristics and the kind of actionable sought by developers from their information contacts. Using developer experience as a grouping variable this research explores the differences in the knowledge networks and the information needs of differences at two different levels—entry-level developers vs. the more experienced developers. Clearly, more empirical research is warranted to validate the study findings and to further our understanding of personal knowledge networks and knowledge-seeking behaviors of developers.

REFERENCES

Adler, P. S., & Kwon, S. W. (2002). Social Capital: Prospects for a New Concept. *Academy of Management Review, 27*(1), 17–40. doi:10.5465/amr.2002.5922314

Ågerfalk, P., & Fitzgerald, B. (2006). Flexible and Distributed Software Processes: Old Petunias in New Bowls? *Communications of the ACM, 49*(10), 27–34.

Alavi, M., & Leidner, D. E. (2001). Review: Knowledge Management and Knowledge Management Systems: Conceptual Foundations and Research Issues. *Management Information Systems Quarterly, 25*(1), 107–136. doi:10.2307/3250961

Allen, T. J. (1977). *Managing the Flow of Technology*. Cambridge, MA: MIT press.

Ambler, S. W. (2004). *The Object Primer: Agile Model-Driven Development with UML 2* (3rd ed.). Cambridge, UK: Cambridge University Press. doi:10.1017/CBO9780511584077

Assimakopoulos, D., & Yan, J. (2006). Sources of Knowledge Acquisition for Chinese Software Engineers. *R & D Management, 36*(1), 97–106. doi:10.1111/j.1467-9310.2005.00418.x

Aurum, A., Daneshgar, F., & Ward, J. (2008). Investigating Knowledge Management Practices in Software Development Organisations - An Australian Experience. *Information and Software Technology, 50*(6), 511–533. doi:10.1016/j.infsof.2007.05.005

Aurum, A., Jeffery, R., Wohlin, C., & Handzic, M. (2003). *Managing Software Engineering Knowledge*. New York, NY: Springer-Verlag. doi:10.1007/978-3-662-05129-0

Baker, W., & Dutton, J. E. (2006). Enabling Positive Social Capital in Organizations. In J. E. Dutton & B. Ragins (Eds.), *Exploring Positive Relationships at Work: Building a Theoretical and Research Foundation* (pp. 325–345). Hillsdale, N.J.: Lawrence Erlbaum, Inc.

Baker, W. E., & Faulkner, R. R. (2004). Social networks and loss of capital. *Social Networks, 26*(2), 91–111. doi:10.1016/j.socnet.2004.01.004

Bandura, A. (1969). Social-learning theory of identificatory processes. In D.A. Goslin (Ed.), Handbook of Socialization Theory and Research (Ch. 3). Rand McNally & Company.

Basili, V., Caldiera, G., & Rombach, H. (1994). *Experience Factory Encyclopedia of Software Engineering* (Vol. 1, pp. 469–476). Malden, MA: John Wiley.

Baskerville, R., & Pries-Heje, J. (2004). Short Cycle Time Systems Development. *Information Systems Journal, 14*(3), 237–264. doi:10.1111/j.1365-2575.2004.00171.x

Batra, D., VanderMeer, D., & Dutta, K. (2011). Extending agile principles to larger, dynamic software projects: A theoretical assessment. *Journal of Database Management, 22*(4), 73–92. doi:10.4018/jdm.2011100104

Beck, K., & Andres, C. (2005). *Extreme Programming Explained: Embrace Change*. Addison-Wesley.

Berends, H. (2005). Exploring knowledge sharing: Moves, problem solving and justification. *Knowledge Management Research and Practice, 3*(2), 97–105. doi:10.1057/palgrave.kmrp.8500056

Birk, A., Dingsøyr, T., & Stålhane, T. (2002). Postmortem: Never Leave a Project Without it. *IEEE Software, 19*(3), 43–45. doi:10.1109/MS.2002.1003452

Björklund, T. A. (2013). Initial mental representations of design problems: Differences between experts and novices. *Design Studies, 34*(2), 135–160. doi:10.1016/j.destud.2012.08.005

Bjørnson, F. O., & Dingsøyr, T. (2005). A Study of a Mentoring Program for Knowledge Transfer in a Small Software Consultancy Company. *Paper presented at the 6th International Conference, PROFES*, Oulu, Finland. Academic Press. 10.1007/11497455_21

Bjørnson, F. O., & Dingsøyr, T. (2008). Knowledge Management in Software Engineering: A Systematic Review of Studied Concepts, Findings and Research Methods Used. *Information and Software Technology, 50*(11), 1055–1068. doi:10.1016/j.infsof.2008.03.006

Boehm, B., & Turner, R. (2005). Management Challenges to Implementing Agile Processes in Traditional Development Organizations. *IEEE Software, 22*(5), 30–39. doi:10.1109/MS.2005.129

Bourdieu, P. (1986). The Forms of Capital. In J. G. Richardson (Ed.), *Handbook of Theory and Research for the Sociology of Education* (pp. 241–258). New York: Greenwood.

Bourgeois, L. J. III, & Eisenhardt, K. M. (1988). Strategic Decision Processes in High Velocity Environments: Four Cases in the Microcomputer Industry. *Management Science, 34*(7), 816–835. doi:10.1287/mnsc.34.7.816

Brown, J. S., & Duguid, P. (1991). Organizational Learning and Communities-of-Practice: Toward a Unified View of Working, Learning, and Innovation. *Organization Science, 2*(1), 40–57. doi:10.1287/orsc.2.1.40

Buono, A., & Poulfelt, F. (2005). *Challenges and issues in knowledge management.* Greenwich, CT: Information Age Pub. Inc.

Bush, A. A., & Tiwana, A. (2005). Designing Sticky Knowledge Networks. *Communications of the ACM, 48*(5), 66–71. doi:10.1145/1060710.1060711

Chang, K., Yen, H.-W., Chiang, C.-C., & Parolia, N. (2013). Knowledge contribution in information system development teams: An empirical research from a social cognitive perspective. *International Journal of Project Management, 31*(2), 252–263. doi:10.1016/j.ijproman.2012.06.005

Chase, R. (1997). The Knowledge-Based Organization: An International Survey. *Journal of Knowledge Management, 1*(1), 38–49. doi:10.1108/EUM0000000004578

Cockburn, A. (2000, Oct). Characterizing People as Non-Linear, First Order Components in Software Development. *Paper presented at the 4th International Multi-Conference on Systems, Cybernetics and Informatics*, Orlando, FL. Academic Press.

Coleman, J. S. (1988). Social Capital in the Creation of Human Capital. *American Journal of Sociology, 94*, S95–S120. doi:10.1086/228943

Cross, R., & Sproull, L. (2004). More Than an Answer: Information Relationships for Actionable Knowledge. *Organization Science, 15*(4), 446–462. doi:10.1287/orsc.1040.0075

Cui, X. (2017). In-and extra-role knowledge sharing among information technology professionals: The five-factor model perspective. *International Journal of Information Management, 37*(5), 380–389. doi:10.1016/j.ijinfomgt.2017.04.011

Davenport, T. H., Long, D., & Beers, M. C. (1998). Successful Knowledge Management Projects. *MIT Sloan Management Review, 39*(1), 43–57.

de Souza, É. F., de Almeida Falbo, R., & Vijaykumar, N. L. (2015). Knowledge management initiatives in software testing: A mapping study. *Information and Software Technology, 57*, 378–391. doi:10.1016/j.infsof.2014.05.016

Demarest, M. (1997). Understanding Knowledge Management. *Long Range Planning, 30*(3), 374–384. doi:10.1016/S0024-6301(97)90250-8

Desouza, K. C. (2003a). Barriers to effective use of knowledge management systems in software engineering. *Communications of the ACM, 46*(1), 99–101. doi:10.1145/602421.602458

Desouza, K. C. (2003b). Facilitating tacit knowledge exchange. *Communications of the ACM, 46*(6), 85–88. doi:10.1145/777313.777317

Desouza, K. C., Awazu, Y., & Baloh, P. (2006). Managing Knowledge in Global Software Development Efforts: Issues and Practices. *IEEE Software, 23*(5), 30–37. doi:10.1109/MS.2006.135

Devanbu, P., Zimmermann, T., & Bird, C. (2018). Belief and Evidence: How Software Engineers Form Their Opinions. *IEEE Software, 35*(6), 72–76. doi:10.1109/MS.2018.4321246

Dingsøyr, T. (2005). Postmortem reviews: Purpose and approaches in software engineering. *Information and Software Technology, 47*(5), 293–303. doi:10.1016/j.infsof.2004.08.008

Dingsøyr, T., Bjørnson, F. O., & Shull, F. (2009). What Do We Know about Knowledge Management? Practical Implications for Software Engineering. *IEEE Software, 26*(3), 100–103. doi:10.1109/MS.2009.82

Dingsøyr, T., & Conradi, R. (2002). A Survey of Case Studies of the Use of Knowledge Management in Software Engineering. *International Journal of Software Engineering and Knowledge Engineering, 12*(4), 391–414. doi:10.1142/S0218194002000962

Dingsøyr, T., & Røyrvik, E. (2001). Skills Management as Knowledge Technology in a Software Consultancy Company. In K.-D. Althoff, R. Feldmann, & W. Müller (Eds.), Advances in Learning Software Organizations (pp. 96-103): Springer. doi:10.1007/3-540-44814-4_10

Dingsøyr, T., & Smite, D. (2014). Managing knowledge in global software development projects. *IT Professional, 16*(1), 22–29. doi:10.1109/MITP.2013.19

Doherty, N. F., & King, M. (2005). From technical to socio-technical change: Tackling the human and organizational aspects of systems development projects. *European Journal of Information Systems, 14*(1), 1–5. doi:10.1057/palgrave.ejis.3000517

Dutton, J., & Heaphy, E. (2003). The Power of High Quality Connections. In K. Cameron, J. Dutton, & R. Quinn (Eds.), *Positive Organizational Scholarship* (pp. 263–278). San Francisco, CA: Berrett Koehler.

Earl, M. (2001). Knowledge management strategies: Toward a taxonomy. *Journal of Management Information Systems, 18*(1), 215–233. doi:10.1080/07421222.2001.11045670

Edmondson, A. (1999). Psychological safety and learning behavior in work teams. *Administrative Science Quarterly, 44*(2), 350–383. doi:10.2307/2666999

Ehrhardt, K., & Ragins, B. R. (2019). Relational Attachment at Work: A Complementary Fit Perspective on the Role of Relationships in Organizational Life. *Academy of Management Journal, 62*(1), 248–282. doi:10.5465/amj.2016.0245

Eisenhardt, K. M. (1989). Building theories from case-study research. *Academy of Management Review, 14*(4), 532–550. doi:10.5465/amr.1989.4308385

Erden, Z., von Krogh, G., & Nonaka, I. (2008). The quality of group tacit knowledge. *The Journal of Strategic Information Systems, 17*(1), 4–18. doi:10.1016/j.jsis.2008.02.002

Faraj, S., & Sproull, L. (2000). Coordinating Expertise in Software Development Teams. *Management Science, 46*(12), 1554–1568. doi:10.1287/mnsc.46.12.1554.12072

Fitz-Enz, J. (1978). Who is the DP Professional? *Datamation, 24*(9), 124–128.

Fredrickson, B. L. (1998). What good are positive emotions? *Review of General Psychology, 2*(3), 300–319. doi:10.1037/1089-2680.2.3.300

Gallagher, K. P., Kaiser, K. M., Simon, J. C., Beath, C. M., & Goles, T. (2010). The requisite variety of skills for IT professionals. *Communications of the ACM, 53*(6), 144–148. doi:10.1145/1743546.1743584

Gallivan, M. J., & Keil, M. (2003). The user–developer communication process: A critical case study. *Information Systems Journal, 13*(1), 37–68. doi:10.1046/j.1365-2575.2003.00138.x

Galunic, C., Ertug, G., & Gargiulo, M. (2012). The positive externalities of social capital: Benefiting from senior brokers. *Academy of Management Journal, 55*(5), 1213–1231. doi:10.5465/amj.2010.0827

Ghobadi, S., & D'Ambra, J. (2012). Coopetitive relationships in cross-functional software development teams: How to model and measure? *Journal of Systems and Software, 85*(5), 1096–1104. doi:10.1016/j.jss.2011.12.027

Gittell, J. F. (2003). *The Southwest Airlines Way: Using the Power of Relationships to Achieve High Performance*. New York, NY: McGraw-Hill.

Gold, A. H., Malhotra, A., & Segars, A. H. (2001). Knowledge Management: An Organizational Capabilities Perspective. *Journal of Management Information Systems, 18*(1), 185–214. doi:10.1080/07421 222.2001.11045669

Gopal, A., & Gosain, S. (2010). The role of organizational controls and boundary spanning in software development outsourcing: Implications for project performance. *Information Systems Research, 21*(4), 960–982. doi:10.1287/isre.1080.0205

Gouldner, A. W. (1960). The Norm of Reciprocity. *American Journal of Sociology, 25*(2), 161–178. doi:10.2307/2092623

Grabher, G., & Ibert, O. (2006). Bad company? The ambiguity of personal knowledge networks. *Journal of Economic Geography, 6*(3), 251–271. doi:10.1093/jeg/lbi014

Granovetter, M. (1985). Economic Action and Social Structure: The Problem of Embeddedness. *American Journal of Sociology, 91*(3), 481–510. doi:10.1086/228311

Granovetter, M. S. (1992). Problems of Explanation in Economic Sociology. In N. Nohria & R. Eccles (Eds.), *Networks and Organizations: Structure, Form and Action* (pp. 25–56). Boston, MA: Harvard Business School Press.

Guest, G., Bunce, A., & Johnson, L. (2006). How Many Interviews Are Enough?:An Experiment with Data Saturation and Variability. *Field Methods, 18*(1), 59–82. doi:10.1177/1525822X05279903

Hansen, M. T. (1999). The Search-Transfer Problem: The Role of Weak Ties in Sharing Knowledge Across Organization Subunits. *Administrative Science Quarterly, 44*(1), 82–111. doi:10.2307/2667032

Hansen, M. T., Nohria, N., & Tierney, T. (1999). What's Your Strategy for Managing Knowledge? *Harvard Business Review, 77*(2), 106–116.

Hertzum, M. (2014). Expertise seeking: A review. *Information Processing & Management, 50*(5), 775–795. doi:10.1016/j.ipm.2014.04.003

Hill, C. A. (1991). Seeking Emotional Support: The Influence of Affiliative Need and Partner Warmth. *Journal of Personality and Social Psychology, 60*(1), 112–121. doi:10.1037/0022-3514.60.1.112

Hoegl, M., Parboteeah, K. P., & Munson, C. L. (2003). Team-Level Antecedents of Individuals' Knowledge Networks. *Decision Sciences*, *34*(4), 741–770. doi:10.1111/j.1540-5414.2003.02344.x

Ibarra, H. (1993). Network Centrality, Power, and Innovation Involvement: Determinants of Technical and Administrative Roles. *Academy of Management Journal*, *36*(3), 471–501.

Johannisson, B. (1998). Personal networks in emerging knowledge-based firms: Spatial and functional patterns. *Entrepreneurship and Regional Development*, *10*(4), 297–312. doi:10.1080/08985629800000017

Kahn, W. A. (1990). Psychological conditions of personal engagement and disengagement at work. *Academy of Management Journal*, *33*(4), 692–724.

Kahn, W. A. (2007). Meaningful Connections: Positive Relationships and Attachments at Work. In J. E. Dutton & B. R. Ragins (Eds.), *LEA's organization and management series. Exploring positive relationships at work: Building a theoretical and research foundation* (pp. 189–206). Mahwah, NJ: Lawrence Erlbaum Associates Publishers.

Kalliamvakou, E., Bird, C., Zimmermann, T., Begel, A., DeLine, R., & German, D. M. (2019). What makes a great manager of software engineers? *IEEE Transactions on Software Engineering*, *45*(1), 87–106. doi:10.1109/TSE.2017.2768368

Kautz, K., & Kjærgaard, A. (2007). Towards an integrated model of knowledge sharing in software development: Insights from a case study. *International Journal of Knowledge Management*, *3*(2), 91–117. doi:10.4018/jkm.2007040105

Kautz, K., & Thaysen, K. (2001). Knowledge, learning and IT support in a small software company. *Journal of Knowledge Management*, *5*(4), 349–357. doi:10.1108/EUM0000000006532

Keil, M., & Carmel, E. (1995). Customer-Developer Links in Software Development. *Communications of the ACM*, *38*(5), 33–44. doi:10.1145/203356.203363

Komi-Sirvio, S., Mantyniemi, A., & Seppanen, V. (2002). Toward a practical solution for capturing knowledge for software projects. *IEEE Software*, *19*(3), 60–62. doi:10.1109/MS.2002.1003457

Kwon, S.-W., & Adler, P. S. (2014). Social capital: Maturation of a field of research. *Academy of Management Review*, *39*(4), 412–422. doi:10.5465/amr.2014.0210

Labianca, G., Umphress, E., & Kaufmann, J. (2000). A preliminary test of the negative asymmetry hypothesis in workplace social networks. *Paper presented at the 60th Annual Meeting of the Academy of Management*, Toronto. Academic Press.

Leana, C. R. III, & Van Buren, H. J. (1999). Organizational Social Capital and Employment Practices. *Academy of Management Review*, *24*(3), 538–555. doi:10.5465/amr.1999.2202136

Lee, A. S., & Baskerville, R. L. (2003). Generalizing Generalizability in Information System Research. *Information Systems Research*, *14*(3), 221–243. doi:10.1287/isre.14.3.221.16560

Lee, H., & Choi, B. (2003). Knowledge management enablers, processes, and organizational performance: An integrative view and empirical examination. *Journal of Management Information Systems*, *20*(1), 179–228. doi:10.1080/07421222.2003.11045756

Levin, D. Z., & Cross, R. (2004). The Strength of Weak Ties You Can Trust: The Mediating Role of Trust in Effective Knowledge Transfer. *Management Science, 50*(11), 1477–1490. doi:10.1287/mnsc.1030.0136

Lewis, J. D., & Weigert, A. (1985). Trust as a social reality. *Social Forces, 63*(4), 967–985. doi:10.1093f/63.4.967

Liu, D., Ray, G., & Whinston, A. B. (2010). The interaction between knowledge codification and knowledge-sharing networks. *Information Systems Research, 21*(4), 892–906. doi:10.1287/isre.1080.0217

Long, Y., & Siau, K. (2007). Social network structures in open source software development teams. *Journal of Database Management, 18*(2), 25–40. doi:10.4018/jdm.2007040102

Long, Y., & Siau, K. (2008). Impacts of social network structure on knowledge sharing in open source software development teams. *AMCIS 2008 Proceedings*. Academic Press.

Luna-Reyes, L. F., Zhang, J., Gil-García, J. R., & Cresswell, A. M. (2005). Information Systems Development as Emergent Socio-Technical Change: A Practice Approach. *European Journal of Information Systems, 14*(1), 93–105. doi:10.1057/palgrave.ejis.3000524

McAllister, D. J. (1995). Affect-and cognition-based trust as foundations for interpersonal cooperation in organizations. *Academy of Management Journal, 38*(1), 24–59.

Mehta, N., Hall, D., & Byrd, T. (2014). Information technology and knowledge in software development teams: The role of project uncertainty. *Information & Management, 51*(4), 417–429. doi:10.1016/j.im.2014.02.007

Méndez-Durón, R., & García, C. E. (2009). Returns from social capital in open source software networks. *Journal of Evolutionary Economics, 19*(2), 277–295. doi:10.100700191-008-0125-5

Millen, D. R., Fontaine, M. A., & Muller, M. J. (2002). Understanding the Benefit and Costs of Communities of Practice. *Communications of the ACM, 45*(4), 69–73. doi:10.1145/505248.505276

Mintzberg, H. (1973). *The Nature of Managerial Work*. New York, NY: Harper & Row.

Mitchell, S. M., & Seaman, C. B. (2016). Could removal of project-level knowledge flow obstacles contribute to software process improvement? A study of software engineer perceptions. *Information and Software Technology, 72*, 151–170. doi:10.1016/j.infsof.2015.12.007

Moran, P. (2005). Structural vs. Relational Embeddedness: Social Capital and Managerial Performance. *Strategic Management Journal, 26*(12), 1129–1151. doi:10.1002mj.486

Myers, C. G. (2018). Coactive vicarious learning: Toward a relational theory of vicarious learning in organizations. *Academy of Management Review, 43*(4), 610–634. doi:10.5465/amr.2016.0202

Nahapiet, J., & Ghoshal, S. (1998). Social Capital, Intellectual Capital, and the Organizational Advantage. *Academy of Management Review, 23*(2), 242–266. doi:10.5465/amr.1998.533225

Nerur, S., & Balijepally, V. (2007). Theoretical Reflections on Agile Development Methodologies. *Communications of the ACM, 50*(3), 79–83. doi:10.1145/1226736.1226739

Newell, S. (2004). Enhancing Cross-Project Learning. *Engineering Management Journal*, *16*(1), 12–20. doi:10.1080/10429247.2004.11415234

Nonaka, I. (1994). Dynamic Theory of Organizational Knowledge Creation. *Organization Science*, *5*(1), 14–37. doi:10.1287/orsc.5.1.14

Organ, D. W. (1988). *Organizational citizenship behavior: The good soldier syndrome*: Lexington Books/ DC Heath and Com.

Oshri, I., van Fenema, P., & Kotlarsky, J. (2008). Knowledge transfer in globally distributed teams: The role of transactive memory. *Information Systems Journal*, *18*(6), 593–616. doi:10.1111/j.1365-2575.2007.00243.x

Ozer, M., & Vogel, D. (2015). Contextualized relationship between knowledge sharing and performance in software development. *Journal of Management Information Systems*, *32*(2), 134–161. doi:10.1080/07421222.2015.1063287

Paré, G. (2004). Investigating Information Systems With Positivist Case Study Research. *Communications of AIS*, *13*, 233–264.

Patnayakuni, R., Rai, A., & Tiwana, A. (2007). Systems Development Process Improvement: A Knowledge Integration Perspective. *IEEE Transactions on Engineering Management*, *54*(2), 286–300. doi:10.1109/TEM.2007.893997

Pelz, D., & Andrews, F. (1966). *Scientists in Organizations: Productive Climates for Research and Development*. New York, NY: Wiley.

Petter, S., Mathiassen, L., & Vaishnavi, V. (2007). Five Keys to Project Knowledge Sharing. *IT Professional*, *9*(3), 42–46. doi:10.1109/MITP.2007.44

Pfeffer, J., & Sutton, R. I. (2000). *The knowing-doing gap*. Boston, MA: Harvard Business School Press.

Podolny, J. (1992). Interview with John Clendenin [video]. Stanford, CA: Stanford Business School.

Polanyi, M. (1966). *The Tacit Dimension*. New York: Anchor Day Books.

Poppendieck, M., & Poppendieck, T. (2006). *Implementing Lean Software Development: From Concept to Cash*. Addison-Wesley Professional.

Powell, W. W. (1998). Learning From Collaboration: Knowledge and Networks in the Biotechnology and Pharmaceutical Industries. *California Management Review*, *40*(3), 228–240. doi:10.2307/41165952

Putnam, R. D. (1993). The Prosperous Community: Social Capital and Public Life. *The American Prospect*, *4*(13), 35–42.

Reagans, R. (2011). Close encounters: Analyzing how social similarity and propinquity contribute to strong network connections. *Organization Science*, *22*(4), 835–849. doi:10.1287/orsc.1100.0587

Robillard, P. N. (1999). The Role of Knowledge in Software Development. *Communications of the ACM*, *42*(1), 87–92. doi:10.1145/291469.291476

Robinson, M. A. (2010). An empirical analysis of engineers' information behaviors. *Journal of the American Society for Information Science and Technology, 61*(4), 640–658.

Ruggles, R. (1998). The State of the Notion: Knowledge Management In Practice. *California Management Review, 40*(3), 80–89. doi:10.2307/41165944

Rus, I., & Lindvall, M. (2002). Knowledge Management in Software Engineering. *IEEE Software, 19*(3), 26–38. doi:10.1109/MS.2002.1003450

Ryan, S., & O'Connor, R. V. (2009). Development of a team measure for tacit knowledge in software development teams. *Journal of Systems and Software, 82*(2), 229–240. doi:10.1016/j.jss.2008.05.037

Ryan, S., & O'Connor, R. V. (2013). Acquiring and sharing tacit knowledge in software development teams: An empirical study. *Information and Software Technology, 55*(9), 1614–1624. doi:10.1016/j.infsof.2013.02.013

Safdar, U., Badir, Y. F., & Afsar, B. (2017). Who can I ask? How psychological safety affects knowledge sourcing among new product development team members. *The Journal of High Technology Management Research, 28*(1), 79–92. doi:10.1016/j.hitech.2017.04.006

Seibert, S. E., Kraimer, M. L., & Liden, R. C. (2001). A Social Capital Theory of Career Success. *Academy of Management Journal, 44*(2), 219–237.

Simonin, B. L. (1999). Ambiguity and the Process of Knowledge Transfer in Strategic Alliances. *Strategic Management Journal, 20*(7), 595–623. doi:10.1002/(SICI)1097-0266(199907)20:7<595::AID-SMJ47>3.0.CO;2-5

Spender, J. C. (1996). Making Knowledge the Basis of a Dynamic Theory of the Firm. *Strategic Management Journal, 17*(S2), 45–62. doi:10.1002mj.4250171106

Su, C., & Contractor, N. (2011). A multidimensional network approach to studying team members' information seeking from human and digital knowledge sources in consulting firms. *Journal of the American Society for Information Science and Technology, 62*(7), 1257–1275. doi:10.1002/asi.21526

Subramaniam, M., & Youndt, M. A. (2005). The Influence of Intellectual Capital on the Types of Innovative Capabilities. *Academy of Management Journal, 48*(3), 450–463. doi:10.5465/amj.2005.17407911

Swan, J., Newell, S., Scarbrough, H., & Hislop, D. (1999). Knowledge management and innovation: Networks and networking. *Journal of Knowledge Management, 3*(4), 262–275. doi:10.1108/13673279910304014

Taylor, M. (1982). *Community, anarchy, and liberty*. New York, NY: Cambridge University Press. doi:10.1017/CBO9780511607875

Thompson, M. (2005). Structural and Epistemic Parameters in Communities of Practice. *Organization Science, 16*(2), 151–164. doi:10.1287/orsc.1050.0120

Tsai, W., & Ghoshal, S. (1998). Social Capital and Value Creation: The Role of Intrafirm Networks. *Academy of Management Journal, 41*(4), 464–476.

van der Rijt, J., Van den Bossche, P., van de Wiel, M. W., De Maeyer, S., Gijselaers, W. H., & Segers, M. S. (2013). Asking for help: A relational perspective on help seeking in the workplace. *Vocations and Learning*, *6*(2), 259–279. doi:10.100712186-012-9095-8

Van Wijk, R., Jansen, J. J. P., & Lyles, M. A. (2008). Inter- and Intra-Organizational Knowledge Transfer: A Meta-Analytic Review and Assessment of its Antecedents and Consequences. *Journal of Management Studies*, *45*(4), 830–853. doi:10.1111/j.1467-6486.2008.00771.x

VanWijk, R., Jansen, J. J., & Lyles, M. A. (2008). Inter-and intra-organizational knowledge transfer: A meta-analytic review and assessment of its antecedents and consequences. *Journal of Management Studies*, *45*(4), 830–853. doi:10.1111/j.1467-6486.2008.00771.x

Wagner, C., & Bolloju, N. (2005). Supporting knowledge management in organizations with conversational technologies: Discussion forums, weblogs, and wikis. *Journal of Database Management*, *16*(2), I.

Walz, D. B., Elam, J. J., & Curtis, B. (1993). Inside a software design team: Knowledge acquisition, sharing, and integration. *Communications of the ACM*, *36*(10), 63–77. doi:10.1145/163430.163447

Wenger, E. C., & Snyder, W. M. (2000). Communities of Practice: The Organizational Frontier. *Harvard Business Review*, 139–145.

Wohlin, C., Šmite, D., & Moe, N. B. (2015). A general theory of software engineering: Balancing human, social and organizational capitals. *Journal of Systems and Software*, *109*, 229–242. doi:10.1016/j.jss.2015.08.009

Xu, Y., Kim, H.-W., & Kankanhalli, A. (2010). Task and social information seeking: Whom do we prefer and whom do we approach? *Journal of Management Information Systems*, *27*(3), 211–240. doi:10.2753/MIS0742-1222270308

Xu, Y., Zhang, C., & Zhang, C. (2010). Information seeking in an information systems project team. *IEEE Transactions on Professional Communication*, *53*(4), 370–381. doi:10.1109/TPC.2010.2044620

Yang, S.-C., & Farn, C.-K. (2009). Social capital, behavioural control, and tacit knowledge sharing—A multi-informant design. *International Journal of Information Management*, *29*(3), 210–218. doi:10.1016/j.ijinfomgt.2008.09.002

Ye, Y. (2005). Dimensions and forms of knowledge collaboration in software development. *Paper presented at the 12th Asia-Pacific Software Engineering Conference, APSEC '05*. Academic Press. 10.1109/APSEC.2005.62

Ye, Y., Yamamoto, Y., & Kishida, K. (2004). Dynamic community: a new conceptual framework for supporting knowledge collaboration in software development. *Paper presented at the 11th Asia-Pacific Software Engineering Conference*. Academic Press.

Yin, R. K. (2001). *Case Study Research: Design and Methods* (3rd ed.). Thousand Oaks, CA: Sage Publications.

Yli-Renko, H., Autio, E., & Sapienza, H. J. (2001). Social Capital, Knowledge Acquisition, And Knowledge Exploitation In Young Technology-Based Firms. *Strategic Management Journal*, *22*(6/7), 587–613. doi:10.1002mj.183

Young, G. J., Charns, M. P., & Shortell, S. M. (2001). Top Manager and Network Effects on the Adoption of Innovative Management Practices: A Study of TQM in a Public Hospital System. *Strategic Management Journal*, 22(10), 935–951. doi:10.1002mj.194

Yuan, M., Zhang, X., Chen, Z., Vogel, D. R., & Chu, X. (2009). Antecedents of coordination effectiveness of software developer dyads from interacting teams: An empirical investigation. *IEEE Transactions on Engineering Management*, 56(3), 494–507. doi:10.1109/TEM.2008.927819

Zhou, M., & Mockus, A. (2010). Developer fluency: achieving true mastery in software projects. *Paper presented at the eighteenth ACM SIGSOFT international symposium on Foundations of software engineering*, Santa Fe, NM. ACM Press. 10.1145/1882291.1882313

This research was previously published in the Journal of Database Management (JDM), 30(4); pages 41-80, copyright year 2019 by IGI Publishing (an imprint of IGI Global).

APPENDIX

Questionnaire Items for Some Relational Social Capital Dimensions of Software Developers [Adapted from Levin and Cross (2004) and Hansen (1999)]

Tie-strength: Prior to seeking information/advice from this person on this project

A.   How close was your working relationship?
      1. very close   2. close   3. somewhat close   4. not sure
      5. somewhat distant   6. distant   7. very distant
B.   How often did you communicate?
      1. daily   2. twice a week   3. once a week   4. twice a month   5. once a month
      6. once every 2nd month   7. once every 3rd month (or never)
C.   C. To what extent did you typically interact with this person?
      1. to no extent   2. to a very little extent   3. to a little extent   4. to some extent
      5. to a reasonable extent   6. to a great extent   7. to a very great extent

Friendship: Prior to seeking information/advice from this person on this project

A.   I would have felt awkward talking to this person about a non-work related problem
      1. strongly disagree   2. disagree   3. somewhat disagree   4. not sure
      5. somewhat agree   6. Agree   7. strongly agree
B.   I knew this person well outside of work-related areas
      1. strongly disagree   2. disagree   3. somewhat disagree   4. not sure
      5. somewhat agree   6. Agree   7. strongly agree

Availability: Prior to seeking information/advice from this person on this project

A.   It would generally be hard for me to get in touch with this person
      1. strongly disagree   2. disagree   3. somewhat disagree   4. not sure
      5. somewhat agree   6. Agree   7. strongly agree
B.   in general I could find this person if I wanted to talk to him or her
      1. strongly disagree   2. disagree   3. somewhat disagree   4. not sure
      5. somewhat agree   6. Agree   7. strongly agree
C.   This person would usually be around if I were to need him or her
      1. strongly disagree   2. disagree   3. somewhat disagree   4. not sure
      5. somewhat agree   6. Agree   7. strongly agree

Chapter 65
Team Characteristics Moderating Effect on Software Project Completion Time

Niharika Dayyala
(iD) https://orcid.org/0000-0003-3128-9954
Illinois State University, USA

Kent A. Walstrom
Illinois State University, USA

Kallol K. Bagchi
(iD) https://orcid.org/0000-0002-5821-4349
The University of Texas at El Paso, USA

ABSTRACT

This study highlights the importance of human factors in software projects developed in capability maturity model (CMM) level software development environments. While software process initiatives help streamline the development process, people factors can influence project outcomes. Using data procured from the International Software Benchmarking Standard Group, the effects of team turnover, team heterogeneity, and team member work experience were examined as they moderate project elapsed time for software projects developed in CMM level software development environments. Team member work experience and team functional heterogeneity were found to have significant moderating effects on project elapsed time to completion. The turnover of members on the team did not have a significant moderating effect on project elapsed time to completion. Previous studies have examined the benefits of raising the level of maturity as identified by the capability maturity model. This study identifies the importance of human factors as they moderate project success.

DOI: 10.4018/978-1-6684-3702-5.ch065

1. INTRODUCTION

The Capability Maturity Model (CMM) is a framework developed by the Software Engineering Institute (SEI) for assessing the maturity of the software development process of organizations. The Capability Maturity Model Integration (CMMI) evolved from the CMM by addressing the integration issues with multiple development models in an organization. CMMI was widely adopted after its release in 2002 (Latif et al., 2019). The CMM and CMMI frameworks describe the key elements to make the software development process manageable, measurable, predictable and repeatable (Örgün et al., 2018). The frameworks facilitate improvement and optimization in the information systems development process in an organization. This staged five level model was built on the proposition that the quality of the software product depends on the quality of the software development and maintenance processes (Söylemez & Tarhan, 2018). The five staged model for CMM and CMMI recommend practices in the process areas to enhance software development and maintenance capabilities (Cuenca et al., 2013). According to Curtis (2019), higher level maturity ratings in an organization leads to better software development than organizations with a lower level of maturity rating.

Despite the existence of various quality centric methods and process improvement techniques many software projects result in systems that do not function as intended, are not used, or are not delivered on time (Khan & Keung, 2016; Lu et al., 2011). Process improvement may not be the complete answer to improving project performance.

AlQaisi et al., (2017) propose that people and teams can shape the sociotechnical environment that exists in software development. The authors state that human related factors on software engineering have first order effect on software development outcomes. According to Yilmaz et al., (2017) team personnel factors are key elements that impact the effectiveness and productivity of software teams. Luna-Reyes et al., (2005) note that a substantial percentage of Information System (IS) failures are due to social and organizational factors, not just technical factors. According to Lu et al., (2011), team composition, dynamics, and interaction of team members are the most important aspects influencing IS development project success. Some of the important characteristics of teams include: work experience of team members; qualification of team members; and a sustainable mix of internal and external team members (Bloch et al., 2012).

Despite the importance of human factors and teams in software development, there is lack of progress in understanding these (Capretz et al., 2017; Almomani et al., 2018). Capretz et al., (2017) and Hoegl & Parboteeah (2007) highlight the presence of only a few qualitative and quantitative investigations about the role of team members and team characteristics. Muñoz et al., (2016) note that software development processes have major influences on the software team's performance. Therefore, the purpose of this study is to examine the moderating effects of team characteristics on project elapsed time of software development in the context of CMM/CMMI level software development environments.

Acquiring the right talent, retaining talent, workforce allocation and planning for critical work positions is a priority for software development managers. To fully utilize the capabilities of the workforce and for successful project completion. Several project factors may influence the success of a software development project. In this study, the focus is how team related factors impact software project outcomes when developers use CMM/CMMI level software development practices. Results from this study can benefit software development practitioners in making the right decisions about staffing teams and assisting team management. This study fits topics covered in the International Journal of Information

Technologies and Systems Approach (IJITSA). It examines the research intersection of the CMM software process framework and the Systemic design of Information Technology (IT) systems.

2. LITERATURE REVIEW

2.1. Project Performance in Information Systems Development

Generally, software projects have multiple outcomes (Langer et al., 2014); hence, several researchers in previous studies have measured project performance using various metrics such as costs, elapsed time, productivity, and quality. In a study by Alla et al., (2017), the authors incorporated cost variation and project schedule variation to determine the relationship between business requirements documentation and software project success. Langer, et al. (2014) used cost performance (actual expenses incurred in projects) and client satisfaction (actual rating for customer satisfaction of a project) to measure project performance. Han (2014) used four measures to estimate project performance: quality, time, customer satisfaction and budget to determine how the different categories of risks affect project performance measures. Athavale & Balaraman (2013), used project performance measures such as quality and quantity of work completed in a unit time (productivity) to develop a human behavioral modeling simulation to demonstrate how human aspects affect task performance in software project development. A successful software project requires the accurate prediction of size, effort and elapsed time for development (Lopez-Martin et al., 2017).

For the purpose of this study elapsed time was selected as the process performance metric. Elapsed time denotes the time taken for the completion of software project (ISBSG, 2016).

2.2. The Capability Maturity Model (CMM) and Capability Maturity Model Integration (CMMI)

The Capability Maturity Model research to date has focused on the factors impacting its adoption (Sharma & Sangal, 2019; Alsawalqah et al., 2019), the after effects of implementing maturity models in the software development process (Bushuyev & Verenych, 2018; Khan et al., 2018; Örgün et al., 2018), case studies on the adoption of process maturity (Buss, 2018) and research reports on the impact on productivity, cycle time, and quality (Paulk, 2009). El Emam and Koru (2008) found that organizational maturity, methodology, and project management experience would affect project success. Örgün et al., (2018) found software development productivity increased due to the reduction of rework in a CMMI level 5 organization. Lee et al., (2017) observed that a firm's absorptive capacity on software process initiative implementation can reduce development cycle time, reduce cost and increase customer satisfaction. Galin & Avrahami (2006) analyzed 19 research studies published about CMM. They concluded project performance improved consistently for seven software development performance metrics when CMM/CMMI principles were used.

2.3. Human Factors in Information Systems Development

Previous research has shown teams staffed with the right people are more likely to be efficient and effective. Cuevas et al., (2018) note that teams and team construction are of key importance in achieving the objectives of process improvement. Although team characteristics have been deemed important by prior researchers, empirical investigations are few (Hoegl & Parboteeah, 2007). In particular, there are few studies that examined the important traits of IS professionals in team contexts (Siau et al., 2010). Hence, there is a need to explore the effect of team characteristics on software project outcomes (Colomo-Palacios et al., 2012).

This study specifically focusses on the team characteristics of team turnover, team functional heterogeneity, and team member work experience. These three characteristics were identified as important moderators that can impact project outcomes of CMM/CMMI level software projects.

2.4. Team Turnover

Turnover (voluntary and involuntary attrition) in the software industry is a challenging problem. Retaining experienced developers is impacted by leaves of absences, retirements and turnover (Šmite et al., 2017). Turnover should be reduced as much as possible to maintain the momentum and motivation of a team (Ebert et al., 2008). Alqadri et al., (2020) note staff turnover in Software Process Initiative (SPI) implementation can increase the costs of hiring replacement staff. Turnover also creates loss of knowledge adversely impacting the project costs and schedules. Employee turnover is a major challenge in software teams because of the knowledge gap arising from planned and unplanned resource releases (Sundararajan et al., 2017). Korrapati & Eedara (2010) stated that in 1999, the software industry had responded to the problem of turnover by increasing the salaries of professionals, this in turn, increased productivity. Low absenteeism and low turnover were indirect benefits for Raytheon when it achieved higher productivity upon evolving from level 1 to levels 2 and 3 of the CMM (Ramanujan & Kesh, 2004). In an exploratory case study of a large-scale distributed software development project at Erickson, Britto et al., (2016) found team turnover negatively correlated to team performance and productivity. Therefore, high turnover can adversely impact project outcomes even though the projects implement the best processes. In this study, both voluntary and involuntary departures causing turnover in a team are considered. Such was termed as team turnover. Thus, the following hypothesis was proposed.

Hypothesis 1: As the CMM level of a software project increases the elapsed time to project completion will decrease. This decrease will be moderated by team turnover such that as team turnover increases elapsed time to project completion will increase.

2.5. Team Functional Heterogeneity

In this study, heterogeneity is measured as the team members belonging to different functional levels of an organization. Software development is complex. It needs the expertise and skills of individuals from different functional areas of an organization such as technical, process, domain and product (Šmite et al., 2017). Team members from a greater number of functional levels indicates higher heterogeneity in the team. Prior studies about the relationship between heterogeneity and project performance have yielded mixed findings. Some researchers observed that heterogeneity in teams gave more positive outcomes than homogeneity in teams and the reverse was true for other studies. A study by Anderson et al., (2019) indicated that homogeneous teams performed well in the initial phases of software development, but over time heterogeneous teams performed much better. According to Lassak, et al. (2017), software organizations form heterogeneous teams to increase efficiency and competitive advantage by leveraging the creativity and flexible adaptation capabilities of team members. On the other hand, broader participation of team members with heterogeneous skillsets in a software development team poses challenges in the form of greater training, code walkthroughs, reviews which may trigger team conflicts, communication and coordination issues (Kudaravalli et al., (2017). However, most of the studies have focused on the top management team heterogeneity but not at the development team level. In this study, the functional heterogeneous team includes software developers, support groups, users, testing groups and other project stakeholders. Therefore, the following hypothesis was proposed.

Hypothesis 2: As the CMM level of a software project increases the elapsed time to project completion will decrease. This decrease will be moderated by team functional heterogeneity such that as team functional heterogeneity increases elapsed time to project completion will increase.

2.6. Team Experience

Understanding the role of work experience in software development is essential because workforce costs constitutes the largest component of software project development costs (Fong Boh et al., 2007). Software developers practice their craft based on their training and work experience (Devanbu et al., 2016). Hence, work experience is an important factor for better project outcomes. According to Bloch, et al. (2012), the right team would understand both business and technical concerns, which is why companies must assign a few high-performing and experienced experts for the length of the program. When considering similar complexity of projects, experienced developers introduce lesser defects compared to developers who are unfamiliar with previous projects in an organization (Tsunoda et al., 2018). Cataldo et al., (2008) noted that experienced software development personnel in different dimensions like tools, domain area, and programming can be more productive and can shorten the development time for a project. High management and staff experience contributed 120 percent to productivity while efficient methods/process contributes only 35 percent (Adolph et al., 2012). Fong Boh, et al. (2007) analyzed whether individuals, groups, and organizational units learn from experience in software development and further examined if experience improves productivity. They found that specialization and diverse experience enhances productivity. To understand the importance of work experience in software development projects the following hypothesis was proposed.

Hypothesis 3: As the CMM level of a software project increases the elapsed time to project completion will decrease. This decrease will be moderated by team experience such that as team experience increases elapsed time to project completion will decrease.

2.7. Research Model

The central idea of the study is that the higher the CMM level of the development process the lower the elapsed time to project delivery. It is hypothesized that this relationship will be moderated by the software development team characteristics. Hence, the research model explores the moderation effects of: team turnover rate, team functional heterogeneity, and team work experience on elapsed time to project delivery (Dayyala, 2017). Figure 1 displays the expected nature of effect between the constructs of the study.

Figure 1. Research Model for the Study

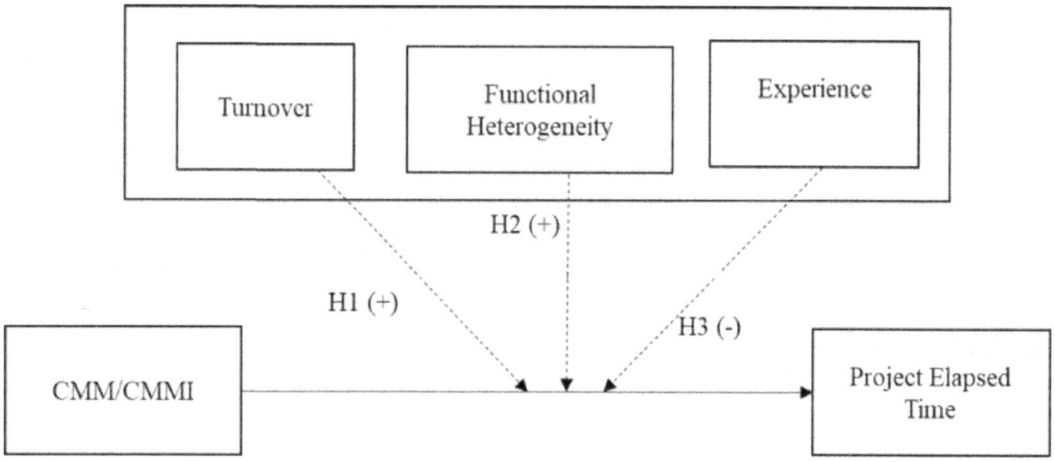

This study examines the following hypotheses:

H1: As the CMM level of a software project increases the elapsed time to project completion will decrease. This decrease will be moderated by team turnover such that as team turnover increases elapsed time to project completion will increase.

H2: As the CMM level of a software project increases the elapsed time to project completion will decrease. This decrease will be moderated by team functional heterogeneity such that as team functional heterogeneity increases elapsed time to project completion will increase.

H3: As the CMM level of a software project increases the elapsed time to project completion will decrease. This decrease will be moderated by team experience such that as team experience increases elapsed time to project completion will decrease.

3. DATA AND METHODOLOGY

3.1. Data

Data was procured from the International Software Benchmarking Standard Group (ISBSG) Corporate Release repository. The repository comprises data of about 5700 software projects that were either newly developed or enhanced between 1989 and 2012. The software projects belong to a wide range of business areas collected from twenty different countries. Data in the ISBSG repository was reported by software organizations and industry leaders on a voluntarily basis. For the purpose of this study, 279 software development projects developed with CMM/CMMI (124 CMM and 155 CMMI) practices between 1999 and 2011 are identified. Among the software projects used for the study CMM practices were adopted for projects developed between 1999 to 2009 and CMMI practices were adopted for projects between 2003 and 2011. The study combines the CMM and CMMI projects to test the moderation effects of team characteristics on the relation between CMM/CMMI level (level 1, level 2, level 3, level 4, level

5) and the project elapsed time. Variables that quantify the team characteristics such as team turnover, team work experience and team heterogeneity were identified from the dataset to perform the analysis.

3.2. Project Elapsed Time

The dependent variable used in the research model is project elapsed time to completion. Project elapsed time is an important measure for every business especially software development since it helps to make decisions about the project cost and plan resources to deliver the project to the stakeholders (ISBSG). According to the ISBSG, project elapsed time is total time taken for the completion of the project in months.

3.3. CMM/CMMI Level

CMM level indicates the CMM/CMMI level (1, 2, 3, 4 or 5) of the software development process followed for a project. As shown in Table 1.

Table 1. Distribution of Projects Based on the CMM/CMMI Level

CMM/CMMI	No. of Projects
level 1	6
level 2	136
level 3	60
level 4	9
level 5	68

3.4. Team Turnover

Team turnover represents the number of team member removals and additions to a software development team during the length of the software development process. Turnover on a software team can occur due to decisions by top management or due to decisions of team members. Voluntary turnover decisions could range from project managers to project personnel. The study considers turnover occurring due to any abnormal replacements due to the illness, nonperformance and voluntary resignations of the team members. Team turnover is a formative construct measured with two attributes: number of unexpected changes in the project manager and number of unexpected changes in the project personnel in the project duration.

3.5. Team Heterogeneity

Team heterogeneity is the functional heterogeneity existing in the software team. Software development requires personnel from different functional areas or levels to work as a team. The team heterogeneity construct in this study is measured using four resource levels. It is measured using a single item attribute which includes all the people whose time is included in the work effort for a project. Level 1 includes all the software development team personnel (e.g., project team, project management, project administration). Level 2 includes Level 1 personnel plus all development team support personnel (e.g., database management, data administration, quality assurance, data security, standards support, audit & control, technical support. Level 3 includes Level 2 personnel plus computer operations personnel (e.g., software support, hardware support, information center support, computer operators, network administration). Level 4 includes Level 3 personnel plus end users or clients (e.g., user liaisons, user training time, application users and/or clients).

3.6. Work Experience

Work experience is measured by the number of years of prior work experience of team members involved in the software development process. Software development teams are primarily comprised of project managers, developers, business analysts, etc. In this study work experience is a formative construct measured using two variables: average work experience of team members in software development and average prior work experience of team members in the business area of the project.

3.7. Structural Equation Modeling

Structural Equation Modeling (SEM) is employed to test the hypotheses about the moderation effects of team characteristics on project elapsed time. WARPPLS 5 (Kock, 2015) software is used to test the model. The research model was tested in two stages. In the first stage, the model is tested only for main effects (Model 1). In the second stage, the model is tested for both the main and the moderation effects (Model 2). The analysis of the results from the SEM analysis was performed in two stages. In the first stage, the overall fit of the model was tested using the model fit indices suggested by (Kock, 2015) and the measurement model is validated using the convergent and discriminant validity. In stage two, the structural model is analyzed to test the hypotheses and the path coefficients for the relationships between the exogenous (path arrows pointing outwards and none leading to it) and the endogenous variables (variables have at least one path leading to it or dependent variables).

4. RESULTS

The model fit indices from the PLS analysis for the Model 1 and Model 2 are shown in Table 2.

According to Kock (2015), it is recommended that the P-values for the Average path coefficient (APC), Average R-squared (ARS) and Average Adjusted R-squared (AARS) all be equal to or lower than 0.05; that is, significant at the 0.05 level for model fit and quality. Both Model 1 and Model 2 satisfy this condition. It can also be observed that the average R-square and average adjusted R-square increase after moderation effects are added to the model. This shows that the model with the moderation effects (Model 2) (ARS=0.32; AARS=0.31) has a better fit compared to the main effects model (Model 1) (ARS =0.24; AARS=0.23). The Tenenhaus GoF (GoF) index is a measure of a model's explanatory power. For both the models, results show that the GoF value is greater than 0.36 indicating they have high explanatory power. Compared to the main effects model (Model 1), the moderation effects model (Model 2) has higher explanatory power. Thus, both models are stable with Model 2 explaining a greater amount of variance and with high explanatory power.

Table 2. Model fit indices

Model fit indices	Model 1	Model 2	Recommended value
Average path coefficient (APC)	0.18; P=0.002	0.15; P=0.002	p<0.05
Average R-squared (ARS)	0.24, P<0.001	0.32, P<0.001	p<0.05
Average adjusted R-squared (AARS)	0.23, P<0.001	0.31, P<0.001	p<0.05
Average block VIF (AVIF)	1.19	1.41	acceptable if <= 5, ideally <= 3.3
Average full collinearity VIF (AFVIF)	1.28	1.61	acceptable if <= 5, ideally <= 3.3
Tenenhaus GoF (GoF)	0.48	0.54	small >= 0.1, medium >= 0.25, large >= 0.36
Sympson's paradox ratio (SPR)	1	1	acceptable if >= 0.7, ideally = 1
R-squared contribution ratio (RSCR)	1	1	acceptable if >= 0.9, ideally = 1
Statistical suppression ratio (SSR)	1	1	acceptable if >= 0.7
Nonlinear bivariate causality direction ratio (NLBCDR)	1	0.93	acceptable if >= 0.7

Further analysis was performed in two steps. Firstly, the measurement models were validated using convergent and discriminant validity. Secondly, the path coefficients of the structural model were analyzed to test the hypothesis.

4.1. Measurement Model

The research model was tested for convergent validity using confirmatory factor analysis with the factor loadings and cross-loadings. The P-values associated with the factor loadings must be less than or equal to 0.05; and the factor loadings must be greater than or equal to 0.5 (Hair et al., 1998; Kock, 2015). Results from the confirmatory factor analysis for Model 2 indicate that all the measurement items load well into their corresponding latent constructs without any notable cross-loadings as shown in Table 3.

Discriminant validity was used to measure the quality of the research model. This was done by comparing the average variance extracted to the correlations among the latent variables. According to Fornell & Larcker (1981) and Nunnally & Bernstein (1994) discriminant validity can be confirmed if the square root of average variance extracted of a latent variable is greater than the correlation with any other latent variable. Correlation between latent constructs and average variance extracted (AVE) for Model 2 are shown in Table 4. The table indicates that the AVE is greater than the correlations between the constructs thus showing evidence of discriminant validity.

Reliability of the constructs is measured using the composite reliabilities of the latent variables. Fornell & Larcker (1981) and Nunnally & Bernstein (1994) note that the composite reliabilities of latent variables need be greater than 0.7 for construct reliability. Composite reliabilities for the constructs of the study are found acceptable as shown in Table 5. The Value Inflation Factors (VIF) for both Model 1 and Model 2 were also tested (VIF < 2.5 is desirable) to check for multicollinearity issues between the latent variables (Hair et al., 1998). Results show that there are no multicollinearity issues between the latent variables (VIF of Model 1 = 1.19 and Model 2 = 1.41).

Table 3. Normalized Combined Loadings and Cross Loadings of Measurement Items into the Latent Constructs (Model 2)

Measurement items	P-Value	Elapsed time	Heterogeneity	Experience	Turnover	CMM
Project Elapsed time	<0.001	1	0	0	0	0
No. of Resource level	<0.001	0	1	0	0	0
IT developer experience	<0.001	0.02	-0.02	**0.78**	0.13	-0.05
Business Area experience	<0.001	-0.02	0.02	**0.78**	-0.13	0.05
Personnel changes	<0.001	0.03	0.005	-0.01	**0.83**	-0.09
Manager changes	<0.001	-0.03	-0.005	0.01	**0.80**	0.09
CMM level	<0.001	0	0	0	0	1
For convergent validity, P values associated with the loadings be equal to or lower than 0.05; and that the loadings be equal to or greater than 0.5						

Table 4. Inter Construct Correlations and Discriminant Validity of Latent Constructs (Model 2)

Constructs	Elapsed time	Heterogeneity	Experience	Turnover	CMM/CMMI
Elapsed time	**1**				
Team heterogeneity	-0.07	**1**			
Experience	0.14	0	**0.94**		
Team turnover	0.24	0.04	0.57	**0.86**	
CMM/CMMI	-0.2	-0.15	-0.16	-0.04	**1**
Inter construct Correlations Table: Diagonal elements in the correlation of constructs matrix are the square root of the average variance extracted. For adequate discriminant validity, diagonal elements (Composite reliability) should be greater than corresponding off-diagonal elements.					

Table 5. Composite reliability of the Latent Constructs (Model 2)

Constructs	Composite Reliability
Elapsed time	1
Team heterogeneity	1
Experience	0.94
Team turnover	0.86
CMM/CMMI	1

4.2. Structural Model

PLS-SEM results show that the average adjusted R square for Model 1 was 0.23 and Model 2 was 0.31. The difference in R-square between Model 1 and Model 2 was 0.08, the difference in R-square indicates the presence of moderation effects. It is evident from the model fit indices of the PLS analysis that there was an increase in the explained variance when the moderation effects are added to the model in addition to the main effects. This increase shows that team characteristics moderate the relation between CMM level and project elapsed time. Furthermore, the moderation effects were analyzed visually using simple slope analysis suggested by Aiken and West (1991) and Dawson (2014). Table 6 shows the path coefficients of the structural models.

Table 6. Results from PLS analysis for Project Elapsed Time as dependent Variable

Path	Model 1(Main effects)	Model 2 (Main and Moderator effects)
CMM→PET	-0.37***	-0.31***
Experience→PET	0.03	0.06
Team functional heterogeneity→PET	-0.08*	-0.11**
Team turnover→PET	0.26***	0.27***
CMM*experience→PET		0.09**
CMM*functional heterogeneity→PET		0.22***
CMM* turnover→PET		-0.01
R squared	**0.24**	**0.32**
CMM = Maturity of software project process; PET = Project Elapsed Time; *** = significant at < 0.01; ** = significant at < 0.05; * = significant at < 0.1;		

Figure 2 displays the research model with the results.

Figure 2. Results of the Research Model

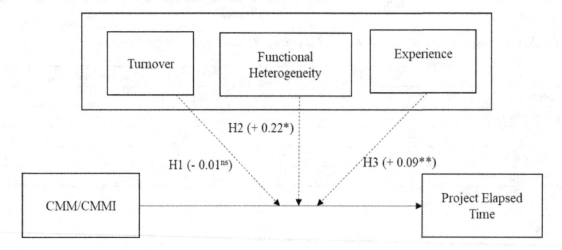

It is observed from the main effects model (Model 1) the CMM level under which a software project is developed significantly impacts (β= -0.37; p<0.01) the project elapsed time to delivery. In particular, it shows that higher CMM levels in the software development process can significantly reduce the overall time to delivery of projects.

Model 1 also shows increased team turnover (β= 0.26; p<0.01) significantly increases project elapsed time.

Model 1 also shows that greater team functional heterogeneity (β= -0.08; p=0.09) significantly reduces project elapsed time. It shows that projects developed using team members from different functional background take less time to completion.

Model 1 further shows that team work experience (β= 0.03; p=0.32) did not have any significant impact on project elapsed time.

Figure 3. Moderation Effects of Team Characteristics on Project Elapsed Time in CMM/CMMI Projects

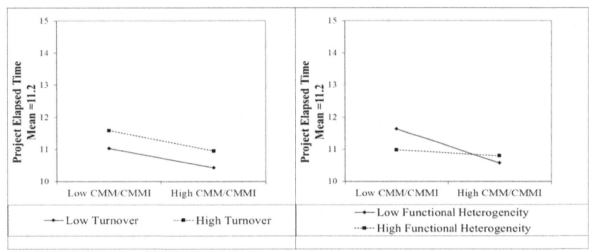

Graph A: Team turnover as moderator   Graph B: Team Functional Heterogeneity as moderator

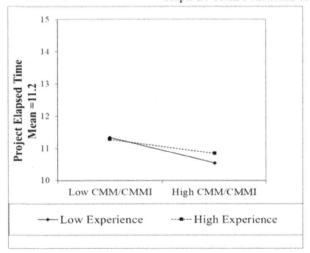

Graph C: Team Experience as moderator

The moderation effects (Model 2) are graphically displayed in Figure 3 (Graph A, Graph B, and Graph C) (Aiken et al., 1991) to understand the nature of the moderation effects of the team attributes used in the study.

The dependent variable project elapsed time is shown along the vertical axis, while the maturity level of the project is shown along the horizontal axis. After the moderation effects of the team characteristics are introduced, it was found that team work experience (β= 0.09; p=0.07) and team functional hetero-geneity (β= 0.22; p<0.01) have significant moderation effects on the project elapsed time. Thus, stating that high or low values of team functional heterogeneity and team work experience have the moderating effect of increasing or decreasing project elapsed time in CMM level projects. Team turnover (β= -0.01; p<0.41) did not have any significant moderation effect suggesting that high and low values of team turnover do not make any difference on project elapsed time. Results from the Model 2 also indicate that team functional heterogeneity partially moderates whereas team work experience fully moderates the relation between CMM and project elapsed time. This is evident because the main effect of team work experience is insignificant after the introduction of the moderation effect.

All three graphs in Figure 3 (Graph A, Graph B, and Graph C) show that higher CMM maturity levels correspond to reduced project elapsed time to completion. This reduction can be observed from the negative slope of the trend lines that depict the relation between CMM level and project elapsed time. However, the results show that the negative effect differs with the low and high values of the two team characteristics: team work experience and team functional heterogeneity which can be understood from the difference in the slope of the lines that represent high and low values of the team characteristics.

In Figure 3, Graph A, the effect of the CMM level of a software project on the project elapsed time for low and high value of team turnover in a software project is projected. The graph shows that the CMM level of the software project has a strong negative relationship with elapsed time, yet, this relation does not differ between teams having high and low turnover due to the insignificant results from the PLS analysis. Thus, Hypothesis H1 is not supported.

In Figure 3, Graph B the effect of the CMM level of a project on the project elapsed time of a software project for low and high values of team functional heterogeneity is shown. This graph shows that higher CMM levels of the software project results in reduced elapsed time and the negative effect is different for high and low team functional heterogeneity. The negative effect is stronger (steep slope) when the teams have less functional heterogeneity. Thus, Hypothesis H2 is supported.

Figure 3, Graph C shows the negative effect of CMM level of a software project on the project elapsed time for low and high levels of team experience. However, the negative effect is found to be stronger when the teams have less experienced members in a team. Thus, Hypothesis H3 is not supported. The summary of results of the hypotheses for project elapsed time as the dependent variable is shown in Table 7.

5. DISCUSSION

5.1. Capability Maturity Model Level

Software process improvement initiatives have become integral components of software development organizations. This study showed support for previous findings (Curtis, 2019; Lee et al., 2017) that an increase in the CMM level of an organization increases the success of software projects. Specifically, empirical support that CMM level can help reduce the elapsed time of a software development project was confirmed. CMM levels in software organizations ensure that any changes that are introduced in the software development process are implemented in a structured manner and the amount of rework in organizations is reduced by identifying common processes (Örgün et al., 2018). Thorough performance evaluations in CMM level organizations help them sustain the software development success rate. This success rate increases as software organizations rise to higher levels of CMM maturity.

Table 7. Results of Hypotheses for Project Elapsed Time

	Hypotheses for Project Elapsed Time	Result
H1	As the CMM level of a software project increases the elapsed time to project completion will decrease. This decrease will be moderated by team turnover such that as team turnover increases elapsed time to project completion will increase.	Non-Significant
H2	As the CMM level of a software project increases the elapsed time to project completion will decrease. This decrease will be moderated by team functional heterogeneity such that as team functional heterogeneity increases elapsed time to project completion will increase	Supported
H3	As the CMM level of a software project increases the elapsed time to project completion will decrease. This decrease will be moderated by team experience such that as team experience increases elapsed time to project completion will decrease.	Significant but not supported

5.2. Human Factors

In addition, support was found for team factors playing a role in the success or failure of software projects developed by CMM level organizations. Many organizations ignore the effects of human factors and highlight the need for software development process initiatives (Ply et al., 2012). However, this study supports the finding of Muñoz et al., (2016) that the success of software process improvement initiatives depends on human aspects. This is supported by the significant moderation effects of team characteristics on CMM and the software project elapsed time to completion.

5.3. Team Turnover

The moderation effect of team turnover on software projects did not have a significant effect on project elapsed time. Losing team members can disrupt the functioning of teams. However, in projects that follow CMM development practices there is not much difference between teams with high turnover and low turnover. Turnover in this study not only considers replacements that occurred in a project due to the voluntary exit of employees due to resignations or transfers but also considers replacement due to illness, maternity leave, and nonperformance. Turnover caused due to nonperformance or under performance can lead to new opportunities by introducing new knowledge and also change existing routine practices in the team. Non-significant difference between high and low values of turnover on the CMM-project elapsed time relationship could be because of the standardized development process in CMM level organizations. Less time is needed for replacements to understand the work in progress. They are familiar with the existing process (Lee et al., 2013). Therefore, team replacements do not always lead to bad consequences as team performance can be sustained with well-planned CMM practices.

5.4. Team Functional Heterogeneity

Results from this study suggest that large functional heterogeneity in teams can be detrimental to software project development. It can increase the elapsed time to completion of the software project. The moderation effects show that teams having high functional heterogeneity will increase the elapsed time to completion. Functional heterogeneity in software projects is common and is required in most software teams. The development of software components require support from members that are experts in different functionalities such as database administrators, network administrators, computer operators, the end users and clients. Involving people from different functionalities during the development phase can lead to misunderstandings and communication issues as each person can understand the project intricacies at a different level. Previous studies also support that functional heterogeneity drives conflict as people have different understanding of the task priorities, assumptions about future events and understanding of various options about preforming tasks thus leading to task conflict and ultimately affecting performance (Kudaravalli et al., (2017). Although functional heterogeneity has benefits in the form of information sharing and creativity empowerment (Srikanth et al., 2016), it can reduce the productivity and increase the elapsed time of the project. Therefore, involving people from different functional diversities may not be a good idea as it can slow the time to project delivery.

5.5. Team Member Work Experience

The impact of work experience on project elapsed time was found to contradict the general expectation that it would reduce the elapsed time. It was found that projects having highly experienced team members resulted in higher overall elapsed time of the project. This might be explained due to the fact that experienced members are mostly involved in complex projects (Tsunoda et al., 2018) as well as many activities such as in project update sessions, resolving issue of other projects that they are involved in and training new developers. This leaves them with less time to work on a particular project and in turn increases the elapsed time to completion of one particular project. Although they may be effective, they cannot control the other activities that act as hindrances which can ultimately extended timelines for the projects.

Findings about work experience suggest that software development teams should be comprised of both experienced and less experienced developers to complete a project in a timely fashion. Although experienced members can be beneficial to the software project, having too many highly experienced staff can lead to exceeded timelines of project delivery. Therefore, teams having a mix of highly experienced and less experienced professionals can fare better in software development teams.

5.6. Managerial Implications

This research has important implications for managers with regard to staffing in the CMM level software development organizations. Findings from this study suggest that people factors, along with process factors, play a significant role in the success of software development projects. While process controls applied through the software process improvement initiatives such as CMM/CMMI can reduce the overall time for development, improper staffing can increase the time to project completion. The study suggests software development managers take care when staffing projects.

Organizations should adopt CMM Level capabilities for software development. Increasing CMM capabilities will reduce elapsed time to project completion all other things being equal. Once adopted, the organizations should raise their CMM Level of capabilities to further reduce project time. Once obtained, these capabilities should be strictly applied to each software project they develop.

Human factors do matter in the development process. Software development managers need to plan and assess the risks and benefits of: having experienced staff members, an increased turnover rate, and the existence of functional heterogeneity in a development team.

Software project managers should not be overly concerned about the turnover rate on teams during the development process. This study suggests managers monitor and track project activities and milestones. Looking to eliminate non-performing or underperforming employees to keep the project on time since employee turnover in CMM level projects is not a big concern. In turn, the software project can benefit from including fresh ideas and better performing employees.

This study suggests managers balance the proportion of highly experienced professionals with the proportion of less experienced professionals. The skillset of the highly experienced members is essential in resolving bottlenecks during the development process. However, a team consisting of only highly experienced professionals may increase the time of the project due to their possible involvement in many projects. Their expertise may be required in many projects. Whereas less experienced professional may be focused on a particular project. They often have the motivation to learn new things and usually have a desire to showcase their abilities.

This study also suggests managers control team functional heterogeneity levels. Although heterogeneity can enhance creativity, it can increase the time to completion. Different levels of functional heterogeneity may be better utilized at different phases of the project. For instance, many levels may be involved in the initial feasibility study. Levels of heterogeneity could then fluctuate through the remaining development phases. Or perhaps the number of participants from each level could be evaluated at each phase of development allowing for adjustments in heterogeneity.

5.7. Limitations and Future Research

This study focused on the moderation effects of team characteristics in CMM/CMMI level software projects. The software development projects used in the study were developed with either CMM or CMMI process improvement techniques. Due to data limitations an analysis for different types and versions of CMMI could not be performed. A plausible future study is to expand the current research to analyze the moderation effects of team characteristics in different types of CMMI practices such as CMMI-DEV (development), CMMI-SVC (services), CMMI-ACQ (acquisition).

CMMI has also evolved over the years with the release of different versions such as CMMI 1.2, CMMI 1.3, CMMI 2.0. The study can be adopted to understand the differences in the moderation effects of team characteristics in different versions of CMMI. Another avenue for future research is to compare the results from the current study with projects developed in the recent years and understand the temporal differences in the moderation effects of team characteristics. Software development is a complex process which incorporates the combined elements of people, processes, and technology. Hence, several factors can impact project outcome. This research can be expanded by incorporating other understudied aspects of development related to people, processes and technology.

6. CONCLUSION

Higher CMM level projects can be delivered faster when fewer organizational functional levels are involved. Projects can also benefit from having less experienced team members involved. Therefore, managers of software development teams must support the teams and foster a suitable environment. Turnover of team members does not significantly impact project results. These factors worked together to deliver a project in less time. It can no longer be said that a high CMM level maturity process is sufficient for a highly successful project but managing the human factors of the team involved in the project is also important.

REFERENCES

Adolph, S., Kruchten, P., & Hall, W. (2012). Reconciling perspectives: A grounded theory of how people manage the process of software development. *Journal of Systems and Software*, *85*(6), 1269–1286. doi:10.1016/j.jss.2012.01.059

Aiken, L. S., West, S. G., & Reno, R. R. (1991). Multiple regression: Testing and interpreting interactions. *Sage (Atlanta, Ga.)*.

Alla, S., Pazos, P., & DelAguila, R. (2017). The Impact of Requirements Management Documentation on Software Project Outcomes in Health Care. In *IIE Annual Conference. Proceedings. Institute of Industrial and Systems Engineers* (pp. 1419-1423). Academic Press.

Almomani, M. A., Basri, S., & Gilal, A. R. (2018). Empirical study of software process improvement in Malaysian small and medium enterprises: The human aspects. *Journal of Software: Evolution and Process*, *30*(10), e1953.

Alqadri, Y., Budiardjo, E. K., Ferdinansyah, A., & Rokhman, M. F. (2020). The CMMI-Dev Implementation Factors for Software Quality Improvement: A Case of XYZ Corporation. In *Proceedings of the 2020 2nd Asia Pacific Information Technology Conference* (pp. 34-40). 10.1145/3379310.3379327

AlQaisi, R., Gray, E., & Steves, B. (2017). *Software systems engineering: A journey to contemporary agile and beyond, do people matter?* BCS.

Alsawalqah, H., Alshamaileh, Y., Al-Shboul, B., Shorman, A., & Sleit, A. (2019). Factors Impacting on CMMI Acceptance Among Software Development Firms: A Qualitative Assessment. *Modern Applied Science*, *13*(3), 170. doi:10.5539/mas.v13n3p170

Anderson, G., Keith, M., Albrecht, C., Spruill, A., & Pettit, C. (2019). Optimizing Software Team Performance with Cultural Differences. *Proceedings of the 52nd Hawaii International Conference on System Sciences*. 10.24251/HICSS.2019.003

Athavale, S., & Balaraman, V. (2013). Human behavioral modeling for enhanced software project management. *7th International Conference on Software Engineering*, 15-17.

Bloch, M., Blumberg, S., & Laartz, J. (2012). Delivering large-scale IT projects on time, on budget, and on value. *Harvard Business Review*.

Britto, R., Šmite, D., & Damm, L. O. (2016). Experiences from measuring learning and performance in large-scale distributed software development. In *Proceedings of the 10th ACM/IEEE International Symposium on Empirical Software Engineering and Measurement* (pp. 1-6). 10.1145/2961111.2962636

Bushuyev, S., & Verenych, O. (2018). Organizational maturity and project: Program and portfolio success. In *Developing Organizational Maturity for Effective Project Management* (pp. 104–127). IGI Global. doi:10.4018/978-1-5225-3197-5.ch006

Buss, T. F. (2018). The adoption and transformation of capability maturity models in government. In *Encyclopedia of Information Science and Technology* (4th ed., pp. 3526–3537). IGI Global.

Capretz, L. F., Ahmed, F., & da Silva, F. Q. B. (2017). *Soft sides of software*. arXiv preprint arXiv:1711.07876

Cataldo, M., Herbsleb, J. D., & Carley, K. M. (2008). Socio-technical congruence: A framework for assessing the impact of technical and work dependencies on software development productivity. *Proceedings of the Second ACM-IEEE International Symposium on Empirical Software Engineering and Measurement*, 2-11. 10.1145/1414004.1414008

Colomo-Palacios, R., Casado-Lumbreras, C., Soto-Acosta, P., Misra, S., & García-Peñalvo, F. J. (2012). Analyzing human resource management practices within the GSD context. *Journal of Global Information Technology Management*, *15*(3), 30–54. doi:10.1080/1097198X.2012.10845617

Cuenca, L., Boza, A., Alemany, M., & Trienekens, J. J. (2013). Structural elements of coordination mechanisms in collaborative planning processes and their assessment through maturity models: Application to a ceramic tile company. *Computers in Industry*, *64*(8), 898–911. doi:10.1016/j.compind.2013.06.019

Cuevas, G., Calvo-Manzano, J. A., & García, I. (2018). Some key topics to be considered in software process improvement. In *Computer Systems and Software Engineering: Concepts, Methodologies, Tools, and Applications* (pp. 134–160). IGI Global. doi:10.4018/978-1-5225-3923-0.ch006

Curtis, B. (2019). Organizational Maturity: The Elephant Affecting Productivity. In Rethinking Productivity in Software Engineering (pp. 241-250). Apress.

Dawson, J. F. (2014). Moderation in management research: What, why, when, and how. *Journal of Business and Psychology*, *29*(1), 1–19. doi:10.100710869-013-9308-7

Dayyala, N. (2017). *Essays on Software Development Projects: Impact Of Social And Technological Factors On Project Performance And Co-Diffusion Of Software Sourcing Arrangements*. Open Access Theses & Dissertations. 631.

Devanbu, P., Zimmermann, T., & Bird, C. (2016). Belief & evidence in empirical software engineering. In *2016 ACM 38th International Conference on Software Engineering* (pp. 108-119). IEEE. 10.1145/2884781.2884812

Ebert, C., Murthy, B. K., & Jha, N. N. (2008). Managing risks in global software engineering: Principles and practices. *2008 IEEE International Conference on Global Software Engineering*, 131-140. 10.1109/ICGSE.2008.12

El Emam, K., & Koru, A. G. (2008). A replicated survey of IT software project failures. *Software, IEEE*, *25*(5), 84–90. doi:10.1109/MS.2008.107

Fong Boh, W., Slaughter, S. A., & Espinosa, J. A. (2007). Learning from experience in software development: A multilevel analysis. *Management Science, 53*(8), 1315–1331. doi:10.1287/mnsc.1060.0687

Fornell, C., & Larcker, D. F. (1981). Evaluating structural equation models with unobservable variables and measurement error. *JMR, Journal of Marketing Research, 18*(1), 39–50. doi:10.1177/002224378101800104

Galin, D., & Avrahami, M. (2006). Are CMM program investments beneficial? analyzing past studies. *IEEE Software, 23*(6), 81–87. doi:10.1109/MS.2006.149

Hair, J. F., Anderson, R. E., Tatham, R. L., & William, C. (1998). *Multivariate data analysis*. Academic Press.

Han, W. (2014). Validating differential relationships between risk categories and project performance as perceived by managers. *Empirical Software Engineering, 19*(6), 1956–1966. doi:10.100710664-013-9270-z

Hoegl, M., & Parboteeah, K. P. (2007). Creativity in innovative projects: How teamwork matters. *Journal of Engineering and Technology Management, 24*(1), 148–166. doi:10.1016/j.jengtecman.2007.01.008

ISBSG. (2016). *Glossary of variables*. http://isbsg.org/wp-content/uploads/2016/10/ISBSG-Glossary_of_Terms-for-DE-and-MS.pdf

ISBSG. (n.d.). *Source of software development project data*. https://isbsg.org/project-data

Khan, A. A., & Keung, J. (2016). Systematic review of success factors and barriers for software process improvement in global software development. *IET Software, 10*(5), 125–135. doi:10.1049/iet-sen.2015.0038

Khan, A. A., Keung, J., Hussain, S., Niazi, M., & Kieffer, S. (2018). Systematic literature study for dimensional classification of success factors affecting process improvement in global software development: Client–vendor perspective. *IET Software, 12*(4), 333–344. doi:10.1049/iet-sen.2018.0010

Kock, N. (2015). *WarpPLS 5.0 user manual*. ScriptWarp Systems.

Korrapati, R., & Eedara, V. S. (2010). A study of the relationship between software project success and employee job satisfaction. In *Proceedings of Allied Academies International Conference*. Academy of Information and Management Sciences.

Kudaravalli, S., Faraj, S., & Johnson, S. L. (2017). A Configural Approach to Coordinating Expertise in Software Development Teams. *Management Information Systems Quarterly, 41*(1), 43–64. doi:10.25300/MISQ/2017/41.1.03

Langer, N., Slaughter, S. A., & Mukhopadhyay, T. (2014). Project managers' practical intelligence and project performance in software offshore outsourcing: A field study. *Information Systems Research, 25*(2), 364–384. doi:10.1287/isre.2014.0523

Lassak, S., Przybilla, L., Wiesche, M., & Krcmar, H. (2017). Explaining How Agile Software Development Practices Moderate the Negative Effects of Faultlines in Teams. *Australasian Conference on Information Systems*.

Latif, A. M., Khan, K. M., & Duc, A. N. (2019). Software Cost Estimation and Capability Maturity Model in Context of Global Software Engineering. In *Human Factors in Global Software Engineering* (pp. 273–296). IGI Global.

Lee, G., Espinosa, J. A., & DeLone, W. H. (2013). Task environment complexity, global team dispersion, process capabilities, and coordination in software development. *IEEE Transactions on Software Engineering, 39*(12), 1753–1771. doi:10.1109/TSE.2013.40

Lee, J. C., Chen, C. Y., & Shiue, Y. C. (2017). The moderating effects of organizational culture on the relationship between absorptive capacity and software process improvement success. *Information Technology & People, 30*(1), 47–70. doi:10.1108/ITP-09-2013-0171

Lopez-Martin, C., Banitaan, S., Garcia-Floriano, A., & Yanez-Marquez, C. (2017). Support vector regression for predicting the enhancement duration of software projects. In *2017 16th IEEE International Conference on Machine Learning and Applications* (pp. 562-567). IEEE. 10.1109/ICMLA.2017.0-101

Lu, Y., Xiang, C., Wang, B., & Wang, X. (2011). What affects information systems development team performance? an exploratory study from the perspective of combined socio-technical theory and coordination theory. *Computers in Human Behavior, 27*(2), 811–822. doi:10.1016/j.chb.2010.11.006

Luna-Reyes, L. F., Zhang, J., Gil-García, J. R., & Cresswell, A. M. (2005). Information systems development as emergent socio-technical change: A practice approach. *European Journal of Information Systems, 14*(1), 93–105. doi:10.1057/palgrave.ejis.3000524

Muñoz, M., Mejia, J., Peña, A., & Rangel, N. (2016, September). Establishing effective software development teams: an exploratory model. In *European Conference on Software Process Improvement*, (pp. 70-80). Springer.

Nunnally, J. C., & Bernstein, I. (1994). The assessment of reliability. *Psychometric Theory, 3*(1), 248–292.

Örgün, P., Güngör, D., Kuru, Y. Y., Metin, Ö. O., & Yılmaz, M. (2018). Software development overall efficiency improvement in a CMMI level 5 organization within the scope of a case study. In *2018 3rd International Conference on Computer Science and Engineering*, (pp. 258-263). IEEE. 10.1109/UBMK.2018.8566252

Paulk, M. C. (2009). A history of the capability maturity model for software. *ASQ Software Quality Professional, 12*(1), 5–19.

Ply, J. K., Moore, J. E., Williams, C. K., & Thatcher, J. B. (2012). IS employee attitudes and perceptions at varying levels of software process maturity. *Management Information Systems Quarterly, 36*(2), 601–624. doi:10.2307/41703469

Ramanujan, S., & Kesh, S. (2004). Comparison of knowledge management and CMM/CMMI implementation. *The Journal of American Academy of Business, Cambridge, 4*(1/2), 271–275.

Sharma, P., & Sangal, A. L. (2019). Investigating the factors which impact SPI implementation initiatives in software SMEs—A systematic map and review. *Journal of Software: Evolution and Process, 31*(7), e2183.

Siau, K., Tan, X., & Sheng, H. (2010). Important characteristics of software development team members: An empirical investigation using repertory grid. *Information Systems Journal, 20*(6), 563–580. doi:10.1111/j.1365-2575.2007.00254.x

Šmite, D., Moe, N. B., Šāblis, A., & Wohlin, C. (2017). Software teams and their knowledge networks in large-scale software development. *Information and Software Technology, 86*, 71–86. doi:10.1016/j.infsof.2017.01.003

Söylemez, M., & Tarhan, A. (2018). Challenges of software process and product quality improvement: Catalyzing defect root-cause investigation by process enactment data analysis. *Software Quality Journal, 26*(2), 779–807. doi:10.100711219-016-9334-6

Srikanth, K., Harvey, S., & Peterson, R. (2016). A dynamic perspective on diverse teams: Moving from the dual-process model to a dynamic coordination-based model of diverse team performance. *The Academy of Management Annals, 10*(1), 453–493. doi:10.5465/19416520.2016.1120973

Sundararajan, S., Bhasi, M., & Pramod, K. V. (2017). Managing software risks in maintenance projects, from a vendor perspective: A case study in global software development. *International Journal of Information Technology Project Management, 8*(1), 35–54. doi:10.4018/IJITPM.2017010103

Tsunoda, T., Washizaki, H., Fukazawa, Y., Inoue, S., Hanai, Y., & Kanazawa, M. (2018). Developer Experience Considering Work Difficulty in Software Development. *International Journal of Networked and Distributed Computing, 6*(2), 53–62. doi:10.2991/ijndc.2018.6.2.1

Yilmaz, M., O'Connor, R. V., Colomo-Palacios, R., & Clarke, P. (2017). An examination of personality traits and how they impact on software development teams. *Information and Software Technology, 86*, 101–122. doi:10.1016/j.infsof.2017.01.005

This research was previously published in the International Journal of Information Technologies and Systems Approach (IJITSA), 14(1); pages 174-191, copyright year 2021 by IGI Publishing (an imprint of IGI Global).

Chapter 66
Co–Diffusion Effects in Software Sourcing Arrangements

Niharika Dayyala
https://orcid.org/0000-0003-3128-9954
Illinois State University, USA

Faruk Arslan
https://orcid.org/0000-0002-2094-8371
New Mexico State University, USA

Kent A. Walstrom
Illinois State University, USA

Kallol K. Bagchi
https://orcid.org/0000-0002-5821-4349
The University of Texas at El Paso, El Paso, USA

ABSTRACT

This study analyzes the temporal diffusion of software sourcing arrangements by applying innovation diffusion theories. The study tests the co-diffusion effects 1) between onshoring and offshoring and 2) between insourcing and outsourcing. The results from the analysis indicate the existence of one-way complementary co-diffusion effects between on-shoring and offshoring and between outsourcing and in-housing. Positive, significant effects of innovation were found for in-housed, on-shored, and offshored software projects. Furthermore, a negative, significant effect of imitation was found for outsourced software projects. Indications were co-diffusion effects are stronger than diffusion effects.

INTRODUCTION

Software sourcing is a multi-faceted phenomenon that enables enterprises to obtain software solutions in a cost-effective manner (Naik, 2016). Software sourcing has evolved from developing software within a country and a within a firm through insourcing and onshoring to innovative sourcing models such as

DOI: 10.4018/978-1-6684-3702-5.ch066

outsourcing and offshoring (Dayyala, et al., 2017). These sourcing models can be broadly classified based on geography: onshoring and offshoring and based on the extent of externalization: insource and outsource (Tate & Bals, 2017). Onshoring is when software development activity is performed in a domestic country and offshoring is when software development activity is performed in a foreign country. While the insourcing can be conceptualized as the allocation or reallocation of resources internally within an organization to develop software, outsourcing can be defined as allocating or reallocating the software development activities internal to an organization, to an external source (Schniederjans, et al., 2015). Several other sourcing options have emerged based on the combination of geography and externalization of software development activities as shown in Figure 1 (Contractor, et al., 2010; Foerstl, et al., 2016). Each software sourcing strategy has its own adoption pattern over time depending on the benefits and drawbacks as perceived by the adopters. Angst, et al. (2017) note that very little is known about software sourcing trends and the rationale for pursuing one sourcing strategy over the other. Inconsistencies in adoption trends can be better understood with diffusion studies that incorporate temporal effects (Manning, et al., 2018). Specifically, diffusion studies explain the channels through which an innovation spreads over time (Rogers, 2010). Bucklin and Sengupta (2003) note that the introduction and adoption of innovations may not only deliver the envisioned benefits but might affect the diffusion of other existing or potential innovation adoptions due to interactions between them. The authors called this phenomenon "the co-diffusion effect". Given the co-existence of several sourcing phenomena we expect that the innovative sourcing strategies may exert co-diffusive interactions on the adoption patterns of traditional sourcing strategies impacting the adoption pattern over time. This study analyzes the diffusion and co-diffusion effects between 1) onshoring and offshoring and 2) insourcing and outsourcing.

Figure 1. Software sourcing models

	ONSHORE	OFFSHORE
OUTSOURCE	Onshore Outsourcing (outsourced within the country)	Offshore Outsourcing (Outsourced to a foreign country)
INSOURCE	Onshore Insourcing (Within the organization within the country)	Offshore Insourcing (Within the organization but in a foreign country)

Geographical distance increases →

Externalization increases ↑

Software sourcing research is well documented in the literature, with researchers performing several cross-sectional studies to understand the motivation of adoptions, sourcing decisions, outcomes, and risks (Liang, et al., 2016). However, the study of the diffusion of software sourcing analyzing the spread of software sourcing over time is limited (Lewin & Volberda, 2011; Mann, et al., 2015, Angst, et al. 2017). Scholars indicate the need for Information Systems (IS) sourcing research to move beyond snap-shot studies and incorporate temporal effects to understand the evolution and development of software sourcing options (Alsudairi & Dwivedi, 2010; Madsen, 2017; Manning, et. al., 2018). Despite the call for diffusion studies in IS literature, there are very few existing studies that study the time-based spread of the software sourcing phenomenon. Some noteworthy studies that applied innovation diffusion models to understand the temporal spread of software sourcing are done by Chakrabarty (2006); Chaudhury & Bharati, (2008); Hu, Saunders, & Gebelt (1997); Loh & Venkatraman (1992); Mann, et al., (2011); and Angst, et al., (2017). These studies analyzed the factors influencing the adoption of information systems outsourcing by identifying it as an innovation. Nevertheless, the application of diffusion studies to analyze the co-diffusive interactions between sourcing options do not exist.

This study focuses on the broader classification of software sourcing options based on geography and perceived externalization. It is expected that sourcing strategies such as outsourcing and offshor-ing can exert co-diffusive effects on traditional sourcing strategies such as insourcing and onshoring, respectively. Research analyzing the co-diffusive effects between software sourcing phenomena was not found. Hence, this study will contribute to the overall software sourcing literature by exploring the temporal co-diffusive effects of the software sourcing arrangements. Application of co-diffusion studies and innovation diffusion models in software sourcing can help understand the channels through which software sourcing phenomena spread over time as well as explain the co-diffusive interactions between the sourcing arrangements. Especially, understanding the interactions between different sourcing options can help the software development project leaders to pursue a strategic portfolio approach to software sourcing to address complex global software development projects as well as projects running concurrently.

In summary, the purpose of this study is to examine the diffusion and co-diffusion effects of software sourcing arrangements. It examines the existence of co-diffusion effects and the nature of the co-diffusion effects between software sourcing options 1) onshoring and offshoring (software sourcing classification based on geography) and 2) insourcing and outsourcing (software sourcing classification based on the extent of externalization).

BACKGROUND

Diffusion in Information Systems (IS)

Diffusion research in information systems (IS) has accumulated an impressive body of knowledge. Over the years, diffusion of innovation theory acted as a foundation for steering research on innovation acceptance and adoption (Lai, 2017). According to innovation diffusion theory (Rogers, 2010, p. 5), *"Diffusion is the process in which an innovation is communicated through certain channels over time among the members of a social system"*. Diffusion studies analyze how fast or slow ideas, products, in-novations, and opinions take off and spread into society (Valente, 1995). They facilitate the prediction of sales growth of new products and innovations (Peterson & Mahajan, 1978) using quantitative and qualitative methods. The communication channel is the means by which the message about innovation characteristics spread from one individual to the other. Communication channels can influence the decision to adopt or reject a new idea. Communication channels can be mass media channels (external influence channels) or interpersonal communication/word of mouth (internal influence channels) among peers. While internal influence portrays the imitation and learning dynamics of interpersonal communication between adopters and potential adopters, external influence depicts guiding forces from outside other than the adopters (e.g. mass media /consulting companies) (Teng, et al., 2002). The time element is the time taken to make a decision to adopt or reject the new idea and the social system is the set of inter-related units engaged in making the decision about adopting a new innovation.

Innovation diffusion studies facilitate understanding of innovations, communication channels through which innovation take place, types of social systems, adopter categories, and stages of innovation diffusion. Beynon-Davies & Williams (2003) identified information systems (IS) development methods as knowledge-based innovation systems. The authors used innovation diffusion theory to study the influence channels of IS development methods. The authors found the Computerization Movement Organization (CMO)'s external influence and the recruitment of members to such organizations along with links to other CMO's through internal and external consultants promoted the diffusion of IS development methods. Zhu, et al., (2006) studied the determinants of post-adoption usage of innovation diffusion using innovation characteristics (relative advantage, compatibility, costs and security concern) and contextual factors (technology competence, organization size, competitive pressure and partner readiness). The authors noted innovation diffusion can better be understood with a combination of innovation and contextual factors rather than by studying them separately. The authors also stated economic and regulatory factors can result in uneven innovation diffusion. Garg, et al., (2011) developed an empirical approach for measuring information diffusion and discovery in online social networks that have measurement challenges. The authors tested this scenario on the online music community with data from 4000 online users. They found peers in such online communities significantly increased the discovery of new music. Low, et al., (2011) investigated the determinants of cloud computing adoption using a sample of 111 Taiwanese high-tech firms. Their empirical research model leveraged the Technology-Organization-Environment (TOE) framework and Roger's diffusion of innovation model antecedents. The authors concluded the size of the organization, perceived relative advantage of cloud computing, top management support, competitive and trading partner pressures can influence cloud computing adoption and usage at the firm level. Miranda, et. al., (2016) explored the adoption process of enterprise resource planning (ERP) systems in non-profit organizations and found that the decision to adopt follows a non-linear pattern. Lee and Huh (2017) applied innovation diffusion models to a better understand replacement and repeat purchases of south Korea mobile handset market.

Diffusion Studies in Software Sourcing

Prior research has generated considerable knowledge on the dynamics of software sourcing. IS scholars have explored various software sourcing options to find factors that influence software sourcing adoption in organizations. In addition, they identified factors that influence the choice of software sourcing. They also looked at the benefits of adoption, risks, and impacts on performance (Lacity, et al., 2010; Liang, et al., 2016; Schneider & Sunyaev, 2016). Other scholars investigated client-vendor relationship, project management, communication and coordination between the client and vendor, and choosing vendor locations in cases of offshoring (Bapna, et al., 2010; Han, et al., 2013; Khan, et al., 2011). IS scholars have noted software sourcing literature has accumulated a number of "snapshot" studies. There is now a need to study the diffusion of software sourcing over time (Alsudairi & Dwivedi, 2010; Lewin & Volberda, 2011; Mann, et al., 2015, Madsen, 2017; Angst, et al. 2017; Manning, et. al., 2018).

Scholars identified IS outsourcing as an innovative governance mechanism (Loh & Venkatraman, 1992; Hu et al., 1997). In the early 1990's, innovation diffusion theories were adopted to study the diffusion phenomenon of software sourcing arrangements. One of the oldest and most notable studies was authored by Loh & Venkatraman (1992). This study was conducted during the time when IT outsourcing had emerged as a promising innovation in an organization's IT strategy. The authors used innovation diffusion theories to explore the outsourcing phenomenon by obtaining information about 60 outsourcing contracts during 1988 to 1990. The authors found outsourcing diffusion was the result of only internal influence channels. The study also considered the Kodak effect (an announcement by IBM that the work of Kodak was outsourced leading to the consideration of IT outsourcing as a serious strategic choice for firms) as a critical event and explored the strength of internal influence channels post and pre-Kodak effect. The authors found internal influence was more pronounced post-Kodak and not pre-Kodak.

Results from this study suggested IT outsourcing mainly occurs through imitation where organizations mimic other organizations. But, a similar study of influence sources on IS outsourcing conducted by Hu et al. (1997) revealed contrasting findings. The authors used a sample of 175 firms that outsourced IS functions during the period from 1985 to 1995 to identify the best diffusion model for characterizing the diffusion of IS outsourcing. Results from this study contradicted the conclusions of Loh & Venkatraman (1992) that IS outsourcing diffusion is the result of mixed influence (both external and internal influences) and that the Kodak effect did not exist in the IS diffusion process. The authors empirically found evidence that external influence in the outsourcing decision was prominent and this influence is exerted aggressively on managers by vendors and extensive information available in the trade press. The authors also found decision makers were influenced by communication among organizations and managers that may be considering or have adopted IS outsourcing.

In an analysis of case studies of offshore outsourced projects, Chakrabarty (2006) noted the offshore outsourcing phenomenon can be considered as an organizational or administrative innovation process that is adopted by various clients and vendors. Chaudhury & Bharati (2008) used innovation diffusion theory and institutional theory to conceptualize the factors that contribute to the adoption of IT services outsourcing by small and medium enterprises. The authors performed a literature survey and proposed that the adoption rate of IT sourcing by vendors depends on three important factors 1) innovation profile features such as relative advantage and complexity of services, 2) innovator profile of vendor such as prestige level, firm size, education level, and 3) field level characteristic such as interfirm connections and service professionalism. The authors offered well-reasoned propositions, but empirical analysis was not performed by researchers to validate the propositions.

Research by Mann, et al., (2011) modeled the diffusion of outsourcing via announcements about IT outsourcing arrangements exceeding 1 billion US dollars. They used the time period 1999 to 2007 and found the mixed influence model best explained the IT outsourcing diffusion. The authors identified the presence of contagion effects in the diffusion of IT outsourcing. Contagion effects, as considered by the authors, were effects such as large, expensive, mega-deals acting as precipitating events for outsourcing adoption. In addition, large firms acting as examples for small firms by reducing inhibitions about outsourcing adoption. Internal communication channels also played an important role in IT outsourcing diffusion.

Based on previous studies, it is evident software sourcing arrangements can be considered as an organizational and an administrative innovation in line with Rogers' definition of innovation which can be any practice, product, reform or idea (Rogers, 2010). Therefore, all software sourcing arrangements: insourcing, outsourcing, offshoring and onshoring can be considered as organizational innovations.

Lewin and Volberda (2011) discussed the emergence of global sourcing of business services. The authors reviewed the decision to offshore work and the overall growth of business service offshoring. The authors state there is no international business theory that can explain how and why firms offshore. The authors also note that prior research had not addressed the interrelationships between firm level offshore decisions. They suggest future research focus on co-evolutionary models of offshoring since the offshoring dynamic is not an outcome of strategic decisions or environmental selection but a joint outcome of emergence, managerial intention, and environmental effects.

In a quantitative interdisciplinary study, Mann, et al., (2015) employed space-time clustering techniques to discover the process underlying the diffusion of IT outsourcing across firms within the U.S from 2000 to 2010. They employed spatial, temporal, and industrial nearness to explore the increasing use of IT outsourcing in the United States with data that appeared in the media on IT outsourcing announcements. The study revealed that diffusion of outsourcing happens more in urban economies and firms of larger size. Madsen (2017) used explorative and qualitative methods to explore the diffusion trajectory of outsourcing. The study analyzed a broad range of studies and data from existing literature on outsourcing and found that outsourcing continues to be a widely used strategy but in the long run there could be a dip in the future popularity due to the low satisfaction levels experienced by the users.

Angst, et el., (2017) applied longitudinal modeling to empirically evaluate the IS sourcing strategies of US hospitals from 2006 to 2013. This study explored the organizational antecedents influencing the rate at which they choose one sourcing option over another. Results from the study revealed that US hospitals tend to adopt single sourcing strategy and that the formal and internal dynamics determine this trend. Manning, et al., (2018) analyzed how the rationale for governance choices vary in firms with time of adoption of global services sourcing. This study revealed that greater institutional distance favors external governance decision. Also, prior outsourcing experiences of other client firms in the same host country matter in governance choices.

Co-Diffusion Studies

Bucklin & Sengupta (1993, p.148) define co-diffusion as *"the interaction between the demands of innovations that have separate adoption tracks and sometimes co-diffusion effects between innovations are stronger than innovation effects"*. There is considerable prior research on diffusion of IT innovations. However, few studies analyzed the diffusion of software sourcing over time (Loh and Venkatraman, 1992; Hu, et al., 1997; Chakrabarty, 2006; Chaudhury and Bharati, 2008; Mann, et al., 2011). Most researchers investigated innovations as if they were independent of each other (Colombo & Mosconi, 1995; Rogers, 2010; Ladrón-de-Guevara & Putsis, 2015). But it is important to understand that innovations diffuse interdependently. Diffusion studies explain diffusion variables independently. In reality, these variables exert potentiating or mitigating effects on the process of diffusion interactively. The relative weight of each variable may change according to the circumstances surrounding the innovation and its context (Wejnert, 2002).

It is important to note the diffusion effect is not the sole reason for dissemination of innovation. Products seldom are unaffected by other existing or new products. Some products have diffusive interactions with other existing or new products. The introduction of an innovation not only delivers expected benefits but might affect the diffusion of another existing or new innovation due to interactions between them known as co-diffusion effects. Sometimes co-diffusion effects between innovations are stronger than innovation effects.

Mahajan & Peterson (1985) extended the basic diffusion model proposed by Bass (1969) to incorporate co-diffusion effects. They tested the diffusion models to understand the co-diffusion effect between black and white, and color television. The authors found complementary and substitutive effects between the two innovations. The parameter estimates from the co-diffusion model suggested growth in sales of color televisions had a substitutive effect on sales of black and white television. The parameter estimates also indicated the growth of black and white television sales had a complementary effect on color television sales.

Bucklin & Sengupta (1993) highlighted the phenomenon of co-diffusion, and they posit diffusion of complementary innovations cannot be studied in isolation. The authors found that Universal Product Code (UPC) symbols printed on packages of stocked items and laser scanners in supermarkets have an asymmetric two-way complementary co-diffusion effect. Colombo & Mosconi (1995) suggested single equation models, which do not consider technological interactions are erroneous, suffering from omitted variables. This casts serious questions about studying individual innovations in isolation.

Kim, et al., (2000) developed a dynamic model that captures both inter-product category effects and technological substitution within a broadened concept of a competitive IT market. They asserted empirically that sales of one related product category have an impact on another's market potential and, consequently, affects its market growth suggesting the existence of co-diffusion effects. Volberda & Lewin (2003) performed a co-evolutionary analysis between firms and suggest that adaptation and selection of innovations are not orthogonal forces but are fundamentally interrelated. They affirm that co-evolution explains the longitudinal time series adaptation within a historical context where changes in any one variable may be caused endogenously by changes in the other.

Dewan, et al. (2010) examined the cross-country diffusive interactions of personal computers and internet access by applying co-diffusion theories. The authors found co-diffusive effects were two-way complementary in nature and the impact of personal computers on internet access was stronger in developing countries compared to developed ones. They identified that owning a computer provided a boost to the rate of diffusion of the co-diffusive effect of internet access. Their findings suggest investing in older generations of IT will bring greater diffusion benefits to newer technologies.

Niculescu & Whang (2012) explored the parallel market evolution of mobile wireless voice and wireless data services and examined the differences and interactions between the associated adoption processes in the Japanese wireless market. The authors used a discrete-time multiproduct model that accounted for diffusion effects and dynamic evolution of the services. They observed the existence of both direct network/imitation effects as well as two-way positive co-diffusion effects at the speed of adoption level. They found the willingness of voice consumers to consider adopting data services positively related to both time and penetration of 3G handsets among voice services adopters. The results suggest mobile content service providers should coordinate and strategize their offerings.

Jin-Xing, et al., (2013) analyzed co-diffusion patterns of mobile instant messaging (IM) services and the desktop IM service of China Mobile. They applied co-diffusion models proposed by Mahajan and Peterson (1985) using Non-Linear Seemingly Unrelated Regression (NL-SUR). Their results showed the ease of use of desktop IM led to a higher rate of diffusion of desktop IM, with stronger innovation and imitation effects. Their co-diffusion analysis revealed mobile IM service and desktop IM service are both complementary and substitutive in nature. Mobile IM has a substitutive effect on desktop IM whereas desktop IM has a complementary effect on Mobile IM.

Westland, et al., (2016) analyzed the process of substitution as older technology is gradually replaced by newer technologies. They applied the Bass mathematical articulation of Rogers's diffusion model on data from 2007 to 2011. They analyzed the substitutive, complementary and network effects of three complementary instant messaging services provided by China mobile. They found the adoption of short message services and multimedia instant messaging or simultaneous adoption of the two services negatively impacted the instant messaging on personal computers adoption rate. A similar study was performed by Yu, et al., (2016) to analyze the relationship between over the top messaging service and the short messaging service in emerging economies. The study found that over the top messaging service diffuses much faster than short messaging service with a complementary diffusive effect in the early stages of diffusion.

In a recent study by Jensen (2017), co-diffusion theory was adapted to understand the impact of technology on behavior change. The author developed co-diffusion of technology and behavior and implemented in an agent-based model. This study analyzed the impact of behavior-changing feedback devices on energy-consumption behavior. Lazzati (2018) applied co-diffusion theory to identify the optimal number of technology units to be distributed in order to maximize the diffusion process of two newly introduced complementary technologies. In particular, the author used co-diffusion theory to find the best allocation of the technology units to individuals who were connected through a social network.

Research Gap

Previous diffusion and co-diffusion studies provide valuable insights for developers, users and providers of innovations about the dynamics of adoption patterns, influence channels, and contagion effects. The existing literature on diffusion has largely focused on diffusion as an independent process ignoring the complementarities of diffusion (Ladrón-de-Guevara & Putsis, 2015). A review of existing diffusion, co-diffusion, and software sourcing literature reveal that existing studies were mostly designed to examine the trends of adoption of software sourcing at a specific moment ignoring the temporal aspects. Recent changes in trends of outsourcing and offshoring in the form of nearshoring (relocate previously offshored activities to a neighboring country of the home country) and back shoring (relocate previously offshored activities to the home country) heighten the need to reevaluate the adoption trends of existing and prevalent sourcing options such as outsourcing and offshoring. This study attempts to fill this gap by answering the following research questions.

Research Question 1: Do co-diffusion effects exist between 1) onshoring and offshoring 2) insourcing and outsourcing.

Research Question 2: What is the nature of the co-diffusion effects between 1) offshoring – onshoring and 2) insourcing – outsourcing?

Hypotheses

A systematic review of the extant literature reveals that several factors are affecting the software sourcing decisions (Hanafizadeh & Zareravasan, 2020). These factors range from technology factors such as asset specificity, perceived cost savings, organizational factors such as availability of required skills, to environmental factors such as competitive pressures (Hanafizadeh & Zareravasan, 2020). While outsourcing tends to reduce costs (Abramovsky & Griffith, 2006) and enable an organization to access technical talent not available internally (Lacity & Willcocks, 1998; Levina & Ross, 2003), some organizations may opt to insource certain software development activities. The reasons behind this decision may include perceived security risk of outsourcing a specific activity (Hanafizadeh & Zareravasan, 2020), complexity related to contract governance issues, and pricing mechanisms, (Hanafizadeh & Zareravasan, 2018), as well as the need for higher levels of operational control of the development project (Naik, 2016). Some organizations choose to retain some capability and capacity in-house for strategic purposes and outsource peripheral activities (Harland, et al., 2005). Organizations' potential to generate benefits from both insourcing and outsourcing in software development projects, can result in a two-way complementary effect for insourcing and outsourcing. Given this, we postulate the following hypotheses:

H$_1$: The co-diffusion effect of insource software development on outsourcing software development is complementary.

H$_2$: The co-diffusion effect of outsourcing software development on insource software development is complementary.

Information Technology managers are always under pressure to deliver projects on time while maintaining project costs (Carmel & Agarwal, 2006). It is observed that onshore employees typically do not accept a lower salary or are less willing to relocate offshore (Chua & Pan, 2008). Thus, managers may choose an offshore sourcing strategy for the cost-benefit of their projects. However, recent literature on information technology offshoring points our several concerns, such as political, legal, social, and economic issues (Hanafizadeh & Zareravasan, 2020). Lack of adequate telecommunication and electricity infrastructure, technical expertise, and experience in the country, where the software development activities are offshored, can pose challenges to the organization offshoring its software development activities (Nahar & Kuivanen, 2010). Furthermore, offshoring software development activities can exacerbate the information security risks for an organization (June & Meiga, 2010) in addition to posing management problems due to cultural and geographical distances (Haried & Dai, 2011). Given the perceived advantages and challenges, IT leadership may want to maximize the benefits of each software sourcing options, while controlling for their challenges, hence resulting in two-way complementary effect between onshoring and offshoring. Therefore, we postulate the following hypotheses:

H$_3$: The co-diffusion effect of onshoring software development on offshoring software development is complementary.

H$_4$: The co-diffusion effect of offshoring software development on onshoring software development is complementary.

METHODOLOGY

Data was obtained from the International Software Benchmarking Standards Group (ISBSG) Corporate Release and Release 13 software project repository containing information on software projects developed in 20 different countries. ISBSG is a dataset about completed software development and enhancement projects which helps organizations make better decisions, based on objective data instead of subjective opinions (ISBSG). The Corporate Release contains data about software projects developed between 1989 and 2012. The Corporate Release database contains additional information about country of origin and country of effort of the software projects, hence this data was used to analyze co-diffusion effects between onshore (developed within same country as the origin) and offshored projects (developed in a foreign country different from the origin). Release 13 contains data about software projects developed between 1989 and 2014. This data set was used to analyze co-diffusion effects between insource (development team belongs to the same organization) and outsourced (developed team in a different organization) software projects. The data in the repository was reported voluntarily by various software organizations and industry and leaders. It has also been validated based on ISBSG quality guidelines and was used in some of the previous studies (Alkhatib, et al., 2018; Fernández-Diego, et al., 2018; Mustapha & Abdelwahed, 2019; Vogelezang, et al., 2019; Bhardwaj, et al., 2019; Shah, et al., 2020). For the purpose of the diffusion analysis, timeseries data was identified from the ISBSG dataset with the year of software development project start date. Using the start date of a project, the number of projects adopting a specific sourcing arrangement for each year was identified. Table 1 shows the total number of software projects developed with a specific type of software sourcing arrangement.

Table 1. Number of projects

Software Sourcing	Number of Projects (n)	Number of Time Periods (T)	Projects Developed Between Time Period
Onshore	2814	23	1991-2013
Offshored	167		
Insource	1269	21	1991-2011
Outsourced	1297		

The cumulative number of software projects that adopted each of the four software sourcing arrangements over the years is displayed in Figure 2. The cumulative adoption data is used to perform co-diffusion analysis using the software package SHAZAM. SHAZAM tests econometric and statistical models. Since the system of equations representing the temporal diffusion process and the co-diffusion process are non-linear equations which have auto correlated errors, Non-Linear - Seemingly unrelated regression (NL-SUR) was used.

NL-SUR is used to estimate (a) the coefficient of external influence or the innovation parameter, (b) coefficient of internal influence or the imitation parameter and (c) the coefficient of co-diffusion consistent with the literature (Dewan, et al., 2010; Jin-Xing et al., 2013; Cho, 2015). NL-SUR with SHAZAM estimates the coefficients for a set of nonlinear equations using a variable metric method (Diana, et al., 2011).

Co-Diffusion Effects

When innovations diffuse, they do not diffuse in a vacuum. They have positive or negative influence on the diffusion of other innovations (Peterson & Mahajan, 1978). Peterson & Mahajan, (1978) introduced a variant of the Bass diffusion model (Bass, 1969) incorporating multiple innovations. This variant was developed because the diffusion of a single innovation (new or existing) is not a self-reliant phenomenon. Seldom is an innovation uninfluenced. A strong relationship may exist between two innovations over a long period of time.

Figure 2. Cumulative adoption over the years

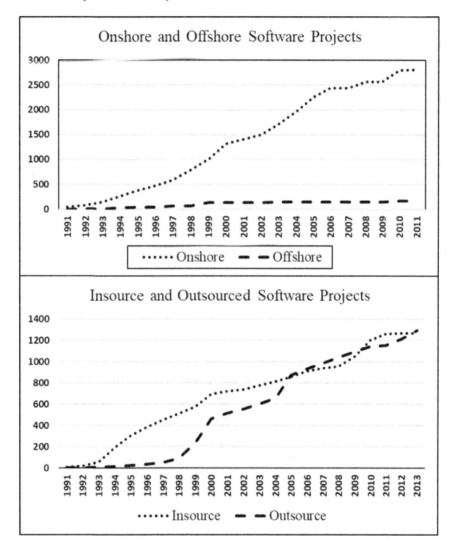

The rate of diffusion for the Bass diffusion model when co-diffusion effects are considered (Bucklin & Sengupta, 1993) is shown in Equation 1 and Equation 2:

$$\frac{dN_1(t)}{dt} = \left[a + bN_1(t) + cN_2(t)\right]\left[m - N_1(t)\right] \tag{1}$$

The cumulative penetration ratio is shown in Equation 4:

$$\frac{dF_1(t)}{dt} = \left[a + bF_1(t) + cF_2(t) \right]\left[1 - F(t) \right] \tag{2}$$

where:

- N1 (t) is the cumulative adoption and F1 (t) is penetration ratio of innovation 1 at time t;
- N2 (t) is the cumulative adoption and F2 (t) is penetration ratio of innovation 2 at time t;
- F1 (t)=N1(t)/m;
- Parameter 'a' is the coefficient of external influence or the innovation parameter;
- Parameter 'b' is the coefficient of internal influence or the imitation parameter;
- Parameter 'c' is the coefficient of co-diffusion which represents the impact of innovation2 on innovation1;
- Parameter 'm' is the maximum potential adopters.

The diffusive interactions of two products can be represented using Equations 3 and Equation 4:

$$innovation1 - F_1(t) = a1 + \left(b1 - a1 + 1 \right) * F_1(t-1) - b1 * F_1^2(t-1) + c1 * F_2(t) - c1 * F_1(t-1) * F_2(t-1) \tag{3}$$

$$innovation2 - F_2(t) = a2 + \left(b2 - a2 + 1 \right) * F_2(t-1) - b2 * F_2^2(t-1) + c2 * F_1(t) - c2 * F_2(t-1) * F_1(t-1) \tag{4}$$

The external influence/innovation effects indicated by parameter 'a' occur through mass media channels, characteristics of the innovation and external agents whereas the internal/imitation effects indicated by parameter 'b' occur through interpersonal communication between adopters and potential adopters. Co-diffusion effects are represented by 'c' which depict the impact of other related, yet independent innovations present in the social system. Estimating the parameters in the equations above, assists in understanding the strength of the impact of each of the influence channels on innovation adoption. The co-diffusion parameters 'c1' and 'c2' capture two types of effects (Dewan, et al., 2010). For instance, in Equation 3, when c1 > 0, it indicates a complementary effect of innovation2 on innovation1 and when c1 < 0, it indicates a substitutive effect of innovation 2 on innovation 1. The co-diffusion effect can be symmetric as well as asymmetric. When both c1 and c2 are positive, a two-way complementary effect exists between the two innovations. The complementary effect indicates that increased adoption of one innovation enhances the adoption of the other over time and vice versa. A good example for this is the adoption of washers and dryers. When both c1 and c2 are negative, a two-way substitutive effect exists between the two innovations. The substitutive effect indicates that increased adoption of one innovation reduces the adoption of the other. A good example for this is the competition between different brands of automobiles.

FINDINGS

The parameter estimates of the co-diffusion analysis of the study are shown in Table 2 and Table 3. Table 2 shows a one-way complementary effect between insourcing and outsourcing. There is a significant, complementary effect of insourcing on outsourced software projects (c2= 0.2307 significant at p<0.05). Thus, hypothesis H1 is supported.

Table 2. Diffusion and co-diffusion coefficients for insourcing and outsourcing co-diffusion analysis

Software Sourcing	Number of Time Periods (T)	Parameter	Coefficient	Standard Error	T-Statistic
Insource (Innovation 1)	23	a1	0.0061**	0.0021	2.9509
		b1	0.0187	0.0727	0.2573
		c1	-0.0279	0.0637	-0.4392
Outsource (Innovation 2)	23	a2	-0.0005	0.0025	-0.2268
		b2	-0.1612 **	0.0767	-2.1011
		c2	0.2307**	0.087	2.6538
*significant at 0.1 level; ** significant at 0.05 level; ***significant at 0.001 level					

Table 3. Diffusion and co-diffusion coefficients between onshore and offshore co-diffusion analysis

Software Sourcing	Number of Time Periods (T)	Parameter	Coefficient	Standard Error	T-Statistic
Onshore (Innovation 1)	21	a1	0.0076**	0.0029	2.6317
		b1	-0.0706	0.0572	-1.2335
		c1	1.9797**	0.8122	2.4372
Offshore (Innovation 2)	21	a2	0.0013**	0.0006	2.348
		b2	-0.0669	0.1455	-0.459
		c2	0.0012	0.0097	0.1241
*significant at 0.1 level; ** significant at 0.05 level; ***significant at 0.001 level					

There is an insignificant, substitutive effect of outsourcing on insource software projects (c1= -0.0279). There is no significant complementary co-diffusion effect of outsourcing on insourcing. Thus, hypothesis H_2 is not supported.

Table 3 shows a one-way complementary effect between onshoring and offshoring. There is a complementary effect of onshoring on offshoring software projects (c2= 0.0012), however this effect is not statistically significant. Thus, hypothesis H_3 is not supported.

There is a significant complementary effect of offshoring on onshore software projects (c1= 1.9797 significant at p<0.05). Thus, hypothesis H_4 is supported.

Table 2 further shows a positive, significant but small effect of innovation (external influence) for insourced software projects (a1 = 0.0061 significant at p<0.05). Table 3 shows significant but small effect of innovation for onshore software projects (a1 = 0.0076 significant at p<0.05), and offshored software projects (a2 = 0.0013 significant at p<0.05). There is no statistically significant effect of external influence on outsourced software projects. On the contrary, there is a statistically significant negative effect of imitation (internal influence) for outsourced software projects (b2 = -0.1612 significant at p<0.05).

DISCUSSION

Figure 2 showed a steady increase in the number of projects completed insourced and outsourced over the 23-year time period from 1991 to 2013. However, those projects were increasingly completed onshore. There was a small but steady number of projects completed offshore. In fact, Table 1 shows that in the period from 1991 to 2011 a total of 167 projects were completed offshore, while 2814 were completed onshore. This shows a steady favoritism of onshore development over offshore development. Table 1 also shows that during that time frame there was a nearly equal preference to develop projects insource (n=1269) and to outsource project development (n=1297).

Results suggest the existence of a one-way complementary co-diffusion effect between insource and outsource software sourcing. Further analysis of the results suggest that insource diffusion occurs only due to the external influences whereas outsourcing diffusion is the result of both the internal effects and the co-diffusion effects. Insource diffusion is a traditional software development method which is generally chosen if the organization has the capacity to take on additional IT development responsibility and/or if the system designed enables a competitive differentiator for the organization. The spread of insourcing adoption occurs through the external influences due to the information obtained from mass media and trade press about insourcing success or failures.

Outsourcing diffusion occurs mainly by co-diffusion effects and internal influences. The internal influence is due to imitation effects through interpersonal communication between managers/firms who have adopted or are planning to adopt outsourcing. Diffusion of outsourcing through internal influence is in line with Manning, et al., (2018) findings that clients rely more on the success stories of their peers when making a decision to outsource a project. Results also suggest a higher adoption of insourcing enhances the adoption of outsourcing. This may be possible because higher insourcing indicates more organizations are looking forward to implementing new technologies to automate their process. Thus, an influx of insource development indicates a higher dependency on IT assets within an organization. Higher dependency on IT assets automatically increases the number of software development projects requiring dedicated experts who can work on these projects quickly with increased efficiency and less risk. One way this can be achieved is through outsourcing (Ali & Khan, 2016). Thus, a higher adoption of insourcing increases the adoption of outsourcing.

Outsourcing has other added benefits where non-IT organizations can focus on their core competencies by outsourcing their IT work. Given the added benefits of outsourcing there will be an increase in outsourcing adoption. The reverse relationship, the effect of outsourcing on insource projects was found to be negative, but not significant. Thus, in the near future it can be expected the adoption of both insourcing and outsourcing will increase. Results from the current study support the findings by Tiwana, & Kim (2016) that there is a growing trend to concurrently insource and outsource the same information technology (IT) activities. This trend exists since insourcing capabilities can complement outsourcing capabilities when client's in-house IT development abilities complement those of its vendors.

Analysis of the results of onshore and offshore sourcing effects suggest both onshore diffusion and offshore diffusion occur due to external influences. Such as information obtained in the trade press and mass media communication channels, but not through interpersonal communication between current and potential adopters. Results also suggest higher adoption of onshore sourcing does not impact offshoring adoption. Whereas higher adoption of offshoring enhances the adoption of onshoring. The co-diffusion effect of offshoring on onshoring was complementary as expected.

Offshore sourcing has become increasingly popular and important in reducing the costs of software development. Offshoring can provide low-cost labor. It provides access to world class expertise to develop software, but it also creates uncertainties in the IT workforce leading to the failure of offshored projects (Zafar, et al., 2018). Offshore development adds new facets to development such as culture, distance, time, space, challenges in communication channels and infrastructure that can complicate development leading to project failures (Khan & Khan, 2017). The downside of offshoring may be missed deadlines, dissatisfied users, and failure to reduce development costs. Many organizations have faced offshoring failures due to various issues such as cultural clashes, communication issues, inability to build necessary social and human capital, challenges with domain knowledge, lack of commitment of external developers (Moe et al., 2014). Smite & Wohlin (2011) found offshoring experiences of organizations resulted in failures due to challenges faced by companies, thus indicating that offshoring software development can be challenging. Vithana et. al., (2018) note companies have realized cost savings are small and problems are bigger compared to co-located development. Thus, the results of this study strengthen the argument provided by previous scholars that offshoring is slowly declining thus increasing the use of onshore software development.

Managerial Implications

The complementary effect of insourced software projects on outsourced projects, as well as the complementary effect of offshoring on onshoring software projects, has specific managerial implications. For example, for time-sensitive projects, IT managers can successfully design 24/7 software development shops by offshoring activities such as quality control and testing to countries, which are located in alternative time zones. Let's say our development team is located in the United States, and our quality control/ testing team is located in India, which is in an alternative time zone and considered to be a "mature" offshoring destination per Carmel and Tija (2005). The U.S. development team can design and code throughout the day and provide the code to the testing environment before leaving work for the day. The Indian quality control and testing team can test the provided code when it is night time in the United States. When the U.S. team arrives at work in the morning the test results would have be compiled and reports waiting. This type of onshoring and offshoring configuration can facilitate the achievement of aggressive project timelines.

Tiwana, & Kim (2016) note that IT managers must shift their thought process from insource or outsource to insource and outsource. Given the observed complementary effect of insourcing software projects on outsourcing software projects, IT management can pursue a portfolio approach in managing IT projects. IT management can define which projects or project activities are critical to the achievement or sustainment of competitive advantage for the organization and keep these insource while outsourcing remaining projects or project activities.

Research Limitations and Future Research

This study focused on co-diffusion analysis of sourcing options for software development projects developed in multiple countries. Due to data limitation we could not apply the co-diffusion studies to other types of sourcing arrangements. We identify this as a potential area of research where the current study can be expanded to analyze co-diffusion effects between other combinations of sourcing arrangements such as onshore outsourcing, offshore outsourcing, onshore insourcing and offshore insourcing. Our study does not take into consideration country-level contextual factors, which may affect the diffusion and co-diffusion process. Hence, co-diffusion effects should be tested within and outside a country to understand the diffusion process for a specific country. Furthermore, our research does not include project size in the evaluation of co-diffusion effects. Future research test how co-diffusion trends vary between large and small sized projects. Future studies could also be expanded to test co-diffusion effects of other development aspects like software development methodologies such as waterfall development or agile development. Other technological aspects used in the software development process should also be studied using co-diffusion models.

CONCLUSION

This study considers software sourcing arrangements such as offshoring and outsourcing as strategic organizational innovation and analyzes the temporal diffusion of software sourcing arrangements by applying innovation diffusion theories. Specifically, the study tests the existence of co-diffusion effects of related yet independent innovations that have separate adoption tracks: 1) between onshoring and offshoring, and 2) between insourcing and outsourcing. The results from the analysis indicate the existence of complementary co-diffusion effects between onshoring and offshoring. It also indicated co-diffusion effects are stronger than diffusion effects.

The co-diffusion effect of insource development on outsourced project development was found to be one-way complementary. Indicating that insource diffusion occurs only due to external influences whereas outsourcing diffusion is the result of both internal effects and co-diffusion effects. The co-diffusion effect indicates the higher adoption of insourcing enhances the adoption of outsourcing. Organizations prefer insourcing development over outsourcing development. However, the more an organization insources the development of projects, the more the organization will adopt outsourcing. Organizations need to understand how to best utilize insourcing and outsourcing options. Determining which part of a development project can best be performed by each phenomenon.

The co-diffusion effect of onshore development on offshore development was found to be significantly, one-way complimentary. This indicates the higher adoption of onshore sourcing does not impact offshoring adoption, whereas higher adoption of offshoring enhances the adoption of onshoring. Organizations prefer onshoring development over offshoring development. In fact, the more an organization offshores development projects, the more the organization will gravitate toward onshoring their development projects. Organizations need to understand how to best utilize onshoring and offshoring options.

Finally, it can be concluded that organizations will increasingly use both outsourcing and onshoring options. They should be considered as prospective sourcing options given the positive impact from insource and offshore sourcing.

In addition, it was found that innovation had a statistically significant, positive effect on insourcing, onshoring, and offshoring. While imitation had a statistically significant negative effect on outsourcing.

Clearly, the use of one type of sourcing impacts the use of other sourcing options. Furthermore, internal and external information scanning provides insight into where and when to adopt a particular sourcing option. With the increase in options available for software development, organizations need to create decision criteria to determine how to best utilize each option.

REFERENCES

Abramovsky, L., & Griffith, R. (2006). Outsourcing and offshoring of business services: How important is ICT? *Journal of the European Economic Association, 4*(2-3), 594–601. doi:10.1162/jeea.2006.4.2-3.594

Ali, S., & Khan, S. U. (2016). Software outsourcing partnership model: An evaluation framework for vendor organizations. *Journal of Systems and Software, 117*, 402–425. doi:10.1016/j.jss.2016.03.069

Alkhatib, G., Al-Sarayrah, K., & Abram, A. (2018, December). Exploring ISBSG R12 Dataset Using Multi-data Analytics. In *International conference on the Sciences of Electronics, Technologies of Information and Telecommunications*, (vol. 1, pp. 131-143). Springer.

Alsudairi, M., & Dwivedi, Y. K. (2010). A multi-disciplinary profile of IS/IT outsourcing research. *Journal of Enterprise Information Management, 23*(2), 215–258. doi:10.1108/17410391021019787

Angst, C. M., Wowak, K. D., Handley, S. M., & Kelley, K. (2017). Antecedents of information systems sourcing strategies in US hospitals: A longitudinal study. *Management Information Systems Quarterly, 41*(4), 1129–1152. doi:10.25300/MISQ/2017/41.4.06

Bapna, R., Barua, A., Mani, D., & Mehra, A. (2010). Research commentary—Cooperation, coordination, and governance in multisourcing: An agenda for analytical and empirical research. *Information Systems Research, 21*(4), 785–795. doi:10.1287/isre.1100.0328

Bass, F. M. (1969). A new product growth for model consumer durables. *Management Science, 15*(5), 215–227. doi:10.1287/mnsc.15.5.215

Beynon-Davies, P., & Williams, M. D. (2003). The diffusion of information systems development methods. *The Journal of Strategic Information Systems, 12*(1), 29–46. doi:10.1016/S0963-8687(02)00033-1

Bhardwaj, M., Rana, A., & Sharma, N. K. (2019). How software size influence productivity and project duration. *Iranian Journal of Electrical and Computer Engineering, 9*(3), 2088–8708. doi:10.11591/ijece.v9i3.pp2006-2017

Bucklin, L. P., & Sengupta, S. (1993). The co-diffusion of complementary innovations: Supermarket scanners and UPC symbols. *Journal of Product Innovation Management, 10*(2), 148–160. doi:10.1111/1540-5885.1020148

Carmel, E., & Agarwal, R. (2006). *The maturation of offshore sourcing of information technology work. Information systems outsourcing.* Springer.

Carmel, E., & Tjia, P. (2005). *Offshoring information technology: Sourcing and outsourcing to a global workforce*. Cambridge University Press.

Chakrabarty, S. (2006). Real-life case studies of offshore outsourced IS projects: Analysis of issues and socio-economic paradigms. Outsourcing and Offshoring in the 21st Century: A Socio-Economic Perspective, 248-281.

Chaudhury, A., & Bharati, P. (2008). IT outsourcing adoption by small and medium enterprises: A diffusion of innovation approach. AMCIS 2008 Proceedings, 390.

Cho, D. (2015). An empirical analysis of smartphone diffusions in a global context. *Journal of Contemporary Eastern Asia, 14*(1), 45–55. doi:10.17477/jcea.2015.14.1.045

Chua, A. L., & Pan, S. L. (2008). Knowledge transfer and organizational learning in IS offshore sourcing. *Omega, 36*(2), 267–281. doi:10.1016/j.omega.2006.06.008

Colombo, M. G., & Mosconi, R. (1995). Complementarity and cumulative learning effects in the early diffusion of multiple technologies. *The Journal of Industrial Economics, 43*(1), 13–48. doi:10.2307/2950423

Contractor, F. J., Kumar, V., Kundu, S. K., & Pedersen, T. (2010). Reconceptualizing the firm in a world of outsourcing and offshoring: The organizational and geographical relocation of high-value company functions. *Journal of Management Studies, 47*(8), 1417–1433. doi:10.1111/j.1467-6486.2010.00945.x

Dayyala, N., Bagchi, K., & Mandal, P. (2017). Software development productivity in different sourcing arrangements. In *Entrepreneurship in technology for ASEAN* (pp. 111–125). Springer. doi:10.1007/978-981-10-2281-4_9

Dewan, S., Ganley, D., & Kraemer, K. L. (2010). Complementarities in the diffusion of personal computers and the internet: Implications for the global digital divide. *Information Systems Research, 21*(4), 925–940. doi:10.1287/isre.1080.0219

Diana, W., Kenneth, J. W., David, B., & Madeleine, G. (2011). *SHAZAM reference manual*. Retrieved from http://store.econometrics.com/shazam/shazam_reference_manual_11_interior.pdf

Erber, G., & Sayed-Ahmed, A. (2005). Offshore outsourcing. *Inter Economics, 40*(2), 100–112. doi:10.100710272-005-0141-8

Fernández-Diego, M., & González-Ladrón-de-Guevara, F. (2018). Application of mutual information-based sequential feature selection to ISBSG mixed data. *Software Quality Journal, 26*(4), 1299–1325. doi:10.100711219-017-9391-5

Foerstl, K., Kirchoff, J. F., & Bals, L. (2016). Reshoring and insourcing: Drivers and future research directions. *International Journal of Physical Distribution & Logistics Management, 46*(5), 492–515. doi:10.1108/IJPDLM-02-2015-0045

Garg, R., Smith, M. D., & Telang, R. (2011). Measuring information diffusion in an online community. *Journal of Management Information Systems, 28*(2), 11–38. doi:10.2753/MIS0742-1222280202

Han, H., Lee, J., Chun, J. U., & Seo, Y. (2013). Complementarity between client and vendor IT capabilities: An empirical investigation in IT outsourcing projects. *Decision Support Systems*, *55*(3), 777–791. doi:10.1016/j.dss.2013.03.003

Hanafizadeh, P., & Zare Ravasan, A. (2018). An empirical analysis on outsourcing decision: The case of e-banking services. *Journal of Enterprise Information Management*, *31*(1), 146–172. doi:10.1108/JEIM-11-2016-0182

Hanafizadeh, P., & Zareravasan, A. (2020). A Systematic Literature Review on IT Outsourcing Decision and Future Research Directions. *Journal of Global Information Management*, *28*(2), 1–42. doi:10.4018/JGIM.2020040108

Haried, P., & Dai, H. (2011). The evolution of information systems offshoring research: A past, present and future meta analysis review. *Journal of International Technology and Information Management*, *20*(1), 5.

Harland, C., Knight, L., Lamming, R., & Walker, H. (2005). Outsourcing: Assessing the risks and benefits for organizations, sectors and nations. *International Journal of Operations & Production Management*, *25*(9), 831–850. doi:10.1108/01443570510613929

Hu, Q., Saunders, C., & Gebelt, M. (1997). Research report: Diffusion of information systems outsourcing: A reevaluation of influence sources. *Information Systems Research*, *8*(3), 288–301. doi:10.1287/isre.8.3.288

ISBSG. (n.d.). *Source of software development project data*. https://isbsg.org/project-data

Jensen, T. (2017). *Simulating co-diffusion of innovations: Feedback technology & behavioral change* (Dissertation). Delft University of Technology.

Jin-Xing, H., Xinping, X., & Siqing, S. (2013). *Mobile operator's dilemma: An exploratory study on the co-diffusion of mobile IM and desktop IM of china mobile*. Paper presented at the E-Business Engineering (ICEBE), 2013 IEEE 10th International Conference On.

June, W., & Meiga, L. N. (2010). Information technology offshore outsourcing security risks and safeguards. *Journal of Information Privacy and Security*, *6*(3), 29–46. doi:10.1080/15536548.2010.10855892

Khan, A. I., Qurashi, R. J., & Khan, U. A. (2011). *A comprehensive study of commonly practiced heavy and light weight software methodologies*. arXiv Preprint arXiv:1111.3001

Khan, S. U., & Khan, A. W. (2017). Critical challenges in managing offshore software development outsourcing contract from vendors' perspectives. *IET Software*, *11*(1), 1–11. doi:10.1049/iet-sen.2015.0080

Kim, N., Chang, D. R., & Shocker, A. D. (2000). Modeling intercategory and generational dynamics for a growing information technology industry. *Management Science*, *46*(4), 496–512. doi:10.1287/mnsc.46.4.496.12059

Lacity, M. C., Khan, S., Yan, A., & Willcocks, L. P. (2010). A review of the IT outsourcing empirical literature and future research directions. *Journal of Information Technology*, *25*(4), 395–433. doi:10.1057/jit.2010.21

Ladrón-de-Guevara, A., & Putsis, W. P. (2015). Multi-market, multi-product new product diffusion: Decomposing local, foreign, and indirect (cross-product) effects. *Customer Needs and Solutions*, 2(1), 57–70. doi:10.100740547-014-0032-x

Lai, P. C. (2017). The literature review of technology adoption models and theories for the novelty technology. *JISTEM-Journal of Information Systems and Technology Management*, 14(1), 21–38. doi:10.4301/S1807-17752017000100002

Lazzati. (2018). *Co-Diffusion of Technologies in Social Networks*. Available at SSRN 3204664

Lee, C. Y., & Huh, S. Y. (2017). Technology forecasting using a diffusion model incorporating replacement purchases. *Sustainability*, 9(6), 1038. doi:10.3390u9061038

Levina, N., & Ross, J. W. (2003). From the vendor's perspective: Exploring the value proposition in information technology outsourcing. *Management Information Systems Quarterly*, 27(3), 331–364. doi:10.2307/30036537

Lewin, A. Y., & Volberda, H. W. (2011). Co-evolution of global sourcing: The need to understand the underlying mechanisms of firm-decisions to offshore. *International Business Review*, 20(3), 241–251. doi:10.1016/j.ibusrev.2011.02.008

Liang, H., Wang, J. J., Xue, Y., & Cui, X. (2016). IT outsourcing research from 1992 to 2013: A literature review based on main path analysis. *Information & Management*, 53(2), 227–251. doi:10.1016/j.im.2015.10.001

Loh, L., & Venkatraman, N. (1992). Diffusion of information technology outsourcing: Influence sources and the kodak effect. *Information Systems Research*, 3(4), 334–358. doi:10.1287/isre.3.4.334

Low, C., Chen, Y., & Wu, M. (2011). Understanding the determinants of cloud computing adoption. *Industrial Management & Data Systems*, 111(7), 1006–1023. doi:10.1108/02635571111161262

Madsen, D. O. (2017). Examining the popularity trajectory of outsourcing as a management concept. *Problems and Perspectives in Management*, 15(2), 178–196. doi:10.21511/ppm.15(2-1).2017.02

Mahajan, V., & Peterson, R. (1985). *Models for innovation diffusion*. Sage Publication. doi:10.4135/9781412985093

Mann, A., Folch, D. C., Kauffman, R. J., & Anselin, L. (2015). Spatial and temporal trends in information technology outsourcing. *Applied Geography (Sevenoaks, England)*, 63, 192–203. doi:10.1016/j.apgeog.2015.06.018

Mann, A., Kauffman, R. J., Han, K., & Nault, B. R. (2011). Are there contagion effects in information technology and business process outsourcing? *Decision Support Systems*, 51(4), 864–874. doi:10.1016/j.dss.2011.02.005

Manning, S., Massini, S., Peeters, C., & Lewin, A. Y. (2018). The changing rationale for governance choices: Early vs. late adopters of global services sourcing. *Strategic Management Journal*, 39(8), 2303–2334. doi:10.1002mj.2795

Miranda, M. Q., Farias, J. S., de Araújo Schwartz, C., & de Almeida, J. P. L. (2016). Technology adoption in diffusion of innovations perspective: Introduction of an ERP system in a non-profit organization. *RAI Revista de Administração e Inovação, 13*(1), 48–57. doi:10.1016/j.rai.2016.02.002

Moe, N. B., Šmite, D., Hanssen, G. K., & Barney, H. (2014). From offshore outsourcing to insourcing and partnerships: Four failed outsourcing attempts. *Empirical Software Engineering, 19*(5), 1225–1258. doi:10.100710664-013-9272-x

Mustapha, H., & Abdelwahed, N. (2019). Investigating the use of random forest in software effort estimation. *Procedia Computer Science, 148*, 343–352. doi:10.1016/j.procs.2019.01.042

Nahar, N., & Kuivanen, L. (2010). An integrative conceptual model of Vietnam as an emerging destination for offshore outsourcing of software development for Finnish companies. *Journal of International Technology and Information Management, 19*(3), 3.

Naik, N. (2016). Crowdsourcing, open-sourcing, outsourcing and insourcing software development: A comparative analysis. In *2016 IEEE Symposium on Service-Oriented System Engineering (SOSE)* (pp. 380-385). IEEE. 10.1109/SOSE.2016.68

Niculescu, M. F., & Whang, S. (2012). Research Note—Co-Diffusion of wireless voice and data services: An empirical analysis of the Japanese mobile telecommunications market. *Information Systems Research, 23*(1), 260–279. doi:10.1287/isre.1100.0346

Peterson, R. A., & Mahajan, V. (1978). Multi-product growth models. *Research in Marketing, 1*(20), 1–23.

Rogers, E. M. (2010). *Diffusion of innovations*. Simon and Schuster.

Schneider, S., & Sunyaev, A. (2016). Determinant factors of cloud-sourcing decisions: Reflecting on the IT outsourcing literature in the era of cloud computing. *Journal of Information Technology, 31*(1), 1–31. doi:10.1057/jit.2014.25

Schniederjans, M. J., Schniederjans, A. M., & Schniederjans, D. G. (2015). *Outsourcing and insourcing in an international context*. Routledge. doi:10.4324/9781315701936

Shah, M. A., Jawawi, D. N., Isa, M. A., Younas, M., Abdelmaboud, A., & Sholichin, F. (2020). Ensembling Artificial Bee Colony with Analogy-Based Estimation to Improve Software Development Effort Prediction. *IEEE Access: Practical Innovations, Open Solutions, 8*, 58402–58415. doi:10.1109/ACCESS.2020.2980236

Smite, D., & Wohlin, C. (2011). A whisper of evidence in global software engineering. *IEEE Software, 28*(4), 15–18. doi:10.1109/MS.2011.70

Tate, W. L., & Bals, L. (2017). Outsourcing/offshoring insights: Going beyond reshoring to rightshoring. *International Journal of Physical Distribution & Logistics Management, 47*(2/3), 106–113. doi:10.1108/IJPDLM-11-2016-0314

Teng, J. T., Grover, V., & Guttler, W. (2002). Information technology innovations: General diffusion patterns and its relationships to innovation characteristics. *IEEE Transactions on Engineering Management, 49*(1), 13–27. doi:10.1109/17.985744

Tiwana, A., & Kim, S. K. (2016). Concurrent IT sourcing: Mechanisms and contingent advantages. *Journal of Management Information Systems, 33*(1), 101–138. doi:10.1080/07421222.2016.1172456

Valente, T. W. (1995). *Network models of the diffusion of innovations* (No. 303.484 V3).

Vithana, V. N., Asirvatham, D., & Johar, M. G. M. (2017). Investigating the Issues of Using Agile Methods in Offshore Software Development in Sri Lanka. In *Asian Conference on Intelligent Information and Database Systems*, (pp. 515-523). Springer. 10.1007/978-3-319-56660-3_44

Vogelezang, F., & van Heeringen, H. (2019). Benchmarking: Comparing Apples to Apples. In Rethinking Productivity in Software Engineering, (pp. 205-217). Apress.

Volberda, H. W., & Lewin, A. Y. (2003). Co-evolutionary dynamics within and between firms: From evolution to co-evolution. *Journal of Management Studies, 40*(8), 2111–2136. doi:10.1046/j.1467-6486.2003.00414.x

Wejnert, B. (2002). Integrating models of diffusion of innovations: A conceptual framework. *Annual Review of Sociology, 28*(1), 297–326. doi:10.1146/annurev.soc.28.110601.141051

Westland, J. C., Hao, J. X., Xiao, X., & Shan, S. (2016). Substitutes, complements and network effects in instant messaging services. *Networks and Spatial Economics, 16*(2), 525–543. doi:10.100711067-015-9287-5

Yu, Y., Hao, J. X., Zuo, M., Shan, S., & Westland, C. (2016). *Co-Diffusion of Mobile Operator's OTT and SMS Messaging Services in Emerging Economies.* AMCIS.

Zafar, A. A., Saif, S., Khan, M., Iqbal, J., Akhunzada, A., Wadood, A., Al-Mogren, A., & Alamri, A. (2018). Taxonomy of factors causing integration failure during global software development. *IEEE Access: Practical Innovations, Open Solutions, 6*, 22228–22239. doi:10.1109/ACCESS.2017.2782843

Zhu, K., Dong, S., Xu, S. X., & Kraemer, K. L. (2006). Innovation diffusion in global contexts: Determinants of post-adoption digital transformation of European companies. *European Journal of Information Systems, 15*(6), 601–616. doi:10.1057/palgrave.ejis.3000650

This research was previously published in the Information Resources Management Journal (IRMJ), 33(4); pages 33-52, copyright year 2020 by IGI Publishing (an imprint of IGI Global).

Chapter 67

Measuring Software Development Project Performance:
A Case Study on Agıle KPI's for Software Start-Ups

Nihan Yildirim
Istanbul Technical University, Turkey

Semih Ersöz
Aalto University, Finland

Bilal Altun
Karlsruher Institut für Technologie, Germany

ABSTRACT

Adopting agile methodologies to software development processes helps software companies to sustain their growth through efficiency for long term. In the digital transformation era, Industry 4.0 as part of High-Tech Strategy 2020 for Germany involves agile principles and brings the latest technological trends in production process. The purpose of this chapter is to design a proper agile project management performance measurement model for start-up software companies. First, all key performance indicators related to agile development in the literature have been listed. Then KPIs that are provided from literature review with content analysis have been reviewed and categorized by expert opinions that were collected through in-depth interviews. Seven strategic KPIs and their data collection systems are defined and designed. Lastly, process and data collection improvements are recommended in order to sustain agile development measurement model.

DOI: 10.4018/978-1-6684-3702-5.ch067

INTRODUCTION

Managing projects with high obscurity level is one of the most strenuous tasks in software project management. Since it has been clearly understood that traditional methodology undercuts the efficiency of software projects, a more iterative and flexible project management methodologies started to proliferate in the industry. The implementation of agile methods to IT project management approach produced compelling results of the outputs of the companies. In recent decades, adopting agile methodologies to software development process helps software companies to sustain their growth through efficiency for the long term. On the other hand, in digital transformation era, Industry 4.0 which involves agile principles brought the agility topic into the research agenda again by raising the need for case studies on applying agile principles in SMEs. As agile approach is interdisciplinary and brings flexibility to organizations, it becomes an aid tool to be utilized for converging processes for higher performance in transformation periods.

In the digital transformation era, software development projects face the challenge of rapidly changing user requirements, increasing technology push, time pressure on product delivery and frequent releases. Hence, effective performance measurement in agile software development has become a significantly rising topic where researchers and practitioners intensely explore feasible and adaptable approaches.

However, flexible and chaotic nature of agile methods refrains companies from measuring the performance as successful as they used to do. Consequently, taking actions becomes harder without clear performance monitoring. Especially during digital transformation projects, agility and lean approaches in project management are expected to be utilized for rapid convergence to new technologies, and hence will require high-level monitoring and performance measurement methodologies of projects.

The purpose of this study is to design a proper Agile Project Management performance measurement model for start-up companies in software business by defining strategic KPIs, measuring defined KPIs and evaluating the results.

As a case study, a midsized software company which evolved in ITU innovation and entrepreneurship ecosystem and operates like a startup in ITU Teknokent, a technology development zone in Turkey, is going through a transformation stage from being a start-up to an important corporation in the international market. Having a structured, well designed agile project management performance measurement model is one of the most pivotal steps for this kind of company. On one hand, it is necessary for staying competitive in the global market on the other hand; technology development zone administration requires performance measurement data to evaluate the companies' performances periodically. Research Model is presented in Appendix A.

In summary, the introduced Agile Project Management Performance Measurement Model aims to support start-up software companies' efforts of growing in the global market with a well-structured and sustainable infrastructure. In addition to that, this chapter aims to help to create an Agile Project Management Performance Measurement Framework for the midsized software companies that operate in developing countries with scarce resources.

BACKGROUND

Theoretical background is presented in the following sections. Background section has two parts: (i) Project Management Methodologies in Software Development and (ii) Performance Measurement in

Software Development Projects. In these sections, sub-topics are presented in a deductive manner, from general terms to specific terms about agile KPI's for performance measurement in software development projects. After giving brief information on the Project Management Methodologies in Software Development, we focus on the Agile Project Management Methodology and, for being the most popular and most widely researched Agile methodology, we provide insights about SCRUM method.

In the second section, we provide basic concepts and definitions about Performance Measurement in software projects, and then we present the characteristics of Key Performance Indicators that are the major tools for tangible performance measurement. Referring to Agile Measurement Principles, we combine Agility and KPI concepts in the subsection of "Agile KPI's.

Project Management Methodologies in Software Development

As Schwalbe (2011) stated, topics and focus area of project management sharply changed in previous decades. Before the 1980s, project management primarily focused on providing schedule and resource data to top management in the military, computer, and construction industries but today project management involves various industries (Schwalbe, 2011). Improvements in Information and Communication technologies like computer hardware, software, networking and emergence of interdisciplinary, global teams radically changed the project environment.

As the number and complexity of projects continue to increase, critical issues about project management also evolved. As Schwalbe (2011) underlined, the success rate of information technology projects has more than doubled since 1995, but still only about a third are successful in meeting scope, time, and cost goals. Flexible and disciplined project management approaches became critical for business success.

In previous decades, various software development approaches have been introduced (Abrahamsson et al., 2002). These software development methodologies which can be classified as heavyweight (suitable for projects where requirements are more constant and complex) and lightweight (suitable for projects where specs are likely to change rapidly, hence require incremental approach and iterations for flexibility) (Despa, 2014). Some of these major methodologies are defined below:

- First described by Royce (1970), Waterfall methodology in software development is the most commonly used, linear sequential SW development project management process which emphasized meticulous planning and comprehensive documentation (Despa, 2014).
- Prototyping methodology entails building a demo version of the software product with critical functionality where initial specifications are defined only to provide sufficient information to build a prototype (Despa, 2014). Prototyping evolved from increasing product specification definition needs and it uses the prototype to refine specifications by taking it as a baseline for communication between the project team and project owner (Cooling and Hughes, 1989).
- Iterative and incremental software development methodology relies on building the software application one step at the time in the form of an expanding model (Larman and Basili, 2003). The process is repeated until the model becomes a fully functional application that meets all requirements (Despa, 2014).
- Rapid application development is a development lifecycle designed to take advantage of powerful software development (Martin, 1991). By imposing less emphasis and encouraging faster development, and higher quality results than the traditional methodologies are achieved.

- Extreme programming uses smaller more manageable chunks than conventional software development process (Despa, 2014) and reduces the cost of changing software by performing limited planning, analysis and design activities in software development process (Beck, 1999; Despa, 2014). The introduction of the extreme programming method is taken as the starting point for agile software development approaches (Abrahamsson et al., 2002).
- Agile development methodologies and especially Scrum methods enable incrementally building software in complex environments (Rising and Janoff, 2000). Software requirements are formulated and prioritized by the product owner (Despa, 2014). The "Agile Movement" in the software industry started with the publication of Agile Software Development Manifesto by a group of software experts in 2001 (Beck et al. 2001; Cockburn 2002). Agile methods recognize people as the primary drivers of project success, coupled with an intense focus on effectiveness and maneuverability (Highsmith and Cockburn, 2001).
- Other methods such Crystal Methods (Cockburn 2000), Feature-Driven Development (Palmer and Felsing 2002), and Adaptive Software Development (Highsmith 2000) then belonged to Agile methods family (Abrahammson et al., 2002).

Among these, Agile Development Methodologies became increasingly popular by their advantages for minimizing the risks associated with the planning process and development of software solutions (Georgiev and Stefanova, 2014). In fact, these developments in software development methodologies reshaped the project management practices in software projects, and they even had been infectious to other project management practices.

On the other hand, as Spundak (2014) discussed, there is a need for hybrid approaches which intend to combine traditional waterfall, prototyping, agile methods of project management. For this, the practitioners should define the needed detail level for the definition and control mechanism of the project and then adapt the appropriate methodology in the required project management framework. Similar to "Agile with Discipline" methodology of IBM which incorporates components of agile development into a more structured approach to project management through providing sufficient documentation and timelines with flexibility, hybrid approaches can leverage the advantages of Agile with the strengths of traditional practices (Adelakun et al., 2017).

Agile Project Management in Software Development

Today's dynamic business environment is forces organizations to constantly change their software requirements to adjust to new environments. As well as welcoming changing requirements, fast delivery of software products are expected. In this aspect, traditional plan-driven developments fail to meet up these requirements. Agile software development brings its own set of novel challenges that must be addressed to satisfy the customer through early and continuous delivery of the valuable software (Beck et al., 2001; The Twelve Principles of Agile Software, 2001). Agile development model (Figure 1) includes the initiation of the project and definition of initial requirements, then continues with development cycles that includes integration and test phases in between. After the completion of the review-feedback-approval phases, frequent releases takes place. In the lack of approval, after the change and adjustment phases, next iteration starts (Agile Manifesto, 2002). Including a set of software development methods based on iterative and incremental development process, agile system development methods emerged as a response to the inability of traditional plan-driven approaches to handle rapidly changing environments (Highsmith, 2002).

Figure 1. Agile Development Model
(Agile Manifesto, 2002)

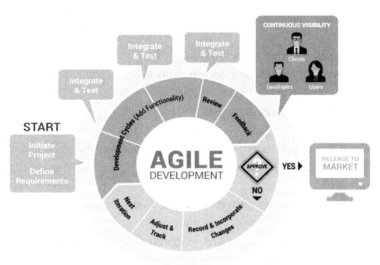

Agility is the ability to sense and respond to business prospects in order to stay inventive and aggressive in an unstable and rapidly shifting business environment (Highsmith, 2002). As can be seen from Table 1, The uniqueness of this approach is about the agility of the development process, development teams, and their environment. Agile teams consist of multi-skilled individuals. The development teams also have on-site customers with substantial domain knowledge to help them better understand the requirements (Abrahamson, Solo, Ronkainen, & Warsta, 2002). Multiple short development cycles also enable teams to accommodate request for change and provide the opportunity to discover emerging requirements.

Table 1. Agile Approach summary

Agile Approach
Iterative; The evolutionarydelivery model
Adaptive
Emergent, rapid change, unknown -Discovered during the project
Self-organizing teams
Client onsite and considered as a team member

Working definitions of agile methodologies can be summarized as a group of software development processes that must be iterative (take several cycles to complete), incremental (not deliver the entire product at once), self-organizing (teams determine the best way to handle work), and emergent (processes, principles and work structures are recognized during the project rather than predetermined). In 2001, seventeen well-respected experts of agile methodology formed an Agile Alliance to better promote their views and wrote the Agile Software Development Manifesto. The basic ideas of the philosophy are introduced through four basic values (Agile Manifesto, 2002);

- Individuals and interactions over processes and tools
- Working software over comprehensive documentation
- Customer collaboration over contract negotiation
- Responding to change over following a plan

Apart from the Agile Manifesto, there is also a set of principles which determine that what is to be agile (The Twelve Principles of Agile Software, 2001);

- Highest priority is to satisfy the customer through early and continuous delivery of valuable software.
- Welcome changing requirements, even late in development. Agile processes harness change for the customer's competitive advantage.
- Deliver working software frequently, from a couple of weeks to a couple of months, with a preference to the shorter timescale.
- Business people and developers must work together daily throughout the project.
- Projects are built around motivated individuals, give them the environment and support they need, and trust them to get the job done.
- The most efficient and effective method of conveying information to and within a development team is the face-to-face conversation.
- Working software is the primary measure of progress.
- Agile processes promote sustainable development. The sponsors, developers, and users should be able to maintain a constant pace indefinitely.
- Continuous attention to technical excellence and good design enhances agility.
- Simplicity--the art of maximizing the amount of work not done--is essential.
- The best architectures, requirements, and designs emerge from self-organizing teams.
- At regular intervals, the team reflects on how to become more effective, then adjusts its behavior.

In the latest report of Collab.Net (2018) on the State of Agile in organizations, the reasons with increasing trend for adopting agile methods in companies are listed as accelerating software delivery, enhancing delivery predictability, improving IT/Business alignment and reducing project cost. According to the same report, the use of Kanban, product road mapping and portfolio planning had been among the rising agile techniques.

A Favorable Agile Software Development Methodology: SCRUM

Among different types of methodologies and Frameworks in AGILE like Dynamic systems development method (DSDM) or Rapid Application Development (RAD), SCRUM is a process which project team focus on delivering the highest business value in shortest time and the development team works as a unit to reach a common goal as opposed to a "traditional, sequential approach" (Jeldi and Chavali, 2013). It primarily deals with problems at the team level and aims to improve teamwork effectiveness by guiding teams to be self-directing.

Despite the Scrum Alliance (2015) states that Scrum is an agile framework for completing complex projects, Scrum is originally designed for small organizations and teams, hence for multiple site and multiple team projects may face some challenges in implementing Scrum.

The Scrum approach has been developed for managing the system development process. It is an empirical approach applying the ideas of industrial process control theory to systems development resulting in reintroduction of the ideas of flexibility, adaptability and productivity (Schwaber and Beedle 2002). The rules of Scrum bind together the events, roles, and artifacts, governing the relationships and interaction between them (Schwaber and Sutherland, 2013). Hence Scrum is more likely to be a project management framework.

"Scrum Flow Framework" (shown in Figure 2) has the following components (Paul and Singh, 2012; Jeldi and Chavali, 2013; Scrum Alliance, 2015; Open View, 2016):

- A product owner creates a prioritized wish list called a product backlog.
- During sprint (short period of time, usually between 1 to 4 weeks, to complete a whole iterative project cycle) planning, the team pulls a small chunk from the top of that wish list, a sprint backlog, and decides how to implement those pieces.
- The team has a certain amount of time — a sprint (usually two to four weeks) — to complete its work, but it meets each day to assess its progress (daily Scrum).
- Along the way, the Scrum Master keeps the team focused on its goal.

Figure 2. Scrum Flow Framework
(Paul and Singh, 2012)

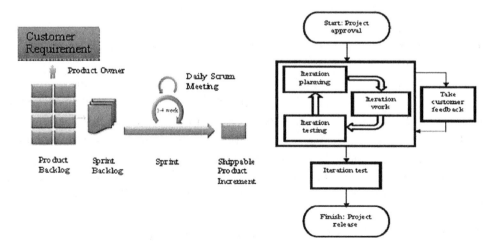

- At the end of the sprint, the work should be potentially shippable: ready to hand to a customer, put on a store shelf, or show to a stakeholder.
- The sprint ends with a sprint review and retrospective.
- As the next sprint begins, the team chooses another chunk of the product backlog, begins working again.

Scrum roles are categorized as "Scrum Team", "Scrum Master" and "Scrum Product Owner" (The Scrum Institute, 2018; Schwaber and Sutherland, 2013).

- The Scrum Master is responsible for ensuring Scrum is understood and enacted; act as a servant-leader for the Scrum Team. Scrum Master ensures that the Scrum Team adheres to Scrum theory, practice, rules.
- The Development Team consists of professionals who do the work of delivering a potentially re-leasable Increment of "Done" product at the end of each Sprint. Only members of the Development Team create the Increment. Development Teams are structured and empowered by the organization to organize and manage their own work, so that the synergy optimizes the Team's overall efficiency and effectiveness.
- The Product Owner is responsible for maximizing the value of the product and the work of the Development Team. How this is done may vary widely across organizations, Scrum Teams, and individuals. The Product Owner is the sole person responsible for managing the Product Backlog.

Performance Measurement in Software Development Projects

Performance measurement can be defined as a process that includes data collection, data analysis and declaration of the results of the performance of a specific individual, group, organization, system or component. Performance measurement systems come across with different challenges. Eccles (1991) mentions 5 activities for reinforcing the strategies of the company by using performance measurement in his article called "The Performance Measurement Manifesto":

- Developing an information architecture
- Putting the technology in place to support this architecture
- Aligning bonuses and other incentives with the new system
- Drawing on outside resources
- Designing an internal process to ensure the other four activities occur

Within this broad perspective, measuring performance in software development projects includes production performance (delivery to customer) and process performance (efficiency of Process) (Liang et al., 2007). Project performance in projects today deal not only with hard aspects such as financial, schedule, and quality (Pollack, 2007) but also with soft dimensions such as communication, team engagement, cohesion (Ravindranath, 2016, Kerzner, 2013).

One of the most important sources on "Project success factors" is the framework of characteristics, definitions and measurement techniques that were introduced by Pinto and Slevin (1986, 1988) in three dimensions of technical validity, organizational validity, and organizational effectiveness with those of time, cost, performance and client satisfaction on projects. Some highlighted success factors from this framework are project mission, top management support, project schedule/plan, client consultation, personnel, technology to support the project, client acceptance, and also some factors that inspired agile project management such as monitoring and feedback, channels of communication, and troubleshooting expertise.

Key Performance Indicators: Major Tools to Make Performance Measurement Tangible

Key Performance Indicators (KPIs) are one of the most widely used performance measurement techniques. However, the definition of KPI can be controversial due to the purpose of its use. According to Bauer (Figure 3), *KPIs are quantifiable metrics which reflect the performance of an organization in achieving its goals and objectives.* Therefore, KPIs should be in accordance with the organization's vision, strategy and objectives. Some approaches have been developed for a long time ago in order to ensure the conformance of metrics with the organization. One of the most respected frameworks in that context is GQM (Goal, Question, and Metric) that links metrics to specific strategic objectives in order to justify the metrics.

Figure 3. Strategic Alignment Pyramid
(Bauer,2004: KPIs - Metrics That Drive Performance Management,

As Crispin & Gregory (2011) states that metrics should be considered as a factor for motivating rather than degrading team's morale. In addition to that, the right set of metrics helps organizations to monitor its performance and provide the conformity level of keeping track of goals. Selection of what to measure is a pivotal step in creating a measurement model. The KPI set should be designed by considering the main purpose of measurement. The organization should be concerned that the designed measurement system does not lead to the dysfunction of the organization. In some cases, teams try only to improve the outcome of an indicator and fail to prioritize the organizations' original goal.

Agile Measurement Principles

Measuring levels should be carefully considered during the design of the measurement model. While measuring the lower levels can cause an increase in dysfunction, limiting the measurement level may hinder the potential of the model.

Poppendieck (2011) and Austin (1996) introduce the concept called "Measure Up" which refers not to measure levels which are lower than the team level. Another related concept was introduced by Guckenheimer which is called "Value Up" that supports to focus on the customer value. Traditional effort-based measurement models become obsolete since agile development requires a flexible and customer value oriented organizational structure. Hartmann suggests a set of more specific criteria in order to define a successful agile metric (Hartmann, 1993);

- Supports and encourages lean and agile principles
- Measures outcome, not output
- Follows trends, not numbers
- Answer a particular question for a real person
- Belongs to a small set of KPIs
- Is easy to collect
- Reveals, rather than conceals, its context and significant variables
- Provides information to discussions about performance
- Provides feedback on a frequent and regular basis
- Reassures ‖good-enough‖ quality

Agile KPI's

Key performance indicator (KPI) in software development aims to measure some features of the current software activities and the processes. Measurement results are important for the organization to make better products and to improve current ongoing processes. The feedbacks that get after correct measurements help to predict the future quality of products. First of all, measurable metrics need to be identified, defined and included in performance measurement systems. Agile software project performance is mostly dependent on monitoring and control mechanisms (Cheng et al., 2009). Agile metrics create a common ground between the expectations from the project and software development processes, and as well they act as communication tools which enable the progress monitoring by different stakeholders (Broadus, 2013). According to agile principles like iterative development, accepted change, and adjustable requirements, the agile metrics are analyzed more frequently and require some set of tailor-made metrics rather than metrics used in traditional project monitoring (Broadus Iii, 2013; Hariharan and Arpasuteera, 2017).

Agile metrics generally focus on value-added to the customers by using customer deliverables against time, cost and quality. Cheng et al. (2009) categorized some agile metrics in team, task and quality dimensions by combining both hard and soft aspects. On the other hand, Broadus Iii (2013) classified Agile KPI's or metrics by velocity, Burn up, Burn down, Running Tested Features, Defect Density. These metrics are perceived as hard dimension because of quantitative attributes (Pollack, 2007). However, there is a need for hybrid metrics like customer satisfaction KPI, which can combine time, cost, quality and effective communication (Kerzner, 2013). When using the right set of Agile KPI's one can gain insight into how Agile working contributes to team performance and organizational performance as a whole. As well, Agile KPI measurement performance is valuable to have quantitative arguments following from these KPI's (Levels, 2016).

A Primary Concern When Setting Key Performance Indicators: Dysfunction in Measurement Systems

As explained above, the purpose of the measurement systems is to get some feedback in order to improve a process, product or project. The dysfunction of the measurement system happens when the performance index improves but there is no improvement of the process, product or project. Performance measurement initiatives may also inadvertently induce a range of unintended and dysfunctional side-effects (Aryankhesal et al., 2013). In agile project management, traditional performance metrics measures may not work within agile teams causing dysfunction (Galen, 2012). Metrics dysfunction is a metric whose collection influences the very behavior being measured—leading to metrics dysfunction (like the number of bugs corrected which depends to the number of bugs that can be manipulated by the developer) (Austin, 1996).

In this context, Austin (1996) categorized the metrics by their intention as motivating and informative measurement: While informational metrics are used only to get some insights from the development team, motivational metrics have a purpose to create positive organizational change among those being measured. As Austin (1996) stated, motivational metrics have a higher risk to create dysfunction since measuring every relevant aspect of the work in the software development process is a challenging issue. Target setting for performance measurements also bears the same risk as motivational measurement (Poppendieck and Poppendieck, 2011). In order to avoid the misuses of measuring systems, informational purposes should be used with hard-to-deceive metrics while a high level of trust is achieved within the organization. As Poppendieck and Poppendiek (2011) explained, target setting for the organizations, teams or people has the same risk of dysfunction.

THE CASE STUDY FROM A SOFTWARE STARTUP COMPANY: ANALYSIS OF THE "AS-IS" STATE (CURRENT PRACTICE) OF AGILE PROJECT MANAGEMENT AND PERFORMANCE MEASUREMENT

In this Case Study Section, which is the contributive application of this chapter, there are two subsections which reflect two phases (analysis and design) of a typical system development process (i) Analysis of the As-Is State of the Agile Project Management and Performance Measurement of the studied company and, (ii) Proposed Design for To-Be State Agile KPI Set for the studied Company. In accordance with the structuring in the Background section, Case Study sections also have sub-topics for Project Management Practices and Project Performance Measurement Practices for both phases of As-Is and To-Be. Research Model which clarifies the flow of the research is presented in Appendix A.

Current Agile Project Management Practices in Software Development

Studied Software Start-Up Company has been using scrum methodology in technical teams. Although the Scrum Guide states that product owner should participate to all planning meetings, some of the projects are carried out without the customer participation since some of the clients are not competent in agile methodology. In that case, project manager and analyst of the project plays the product owner role during the scrum meetings. On the other hand, every team member in is trained about scrum methods. Therefore, there is no vital impediment that undermines agile processes in internal projects. In addition, agile processes are supported company-wide. Sales and Human Resources departments are trying to adopt the latest agile software development processes within their routine tasks.

Sprints are planned to be 2 weeks and start with sprint planning meetings. At the beginning of every project, longer and more detailed release planning meetings are carried out. After the user requirements transformed into user stories by the analyst of the project, members of the scrum team list the product backlog items in the initial release planning meeting. The backlog items at that level are described as "epic" which refers to its complexity and the necessary amount of resources to complete that task. During the sprint planning meetings, product backlog items are defined and divided into more basic and simple tasks. Every task which is defined during this meeting can be completed by one individual team member. At the end of the sprint planning meeting, sprint backlog items, tasks that are planned to complete during 2-week sprint, are listed into the online scrum planning tool.

- **Development Process During Sprint:** After the sprint tasks are listed on to the scrum planning tool, every team member (developer) chooses the task that he/she starts to carry out. That process transforms the user stories into the code parts. Developers write the codes in Visual Studio and upload these files to the version control system. Codes are merged into the main branch after a peer developer controls and accepts the merge request. After all the sprint backlog items are completed, merged codes are transferred to Build / CI Server. Codes are merged with the main branch of the codes which are developed earlier. Those codes are transferred into Deploy Server and Test Server to be tested in company environment by the tester. At the end of the process, codes are deployed into the Production Server of the customer by the release manager (Figure 4).

Figure 4. Start-Up's Software Development Process

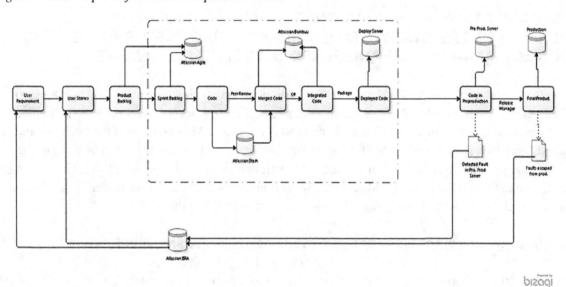

- **Retrospective Meeting at the End of Sprint:** The team organizes another meeting at the end of the sprint in order to evaluate the efficiency and effectiveness of the sprint. 3 basic questions given below are answered and argued during the retrospective meetings. After the end of the sprint, sprint planning meeting are held to keep the incremental project development process:
  - ○ What did we do well, that if we don't discuss we might forget?
  - ○ What did we learn?
  - ○ What should we do differently next time?
  - ○ What still puzzles us?

Current Agile Project Performance Measurement Practices and KPI's

Software Start-Up Company decided to develop an in-house measurement system for its technical teams 2 years ago. The model has been developed with limited resources in a limited time. Although the system satisfied the requirements at that time, it was not improved in order to keep in pace with the changes and developments of the technical teams. Consequently, measurement system started to become obsolete with every change in the organization.

For instance, a part of the measurement system was designed to monitor whether all teams use an online scrum tool. The purpose of this KPI is to make every technical team to use online scrum planning tools, however, it became unnecessary after every team got used to online scrum tool. KPIs that are measured by Quality and Internal Audit Department are shown in Table 2. The current measurement practices of Software Start-Up Company are carried out by the Quality and Internal Audit Department. 5 KPIs are measured from 3 different data collection points. While data from version control system is collected automatically, other 2 data collection points do not have any automation. The data collection and analysis are carried out quarterly. The analysis of the quarterly KPI results is reported to the top management with a graphical summary. In addition to that, a different version of the report is prepared if the top management wants to share some of the results with the technical teams and project managers. The measurements are carried out both company and team levels.

Table 2. Current Measurements of Software Start-up

KPI	Explanation	Data Collection System
Version Tag Usage Rate	Number of Taged Modules / Number of Total Modules	Automated Data Collection From Version Control System
Branching Struture Quality	Number of Modules with 2 Branches/ Number of Total Modules	Automated Data Collection From Version Control System
Peer Review Rate	Number of Modules with merge request/ Number of Total Modules	Automated Data Collection From Version Control System
Documentation	Number of Prepared Documents/ Number of Required Documents	Manual Data Collection From Wiki Based Collaboration Tool
Scrum Tool Usage Rate	Number of Teams currently use a scrum tool / Total Number of Teams	Manual Data Collection From Scrum Tools

PROPOSED DESIGN FOR AGILE KEY PERFORMANCE INDICATOR SET FOR THE ANALYSED SOFTWARE START UP COMPANY (TO-BE STATE)

Definition of Total Agile KPI's Set: Understanding the "Theoretical Base" Through Literature Research

Before defining the metrics for a specific organization, designer of an agile project performance measurement system should focus on which metrics of hard and soft aspects are measured, keeping the actual aim at the end of this measurement process. Chosen metrics should fit the project type, organization strategy, resources and constraints of the organization and the project team to avoid negative consequences and dysfunctional impacts on the project measurement process.

For responding to these needs, we aimed to propose a list of "widely accepted and practiced" and adaptable KPI's for the studied software start-up company. For this aim we conducted a content analysis on literature and published theoretical/practical background (23 different major articles and books on "Agile Software Development Performance measurement") to gather information on currently known agile KPI's and measures. In the end of content analysis, a total of 99 KPI's are found and listed. The referred sources are listed below by their categories of topic:

- *Agile SW Development Method:* Abrahamsson et al.,2002; Duvall et al.,2007; Scrum Alliance, 2015.
- *Performance Measurement in Software Development*: Basili, 1994; Eccles, 1991; Gopal, 2002; Gustaffsonn, 2011; Hartmann and Dymond, 2006; Hughes, 2000; Upadhaya et al., 2014; Blackburn, 2015; Montequin et al, 2013; Elahe et al., 2014, Cheng et al., 2009, Broadus Lii, 2013, Andersson, 2010, Poppendieck and Poppendieck, 2008., Andersson, 2010
- *Software Metrics*: Fenton and Pfleeger, 1997; Grady, 1992; Kitchenham, 1996; Mannila, 2013; Umarji and Seaman, 2008; Rawat et al., 2012; U.S. Department of Defense, 2018; Cleff A., 2010
- *Testing Performance*: Crispin & Gregory, 2010; Shahid et al., 2011.
- Andersson, D. J. 2010. Kanban, successful evolutionary change for your technology business. 1st printing. Sequim, WA: Blue Hole Press.

Referring to classification of Mannila (2013), the collected measurements and usage categories are summarized in summary table as type, level, period, scope and Frequency. Definition of measurement categories are shown in Table 3:

Table 3. Measurement Definition Table

Category	Explanation	Metrics
Scope:	Defines the measurement scope like what is measured.	story point, user story, feature
Period:	Defines the time period of the measurement	week, sprint, month, quarter, 6 months, year
Level:	Defines the organization level in which the measurement is followed	team, value stream, site, product, release
Type:	Defines the type of measurement (number, ratio, etc.).	number, ratio (%), trend, cumulative, correlation
Frequency:	Defines the commonality and reference/usage intensity target of the measure	how many times a measurement was introduced or promoted in the source data

In the second round of Content Analysis, frequencies of 99 KPI's that are listed in Appendix B are counted. Adapted from the approach of Mannila (2013) among these KPIs the ones which appeared in more than 3 different sources in literature were identified and listed in Table 4.

DEFINITION OF ENHANCED KPI SET

The KPIs that appeared in more than 3 different sources in literature were identified by content analysis. After the literature research, several interviews have been made with 3 experts (software engineers with 10 years of experience) on Agile Performance Measurement Methods. Experts rated the priority of each KPI that were derived from literature. These KPIs have been discussed and categorized as "must have" and "nice to have" KPI set in accordance with their frequency of being mentioned in previous literature and with the ratings of the experts. KPI's which had been both highly (>5) mentioned in literature and rated high (3) by the experts, but those not being used currently by the studied software start-up company are selected as "Must have" KPIs (Table 5). As well, KPIs which have been both highly (>5) mentioned in literature and rated medium (3) by the experts, but those not being used currently by the studied software start-up company are selected as "Nice to have" KPIs (Table 6).

Table 4. KPI List and Expert ratings

Key Performance Indicator	Frequency in Literature (Mannila, 2013)	Expert Rating (1:Low 2:Medium 3:High)	Current use in Company
Feature Development			
Number of features available for releasing	13	3	Yes
Number of features available in planned release date	7	3	Yes
Feature cycle time (days) correlation to the work amount	5	3	Yes
Quality of Team Planning			
Content stability (added/removed items)	6	2	No
Used hours per planned items in priority order	6	1	No
Quality of User Stories			
User story average cycle time - from started to done	6	1	No
User Story Deployment			
Accepted user stories (potentially shippable content)	13	1	No
Team Velocity			
Team velocity versus capacity	6	2	No
Team commitment keeping ratio (on time delivery)	5	2	No
Green Build Ratio (MUST HAVE)			
Product CI and automated test case success	**8**	**3**	Yes
Test Case Amounts			

continues on following page

Table 4. Contined

Manual and automated acceptance tests/total test cases, report showing the ratio of automated tests	12	3	Yes
Unit test coverage for the developed code (%), number of passing tests – way towards (A)TDD	**9**	**3**	No
Fault Source			
Faults found by customer, escaping from production	**8**	**3**	No
Number of Faults			
New/closed/open faults by priority level (critical, major, minor)	13	3	Yes
Customer Care Cases			
New customer cases (faults).	4	1	
Open customer cases (faults)	4	1	
Multitasking in time usage			
Sprint work flow diagram for user stories under the work, cumulative view to "not started", "ongoing" and "done" tasks in a sprint. Indicates if a team has silos and impediments	**6**	**3**	No
Sprint workflow diagram for features under the work, cumulative view to multitasking in the team. Number of items in the process and if the team works together on the same tasks	6	3	No
Sprint burn-down/-up			
Sprint burn-down chart for tracking of team level work progress, work remaining	*10*	*2*	No
Release burn-down/-up			
Release burn-down chart for tracking work progress in a release (story points - sprints), if the project or release is "on schedule"	7	3	Yes
Feature effort estimation accuracy, original versus team vs. real work	5	2	No

Must Have KPIs

The KPIs in "Must Have" category are needed to be on the measurement model even though the company does not have the measurement capability. Therefore, "Must Have" KPI set has been studied in order to verify the measurement capability of the company (Table 5). Also, each "Must Have" KPI is analyzed if the company can measure it within its current data collection system and its current agile processed in Table 6. Secondly, KPIs which cannot be measured because of the current agile processes is explained. In addition to the explanation, necessary process improvements have been recommended to the company as well.

The detailed explanations of KPI's that are recommended for being used in Agile Software Project Management framework of the studied company is given in Table 6 with their KPI Explanation, "Category", "Type", "Level", "Period" and "Scope". Definitions of each KPI and related "Process Improvement Recommendations" are also presented in the following sections.

Table 5. Must Have KPIs

No.	Key Performance Indicator	Measurement Capability of Company
1.	**Green Build Ratio:** Product CI and automated test case success (regression steps)	Process Improvement is Needed
2.	**Test Case Amounts**: Unit test coverage for the developed code (%)	Capable
3.	**Fault Source**: Faults found by customer, escaping from production	Data Collection Improvement Needed
4.	**Multitasking in time usage**: Sprint workflow diagram for user stories under the work, cumulative view to "not started", "ongoing" and "done" tasks in a sprint. Indicates if a team has silos and impediments	Capable

Table 6. Explanations and Classification of Must Have KPIs

KPI Explanation	Category	Type	Level	Period	Scope
1. Product CI and automated test case success (upgrade, smoke, regression steps)	Green Build Ratio	Ratio	Team	Sprint	Feature
2. Unit test coverage for the developed code (%)	Test Case Amounts	Ratio	Team	Sprint	Feature
3. Faults found by customer, escaping from production	Fault Source	Number & Trend	Product	Quarter	Feature
4. Sprint work flow diagram for user stories under the work, cumulative view to "not started", "ongoing" and "done" tasks in a sprint. Indicates if a team has silos and impediments	Multitasking in time usage	Ratio	Team	Sprint	User Story

The process improvement recommendations are also shown in Figure 5 more accurately.

Figure 5. Recommended Process Improvement

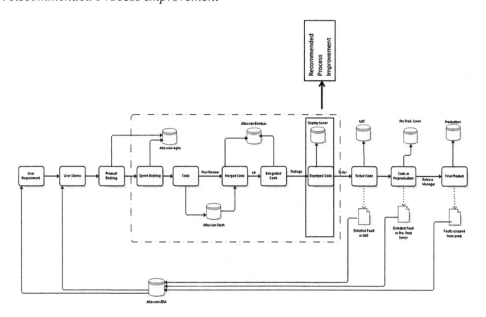

- **Green Build Ratio: Continuous Integration-** Continuous Integration is a software development practice where members of a team integrate their work frequently; where each integration is verified by an automated build by including some test like regression test cycle and smoke test cycle to detect integration errors as quickly as possible. Many teams find that this approach leads to significantly reduced integration problems and allows a team to develop cohesive software more rapidly (Fawler, 2006).

As summarized by Collab.NET (2012) the flow of continuous integration's iterative cycle at a high level is: "**monitor, check out, build, test and release; with a feedback mechanism**": *"The flow of continuous integration requires that the team monitors the code base for any changes. Once a change occurs it needs to be checked out, built, and tested for quality. If successful and no defects are detected, it is released to a central storage repository or release area. If something does go wrong during the build process or a defect is detected, the team needs to know immediately that something went wrong so that this can be resolved quickly. Therefore, there needs to be a built-in feedback mechanism"* (collab. NET, 2012). Continuous Integration brings multiple benefits to the organization (Duvall et al., 2007):

- Increase visibility which enables greater communication
- Spend less time debugging and more time adding features
- Stop waiting to find out if your code's going to work
- Reduce integration problems allowing you to deliver software more rapidly

Process Improvement Recommendation: The studied software company must also improve their Green Build Ratio measurement and monitoring practices in accordance with the above given iterative cycle.

- **Unit Test Coverage:** Unit testing is a software testing method by which individual units of source code are tested to determine whether they are fit for use hence it forms the basis for component testing (Laudon and Laudon, 2011). The goal of unit testing is to isolate each part of the program and show that the individual parts are correct. Test coverage (also referred to by some as code coverage) is one of many metrics that are commonly used to give a statistical representation of the state of the code written for a certain piece of software (Shahid et al., 2010).

Process Improvement Recommendation: In order to measure automated test case success, Software Company needs to improve its testing processes since there is no data point in the current process. After the code is deployed, an additional testing process can be carried out on User Acceptance Testing server. Although UAT done also by the customer, adding an extra internal testing process will help company to increase its automated test case success with the data verification.

Faults Found by Customer

For this KPI measurement there are two types of questions; (I) "How many new customer defect reports have been received during the month?" and (II) "How many customer defect reports are open at the end of the month at the time the calculation is done?". The number of reported customer defect reports gives an indication whether internal testing is effective, and the overall testing process is done well. From Figure 6, we can see different types of defects and error that are categorized in 4 requirements. The defects in **Requirement 4** were introduced during the definition of the requirements; the product has been designed and built to meet that flawed requirements definition. If the product is tested for meeting requirements, it will pass its tests but may be rejected by the customer. Defects

Figure 6. Fault Category Chart

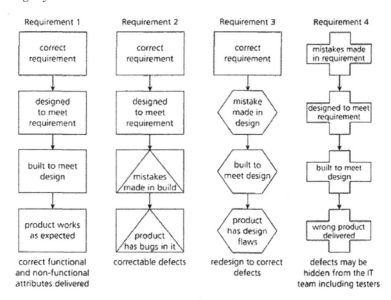

Process Improvement: To establish a software measurement environment, the software organization must define a data collection process and recording media.

- **Sprint Work Flow Diagram: S**print work flow diagrams (Figure 7) shows the pace of work, how much work is done, the status of ongoing, and backlog steps Furthermore, to gain insight into a portfolio of features, scenarios, or user experiences, product owners and program managers can map user stories to features. By sprint work flow diagrams team members can see clearly what is going on in the current work; the plans of next step can be mapped according to these diagrams; process can be graphed as cumulatively. As Petersen and Wohlin (2010) explained, in cumulative work flow diagrams *"The x-axis shows the time-line and the y-axis shows the cumulative number of requirements having completed different phases of development. The area between those two lines is the number of incoming requirements to be detailed."*

The workflow (Figure 8) shows the progression and regression of work that team members will perform. From this flow diagram team can analyze the status of sprint when new items are added and removed; and also observe the commitment of a team member when the new features those are added/ removed to the process. The results of this activity can be an asset to measure the quality of agile process.

Process Improvement Recommendation: The studied company should apply sprint cumulative work flow diagrams and establish a process for added and removed items in the backlog to increase the effectiveness in their project monitoring activities.

Figure 7. An Example of Cumulative Work Flow Diagram
(Petersen and Wohlin, 2010)

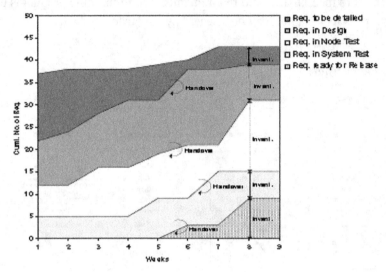

Figure 8. Process of Added/Removed Items

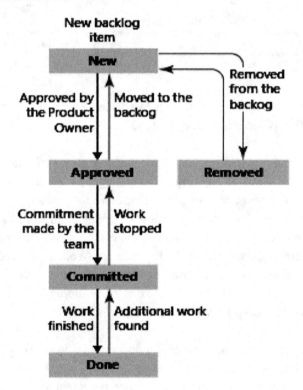

Nice to Have KPIs

KPIs in "Nice to Have" category provide valuable information to agile project performance measurement models. However, according to those KPIs are not pivotal for the model to provide a clear agile measurement results. Consequently, only the KPIs that the company is capable of measuring in Table 7 will be added to the measurement model.

Table 7. Nice to Have KPIs

No.	Key Performance Indicator	Measurement Capability of Company
1.	Feature Development	
	Number of features available for releasing	Data Collection Improvement is Needed
	Quality of Team Planning	
2.	Content stability (added/removed items)	Capable
3.	Used hours per planned items in priority order	Data Collection Improvement is Needed
	Quality of User Stories	
4.	User story average cycle time - from started to done	Data Collection Improvement is Needed
	User Story Deployment	
5.	Accepted user stories (potentially shippable content)	Process Improvement is Needed
	Team Velocity	
6.	Team velocity versus capacity	Capable
7.	Team commitment keeping ratio (on time delivery)	Data Collection Improvement is Needed
	Multitasking in time usage	
8.	Sprint work flow diagram for features under the work, cumulative view to multitasking in the team. Nr of items in process, if the team works together on the same tasks	Data Collection Improvement is Needed
	Sprint burn-down/-up	
9.	Sprint burn-down chart for tracking of team level work progress, work remaining	Capable
	Release burn-down/-up	
10.	Release burn-down chart for tracking work progress in a release (story points - sprints), if the project or release is "on schedule"	Data Collection Improvement is Needed
11.	Feature effort estimation accuracy, original versus team versus real work	Data Collection Improvement is Needed

The detailed explanations of "Nice to Have KPI's that are recommended for being used in Agile Software Project Management framework of the studied company is given in Table 8 with their KPI Explanation, "Category", "Type", "Level", "Period" and "Scope". Definitions of each KPI and related "Process Improvement Recommendations" are also presented in the following sections.

- **Content Stability:** According to Schwaber and Sutherland (2013), definitions of Product Backlog and Sprint Backlog are as follows:

Table 8. Content Stability Summary

KPI Explanation	Category	Type	Level	Period	Scope
B1.Content stability (added/removed items)	Quality of Team Planning	Ratio	Team	Sprint	User Story
B2.Team velocity versus capacity	Team Velocity	Ratio & Trend	Team	Sprint	User Story
B3.Sprint burn-down chart for tracking of team level work progress, work remaining	Sprint burn-down/-up	Number	Team	Sprint	User Story

- The Product Backlog is an ordered list of everything that might be needed in the product and is the single source of requirements for any changes to be made to the product. All items in the Product Backlog are prioritized and sorted by business value. The top priority items that are selected for development during Sprint Planning drive the next development activities.

- *The Sprint Backlog is the set of Product Backlog items selected for the Sprint plus a plan for delivering the product Increment and realizing the Sprint Goal. The Sprint Backlog is a forecast by the team in sprint planning meeting and is about what functionality will be in the next increment and the work needed to deliver that functionality. In the Sprint Backlog, the Team plans the necessary tasks to implement the items selected from the Product Backlog in Sprint Planning. Estimations are set and Sprint Backlog is updated by the development team during the Sprint. As the work is done, the Development Team may find that more, less or different tasks are needed. To minimize delays and encourage flow, the team should strive to have no more than one item blocked at a time. "*

As shown in the Figure 9, a well-organized team plan is needed for content stability. Otherwise, tasks which are not started yet will be much more and the same situation will be in process and done parts. Thus, adding and removing items in our sprint planning will affect schedule performance. By this KPI quality of team planning can be measured by completion time for releasing of the product.

Figure 9. Scrum Board Flow Diagram
(Kniberg, 2009)

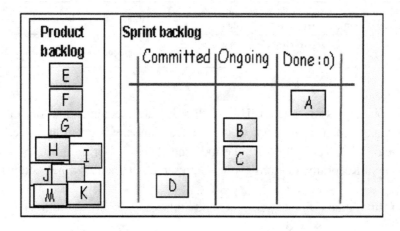

- **Team Velocity vs. Capacity:** The team's velocity is defined as the number of story points delivered per iteration (sprint). Less capacity means fewer products delivered (Manilla, 2013; Gustaffson, 2011; Leffingwell, 2008). The team should have a realistic workload. Hence, team must perform both velocity planning and capacity planning which are related to each other. An efficient team velocity and capacity planning schedule is a valuable asset for performance evaluation by determining an input for this KPI. An effective Team Velocity vs. Capacity planning schedule can be designed as follows:
- Each team member registers the number of hours they have worked per user story on a daily basis.
- At the end of the sprint, we should calculate the total amount of worked hours.
- Number of delivered story points Per worked hours gives the sprint's velocity: man-hours per story point.
- Before the next sprint planning session, the availability of the individual team members during that sprint should be determined and summarized in available man-hours. Then, the available man-hours are divided by the velocity (expressed in man-hours per story point) to know the amount of story points to be delivered by the next sprint.

As a KPI metric, we can define the performance measurement of team velocity-capacity by using the formula which is "$CBV = SP$ (Number of story points) $/DC$ (Delivered capacity: DC).

- **Sprint Burn-Down Chart:** This chart shows the remaining work in a sprint backlog and the duration of task completion by the team, and it predicts when team will achieve the goals of the sprint. Raw data is provided from the sprint backlog. The horizontal axis shows days in a sprint, and the vertical axis measures the amount of remaining work to complete the tasks in the sprint (Figure 10). By this graph, team working performance can be used as a useful KPI to evaluate and analyze organizational performance. As Kniberg (2009) defines:"*A sprint burndown chart shows, on a daily basis, how much work remains in the current iteration. The unit of the Y-axis is the same as the unit used on the sprint tasks. Typically hours or days (if the team breaks backlog items into tasks) or story points (if the team doesn't). In Scrum, sprint burndown charts are one of the primary tools for tracking the progress of an iteration. Release burndown charts which follow the same format at a release level can also be used– showing how many story points are left in the product backlog after each sprint.*

CONCLUSION

As software projects become more complex day by day, static project management methodologies cannot respond to its demanding challenges. Object-oriented methodologies are introduced to the software industry in order to satisfy the demands of obscure projects. Agile development, one of the most popular object-oriented PM solution in the software industry, can be currently considered as the best option for complex projects in software industry. Although companies started to define generally accepted agile frameworks, there is not any generally accepted agile measurement model. Therefore, monitoring and measuring agile processes is one of the biggest challenges for the companies that started to implement agile development processes. The aim of the project is to design a performance measurement model for Software Start-Up Company's software projects which are managed by agile methods.

Figure 10. An Example of Sprint Burn down Chart
(Kniberg, 2009)

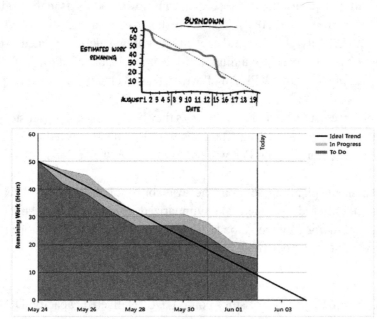

Firstly, current literature about the topic has been researched and 99 different key performance indicators have been listed (in Appendix B). Then, KPIs that is observed in more than 3 sources has been listed to further inspection. After that, expert interviews have been made in order to put KPIs into "must have" and "nice to have" category. On the other hand, the company has been studied in order to implement the measurement model. In that context, current measurement practices and current agile development processes have been investigated.

The next step was the evaluation of Software Start-Up Company's measurement capability of recently selected KPIs. In this step, a data collection system improvement and a process improvement have been recommended to the company. KPIs in nice to have category are evaluated if the company have the capability to measure them. Only the KPIs that can be measured by the current process and data collection system are included to measurement model. Lastly, data collection system is designed by matching data sources to key performance indicators.

The model is designed specifically for Software Start-Up Company, however it can be generalized in industry level under some constraints. Those constraints are;

- **Company Structure:** The numbers of projects a developer works on at the same time make the measurement of KPIs difficult.
- **Agility Level:** Different level in agile process implementation requires different key performance indicators. Therefore, the measurement model cannot be completely utilized by the companies that just started to implement agile methodologies to their processes.
- **Agile Development Management Tools:** Agile Development requires a high level of coordination between the process management tools. Therefore, the companies that do not have an integrated set of modules, measuring those KPIs would be very difficult.

In literature, there is limited resources on a validated list of Agile Performance Indicators and there is still room for research in proposing recommended models on filtering the current KPI sets that can reflect the needs and conditions of the practicing organizations. We aimed to contribute to closing the gap between the practical needs of practitioners and the theoretical background. These KPI Sets and the selection model which we used (detailed scanning of secondary data sources and literature for creating KPI set; filtering KPIs by their frequency in sources; creating practical classifications of KPI sets, collecting expert opinions for classifying KPIs by being "must have" and "nice to have").

The recent model can be improved by benchmarking. During the design of the model, benchmarking with similar companies has not been used. However, it can improve the quality of the measurement model for further studies. In addition to that, an AHP model could be integrated to expert review phase of the study.

REFERENCES

Abrahamsson, P., Solo, O., Ronkainen, J., & Warsta, J. (2002). Agile Software Development Methods: Review and analysis. VTT Technical Research Centre of Finland Publication.

Adelakun, O., Garcia, R., Tabaka, T. & Redar, L. (2017). Hybrid Project Management: Agile with Discipline. *CONF-IRM 2017 Proceedings*. Retrieved from http://aisel.aisnet.org/confirm2017/14

Andersson, D. J. (2010). *Kanban, successful evolutionary change for your technology business. 1st printing*. Sequim, WA: Blue Hole Press.

Aryankhesal, A., Sheldon, T. A., Mannion, R., & Mahdipour, S. (2015). The dysfunctional consequences of a performance measurement system: The case of the Iranian national hospital grading programme. *Journal of Health Services Research & Policy*, 20(3), 138–145. doi:10.1177/1355819615576252 PMID:25784632

Austin, R. D. (1996). *Measuring and Managing Performance in Organizations*. DorsetHouse Pub.Co.

Basili, H. (1994). The goal question metric approach. Encyclopedia of Software Engineering.

Beck, K. (1999). Embracing change with extreme programming. *Computer*, 32(10), 70–77. doi:10.1109/2.796139

Beck, K., Beedle, M. A., Bennekum van, A., Cockburn, W., Cunningham, M., Fowler, J., … Thomas, D. (2001). *Manifesto for Agile Software Development*. Retrieved from http://AgileManifesto.org

Blackburn, T. (2015). *Key Performance Measures in a Lean Agile Program*. Speech to Office of the Under Secretary of Defense for Acquisition, Technology and Logistics. Retrieved from https://www.acq.osd.mil/evm/resources/AgileFeb2015/9%20Blackburn_Key%20Performance%20Measures%20in%20a%20Lean%20Agile%20ProgramOriginal.pdf

Broadus, W. A., III. (2013). Stakeholder Needs and Expectations: Planning Your Agile Project and Program Metrics. *Defense AT&L, 42*, 50-54.

Cockburn, A. (2000). *Writing Effective Use Cases*. The Crystal Collection for Software Professionals, Addison-Wesley Professional.

Cockburn, A. (2002). *Agile Software Development*. Boston: Addison-Wesley.

Collab.NET. (2012). *Building Value with Continuous Integration*. Report, CA, USA.

Collab.Net. (2018). *12th State Of Agile Report*. Retrieved from https://explore.versionone.com/state-of-agile/versionone-12th-annual-state-of-agile-report

Cooling, J. E., & Hughes, T. S. (1989). The emergence of rapid prototyping as a realtime software development tool. *Proceedings of the Second International Conference on Software Engineering for Real Time Systems*, 60-64.

Crispin, L., & Gregory, J. (2010). *Agile testing* (6th ed.). Addison-Wesley.

Despa, M.L. (2014). Comparative study on software development methodologies. *Database Systems Journal, 5*(3), 37-56.

Duvall, P., Matyas, S., & Glover, A. (2007). *Continuous Integration: Improving Software Quality and Reducing Risk* (1st ed.). Addison-Wesley.

Eccles, G. R. (1991). The Performance Measurement Manifesto. *Harvard Business Review*. Retrieved from https://hbr.org/1991/01/the-performance-measurement-manifesto

Elahe, M. F., & Mahmud, S. M. H. (2014). Efficiency of scrum the most widely adopted method for agile software development. *IOSR Journal of Computer Engineering, 16*(6), 70–73.

Fenton, N., & Pfleeger, S. L. (1997). *Software metrics: A rigorous and practical approach*. Boston: PWS.

Fowler, M. (2006). *Continous Integration*. Retrieved from https://martinfowler.com/articles/continuousIntegration.html)

Galen, R. (2012). *The Agile Project Manager—The 'Essence' of Agile Metrics*. Retrieved from http://rgalen.com/agile-training-news/2012/6/2/the-agile-project-managerthe-essence-of-agile-metrics.html

Georgiev, V., & Stefanova, K. (2014). Software Development Methodologies for Reducing Project Risks. *Economic Alternatives, 2*, 104-113.

Gopal, A. (2002). Measurement Programs in Software Development: Determinants of Success. IEEE Trans. Softw. Eng., 28, 863-875.

Grady, R. B. (1992). *Practical software metrics for project management and process improvement*. Upper Saddle River, NJ: Prentice-Hall.

Gustaffsonn, M. (2011). *Model of Agile Software Measurement: A Case Study* (Master of Science Thesis). Chalmers University of Technology, University of Gothenburg.

Hariharan, B., & Arpasuteera, P. (2017). *Combining Hard and Soft Aspects in Project Performance Measurement - A Qualitative Research Undertaken in an Agile Software Development Project Scenario* (Master's Thesis). Chalmers University of Technology, Göteborg, Sweden.

Hartmann, D., & Dymond, R. (2006). Appropriate Agile Measurement: Using Metrics and Diagnostics to Deliver Business Value. *AGILE Conference*, 0, 126-134. 10.1109/AGILE.2006.17

Highsmith, J., & Cockburn, A. (2001). Agile Software Development: The Business of Innovation. *Computer, 34*(9), 120–122. doi:10.1109/2.947100

Highsmith, J. A. (2000). *Adaptive Software Development: A Collaborative Approach to Managing Complex Systems*. New York, NY: Dorset House Publishing.

Highsmith, J. A. (2002). *Agile software development ecosystems*. Addison-Wesley Professional.

Hughes, A. (2000). *Practical software measurement*. Cambridge, UK: McGraw-Hill.

Jeldi, N.P., & Chavali, N.K.M. (2013). Software Development Using Agile Methodology Using Scrum Framework. *International Journal of Scientific and Research Publications, 3*(4).

Kitchenham, B. A. (1996). *Software metrics: measurement for software process improvement*. Cambridge, MA: Blackwell.

Kniberg, H. (2009). *Kanban vs Scrum: How to make the most of both, Minibook, InfoQ, Crisp, SE*. Retrieved from http://www.infoq.com/minibooks/kanban-scrum-minibook

Larman, C., & Basili, V. R. (2003). Iterative and Incremental Development: A Brief History. *Computer, 36*(6), 47–56. doi:10.1109/MC.2003.1204375

Leffingwell, D. (2008). *Scaling software agility, best practices for large enterprises. 2nd printing*. Boston, MA: Addison-Wesley.

Levels, N. (2016). *Agile and KPI's, friends or enemies?* Gladwell Academy. Retrieved from https://www.gladwell.nl/wp-content/uploads/2016/03/4.-Agile-kpis-vrienden-of-vijanden.pdf

Mahnic, V. (2014). *Improving Software Development through Combination of Scrum and Kanban*. Recent Advances in Computer Engineering, Communications and Information Technology.

Mannila, J. (2013). *Key Performance Indicators in Agile Software Development* (BS thesis). Satakunta University of Applied Sciences.

Martin, J. (1991). *Rapid application development*. Macmillan Publishing.

Montequin, V. R., Fernández, F. O., Perez, C. A., & Balsera, J. V. (2013). Scorecard and KPIs for monitoring software factories effectiveness in the financial sector. *International Journal of Information Systems and Project Management, 1*(3), 29–43.

Open View. (2016). *Executive's Guide to Scrum*. Author.

Palmer, S. R., & Felsing, J. M. (2002). *A Practical Guide to Feature-Driven Development*. Academic Press.

Paul, S., & Singh, K. J. (2012). Be Agile: Project Development With Scrum Framework. *Journal of Theoretical and Applied Information Technology, 40*(1), 105–112.

Permana, P. A. G. (2015). Scrum Method Implementation in a Software Development Project Management (IJACSA). *International Journal of Advanced Computer Science and Applications, 6*(9), 198–204.

Petersen, K., & Wohlin, C. (2010). Measuring the flow in lean software development. *Software, Practice & Experience, 41*(9), 975–996. doi:10.1002pe.975

Pinto, J. K., & Slevin, D. P. (1988). Project success: Definitions and measurement techniques. *Project Management Journal, 19*(1), 67–73.

Poppendieck, M., & Poppendieck, T. (2009). *Leading Lean Software Development: Results Are not the Point* (6th ed.). Addison-Wesley.

Rawat, M. S., Mittal, A., & Dubey, S. K. (2012). Survey on Impact of Software Metrics on Software Quality, (IJACSA). *International Journal of Advanced Computer Science and Applications, 3*(1), 2012.

Rising, L., & Janoff, N. S. (2000). The Scrum Software Development Process for Small Teams. *IEEE Software, 17*(4), 26–32. doi:10.1109/52.854065

Royce, W. W. (1970). Managing the development of large software systems: Concepts and techniques. *IEEE WESCON, 26*(8), 1–9.

Schwaber, K., & Beedle, M. (2002). *Agile Software Development With Scrum.* Upper Saddle River, NJ: Prentice-Hall.

Schwaber, K., & Sutherland, J. (2013). *The Scrum Guide™, The Definitive Guide to Scrum: The Rules of the Game, Scrum.org.* Creative Commons License.

Schwalbe, K. (2011). Information technology project management (6th ed.). Cengage Learning.

Scrum Alliance. (n.d.). Retrieved from https://www.scrumalliance.org/why-scrum/

Shahid, M., Ibrahim, S., & Mahrin, M. N. (2011). *A Study on Test Coverage in Software Testing.* In IACSIT, 2011, International Conference on Telecommunication Technology and Applications, Singapore.

Spundak, M. (2014). Mixed agile/traditional project management methodology – reality or illusion? *Procedia – Social and Behavioral Sciences (Science Direct), 119*, 939-948.

The Manifesto for Agile Software Development. (n.d.). Retrieved from http://agilemanifesto.org/

Umarji, M., & Seaman, C. (2008). Why do programmers avoid metrics? *Proceedings of the 2nd ACM-IEEE International symposium on Empirical SW Engineering & Measurement.*

Upadhaya, B., Munir, R., & Blount, Y. (2014). Association between Performance Measurement Systems and Organizational Effectiveness. *International Journal of Operations & Production Management, 34*(7), 2–2. doi:10.1108/IJOPM-02-2013-0091

U.S. Department of Defense. (2018). *Defense Innovation Board Metrics for Software Development Version 0.9.* Retrieved from https://media.defense.gov/2018/jul/10/2001940937/-1/-1/0/dib_metrics_for_software_development_v0.9_2018.07.10.pdf

APPENDIX A

Research Model

Figure 11.

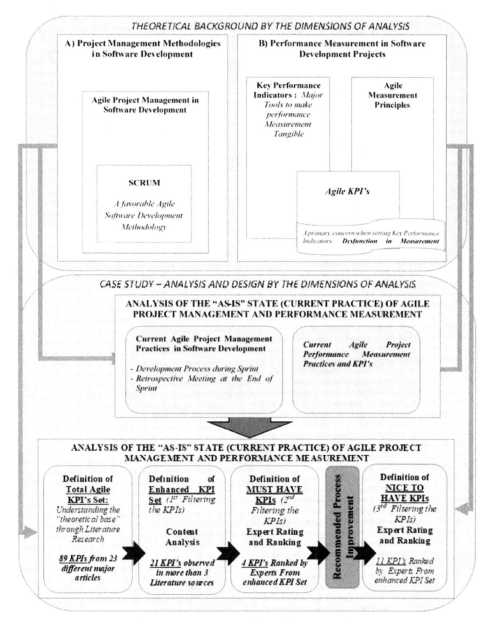

APPENDIX B

Key Performance Indicators (99 KPIs) Derived From Literature

Figure 12a.

Nr.	KPI
1	Cumulative Flow Diagrams
2	Control Charts
3	Percent Complete and Accurate
4	Flow Efficiency
5	Time Blocked per Work Item
6	Blocker Clustering
7	Escaped Defects
8	Escaped Defect Resolution Time
9	Release Success Rate
10	Release Time
11	Time Since Last Release
12	Cost Per Release
13	Release Net Promoter Score
14	Release Adoption / Install Rate
15	Customer / Business Value Delivered
16	Risk Burndown
17	Push / Pull
18	Product Forecast
19	Product Net Promoter Score
20	User Analytics
21	Test Coverage
22	Build Time
23	Defect Density
24	Code Churn
25	Code Ownership
26	Code Complexity
27	Coding Standards Adherence
28	Crash Rate
29	Team Happiness / Morale
30	Learning Log
31	Team Tenure
32	Phone-a-Friend Stats
33	Whole Team Contribution
34	Transparency (access to data, access to customers, sharing of learning, successes and
35	Product delivery/lead time precision
36	Number of innovations/ideas in different phases - Idea, Prototype,
37	Pilot, Production
38	Cost/off-shoring savings (euros)
39	Service level/incident resolution – as per service level agreements.
40	Planning/detailed planning horizon – time in future when less than
41	80% of people are covered by detailed committed plan.
42	Planning/backlog horizon (months)
43	Quality - defect count per iteration
44	Quality/technical Debt
45	Quality/faults-slip-through
46	Predictability/velocity - delivery capacity, velocity for productivity
47	Predictability/running automated tests – counts test points
48	Value/customer satisfaction survey
49	Value/business value delivered
50	Lean/lead time – from concept-to-cash
51	Lean/work in progress
52	Lean/queues – the cost of delay of the items in the queues
53	Mini-waterfall level inside a team and sprint
54	Feature component cycle time "from concept to cash" (days).
55	TDD usage per sprint per team/value stream (hours).
56	User story check list (definition of done) compliance level/ratio (%)
57	Pair programming usage per sprint per team/value stream (hours).
58	Team test automation versus manual testing/total testing per sprint
59	Planned testing hours versus implementation hours ratio

Figure 12b.

60	Number of passing test cases (unit, functional, user story, GUI, load),
61	Number of implemented methods per a sprint, trend.
62	Test coverage on code/methods per a sprint, trend.
63	Number of defects reported by priority per week.
64	Defect in- and outflow (amount) per week/sprint/month
65	Team work progress during a sprint by using burn-down chart and estimated versus actu
66	Reported defects over a time, per week/sprint/month.
67	Amount of sprint deliverable re-factored and coded to standards
68	Amount of sprint deliverable unit tested, coverage results per each sprint
69	Sprint deliverable have passing, automated, acceptance tests.
70	Coverage report showing the ratio of automated tests.
71	Project work flow diagram for tasks under the work at the moment,
72	Sprint work flow diagram for tasks under the work at the moment,
73	Average lead time from starting a feature until it is finished
74	Work in process (WIP) diagram, shows the work in process.
75	Lead time
76	Due date performance - item/feature delivered in time.
77	Throughput – number of items delivered in a given time period
78	Issues and blocked work items – a cumulative flow diagram
79	Flow efficiency – the lead time against used time
80	Initial quality – number of escaped defects as a percentage of total WIP
81	Bugs/feature each day in a sprint).
82	Automated acceptance test coverage in %
83	Continuous build success rate in %
84	Developers integrate code multiple times per day, average
85	Re-factoring work ratio in a sprint
86	Code review implementation ratio
87	Level of pair programming, hours used per sprint
88	Team velocity versus capacity in a sprint
89	Value feature points delivered per sprint
90	Release date percentage, promised/actual content
91	Number of defects and normalized defects in a sprint
92	Support calls and normalized support calls in a sprint
93	Limit work to capacity: feature development time in sprints when team velocity
94	Cycle time of deployed features, number of features per time division
95	Request age (age of active customer requests)
96	Customer request arrival rate per week
97	Cycle time from concept to cash.
98	Financial return.
99	Customer satisfaction

Chapter 68
The Influence of the Application of Agile Practices in Software Quality Based on ISO/IEC 25010 Standard

Gloria Arcos-Medina

Escuela Superior Politécnica de Chimborazo, Ecuador; Universidad Nacional Mayor de San Marcos, Perú

David Mauricio

(iD) https://orcid.org/0000-0001-9262-626X

Universidad Nacional Mayor de San Marcos, Perú

ABSTRACT

Agile practices are activities or procedures that are applied during the software development process in order to improve its quality and productivity. The objective of this study is to determine the influence of agile practices on software quality. For this purpose, a model composed of 4 groups of agile practices and 8 quality characteristics according to the ISO/IEC 25010 standard has here been proposed. The results of 146 questionnaires addressed to people involved in the software development process show that the application of agile engineering and project management practices have a significant positive influence on the quality attribute functionality. On the other hand, project management practices have a low impact on the quality characteristics of compatibility, portability, security, and usability.

1. INTRODUCTION

While software is essential in all areas of the modern world, software development itself has yet to become a perfect process. Despite efforts to employ software engineering methodologies, software development has not been consistently successful, as evidenced by the high rates of delayed, abandoned, or rejected software projects. Several investigations indicate that the success factors of a project can be linked to the

DOI: 10.4018/978-1-6684-3702-5.ch068

cost, delivery time, scope, and quality (Agarwal & Rathod, 2006; Chow & Cao, 2008; de Wit, 1988). Therefore, lack of quality directly contributes to the failure of a project.

Agile methodologies were disseminated in order to improve software quality and respond more easily to changes. Unfortunately, the results verify that this goal has not yet been achieved and that the lack of quality in software continues to be worrisome. Quality is undoubtedly the most important element of a software project (Xu, 2009). Agile software processes, such as eXtreme Programming (XP) and Scrum, rely on best practices that are expected to improve software development quality. It can be said that best practices aim to introduce software quality assurance (SQA) into a project (Sagheer, Zafar, & Sirshar, 2015).

There are various studies that have contributed to identifying the agile practices and quality characteristics that influence agile development (Bermejo et al., 2014; Gorla & Lin, 2010; Opelt & Beeson, 2008; Subramanyam & Prasad, 2013; Versionone, 2017; Xu, 2009). In addition, research has been carried out to analyze the relationship between agile practices and quality (Bougroun, Zeaaraoui, & Bouchentouf, 2014; Curcio, Malucelli, Reinehr, & Paludo, 2016; Gorla & Lin, 2010; Santos, 2011). In such research, the concept of quality has been analyzed as a whole. However, individual quality characteristics and how agile practices affect each of them have not been considered. That information is vital for project managers to be able to prioritize the practices that contribute to software quality.

In this paper, a conceptual model is introduced to identify the practices that influence the quality characteristics of the software development process by applying agile methodologies. The proposed model consists of four categories of agile practices, eight quality characteristics based on the ISO/IEC 25010 standard (ISO/IEC, 2005), and 13 relationships between agile practices and quality characteristics. The four categories of agile practices that were included are teamwork, project management, engineering, and test. The model was validated through surveys administered to 146 people who implement agile methodologies in the software development process.

The remainder of this paper is organized into 4 sections. Section 2 includes a theoretical framework of agile methodologies, agile practices, and software quality, and it climaxes with the motivation for this work. Section 3 details the proposed model, as well as the strategy employed for the collection of information. Section 4 presents the results of the study. In Section 5, we realize a discussion of the results, and finally, the conclusions of the work are presented.

2. BACKGROUND

2.1 Agile Methodologies and Practices

In February 2001, the term "agile" was applied for the first time to software development. A group of 17 experts from the software industry participated in the meeting where that software term was born. Its objective was to propose the values and principles that would allow teams to quickly develop software that can respond to changes that may arise throughout the project (Muñoz, Velthuis, & Rubia, 2010). After the meeting, The Agile Alliance was created. The Agile Alliance is a non-profit organization dedicated to promoting concepts related to agile software development and helping organizations to adopt those concepts. The starting point was the Agile Manifesto, a document that summarizes the agile philosophy. Although the creators and promoters of the most popular agile methodologies subscribe to the Agile Manifesto and principles, each methodology has its own characteristics and emphasizes one or more distinct aspects. On the other hand, Abrahamsson et al. (2017) say "The focal aspects of light and agile methods are simplicity and speed". They also assert that a development method is agile when it is incremental, cooperative, straightforward, and adaptive.

Among the methodologies that best represent agile principles are XP, Scrum Crystal Methodologies, Dynamic Systems Development Method (DSDM), Adaptive Software Development (ASD), Feature-Driven Development (FDD), and Lean Development (LD) (García-Mireles, Moraga, García, & Piattini, 2015). Agile methodologies base their process on the application of agile practices, that is, activities or procedures oriented around the development of highly productive projects. XP and Scrum are the most accepted methodologies for the development of agile software (Versionone, 2017). Scrum, XP, and a hybrid methodology between the two are utilized by 69% of all software developers.

These methodologies use multiple agile practices. For example, Xu (2009) lists 12 agile practices for XP, the planning game, small release, Metaphor, simple design, testing, refactoring, pair programming, collective ownership, continuous integration, 40-hour week, on-site customer, and coding standards. The main agile practices used by Scrum are iterative and incremental development, project planning, team empowerment, task-oriented project progress control, change management, retrospectives, "post-mortem" analysis at the end of each iteration, and the use of timeboxing for all Scrum activities (Schwaber & Sutherland, 2013).

Agile Practices have been the subject of much research, for instance, Henriksen and Pedersen (2017), determined that 15 practices are most important to achieve project success. McHugh, Conboy and Lang (2012) analyzed the impact of three agile practices on trust in software project teams.

A previous study made it possible to identify 93 distinct agile practices compiled from the literature reviewed. They have been classified into four categories and serve as the basis for selecting the practices included in this study. A list of the compiled practices can be found in Appendix A.

2.2 Software Quality

The IEEE Glossary of Software Engineering Terminology defines quality assurance in two ways. (1) "A planned and systematic pattern of all actions necessary to provide adequate confidence that the item or product conforms to established operational, functional, and technical requirements." (2) "A set of activities designed to evaluate the process by which products are developed or manufactured". From an agile perspective, as Ambler (2005) considers agile quality to be a result of practices such as effective collaborative work, incremental development, and iterative development as implemented through techniques such as refactoring, test-driven development, agile model-driven development, and effective communication techniques.

Quality models are generally composed of quality characteristics which, in turn, include quality sub-characteristics that are able to be measured to determine the quality of software. One of the main contributors to the definition of software quality standards is the ISO 9126 standard from the year 1991. Later, in the year 2001, this standard was replaced by two related standards, the ISO/IEC 9126, which defines quality characteristics and software quality metrics, and the ISO/IEC 14598 standard, which outlines the evaluation of software products (Estayno, Dapozo, Cuenca Pletsch, & Greiner, 2009). The ISO/IEC 9126 standard consists of four parts, quality model, external metrics, internal metrics, and metrics of quality in use, and six characteristics, functionality, reliability, usability, efficiency, maintainability, and portability.

The most current standard is represented by the ISO 25000: 2005 standards, known as SQuaRE (Software Quality Requirements and Evaluation). It is based on ISO 9126 and ISO 14598 and can be broken down into five topics: a) Quality Management (2500n), b) Quality Model (2501n), c) Quality Measures (2502n), d) Quality Requirements (2503n), and e) Quality Assessment (2504n).

2.3 Motivation

The four areas included in this research are identified in this section. Each contributes to aspects related to the quality of the agile development process. They have been addressed from different points of view, as summarized in Table 1.

Table 1. Areas covered by quality aspects

No.	Areas identified in the related research	Authors
1	Agile practices and their relationship to quality.	(Bougroun et al., 2014; Curcio et al., 2016; Gorla & Lin, 2010; Henriksen & Pedersen, 2017; Santos, 2011; Xu, 2009).
2.	Identification of quality characteristics.	(Christensen, Hansen, & Lindstrøm, 2010; Khomh & Guéhéneuc, 2008; Mnkandla & Dwolatzky, 2006; Ran, Zhuo, & Jianfeng, 2009; Sagheer et al., 2015).
3.	Software development process and quality characteristics.	(Arvanitou, Ampatzoglou, Chatzigeorgiou, Galster, & Avgeriou, 2017; Sfetsos & Stamelos, 2010; Singh & Gautam, 2016).
4.	Relationship of agile practices to quality characteristics	(Bhasin, 2012; Rico, 2008).

In Area 1, the concept of quality has been analyzed as a whole, without considering quality characteristics and how each agile practice influences it.

A large number of the studies corresponding to Area 2 have contributed to identifying quality characteristics that exert an influence on agile development. However, no research has been found that analyzes the influence of the identified characteristics on the application of agile practices.

In Area 3, a study conducted by Singh & Gautam (2016) on the impact of the Software Development Process on Software Quality can be seen. This study divides the development process into four stages: Requirement, Design, Coding, and Testing. Those stages are then associated with several characteristics and quality sub-characteristics based on a literature review. However, these characteristics do not apply to a specific standard. A similar work was carried out by Arvanitou et al. (2017), and it recognized seven stages of software development: Project management, Requirements, Design, Implementation, and Maintenance. Sfetsos and Pamelos (2010), presented the initial results of a systematic review evaluating quality approaches and metrics, according to ISO/IEC 12207 and ISO/IEC 9126 standards, in agile practices; but the results do not include a quality characteristic analysis according with the standard.

According to Rico (2008), a study found in Area 4, Agile methods are characterized by factors of iterative development, which exercise a positive influence on the quality of website design and customer feedback which, in turn, positively influences privacy and security. On the other hand, Bhasin (2012) considers aspects of agile development to improve quality in terms of defect reduction, early defect detection, cycle time improvement, and code quality. The study considers some agile practices as control variables. However, it was not based on the software quality characteristics proposed by the ISO/IEC 25010 standard.

It is important to distinguish the key agile practices that contribute to the achievement of quality characteristics in software so that project managers are able to prioritize the application of these practices for their work team and thus develop a quality product that meets established standards.

3. CONCEPTUAL MODEL

The purpose of the proposed conceptual model found in this study is to determine which agile practices have a positive or negative influence on the software quality. The structure of the proposed model is presented in Figure 1, where the following components are displayed.

a. Component 1: Agile practices applied in the agile software development process. They are repre-sented in the first part of the figure through 17 agile practices and their respective categories.
b. Component 2: Quality features based on the ISO/IEC 25010 standard. They are represented in the second part of the figure as Software Quality Characteristics.
c. Component 3: Hypotheses that represent the impact of agile development practices on the software quality characteristics. They are presented in dotted lines in figure.

Figure 1. A conceptual model to determine the impact of agile practices on the quality of a software development process

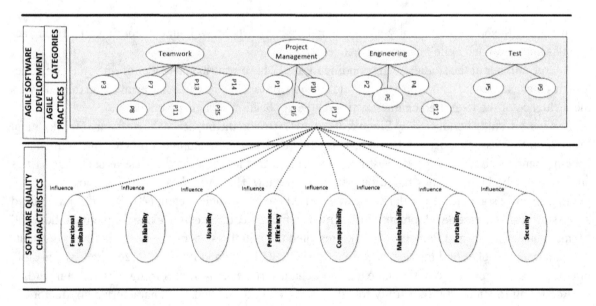

3.1 Component 1: Agile Practices

The model consists of 17 practices or actions used in the software development process based on the most frequently adopted agile methodologies. Despite the variations between the different agile methodologies, a set of practices that are common to most of them has been identified. The selected practices are based on a research study conducted by Xu (2009), from which 11 practices have been ascertained, The Planning Game, Small release, Simple design, Testing, Refactoring, Pair Programming, Collective ownership, Continuous integration, 40-hour week, On-site customer, and Coding standards. Xu cites these practices from the perspective of quality management in XP. According to the last five annual state of agile reports (Versionone, 2017), daily standup and retrospectives are included within the top five agile techniques. Therefore, these practices were included in our paper. In the study by Diebold & Dahlem (2014), Timeboxing was considered the most utilized agile practice, so it also was also included in this paper.

From that same study, the following practices were included. Monitoring progress: All the planning carried out within the projects must be controlled. Small cross-functional teams - Multifunctional teams: This aspect emphasizes the importance of teamwork within the agile methodology. In addition, the practice of self-organizing teams was selected from the study produced by Ahmed et al. (2010).

Table 2 presents the practices that served as the basis for this study. These practices have been grouped into categories in order to facilitate the present study. PTW, Teamwork Practices, relate to the work method and characteristics of the work team for an agile project. The PMP, Project Management Practices, group of practices are related to project management derived from the functions of the project manager and organizational culture. PENG, Engineering Practices, examine agile practices relevant to the realization of good software design and coding. Finally, PTEST, Testing Practices, reflect two important agile practices for the execution of tests that ensure the internal quality of the software.

3.2 Component 2: Quality Characteristics

The proposed model considers eight quality characteristics from the ISO/IEC 25010 standard and they are presented in Table 3. These characteristics determine the internal quality of the software which depends directly on its development process.

3.3 Component 3: Relationships

The model expresses the relationships between agile practices and quality characteristics. Utilizing the four categories of agile practices and the eight characteristics of quality analyzed in this model, a standardized residuals analysis has been conducted for the 32 relationships generated between the practices and characteristics. In some of the relationships between the agile practice and a quality characteristic, the analysis does not provide sufficient evidence to reject the null hypothesis. Likewise, there is not sufficient evidence to accept the null hypothesis. Consequently, only 13 derived hypotheses were generated. They are revealed in Table 4 and supported in subsections 3.3.1 to 3.3.4. These hypotheses have been coded as *Hi.j*, *i* being the practice analyzed and *j* the characteristic of quality influences. For example, hypothesis H3.2 corresponds to the relationship between the practice 3, *Engineering practices* (PENG), and characteristic 2, *Reliability (ARELI)*.

Table 2. Classification of agile practices

ID	Category	Practice No.	Agile Practices
PTW	Teamwork	P1	Pair Programming
		P2	On-site customer
		P3	Stand up meetings
		P4	Self-Organizing teams
		P5	Multifunctional teams
		P6	Retrospectives
		P7	Collective code ownership
PMP	Project Management	P8	Planning games
		P9	Monitoring Progress
		P10	40 hours per week
		P11	Timeboxing
PENG	Engineering	P12	Small releases
		P13	Simple design
		P14	Refactoring
		P15	Coding standards
PTEST	Test	P16	Unit Test
		P17	Continuous integration

Table 3. Quality characteristics based on the ISO / IEC 25010 standard

ID	Characteristics	Description
AFUN	Functional Suitability	Set of attributes related to the existence of software functions and their specific properties.
ARELI	Reliability	Attributes that represent the software's ability to maintain its level of performance under certain conditions and for a set period of time.
AUSAB	Usability	Attributes that are related to the effort required to learn the management of an application, work with it, and achieve the expected results.
APEF	Performance Efficiency	Set of attributes that represent the relationship between the level of software performance and the amount of hardware and software resources used under established conditions.
ACOMP	Compatibility	The capability of two or more systems or components to exchange information and/or perform their required functions while sharing the same hardware or software.
AMAIN	Maintainability	Set of attributes related to the effort required to make modifications.
APORT	Portability	Attributes that represent the ability of the software to be transferred from one environment to another.
ASEC	Security	The degree of protection of the information and data that cannot be read or modified by unauthorized persons or systems.

3.3.1 Set of Hypotheses, Category of Agile Practices: Teamwork

The category of *Teamwork Practices* can exert a significant influence on the quality characteristic of *Functional Suitability,* no doubt due to the application of practices such as On-site customer, stand up meetings, retrospectives, and collective code ownership that contribute to obtaining complete functionality and compatible software. Consequently, the following hypothesis proposed.

H1.1 "There is a significant influence that Teamwork practices exert on Functional Suitability."

3.3.2 Set of Hypotheses, Category of Agile Practices: Project Management

The category *Project Management Practices* include practices related to planning, monitoring, working hours, and timeboxing which do not exert a direct influence on the quality characteristics of the resulting software. Nevertheless, correct planning and the monitoring of the compliance with user requirements does contribute to obtaining correct functionality. For this reason, the following hypothesis has been proposed.

H2.1 *"There is a significant influence that Project Management practices exert on Functional Suitability."*

3.3.3 Set of Hypotheses Category of Agile Practices: Engineering

The category *Engineering practices* includes the application of software *Small releases, Simple design, Refactoring,* and *Coding standards.* These factors contribute to the correct construction of software in the analysis, programming, and coding stages of software development and therefore we will help to produce software that meets quality characteristics. The quality characteristic of *Portability* has been omitted in this hypothesis set for the reason that *Engineering practices* do not contribute significantly to the *installability and replaceability* of software. Based on the above, the following seven hypotheses have been suggested.

H3.1, H3.2, H3.3, H3.4, H3.5, H3.6, and H3.8 *"There is a significant influence that Engineering practices exert on Functional Suitability, Reliability, Usability, Performance, Efficiency, Compatibility, Maintainability, and Security."*

3.3.4 Set of Hypotheses Category of Agile Practices: Testing

The practices corresponding to the *Testing* category are extremely important in all stages of the software development process as they guarantee reliability and customer satisfaction when delivering the final product. The objective of testing practices is to find errors starting from the beginning of software development and therefore, contribute to producing a quality product. We have prioritized the influence of the application of these practices on four quality characteristics, *Functional Suitability, Reliability, Performance Efficiency,* and *Portability*, which have been expressed in hypotheses H4.1, H4.2, H4.4, and H4.7. Although the other characteristics are important, they are a consequence of the application of all the agile practices.

H4.1, H4.2, H4.4, and H4.7 *"There is a significant influence that Testing practices exert on Functional Suitability, Reliability, Performance Efficiency, and Portability."*

Table 4. Hypotheses categories

Agile Practices	Quality characteristics							
	Functionality	Reliability	Usability	Performance Efficiency	Compatibility	Maintainability	Portability	Security
PTW	H1.1							
PMP	H2.1							
PENG	H3.1	H3.2	H3.3	H3.4	H3.5	H3.6		H3.8
PTEST	H4.1	H4.2		H4.4			H4.7	

4. RESEARCH METHOD

4.1 Information Gathering Process

This research is framed within an organizational context, analyzing companies and institutions that develop software in Ecuador. This study used a survey conducted via the web using the Google Forms tool over a period of four months, from October 2016 to January 2017.

In 2015, there were 457 entities from both public and private sectors who were involved in activities related to software publishing, computer programming activities, computer consultancy and computer facilities management activities, and other information technology and computer service activities, corresponding to International Standard Industrial Classification of All Economic Activities codes J5820, J6201, J6202, J6209. From those 362 were categorized as small entities, 83 as medium and 12 as large. The data was obtained from Ecuadorian National Statistics and Census Institute Open Data. The survey was directed to 387 individuals from those entities who are involved in software development process employing agile methodologies. Practitioners were selected from databases of software development companies, as well as from the records of graduates of postgraduate programs in Software Engineering and Applied Computing from the country's universities. 155 individuals responded to the survey. The objective of the survey was to ascertain their viewpoint towards the influence of the application of agile practices on software quality.

The survey was set up into 3 sections. Section 1: General Data (8 questions), Section 2: Perception of how agile practices influence the quality characteristics of the resulting software (8 questions), and Section 3: Other Related Aspects (2 questions) to the user experience regarding quality and the application of agile practices. The questions in Section 1 were related to which agile methodologies are employed and the role they have played in software development projects. There were diverse responses since this information and the answers produced can vary according to the project to which the agile methodologies are applied. The questions in section 2 were evaluated utilizing the Likert scale, a scale of five values: 1-No influence, 2-Low influence, 3-Medium influence, 4-High influence and 5-Complete influence. The survey was implemented in the Spanish language. A translation of the survey into English is available in Appendix B.

Once the survey was prepared, a pilot test was carried out to a) ensure the validity of the survey, confirming that it measures what it should measure and that it is in accordance with the hypotheses proposed, b) analyze the wording of the questions to confirm that it was understandable for the respondents, c) detect unexpected values from the variables, flows of erroneous questions and other aspects, and d) determine if the duration of the questionnaire was adequate. For this, a group of five experts familiar with the topic, two professors and three Ph.Ds., were selected. As a result of the pilot test, some corrections were suggested to improve the survey, including concepts of the variables considered in the questions to avoid misinterpretation and introducing additional questions to ensure that the answers were consistent with the responders' experience with agile practices.

Once the information was obtained, the surveys were validated in order to eliminate inconsistencies and resolve, as far as possible, problems with the data collected. The main criterion of eligibility for the respondents to the answers was that the participants have indeed applied Agile Software Development Methodologies. Based on that criterion, the number of valid questionnaires was reduced to 146. The valid questionnaires were subjected to the coding of the variables under study.

4.2 The Applied Methodology to Analyze The Results

The approach to data analysis was quantitative. The results were arranged to statistically analyze the data collected in Sections 1 and 3 of the survey, which are related to the objective of this study and are applied to all values collected from the variables studied. The following analyses were performed:

a) Descriptive statistics were elaborated to know the demographic characteristics of the respondents.
b) The reliability and validity test used Cronbach's alpha to determine the reliability of the internal consistency of the instrument to ensure that the items measured on the Likert scale measure the same constructs and are highly correlated.
c) The examination of standardized residuals was an analysis conducted of all the answers, relating categories of agile practices and characteristics of software quality, based on Section 3 of the survey.

To analyze the independent hypothesis of the variables representing the rows and columns of a table, it is necessary to identify the value of each cell of the table (for each respondent, r), and define as a probability a standard normal deviate that exceeds the adjusted residual as a specific percentage.

The procedure suggested by Haberman (1973) as adapted. It involves an examination of standardized residuals, e_{ij}, as follows,

$$e_{ij} = \frac{a_{ij} - \bar{a}}{\sqrt{\bar{a}}}$$

where a_{ij} is the value given for the respondent to each cell in the formed contingency table and $\bar{a}$ is the mean of all values given by the respondent, the expected value. For each e_{ij}, the variance is estimated by:

$$v_{ij} = \left(1 - \frac{n_{i.}}{N}\right)\left(1 - \frac{n_{.j}}{N}\right)$$

where $n_{i.}$ and $n_{.j}$ are the sum of all the a values for row i and column j respectively, and N is the sum of all a_{ij} values. Thus, for each cell in the contingency table we are able to compute an adjusted residual, d_{ij} where:

$$d_{ij} = \frac{e_{ij}}{\sqrt{v_{ij}}}$$

Finally, for all respondents, the terms d_{ij} are normally adjusted as:

$$d_{ij}' = \frac{d_{ij}}{\sigma_r}$$

where σr is the standard deviation of all $d i_{.j.}$

When the variables forming the contingency table are independent, the terms d_{ij}' are normally distributed with a mean of 0 and standard deviation of 1. We may then compare the absolute values of the entries with the standard normal deviate (z) using the Stanine method of scaling (Zucker, 2003). The basis for obtaining stanines is that a normal distribution is divided into nine intervals, each of which has a width of 0,5 standard deviation excluding the first and the last which are the remainder of the tails of the distribution. The mean value lies at the center of the fifth interval. The qualitative description used for the nine stanines are related on Figure 2.

Finally, a test of the hypotheses was carried out to determine which relationships were accepted and rejected, which agile practices exert an influence on the characteristics of software quality.

5. RESULTS

The approach to the data analysis was quantitative and based on closed-ended questions. Based on the survey, the data we obtained were summarized as a percentage, which are presented in Appendix C.

5.1 Descriptive Statistics

The information was collected from the 146 respondents, of whom 27,4% were women, and 72,6% were men. Most of them, 76%, work in companies whose main activity is software development. There were also 6,8% of the respondents working in institutions of higher education and another 6,4% of respondents that belong to financial institutions. The remaining percentage was distributed among the telecommunications, health, and tourism industries and government institutions. The size of the companies where the majority of the respondents work, 52,8%, corresponded to small businesses of less than 20 employees. 32,8% work in companies that have less than 50 employees, and 14,4% work in companies with more than 50 employees.

Figure 2. Stanines defined descriptively

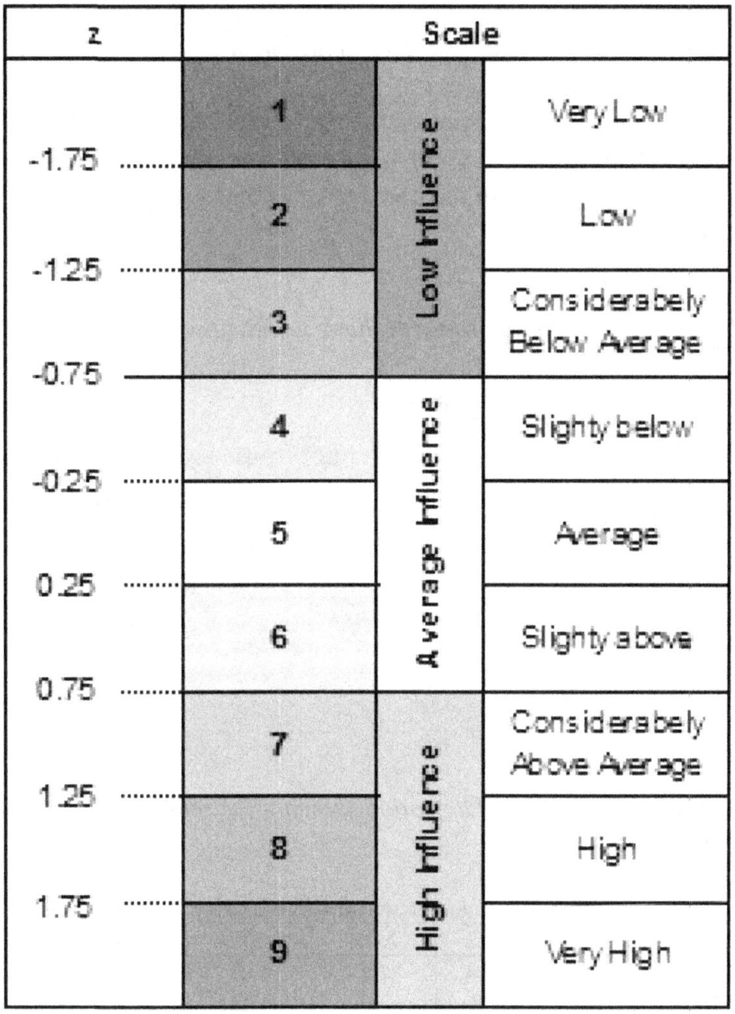

z	Scale		
	1		Very Low
-1.75	2	Low Influence	Low
-1.25	3		Considerabely Below Average
-0.75	4		Slighty below
-0.25	5	Average Influence	Average
0.25	6		Slighty above
0.75	7		Considerabely Above Average
1.25	8	High Influence	High
1.75	9		Very High

As shown in Figure 3(a), 59,69% of respondents utilize the Scrum methodology, followed by XP and XP/Scrum hybrids with 21,99% and 9,95%, respectively. The remaining percentage belong to responders who use other methodologies such as Agile Unified Process (AUP), Feature-Driven Development (FDD), or proprietary methodologies adapted by their companies.

Figure 3(b) reveals that 47,40% of the responders were software developers who have experience using agile methodologies, followed by Project Managers, IT staff, and Product Owners with 17,92%, 11,56%, 10,98%, respectively. The respondents who have a profile as testers correspond to only 4,05%. Others identified themselves as systems analysts, business analysts, and agile coaches, and they represented 8,09% of the respondents.

Figure 4 shows the statistics corresponding to the mean and standard deviation, by means of a heat map, of the 32 variables that relate the agile practices (columns) with the quality characteristics (rows). There, it can be seen that the relationship PTW-AFUNC has the highest average of 4,14, with a standard deviation of 0,983, in dark green, which implies that most of the participants in this survey agree that teamwork practices exerts a strong positive influence on the characteristic of functionality. On the other hand, the PMP-ACOMP relationship has the lowest average of 3,46 and a standard deviation of 1,238, in dark red, which indicates that the agile *project management practice* has a weak influence on the *compatibility* characteristic.

Table 5 shows a summary of the statistics of the study variables. The mean value of the items is 3,844, with a range of 0,726 between 3,418 and 4,144 from a total of 32 items considered, using a 4 x 8 contingency table. The mean variance of the items is 1,177 and a range of 0,705 between a minimum and maximum of 0,850 and 1,555.

Figure 3. Used agile methodologies and profile of the respondents

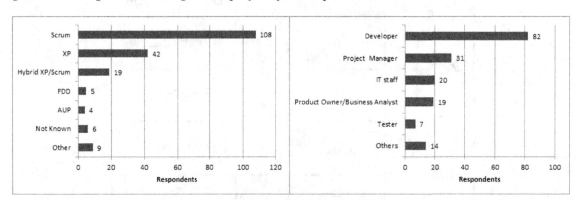

Figure 4. Heat map of mean and standard deviation showing the relationships between agile practices and characteristics of quality

Agile Practices	Characteristics of quality							
	AFUN	ARELI	AUSAB	APEF	ACOMP	AMANT	APORT	ASEC
PTW	4,14 ±0,983	3,86 ±0,996	3,84 ±1,133	3,9 ±1,106	3,77 ±1,161	3,91 ±1,043	3,6 ±1,142	3,87 ±1,097
PMP	3,88 ±0,975	3,7 ±1,147	3,55 ±1,187	3,69 ±1,067	3,46 ±1,238	3,68 ±1,132	3,42 ±1,247	3,6 ±1.178
PENG	4,09 ±0,996	4,02 ±0,972	4,07 ±0,922	4 ±1,05	3,92 ±1,064	3,97 ±1,053	3,93 ±1,048	3,98 ±1.02
PTEST	4,07 ±1,001	4 ±1,044	3,88 ±1,099	4,01 ±1,089	3,77 ±1,1	3,88 ±1,073	3,7 ±1,217	3,87 ±1.039

5.2 Reliability and Validity Test

To test the reliability of the internal consistency of the collected data, we use Cronbach's Alpha, which uses values between 0 (a consistent variance cannot be explained) and 1 (the variance is consistent). A higher value of the Cronbach's Alpha would indicate a greater reliability or accuracy of the statistical inferences of the data. Acceptable values for Cronbach's Alpha begin at 0,70 (Bland & Altman, 1997; DeVellis, 2016; Nunnally & Bernstein, 1994). In Table 6, we can see that Cronbach's Alpha for the 24 variables analyzed was 0,976. This indicates that the internal consistency of the data is highly reliable.

Table 5. Summary of the item statistics

	Mean	Minimum	Maximum	Range	Maximum / Minimum	Variance	Number of items
Media of the items	3,844	3,418	4,144	0,726	1,12	0,034	32
Variance of the items	1,177	0,850	1,555	0,705	1,829	0,031	32

Table 6. Reliability statistics for the 32 variables analyzed

Cronbach´s Alpha	Cronbach´s Alpha based on standardized items	N. of items
0,975	0,976	32

5.3 Analysis of Adjusted Residuals

Figure 5 shows the adjusted residuals in the form of a heat map. The darker green color corresponds to the highest ratings from the respondents (high influence) and the darker red color corresponds to the lowest ratings from the respondents (low influence). The significance is represented by the Stanines (scale of 1-9) as seen in Figure 2. The results show the significant influence of Teamwork practices (PTW) on the characteristic of functionality quality (AFUN) is the highest with a residual adjustment of 1,63, which corresponds to a value of 8 on the Stanines scale. Other agile practices that positively influence functionality are engineering (PENG) and testing (PTEST). According to the results obtained, the attribute of functionality is positively affected by 75% of the categories of agile practices analyzed.

Another important outcome indicated by the study is that project management practices presents a negative value in 87,5% of the characteristics analyzed. The negative value is seen to be greater in the portability attribute, followed by the characteristics of compatibility, usability, and security. This means that project management appears to have a very low influence on these quality characteristics.

5.4 Test of Hypothesis

Table 7 summarizes the results detailed in this section. Of the 13 hypotheses proposed, 4 are null hypotheses (H2.1, H3.5, H3.6 and H3.8), because the *d'* value is between -0,75 and 0,75 and these values are not consequential enough to reject the null hypothesis which indicates that an average influence is found. The other nine hypotheses can be confirmed as true, meaning the influence of agile practices on characteristics of quality is high enough or low enough to reject the null hypothesis. Hypotheses H1.1, H3.1, H4.1, H3.2, H4.2, H3.3, H3.4, and H4.4 exert an above average influence. The results confirm that the only significantly lower influence was produced by the agile testing practices on the quality characteristic of Portability (H4.7). The remaining hypotheses show the agile practice exerts a below average or null influence on the characteristic of quality.

Figure 5. Heat map of adjusted residuals between agile practices and characteristics of quality

Agile Practices	Characteristics of quality							
	AFUN	ARELI	AUSAB	APEF	ACOMP	MANT	PORT	ASEC
PTW	**1,63** (8)	0,064 (5)	-0.048 (5)	0,287 (6)	-0,381 (4)	0,361 (6)	-1,343 (2)	0,138 (5)
PMP	0,174 (5)	-0.783 (3)	-1,591 (2)	-0,82 (3)	-2,065 (1)	-0,893 (3)	-2,282 (1)	-1,333 (2)
PENG	**1,34** (8)	0,962 (7)	**1,222** (7)	0,85 (7)	0,437 (6)	0,662 (6)	0,474 (6)	0,737 (6)
PTEST	**1,222** (7)	0,846 (7)	0,213 (5)	**0,921** (7)	-0,382 (4)	0,213 (5)	-0,789 (3)	0,138 (5)

Table 7. Results of hypothesis testing

Agile Practices	Characteristics of Quality							
	Functionality	Reliability	Usability	Performance Efficiency	Compatibility	Maintainability	Portability	Security
PTW	H1.1+							
PMP	H2.1							
PENG	H3.1+	H3.2+	H3.3+	H3.4+	H3.5	H3.6		H3.8
PTEST	H4.1+	H4.2+		H4.4+			H4.7-	

Figure 6 shows the categories of agile practices that have a significant influence on characteristics of quality and the value obtained according to Section 5.3. As can be observed, the category of Project management practices has been eliminated for the reason that it does not exert any significant influence on any of the characteristics of quality. Likewise, the results show that the quality characteristics of Maintainability, Security, and Compatibility are not significantly influenced by the application of the categories of agile practices analyzed.

6. DISCUSSION

6.1 Influence of Agile Practices on Software Quality

Teamwork practices exert a significantly positive influence on the quality characteristic of Functional Suitability. This result is accomplished through the application of practices such as On-site customer, stand up meetings, retrospectives, and collective code ownership, which all contribute to obtaining complete and correct functionality of the software. Furthermore, it has been observed that these practices have a significantly low influence on the Portability characteristic, that is, the software's adaptability, installability, and replaceability, in view of the fact that they do not rely on the utilization of teamwork practices. In like manner, the other quality characteristics are not significantly influenced by this group of practices.

From the quantitative data obtained in our study, it has been proven that three groups of agile practices, Engineering practices, Teamwork practices, and Testing practices, have a significant positive influence on the quality attribute Functionality. Contrastingly, the application of Project management practices has a low influence on all quality characteristics except the Functionality characteristic, on which it exerts an average influence. Although the other practices analyzed also exert a level of influence that is high, medium, or low on the quality characteristics, the values obtained are not significant enough to

Figure 6. Final model of the categories of agile practices and their influence on quality characteristics, based on the ISO/IEC 25010 standard

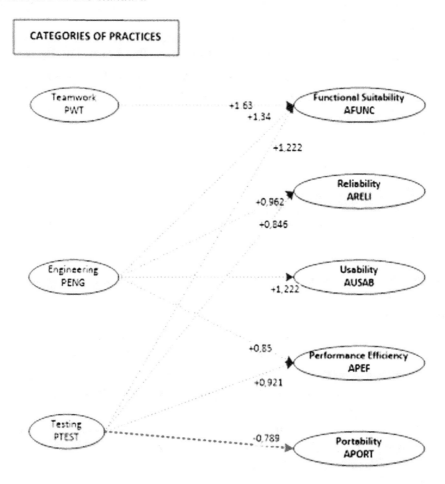

be considered. This implies that although agile practices are applied in a software development project, their influence on those specific quality characteristics of the software will not change.

Testing practices have been proven to exercise a high positive influence on functionality, reliability, and performance efficiency, and an average influence on usability, maintainability, and security. These results are to be expected since the first group of characteristics is directly related to the design and programming of the software and the second group to the operation of the system. It is also evident that testing practices have little effect on portability.

According to the hypotheses, there are three quality characteristics that are not influenced significantly by agile practices. They are compatibility, maintainability, and security. However, agile engineering practices do exert an average positive influence on those same characteristics.

In the literature review conducted by Singh & Gautam (2016), it was determined that all quality attributes are important. However, maintenance capacity could be considered as the most important attribute for software products because software maintenance is the process of refining the software to ensure it continues to meet the needs of the business. It also states that the maintainability of the software allows for the improvement of performance and other attributes over time.

Based on this analysis, every phase of software development is necessary for software quality. However, the software design phase should be considered as the most important phase. In our study, Engineering Practices was proven to exert a medium influence on maintainability. In addition, this group of practices involves aspects related to design, such as small releases, simple design, coding standards and refactoring, which exert a high influence on the characteristics of Functionality, Reliability, Usability, and Performance efficiency, and exercise an average influence on the attributes of Compatibility, Maintainability, and Security. These results coincide with the statements made by Singh & Gautam.

6.2 Limitations

This study uses the survey technique to obtain its results. Therefore, it is subject to the following limitations:

1. The type and size of the projects were not considered. Such aspects could modify the results of this study because the level of application of agile practices will differ depending on the type and size of the project.
2. A small percentage, 16,44%, of the responders use agile methodologies different from Scrum and XP, as shown in Figure 3a. Consequently, the results may demonstrate a bias towards the practices used by these methodologies.
3. According to a study carried out by the Ecuadorian Software Association in 2015, in Ecuador, 22% of the software development companies had more than 50 employees. Only 14,4% of the responders to the survey belonged to this classification of companies and it cannot be demonstrated that this sample incorporates all existing companies. A gap in the results may be possible.
4. The sample was limited to those involved in the software development process in Ecuador. Although all possible responders were contacted through social networks and email, in comparison, the sample utilized in the study is small. We must take into account that the agile community in this country has more than 700 followers. A larger sample size could provide a more robust statistical calculation and more accurate analysis.
5. The specific practices corresponding to each practice category were not analyzed. However, the questionnaire did indicate which practices were considered in each category. This aspect may not have been regarded correctly by the responders, which could affect the results.

7. CONCLUSION

In this study, we have analyzed the influence of four categories of agile practices, Teamwork, Project Management, Engineering, and Testing, on eight quality characteristics, Functional Suitability, Reliability, Usability, Performance Efficiency, Compatibility, Maintainability, Portability and Security, based on the ISO/IEC 25010 standard.

This work has shown that 9 of the 13 proposed hypotheses indicate the significant influence agile practices have on quality characteristics. The results obtained from a survey administered to 146 responders involved in the software development process in Ecuador identified the following Agile practices as having high influence on characteristics of software quality: Teamwork practices exert a considerable influence on the quality feature of functionality. Engineering practices exert a substantial influence on the characteristics of functionality, reliability, usability, and performance efficiency. Testing practices exert a significant influence on the characteristics of functionality, reliability, and performance efficiency. In addition, a low influence of agile testing practices on the portability characteristic was ascertained.

In this paper, agile practices have been grouped into four categories. Therefore, the information obtained in this analysis can serve as a basis for future studies, such as understanding the influence of the practices that correspond to each category on the characteristics and sub-characteristics of quality. In addition, practices that have a significant influence on the quality of the software development process could be monitored in existing projects in order to ratify or refute the results obtained. In this work, the survey was not directed to very small entities, which could be considered in the future for determining the influence of agile practices on software quality according to standard ISO/IEC 29110: Systems and Software Life Cycle Profiles and Guidelines for Very Small Entities (VSEs).

The size of the selected sample is reasonable to obtain a satisfactory conclusion for the software industry of Ecuador. Concurrently, we do not intend to generalize our findings to other countries and regions. For this reason, the demographic information of the participants has been included, so that this study may be tested in other contexts.

REFERENCES

Abrahamsson, P., Salo, O., Ronkainen, J., & Warsta, J. (2017). Agile Software Development Methods: Review and Analysis. Retrieved from http://arxiv.org/abs/1709.08439

Agarwal, N., & Rathod, U. (2006). Defining 'success' for software projects: An exploratory revelation. *International Journal of Project Management*, 24(4), 358–370. doi:10.1016/j.ijproman.2005.11.009

Ahmed, A., Ahmad, S., Ehsan, N., Mirza, E., & Sarwar, S. Z. (2010). Agile software development: Impact on productivity and quality. *Proceedings of the 2010 IEEE International Conference on Management of Innovation and Technology (ICMIT)* (pp. 287–291). IEEE. 10.1109/ICMIT.2010.5492703

Ambler, S. (2005). Quality in an agile world. *Software Quality Professional*, 7(4), 34.

Arvanitou, E. M., Ampatzoglou, A., Chatzigeorgiou, A., Galster, M., & Avgeriou, P. (2017). A mapping study on design-time quality attributes and metrics. *Journal of Systems and Software*, 127, 52–77. doi:10.1016/j.jss.2017.01.026

Bermejo, P. H. de S., Zambalde, A. L., Tonelli, A. O., Souza, S. A., Zuppo, L. A., & Rosa, P. L. (2014). Agile Principles and Achievement of Success in Software Development: A Quantitative Study in Brazilian Organizations. *Procedia Technology*, 16, 718–727. doi:10.1016/j.protcy.2014.10.021

Bhasin, S. (2012). Quality Assurance in Agile: A Study towards Achieving Excellence. Proceedings of the 2012 AGILE India (AGILE INDIA) (pp. 64–67). Academic Press. doi:10.1109/AgileIndia.2012.18

Bland, J. M., & Altman, D. G. (1997). Statistics notes: Cronbach's alpha. *BMJ (Clinical Research Ed.)*, *314*(7080), 572. doi:10.1136/bmj.314.7080.572 PMID:9055718

Bougroun, Z., Zeaaraoui, A., & Bouchentouf, T. (2014). The projection of the specific practices of the third level of CMMI model in agile methods: Scrum, XP and Kanban. *Proceedings of the 2014 Third IEEE International Colloquium on Information Science and Technology (CIST)* (pp. 174–179). IEEE. doi:10.1109/CIST.2014.7016614

Chow, T., & Cao, D.-B. (2008). A survey study of critical success factors in agile software projects. *Journal of Systems and Software*, *81*(6), 961–971. doi:10.1016/j.jss.2007.08.020

Christensen, H. B., Hansen, K. M., & Lindstrøm, B. (2010). Lightweight and Continuous Architectural Software Quality Assurance Using the aSQA Technique. In M. A. Babar & I. Gorton (Eds.), *Software Architecture* (pp. 118–132). Springer. doi:10.1007/978-3-642-15114-9_11

Curcio, K., Malucelli, A., Reinehr, S., & Paludo, M. A. (2016). An analysis of the factors determining software product quality: A comparative study. *Computer Standards & Interfaces*, *48*, 10–18. doi:10.1016/j.csi.2016.04.002

de Wit, A. (1988). Measurement of project success. *International Journal of Project Management*, *6*(3), 164–170. doi:10.1016/0263-7863(88)90043-9

DeVellis, R. F. (2016). *Scale development: Theory and applications* (Vol. 26). Sage publications.

Diebold, P., & Dahlem, M. (2014). Agile Practices in Practice: A Mapping Study. *Proceedings of the 18th International Conference on Evaluation and Assessment in Software Engineering* (pp. 30:1–30:10). New York: ACM. 10.1145/2601248.2601254

Estayno, M. G., Dapozo, G. N., Cuenca Pletsch, L. R., & Greiner, C. L. (2009). Modelos y métricas para evaluar calidad de software. *Proceedings of the XI Workshop de Investigadores en Ciencias de la Computación*. Academic Press. Retrieved from http://sedici.unlp.edu.ar/handle/10915/19762

García-Mireles, G. A., Moraga, M. Á., García, F., & Piattini, M. (2015). Approaches to promote product quality within software process improvement initiatives: A mapping study. *Journal of Systems and Software*, *103*, 150–166. doi:10.1016/j.jss.2015.01.057

Gorla, N., & Lin, S.-C. (2010). Determinants of software quality: A survey of information systems project managers. *Information and Software Technology*, *52*(6), 602–610. doi:10.1016/j.infsof.2009.11.012

Haberman, S. J. (1973). The Analysis of Residuals in Cross-Classified Tables. *Biometrics*, *29*(1), 205. doi:10.2307/2529686

Henriksen, A., & Pedersen, S. A. R. (2017). A qualitative case study on agile practices and project success in agile software projects. *The Journal of Modern Project Management*, *5*(1). doi:10.19255/jmpm230

ISO/IEC. (2005). ISO/IEC 25000:2005 - Software Engineering -- Software product Quality Requirements and Evaluation (SQuaRE) -- Guide to SQuaRE. Retrieved from http://www.iso.org/iso/home/store/catalogue_tc/catalogue_detail.htm?csnumber=35683

Khomh, F., & Guéhéneuc, Y.-G. (2008). DEQUALITE: Building Design-based Software Quality Models. *Proceedings of the 15th Conference on Pattern Languages of Programs* (pp. 2:1–2:7). New York: ACM. doi:10.1145/1753196.1753199

Manjunath, K. N., Jagadeesh, J., & Yogeesh, M. (2013). Achieving quality product in a long term software product development in healthcare application using Lean and Agile principles: Software engineering and software development. *Proceedings of the 2013 International Multi-Conference on Automation, Computing, Communication, Control and Compressed Sensing (iMac4s)* (pp. 26–34). doi:10.1109/iMac4s.2013.6526379

Marrington, A., Hogan, J. M., & Thomas, R. (2005). Quality assurance in a student-based agile software engineering process. *Proceedings of the 2005 Australian Software Engineering Conference* (pp. 324–331). Academic Press. 10.1109/ASWEC.2005.38

McHugh, O., Conboy, K., & Lang, M. (2012). Agile Practices: The Impact on Trust in Software Project Teams. *IEEE Software, 29*(3), 71–76. doi:10.1109/MS.2011.118

Mirnalini, K., & Raya, V. R. (2010). Agile - A software development approach for quality software. *Proceedings of the 2010 International Conference on Educational and Information Technology (ICEIT)* (*Vol. 1*, pp. V1-242-V1-244). Academic Press. 10.1109/ICEIT.2010.5607732

Mnkandla, E., & Dwolatzky, B. (2006). Defining Agile Software Quality Assurance. *Proceedings of the International Conference on Software Engineering Advances* (pp. 36–36). Academic Press. 10.1109/ICSEA.2006.261292

Mundra, A., Misra, S., & Dhawale, C. (2013). Practical Scrum-Scrum Team: Way to Produce Successful and Quality Software. *Proceedings of the 2013 13th International Conference on Computational Science and Its Applications (ICCSA)* (pp. 119–123). Academic Press. doi:10.1109/ICCSA.2013.25

Muñoz, C. C., Velthuis, M. G. P., & de la Rubia, M. Á. M. (2010). *Calidad del producto y proceso software*. Editorial Ra-Ma.

Nunnally, J., & Bernstein, L. (1994). *Psychometric theory*. New York: McGraw-Hill, Inc.

Opelt, K., & Beeson, T. (2008). Agile Teams Require Agile QA: How to Make it Work, An Experience Report. Proceedings of the Agile Conference AGILE '08 (pp. 229–232). Academic Press. doi:10.1109/Agile.2008.59

Ran, H., Zhuo, W., & Jianfeng, X. (2009). Web Quality of Agile Web Development. *Proceedings of the IITA International Conference on Services Science, Management and Engineering SSME '09* (pp. 426–429). 10.1109/SSME.2009.112

Rico, D. F. (2008). Effects of Agile Methods on Website Quality for Electronic Commerce. *Proceedings of the 41st Annual Hawaii International Conference on System Sciences* (pp. 463–463). IEEE Press. 10.1109/HICSS.2008.137

Sagheer, M., Zafar, T., & Sirshar, M. (2015). A Framework For Software Quality Assurance Using Agile Methodology. *International Journal of Scientific & Technology Research, 4*(2), 44–50.

Santos, M. de A., Bermejo, P. H. S., Oliveira, M. S., & Tonelli, A. O. (2011). Agile Practices: An Assessment of Perception of Value of Professionals on the Quality Criteria in Performance of Projects. *Journal of Software Engineering and Applications, 04*(12), 700–709. doi:10.4236/jsea.2011.412082

Scharff, C. (2011). Guiding global software development projects using Scrum and Agile with quality assurance. *Proceedings of the 2011 24th IEEE-CS Conference on Software Engineering Education and Training (CSEE T)* (pp. 274–283). IEEE. 10.1109/CSEET.2011.5876097

Schwaber, K., & Sutherland, J. (2013). La Guía de Scrum. Scrum.Org and ScrumInc. Retrieved from http://scrumguides.org/

Sfetsos, P., & Stamelos, I. (2010). Empirical Studies on Quality in Agile Practices: A Systematic Literature Review. *Proceedings of the 2010 Seventh International Conference on the Quality of Information and Communications Technology* (pp. 44–53). Academic Press. 10.1109/QUATIC.2010.17

Singh, B., & Gautam, S. (2016). The Impact of Software Development Process on Software Quality: A Review. *Proceedings of the 2016 8th International Conference on Computational Intelligence and Communication Networks (CICN)* (pp. 666–672). Academic Press. 10.1109/CICN.2016.137

Subramanyam, V., & Prasad, C. G. (2013). Organizational practices that effects Software Quality In Software Engineering process. *International Journal of Engineering Trends and Technology, 2*(3), 25–30.

Sultana, S., Motla, Y. H., Asghar, S., Jamal, M., & Azad, R. (2014). A hybrid model by integrating agile practices for Pakistani software industry. *Proceedings of the 2014 International Conference on Electronics, Communications and Computers (CONIELECOMP)* (pp. 256–262). Academic Press. 10.1109/CONIELECOMP.2014.6808600

Versionone. (2017). 11th Annual State of Agile Report. Retrieved from https://explore.versionone.com/state-of-agile

Xu, B. (2009). Towards High Quality Software Development with Extreme Programming Methodology: Practices from Real Software Projects. *Proceedings of the International Conference on Management and Service Science MASS '09* (pp. 1–4). Academic Press. doi:10.1109/ICMSS.2009.5302042

Zucker, S. (2003). Fundamentals of Standardized Testing. Pearson Assessment Report, 8.

This research was previously published in the International Journal of Information Technologies and Systems Approach (IJITSA), 13(2); pages 27-53, copyright year 2020 by IGI Publishing (an imprint of IGI Global).

APPENDIX 1

Table 8. Summary of agile practices found in the literature

Agile Practices	Source
Category: Teamwork Practices	
Small teams	(Ahmed et al., 2010; Mundra, Misra, & Dhawale, 2013)
Multifunctional teams	(Diebold & Dahlem, 2014)
Multiple teams	(Mundra et al., 2013)
Daily meeting	(Diebold & Dahlem, 2014; Manjunath, Jagadeesh, & Yogeesh, 2013; Mirnalini & Raya, 2010; Mundra et al., 2013)
Stand-up meeting	(Bougroun et al., 2014; Manjunath et al., 2013; Scharff, 2011)
Client on-site	(Scharff, 2011; Xu, 2009)
Pair Programming	(Bougroun et al., 2014; Manjunath et al., 2013; Scharff, 2011; Sultana, Motla, Asghar, Jamal, & Azad, 2014; Xu, 2009)
Agility in team communication	(Bermejo et al., 2014; Scharff, 2011; Sultana et al., 2014; Xu, 2009)
People collaboration capabilities	(Bermejo et al., 2014; Marrington, Hogan, & Thomas, 2005)
Team communication capabilities	(Bermejo et al., 2014; Diebold & Dahlem, 2014)
Competence of individuals	(Bermejo et al., 2014)
Confidence among team members	(Bermejo et al., 2014)
Participation of leaders	(Bermejo et al., 2014)
Leader recognition	(Bermejo et al., 2014; Marrington et al., 2005)
Daily cooperation between business people and developers	(Bougroun et al., 2014)
Frequency of interactions with customers	(Ahmed et al., 2010; Bermejo et al., 2014; Bhasin, 2012; Diebold & Dahlem, 2014; Marrington et al., 2005; Mirnalini & Raya, 2010; Sultana et al., 2014)
Customers motivations	(Bermejo et al., 2014)
Shift work	(Manjunath et al., 2013)
Self-organizing teams	(Ahmed et al., 2010; Scharff, 2011)
Training of professionals	(Ahmed et al., 2010)
Customer satisfaction with the projects	(Bermejo et al., 2014)
Interaction with partners in software development	(Bermejo et al., 2014)
Interaction with external partners	(Bermejo et al., 2014)
Organizational openness to talk	(Bermejo et al., 2014)
Agility in design decisions	(Bermejo et al., 2014; Scharff, 2011)
Team autonomy in projects	(Bermejo et al., 2014)
Multiple location teams	(Mundra et al., 2013)
Customer training	(Bermejo et al., 2014)
Knowledge transfer	(Diebold & Dahlem, 2014; Manjunath et al., 2013)
Learning loop	(Diebold & Dahlem, 2014)
Project charter	(Sultana et al., 2014)

Agile Practices	Source
Useful documentation for the team	(Bermejo et al., 2014)
Useful documentation for the customer	(Bermejo et al., 2014)
Retrospective /feedback	(Bhasin, 2012; Bougroun et al., 2014; Manjunath et al., 2013; Scharff, 2011; Sultana et al., 2014; Xu, 2009)
Collective ownership code	(Xu, 2009)
Category: Engineering Practices	
Zero Technical debts	(Manjunath et al., 2013)
Product Vision	(Diebold & Dahlem, 2014)
Sprints	(Bougroun et al., 2014)
User story	(Manjunath et al., 2013; Mundra et al., 2013; Scharff, 2011)
Metaphor	(Xu, 2009)
CRC cards	(Manjunath et al., 2013; Opelt & Beeson, 2008)
QA story card	(Opelt & Beeson, 2008)
Scenarios	(Bhasin, 2012; Mirnalini & Raya, 2010)
Coding standards	(Manjunath et al., 2013; Marrington et al., 2005; Scharff, 2011; Sultana et al., 2014; Xu, 2009)
Simple design	(Ahmed et al., 2010; Bougroun et al., 2014; Manjunath et al., 2013; Marrington et al., 2005; Sultana et al., 2014; Xu, 2009)
Flexibility to changes	(Ahmed et al., 2010; Bermejo et al., 2014; Scharff, 2011; Sultana et al., 2014)
Environmental configuration	(Bermejo et al., 2014)
Requirements captured at high level	(Scharff, 2011)
Quality check	(Diebold & Dahlem, 2014)
Continuous specification analysis	(Diebold & Dahlem, 2014)
Reduced documentation	(Ahmed et al., 2010)
Sprint Document	(Sultana et al., 2014)
Review document	(Sultana et al., 2014)
Design document	(Sultana et al., 2014)
Business Case document	(Sultana et al., 2014)
Automatic generation of documentation	(Manjunath et al., 2013)
Feasibility report	(Sultana et al., 2014)
Small releases	(Bougroun et al., 2014; Mirnalini & Raya, 2010; Sultana et al., 2014; Xu, 2009)
Refactoring	(Ahmed et al., 2010; Bhasin, 2012; Diebold & Dahlem, 2014; Scharff, 2011; Sultana et al., 2014; Xu, 2009)
Category: Project Management Practices	
Study of business objective	(Scharff, 2011)
Burndown charts	(Manjunath et al., 2013; Scharff, 2011)
Kanban	(Bougroun et al., 2014)
Planning games	(Mirnalini & Raya, 2010; Scharff, 2011; Xu, 2009)
Velocity team	(Manjunath et al., 2013; Scharff, 2011)

Agile Practices	Source
Early Estimation	(Sultana et al., 2014)
Iteration planning meeting	(Bougroun et al., 2014; Manjunath et al., 2013; Mirnalini & Raya, 2010; Mundra et al., 2013; Opelt & Beeson, 2008; Scharff, 2011; Sultana et al., 2014)
Outcome review	(Scharff, 2011)
Review of requirements with product Owner and team	(Bougroun et al., 2014)
Risk Analysis	(Sultana et al., 2014)
Code review	(Sultana et al., 2014)
Project scope	(Bermejo et al., 2014)
Quality of projects	(Bermejo et al., 2014)
Term projects	(Bermejo et al., 2014)
Release Planning	(Manjunath et al., 2013; Mundra et al., 2013; Opelt & Beeson, 2008; Scharff, 2011)
Incremental delivery	(Diebold & Dahlem, 2014; Sultana et al., 2014)
Version Control	(Sultana et al., 2014)
Prioritized Requirements	(Bhasin, 2012; Scharff, 2011; Sultana et al., 2014)
Risk reduction with external partners	(Bermejo et al., 2014)
Time boxing	(Diebold & Dahlem, 2014)
Monitoring Progress	(Diebold & Dahlem, 2014)
40-hour week	(Xu, 2009)
Category: Testing Practices	
Test early and often	(Bhasin, 2012; Scharff, 2011; Xu, 2009)
Continuous integration	(Bhasin, 2012; Bougroun et al., 2014; Diebold & Dahlem, 2014; Manjunath et al., 2013; Sultana et al., 2014)
Screening bugs	(Manjunath et al., 2013)
Functional test	(Bougroun et al., 2014; Opelt & Beeson, 2008)
System tests	(Sultana et al., 2014; Xu, 2009)
Integration tests	(Sultana et al., 2014)
Test Driven Development	(Bhasin, 2012; Opelt & Beeson, 2008; Sultana et al., 2014)
Unit tests	(Manjunath et al., 2013; Marrington et al., 2005; Opelt & Beeson, 2008; Sultana et al., 2014; Xu, 2009)
Acceptance tests	(Bhasin, 2012; Mirnalini & Raya, 2010; Scharff, 2011; Sultana et al., 2014),
Validation	(Diebold & Dahlem, 2014)
Audits	(Scharff, 2011)
Prioritizing Bugs	(Opelt & Beeson, 2008)

APPENDIX 2

Survey

Determination of the factors and attributes that influence the quality of the software development process that applies agile methodologies.

This survey is aimed to software development teams that apply agile methodologies.

Your answers are anonymous and will be used strictly for investigative purposes.

The Survey have 3 sections. Section 1 is related to the characterization of the company and the people who complete the questionnaire. Section 2 helps to determine the influence of agile practices on software quality attributes. And Section 3 contains questions that complement the study.

Thanks for your participation!

Section 1: General Data.

1.1 Does the company you work for use agile methodologies for software development? If your answer is NO, do not fill out this questionnaire.

Yes;   No

1.2 Which agile methodologies does the company use?

Scrum;   XP;   FDD;   Agile UP;   Hybrid XP/Scrum;   Do not know;   Other.

1.3 What is your position in the company?

Project Chief;   Software developer;   Owner;   IT Personal;   Tester;   Other.

1.4 Gender

Male;   Female.

1.5 How many people make up the development team in your company?

<10;   10-19;   20-29;   30-39;   40-49;   >50

1.6 What is the company's core business?

Software development;   Financial services;   Professional services;   Health;

Public Institution;   Education;   Telecommunication;   Insurance;   Other.

1.7 Where is the company's head office located?

(open answer)

1.8 Where are you currently working?

(open answer)

Section 2. Relationships between agile practices and quality attributes

Evaluate on a scale of 1 to 5 (1: No influence, 5: High influence)

Functionality:

Degree to which a product or system provides functions that meet stated and implied needs when used under specified conditions.

2.1 What influence do the following agile practices have on software FUNCTIONALITY:

Teamwork:	1; 2; 3; 4; 5
Project Management	1; 2; 3; 4; 5
Engineering	1; 2; 3; 4; 5
Testing	1; 2; 3; 4; 5

Reliability:

Degree to which a system, product or component performs specified functions under specified conditions for a specified period of time.

    2.2 What influence do the following agile practices have on software RELIABILITY:

Teamwork:	1; 2; 3; 4; 5
Project Management	1; 2; 3; 4; 5
Engineering	1; 2; 3; 4; 5
Testing	1; 2; 3; 4; 5

Usability:

Degree to which a product or system can be used by specific users to achieve specified goals with effectiveness, efficiency, and satisfaction in a specified context of use.

    2.3 What influence do the following agile practices have on software USABILTY:

Teamwork:	1; 2; 3; 4; 5
Project Management	1; 2; 3; 4; 5
Engineering	1; 2; 3; 4; 5
Testing	1; 2; 3; 4; 5

Performance efficiency:

Performance relative to the amount of resources used under stated conditions.

    2.4 What influence do the following agile practices have on software PERFOMANCE EFFICENCY:

Teamwork:	1; 2; 3; 4; 5
Project Management	1; 2; 3; 4; 5
Engineering	1; 2; 3; 4; 5
Testing	1; 2; 3; 4; 5

Maintainability:

Degree of effectiveness and efficiency with which a product or system can be modified by the intended maintenance team.

    2.5 What influence do the following agile practices have on software MAINTAINABILITY:

Teamwork:	1; 2; 3; 4; 5
Project Management	1; 2; 3; 4; 5
Engineering	1; 2; 3; 4; 5
Testing	1; 2; 3; 4; 5

Portability:

Degree of effectiveness and efficiency with which a system, product, or component can be transferred from one hardware, software or other operational or usage environment to another.

    2.6 What influence do the following agile practices have on software PORTABILITY:

Teamwork:	1; 2; 3; 4; 5
Project Management	1; 2; 3; 4; 5
Engineering	1; 2; 3; 4; 5
Testing	1; 2; 3; 4; 5

Security:

Degree to which a product or system protects information and data so that persons or other products or systems have the degree of data access appropriate to their types and levels of authorization.

2.7 What influence do the following agile practices have on software SECURITY:

Teamwork:	1; 2; 3; 4; 5
Project Management	1; 2; 3; 4; 5
Engineering	1; 2; 3; 4; 5
Testing	1; 2; 3; 4; 5

Compatibility

Degree to which a product, system, or component can exchange information with other products, systems, or components, and/or perform its required functions, while sharing the same hardware or software environment.

2.8 What influence do the following agile practices have on software COMPATIBILITY:

Teamwork:	1; 2; 3; 4; 5
Project Management	1; 2; 3; 4; 5
Engineering	1; 2; 3; 4; 5
Testing	1; 2; 3; 4; 5

Section 3. Other related aspects.

3.1 Choose one or more agile practices you apply to software development.

Pair programming; on-site costumer; stand up meetings; multifunctional teams; self-organizing teams; retrospectives; collective code ownership; planning games; monitoring progress; 40 hours per week; Timeboxing; simple design; small releases; refactoring; coding standards; testing, continuous integration

3.2 Does the company apply quality control to the software development process?

Yes;   No;   Partially

APPENDIX 3

Table 9. Summary obtained from survey data regarding the influence of agile practices on characteristics of quality

Practice	Characteristic	1 (%)	2 (%)	3 (%)	4 (%)	5 (%)
FDİS	ACOMP	3	7	19	35	36
	AEFİ	3	5	20	32	40
	AFİAB	1	5	21	34	38
	AFUNC	2	3	23	27	45
	AMAIN	3	5	20	34	38
	APORT	1	9	23	28	38
	ASEC	2	7	20	34	38
	AUSAB	0	6	21	34	40
Subtotal FDİS		*2.1*	*6.0*	*20.8*	*32.1*	*39.0*
FGP	ACOMP	10	13	17	40	20
	AEFİ	4	8	27	35	25
	AFİAB	5	10	21	35	28
	AFUNC	1	9	19	42	29
	AMAIN	5	11	23	34	27
	APORT	11	13	18	38	19
	ASEC	7	11	23	34	25
	AUSAB	7	14	21	36	23
Subtotal FGP		*6.3*	*11.1*	*21.3*	*36.6*	*24.7*
FTE	ACOMP	6	9	17	37	31
	AEFİ	4	8	19	33	36
	AFİAB	3	7	21	42	28
	AFUNC	1	5	17	29	47
	AMAIN	3	9	16	40	33
	APORT	5	11	27	31	25
	ASEC	2	12	18	32	36
	AUSAB	4	10	20	32	35
Subtotal FTE		*3.6*	*8.8*	*19.3*	*34.4*	*33.8*
FTEST	ACOMP	6	8	14	47	25
	AEFİ	3	7	17	30	42
	AFİAB	4	2	23	31	40
	AFUNC	3	4	18	34	41
	AMAIN	4	7	18	38	33
	APORT	9	5	23	32	31
	ASEC	3	5	26	33	33
	AUSAB	5	4	21	35	34
Subtotal FTEST		*4.8*	*5.2*	*20.2*	*34.8*	*34.9*

Chapter 69
A Decision Making Paradigm for Software Development in Libraries

Harish Maringanti
University of Utah, USA

ABSTRACT

Framing a technology question as a simple choice between developing an in- house application system and off-the- shelf proprietary system, or simply put, as a choice between build and buy, runs the risk of ignoring myriad options available in between the two extremes. In this era of cloud computing and run anything-as- a-service model, the very notion of developing an in-house application would raise a few eyebrows among C- level executives. How then can academic libraries, under mounting pressure to demonstrate their value (Oakleaf, 2010), justify investments in software development in particular? What follows in these sections is a brief discussion on the importance of investing in software development in libraries, three mini-case studies demonstrating the wide possibilities of integrating software development in library operations and a non- prescriptive model to assess which projects may be worth pursuing from the software development standpoint.

INTRODUCTION

Framing a technology question as a simple choice between developing an in-house application system and off-the-shelf proprietary system, or simply put, as a choice between build and buy, runs the risk of ignoring myriad options available in between the two extremes. As Langer puts it – "Choices of whether to make or buy do not necessarily need to be binary, that is, one or the other, but rather could end up as a hybrid decision. For example, an organization can develop its own application using open source within its application development strategy or it can license a third-party product that also contains open source." (Langer, 2016). In this era of cloud computing and run anything-as-a-service model, the very notion of developing an in-house application would raise a few eyebrows among C-level execu-

DOI: 10.4018/978-1-6684-3702-5.ch069

tives. How then can academic libraries, under mounting pressure to demonstrate their value (Oakleaf, 2010), justify investments in software development in particular? What follows in these sections is a brief discussion on the importance of investing in software development in libraries, three mini-case studies demonstrating the wide possibilities of integrating software development in library operations and a non-prescriptive decision making paradigm to assess which projects may be worth pursuing from the software development standpoint.

Why Invest in Software Development?

Traditionally, businesses looked at IT systems as "black boxes" where it really did not matter what the interior looked like as long as those systems were able to deliver the value to the customer. Libraries were no different - one look at the literature points to a rich history behind library automation where proprietary systems played a major role (Breeding, 2006; Andrews, 2007). In the initial years, the focus was on automation where libraries cared about automating as many internal operations as possible. And as the years progressed, the expectations from such systems only increased to a point where automation alone wasn't sufficient anymore - integration between the automated components was expected. It can be seen in the natural progression of the vernacular from Automated Library System (ALS) to the Integrated Library System (ILS) (Kinner, & Rigda, 2009). Somewhere along, a big "mental shift" happened in libraries' thinking - the realization that technology could be leveraged not only to optimize the internal operations but also to drive innovation and deliver value to the users. As libraries demanded more of the vendors, the vendors responded by opening up the "black boxes" to give libraries some control over what and how things could be developed. Libraries, in turn, began responding to the local needs by hacking and developing tools on top of ILSes, where feasible.

But, libraries' future is not just in ILSes anymore - a remarkable array of new services are being developed. From generic institutional repositories to specialized subject-based data repositories, from offering mediated access to commodity collections to opening up access to troves of unique special collections - in every facet of the new and emerging programs, one can see the influence of technology driving the future. Though vendors have been great collaborators and partners in working with the libraries to support and sustain traditional library operations, it is imperative for the libraries to take control of their future and make investments in technology to support new and emerging services. Tyler Walters and Katherine, urge research libraries to "Be a doer, not a broker" and to "bring these services in-house (e-publishing services, hosting and curating digital archives, datasets) and seize the moments of opportunity as they arise" (Walters, & Skinner, 2011). Another important way in which developers (within libraries) can be a great asset is by looking out for solutions to solve what were once traditional library problems. Dan Chudnov expressed this sentiment eloquently - "The very notion of what has defined "library automation" for the past 30 years will shrink to mean primarily legacy operations; more and more of our critical systems, standards, and services will come to be supported by solutions developed outside of our community, and customized and optimized within it" (Gordon, 2007). Libraries need to invest in software development activities so that employees can implement this "outside-in" strategy to bring in solutions to solve current library problems from other fields.

THREE CASE STUDIES

This section will discuss 3 short case studies covering the gamut of software development projects - starting with hacking "black box" vendor systems to using APIs to develop custom functionality on top of proprietary systems, and from making simple customizations to open source systems to developing a custom application. It lays the groundwork for the last section, in which the author proposes a framework that IT managers can use to develop a strategy that outlines where the software development resources are best invested for maximum benefit.

One of the two axes that will be part of the matrix, will be introduced in this section – Y-axis or the build-buy axis. The two ends of extremes on this axis are vendor driven solutions (buy) and custom built, in-house solutions (build). That is as we move along the axis, more and more custom development would be involved. We start with a case study (#1) that is closer to the "buy" solution and end with a case study (#3) that is closer to the "build" solution. These case studies are presented from the perspective of a developer and in some cases, manager of a small development team.

Case Study 1

This case study discusses the progression of "hacks" that were developed on a proprietary Integrated Library Systems catalog. The complexity of the implementation gets simpler with each example, even though the impact of the functionality remains the same. Before Library vendors started offering cloud based platforms for ILSes, there was widespread dissatisfaction with the way the Online Public Access Catalogs (OPAC) worked. Roy Tennant's quip about "applying lipstick on pig" (Tennant, 2005) summarizes the extent to which the catalogs were broken. During the same time, several innovative projects started looking at enhancing the catalogs or totally rebuilding the functionality from scratch. At Kansas State University, a decision was made to enhance the catalog through various manageable hacks:

1. **Removing the Leading Article:** Catalogs were notorious for choking on the leading articles when searches were performed. Just when majority of Library users were getting used to the google-way of finding things (mid 2000s), library catalogs still suffered from lack of attention given to the user experience part. Asking users to not type in leading articles in their searches was never a good strategy. In spite of hammering the point through library instruction sessions, search logs revealed a big problem with this functionality. Because the focus was on automating functionality for staff, not much attention was paid to how catalogs were built. Customizing the catalogs in the pre-API era required applying band-aid solutions. To fix the leading article issue, the author wrote a simple javascript that would parse the text entered in the search box and get rid of the leading article. Though the solution required only a few lines of code, it had to be thoroughly tested and modified to work across a variety of browsers and platforms. Furthermore, such hacks had to be manually ported to newer versions, and there was no guarantee that the same code could work.

2. **Adding SMS Functionality in the Catalog:** This functionality was added to the catalog when users started using mobile devices to interact with library services. There were two main reasons why this feature was a welcome addition - Library catalogs were not mobile friendly and the wifi/cellular coverage in the stacks was problematic - users were likely to lookup the information elsewhere, but, wanted an easy way to note it down. Offering a link, that when clicked, would send the bibliographic information along with the call number as a text message turned out to be a useful

solution. The catalog had evolved to using xml and xslt - adding and maintaining this feature was a lot easier using xslt. Porting the code to newer versions was a lot more stable, as, there was less dependence on the user's environment (browser, platform).

3. **Integration With Quasi-Portal:** As campus portal systems evolved to aggregate important student-centered information into one system, Library could leverage this opportunity to push out relevant information pertaining to a student into these systems. One such effort to push out time sensitive information (returns, dues) was undertaken at this University. Luckily, the implementation was much easier, thanks to a well-developed Application Programming Interface (API) by that time. The system would return fines, books due information to the user upon receiving user's unique ID. The users had to sign into only one campus system, and all the important notifications from various departments, including library, was made available in one system. There was not an issue with porting the functionality to newer versions of the catalog, as the functionality was only tied to the catalog's API. As long as the API remained study, no code had to be re-written.

Team

The author worked in a small team comprising of web development librarian, instruction librarian and a staff specialist to identify priorities, implement the code and publicize the enhancements.

Assessment

All these enhancements were huge successes - the leading article fix was reused in future versions of the catalog and other systems (libx); sms feature was used over 12,000 time in less than 18 months; and traffic from the central portal-like system to the library catalog increased after rolling out the notifications feature.

Discussion

All the three examples were enhancements done to a very mature and well known library service - catalog. The enhancements themselves represent a steady progression and improvement in the product i.e, starting with hacking interfaces that were really not set to be customized to adding functionality in a structured way that vendors facilitated. All the librarians, and staff working at the reference desk were aware of the issues and they developed workarounds that became part & parcel of library instruction. The reason for successes:

1. **Mature Services, Need Already Identified:** The author, as a programmer, focused solely on implementing the solution. Because the author worked in a team comprising of knowledgeable folks who understood the problem, articulated the need, took it upon themselves to publicize the solution, the end result was a huge success.
2. **Structure/Staffing:** Though it was a single programmer, these mini hacks were made possible because of the collaboration between the programmer, web development librarian and others. It was an organic development process that did not rely on any formal departmental structures, but rather, on the notion that things needs to be made easier for the Library users.

3. **Hacks Rather Than Full-Fledged Systems:** The programmer could focus exclusively on adding mini functions rather than developing a full-fledged system. The Library relied on the vendor to deliver core functionality that employees relied on and the development resources could be catered to public facing functionality. As Roy Tenant (2005) had suggested, rather than asking vendors for small enhancements, the library added enhancements themselves and reserved bigger requests for the vendor.

4. **Organizational Barriers:** There was little to no organizational resistance to add these features. Catalog was a well-known entity, and many departments within the Library were accustomed to the issues existent within the catalog at that time - so, any enhancements were welcome. There were no clear stakeholders/advocates for the catalog within the library - IT, public services, cataloging department - all had various roles but none of them had all the knowledge and expertise to identify and implement these features in the catalog all by themselves. Collaboration was key and the desire to fix catalog issues was so strong in the organization that, not having a strong advocate, did not matter.

Case Study 2

This case study discusses projects that involved customizing open source applications:

1. **Authorization Scheme Built in Dspace:** Dspace was starting to be used as Institutional repository, initially to archive electronic theses and dissertations, but later to archive faculty's creative output. There was a need to identify user's affiliations to academic departments and to provision user's access to pre-defined set of collections for deposit. Dspace lacked this functionality but, because, it was an open source application, developers could look under the hood and add functionality as was needed. A set of java classes were developed that could lookup user's department affiliation from campus's central authentication and authorization system and integrate it with Dspace. When users are signed into their accounts, they had access to their department's collections without having to go through a manual approval process. Porting this feature to newer versions of Dspace turned out to be a nightmare because the code was deeply tied to the rest of the system and any small changes elsewhere warranted changes to this custom code.

2. **Database of Databases in Wordpress:** There was a need expressed to add descriptions to each research database that the institution subscribed to, and to give users the ability to search within the descriptions and narrow down their database selections. A simple solution was created on top of Wordpress, where by, library faculty could add descriptions, tags, keywords to each database. Users could narrow down the databases by either searching for descriptions or by navigating the tags, and categories. Because of the tags, categories and availability of RSS feeds, the content could be reused and linked to from various other systems without much difficulty.

3. **Bulk Ingest Content Into Dspace:** Though Dspace had the bulk ingest capability, content had to be packaged in a standard way to make this happen. There were several projects where metadata for the content to be ingested was already available in different systems - for example, as MARC records in the ILS, or in MS-Access database, or in excel spreadsheets. The software development team developed a set of scripts that would extract the metadata from these systems, match them up with the digitized files, and package the content in a way that Dspace needed. The team was able to reuse the scripts for each type of data source.

Team

The team comprised of a programmer, systems administrator and a key stakeholder (repository manager, faculty liaison for databases). Whereas the programmer led the actual code development in two cases described above, systems administrator led the code development on the 3rd one. In-house developers were able to mentor systems administrator in the actual code development, thereby increasing the organizational capacity to undertake software development tasks.

Assessment

All the projects were successful judging by whether the original goals of each project were met. The team had good success ingesting materials into Dspace (thousands of records at a time) without having to do it manually or without having to rekey metadata that was already available in other systems. With database of databases, library faculty was able to add meaningful information to the system and users began using tags and categories to narrow down their database selection.

Discussion

A key decision that a development team might encounter during such projects is whether to add functionality to the system itself or to develop that piece of code outside of the system. The decision of course hinges on what other projects are being worked on or other systems are being used locally, but having a dedicated developer who can develop such a strategy always helps. Key takeaways:

1. **Roles and Responsibilities:** Roles and responsibilities were very clear when working with OS projects. Software developers were technical leads whereas repository managers or faculty/department liaisons were project managers for these projects.
2. **Communication:** Because the roles were very well defined, communication was never an issue. It added a few additional steps before the applications could be made live, but, sacrificing speed of development for communication was ok in these cases.
3. **Standards, Policies, and Governance:** A lot more time was spent bringing the right set of stakeholders to the table, creating working groups to evaluate viable options, and making the final decisions. Some of the questions that had to be considered before selecting an open source application included - the type of adoption that application had in libraries, number of contributors to the code, frequency of code contributions to the application (active, passive), code contributors' engagement with the community, and type of skills needed to support the application.

Case Study 3

This case study discusses the applications that were built in-house:

1. **GRA Croplands Research Database:** This database of literature about greenhouse gases and croplands supports the Global Research Alliance (GRA) Croplands Group's mission of reducing greenhouse gas intensity and improving overall production efficiency of cropland systems. The database contains literature about greenhouse gases and many different crops located in various

climates. In addition to journal articles, the content also included conference papers, white papers, videos, data sets, and other useful research files. The database served as a place to preserve grey literature that might be difficult to find on the Internet or that might disappear over time (Olsen, Baillargeon, & Maringanti, 2012). The project team started with a small amount of data to understand challenges involved in editing the data, in identifying and correcting any copyright issues and identifying efficient solutions. In the first phase of the project, features that benefited both the end users and the staff were added to the system. Simple user interface enhancements, such as, listing the controlled vocabulary options as drop downs, cut down on data entry mistakes. Several tools were made available to staff to prepare data for ingestion. The technology stack used to develop the pilot project included Apache, PHP, MySQL and Solr.

2. **Workflow Management System:** Institutional Repository (IR) at Kansas State, K-REx, initially began as a platform for students to electronically deposit their theses, dissertations, and reports. After a few years, library started capturing faculty research and publications in the IR. Based on initial pilot projects, it was clear that libraries would have to devote staff resources to do the submissions and also to process the submissions. Each submission had to go through a set of standard steps and individual staff members were responsible for each step. The standard steps included - contacting the faculty member to get permission to archive their research in the IR, check for copyright permission with the publisher, add metadata and finally submit it for ingestion into the repository. A simple tracking system was needed to track each submission as it went through these steps, one-at-a-time. What started as a tracking system evolved into a complete Workflow Management System (WMS) that had a range of features in it - library staff could do most of their work related to the IR submissions in this system and, at the end, simply submit the record to IR without ever logging into IR. The system was developed using Apache, PHP, and MySQL.

Team

In both the cases, the programming team comprised of IT manager and programmer, worked very closely with the project partners. In the first case, the project partners were librarians who wanted to expand their department's outreach efforts by collaborating with other departments on campus. In the latter case, the project partners included repository manager, staff and librarians across a few departments within the library.

Assessment

The GRA croplands research database has been a huge success. More and more data is being added to the system, even after the original creators left the University. Debbie and Jenny, who worked with programming team on the WMS, wrote - "The workflow management system has been a great success, allowing easy handoffs between several individuals in two different departments and expanding to provide greater efficiency as processes develop. The system was designed with tools to simplify operations, such as the RefWorks interface, and the ability to add new features as needed, such as the publisher data. This flexibility provides the means of increasing both the capacity as well as the efficiency of the overall operation" (Madsen, & Oleen, 2013).

Discussion

Both of the above examples demonstrate the importance of having programming expertise within the Library. One was more focused on improving staff workflows (WMS) whereas the other project created a unique opportunity for the library to be an equal partner with the a respected faculty member on campus. It increased the profile of the library on campus and created more opportunities for the library to partner with faculty on campus on more innovative projects.

The 3 case studies follow a distinct pattern in terms of a direct correlation between the depth and complexity of the coding that was required and the size of the software development team. That is, most of the minor enhancements that were developed on top of the vendor systems happened when the software development team size was small (only 1). Gradually, as more resources were added to the team (with an additional programmer and a systems administrator), the development team could undertake complex projects and pursue innovative projects that needed custom applications to be built. Key lessons that resonate across all the case studies include:

1. **Communication:** It does not matter how talented the developers are - IT staff can no longer rely simply on their technical expertise (Trubitt, & Muchane, 2008). Communication is the responsibility of the software development manager and key library faculty who collaborate on projects. The more a developer's time could be dedicated to the development activities (and not administrative duties), the more projects could be finished in a timely manner. It does put responsibility of advocating for the projects, and championing the outcomes onto others, but it plays to the strengths of individuals.
2. **Culture:** The more the interaction between the IT staff and librarians the better. By working with each other, it helps to close the gaps in terminology, and understand motivations behind each type of position. IT specialist need to recognize that the time spent in meetings are important as bulk of the project's success depends on buy-in, relating to strategic goals and ensuring that right amounts are resources are allocated for the project's continued success. Librarians need to recognize that software development is not a commodity, it is a creative and intellectual process, and IT specialists need to be recognized and acknowledged for the work they create.
3. **Team Size and Structure:** Not one model or method will work in every case. Successful projects depend on the ability of the leadership to discern the right structure in each case. For example, grouping all the programmers in one group has merits but care needs to be taken so that each programmer spends enough time interacting with staff outside of IT to learn relevant subject matter.

SOFTWARE DEVELOPMENT DECISION MATRIX

The case studies discussed above were presented from the perspective of a developer. An organization can inventory the IT projects on the build-buy spectrum and assess its current IT strengths and plan future projects. For example, if the projects are more leaning on the buy end of the axis but future projects point to build approach, then managers need to think about creating support systems for build approach. If more IT projects are on the build end of the axis and the future projects point to buy approach, then the organization may need to hire for different skillsets i.e, rather than hiring software developers, the organization may need to hire system analysts. Langer built on the work of others and outlines reasons on when to support buy approach (cost, time to market, political environment, staff skillset, architectural differences) and when to support build approach (availability of software developers, adapt to changing business needs, competitive advantage, poor quality of prior packaged software). While these reasons give a good insight into when to choose either of the strategies, they do not complete the picture in a business context. Whether the build or buy decision needs to be made at the strategic or operational level (Inman, et al, 2011), analyzing it in the context of business functions is critical for IT managers. To do this, we will now add a second dimension to the decision making paradigm – the second axis called the internal-external axis. The two ends of extremes along the X-axis are internal facing applications and external facing applications. By internal, these applications are primarily geared to automate a functionality that would help library employees in their day-to-day operations. External facing applications are the library online services that users can interact with directly without engaging with any library employees.

Marty Cagan introduces a simple terminology to differentiate between internal and external applications - IT software and Product software. IT software, being internal focused, doesn't have the same set of expectations that Product software carries. For example, if there is an issue with IT software, employees can deal with it. But if there is an issue with the Product software then it reflect very poorly on the organization. She summarizes the difference between these two softwares as - "The truth is that most product software has a much higher bar in terms of the definition, design, implementation, testing, deployment and support than is necessary than most IT software. It's also true that salaries usually reflect this. Finding people with the necessary product software experience is much harder than finding IT experience." Given this reality, it is imperative that Product software projects are approached in a much different way than the traditional IT software projects. One of her recommendations is - "If you can outsource or buy off-the-shelf any of your true IT software (internal-facing software) you should do so, so that you can put your best people, time and mind-share on the customer-facing software" (Cagan, 2008).

It is useful to refer to two related concepts in this regard - Ledeen's "Core Vs Context" and Langar's "Driver/Supporter". These concepts introduce vocabulary that parallels the IT and Product software definitions. Ledeen discusses "core vs context" as one of the criterion to employ while choosing between the build and buy approach. He suggests that "Core activities are those that contribute directly to the organizations differentiation and value creation. Context is everything else." (Ledeen, 2014), in other words, core is "Product software" whereas context is "IT software". Langar employs his "driver/supporter" theory to decide between build and buy approach - "to summarize Driver/Supporter, there are essentially two types of generic functions performed by departments in organizations: driver functions and supporter functions... drivers are defined as those units that engaged in frontline or direct revenue generating activities. Supporters are units that did not generate obvious direct revenues but, rather, were designed to support frontline activities." (Langar, 2016).

For academic libraries that are planning to get into software development, a simple framework is proposed that will outline how to think about prioritizing projects based on available development resources. It is by no means a prescriptive model, but a model that can be used in the planning process to answer questions regarding important software development investments.

The two-dimensional model shown in Figure 1 is one possible way to map all the software development projects that are undertaken in the Library. The two ends of extremes along the X-axis are internal facing applications and external facing applications. Borrowing Ledeen and Langar's terminologies, internal facing applications can also be labeled as "context" or "supporter" applications, while external applications can be labeled as "core" or "driver" applications. The two ends of extremes on the Y-axis are completely vendor driven solutions and custom built, in-house solutions. That is as we move along the axis, more and more custom development would be involved. There are four quadrants in the figure, numbered from 1 through 4.

Figure 1. Two dimensional model

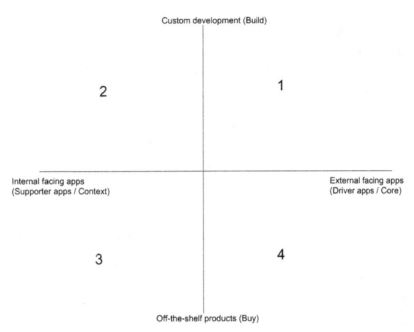

IT leadership and management can use this matrix to audit their current application stack inventory and overlay their software developments projects on top. It can give a visual representation of where they are investing most of their software development (human) and financial (operating or capital IT expenses) resources. IT leaders need to engage library leadership in discussions related to future library priorities and develop a robust application strategy. This is important because IT is still not well integrated into the functioning of research libraries (Roger, 2016 & Hinchliffe, 2016). According to recent S+R report (Roger, 2016), several IT structural models exist within academic libraries. It shows how IT is sometimes is still nascent and libraries are struggling to accommodate IT. It is in this context, that IT managers or directors need to engage library leadership very effectively. Without getting into the nuts and bolts of software development, library leadership can advise IT leaders on how to redistribute resources (or add resources) based on strategic goals. IT leaders can help develop key drivers for each quadrant that can guide the strategy discussions internally.

This chart would give the leadership a yardstick to measure whether IT projects are in alignment with their definition of IT. If IT is viewed mainly as an internal organization then, it is likely that majority of the projects on the chart might fall on the left quadrants (#2,#3) on the chart. As long as the leadership wants it that way, it is fine. But, if leadership wants IT to lead new public facing initiatives and the chart is leaning to the left side of the chart, then it shows a real need to change the approach of IT.

Key Drivers

Assuming that an IT manager has a finite operating budget, a finite set of software development resources, and a set of business problems to solve, the matrix can help in shaping the local application development strategy:

- **When to Choose Custom Development for External Applications (Quadrant #1 in Figure 1; Product Software):** If no existing product in the market can solve a current business need, or if an off-the-shelf product that meets the needs is prohibitively expensive, then one could advocate for custom developing a solution. It is quite normal for institutions to develop custom solutions in what they may see as emerging areas – these areas are relatively new in that workflows, processes and features may not have matured to the point that vendors could implement a common set of features to address the needs across the board. Custom development of digital asset management systems and tools, and emerging custom library catalogs built on black light before the discovery tools became a norm, are some examples in this category. Put it differently, emerging areas have the potential to change the relationship between libraries and academic units – Langer argues that IT needs to be a "driver" in such cases (Langar, 2016). Research data management, Digital Humanities, Digital Scholarship - all are additional examples of areas where Libraries could take the Product Software approach. Langer's conclusion for implementing driver applications is to handle it in-house i.e, employ custom development (build) and Ledeen also concluded that "custom solution for core" approach has ample evidence in his research (Ledeen, 2014). Key success factors: Success in developing custom products hinges on availability of highly skilled developers, product managers reporting through appropriate lines who can communicate information back and forth between stakeholders, end users and the developers (structure), and support from library leadership (alignment with strategy).
- **When to Choose Custom Development for Internal Applications (Quadrant #2 in Figure 1):** The same criteria used above apply in this case, but managers may impose additional restrictions on the budget for internal needs. Marty Cagan makes a great case for investing important resources in the Product Software side of the house – in similar vein libraries need to avoid spending development resources for internal applications, unless it is absolutely necessary. Rather than look at the internal needs in isolation, libraries need to be willing to look at the overall context (strategy, structure) and change their workflows and processes to accommodate existing off-the-shelf products, if they are affordable. Workflow Management System (WMS) discussed as part of case study 3 in the earlier section, falls under this quadrant. There were no off-the-shelf products that addressed the local needs at that point in time. One point to consider is to collaborate with other institutions before embarking on development projects for internal needs – it is likely that, such needs may exist for other institutions and it is always better to collaborate and pool resources together, rather than going solo on such projects. The urgency of the need and the scale of the project will dictate whether a community can be created around such a product.
- **When to Buy Off-the-Shelf Products for External Applications (Quadrant #4 in Figure 1):** If off-the-shelf product exist that meet the requirements and is affordable enough, then, libraries should take this route. If they need the ability to customize the product then those requirements need to be reflected in the specifications list. Libraries always need to develop an exit strategy when considering proprietary products – by having a robust exit strategy they can avoid vendor

lock-in and will be better prepared to engage with new vendors in the market for possible solutions. If off-the-shelf products exist, but are expensive, and local development resources are not sufficient to undertake the development, then library leadership could either re-allocate resources from other areas or make a case for more funding from campus administration. What approach one takes will depend on the need that the product can fulfill.

- **When to Buy Off-the-Shelf Products for Internal Applications (Quadrant #3 in Figure 1):** In cases where off-the-shelf products are affordable and can meet the requirements then libraries should consider taking this approach.

Figure 2 shows an overlay of the case studies on the matrix along with key decision drivers for each quadrant. IT managers need to identify strengths, prioritize local needs and invest their resources appropriately to derive maximum benefits. Going through the exercise of mapping their current applications onto this matrix would help IT managers visualize their current application portfolio. If most of their budget and local development resources are weighed heavily on the left side of the matrix (internal facing), it is a clear indication that they have to modify their strategy to become more user-centric (external facing).

Figure 2.

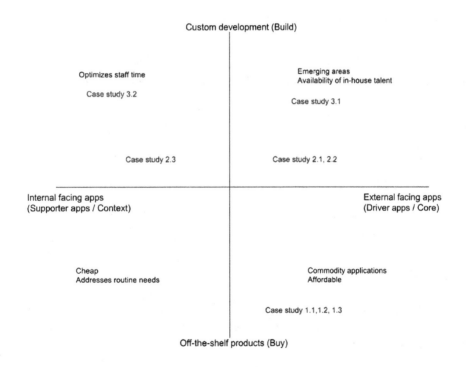

CONCLUSION

Developing institutional capacity to create in-house tools is an important strategic direction for Libraries. While every tool has a finite shelf life, the knowledge gained by developing tools in-house, can be invaluable. It will help libraries - to be doers than mediators, to think critically about their local resources and to drive key emerging initiatives without being excessively dependent on vendors. All software development projects are not created equal – prioritizing projects and committing to invest resources in projects is an important decision that needs to be driven by institutional priorities. Libraries need to develop application development strategy that can help guide decisions on when to develop locally or when to look for off-the-shelf products or some combination of the two. The author proposed a non-prescriptive decision making model in this chapter in the hopes of adding another perspective to this important topic.

REFERENCES

Andrews, M. (2007). Changing Markets, changing relationships. *Library Hi Tech*, 25(4), 562–578.

Breeding, M. (2006). Reshuffling the deck. *Library Journal*, 131(6), 40–50.

Cagan, M. (2008, July 6). Moving from an IT to a Product Organization. Retrieved from http://www.svpg.com/moving-from-an-it-to-a-product-organization

Gordon, R. S. (Ed.). (2007). *Information tomorrow: reflections on technology and the future of public and academic libraries*. Information Today, Inc.

Hinchliffe, L. J., & Askey, D. From Invasive to Integrated: Information Technology and Library Leadership, Structure, and Culture.

Inman, R. A., Sale, R. S., Green, K. W., & Whitten, D. (2011). Agile manufacturing: Relation to JIT, operational performance and firm performance. *Journal of Operations Management*, 29(4), 343–355.

Kinner, L., & Rigda, C. (2009). The integrated library system: From daring to dinosaur? *Journal of Library Administration*, 49(4), 401–417. doi:10.1080/01930820902832546

Langer, A. M. (2016). Build Versus Buy. In Guide to Software Development (pp. 37-48). Springer London.

Ledeen, K. S. (2014). Build v. buy: a decision paradigm for information technology applications.

Madsen, D. L., & Oleen, J. K. (2013). Staffing and workflow of a maturing institutional repository. *Journal of Librarianship and Scholarly Communication*, 1(3), 1–12. doi:10.7710/2162-3309.1063

Oakleaf, M. (2010). *The value of academic libraries: A comprehensive research review and report*. Assoc. of College & Research Lib.

Olsen, L., Baillargeon, T., & Maringanti, H. (2012). Developing an open access croplands research database through global collaboration. *Journal of Agricultural & Food Information*, 13(1), 35–44. doi:10.1080/10496505.2012.639272

Schonfeld, R. C. (2016). Organizing the work of the Research Library.

Tennant, R. (2005, April 15). Digital Libraries: "Lipstick on a Pig." Retrieved from http://lj.libraryjournal.com/2005/04/ljarchives/digital-libraries-lipstick-on-a-pig/

Trubitt, L., & Muchane, M. (2008). In plain English, please: Effective IT communications. *EDUCAUSE Quarterly, 31*(2), 62.

Walters, T., & Skinner, K. (2011). *New roles for new times: Digital curation for preservation.* Association of Research Libraries.

This research was previously published in Developing In-House Digital Tools in Library Spaces; pages 59-75, copyright year 2018 by Information Science Reference (an imprint of IGI Global).

Chapter 70
Quality Assurance Issues for Big Data Applications in Supply Chain Management

Kamalendu Pal

https://orcid.org/0000-0001-7158-6481

City, University of London, UK

ABSTRACT

Heterogeneous data types, widely distributed data sources, huge data volumes, and large-scale business-alliance partners describe typical global supply chain operational environments. Mobile and wireless technologies are putting an extra layer of data source in this technology-enriched supply chain operation. This environment also needs to provide access to data anywhere, anytime to its end-users. This new type of data set originating from the global retail supply chain is commonly known as big data because of its huge volume, resulting from the velocity with which it arrives in the global retail business environment. Such environments empower and necessitate decision makers to act or react quicker to all decision tasks. Academics and practitioners are researching and building the next generation of big-data-based application software systems. This new generation of software applications is based on complex data analysis algorithms (i.e., on data that does not adhere to standard relational data models). The traditional software testing methods are insufficient for big-data-based applications. Testing big-data-based applications is one of the biggest challenges faced by modern software design and development communities because of lack of knowledge on what to test and how much data to test. Big-data-based applications developers have been facing a daunting task in defining the best strategies for structured and unstructured data validation, setting up an optimal test environment, and working with non-relational databases testing approaches. This chapter focuses on big-data-based software testing and quality-assurance-related issues in the context of Hadoop, an open source framework. It includes discussion about several challenges with respect to massively parallel data generation from multiple sources, testing methods for validation of pre-Hadoop processing, software application quality factors, and some of the software testing mechanisms for this new breed of applications

DOI: 10.4018/978-1-6684-3702-5.ch070

INTRODUCTION

All business today understands the value and importance of building an effective supply chain, as part of organizational growth and profitability (Pal, 2017). A supply chain is a network of suppliers, factories, warehouses, distribution centers and retailers, through which raw materials are procured, transformed into intermediate and finished products, and finally delivered the finished products to customers. In this way, a supply chain consists of all the activities associated with the flow and transformation of raw materials stage, through to the end-customers; and as well as the associated information flows. Supply Chain Management (SCM) is a set of synchronized decision and activities, utilized to effectively integrate all relevant business processes to deliver the right products, to the right locations, and at the right time, to optimize system wide costs while satisfying customer service level. Information and Communication Technology (ICT) applications have ushered enormous opportunities to retail supply chain management; and helping it to grow at faster pace. Figure 1 shows a simple diagrammatic representation of a retail supply chain, which highlights some of the main internal business activities.

In addition, retail businesses are evolving into new forms based on knowledge and networks in response to a globalized environment characterized by indistinct organizational boundaries and fast-paced change. These enterprises have understood the importance of enforcing performance tracking of the goals defined by their corporate strategy through metrics-based management (Kaplan & Norton, 1993). The strategic fit requires that a retailer's supply chain achieve the balance between responsiveness and efficiency that best support the business's competitive strategy. A supply chain's performance in terms of responsiveness and efficiency is best on interaction between the following logistical cross-functional drivers of business: demand forecasting, warehousing, scheduling, delivery, inventory planning, and distribution. The performance drivers and some of the related issues are highlighted in Figure 1. Demand forecasting helps more accurate estimation of demand by accessing data of sales, market trends, competitor analysis, and relevant local and global economic factors. Warehousing deals with real-time Big Data-based analysis within the Enterprise Resource Planning (ERP) system and identifying inventory levels, delivery miss-matches, and incoming deliveries. Scheduling plays an important role in SCM. It could help directly increasing visibility of inventory levels, demand, and manufacturing capacity; hence more accurate and distributed scheduling is necessary for global SCM.

Increased internationalization of retail business is changing the operational practices of global retail supply chains, and many retailers have adopted new models, either by outsourcing or by establishing business-alliances in other countries. Globalization has also led to changes in operational practices, where products are manufactured in one part of the world and sold in another. The retail supply chain has become more global in its geographical scope; the international market is getting more competitive and customer demand oriented. Customers are looking for more variety as well as better quality products and services.

Increased customer demand, fierce competitive market conditions, structural complexity of global operations, corporate aspiration of customer satisfying products and services, advances in technological innovation, ICT, have added extra challenges in designing and managing retail supply chains. Over the years, the concepts and practices of SCM have undergone many changes that have been reflected in its '*constantly evolving*' nature. From its initial cost efficiency focus to modern responsive and agile nature, SCM has witnessed a transformational change at the operational frontier. To survive under unpredictable business environment, it has become imperative to function with information driven strategies wherein collaborative business practice among supply chain partners is one of the crucial success factors.

Figure 1. A simple diagrammatic representation of retail supply chain

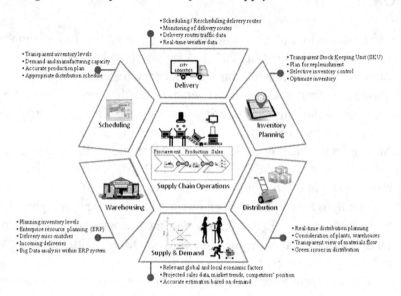

In this way, sharing of business operational information enhances customer services and financial performances by offering correct and relevant real-time information. It also improves supply chain's operational visibility to its collaborative business partners. This also arranges and checks key performance indicators to focus variances and sloppiness and tackles the *bullwhip effect* which is basically happened due to the *mismatch* of demand information while moving from downstream to upstream. However, timely and efficiently an enterprise can formulate an appropriate forward-looking strategy has become a crucial factor in the context of modern SCM. Probing the rich oracles of *Business Intelligence* (BI) and *Business Analytics* (BA) application software, retail enterprises can take the advantages of Big Data-driven insight to work with optimal-lead time and enhance prediction of future to cope-up with uncertainties.

With the rapid evolution and adoption of ICT by the retail industries, deluge of data is being produced all pervasively from each business activity along retail supply chain. This creates a huge chance for retail enterprises to properly use such vast amount of data for making judicious business decisions. As the retail enterprises are changing towards a new kind of ICT laid digital infrastructure, where every object linked with a supply chain is now acting like as a continuous producer of data in structured and unstructured form. This is ushering a new era of digitized supply chain, which can act as an intelligent ICT based decentralized real-time data production system. In this system, the real and virtual worlds are connected through a cyber-physical connectivity wherein the products and machineries independently exchange and respond to information for managing end-to-end processes. It offers a technological platform to agglutinate production technologies and smart process to establish a smart factory. It is providing organizations an unprecedented opportunity to leverage informed supply chain strategy for leveraging competitive advantage. Managing such mega volume of data, commonly referred to as Big Data, is a challenging task. Understanding and tracking of data generation and then processing of data for deriving useful information to operate a smart supply chain stands as the key to success. Analytics thus play a vital role in formulating smart strategies for enhancing the performance of a retail supply chain.

Retail supply chain managers are increasingly seeking to '*win with data*'. They are reliant upon data to gain visibility into expenditure, looking for trends in corporate operational cost and related performance, and support process control, inventory monitoring, production optimization, and process improvement efforts. In fact, many retail businesses are awash in data, with many seeking to capture data analysis as a means for gaining a competitive advantage (Davenport, 2006). In this way, appropriate data capture, data cleaning, and different data analysis techniques are each thought to be part of an emerging competitive area that will transform the way in which retail supply chains are designed and managed. In addition, due to the huge volume of generated data, the fast velocity of arriving data, and the large variety of heterogeneous data, the Big Data-based applications bring new challenges. It is a hard job to test the correctness of a Big Data-based software system due to its enormous size and timeliness. This is an important concern for Big Data-based software system practitioners who are motivated to come up with innovative ways of thinking about how data is produced, organized, and analyzed. Thus, Big Data-based systems quality assurance plays a crucial role.

BIG DATA AND THEIR IMPACT ON SUPPLY CHAIN MANAGEMENT

Big Data is one of the most '*hyped*' terms in the business information systems world now-a-days; however, there is no consensus as to how to define it. The term is often referred to data, which goes beyond the processing capacity of the standard relational database management systems. Moreover, to the aspect that sheer size of Big Data (e.g. an enormous number of transactions, real-time data streams from sensors, mobile devices) is a key factor. This type of data is typically generated by controlled interactions between enterprise and its customers and other internal / external stakeholders through a defined set of enterprise applications and interfaces. The structure of this data is decided in design time and generally relational in nature. For example, data generated by ecommerce, Enterprise Resource Planning (ERP), Customer Relationship Management (CRM), Human Resource Management (HRM), and Accounting Information Systems (AIS) including general ledger are all part of transactional data. In addition, retail business observational data are also part of this deluge of raw information source. This type of data is typically generated by automated machines / sensors as ancillary to the main application data while business processes get executed. The structure of this data through typically decided in design time; but they are non-relational in nature. The examples include data arising from blogs, sensors that monitor specific events, customer call logs in call centers, and so on. There are also issues around how to identify dedicated techniques to analyses this huge volume of data to unlock business critical information from it. Doing so would lead subsequently to important knowledge used to manage the retail supply chain.

This also forms the basis for the most used definition of Big Data, the five V's: Volume, Velocity, Variety, Veracity, Values; and some of the data sources are shown in Figure 2.

- **Volume:** The volume refers to huge amount of information involved. The huge volume of data can be advantageous for the predictive data analytics purpose. In other words, this massive volume of data may enhance the data analysis models by having more business situations available for forecasts and increase the number of factors to be considered in the models making them more realistic. On the other hand, the volume bears potential challenges for data processing infrastructures to deal with enormous amounts of data, when considering its second V-feature – velocity.
- **Velocity:** The velocity, with which data flows into the retail supply chain environment, or the expected response time to the data, is the second V-feature of Big Data. In genuine business environment, Big Data may arrive in high speed in real-time or near real-time. If data arrives too

quickly the information processing infrastructures may not be able to respond timely to it, or even fail to store these data. Such adverse cases may result to data inconsistencies hazards. However, real-time or nearly real-time information makes it possible for a retail business to be much more *agile* than its competitors.

- **Variety:** Data comes from different data sources. In other words, this characteristic refers that data comes in many formats, not falling into the rigid relational structures of SQL (Standard Query Language) databases without loss of information. Some of data stream may be saved as blobs inside traditional data base. The data processing infrastructures for Big Data are referred as NoSQL (i.e. not only SQL). Examples of diverse sources and types of data are typical business documents, transactional records and unstructured data in form of images, videos, HTML web pages, text, email messages, streams from environmental monitoring sensors, GPS (Global Positioning, System) data, click stream from web queries, social media updates, and so on) data, click stream from web queries, social media updates, and so on. Social interaction data is typically gathered from voluntary participation of the stakeholders of a retail business through a defined process or casual interactions. The structure of this data is typically open / free following and not decided in design time of the enterprise processes or applications. This includes feedback from customers, information gathered from social media like Twitter, Google Plus, LinkedIn, Facebook and so on.

Figure 2. The typical types of Big Data application systems

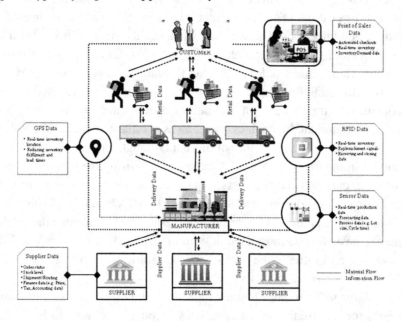

- **Veracity:** This feature defines in relation to two aspects: *data consistency* and *data trustworthiness* in a business environment. Consistency refers to data set must be statistically reliable; and data trustworthiness relates to number of factors (e.g. data origin, data collection and processing methods, facilities within Big Data-based information systems infrastructure). The data must be in a secure environment during the whole of their lifecycle from collection from trusted sources to processing on trusted software systems infrastructure.

- **Value:** The fourth V-feature for Big Data is value. The Big Data Value dimension denotes the potential value of Big Data which first requires processing, to make it useful for retail business decision making purposes. The Value feature bears special importance for retail supply chain design and management point of view.

Big Data is changing the way resources are used within retail business environment. The managerial challenges are immensely acknowledged within academics and practitioners; it is also highlighted that senior decision makers must embrace evidence-based decision-making (McAfee & Brynjolfsson, 2012). Detail analysis and interpretation from Big Data can help those in global retail business to make judicious decisions. In addition, it can help deepening customer engagement, optimize retail operational costs, able to provide business operational risks related warnings, managing resource management appropriately and capitalizing on new source of revenue. This extra demand on Big Data-based software applications for clear insights needs an innovative approach. An approach to find out meaningful value from Big Data-based software processing power as well as abilities to analyses the data (analytics) as well as appropriate skills.

In this way, data manipulation mechanisms transform data into information. Knowledge workers equipped with analytical tool identify pattern in the information and create rules and models, to be used to develop global retail business strategies. Retail enterprises gain wisdom by reviewing the impact of their strategies. Value resides in Big Data, and the insights derived from the data can be leveraged for improved operational competitive advantage. Researchers and practitioners (Davenport & Harris, 2007; Gorman, 2012) define analytics by three categories:

1. **Descriptive Analytics:** These types of analytics prepare and analyses historical data; and identify patterns from samples for reporting trends.
2. **Predictive Analytics:** These types of analytics predict future probabilities and trends; and find relationships in data that may not be clear with descriptive analysis.
3. **Prescriptive Analytics:** These types of analytics evaluate and use innovative ways to operate; consider business operational objectives; and try to mitigate all business constraints.

In addition, International Business Machines (IBM) Corporation provides the definition of Social Media Analytics and Entity Analytics (Dietrich, Plachy, & Norton, 2014). Social media analytics try to analysis data based on pattern embedded in it; and they use data classification and clustering mechanisms. The main characteristic of social media analytic is that data do not originate from within an enterprise; and which are simply considered as transactional data (e.g. data from social media). Entity Analytics focus on sorting and grouping data belonging to the same entity together. Modern computing power permits the analysis of data in a much more quickly, and detailed fashion than ever before.

In a broad range of functional areas within retail supply chain, data is being collected at unprecedented scale. Decisions that previously were based on guesswork, or on painstakingly constructed models of reality, can now be made based on the data itself. Such Big Data analysis now drives nearly every aspect of global retail business. The promise of Big Data-driven decision-making is now being recognized broadly, and there is growing enthusiasm for the research challenges within academics and practitioners. While the potential advantages of Big Data are real and significant, and some initial successes have already been achieved, there remain many technical challenges that must be addressed to fully realize this potential.

RESEARCH IN BIG DATA-BASED SUPPLY CHAIN APPLICATIONS

In recent years Big Data and Business Analytics have attracted burgeoning interest among researchers due their potential in business community (Waller & Fawcett, 2013). Particularly, a research conducted by IBM Institute for Business Value in collaboration with MIT Sloan Review revealed the importance of Big Data to business managers. The subject has been embraced in special journals including Harvard Business Review articles (McAfee & Brynjolfsson, 2012; Davenport & Patio, 2012; Barton & Court 2012); and some articles in MIT Sloan Management Review (Wixom & Ross, 2017). However, despite increasing contributions, Big Data-based software applications in supply chain management (SCM) are still in their infancy.

J R Stock (Stock, 2013) discusses Big Data driven supply chain management related issues in one of his recent publications; and he also proposes that Big Data-based analytics for SCM will allow decision makers to make faster decisions. In an industry survey conducted by Mitsubishi Heavy Industries and consulting company Deloitte (Deloitte & MHI, 2014); supply chain executives were questioned about innovations that drive supply chains. The main objective was to get the views of business executives on emerging technology trends that could dramatically impact supply chains of the future. The survey also identified areas for analytic-based SCM. The Council for Supply Chain Management Consultants published a report on Big Data in SCM, based on interviews with supply chain managers. One of the objectives of this research was to find out best practices in using Big Data for better SCM performance. Many commercial Big Data applications related to SCM are attracted the attention of academics and practitioners (Watson, Lewis, Cacioppo, & Jayaraman, 2013; Davenport, 2006; Davenport & Harris, 2007; McAfee & Brinjals, 2012; Deloitte & MHI, 2016). For example, a few researches work in corporate marketing management are showing tremendous opportunity in Big Data-based business analytics. The number of publications on supply chain network design using Big Data-based business analytics is also growing ceaselessly (Baseness, 2014; Dietrich, Plachy, & Norton, 2014; Swathi, 2012; Siegel, 2013; Watson, Lewis, Cacioppo, & Jayaraman, 2013).

It is evident from research literature review that the critically important organizational functions of SCM will evolve and adapt to Big Data analytics. An industry report (Deloitte & MHI, 2016) expressed a view about the potential of supply chains to deliver massive economic and environmental rewards for society. However, to fulfill this potential, the report suggests technological innovation will need to play a crucial role. Big Data analytics can provide step-change improvements in supply chain visibility, cost savings, and customer service. The key is to not only generate insightful data analysis, but to share it between business partners along retail supply chain so that they can act on it.

To solve a problem, Big Data-based application used intelligent reasoning in automated software environment that helps users apply analytical and scientific methods to business decision making. The software applications that focus on the retail supply chain domain are referred to as retail decision support systems, providing Big Data-based tools to support a user for global supply chain related reasoning process to come up with a solution to a problem. This type of reasoning can be considered an intellectual process by which retail managers use diverse types of artificial intelligence-based inference mechanisms (e.g. rule-based reasoning, case-based reasoning, model-based reasoning, and neutral network-based reasoning) to solve day-to-day operational problems.

Each of these approaches focuses on enriching some aspects of the traditional retail intelligent decision support systems. In addition, these automated software systems regularly make use of models that are expected to be reasonably accurate reflections of real-world work practices. In the term, *reasonably accurate*, one discovers the need of evaluation. The way these models are obtained and deployed across decision-making entities (i.e. *human* and *machine*) can introduce inconsistencies, incompleteness, re-dundancies, as well as problems in coordination. Consequently, there is a clear need for the evaluation of Big Data-based systems that are intended for serious business use.

Moreover, considering both the proliferation of Big Data-based analytics use for global retail business management and the fact that the data upon which these software applications (i.e. analytics) functions rely are often error-prone; there is an important need to assess the *data quality* as it pertains to the field of global retail management. As such, poor data quality can have a direct impact on retail supply chain operational decisions; and this will promote several tangible and intangible losses for global business. Retail operational managers are seeing the problems and impacts attributed to poor *data quality* grow-ing in importance.

Many of the issues in Big Data-based retail supply chain related applications may not be new, but there is an evolving positive view of business analytics that is resulting in significant business transfor-mations. The use of the term business analytics is now becoming standard to communicate the full life cycle of enhanced data-driven business decision making. Big data is the key ingredient in the estimation of many analytical models and the well-known garbage in, garbage out principle continues to apply. In Big Data era, the requirement that data must be accurate remains a critical issue. Data quality assurance is playing key role in different problem domains of supply chain management (e.g. sales forecasting, risk management, raw material procurement system).

BIG DATA-BASED SOFTWARE APPLICATIONS TESTING APPROACH

Testing Big Data-based applications is one of the crucial challenges faced by software development community. This is due to lack of knowledge on what to test; how to test; and how much data to test. In addition, Big Data-based application developers have been facing daunting challenges in creating the best strategies for structured and unstructured data validation; formulating an appropriate software test framework, working with broader use of existing data, integration of new sources of data, and making sure to maintain the standard of in-house quality assurance practices. These challenges are causing in inferior quality of data in production and delayed implementation and increase in total product cost. Robust Big Data-based applications testing strategy need to be defined for validating structured and unstructured data. Additionally, early identification of defects in Big Data-based software helps to mini-mize the overall deployment cost and time to market.

Big Data-based technologies are mainly classified into three distinct types: *file system*, *computing frameworks*, and *tools for analytics*. File system is responsible for the organization, storage, naming, sharing, and protecting files. Big Data-based application frameworks are often categorized into two: *open-source frameworks*, and *commercial frameworks*. Well known open source *frameworks* are - Apache Hadoop (Hadoop, 2017), Spark (Spark, 2017), Storm (Storm, 2017), and S4 (S4, 2017). Google offers Big Query (BigQuery, 2017) to operate on Google Big Table, Amazon support Big Data through Hadoop cluster, and NoSQL support of columnar database using Amazon DynamoDB are the few examples of commercial frameworks. The brief descriptions of the several Big Data tools can be found in academic literatures (Kune, Konugurthi, Agarwal, Chillarige, & Buyya, 2016). Technical details of these technolo-gies are beyond the scope of this chapter.

Different software testing mechanisms (e.g. functional, non-functional) are used along with test data and test environment management to make sure that the data from different sources (e.g. retail business in-house data, data from outside sources) is processed error free and is of good quality to perform analysis. Functional testing mechanisms, like validation of map reduce process, structured and unstructured data validation, data storage validation are essential to make sure that the data is correct, in consistent format, and is of quality assured. Except functional validations other non-functional testing (e.g. *failover* testing, system *performance* testing, *service level agreement* testing) are also play crucial role in Big Data-based applications development.

To discuss different Big Data-based application testing mechanism, this chapter uses an open source software framework (i.e. Hadoop) for explanation purpose. Hadoop uses its own distributed file system, HDFS (Hadoop Distributed File System), which extends the native file system of the host operating system (e.g. UNIX, Linux, Windows). Hadoop is not actually a single product but is instead a growing collection of components and related projects. Figure 3 shows a typical Big Data architecture diagram and highlights the areas where testing should be focused. A brief description of the relevant technical terms in this architecture is explained in Table 1.

Figure 3. A typical Big Data architecture highlighting the areas of testing

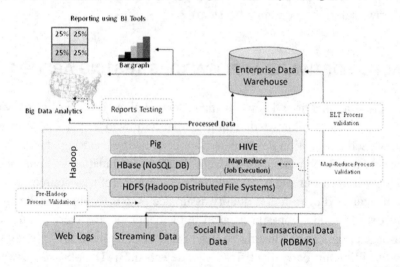

Big Data implementation deals with written complex Pig, Hive programs and running these jobs using Hadoop map educe framework on huge volumes of data across different nodes. Hadoop is a framework that allows for the distribution processing of large data sets across clusters of computers. Hadoop uses Map/Reduce, where the application is divided into many small fragments of work, each of which may be executed or re-executed on any node in the cluster. Hadoop utilizes its own distributed file system, HDFS, which makes data available to multiple computing nodes.

A step-by-step process need to follow in testing Big Data systems, using Hadoop ecosystem. First step loading source data into HDFS involves in extracting the data from different source systems and loading into HDFS. Data is extracted using crawl jobs web data, tools like sqoop for transactional data and then loaded in HDFS by splitting into multiple files. Once this step is completed second step perform map reduce operations involves in processing the input files and applying map and reduce operations to get a desired output. Last setup extracts the output results from HDFS involves in extracting the data output generated out of second step and loading into downstream systems which can be enterprise data warehouse for generating analytical reports or any of the transactional systems for further processing.

Big Data-Based Software Applications Testing

Poor implementation of Big Data-based software applications can lead to poor quality, and delays in testing. Performing functional testing can identify data quality issues that originate in errors with coding or distributed node configuration; effective test data and test environment management ensures that data from a variety of sources is of enough quality for accurate analysis and can be processed without error.

Table 1. Technical description in Hadoop framework

Technical Term	Brief Description
Web Logs	Log files from a web server and based on the values contained in the "Log files", derives indicators about when, how, and by whom a web server is visited.
Streaming Data	Streaming data is data that is generated continuously by thousands of data sources, which typically send in the data records simultaneously, and in small size (order of kilobytes). Streaming data includes a wide variety of data such as log files generated by customers using their mobile device or web-based applications, and so on.
Social Data	Social data is information that social media users publicly share, which includes metadata such as the user's location, language spoken, biographical data and / or shared links. Social data is valuable to marketers looking for customer insights that may increase sales of a particular retail product.
Transactional Data	Transactional data are information directly derived as a result of transactions. Unlike other sorts of data, transactional data contains a time dimension which means that there is timeliness to it and over time.
HDFS	Hadoop uses its own distributed file system, HDFS (Hadoop Distributed File System), which extends the native file system of the host operating system (e.g. UNIX, Linux, Windows).
HBase	Apache HBase is an open source; non-relational database modeled after Google's Bigtable and is written in Java. It runs on top of HDFS. It provides a fault-tolerant way of storing enormous quantities of *sparse data*.
PIG	Apache Pig provides an alternative language to SQL (Structured Query Language), called Pig Latin, for querying data stored in HDFS. Pig does not require the data to be structured as relational database tables.
HIVE	Hive is a software tool that structures data in Hadoop into the form of relational-like tables and allows queries using a subset of SQL.
EDW	Enterprise Data Warehouse (EDW) is a database that stores all information associated with a business. EDW contains data related to areas that the business wants to analyze for business intelligence (BI) operation.

Apart from functional testing, non-functional testing (e.g. performance testing, failover testing) plays a key role in ensuring the scalability of the process. Functional testing is performed to identify functional coding issues and requirements issues, while non-functional testing identifies performance bottlenecks and validates the non-functional requirements. The size of Big Data applications often makes it difficult or too costly to replicate the entire system in a test environment; a smaller environment must be created instead, but this introduces the risk that applications that run well in the smaller test environment behave differently in production.

Therefore, it is necessary that the system engineers are careful when building the test environment, as many of these concerns can be mitigated by carefully designing the system architecture. A proper systems architecture can help eliminate performance issues (such as an imbalance in input splits or redundant shuffle and sort), but, of course, this approach alone doesn't guarantee a system that performs well.

The numerical stability of algorithms also becomes an issue when dealing with statistical or machine learning algorithms. Applications that run well with one dataset may abort unexpectedly or produce poor results when presented with a similar but poorly conditioned set of inputs. Verification of numerical stability is particularly important for customer-facing systems.

Two key areas of the testing problem are: (1) establishing efficient test datasets and; (2) availability of Hadoop-centric testing tools (e.g. PigUnit, Junit for Pig).

Testing should include all four phases shown in Figure 4. Data quality issues can manifest themselves at any of these stages.

Figure 4. Testing phases

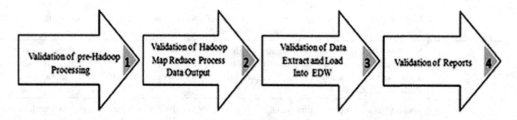

Testing Methods for Validation of Pre-Hadoop Processing

Big Data systems typically process a mix of both structured data (e.g. POS transactions, call detail records, general ledger transactions, and call center transactions). Unstructured data (such as user comments, insurance claims descriptions and web logs) and semi-structured social media data (from sites like Twitter, Facebook, LinkedIn and Pinterest). Often the data is extracted from its source location and saved in its raw or a processed form in Hadoop or another Big Data database management system. Data is typically extracted from a variety of source systems and in varying file formats (e.g. relational tables, fixed size records, flat CSV files with delimiters, XML files, JSON and text files).

The most important activity during data loading is to compare data to ensure extraction has happened correctly and to confirm that the data loaded into the HDFS (Hadoop Distributed File System) is a complete, accurate copy.

Typical Tests Include

1. **Data Type Validation:** Data type validation is customarily carried out on one or more simple data fields. The simplest kind of data type validation verifies that individual characters provided through user input are consistent with the expected characters of one or more known primitive data types as defined in a programming language or data storage and retrieval mechanism.

2. **Range and Constraint Validation:** Simple range and constraint validation may examine user input for consistency with a minimum/maximum range, or consistency with a test for evaluating a sequence of characters, such as one or more tests against regular expressions.
3. **Code and Cross-Reference Validation:** Code and cross-reference validation includes tests for data type validation, combined with one or more operations to verify that the user-supplied data is consistent with one or more external rules, requirements or validity constraints relevant to an organization, context or set of underlying assumptions. These additional validity constraints may involve cross-referencing supplied data with a known look-up table or directory information service.
4. **Structured Validation:** Structured validation allows for the combination of any number of various basic data type validation steps, along with more complex processing. Such complex processing may include the testing of conditional constraints for an entire complex data object or set of process operations with a system.

Testing Methods for Hadoop MapReduce Processes

Hadoop MapReduce: Hadoop MapReduce, as shown in Figure 5, is a software framework for easily written applications that process vast amounts of data (multi-terabyte datasets) in-parallel on large cluster (thousands of nodes) of commodity hardware in a reliable fault-tolerant manner.

Figure 5. Hadoop MapReduce software framework

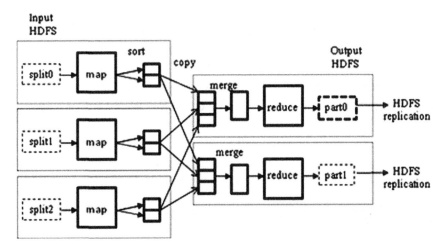

A MapReduce job usually splits the input dataset into independent chunks that are processed by the map tasks in a completely parallel manner. The framework sorts the outputs of the maps, which are then input to the reduce tasks. Typically, both the input and the output of the job are stored in a file system. The framework takes care of scheduling tasks and monitoring them and re-executed the failed tasks.

ETL Process: ETL is a variation of the Extract, Transform, Load (ETL), a data integration process in which transformation takes place on an intermediate server before it is loaded into the target. This capability is most useful for processing the large data set required for BI and BA.

Testing Methods for Data Extract and EDW Loading

The major part of the data warehouse system is data extraction, transformation and loading (ETL). The goal is to extract the data, often from a variety of different systems, and transform it so that it is uniform in terms of format and content, and, finally, to load the data into a warehouse where it can serve as the basis for business intelligence needs.

The integrity of the data must be maintained at every step. It must be stored clearly and concisely without loss and should be accessible to all authorized professionals. So, for the data warehouses to deliver value, they require carful ETL testing to ensure that processes work as required.

The different methods for ETL testing depend on the challenges faced in performing this testing. The following are some of the main challenges to overcome.

- **No User Interface**: In data warehouse testing, no user interface is present by only data and its relations are there. To test this type of data, the ability to look at data, validate data processing rules, and analyze final data output are required. Consequently, knowledge of database query languages like SQL is essential for testers to do this accurately, where traditional manual testing skills are not enough.
- **Huge Volume of Data**: Millions of transactions can be happening every day. It is a challenge to verify the extraction, transformation and loading of that data in the real-time environment as the code is updated.
- **Variety of Sources**: Typically, a wide variety of systems feed daily transactional data to a data warehouse. Some of the data may even come from systems used in cloud computing or hosted by a third party. Similarly, the format and content of the data will vary. It is often a huge challenge to merge the data while making sure that everything gets processed consistently and in relation to each other.
- **Bad or Missing Data**: The information collected from the various source systems may not be complete, may have many special cases requiring exception processing, or may be of poor quality generally.
- **Non-Static Rules**: The source systems will likely change over time because of release upgrades with attendant changes in data content and structure. There should be ways to cope with these changes without having to change the design of the data warehouse.

Testing Methods for Reports

Big Data analytics solutions are built to report and analyze data from data warehouses. They can vary in size and complexity depending on the needs of the business, underlying data stores, number of reports and number of users. The key focus is on validating layout format as per the design mock-up, style sheets, prompts and filter attributes and metrics on the report. Verification of drilling, sorting and export functions of the reports in Web environment is also done. Data generated on the reports should be corrected as per business logic. The test team needs to target the lowest granularity that is present in the data warehouse, understanding each report and the linkages of every field displayed in the report with the schema. Tracing its origin back to the source system is a big challenge and a time-consuming process.

SCOPE AND PROCESS OF BIG DATA APPLICATION QUALITY ASSURANCE

Big Data-based software Quality Assurance (QA) has its roots in assuring the quality of manufactured physical product. In manufacturing product QA is performed by inspecting the product and evaluating its quality near its completion or at various stages of production process. However, software is not as tangible as manufactured engineering products which are much more physical items by nature. But a software product is *'invisible in nature'* and it is characterized by its functionalities. This invisible nature of software product creates extra problems of assessing its quality. In this way, engineering manufactured products are visible, whereas software engineering products are invisible. Majority of the defects in an industrial engineering product can be detected during the manufacturing and fabrication processes. However, defects in software products are invisible that makes its incorrectness identification much harder and as a result software quality assurance is very complex. Moreover, there are additional problems with assessing software quality; and this is attributed to its recent trend of software product design and development. For example, now-a-days software products are often developed by global teams of professional spanning multiple countries, multiple development platforms, and multiple layers of interfaces between software components.

Different academics and practitioners have different views on the source of the software quality attributes. Juran and his fellow practitioners (Juran & Gryna, 1970) define software quality as 'fitness for use' and 'customer impression' and later 'freedom of deficiencies'. A second view is that of Crosby (Crosby, 1979) who defines quality as both the 'conformance to requirements' and 'non-conformance implies defects. A third view is that of Roger Pressman (Pressman, 2000) who states that there are three requirements for software quality, namely 'specific functional requirements', 'adhering to quality standards in the contract' and lastly 'good software engineering practices.

These views on software quality has suggested to approaches of measuring the quality of Big Data-based software applications. The entire process of Big Data-based software development is guided by software engineering techniques and the assessment of the quality of the software is carried out during the quality assurance process. In software engineering, different techniques are used to design and develop software applications based on business requirements. At the same time, software quality assurance (SQA) mechanisms manage quality of software during the software development process. SQA defines and measures the inputs and outputs of the development processes and qualifies the quality of the software in terms of defects. To assess the software quality, it is advantageous to identify what aspect of software need to measure.

Factors that Impact Software Application Quality

McCall (McCall, 1977) has identified three different categories of factors that software quality can come under. The factors are spread over the lifespan of the application and not only its original development. The first set of factors is associated with the original operation of the software product by a user. The second set of factors is directed towards the revision of the product from an existing product to new or enhanced product and how the quality of the original design and code allows for this revision. The last set of factors is concerned with the transaction of the product to another target environment, such as a new database or operating system. The factors are outlined in the Table 2.

In this chapter, software quality assurance (SQA) is considered as a process for the measurement of deliverables and activities during each stage of Big Data-Based software application development lifecycle. The objective of SQA is to quantify the quality of the products and the activities giving rise to them and to guide a quality improvement effort. For discussion, this chapter considers that Big Data-based software applications assurance activities take place at each development stage of the application development lifecycle. The stages are categorized into areas for requirements capture, system design, coding and testing, and finally release.

Table 2. McCalls Quality factors for new software development

Quality Factors for New Software Development s for		
Product Operational	**Product Revision**	**Product Transaction**
Correctness Reliability Efficiency Integrity Usability	Maintainability Flexibility Testability	Portability Reusability Interoperability

In general, Big Data-based application quality assurance refers to the study and application of various assurance process, methods, standards, criteria, and systems to ensure the quality of Big Data system in terms of a set of quality parameters. Figure 6 shows a sample scope of validation for quality assurance of Big Data-based supply chain management applications.

Figure 6. The scope of validation for Big Data application system quality

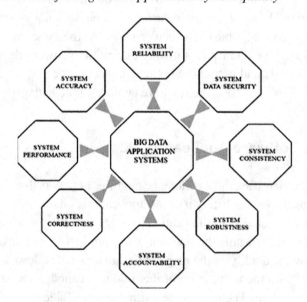

Conventional system quality parameters such as performance, robustness, security, etc., can be applicable to Big Data systems. These are listed below:

- **System Reliability:** Software systems reliability means the ability of an application (e.g. product or service) to perform as expected over time; and this is usually measured in terms of the probability of it performing as expected over time.

Figure 7. A quality test process for Big Data-based application systems

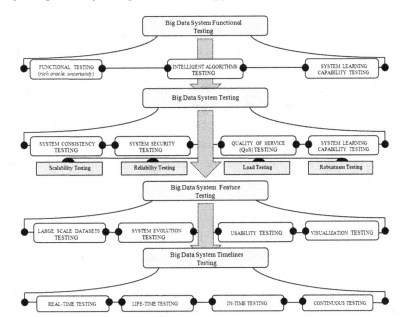

- **System Data Security:** Software systems data security could be used to evaluate the security of Big Data applications indifferent perspectives. Using this criterion, data security could be evaluated in various aspects at various levels of software system application user hierarchy.
- **System Consistency:** The absence of difference, when comparing two or more test case outputs in software testing environment.
- **System Robustness:** System robustness complements correctness. Correctness addresses the behavior of a system in case covered by its specification; robustness characterized what happens outside of the specification. In this way, robustness is the ability of software systems to react appropriately to abnormal conditions.
- **System Accountability:** System accountability quality factor can be divided up into three processes. First, one must identify relevant parties, for what they are accountable, and to whom they are accountable. Second, if a condition verifies for which a party was previously identified as accountable, a forum of some kind convenes to gather the necessary information and passes a judgement as to the accountability of the said party. Third, one must assign positive or negative sanctions to the responsible party.

- **System Correctness:** System correctness is the very essential quality criteria for Big Data analytic applications. It is the quality criteria of software applications to perform their specific tasks, as specified by their specification. If a Big Data-based analytic application does not do what it is meant to do, everything else (e.g. nice graphical user interface, appropriate algorithm to data processing) about it matters little.
- **System Performance:** This quality criterion indicates the performance of the system, such as availability, response time, throughput, scalability, and so on.
- **System Accuracy:** System accuracy criterion indicates the results of Big Data-based software systems as anticipated.

The promise of Big Data-driven decision making is now being recognized broadly, and there is a growing enthusiasm for business analytics quality assurance related testing methods. Heterogeneity, scale, timeliness, and privacy problems with supply chain Big Data impede process at all phases of the pipeline that can create value from this huge data set. The problems start right away during operational data acquisition, data cleaning, and selecting the right data for decision-making software applications. One of the main problems about what data to keep and what data to discard, and how to store that make data to be reliable for the indented applications. Much supply chain operational data today is not natively structured format; for example tweets and blogs are weakly structured pieces of text, while images and video are structured format for storage and display. Therefore, getting the appropriate data set is a challenging task.

Nevertheless, this chapter will highlight a simplistic view of Big Data-based software testing that consists of systems functional testing aspects (e.g. rich oracle, uncertainty), intelligent algorithms testing (e.g. scalability, reliability, load, robustness), and system learning capability testing. A brief over view of Big Data-based software testing is shown in Figure 7.

There are two typical Big Data applications: (a) recommendation systems, and; (b) prediction systems. Figure 8 summarizes the typical quality factors for prediction and recommendation systems in a fishbone diagram, and a brief description of those factors are presented in the next section.

Quality Factors for Prediction Systems

- **System Correctness:** System Correctness is a quality factor used to evaluate the correctness of the Big Data applications. Unlike the conventional system, Big Data applications are hard to validate for correctness. For instance, prediction-related software is mainly developed to make predictions about real world activities. Hence, it is difficult to determine the correct output for those types of software. Correctness is related to the prediction pattern or model. For instance, some models are more likely used to predict point of inflexion values while some other models do well in predicting continuity. Thus, to verify the correctness of the system effectively, engineers need to evaluate the capability of prediction in the specified conditions and environments.
- **System Accuracy:** System Accuracy is used to evaluate if the system yields true (no systematic errors), and consistent (no random errors) results. Some Big Data applications are developed to find previous unknown answers; thereby only approximate solutions might be available. This can be called uncontrollable prediction. Some prediction is used to prevent something happening in the future, and the prediction result will affect actions or behaviours. In turn, those actions can promote the prediction result.

- **System Stability:** System Stability reflects the stability of the system prediction while the environment or data changes. For example, the prediction capability of a system is stable with minor changes when statistical data are acquired from different timeframes.
- **System Consistency:** System Consistency is a quality indicator useful to evaluate the consistency of the targeted system in different perspectives. Due to the inherent uncertainties in system models, some applications do not produce a single correct output for a given set on inputs. This leads to hardly determining the expected behaviours of the software. In such situations, domain-specific experts could provide opinions to support system consistency.

Figure 8. Big Data Application System Quality Factors

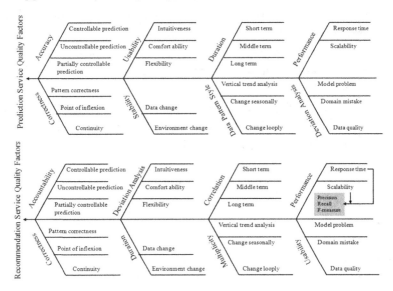

- **Duration:** Duration indicates the expected prediction period. It can measure how up-to-date the data is, and whether it is correct despite the possibility of modifications or changes that impact time and date values. For instance, commonly-used prediction duration in enterprise management can be divided into short term, middle term, and long term.
- **Deviation Analysis:** Deviation Analysis is used to analyze the prediction deviation within an accepted range or confidence interval.
- **System Usability:** System usability is a parameter that indicates how well the Big Data application service can be used. This can be very subjective due to different developers and users having diverse user experiences. The typical usability factors include intuitiveness, comfortability, and flexibility.

This aspect concerns understandability – the users' effort for recognizing the logical concept and its applicability; learnability – the users' effort for learning its application; operability – the users' effort for operation and operation control.

- **System Performance:** System Performance is a distinct quality factor for Big Data application service. It is useful to evaluate how well Big Data is structured, designed, collected, generated, stored, and managed to support large-scale prediction services.

QUALITY FACTORS FOR RECOMMENDATIONS

- **Correctness:** This quality factor reflects if the recommended service or commodity meets the demands of customers. Correctness could be subjective between different persons. Thus, how to measure correctness is still a challenge for quality assurance engineers.
- **Correlation:** This quality factor evaluates the degree of correlation of the recommended service. This involves various recommendation strategies, such as user content-based, behavior-based, and collaboration filtered-based.
- **Multiplicity:** This quality factor refers to the measurements for repeatability of recommended service. For instance, a poor-quality system probably recommends too many repeated or similar commodities to users.
- **Category Coverage:** This indicator is useful to evaluate the coverage rate for diverse categories. This factor measures the completeness of recommendation within a selected domain.
- **Accountability:** This quality parameter is very important and mandatory for both Big Data service applications and users. This could be measured in a quantitative way, such as user rating similarity, domain trust value, domain related degree, and social intimacy degree.
- **Duration:** This factor indicates the expected recommendation period. For instance, commonly-used recommendation duration in enterprise management can be divided into short term, middle term, and long term.
- **Deviation Analysis:** This factor is used to analyze the recommendation deviation within an accepted range or confidence interval.
- **System Usability:** This parameter indicates how well the Big Data application service can be used. This can be very subjective due to different developers and users having diverse user experiences.
- **System Performance:** This is a distinct quality factor for Big Data application service, and it is useful to evaluate how well Big Data is structured, designed, collected, generated, stored, and managed to support large-scale recommendation services.

In addition to the typical applications discussed above, there are more Big Data related applications such as machine learning system, ranking system, and search systems.

SYSTEM VALIDATION METHODS FOR BIG DATA-BASED APPLICATIONS

Software testing process attempt to verify and validate the capability of a software system to meet its required attributes and functionality. This aims at evaluating an attribute or capability of a software system and determining that it meets its required results. Although crucial to software quality and widely deployed by programmers and testers, Big Data-based application systems validation remains an art, due to limited understanding of the principles of software. The difficulties in software testing and validation stems from the complexity of software. The purpose of validation can be quality assurance, verification and reliability estimation.

This section presents the existing software testing methods which have been used to validate several types of Big Data-based applications including intelligent systems, data mining systems, and learning-based systems.

Program-Based Software Testing

Program-based software testing methods have been used in many Big Data-based applications. In this software testing mechanism systematically searches for errors in MapReduce applications and generates corresponding test cases.

Classification-Based Testing

A classification-based testing method to software systems testing usually involves two distinct steps: (a) training a classifier to distinguish failure from successful cases on a select subset of results, and then; (b) applying the trained classifier to identify failures in the main set of results. A resembling reference model is usually used to train a classifier. More specifically, there are techniques for applying pattern classifications to alleviate the test oracle problems.

Oracle Problem in Software Testing

Testing involves examining the behavior of a system to discover potential faults. Given an input for a system, the challenge of distinguishing the corresponding desired, correct behavior from potentially incorrect behavior is called the "test oracle problem". Test oracle automation is important to remove a current bottleneck that inhibits greater overall test automation. Without test oracle automation, the human should determine whether observed behavior is correct.

Machine Learning-Based Software Testing

Software testing is an investigation process which attempts to validate and verify the alignment of a software system's attributes and functionality with its intended goals. Due to this fact, automated testing approaches are desired to reduce the time and cost. Besides, automation can significantly enhance the testing process performance. Several machine learning techniques been used for automated software testing purpose. Particularly, Artificial Neural Networks (ANN), Decision Tree-based algorithms have been used for predicting potential bugs in Big Data-based applications.

Crowd-Sourced Software Testing

Software engineering no longer takes place in small, isolated groups of developers, but increasingly takes place in organizations and communities which involves delegating a variety of tasks to an unknown workforce – the crowd. There is an increasing trend towards globalization with a focus on collaborative methods and infrastructure. Driven by Web 2.0 technologies, organizations can tap into a workforce consisting of anyone with an Internet connection. Customers, or *requesters*, can advertise chunks of work, or tasks, on a crowdsourcing platform, where suppliers (i.e., individual workers) select those task that match their interests and abilities. Several potential benefits have been linked to the use of crowdsourcing in general, and these would also be applicable in the context of software development specifically: *cost reduction, faster time-to-market, higher quality through broad participation*, and usher *open innovation*. It is a cost-effective method to validate a machine-learning based application systems, such as human face recognition system. Currently, crowd-sourced testing has been used in mobile app testing and mobile Teas (Testing as a Service). One good example is test (http://www.utest.com/company).

Crowdsourcing has gained much attention in practice over the last years. Many Big Data-based applications have drawn on this concept for performing different tasks and value creation activities. Nevertheless, despite its popularity, there is still comparatively little well-founded knowledge on crowdsourcing, particularly about crowdsourcing intermediaries.

Model-Based Software Testing

There is an abundance of testing style in the disciple of software engineering. Over the last few decades, many of these have come to be used and adopted by the industry as solutions to address the increasing demand for assuring software quality. Due to popularization of object-oriented design and development of software, models are used for software implementation. There has been a growth in black box testing techniques that are collectively dubbed *model-based testing* (MBT). Model-based testing has recently gained attention with the popularization of models (e.g. UML-based models) in software design and development. Model-based testing or MBT is a general term that signifies an approach that bases common testing tasks such as test case generation and test result evaluation on a model of the application under test.

FUTURE RESEARCH DIRECTIONS

Opportunities are always followed by challenges. On the one hand, Big Data-based supply chain software applications bring many attractive opportunities; and on the other hand, Big Data-based supply chain management applications software are facing a lot of challenges. These challenges can be broadly categorized as Big Data-based software architectural aspects, system hardware performance enhancement related issues, and parallel software testing capabilities. Particularly, Big Data-based supply chain applications testing is the most expensive and critical phase of software development life cycle.

As part of the general Big Data quality assurance research initiative, the current research will continue the concurrency and parallelism issues of Big Data generation and uses in global supply chain business analytics. Therefore, in dealing with this huge amount of data and executing it on multiple nodes of processing is a highly challenging risk of having bad data and even data quality related issues may exist at every stage of design and development. Some of the future research agendas are: (1) increasing need for integration of large volume of data available from multiple sources (e.g. text, video, audio); and this integration forces global supply chain operational provision to have constantly clean and reliable data sets; (2) instant data collection and live deployment are very crucial issues in order to get appropriate business intelligences for a retail business, which can be overcome only by testing the business intelligence software applications before live deployment, and finally; (3) real-time scalability related issues of large amounts of data generated by devices equipped with sensing components along global supply chain. In addition, there are emerging needs for research problems and directions on this subject in terms of quality control models, automated validation methods, approaches, and service platforms as well as TasS (Testing-as-a-service) and test automation techniques.

CONCLUSION

With the advent of big data management technologies and analytics in supply chain management, academics and practitioners are paying much more attention to build high-quality software services for business applications. However, there are increasing quality problems resulting in erroneous data costs in global supply chain industries. Data has always been an integral part of business. Technology transformation has further reinforced this importance. The entrance of social media, mobility, and the Internet of Things (IoT) has not only blurred the lines between online and offline business, but also resulted in the availability of a huge amount of unstructured data related to consumer behavior and interests. With big insights, Big Data could indeed mean big business for supply chain management. However, industry analysts are echoing growing concerns on data quality. Quality Assurance (QA) can offer a solution to the data quality challenge, and a robust and effective QA strategy can deliver big returns from Big Data.

The design and development of Big Data-based software applications have been proven useful in a diverse area of application for solving problem in global supply chain industry – e.g., raw material procurement planning, marketing strategy formulation, and logistics planning. This chapter provides an introductory discussion on Big Data-based business intelligence software systems and their quality assurance related issues; it includes a brief discussion on the appropriate software testing mechanisms for the new breeds of Big Data-based applications.

While Big Data provides solutions to complex business problems like analyzing large volume of data to derive precise answers, analyzing data in motion it processes bigger challenges in testing these scenarios. The data is highly volatile and often unstructured as it is generated from myriad of sources – such as weblogs, radio frequency identification (RFID) devices, sensors embedded in different business applications (e.g. in artifact manufacturing machines, global positioning systems, transportation networks). The quality data plays an important role in all supply chain management applications. The quality of data is recognized as a relevant performance issue in operating processes, business decision-making activities, and business-partners cooperation requirements.

Several initiatives have been lunched in the public and private sectors, with data quality having a leading role. At the same time, information systems have been migrating from a hierarchical / monolithic structure to a networked-based structure. Here the set of potential data sources that organizations can use has dramatically increased in size and scope. The issue of data quality has become more complex and controversial because of this evolution. In network information systems, processes are involved in complex information exchanges and often operate on a priori – input obtained from external sources. Consequently, the overall quality of the data that flows across information systems can rapidly degrade over time if the quality of both processes and information inputs is not controlled. On the other hand, networked information systems offer new opportunities for data quality management, including the availability of a broader range of data sources and the ability to select and compare data from diverse sources. The aim is to detect and correct errors, and thus, improve the overall quality assurance of data, and the business applications based on this data.

Moreover, Big Data is changing definitions and benchmarks for breakthrough technologies. The need to stream and collect real time data from varied data sources and in different formats results in an exponential increase in volume. Further, there is also the need to continuously 'listen' to the stream and sift out irrelevant data. There is no point in responding to a customer tweet after a week, or having dirty, noisy data affecting business decisions.

REFERENCES

Arnold, S. E. (1992). Information manufacturing: The road to database quality. *Database*, *15*(5), 32–39.

Baesens, A. (2014). *Analytics in a big data world: The essential guide to data science and its applications*. Hoboken, NJ: John Wiley & Sons.

Ballou, D. P., & Pazer, H. L. (1985). Modeling data and process quality in multi-input, multi-output information systems. *Management Science*, *31*(2), 150–162. doi:10.1287/mnsc.31.2.150

Ballou, D. P., Wang, R., & Pacer, H. (1998). Modeling information manufacturing systems to determine information product quality. *Management Science*, *44*(4), 462–484. doi:10.1287/mnsc.44.4.462

Battani, C., Cappelli, C., Francians, C., & Maurino, A. (2009). Methodologies for data quality assessment and improvement. *Association for Computing Machinery Computing Surveys*, *41*(3), 1–52.

Blake, R., & Mangiameli, P. (2011). The effects and interactions of data quality and problem complexity on classification. *Association for Computing Machinery Journal of Data and Information Quality*, *2*(2), 1–28. doi:10.1145/1891879.1891881

Cooke, J. A. (2013). Three trends to watch in 2013, Perspective. *Supply Chain Quarterly*, *1*, 11.

Crosby, P. (1995). *Philip Crosby's Reflections on Quality*. McGraw-Hill.

Davenport, T. H., Barth, P., & Bean, R. (2012, Fall). How Big Data is different. *MIT Sloan Management Review*, 22–24.

Davenport, T. H., & Harris, J. G. (2007). *Competing on analytics – the new science of wining*. Boston: Harvard Business School Publishing Corporation.

Davenport, T. H., Harris, J. G., & Morison, R. (2010). *Analytics at work – smart decisions, better results*. Boston: Harvard Business Press.

Davenport, T. H., & Prusiks, L. (2000). *Working knowledge: how organizations manage what they know*. Boston: Harvard Business Press.

Deloitte & MHI. (2014). *The 2014 MHI Annual Industry Report – Innovation the driven supply chain*. Charlotte, NC: MHI.

Deloitte & MHI. (2016). *The 2016 MHI Annual Industry Report – Accelerating change: How innovation is driving digital, always-on Supply Chains*. MHI.

Deming, W. E. (2000). *The New Economics for Industry, Government, Education* (2nd ed.). MIT Press.

Dietrich, B., Plachy, E. C., & Norton, M. F. (2014). *Analytics across the enterprise: How IBM realize business value from big data and analytics.* Boston: IBM Press Books.

Emery, J. C. (1969). *Organizational planning and control systems: Theory and management.* New York: Macmillan.

Hadoop. (2017). Retrieved from http://hadoop.apache.org

Haug, A., & Arlbjorn, J. S. (2011). Barriers to master data quality. *Journal of Enterprise Information Management, 24*(3), 288–303. doi:10.1108/17410391111122862

Haugh, A., Arlbjorn, J. S., & Pedersen, A. (2009). A classification model of ERP system data quality. *Industrial Management & Data Systems, 109*(8), 1053–1068. doi:10.1108/02635570910991292

HBR. (2012, October). Getting Control of Big Data. *Harvard Business Review.*

Huh, Y. U., Keller, F. R., Redman, T. C., & Watkins, A. R. (1990). Data quality. *Information and Software Technology, 32*(8), 559–565. doi:10.1016/0950-5849(90)90146-I

Imminent, A., Pacemen, P., & Alaska, E. (2015). Evaluating the quality of social media data in big data architecture. *IEEE Access: Practical Innovations, Open Solutions, 3,* 2028–2043. doi:10.1109/ACCESS.2015.2490723

Jones-Farmer, L. A., Ezell, J. D., & Hazen, B. T. (2013). Applying control chart methods to enhance data quality. *Technometrics.*

Jurak, J. M., & Godfrey, A. B. (1999). *Juran's Quality Handbook* (5th ed.). McGraw-Hill.

Kahan, B. K., Strong, D. M., & Wang, R. Y. (2002). Information quality benchmarks: Product and service performance. *Communications of the ACM, 45*(4), 184–192. doi:10.1145/505248.506007

Kaplan, R. S., & Norton, D. P. (1993, September). Putting the Balanced Scorecard to Work. *Harvard Business Review,* 4–17.

Kune, R., Konugurthi, P. K., Agarwal, A., Chillarige, R. R., & Buyya, R. (2016). The anatomy of big data computing. *Software, Practice & Experience, 46*(1), 79–105. doi:10.1002pe.2374

Lee, Y. W., Pipino, L., Strong, D. M., & Wang, R. Y. (2004). Process-embedded data integrity. *Journal of Database Management, 15*(1), 87–103. doi:10.4018/jdm.2004010104

Lee, Y. W., Strong, D. M., Kahn, B. K., & Wang, R. Y. (2002). AIMQ: A methodology for information quality assessment. *Information & Management, 40*(2), 133–146. doi:10.1016/S0378-7206(02)00043-5

March, S. T., & Hevner, A. R. (2007). Integrated decision support systems: A data warehousing perspective. *Decision Support Systems, 43*(3), 1031–1043. doi:10.1016/j.dss.2005.05.029

McAfee, A., & Brynjolfsson, E. (2012). Big data: The management revolution. *Harvard Business Review, 90*(10), 61–68. PMID:23074865

Murphy, C., Kaiser, G., Hu, L., & Wu, L. (2008). Properties of machine learning applications for use in metamorphic testing. *Proceeding of the 20th Internal Conference on Software Engineering and Knowledge Engineering (SEKE),* 867-872.

Pal, K. (2017). A Semantic Web Service Architecture for Supply Chain Management. *Procedia Computer Science*, *109C*, 999–1004. doi:10.1016/j.procs.2017.05.442

Parssian, A. (2006). Managerial decision support with knowledge of accuracy and completeness of the relational aggregate functions. *Decision Support Systems*, *42*(3), 1494–1502. doi:10.1016/j.dss.2005.12.005

Pipino, L. L., Lee, Y. W., & Wang, R. Y. (2002). Data quality assessment. *Communications of the ACM*, *45*(4), 211–218. doi:10.1145/505248.506010

Redman, T. C. (1996). *Data Quality for the Information Age*. Norwood, MA: Artech House Publishers.

Ronen, B., & Spiegler, I. (1991). Information as inventory: A new conceptual view. *Information & Management*, *21*(4), 239–247. doi:10.1016/0378-7206(91)90069-E

S4. (2017). Retrieved from http://incubator.apache.org/s4

Sathi, A. (2012). Big data analytics: Disruptive technologies for changing the game. MC Press Online, LLC.

Scannapieco, M., & Catarci, T. (2002). Data quality under a computer science perspective, *Archivi and Computer*, 21-15.

Siegel, E. (2013). *Predictive analytics: The power to predict who will click, buy, lie or die*. Hoboken, NJ: John Wiley & Sons Inc.

Smith, W. B. (1993). Total Customer Satisfaction as a Business Strategy. *Quality and Reliability Engineering International*, *9*(1), 49–53. doi:10.1002/qre.4680090109

Spark. (2017). Retrieved from https://spark.incubator.apache.org

Stock, J. R. (2013). Supply chain management: A look back, a look ahead. *Supply Chain Quarterly*, *2*, 22–26.

Storm. (2017). Retrieved from https://storm.incubator.apache.org

Svilvar, M., Charkraborty, A. & Kanioura, A. (2013). Big data analytics in marketing. OR/MS Today, October 22-25.

Wand, Y., & Wang, R. Y. (1996). Anchoring data quality dimensions in ontological foundations. *Communications of the ACM*, *39*(11), 86–95. doi:10.1145/240455.240479

Wang, R. Y. (1998). A product perspective on total data quality management. *Communications of the Association for Computer Machinery*, *41*(2), 58–65. doi:10.1145/269012.269022

Wang, R. Y., & Kon, H. B. (1993). Towards total data quality management (TDQM). In R. Y. Wanf (Ed.), *Information technology in action: Trends and perspectives*. Englewood Cliffs, NJ: Prentice-Hall.

Wang, R. Y., Storey, V. C., & Firth, C. P. (1995). A framework for analysis of data quality research. *IEEE Transactions on Knowledge and Data Engineering*, *7*(4), 623–640. doi:10.1109/69.404034

Wang, R. Y., & Strong, D. M. (1996). Beyond Accuracy: What data quality means to data consumers. *Journal of Management Information Systems*, *12*(4), 5–33. doi:10.1080/07421222.1996.11518099

Watson, M., Lewis, S., Cacioppo, P., & Jayaraman, J. (2013). *Supply chain network design – applying optimization and analytics to the global supply chain*. FT Press.

Watts, S., Shankaranarayanan, G., & Even, A. (2009). Data quality assessment in context: A cognitive perspective. *Decision Support Systems*, *48*(1), 202–211. doi:10.1016/j.dss.2009.07.012

Williamson, O. (1996). *The Mechanisms of Governance*. New York: Oxford University Press.

Wixom, B. H., & Ross, J. W. (2017). How to Monetize Your Data, MIT Sloan Management Review. *Spring Issue*, *58*(3), 10–13.

Zeithaml, V. A., Berry, L. L., & Parasuraman, A. (1990). *Delivering quality service: Balancing customer perceptions and expectations*. New York: Free Press.

KEY TERMS AND DEFINITIONS

Big Data Analytics: Analytics is the discovery, interpretation, and visualization of meaningful patterns in big data. To do this, analytics use data classification and clustering mechanisms.

Decision-Making Systems: A decision support system (DSS) is a computer-based information system that supports business or organizational decision-making activities, typically resulting in ranking, sorting, or choosing from among alternatives. DSSs serve the management, operations, and planning levels of an organization (usually mid and higher management) and help people make decisions about problems that may be rapidly changing and not easily specified in advance (i.e., unstructured and semi-structured decision problems). Decision support systems can be either fully computerized, human-powered or a combination of both.

Radio Frequency Identification (RFID): This is a wireless technology used to identify tagged objects in certain vicinities. Generally, it has got three main components: a tag, a reader, and a back-end. The tag uses the open air to transmit data via radio frequency (RF) signal. It is also weak in computational capability. RFID automates information collection regarding an individual object's location and actions.

Supply Chain Management: A supply chain consists of a network of key business processes and facilities, involving end users and suppliers that provide products, services and information. In this chain management, improving the efficiency of the overall chain is an influential factor; and it needs at least four important strategic issues to be considered: supply chain network design, capacity planning, risk assessment and management, and performances monitoring and measurement. Moreover, the details break down of these issues need to consider in the level of individual business processes and sub-processes; and the combined performance of this chain. The coordination of these huge business processes and their performance are of immense importance.

This research was previously published in Predictive Intelligence Using Big Data and the Internet of Things; pages 51-76, copyright year 2019 by Engineering Science Reference (an imprint of IGI Global).

Chapter 71
Knowledge Management and Quality Control in Software Outsourcing Projects

Rajorshi Sen Gupta

BITS Pilani, KK Birla Goa Campus, Zuari Nagar, India

ABSTRACT

This article describes how entrepreneurs face critical risks in terms of quality control and knowledge management while outsourcing software development to independent service providers. First, it is recommended that lump-sum payment contracts should be avoided since software development project involves uncertainty. Instead, a variable payment contingent on observed quality can induce the service provider to exert optimal effort on the project. Second, entrepreneurs must not overlook the importance of providing economic incentives. They can protect their intellectual property by withholding critical knowledge and paying information rents in terms of higher than market wages to the service providers. Third, a startling result is that a low wage nation is not necessarily the optimal location to outsource software development projects. Thus, high wage-strong IPR nations might be chosen instead of low wage-weak IPR nations. Finally, the article explains the apparent paradox that software projects are often outsourced to locations that are characterized by weak intellectual property rights regime and high propensity of imitation.

INTRODUCTION

Traditionally, profit seeking business organizations have outsourced non-core production activities like manufacturing outside their own boundaries. Until recently, firm specific core activities were looked upon as sacrosanct areas which firms preferred to keep in-house. However, in the spate of increased competition and tight budget constraints, perceptions are changing and companies are looking to outsource even their core activities. Evidently, outsourcing of specialized services like software development, R&D has become prominent in business supply chains. Software development is a human and knowledge intensive activity (Birk et al., 1999) involving collaboration between several entities. For instance, entrepreneurial

DOI: 10.4018/978-1-6684-3702-5.ch071

software firms are found to outsource development tasks to contract agents; the pharmaceutical industry is extensively outsourcing R&D to independent contract research organizations. More recently, companies are increasingly following the trend of adopting mobile-first and mobile-only strategy. Consequently, mobile application ("app") development industry is a burgeoning area where entrepreneurs are contemplating whether or not to outsource the app development tasks to independent, specialized contractors.

In contrast to manufacturing outsourcing, where client firms might have an established line of product, software development outsourcing is quite different in terms of the risk factors involved. An entrepreneurial start-up may not have an established product. Instead, it is the idea and intellectual property (IP) that plays most important role for software companies. If idea and critical business sensitive knowledge is misappropriated then there is hardly anything that can be done except resorting to time consuming, costly legal proceedings. In the software industry there is severe competition and first mover advantage plays a vital role. Thus, entrepreneurs need to take vital decisions while deciding to outsource the development service to independent contractors. In order to save resources like time and money, entrepreneurial software start-up firms are resorting to outsourcing of software application development service. While doing so, the entrepreneurs face the following practical problems.

It is being observed that several firms are outsourcing software development projects to geographic locations where wages are low but IPR protection is weak and may have prevalent culture of copying client's technologies. For instance, software piracy rate in China is 74% and that in India is 60% which incidentally are the most sought-after IT outsourcing destinations (U.S. Chamber of Commerce, 2016). In contrast, another set of firms choose to outsource their project to locations that are characterized by higher wage yet strong IPR regimes. This creates a puzzle for software entrepreneurial firms while deciding the location of outsourcing their project. Specifically, these firms face a trade-off between wages and IPR regimes. In addition to the problem related to choice of location, firms also face two critical risk factors (agency problems) associated with service outsourcing.

First, the entrepreneur loses control over the software development task being outsourced. This is one of the major issues faced by entrepreneurs while deciding whether or not they should go for outsourcing of development tasks. Since the entrepreneur (client) is outsourcing the development to independent developers; he/she cannot directly control and monitor the activities of the service provider (developer). If not being monitored, there is possibility that the developer might exert less than optimal effort on the outsourcing project. Depending on the task being outsourced, this can lead to severe adverse impact for the client. For instance, if a developer engages in shirking and exerts suboptimal effort on the outsourced project, then the software would not meet the envisaged specification requirements. This could lead to severe quality control problem for the client firm. In a highly competitive market like that of software app market, if the client ends up with an app with less than desirable quality, then it would be impossible to cater to the target audience. Thus, it is critically important for the client to devise certain mechanism that would ensure that the developer exerts desired optimal effort on the outsourced project to meet the functionality specifications.

Knowledge management (KM) and confidentiality is the second major problem that entrepreneurs face when they decide to outsource development tasks to independent service providers. Software companies routinely share their proprietary IP like source codes for testing and debugging and sensitive systems designs for applications development with their contractors. By doing so, these firms expose themselves to the risk of losing their IP. The developer might use the proprietary software of the customer to build a rival product. Likewise, in the context of cloud computing, client firms may lose control over their proprietary data and applications that are located with the provider (Sen, 2013). Cloud operators might take ownership of cloud content that could harm a company (Phelps and Jennex, 2015). This relatively new phenomenon has brought new challenges since multiple clients often share the same physical infrastructure. Hence client firms often end up losing control over their confidential and economically sensitive data to opportunistic service providers. Collaboration involving cloud computing would often necessitate relinquishing considerable control over critical information (WIPO, 2015).

For entrepreneurial software firms, their idea and pre-existing intellectual property (IP) are deemed to be crucial. Only when firms have secured IP rights they can sell or license the developed applications through appropriate distribution channels. Whereas, an entrepreneur would lose the competitive advantage if the proprietary knowledge gets leaked to the competitors. Thus, if application development is being outsourced, appropriate economic strategies would be needed to protect intellectual property embedded in software applications.

As a first step to analyze these problems, the following examples are enumerated to understand the phenomenon of IP misappropriation in software outsourcing engagements.

Example 1: Chen and Bharadwaj (2009) cite the case of Point Solutions Ltd. vs.

Focus Business Solutions Ltd. In 2001, Focus had outsourced software development and review task to Point. While doing so, Focus shared its proprietary codes with Point so that the latter can accomplish the task. After Point had received the contract, it began to develop its own competing software. The rapid development of the competing software by Point was possible because it had access to source code shared by Focus. Focus claimed that it had lost competitive advantage due to the IP misappropriation problem.

Example 2: In 2014, T-Mobile USA, Inc. brought an action against its supplier Huawei Device USA, Inc. and Huawei China for theft of trade secrets, breaches of confidentiality and Non-Disclosure Agreements (TMobile-Huawei Case, 2016). T-Mobile had developed a smart-phone testing robot for the diagnosis and quality control of mobile phone handsets. The company uses the robot when working with handset suppliers such as Huawei to perform quality control and testing. Huawei leveraged its relationship as a phone handset supplier for T-Mobile and got access to T-Mobile's robot technology including its specifications, software and trade secrets. Eventually, Huawei used the stolen technology to develop and improve its own testing robot. Thus, the IP misappropriation led to competition between T-Mobile and Huawei in the handset testing robot market. It is also important to note that the knowledge and IP management problem arose in spite of the fact that T-Mobile's robot, its component parts, its functionality, and software were protected by NDA and confidentiality contracts. T-Mobile was eventually awarded $4.8 million for breach of agreement.

Example 3: SolidWorks Corp., a U.S. based software company had outsourced debugging tasks of its 3D computer aided design (CAD) to Geometric Software Solutions Ltd. in India. An employee of the offshore company stole the program source code and tried to sell it off to SolidWork's competitors. The employee was charged with theft but he might win the case since the source code did not belong to Indian company and therefore the Indian laws would not be applicable (Fitzgerald, 2003). Jolly Technologies, a California based software manufacturer had similar adverse experience when it offshored R&D to an Indian company (Frank, 2005). As an aftermath, Jolly Tech. pulled out R&D activities from India. It is often argued that lack of legal enforcement in offshore locations is the root cause of such misappropriation cases.

Example 4: Tata Consultancy Services (TCS) and Tata America International Corp. misappropriated critical data from Epic Systems while providing service to a mutual client, Kaiser Permanente. TCS had illegally accessed Epic Systems' data while providing the installation and testing service. Eventually it developed competing medical management software called Med Mantra. The software consultancy firm was fined $940 million for stealing Epic's trade secrets (Epic Systems-TCS Case, 2016).

RESEARCH QUESTIONS

In the light of the above problems associated with software development outsourcing, the following research questions are imminent. First, how entrepreneurs can ensure that independent service providers would exert optimal effort on the outsourcing project? This is the quality control problem. Second, what kind of strategies would enable the entrepreneurs to manage their critical proprietary knowledge from being misappropriated by the service providers? Third, given the puzzling trade-off between wages and IPR regimes, how should an entrepreneur choose the location of outsourcing? That is, under what condition the entrepreneur might successfully outsource the project to a location that is characterized by low wage, yet weak IPR regime.

The analysis proceeds as follows. The cases discussed in the context of IP misappropriation problem in software services outsourcing provide the context to develop an economic model. Different scenarios are considered depending on whether the client takes into account the possibility of IP misappropriation and shirking behavior by the service provider. The characteristic features of the optimal contract that solve the agency problems are analyzed. Finally, the problem of choice of location is addressed given the trade-off between wages and IPR regimes.

LITERATURE REVIEW

It is important to understand the motivating factor as to why firms are outsourcing specialized service to independent contract agents. According to Prahalad and Hamel (1990), firms should keep core activities in-house and outsource non-core tasks if there are significant cost advantages. Offshoring of specialized services like R&D is typically attributed to cost savings due to location specific and specialization advantages (Nieto and Rodríguez, 2011). Lewin et al. (2009) find that firms are offshoring innovation activities in order to seek resources like knowledge, qualified workers and efficiency in terms of cost reduction. In the software industry, organizations constantly strive to decrease software project development time and costs. The costs of testing of a software project or product are considerable, as more than 50% of the development effort is spent on testing (Kit, 1995). More recently, firms are outsourcing their business-critical processes using cloud computing model in order to reduce cost and increase efficiency.

While the benefits of outsourcing are pressing, the relatively new phenomenon of outsourcing core services along with legal uncertainty across geographic locations has made KM and IP protection more difficult than ever. Entrepreneurs are realizing that KM and IP protection in outsourcing relationships can be a daunting task. For example, a survey conducted by R&D Magazine (2007) cites IP protection as the main reason firms did not outsource R&D. For an entrepreneur, IP is often the most important asset. As pointed out by Rajan and Zingales (2001), entrepreneurs with unique, critical ideas and superior management techniques form the basis of surplus generating enterprises. Thus, knowledge is being seen as the most strategically-important resource which organizations possess, and a major source of value creation, (Nonaka, 1991; Teece, Pisano & Shuen, 1997). If IP can be easily misappropriated, the ability of entrepreneurs to generate rents from proprietary knowledge becomes limited. Since software development is knowledge intensive activity (Birk et al., 1999) the role of KM is crucial for sustained competitiveness of software development organizations. Teece (2000) had long identified the importance of KM to get the most from an organization's tacit and codified know-how.

According to the extant literature, firms can broadly use the following mechanisms to manage their knowledge and IP in the context of outsourcing. Client firms typically rely on IP and contract laws while engaged in outsourcing. Unfortunately, there is a gap between the current state of IP law and the current state of technology and KM practice. For instance, the modern cloud technology benefits from being borderless, but IP laws are not built to handle issues without clear jurisdictions (Narayanan, 2012). Thus, companies remain vulnerable to loss of IP as they utilize modern networking technology such as cloud storage and collaborative KM systems (Phelps and Jennex, 2015).

As pointed out by Meehan (2006), while outsourcing IT, client firms must transfer IP and expertise to offshore development teams. In some software projects, the client firm may transfer to the offshore team the knowledge of how internal software modules operate. In complex software projects, such as revamping software systems, the client firms ought to transfer the entire code or portions of the code to the offshore team. This information sharing by the client enables the offshore team to gain knowledge of the algorithms and its application. These IP might constitute the client firm's competitive advantage. Under the contracting model, the IP and expertise transferred to the offshore contracting firm are protected to some extent by the contract agreement and the IP laws. However, uncertainty and enforceability of contracts is the key problem. Moreover, some of the transferred expertise is not protectable under contract or IP law, such as the ability to use the client firms' internal software system modules. Under these circumstances, client firms often tend to favor Foreign Direct Investment (FDI) over contracting. Thus, internalization of IT tasks through owned foreign subsidiaries is one route to protect IP. The FDI model provides protection for trade secrets and other IPs through increased workforce coherence (Meehan, 2006).

The extant literature also identifies the importance of compensation structure in curbing opportunistic behavior by outsourcing service providers. Explicitly writing control mechanisms in the contract along with high powered incentives are needed while outsourcing R&D (Ulset, 1996). When compared to typically used lump-sum payments, a revenue sharing contract might be more effective in R&D outsourcing (Lai et al., 2009). Ho (2009) finds that due to competition between client and contractor for R&D results, it may not be possible to write a profitable outsourcing contract. In the context of software outsourcing contracts, client firms typically use legal options like restrictive covenants and rights sharing mechanism to protect their IP (Chen and Bhardwaj, 2009). Unfortunately, legal procedures are known to be time consuming, expensive and often lead to unpredictable outcomes.

In addition to legal solutions, the literature on KM focuses on the technical issues and technology risk assessment in cloud technologies (Phelps and Jennex, 2015). In the KM literature, according to Hansen et al. (1999) there are two primary strategies for knowledge management: the codification strategy and the personalization strategy. In the codification strategy knowledge is codified and stored in databases which can be accessed and used by anyone in the company. In contrast, the personalization strategy involves tacit knowledge, which is shared through direct person-to person contacts. Given this distinction, the KM literature stresses the importance of tacit knowledge. The difficulty of copying tacit knowledge enables tacit knowledge to be the basis of an inimitable competitive advantage (Rebernik and Širec, 2007). The issue of codified knowledge sharing is gaining importance in the context of KM in cloud computing. This requires thorough employee training and control over who can access the data being shared in the cloud. This is a safe way to protect sensitive knowledge from getting abused by a cloud operator or collaborating partner (Phelps and Jennex, 2015). However, the major problem to reduced knowledge sharing is that by limiting what can be shared, the client firm might limit the growth and innovation that make KM and cloud sharing the superior method knowledge development in the first place.

This paper contributes to the literature in the following unique ways. First, the inter-related risk factors related to quality management in association with knowledge and IP protection in the context of software outsourcing have not been analyzed in the existing literature. This paper contributes to the literature by providing economic strategies that entrepreneurs can use to a) protect their proprietary knowledge and b) ensure quality control on outsourced projects while engaging with contract service providers. Second, the literature typically addresses the protection of knowledge that is generated within an outsourcing relationship and ownership of newly created IP (e.g. Phelps and Jennex, 2015). In contrast, the present paper pertains to KM and protection of IP comprising of proprietary, pre-existing knowledge of an entrepreneur. Thirdly, the paper also addresses the apparent puzzle faced by entrepreneurs while choosing the location of outsourcing given the trade-off between low/high wages and weak/strong IPR regimes.

METHODOLOGY

Development of Economic Model

Given the problems of IP misappropriation, quality control and choice of location faced by entrepreneurial firms, an economic model is being developed in this section. A design science research approach is being followed to develop the model by drawing upon the sample cases enumerated in the introductory section. These cases reflect several striking observations in terms of IP misappropriation problem in software service outsourcing. First, the client (principal) shares its existing knowledge like proprietary source codes, trade secrets with an independent service provider (agent). The knowledge sharing is necessary in order to facilitate the contracted outsourcing project. Second, the service provider misappropriates the client's IP towards unilateral economic gain. This is manifested in two ways: either the contractor competes directly with the client by producing competing products or through information leakage to competing firms of the client. The service provider can use the misappropriated knowledge to obtain unfair development and design advantage over the client. Third, IP misappropriation cases can occur anywhere, irrespective of the strength of IPR protection regimes prevailing in a particular location. Thus, the sample cases highlight the inadequacy of legal tools in protecting IP, which calls for complementary economic strategies for KM and IP protection. These issues are the building blocks of the analytical model developed in this section. The objective of developing this model is to design an optimal contract mechanism that software entrepreneurs can use to manage the independent outsourcing service providers. Specifically, the theory of incentives is used to address the two agency problems due to shirking and knowledge misappropriation by the service provider.

A principal–agent model is chosen given the contractual relationship between the two independent entities. Typically, outsourcing of software development take the form of a principal (Customer or Client)– agent (Developer or Vendor) relationship. For instance, the principal would be an entrepreneurial client who is outsourcing software application development and the agent would be an independent

Developer. For the sake of exposition, one might think of the principal to be an entrepreneur who has developed a prototype or alpha version of software. The entrepreneur wants the next (beta) phase of the application to be developed as per the requirements specifications mentioned in the scope of the work. The Developer would provide its service to develop the required software application for the Customer. The intended application could be for various platforms such as mobile, desktop, enterprise software development project. The interaction between the entrepreneur and the service provider involves the following stages:

Stage 1: An entrepreneurial software firm (principal) offers outsourcing contract to a service provider (agent). The agent decides on whether to accept or reject it. The agent agrees to perform the services as an independent developer. As per the agreement, all the materials prepared by the developer under the agreement would be considered as "work for hire" and the exclusive property of the Principal.

Stage 2: The entrepreneur shares existing IP and knowledge relevant to the project with the agent. For example, in the context of software services outsourcing, one might interpret knowledge as source code of the existing software, business know-how and trade secrets of the principal.

Stage 3: The agent decides on how much effort to exert on the outsourcing project. Nevertheless, effort is a non-contractible variable which is the source of quality control problem.

Stage 4: If the agent does not misuse the client's IP then the project concludes. The quality of the software is observed and the payment is made according to the contract terms agreed upon. Instead, if the agent decides to abrogate the contract then it misappropriates the knowledge to produce competing software and starts competing with the principal in the appropriate platform.

Given the structure of the game, the principal faces two types of asymmetric information problems associated with shirking of effort by the agent in Stage3 and misappropriation of knowledge in Stage4. In order to demonstrate how the principal should design the optimal contract, three scenarios are being considered:

Scenario 1: The principal takes into account both knowledge misappropriation and shirking problems. The first best, optimal contract thus developed is referred to as OC.

Scenario 2: The principal does not take into account the knowledge misappropriation problem. However, the principal perceives and takes into account the quality control problem emanating from lack of effort by the agent. The contract developed under this scenario is referred to as QC.

Scenario 3: The principal does not take into account the quality control problem and thus offers a lump-sum fixed payment contract to the agent. However, the principal takes into account the knowledge misappropriation problem. This contract is referred to as LC.

SCENARIO 1

The contract ought to specify the expected functionalities of the software in unambiguous terms. If the software developed by the agent meets all the "specification requirements" as outlined in the scope of work, then the project would be deemed successful. As observed in the real-life examples described earlier, the information, data and knowledge (K) shared by principal plays a critical role on the project outcome. If the project is successful, then the observable high-quality project return would be $\bar{v}(K)$

and the principal agrees to pay H to the agent. Instead, if the application fails to meet all the desired functionalities then the project is not successful and the observable low-quality project return would be $\underline{v}(K)$. In this case, the principal would have to pay $L < H$ to the agent. Thus, the outsourcing contract is essentially contingent on the observed project return. In practical terms, $\{\overline{v}(K), \underline{v}(K)\}$ may be regarded as the key performance indicators. Generally, acceptance testing is conducted by clients to ensure whether the developer is indeed meeting the desired specifications.

Since software development tasks are inherently risky and the agent can only be imperfectly monitored, the principal is most likely to face post-contractual opportunism problem emanating from suboptimal effort exerted by the agent on the outsourcing project. This is particularly true when software outsourcing involves harnessing remote talent from different geographic locations. The agent decides how much effort (e) to exert on the outsourcing project. The principal ought to design the contract in such a way that the agent would exert optimal effort to ensure that the design and functionality of the software meets the desired specifications.

The project outcome depends on the effort exerted by the agent and the knowledge shared by the principal in the following way. The probability of realizing high quality project outcome $\overline{v}(K)$ is $p(e)$; that of realizing low quality project outcome $\underline{v}(K)$ is $1-p(e)$. For the sake of simplifying the analysis, it is assumed that the quality of software and hence project return depends linearly on the level of knowledge shared by the principal so that $\overline{v}(K) = K$. Thus, knowledge sharing by the principal is intended to facilitate the project, which corroborates with the real-life examples enumerated earlier. In case the project fails, however, then the software is of low quality and project return is reduced by a factor $0 < \delta < 1$ so that $\underline{v}(K) = \delta K$ is observed. Essentially this implies that if the agent exerts less effort then the quality of software does not meet the specification requirements which reduce the project return. Also, it is assumed that $p(e)=e$, so that the probability of getting high value project outcome depends linearly on the level of effort exerted by the agent (Laffont and Martimort, 2002).

Thus, if the agent sticks to the OC contract, then the profit of the entrepreneur would be:

$$\pi_1^{OC} = e \cdot \left(\overline{v}(K) - H\right) + \left(1 - e\right) \cdot \left(\underline{v}(K) - L\right) - C(K) \tag{1}$$

where the entrepreneur incurs cost of knowledge sharing as $C(K) = \frac{\gamma}{2}K^2$. The parameter $\gamma > 0$ captures increasing marginal cost of knowledge sharing by the entrepreneur. It is plausible that when the entrepreneur is sharing knowledge with the service provider, there could be communication barriers in offshore locations. Knowledge sharing might also involve extensive training. Typically, client firms have rudimentary ideas at the initial stage. Thus, knowledge itself may be in different stages of flux or transition. Consequently, it may be increasingly difficult to transfer knowledge that is embedded within the organizational structure of the client firm. This aspect of knowledge embeddedness is consistent with the notion of knowledge complexity which can increase the cost of knowledge sharing (Cummings, 2003 and Dixon, 2000). Under the proposed contract, the profit of the agent would be:

$$\pi_2^{OC} = e \cdot H + \left(1 - e\right) \cdot L - c(e) \tag{2}$$

where $c(e)$ denotes the cost incurred by the agent while exerting effort on the project. The agent's cost of developing the software would typically depend on time effort and materials expended on the project. Specifically, the cost function of the agent is assumed to be $c(e) = \frac{1}{2}e^2$. A key feature of software outsourcing project is the uncertainty in terms of project outcome. Thus, the service provider would have to exert effort while adapting with the project and get accustomed to new techniques and requirements as per the project. This explains the increasing marginal cost of exerting effort by the service provider.

The entrepreneur ought to design the contract in such a way that the agent would not have any incentive to misappropriate the shared knowledge. Thus π_2^{OC} must be high enough for the agent to stay with the contract. While designing the contract the entrepreneur would have to ensure that the profit of the agent from the contract exceeds the outside option of the agent which is developed as follows.

Instead of staying with the contract, if the agent decides to develop competing software, then there would be competition between the client and the agent. Essentially, once the IP is misappropriated, both the client and the agent would produce two competing software which are likely to have similar functionalities. Consequently, it might be reasonable to assume that the two competing firms would be producing homogeneous products. Moreover, since the agent gained access to the critical knowledge of the principal and also exerted effort on the project, it might have the first mover advantage. This assumption corroborates along the lines of cases enumerated earlier. By moving first, the misappropriating agent would have an edge over the client in terms of grabbing the market share. Consequently, the competition between the principal and the agent is modeled as Stackelberg competition, where the agent emerges as Leader and the principal becomes a Follower.

The inverse demand function characterizing the market is assumed to be $P=1-Q$ where P denotes the common price charged for the homogeneous product and $Q=q_1+q_2$ denotes the total market quantity produced by the two firms. The profit functions of the competing firms are specified as follows where subscript 1 (2) denotes the variables corresponding to the principal (agent).

The principal firm has already sunk the cost of sharing knowledge with the agent. Consequently, the profit of the principal with marginal cost of production c would be:

$$\pi_1^S = (1-q_1-q_2)q_1 - cq_1 - \frac{\gamma}{2}K^2 + \sigma \tag{3}$$

where σ denotes expected indemnity paid by the agent to the principal. In the present context, legal remedy would be through breach of contract laws. If the project is outsourced to an offshore location where legal protection is weak and uncertain, the indemnity paid by the agent would be very small. In the worst scenario, the principal might not be able to obtain any indemnity from the agent in the absence of legal enforcement. For instance, in California, Non-Compete clauses are often unenforceable (Phelps and Jennex, 2015).

The agent misappropriates the knowledge shared by the principal and produces competing software, albeit at a lower marginal cost. The extent to which marginal cost gets reduced depends on the ability of the agent to learn and integrate the knowledge into its own operation. Thus, if K is the knowledge shared by the principal, then the agent is assumed to assimilate only αK where $0 \leq \alpha \leq 1$ captures the degree of learning ability of the agent. According to KM literature, the recipient must have a critical mass of knowledge and skills to absorb new knowledge (Cohen & Levinthal, 1990). Given the demand, cost and indemnity, the profit of the agent would be:

$$\pi_2^S = (1 - q_1 - q_2)q_2 - (c - \alpha K)q_2 - \sigma \tag{4}$$

The Stackelberg competition between the two firms yield the profits:

$$\pi_1^S = \frac{(1 - c - 2\alpha K)^2}{16} - \frac{\gamma}{2}K^2 + \sigma \tag{5}$$

$$\pi_2^S = \frac{(1 - c + 2\alpha K)^2}{8} - \sigma = \tilde{\pi}_2 - \sigma \tag{6}$$

The proofs are provided in the Appendix. Here $\tilde{\pi}_2$ is the operating profit of the agent which depends on the knowledge shared by the principal. It is important to note that $\dfrac{\partial \tilde{\pi}_2}{\partial K} > 0$. Thus, the entrepreneur must understand that the outside option and hence the behavior of the agent can be controlled through the knowledge sharing mechanism. Evidently, the knowledge sharing decision of the entrepreneur turns out to be critically important. While the knowledge sharing is imperative for the success of the project by affecting the project return, it also affects the outside option of the agent in favorable way.

According to the OC contract, the principal must design the contract that would maximize its profit specified in (1) subject to the participation constraint of the agent:

$$\pi_2^{OC} = eH + \left(1 - e\right)L - \frac{1}{2}e^2 \geq \pi_2^S \tag{7}$$

The participation constraint ensures that it is optimal for the agent to stay with the contract instead of abrogate the contract and engage in Stackelberg competition. Moreover, under Scenario1 the principal has asymmetric information regarding the effort exerted by the agent on the project. Since effort of the agent is an unobserved variable, the principal should anticipate the shirking behavior of the agent and design the contract accordingly. In particular, the contract offered must be incentive compatible for the agent to exert optimal effort on the project. This requirement leads to the Incentive Compatibility Constraint of the agent as follows:

$$e = \max_{e \in [0,1]} \left[eH + \left(1 - e\right)L - \frac{1}{2}e^2 \right] \tag{8}$$

Result 1

If observed project outcome is $\bar{v}$ then the optimal payment would be:

$$H^{OC} = (1-\delta)K_{OC} + \pi_2^S(K_{OC}) - \frac{1}{2}(1-\delta)^2 K_{OC}^2 \qquad (9)$$

Instead, if the observed project outcome is $\underline{v}$ then the payment would be:

$$L^{OC} = \pi_2^S(K_{OC}) - \frac{1}{2}(1-\delta)^2 K_{OC}^2 \qquad (10)$$

The economic intuitions of these results are discussed here. The optimal proposed contract comprises of variable payments that are contingent on the observed project outcomes. Since the principal cannot observe the effort put by the agent, the latter needs to be motivated to exert optimal effort as desired by the principal. Consequently, it is critically important to incentivize high effort exerted by the developer. This is accomplished by offering $H^{OC} > L^{OC}$. The profit of the agent under the proposed optimal contract would be:

$$\pi_2^{OC} = \pi_2^S(K_{OC}) \qquad (11)$$

Result 2

The principal would optimally share knowledge K_{OC} with the agent where:

$$K_{OC} = \frac{2\delta - \alpha(1-c_1)}{2\left[(\gamma + \alpha^2) - (1-\delta)^2\right]} \qquad (12)$$

Given the contractual terms, the marginal benefit of knowledge sharing by the principal is $e\bar{v}'(K) + (1-e)\underline{v}'(K)$ whereas the marginal cost of knowledge sharing is $\gamma K + \frac{\partial \pi_2^S}{\partial K}$. The Stackelberg competition developed earlier demonstrates the favorable impact of knowledge sharing by the principal on the profit of the agent π_2^S. Consequently, a forward looking, rational entrepreneur must take into consideration the impact of knowledge sharing on the agent.

Result 3

Given the proposed contractual terms, the agent would exert optimal effort:

$$e^{OC} = (1-\delta)KO_c \qquad (13)$$

The optimal effort exerted by the agent is obtained by equating the marginal benefit, $(H - L) = \bar{v} - \underline{v}$ with marginal cost, e. Thus, effort exerted by the agent depends on the dispersion of the contractual payments (H–L). The agent would be able to increase the probability of receiving higher payment H only through exerting higher effort on the project. This implies that the principal can incentivize the agent to exert high effort by designing the contractual terms judiciously.

SCENARIO 2

The QC contract is developed in this section. The principal takes into account the quality control problem emanating from suboptimal effort exerted by the agent, but does not take into consideration the possibility of knowledge misappropriation. In this case, while designing the contract the principal would underestimate the outside option of the agent. Specifically, the principal only ensures that the agent receives at least as much as the prevailing market wage, w. Thus, the participation constraint of the agent in this scenario would be:

$$\pi_2^{QC} = e \cdot H + \left(1 - e\right) \cdot L - \frac{1}{2}e^2 \geq w \tag{14}$$

The incentive compatibility constraint (8) of the agent would remain unchanged.

Result 4

The QC contract would entail a variable compensation scheme comprising of:

$$H^{QC} = w + (1 - \delta)K_{QC} - \frac{1}{2}(1 - \delta)^2 K_{QC}^2 \tag{15}$$

$$L^{QC} = w - \frac{1}{2}(1 - \delta)^2 K_{QC}^2 \tag{16}$$

Given the quality control problem emanating from lack of effort by the agent, the principal would offer a contract involving variable payments depending on the observed project outcome. The agent can increase the probability of receiving higher payment $H^{QC} > L^{QC}$ only by putting higher effort. Thus, variable payment scheme would induce the agent to exert higher effort.

Result 5

The knowledge shared by the principal would be:

$$K_{QC} = \frac{\delta}{\gamma - (1-\delta)^2} \qquad (17)$$

It is important to note the key difference between the OC and QC contracts with respect to knowledge shared by the entrepreneur. In principle, the entrepreneur would share knowledge by equating marginal benefit with marginal cost of knowledge sharing. Under QC scenario, the perceived marginal cost of the entrepreneur is γK only. This is due to the fact that the principal is not considering the possibility of knowledge misappropriation. Thus, the principal ends up underestimating the true marginal cost of knowledge sharing and erroneously shares more knowledge with the agent. This excessive knowledge sharing by the principal would eventually facilitate IP misappropriation by the agent.

Result 6

According to the QC, the agent would exert following level of effort:

$$e^{QC} = \bar{v}(K_{QC}) - \underline{v}(K_{QC}) = (1-\delta)K_{QC}$$

It is found that:

$$e^{QC} = (1-\delta)K_{QC} > e^{OC} = (1-\delta)K_{OC} \qquad (18)$$

Since the principal shares more than optimal knowledge, the agent would exert more effort under QC. While this might appear to have a favorable impact on the project, the problem lies in the excessive knowledge sharing that would incentivize the agent to leave the contract and set up a competing firm.

SCENARIO 3

In various outsourcing contracts, a Lump-sum fixed payment T is offered to the developer. What would be the implication of such fixed price contract given the problem in hand? Nonetheless, the entrepreneur is aware of the potential knowledge misappropriation problem; hence takes into consideration the outside option of the agent. As developed in Scenario1, the outside option of the agent would be the profit from Stackelberg competition between the principal and the agent. In this scenario, the profit of the principal would be:

$$\pi_1^{LC} = e \cdot \left(\bar{v}(K) - T\right) + (1-e) \cdot \left(\underline{v}(K) - T\right) - C(K) \qquad (19)$$

The profit of the agent would be:

$$\pi_2^{LC} = e \cdot T + (1-e) \cdot T - c(e) \qquad (20)$$

The principal would maximize profit subject to the participation constraint of the agent:

$$\pi_2^{LC} = e \cdot T + \left(1 - e\right) \cdot T - c(e) > \pi_2^S \tag{21}$$

The incentive compatibility constraint of the agent becomes:

$$e = \frac{\max}{e \in [0,1]} \left[eT + \left(1 - e\right) \cdot T - \frac{1}{2}e^2 \right] \tag{22}$$

Result 7

The LC contract would entail a fixed lump-sum payment:

$$T = \pi_2^S \left(K_{LC}\right) \tag{23}$$

and the knowledge shared by the principal would be:

$$K_{LC} = \frac{2\delta - \alpha\left(1 - c_1\right)}{2\left(\gamma + \alpha^2\right)} \tag{24}$$

Given the lump-sum contract, the agent would exert:

$$e_{LC} = 0 \tag{25}$$

The economic intuition of this result is noteworthy. The incentive compatibility constraint (22) implies that since the agent receives a lump-sum payment, the marginal benefit of exerting effort is zero but the marginal cost of effort is positive. Thus, the agent has no incentive to exert effort on the project.

Result 8

$$e_{QC} > e_{OC} > e_{LC} \tag{26}$$

While LC involves a fixed payment, both QC and OC involve variable payments. The entrepreneur must offer a contract involving variable payments to elicit high effort from the agent. In contrast, a fixed payment type contract would lead to suboptimal effort from the agent. This result demonstrates the efficacy of variable payment over lump-sum payment to incentivize higher effort from the agent.

Result 9

$$K_{QC} > K_{OC} > K_{LC} \tag{27}$$

An important lesson emanates from this result. Software entrepreneurial firms ought to strategically withhold their key knowledge from the developers. How does reduced knowledge sharing mitigate the KM problem? By sharing less knowledge, the entrepreneur is able to reduce $\pi_2^S(K_{OC})$, the outside option of the developer. The proposed OC developed in Scenario1 demonstrates that the entrepreneur would have to pay $\pi_2^S(K_{OC})$ to the service provider in order to deter the two agency problems. In contrast, under QC the entrepreneur shares more knowledge than desirable and also underpaying the developer by paying w. This, unfortunately, is a myopic strategy in the light of the OC.

In the LC contract, since the agent has no incentive to exert effort on the project, the probability of realizing high quality software is reduced to zero. In this case the project return would be:

$$\underline{v}(K_{LC}) = \delta K_{LC} \tag{28}$$

From the perspective of the entrepreneur, LC contract would lead to least project return. Hence the entrepreneur would like to avoid using LC contract whenever the project involves substantial uncertainty. Anticipating this outcome, the entrepreneur would optimally reduce the knowledge shared with the developer to K_{LC}.

Result 10

$$\pi_2^{OC} = \pi_2^S(K_{OC}) > \pi_2^{LC} = \pi_2^S(K_{LC}) > \pi_2^{QC} = w \tag{29}$$

The OC contract entails that the entrepreneur must pay the service provider more than the prevailing market wage rate. This is needed to ensure that the latter exerts optimal effort on the project and does not misappropriate the client's knowledge. In the light of this result, it is important to note the difference between OC and QC in deterring the agency problems. As per the QC, the principal pays only the prevailing market wage w to the agent. From (18) it is observed that the agent would have to exert more effort under QC but is underpaid since the payment is just equal to the wage rate. From the perspective of the agent, w is too low compared to the outside option that could have been earned by setting up a competing firm. Thus, the payment under QC is insufficient to deter the knowledge misappropriation by the agent.

Instead of using the QC, if the entrepreneur uses OC, then the problems associated with shirking and knowledge misappropriation are jointly solved by pushing up the payment of the agent over and above the prevailing wage rate w. The service provider has private information regarding its intent to exert effort and misappropriate knowledge. The entrepreneur faces asymmetric information problem and therefore has to pay incentive payment that exceeds the wage rate. This is the information rent accrued by the service provider. Hence, it can be argued that the IP misappropriation cases are likely to occur when the clients a) share excessive knowledge with their developers and b) the payment is sub-optimally low.

In what sense would the OC be an improvement over the QC and LC? As demonstrated in (28), the LC contract should be avoided by the entrepreneur since the agent would not exert effort and hence project return would be least. Thus, the choice boils down between OC and QC. An entrepreneur would use QC contract when quality control is the dominant motive rather than KM problem. As per QC, the developer is paid according to the prevailing market wage w only. Hence such type of cheap contracts might be favored by the cash-strapped start-up firms. This, however, is erroneous since it overlooks the incentive of the agent to steal the client's knowledge. If the agent has hidden motive to misappropriate the knowledge and start competing with the principal then the profit would actually be $\pi_2^S(K_{OC})$. Such action would be profitable from the perspective of the agent whenever $\pi_2^S(K_{OC}) > w$. In contrast, the OC motivates the developer to exert optimal effort and not misappropriate the knowledge of the client. This is accomplished by pushing up the expected payment of the agent to $\pi_2^{OC} = \pi_2^S(K_{OC})$. Hence the QC would fail to deter the knowledge theft by the agent, whereas the OC would be successful in protecting the knowledge shared by the principal. This demonstrates the efficacy of the OC over QC in solving both the KM and quality control problems. Figure 1 depicts this scenario.

Figure 1. Comparison of payment to agent under OC and QC

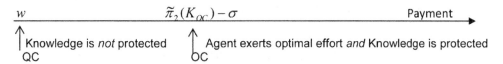

Legend: OC denotes the payment needed according to Scenario 1: Optimal Contract; and QC denotes the payment needed according to Scenario 2: Quality Control

Next, the choice of location problem faced by entrepreneurs is analyzed in this section. Suppose the entrepreneur has option of offshore-outsourcing the project to two different locations, nation I and nation II. The two nations are assumed to be diverse in terms of the prevailing wage rates and the IPR regimes. Specifically, the wage rate is lower in nation I, thus $w^I < w^{II}$. To make the problem interesting, IPR regime is assumed to be stronger in nation II. If prosecution is successful, then the entrepreneur would be able to receive larger indemnity from the agent in nation II as compared to nation I, thus $\sigma^I < \sigma^{II}$.

If the entrepreneur uses QC, then the choice of location is solely determined by wages. Since $w^I < w^{II}$, the entrepreneur would choose nation I as the favored destination for outsourcing the project. However, that would not solve the quality control and KM problems. Instead, if the OC is used then the client must pay the agent according to the optimal contract derived in (11). The payment needed would have to be $\tilde{\pi}_2 - \sigma^I$ in nation I and $\tilde{\pi}_2 - \sigma^{II}$ in nation II. Ceteris paribus, $\sigma^I < \sigma^{II}$ implies that $\tilde{\pi}_2 - \sigma^I > \tilde{\pi}_2 - \sigma^{II}$. Consequently, according to OC, the entrepreneur would have to pay lesser amount to the agent if the project were outsourced to nation II. It is important to note that although the payment needed is less in nation II, the amount is just sufficient to deter the both the KM and quality control problems. Hence the entrepreneur should choose nation II even if it is a high wage nation when compared to nation I. This scenario is presented in Figure 2.

Figure 2. Choice of location according to OC and QC

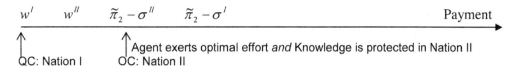

Legend: OC denotes the payment needed according to Scenario 1: Optimal Contract; and QC denotes the payment needed according to Scenario 2: Quality Control

Finally, the practical advantage of OC is demonstrated using the following scenario. To make the choice problem faced by the entrepreneur intriguing and close to reality, nation I is characterized by lower wage but weaker IPR regime. In addition, it is also assumed that service providers have higher propensity to copy technology in nation I. Thus $w^I < w^{II}$, $\sigma I < \sigma II$ and $\alpha I > \alpha^I I$. Conventional wisdom would dictate that the entrepreneur should refrain from outsourcing the project to nation I since IPR is weak and copying culture is more severe in that nation. What would the recommended project location be under OC and QC? Ceteris paribus, Equation (12) implies that the knowledge shared by the principal depends inversely on the intensity of imitation by the agent. Hence according to OC, the principal would share less knowledge with the agent in nation I, whereby $K_{OC}^I < K_{OC}^{II}$. Moreover, according to (6), the operating profit of the agent is increasing in the knowledge shared by the principal, so that $\tilde{\pi}_2(K_{OC}^I) < \tilde{\pi}_2(K_{OC}^{II})$. Then the choice of location can be determined by estimating the value of outside option of the agent. Several cases are possible which are presented in Figure 3.

Figure 3. Choice between Nation I: High wage-strong IPR and Nation II: Low wage-weak IPR

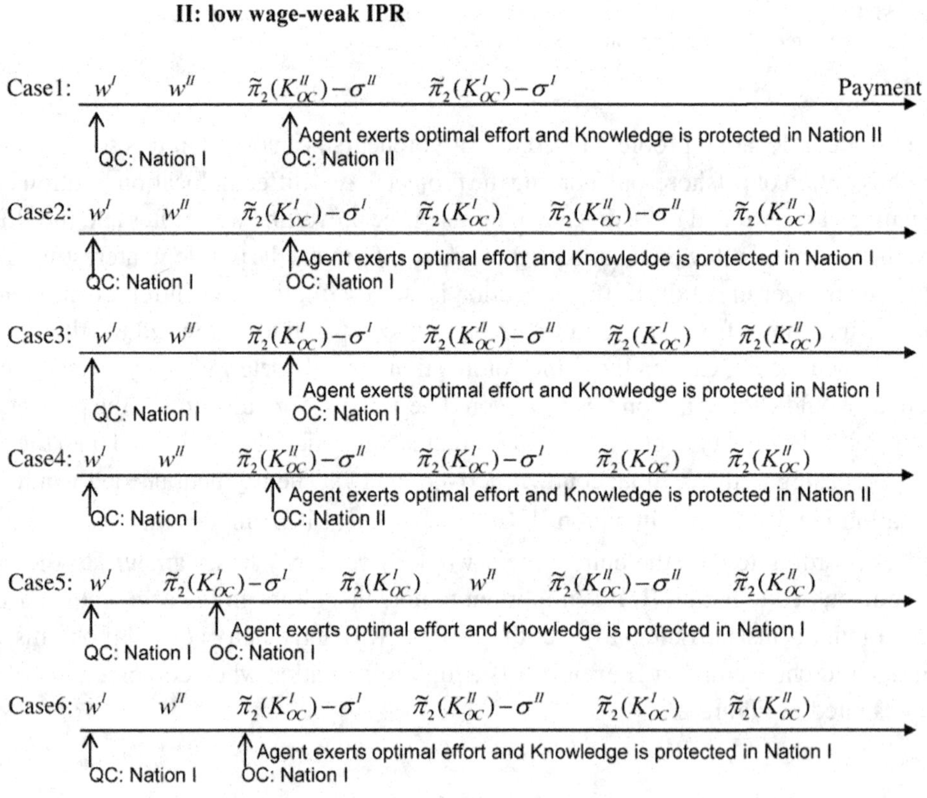

II: low wage-weak IPR

Case1: w^I w^{II} $\tilde{\pi}_2(K_{OC}^{II}) - \sigma^{II}$ $\tilde{\pi}_2(K_{OC}^I) - \sigma^I$ Payment
QC: Nation I — OC: Nation II — Agent exerts optimal effort and Knowledge is protected in Nation II

Case2: w^I w^{II} $\tilde{\pi}_2(K_{OC}^I) - \sigma^I$ $\tilde{\pi}_2(K_{OC}^I)$ $\tilde{\pi}_2(K_{OC}^{II}) - \sigma^{II}$ $\tilde{\pi}_2(K_{OC}^{II})$
QC: Nation I — OC: Nation I — Agent exerts optimal effort and Knowledge is protected in Nation I

Case3: w^I w^{II} $\tilde{\pi}_2(K_{OC}^I) - \sigma^I$ $\tilde{\pi}_2(K_{OC}^{II}) - \sigma^{II}$ $\tilde{\pi}_2(K_{OC}^I)$ $\tilde{\pi}_2(K_{OC}^{II})$
QC: Nation I — OC: Nation I — Agent exerts optimal effort and Knowledge is protected in Nation I

Case4: w^I w^{II} $\tilde{\pi}_2(K_{OC}^{II}) - \sigma^{II}$ $\tilde{\pi}_2(K_{OC}^I) - \sigma^I$ $\tilde{\pi}_2(K_{OC}^I)$ $\tilde{\pi}_2(K_{OC}^{II})$
QC: Nation I — OC: Nation II — Agent exerts optimal effort and Knowledge is protected in Nation II

Case5: w^I $\tilde{\pi}_2(K_{OC}^I) - \sigma^I$ $\tilde{\pi}_2(K_{OC}^I)$ w^{II} $\tilde{\pi}_2(K_{OC}^{II}) - \sigma^{II}$ $\tilde{\pi}_2(K_{OC}^{II})$
QC: Nation I — OC: Nation I — Agent exerts optimal effort and Knowledge is protected in Nation I

Case6: w^I w^{II} $\tilde{\pi}_2(K_{OC}^I) - \sigma^I$ $\tilde{\pi}_2(K_{OC}^{II}) - \sigma^{II}$ $\tilde{\pi}_2(K_{OC}^I)$ $\tilde{\pi}_2(K_{OC}^{II})$
QC: Nation I — OC: Nation I — Agent exerts optimal effort and Knowledge is protected in Nation I

Legend: OC denotes the payment needed according to Scenario1: Optimal Contract; and QC denotes the payment needed according to Scenario 2: Quality Control

Case 1: See Equation (30):

$$w^{I} < w^{II} < \tilde{\pi}_{2}(K_{OC}^{II}) - \sigma^{II} < \tilde{\pi}_{2}(K_{OC}^{I}) - \sigma^{I} \Rightarrow w^{I} < w^{II} < \pi_{2}^{S}(K_{OC}^{II}) < \pi_{2}^{S}(K_{OC}^{I}) \qquad (30)$$

Evidently, the entrepreneur would choose nation I under QC due to lower wage. However, that would not solve the agency problems faced by the entrepreneur.

Under OC, nation II would be chosen since the payment needed is lesser in nation II as $\tilde{\pi}_{2}(K_{OC}^{II}) - \sigma^{II} < \tilde{\pi}_{2}(K_{OC}^{I}) - \sigma^{I}$. Evidently the choice of location becomes markedly different depending on whether QC or OC is being considered. Thus, if the entrepreneur uses QC then the low wage-weak IPR, high imitating nation I would have been chosen. Instead, if the OC is used then high wage-strong IPR, low imitating nation II would be the optimal choice. Therefore, it is not necessarily true that a low wage nation should always be the favored location to outsource software development projects.

Case 2: See Equation (31):

$$w^{I} < w^{II} < \tilde{\pi}_{2}(K_{OC}^{I}) - \sigma^{I} < \tilde{\pi}_{2}(K_{OC}^{I}) < \tilde{\pi}_{2}(K_{OC}^{II}) - \sigma^{II} < \tilde{\pi}_{2}(K_{OC}^{II})$$
$$\Rightarrow w^{I} < w^{II} < \pi_{2}^{S}(K_{OC}^{I}) < \tilde{\pi}_{2}(K_{OC}^{I}) < \pi_{2}^{S}(K_{OC}^{II}) < \tilde{\pi}_{2}(K_{OC}^{II}) \qquad (31)$$

In this case, nation I would be chosen according to both QC and OC. Although the wage payment made under QC would not solve the agency problems as explained earlier. The entrepreneur should choose nation I according to OC because the threshold payment needed to deter the agency problems is lesser in nation I when compared to nation II, since $\tilde{\pi}_{2}(K_{OC}^{I}) - \sigma^{I} < \tilde{\pi}_{2}(K_{OC}^{II}) - \sigma^{II}$.

Case 3: See Equation (32):

$$w^{I} < w^{II} < \tilde{\pi}_{2}(K_{OC}^{I}) - \sigma^{I} < \tilde{\pi}_{2}(K_{OC}^{II}) - \sigma^{II} < \tilde{\pi}_{2}(K_{OC}^{I}) < \tilde{\pi}_{2}(K_{OC}^{II})$$
$$\Rightarrow w^{I} < w^{II} < \pi_{2}^{S}(K_{OC}^{I}) < \pi_{2}^{S}(K_{OC}^{II}) < \tilde{\pi}_{2}(K_{OC}^{I}) < \tilde{\pi}_{2}(K_{OC}^{II}) \qquad (32)$$

Since $w^{I} < w^{II}$ the entrepreneur would choose nation I according to QC

Moreover, since the payment needed to deter the agency problems would be lesser in nation I, the choice would be nation I according to OC as well.

Case2 and Case3 explain the apparently surprising observation that firms often outsource software development projects to locations that are notorious in terms of weak IPR and have high propensity of imitation. In contrast, the strong IPR-low imitating nation II might not be chosen because the payment needed to deter the agency problems would have been higher since $\pi_{2}^{S}(K_{OC}^{I}) < \pi_{2}^{S}(K_{OC}^{II})$. Nevertheless, while the project is being outsourced to nation I, the entrepreneur must ensure that the agent is paid more than the wage rate as per the OC: $w^{I} < \pi_{2}^{S}(K_{OC}^{I})$.

Case 4: See Equation (33):

$$w^I < w^{II} < \tilde{\pi}_2(K_{OC}^{II}) - \sigma^{II} < \tilde{\pi}_2(K_{OC}^I) - \sigma^I < \tilde{\pi}_2(K_{OC}^I) < \tilde{\pi}_2(K_{OC}^{II})$$
$$\Rightarrow w^I < w^{II} < \pi_2^S(K_{OC}^{II}) < \pi_2^S(K_{OC}^I) < \tilde{\pi}_2(K_{OC}^I) < \tilde{\pi}_2(K_{OC}^{II})$$

(33)

In this case, the entrepreneur would choose nation I according to QC However, this cannot deter the agency problems. In contrast, since $\pi_2^S(K_{OC}^{II}) < \pi_2^S(K_{OC}^I)$, the entrepreneur would have to pay lesser amount in nation II in order to avoid the agency problems. Consequently, according to OC, the entrepreneur ought to choose nation II. Thus, similar to Case 1A, the choice of location can be different depending on whether QC or OC is used.

Case 5: See Equation (34):

$$w^I < \tilde{\pi}_2(K_{OC}^I) - \sigma^I < \tilde{\pi}_2(K_{OC}^I) < w^{II} < \tilde{\pi}_2(K_{OC}^{II}) - \sigma^{II} < \tilde{\pi}_2(K_{OC}^{II})$$
$$\Rightarrow w^I < \pi_2^S(K_{OC}^I) < \tilde{\pi}_2(K_{OC}^I) < w^{II} < \pi_2^S(K_{OC}^{II}) < \tilde{\pi}_2(K_{OC}^{II})$$

(34)

Case 6: See Equation (35):

$$w^I < w^{II} < \tilde{\pi}_2(K_{OC}^I) - \sigma^I < \tilde{\pi}_2(K_{OC}^{II}) - \sigma^{II} < \tilde{\pi}_2(K_{OC}^I) < \tilde{\pi}_2(K_{OC}^{II})$$
$$\Rightarrow w^I < w^{II} < \pi_2^S(K_{OC}^I) < \pi_2^S(K_{OC}^{II}) < \tilde{\pi}_2(K_{OC}^I) < \tilde{\pi}_2(K_{OC}^{II})$$

(35)

In these cases, nation I would be chosen according to both QC and OC. The economic logic follows Cases 2 and 3 and therefore not repeated for brevity.

DISCUSSION AND MANAGERIAL IMPLICATIONS

Several important insights emanate from the results obtained in this paper. Recently, the outsourced development of software apps has been undergoing substantial growth. The entrepreneurial start-up firms typically design the software apps but the actual development is outsourced to freelancers or independent contractors. In such a scenario, lack of experience in managing independent contractors can lead to irreversible damages for the companies. Therefore, such entrepreneurs must understand the importance of properly designing the app development contracts. Outsourcing of software development may be pursued only when the clients understand the risks described in this paper and take the following safeguards to mitigate them.

First, the risk factor emanating from non-contractible effort and quality control problem is being considered. It is important to design the contract in such a way that the independent developer acts in the best interest of the client. The payment structure should be such that the developer has incentive to exert optimal effort and develop the software according to envisaged specifications. According to this paper, the agent can be incentivized by providing a variable payment type contract instead of a lump-sum fixed payment contract. In practical terms, the variable payments might be interpreted as milestone based payments based on the quality of software achieved by the developer.

Second, the risk factor related to KM and IP misappropriation is considered. It is critically important to note that the problem of knowledge misappropriation is driven by two reasons: a) excessive knowledge sharing and b) suboptimal payment being made to the service provider. According to the optimal contract developed in this paper, the client can solve this problem by using incentive payment structure and sharing limited knowledge with the agent. In an effort to reduce costs and increase profits, entrepreneurs often tend to pay less that what is needed to deter the problem of IP misappropriation by the agent. If start-up firms use QC contract then they would tend to underpay for the outsourced services by paying only the market wage. In contrast, the OC requires that the independent contractors are paid more than market wage rate, which would dissuade them from stealing knowledge and shirking on the project. Given the asymmetric information problem, entrepreneurs would have to give information rent to the service providers in terms of higher than market wage. In addition to the payment structure, entrepreneurs must share limited knowledge with the independent developers. In software outsourcing projects, for example, entrepreneurs ought to split source code into independent sections, put restrictions on access to databases and share resources with their developers only on a need to know basis. By sharing limited knowledge, the entrepreneur would be able to reduce π_2^S, the outside option of the agent. This, in turn, would reduce the incentive of the agent to walk away from the contractual relationship and setup a competing firm. Thus, the entrepreneur would be able to align the behavior of the agent as optimally desired.

A note of caution is important in the context of knowledge sharing. From a practical standpoint, often it might be difficult for entrepreneurs to withhold knowledge from the service providers. Indeed, extant lawsuits indicate that a lot of knowledge sharing occurs inevitably between principal and agent during a project. In the light of this paper, knowledge sharing by the entrepreneur plays an important role in determining the quality of the project outcome. Therefore, increased knowledge sharing is deemed necessary for the success of a project. This is true, for instance, in software testing projects as observed in the Epic Systems –TCS case, where client ought to share extensive knowledge in terms of source code, system specifications and design documents with the service provider. While an entrepreneur may be unable to withhold knowledge, it must be ensured that the service provider is paid appropriately. In particular, the agent should be paid according to the optimal contract. In the context of knowledge misappropriation, it may be argued that the key distinguishing factor between the unsuccessful projects and successful projects is the payment received by the agent. Suboptimal payment creates incentive for the agent to act according to selfish motive and abrogate the contract.

Third, the knowledge shared by the entrepreneur comprises the heart of the misappropriation problem. In this model α captures the degree to which the supplier can effectively use the knowledge shared by the entrepreneur. From Equation (12), it can be inferred that if the project is being outsourced to a location where copying culture is pervasive, then the entrepreneur ought to share less knowledge with the service provider.

Compared to tacit knowledge, codified knowledge is easier to copy (Teece, 2000). While more of tacit knowledge might be shared, entrepreneurs must share limited codified knowledge with the service providers. What are the factors that would enable a supplier to learn the technology and then use it according to its own benefit? The ability to learn and use the client's know-how is an important factor behind the information leakage problem. Indeed, as Teece (1987) explains, the possibility of leakage of knowledge would depend on the degree to which the suppliers can effectively use the shared know-how. Not all suppliers can assimilate the knowledge shared by the client. The ability to use the knowledge would depend on the absorptive capacity, complementary assets and co-specialized knowledge of the supplier firm. In other words, if a supplier does not possess the required complementary assets/knowledge, it cannot use the knowledge shared by the client effectively to its own benefit.

Fourth, while choosing offshore outsourcing destinations, entrepreneurs often face an important trade-off in terms of wages and IPR protection. According to this paper, the choice problem can be solved by using the OC developed in this paper. Thus, if two locations differ in terms of wage rates of the developers, conventionally the entrepreneur would choose the location with lower wage rate. However, this strategy might be erroneous since it does not take into consideration the optimal payment necessary to deter the KM and quality control problems. While nation I might have lower wages, it does not necessarily imply that the optimal payment required to deter the agency problems would also be lesser in nation I. In contrast, if a high wage nation II is characterized by stronger IPR regime, then it is possible that the optimal payment needed would be lesser in nation II. As demonstrated in Cases 1 and 4, it is plausible that the location with higher wage might be chosen when OC is taken into consideration. This result explains the observed phenomenon of reverse-outsourcing or insourcing, whereby firms have started bringing back offshored projects back to locations where wages are higher, yet IPR is more secured.

Fifth, this paper provides economic justification of a puzzling observation that firms often choose to outsource software development projects to locations that are notorious in terms of protecting IPR and have high propensity to copy clientele technology. For instance, according to a recent study conducted by Global Intellectual Property Center (GIPC), India was ranked the second worst in terms of IPR protection (U.S. Chamber of Commerce, 2016). Does this imply that India should be avoided to outsource software development projects? The answer would depend on the payment needed according to OC developed in this paper. As demonstrated in Cases 2,3 5 and 6, it is plausible that the optimal payment necessary to deter the agency problems is lesser in such location when compared to the optimal payment that would have been required in a high wage location. Thus, entrepreneurial start-ups can determine the location of outsourcing software app development project based on the optimal contract developed in this paper. The key to managing the independent contractors and developers would be through provision of adequate incentives through appropriately designed contracts.

Finally, it is important to discuss future research directions. Often, firms are able to sustain competition through creation of brand loyalty. It would be worthwhile to examine the impact of brand loyalty in deterring knowledge misappropriation and quality problem associated with outsourcing. The theoretical predictions of the present paper can be empirically tested as well.

CONCLUSION

Entrepreneurs face risk of knowledge misappropriation and quality control problems when they outsource software development projects to independent service providers. These problems can be managed by designing the outsourcing contracts judiciously. The following specific conclusions emanate from this paper:

1. How should entrepreneurs choose a location for outsourcing their software development projects? It depends on how much the entrepreneur would have to pay the service provider to deter the agency problems. The optimal payment can vary from one location to another, depending on the strength of IPR regime, wage rates, and factors like persistent copying culture. The entrepreneur

must choose the location that requires the lowest optimal payment. As demonstrated in this paper, it is important to note that the location requiring lowest optimal payment need not be the location where the wage is least;

2. The quality control problem associated with software development outsourcing can be mitigated by designing the optimal contract by including milestone or variable payments contingent on observed project outcomes. Entrepreneurs should avoid using fixed price contracts when the project involves uncertainty;

3. Often, given the pressing objective of cost reduction, firms tend to overlook the importance of providing adequate incentives to independent service providers. Entrepreneurs can protect their IP from being misappropriated by using the optimal contract developed in this paper. This involves a) sharing limited knowledge with service providers and b) paying information rents higher than wage rate.

ACKNOWLEDGMENT

The helpful suggestions from two anonymous Reviewers are gratefully acknowledged.

REFERENCES

Birk, A., Surmann, D., & Althoff, K. (1999). Applications of knowledge acquisition in experimental software engineering. In *Proceedings of the 11th European Workshop on Knowledge Acquisition, Modeling, and Management* (pp. 67-84). 10.1007/3-540-48775-1_5

Chen, Y., & Bharadwaj, A. (2009). An empirical analysis of contract structures in IT outsourcing. *Information Systems Research*, *20*(4), 484–506. doi:10.1287/isre.1070.0166

Cohen, W. M., & Levinthal, D. A. (1990). Absorptive capacity: A new perspective on learning and innovation. *Administrative Science Quarterly*, *35*(1), 128–152. doi:10.2307/2393553

Cummings, J. (2003). *Knowledge sharing: a review of the literature*. The World Bank Operations Evaluation Department. Retrieved from http:/www.worldbank.org/oed

Dixon, N. M. (2000). *Common knowledge: how companies thrive by sharing what they know*. Boston, Mass: Harvard Business School Press.

Epic Systems-TCS Case. (2016). Epic systems win 940 mln us jury verdict in tata trade secret case. Retrieved from https://www.reuters.com/article/us-tata-epic-verdict/epic-systems-wins-940-mln-u-s-jury-verdict-in-tata-trade-secret-case-idUSKCN0XD135

Fitzgerald, M. (2003). Big Savings, Big Risk. *CSO Online*. Retrieved from www.csoonline.com/read/110103/outsourcing.html

Frank, S. J. (2005). Source out, risk in. *IEEE Spectrum*, *42*(4), 60–62. doi:10.1109/MSPEC.2005.1413734

Hansen, M. T., Nohria, N., & Tierney, T. (1999). What's your strategy for managing knowledge? *Harvard Business Review*, *77*(2), 106–116. PMID:10387767

Ho, S. (2009). Information leakage in innovation outsourcing. *R & D Management*, *39*(5), 431–443. doi:10.1111/j.1467-9310.2009.00574.x

Kit, E. (1995). *Software testing in the real world: improving the process*. Reading, MA: Addison-Wesley.

Laffont, J., & Martimort, D. (2002). *The Theory of Incentives- the Principal-Agent Model*. Princeton University Press.

Lai, E. L. C., Riezman, R., & Wang, P. (2009). Outsourcing of innovation. *Economic Theory*, *38*(3), 485–515. doi:10.100700199-007-0326-4

Lewin, A. Y., Massini, S., & Peeters, C. (2009). Why are companies offshoring innovation? The emerging global race for talent. *Journal of International Business Studies*, *40*(6), 901–925. doi:10.1057/jibs.2008.92

Meehan, M. J. (2006). Outsourcing information technology to India: Explaining patterns of foreign direct investment and contracting in the software industry. *Brigham Young University International Law & Management Review*, *2*(2), 285–309.

Narayanan, V. (2012). Harnessing the cloud: International law implications of cloud-computing. *Chicago Journal of International Law*, *12*(2), 783–809.

Nieto, M. J., & Rodríguez, A. (2011). Offshoring of R&D: Looking abroad to improve innovation performance. *Journal of International Business Studies*, *42*(3), 345–361. doi:10.1057/jibs.2010.59

Nonaka, I. (1991). The knowledge-creating company. *Harvard Business Review*, *69*(6), 96–104.

Nonaka, I. (1994). A dynamic theory of organizational knowledge creation. *Organization Science*, *5*(1), 14–37. doi:10.1287/orsc.5.1.14

Phelps, M., & Jennex, M. E. (2015). Ownership of collaborative works in the cloud. *International Journal of Knowledge Management*, *11*(4), 51–68. doi:10.4018/IJKM.2015100103

Phelps, M., & Jennex, M. E. (2015). Yours, mine, or ours: discussing ownership of collaborative works in the cloud. In *Proceedings of the 48th Hawaii International Conference on System Sciences* (pp. 3951-3957). 10.1109/HICSS.2015.473

Prahalad, C. K., & Hamel, G. (1990). The core competence of the corporation. *Harvard Business Review*, *68*, 79–91.

Rajan, R. G., & Zingales, L. (2001). The firm as a dedicated hierarchy: a theory of the origins and growth of firms. *The Quarterly Journal of Economics, 116*(3), 805-851.

R&D Magazine. (2007). R&D outsourcing becomes more strategic. Retrieved from http://rdmag.com

Rebernik, M., & Sirec, K. (2007). Fostering innovation by unlearning tacit knowledge. *Journal of Kybernetes*, *36*(3), 406–419. doi:10.1108/03684920710747039

Sen, J. (2013). Security and privacy issues in cloud computing. In A. Ruiz-Martinez (Ed.), *Architectures and Protocols for Secure Information Technology Infrastructures*. Hershey, PA: IGI Global.

Teece, D. (1987). Capturing value from technological innovation: integration, strategic partnering and licensing decision. In B. Guile & H. Brooks (Eds.), *Technology and Global Industry* (pp. 65–95). Washington: National Academy Press.

Teece, D. J. (2000). Strategies for managing knowledge assets: The role of firm structure and industrial context. *Long Range Planning*, *33*(1), 35–54. doi:10.1016/S0024-6301(99)00117-X

Teece, D. J., Pisano, G., & Shuen, A. (1997). Dynamic capabilities and strategic management. *Strategic Management Journal*, *18*(7), 509–533. doi:10.1002/(SICI)1097-0266(199708)18:7<509::AID-SMJ882>3.0.CO;2-Z

Regmedi.co.uk. (2016). TMobile-Huawei Case. Retrieved from https://regmedia.co.uk/2016/07/06/tmobile_hauwei_robot.pdf

U. S. Chamber of Commerce. (2016). *Global International IP Index*. Fourth edition. Retrieved from http://www.theglobalipcenter.com/wp-content/themes/gipc/map-index/assets/pdf/2016/GIPC_IP_Index_4th_Edition.pdf

Ulset, S. (1996). R&D outsourcing and contractual governance: An empirical study of commercial R&D project. *Journal of Economic Behavior & Organization*, *30*(1), 63–82. doi:10.1016/S0167-2681(96)00842-6

World Intellectual Property Organization (WIPO). (2015). *Protecting intellectual property in the cloud*. Retrieved from http://www.wipo.int/wipo_magazine/en/2015/03/article_0004.html

This research was previously published in the International Journal of Knowledge Management (IJKM), 13(4); pages 31-55, copyright year 2017 by IGI Publishing (an imprint of IGI Global).

APPENDIX

To solve the Stackelberg competitive game, the optimization problem faced by the Follower (Principal) firm is considered first. The Follower would choose q_1 after observing the output q_2 produced by the Leader. The optimization problem of the follower $\dfrac{\partial \pi_1^S}{\partial q_1} = 0$ yields the reaction function of the Follower:

$$q_1 = \frac{1 - q_2 - c}{2}$$

Consequently, the Leader would maximize its profit by taking into consideration the reaction function of the Follower. This leads to:

$$\pi_2^S = \left(1 - \left(\frac{1 - q_2 - c}{2}\right) - q_2\right)q_2 - (c - \alpha K)q_2 - \sigma = \left(\frac{1 - q_2 + c}{2}\right)q_2 - (c - \alpha K)q_2 - \sigma$$

$$\frac{\partial \pi_2^S}{\partial q_2} = 0 \Rightarrow q_2 = \frac{1 + c - 2(c - \alpha K)}{2} = \frac{1 - c + 2\alpha K}{2}$$

Consequently the reaction function of follower yields $q_1 = \dfrac{1 - c - 2\alpha K}{4}$.

Thus $Q = \dfrac{3 - 3c + 2\alpha K}{4}$ and $P = \dfrac{1 + 3c - 2\alpha K}{4}$

which yields the profits of the competing firms:

$$\pi_1^S = (P - c)q_1 - \frac{\gamma}{2}K^2 + \sigma = \frac{(1 - c - 2\alpha K)^2}{16} - \frac{\gamma}{2}K^2 + \sigma$$

and:

$$\pi_2^S = (P - (c - \alpha K))q_2 - \sigma = \frac{(1 - c + 2\alpha K)^2}{8} - \sigma = \tilde{\pi}_2 - \sigma$$

Result 1

The Incentive Compatibility Constraint implies $H\!-\!L\!-\!e\!=\!0 \Rightarrow e\!=\!H\!-\!L$.

   Thus, the Lagrangean is:

$$\ell = \left(H - L\right) \cdot \left(\overline{v}(K) - H\right) + \left(1 - \left(H - L\right)\right) \cdot \left(\underline{v}(K) - L\right) - \frac{\gamma}{2} \cdot K^2$$
$$+ \lambda \cdot \left[\left(H - L\right) \cdot H + \left(1 - \left(H - L\right)\right) \cdot L - 0.5\left(H - L\right)^2 - \pi_2^S(K)\right]$$
$$= \left(H - L\right) \cdot \left(K - H\right) + \left(1 - \left(H - L\right)\right) \cdot \left(\delta K - L\right) - \frac{\gamma}{2} \cdot K^2$$
$$+ \lambda \cdot \left[\left(H - L\right) \cdot H + \left(1 - \left(H - L\right)\right) \cdot L - 0.5\left(H - L\right)^2 - \pi_2^S(K)\right]$$

$$\frac{\partial \ell}{\partial H} = 0 \text{ and } \frac{\partial \ell}{\partial L} = 0 \Rightarrow \left(H - L\right) = (1 - \delta)K \Rightarrow \lambda = 1$$

$$\frac{\partial \ell}{\partial K} = 0 \text{ yields } K = \frac{2\delta - \alpha\left(1 - c_1\right)}{2\left[\left(\gamma + \alpha^2\right) - \left(1 - \delta\right)^2\right]} = K_{OC}$$

specified in (12)

$$\frac{\partial \ell}{\partial \lambda} = 0 \Rightarrow L = \pi_2^S - 0.5\left((1 - \delta)K\right)^2$$

and $(H–L)=(1–\delta)K$ leads to the optimal payments specified in (9) and (10).

Result 4

The Lagrangean for the optimization problem in Scenaio2 is:

$$\ell = \left(H - L\right) \cdot \left(K - H\right) + \left(1 - \left(H - L\right)\right) \cdot \left(\delta K - L\right) - \frac{\gamma}{2} \cdot K^2$$
$$+ \lambda \cdot \left[\left(H - L\right) \cdot H + \left(1 - \left(H - L\right)\right) \cdot L - 0.5\left(H - L\right)^2 - w\right]$$

$$\frac{\partial \ell}{\partial K} = 0 \Rightarrow K = \frac{\delta}{\gamma - (1 - \delta)^2} = K_{QC}$$

$$\frac{\partial L}{\partial \lambda} = 0 \Rightarrow \left(H - L\right) \cdot H + \left(1 - \left(H - L\right)\right) \cdot L - 0.5\left(H - L\right)^2 = w \text{ and } \left(H - L\right) = (1 - \delta)K$$

are solved to obtain the payments specified in (15) and (16).

Result 7

The Lagrangean for the optimization problem specified in Scenario3 is:

$$\ell = e \cdot (K - T) + (1 - e) \cdot (\delta K - T) - \frac{\gamma}{2} \cdot K^2 + \lambda \cdot \left[e \cdot T + (1 - e) \cdot T - 0.5 e^2 - \pi_2^S \right]$$

The incentive compatibility constraint yields $e=0$. Thus:

$$\ell = (\delta K - T) - \frac{\gamma}{2} \cdot K^2 + \lambda \cdot \left[T - \pi_2^S \right]$$

which implies:

$$\frac{\partial \ell}{\partial T} = 0 \Rightarrow \lambda = 1$$

$$\frac{\partial \ell}{\partial K} = 0 \Rightarrow \frac{2\delta - \alpha(1 - c_1)}{2(\gamma + \alpha^2)} = K_{LC}$$

$$\frac{\partial \ell}{\partial \lambda} = 0 \Rightarrow T = \pi_2^S(K_{LC})$$

Chapter 72
Reuse in Agile Development Process

Chung-Yeung Pang

https://orcid.org/0000-0002-7925-4454

Seveco AG, Switzerland

ABSTRACT

Reusability is a clear principle in software development. However, systematic reuse of software elements is not common in most organizations. Application programmers rarely design and create software elements for possible future reuse. In many agile software development processes, the project teams believe that the development of reusable software elements can slow down the project. This can be a misconception. This chapter examines various ways to reuse software. Three approaches to developing reusable software artifacts from 15 years of experience in the agile development process are presented. The first approach is to create generic programs or configurable frameworks that support similar solutions for a variety of use cases and environments. The reuse of patterns is the second approach presented. Another effective way is to use a model-driven approach with model patterns. These approaches help to speed deployment software. The final product is flexible and can easily be adapted to changes. This is one of the main goals of an agile approach.

INTRODUCTION

An experienced programmer would reuse his / her code written for another project whenever a similar function is needed. In fact, people always use the same solution for similar problems. That is why experience can be very valuable. When implementing a new module, a veteran programmer, after years of observation by the author, often cuts out code fragments from old modules that he / she has written and inserts them into the new module. He / she is usually more efficient and productive as he / she already has experience solving similar problems. Transforming this experience into a set of reusable elements that anyone can use would bring great benefits to overall software development. That's what software reuse is all about.

DOI: 10.4018/978-1-6684-3702-5.ch072

With advances of software technologies, there are many packages and libraries containing reusable software elements available commercially or open sources. Different business or system units from large organizations usually provide business domain specific or infrastructure related software components and functions (e.g. a function to retrieve customer data, etc.) for application development. Using these software elements in application development forms the common practice of reuse. With decades of experience working for many large organizations, the author finds that it is not a common practice for application programmers to design and build software elements for possible future. When developers have to meet deadlines and provide functionality, building software elements that can be reused is never a priority. In fact, often one can find programs with hard coded values and algorithm that prevent them from being reused in different context without code changes.

In recent years, the agile software development process has become very popular in the software industry (Ambler, 2010; Larman, 2003). In this approach, the emphasis is on providing working software with the highest business values as a measure of the progress of a software project. It prefers functioning software over documentation and customer collaboration over contract negotiation. As a result, so many developers are simply write ad hoc-style code, even though the agile approach does not exclude the value of analysis and design. For many agile development teams, designing and building reusable software elements are out of the question.

Although agile development practice has great advantages in software development, many projects are still failing (Harlow, 2014; Ismail, 2017). When a software element has high reuse potential through configuration and extension, it is flexible and easily adapt to changes. This actually fulfil the motivation of agile software approach that the end system should be flexible and easy to change. The purpose of this chapter to describe the techniques to design and build reusable software artefacts and demonstrate that they bring many benefits. The development process to provide working software can be speeded up. The end product is flexible and easily adaptable to changes, which is one of the main goals in using an agile approach.

The chapter gives a brief survey of software reuse. It presents the general reusable software artefacts with their motivation, implementation concept, consequences and applicability. Specific approaches to develop reusable software artefacts that evolved out of 15 years of experience of agile development practice are described. The approaches include those for "generic programming and configurable framework", "pattern based reuse" and "model driven approach". The chapter is organized with a first section on the background of agile software development and reusing software. It is followed by a section on reusable software elements. The three approaches mentioned before will be described in three different sections. The chapter ends with sections on the vision for the future and a final conclusion.

BACKGROUND

In the background, the first subsection deals with the history of software development and the agile approach. Following is a subsection on reuse based software engineering.

History of Software Development and Agile Approach

In the early days of software history, programmers tended to develop their programs without documentation in an ad-hoc style. As software systems evolved with features over the years, they were no longer serviceable (Software Crisis, 2010). Software engineers argued that software development should not just be coding. Analysis and design with the right documentation are as important as writing code (Software Engineering, 2010). It has gone the extra mile that much effort has been put into requirements specification and design work, resulting in a tremendous amount of documentation. The author has experienced that a number of projects did not survive the requirement specification analysis phase before the budget was exhausted and no single working software was created.

In 2001, a number of prominent software engineers joined forces to create a Manifesto for Agile Software Development (Agile Manifesto Group, 2001). They were not satisfied with the usual software development practices, especially with the extensive documents nobody would read. They came up with 12 principles. Four main principles related to the context of this chapter are:

- Individuals and interactions over processes and tools.
- Working software over comprehensive documentation.
- Customer collaboration over contract negotiation.
- Responding to change over following a plan.

The agile approach to software development is widespread in the software community. Many agile development methods have been introduced. The most popular are Scrum, Kanban and extreme programming (Stellman & Greene, 2015). In particular, these methods divide the product development work into small increments that minimize the planning and design effort. Iterations are short periods, which usually take one to four weeks. Work software is the primary measure of progress. Program elements from each iteration should be continuously integrated into the system.

The Agile Software Development Manifesto provides only principles for software development. There is no framework for how the development should be done. An agile development method like Scrum provides the blue print of a software development process. However, there is no suggestion on the mechanism how program elements should be developed in each iteration and how they can be continuously integrated into the system.

The 2015 CHAOS report (Hastie & Wojewoda2015) shows that the statistical success rate in agile software development is three times higher than traditional approaches. However, the report also shows that the overall success rate of an agile approach project is only 39%. Despite using the agile approach many projects still fail. This chapter proposes techniques for improving the situation.

Reuse Based Software Engineering

Reuse is a distinct field of study in software engineering. It started with the concept of reusable software components. Early developments in reuse research include the idea of program families and domain analysis concepts (Biggerstaff & Perlis, 1989). Other areas of reuse research include function libraries, methods and tools for domain engineering, design patterns, domain-specific software architecture, components, generators, measurements and experiments, and business and finance (Soora, 2014; Jacobson, et al., 1997). There are also areas of computer science research that are central to reuse: abstract data types and object-oriented methods, programming language theory, software architectures, compilers, models for software development processes, metrics and experiments, and organization theory (Krueger, 1992; Frakes & Kang, 2005; 2015). Reuse can also be applied in the different phases of the software lifecycle, e.g., requirements analysis and specification, software design, implementation, testing and deployment, and product maintenance (Leach, 2011).

There are many approaches to the software reuse concept. In order to organize and place different concepts and models of reuse, a set of conceptual frameworks for the reuse of software has been proposed. Biggerstaff and Richter (1989) propose a framework that divides available reusability technologies into two main groups: composition technologies and generation technologies. Krueger (1992) proposed a framework with four taxonomies for reusable artifacts. The four taxonomies are abstraction, selection, specialization and integration. Another framework developed by Freeman (1987) asked questions such as "what is reused?", "How should it be reused?" and "What is required to enable a successful reuse?". His framework defines five levels of reusable information code fragments, logical structure, functional architecture, external knowledge (e.g. knowledge of application domains and software development), and environmental knowledge related to organizational and psychological issues. Other frameworks are based on forms of reuse such as data, code, and design (Horowitz & Munson, 1984; Jones, 1984). Reusable software artifacts include application systems, subsystems or frameworks, components, modules, objects and functions or procedures.

Reusability is a key principle of software engineering. However, as mentioned earlier, application programmers rarely create their programs considering reuse. For reusable software artifacts to be widely reusable, they must be properly documented so that the software project members can use these software artifacts during development. This type of task rarely has priority in the development process. In an agile approach to software development, such a task does not seem to have business value. The project team could assume that reuse would slow down the deployment of working software. As shown in this chapter, it's a mistake to make reusable software artifacts slow down project progress. Rather, it can accelerate. The final product would be flexible and easy to adapt to changes.

REUSABLE SOFTWARE ELEMENTS

Nobody would start a software project from scratch these days. Reuse happens all the time, though the development team may not even notice it. Business concepts, architectures and experiences are used repeatedly. Reusable software elements include application systems, subsystems or frameworks, components, modules, objects and functions or procedures (Sommerville, 2015, Leach, 2011). This section explains how to reuse these reusable elements in the following subsections. Each subsection would contain description, motivation, implementation approach, consequence and applicability of the various reusable elements.

Function and Object Libraries

The simplest reusable software items are libraries that contain callable functions or procedures. Throughout software development history, there are many libraries that provide system-related issues such as input and output (IO), scientific and mathematical calculations, and more.

With the development of object-oriented programming we have libraries with application interfaces (API). When we code with Java, the SDK provides the most basic classes for many functions. The functions are constantly being improved and expanded. For legacy programming languages like COBOL, system vendors like IBM would provide a variety of features for their infrastructure, such as security, communications, and database.

Apart from the libraries provided by vendors or open sources, it is always advisable to develop features that are used repeatedly within an organization. A good example is a Java function that is constantly used to read a file within the project class paths with a specific filename. It was noted that there were a dozen implementations in a financial institution to resolve and validate an International Bank Account Number (IBAN). The same functions but different approaches have been found in different programs. The functions are usually hard-coded within the module that needs them. For a developer to implement such a feature, he / she must first understand the structure and validation algorithm of IBAN. This usually takes longer than coding the function. Functions like these examples should be placed in reusable function libraries.

In general, a function in libraries performs exactly one function and requires one or more input parameters. Normally only one output is provided. Such a function is relatively easy to implement. Most programming languages, such as Javascript, support the development of callable functions. In Java, a class can contain a list of static methods. Each of these methods would perform a single function. In COBOL, a function would be a callable module. Reusable libraries in COBOL are basically a collection of modules. A callable COBOL module can contain COBOL structures for its input and output. Libraries in object-oriented languages usually contain object classes. Each object (instant of a class) would represent a distinct entity, and it would contain methods for operating its properties. For example, a list object has list properties and methods to handle list items. For programmers to use functions or objects from a reusable library, documentation must be provided. The minimum documentation for a function contains a description of the operation and a description of the input and output parameters. Descriptions of the object and all its public methods are required for a class.

In an agile development approach, creating reusable object or function libraries does not contribute to immediate business value. Such an activity appears to burden the project and not bring the benefit of enterprise-wide software development. Often this is a mistake. Similar functions and objects can be used repeatedly in an application. The multiple development of the same function or object, especially from different developers, would require much more effort than documenting and storing in a reusable library. The document would also help the QA team to test the object or feature. A QA team can test a function, object, or module as a black box. It helps to improve the quality of the software system.

System and Application

Objects and functions are small reusable elements. Systems and applications can be reused to a greater extent. For example, an achieving system can be integrated when documents are needed to be achieved in an application.

The development of a new system may involve the reuse of a number of applications. For example, the integration of an Enterprise Resource Planning (ERP) system, a Management Information System (MIS), a Customer Relationship Management (CRM) system, and financial applications can be a new general-purpose system for a business. Thus, users do not have to enter the same data for each application. It is also more user-friendly to have a unique system than a number of independent applications.

Such integration would require changes and extensions to individual applications. Independent applications usually have their own data structure and database. In an integrated environment, data such as that for customers, sales, bookings, etc. must be exchanged or shared between applications. An author's suggested approach is to provide APIs to transfer shared data to and from each application. It should be avoided to extend an application so that it can access data from another application. An agent can be used for this purpose. The agent can provide a communication channel between applications. In addition, a new GUI may need to be developed to ensure a consistent style and navigation for the various applications. Again, the front-end GUI can communicate with the agent, which sends the requests to the applications and sends the output of the applications back to the front-end GUI.

For more examples such as Software Product Lines, Commercial Off-the-shelf (COTS), and ERP systems, see Sommerville's (2015) book. Many systems and applications are available commercially or in open source. There are also companies that develop their own systems.

Component

In most organizations, there is a development team that is responsible for the software of a particular business domain. The team usually provides a set of software components that can be invoked by any application as needed. Components are reusable elements. They have a higher granularity than functions or objects in a function library and are sometimes considered as subsystems. Typically, they provide a set of services or interfaces through which they can be activated. They would perform most if not all activities related to their business domain. A business architecture typically includes a component model. This model shows the components available from various business units with the services or interfaces they provide. The technical architecture provides mechanisms for calling business components.

All classes of a Java programmed component are usually packaged in a JAR, WAR, or EAR file. In a legacy environment with COBOL, modules of a component are packaged together. In a service-oriented system, components can provide services to consumers. This allows components to work together in a cross-platform environment in an application.

Architecture and Framework

Any working software has an architecture, although it may not have been designed by the development team. When we create a simple website, we use the HTML framework with the HTTP protocol. Designing architectures is not an issue for many agile development teams, especially when building web applications using frameworks like Node.js, Lavavel, Vue.js or CMS frameworks like Drupal and Wordpress. All of these frameworks have a solid architecture. Developers must follow the style, structure, and mechanism that the architectures of these frameworks dictate for the integration of their program elements.

Architecture is very important for a corporate IT system. The architecture must set standards and mechanisms for executing specific actions in an application. Logging and exception handling are a good example. Imagine, with a sales order something goes awry and it has been processed by different components in different systems. It would be a nightmare if customer support helpdesk staff had to investigate the problem based on the different types of logs from different systems.

One big mistake that a project can make is that application programmers need to have a deep understanding of the technical infrastructure. Application programmers should focus on business logic that brings business benefits. A set of reusable infrastructure components should be developed separately. They are usually programmed by system programmers. If application programmers can focus only on business logic without having to worry about the infrastructure, they are much more efficient, ultimately increasing the agility to make changes to the final application.

Software architectures are generally associated with frameworks. A software framework is an abstraction in which software that provides generic functions can be selectively changed by additional user-written code, thereby providing application-specific software. It is a standard method of creating and deploying applications and is a universal, reusable software environment that provides certain functionality as part of a larger software platform to facilitate the development of software applications, products and solutions. Software frameworks may include support programs, compilers, code libraries, tool sets, and Application Programming Interfaces (APIs) that merge all the different components to enable the development of a project or system.

Following an agile development practice, application programmers should be able to create individual program elements and integrate them into the system in small, time-limited iterations. Therefore, the architecture or framework would have to provide a plug-and-play mechanism for integrating program elements. When the application programmers finish a module, the module must be integrated into the business process. This must be possible without having to modify existing modules to forward data and invoke the new module. In fact, without a plug-and-play architecture framework, it is very difficult to perform the agile incremental and iterative development process.

An example of a plug-and-play architecture was presented by Pang (2016) for a legacy IT system with COBOL programs. A Java implementation of an architecture framework is presented in the next section.

GENERIC PROGRAMMING AND CONFIGURABLE FRAMEWORK

The original concept of generic programming is the implementation of an algorithm with elements that have more than one interpretation, depending on parameters that represent types (Meyer, 1988). In the Cambridge dictionary, generic is defined as "relating to a whole group of similar things, not a specific thing." Generic programming deals with the using abstract representations of efficient algorithms, data structures and other software concepts as well as their systematic organization. The goal of generic programming is to express algorithms and data structures in a broad, interoperable form that allows their direct use in software construction.

Generic programming can be applied to all reusable software elements (Kramer & Finkelstein, 1991; Jazayeri et al., 1998). We can have generic systems, applications, architectures and frameworks, services and components, down to generic functions and procedures. In this chapter, generic programming is considered a flexible, monolithic solution that can be used in a variety of applications and environments. It improves extensibility, reusability and compatibility. An in-depth discussion of the full spectrum of generic programming would go beyond the scope of this chapter. This section introduces some general programming techniques that are suitable for agile development. Topics covered are configurable algorithm and framework as well as scripting languages and generic database schema.

Configurable Algorithm and Framework

Generic programming was first supported in programming languages such as ADA. For a function like swapping two elements you can have the following function declaration:

generic type Element_T is private; -- Generic formal type parameter
procedure Swap (X, Y: in out Element_T);

This function can be applied to elements of all kinds. The type is defined dynamically at runtime when the function is used. The generic type is also supported in Java, as shown below for an ArrayList class:

public class ArrayList<E>;

Generic programming is not limited to what a programming language supports in application development. It is also not limited to primitive functions like swap or base class like a list. You can develop an algorithm for one or more activities that require multiple elements and components to work together. The involved elements or components can be configured in a context.

As discussed in the previous section, an agile development process requires a plug-and-play architecture framework. The example presented here is a framework that is based on a finite-state machine in the form of a Java-programmed process control. The steps and processes of the process controller are configured externally. The implementation of such a process controller is shown in the code segment in Figure 1.

The finite-state machine (i.e. the process controller) calls an object based on the actual state and event. An object must provide an event for the transition after completing its task. This event usually depends on the result of the process. If everything is ok, the default event is an "OK" event. This event, along with the status of the process, is used by process control to determine the next object to invoke. This implementation uses the Spring framework. The configuration of the process controller is specified in a text file in JSON (see Figure 2).

For an object to perform its task, input data is always required. The process controller should be generic and not responsible for transferring data to the objects. A data transfer mechanism can be achieved using a data object container. Each object retrieves data objects that provide the input from that container and fills the output data with the output objects that are eventually stored in the container. The application context of Spring framework can be used as a data object container. Figure 3 shows an example of the Java implementation of an object and the retrieval of data objects from the Application Context of the Spring framework.

After implementing an object for a step in the business process in an iteration, the object can be inserted into the configuration of the process controller in the process descriptor file. The design of the business process must ensure that the required data objects are available at runtime when the object is activated by the process controller.

The example above shows the power of generic programming. It shows how a continuous integration of iteratively developed program elements can be achieved. The implementation of the process controller can be used in any business process in any application.

Script Language and Generic Database Schema

In an agile development process, application programmers develop program elements iteratively. Each iteration has a short timeframe and therefore the program elements should be kept rather small. It may happen that the functionality of a program element is small, but the development of the required infrastructure is rather a big task, e.g., designing a database to store persistent data. An application programmer may feel that designing a well-structured database has no business value. Therefore, he / she would save the data in some files without a suitable format. In this case, it would be a nightmare for the other developer who needs to create a search engine for the data.

Figure 1. Implementation of generic process controller using finite state pattern

```java
public void build() throws Exception {
 if (applicationContext == null) {
        applicationContext = new ClassPathXmlApplicationContext("/applicationContext.xml");
 }
 InputStream stream = new ClassPathResource(configName).getInputStream();
 String configData = IOUtils.toString(stream, StandardCharsets.UTF_8);
 JSONParser parser = new JSONParser();
 JSONObject processObj = (JSONObject) parser.parse(configData);
 JSONArray arr = (JSONArray) processObj.get("process");
 String stateEvent = "start";
 if (arr != null) {
  for (Object proc : arr) {
   String state = ((JSONObject) proc).get("state").toString();
   if (stateEvent.equals("start")) {
    startState = state;
   }
   if (processTable == null) {
    processTable = new HashMap<String, BusinessProcess>();
    nextStateTable = new HashMap<String, String>();
   }
   BusinessProcess process = processTable.get(state);
   if (process == null) {
    String name = ((JSONObject) proc).get("name").toString();
    process = (BusinessProcess) applicationContext.getBean(name);
    processTable.put(state, process);
   }
   if (stateEvent.equals("start")) {
    nextStateTable.put(stateEvent, state);
   }
   String event = ((JSONObject) proc).get("event").toString();
   stateEvent = state + " : " + event;
   String nextState = ((JSONObject) proc).get("next state").toString();
   nextStateTable.put(stateEvent, nextState);
  }
 }
}

public String start() throws Exception {
 String stateEvent = "start";
 String state = startState;
 while (!state.equals("exit")) {
  BusinessProcess process = processTable.get(state);
  String event = process.execute(stateEvent);
  if (!state.equals("exit")) {
   state = nextStateTable.get(stateEvent);
   stateEvent = state + " : " + event;
  }
 }
 return stateEvent;
}
```

Figure 2. Process descriptor in JSON

```
{"process": [
  {"state": "validate input", "name": "validate_input", "event": "OK", "next state": "check eligibility"},
  {"state": "validate input", "name": "validate_input", "event": "Invalid Input", "next state": "handle error"},
  {"state": "check eligibility", "name": "check_eligibility", "event": "OK", "next state": "check availability"},
  {"state": "check eligibility", "name": "check_eligibility", "event": "Not Eligible", "next state": "handle error"},
  {"state": "check availability", "name": "check_availability", "event": "OK", "next state": "exit"},
  {"state": "check availability", "name": "check_availability", "event": "Not Available", "next state": "handle error"},
  {"state": "handle error", "name": "handle_error", "event": "OK", "next state": "exit"}
]}
```

Figure 3. Example of data object and its retrieval from spring framework application context

```
public interface OrderCurrData {
    void setISOCode(String iso);
    void setAccount(String account);
    void setAmount(double amount);
    void setBookingText(String bookingText);
    void setCreditDebitFlag(int flag);

    String getISOCode();
    String getAccount();
    double getAmount();
    String getBookingText();
    int getCreditDebitFlag();
}

// Object that sets the data
OrderCurrData outCurrData = (OrderCurrData) applicationContext.getBean("Order Curr Data");
outCurrData.setISOCode(isoCode);
outCurrData.setAccount(accountNo);
...

// Object that gets the data
OrderCurrData inCurrData = (OrderCurrData) applicationContext.getBean("Order Curr Data");
String isoCode = inCurrData.getISOCode();
String accountNo = inCurrData.getAccount();
...
```

Most applications require a proper database design. This task would require a detailed analysis of the affected persistent data and the required search mechanisms. Many modules to be developed in later iterations depend on this design. Therefore, the project requires a pre-defined detail design task that does not conform to the concept of an agile development process. One possible solution is a generic database schema.

In a normal database schema, a table is created for each data structure, whose columns are mapped to the fields of the data structure. This would not work for a generic database schema because it has to process different data structures. One solution to this problem is to use a scripting language such as XML or JSON. Instead of storing each field in a separate column, each entry stores a single text in XML or JSON that contains the entire data structure. In other words, the table-based database effectively becomes a document-based database. Document-based databases are a feature of NoSQL. However, most organizations prefer to use mature and stable relational SQL databases, such as IBM DB2, Oracle, MySQL, etc. instead of NoSQL.

The most common SQL relational databases support the storage and indexing of documents. IBM DB2 provides support for XML and JSON documents. MySQL offers Document Store with X DevAPI for JSON documents. They also support transaction processing for documents. It is possible to create a generic module to handle both basic CRUD operations and transactions for various data structures.

An example with Java is worked out here. This example uses simple old Java objects (POJO) to represent data structures. The persistent data processing capabilities provided by the generic Java object are shown in Figure 4. The basic mechanism includes the following. The data structure represented by the POJO is resolved using Java Reflection. Depending on the requested function, a corresponding JSON document is generated using the data structure as well as the data of the POJO. The metadata such as the name of the data structure and the indexed fields are needed to create a new data structure. The function search allows search criteria written in a script such as "age <30 and gender = m". Other features shown in Figure 4 are quite transparent.

Figure 4. Generic Java persistent object interface

```
public interface SmfwPersistentManager {
    void init();
    void close() throws Exception;
    String startTransaction() throws Exception;
    void commit(String transName) throws Exception;
    void rollback(String transName) throws Exception;
    void close(String transName) throws Exception;

    void setCurrentSchema(String schemaName) throws Exception;
    void createNewDataStructure(String dataStructureName) throws Exception;
    void createIndex(String dataStructureName,
        String indexName, String[] fields) throws Exception;

    void add(String dataStructureName, Object pojo) throws Exception;
    Object find(String dataStructureName, Object pojo) throws Exception;
    void modify(String dataStructureName, Object searchPojo, Object newPojo) throws Exception;
    void delete(String dataStructureName, Object searchPojo) throws Exception;
    List<Object> search(String dataStructureName, String searchCriteria) throws Exception;
}
```

The use of a document-based database has advantages and disadvantages compared to a table-based database. There are a considerable number of articles that explain the two types of database styles (Chan, 2019; Shiff & Rowe, 2018). The main advantage of the document-based database is that the data schema can be flexibly changed without having to change existing data. With the implementation of a generic module (see Figure 4), application programmers do not need to create individual schemas for their data structures. Programmers do not have to worry about database connection and writing SQL statements to their program elements. It is more suitable for agile development processes.

PATTERN BASED REUSE

We live in a world full of patterns. Our habits are nothing more than repeatedly following a series of behavioral patterns. Since the publication of the book by Gamma et al. (1995), software developers have been made aware of patterns that we are constantly using and should be used in software development. A pattern is defined as the solution to a problem in a particular context. A pattern-driven approach would be to identify the problem to be solved and look up the pattern that provides the solution to the problem in the given context.

In software development, there are patterns for the development process, patterns for architectural, structural and behavioral designs, as well as code patterns for implementation and so on. Usage patterns provide a general overview of the use of applications. They help identify the information a business component should deliver and the expected interactions with other components. The pattern-driven approach complements the agile approach to software development in a way that accelerates developmental iterations by avoiding reinventing the wheel at every stage of development.

Patterns can accelerate the development process by providing proven and proven development paradigms. They should be stored in a repository and published so that every developer in the enterprise can access them. This section explains various types of patterns for analysis and business process, architecture and design, and usage and code in the subsections.

Analysis and Business Patterns

In his classic book, Martin Fowler defines a pattern as an "idea that was useful in one practical context and is likely to be useful in others" (Fowler, 1996). He also discusses the analysis paradigm that reflects "conceptual structures of business processes, not actual software implementations." Analysis patterns are conceptual models that capture an abstraction of a typical situation in modeling. They focus on the organizational, social and economic aspects of a system, as these aspects are central to the requirements analysis and the acceptability and usability of the final system (Geyer-Schulz & Hahsler, 2001).

In addition to business processes, under certain circumstances there may be patterns for conducting analysis. An example is the pattern described by Wake (Wake, 2018) for writing and sharing user stories. The Scrum model can also be viewed as a model for an agile software development process.

Identifying reusable patterns in an IT system can be of great value. Business processes, rules, algorithms and data structures are generally refined and proven over the years. They can be very useful for the future development and improvement of applications. They also provide documentation of the system in operation and materials for training business analysts and developers. In fact, the way companies do business always follows certain patterns. They rarely change, though there may be variations in the details. For example, the business process of a customer business order always includes the following four processes, regardless of the product type for the business:

1. Trade order entry.
2. Validation of the trade order after accounts have been selected for settlement and booking.
3. Making an offer with quote and pricing information.
4. Acceptance of the offer for the trade by the client and start of the trade settlement process.

There are also standard patterns for dealing with errors and exceptions when the validation fails or the time for an offer has expired, etc. The trade validation process also includes standard checks for entitlement, availability, credit and amount limits, and so on. When developing a customer order application for a new product, business analysts can follow these patterns to identify the detail requirements of business process steps and include them as tasks in the product backlog in the Scrum development process.

Architectural and Design Patterns

The concept of the design pattern in software development was first described by Gamma et al. al. (Gamma, 1995). It focuses on finding a reusable solution to a common problem in a particular software design context. It is not intended as a ready-made design that application programmers convert directly to source code. It is more a description of how to solve a problem that can be used in many different situations. Developers still have to adapt the design to their specific requirements.

In the classic book by Gamma et al. there are a number of examples of categories such as creation patterns, texture patterns, and patterns of behavior. The use of delegation, aggregation and consultation concepts is well described. In general, you cannot simply pick up one of these examples with source code and use it as it is. For example, consider a design pattern for facet and decor type enhancements presented by Pang (Pang, 2001). In the example he tries to solve the problem that a university member can be a student or an employee. The member can also be both a student and an employee. Depending on the client's use of the college member object, it may be a student or a co-worker. The exact problem does not occur in most business cases. However, presenting a business partner who is both a customer and a supplier is a similar problem. The solution and much of the featured base code can be used after the solution has been tailored to the problem of each business partner.

Patterns presented in the literature are usually for general purposes. In a corporation for a particular business, there are many design patterns that can be reused in multiple applications. They are domain-specific patterns. An example of a domain-specific pattern is a series of activities involved in the booking process of an order (see below):

1. Get the amount decimal places for the respective product from the financial instrument component.
2. Convert the booking amount for the order into a format with the correct decimal places.
3. If the order amount unit is the currency unit of the ledger, use the same amount to post the ledger.
4. If the order amount unit is not the currency unit of the ledger, proceed as follows:
   a. Get the exchange rate from the financial instrument component.
   b. Convert the booking amount to the amount in ledger currency.
   c. Use the converted amount for ledger booking.

Design patterns can also be applied in the software architecture. In fact, there are many well-structured architectural patterns. Some of the most popular are client / server, layer architecture, component-based architecture, event-driven architecture, model-view-controller (MVC), service-oriented architecture (SOA), etc. (Richards 2015). In his book, Fowler presented many patterns for enterprise application architecture (Fowler, 2006). Patterns include object relational mapping, web presentation, concurrency, session state, etc. To design an architecture for an enterprise IT system, it is usually necessary to identify the combination of architectural patterns that meet the requirements (Pang, 2015; Pang, 2016).

Developers should be encouraged to use patterns. They should also be trained to identify the theme and variations of their design and implementation in order to derive patterns that developers can reuse for other applications with similar problems.

Code Patterns and Template

A pattern is usually associated with templates in the form of models or snippets of code. Developers can complete the design or implementation with context-specific elements based on these templates. Note the domain-specific pattern of activities involved in the posting process of a purchase order example in the previous subsection. We can have a code segment as shown in Figure 5.

Figure 5. Code pattern of booking process

```
FinancialInstrument finInst = (FinancialInstrument)
  applicationContext.getBean("FinancialInstrument");
ISOData bookingISOData = finInst.getISOData(${BookingISO});
double bookingAmountDouble = ${OrigAmount} * bookingISOData.getDecimal();
int bookingAmount = (int) Math.round(bookingAmountDouble);

BookingManager bookingManager = (BookingManager)
  applicationContext.getBean(${BookingManager});
bookingManager.setNewBooking();
bookingManager.setAccount(${AccountNo});
bookingManager.setAmount(bookingAmount, bookingISOData.getDecimal());
bookingManager.setBookingText(${BookingText});
bookingManager.setCreditDebitFlag(${CreditDebitFlag});

if (${BookingISO}.equals(bookingISOData.getLedgerISOCode())) {
        bookingManager.setLedgerAmount(bookingAmount, bookingISOData.getDecimal());
} else {
        double ledgerAmountDouble = ${OrigAmount} *
         finInst.getLedgerExchangeRate(${BookingISO}) *
          bookingISOData.getLedgerDecimal();
        int ledgerAmount = (int) Math.round(ledgerAmountDouble);
        bookingManager.setLedgerAmount(ledgerAmount, bookingISOData.getLedgerDecimal());
}
bookingManager.book();
```

The code segment in Figure 5 uses the symbols $ {xxx} as wildcards. With this code segment, developers can replace all placeholders with correct variable names. With available code segments and reusable templates, developers can finish the code with little effort.

REUSE IN MODEL DRIVEN APPROACH

Software development usually starts with modeling. Models provide abstractions of high-level design concepts and enable communication between software users that code alone cannot. These models are drawn on a flipchart or graphically displayed in a CASE tool. After all, these models become programs in one way or another.

The Object Management Group (OMG) attempts to standardize modeling techniques in software development in a Model Driven Architecture (MDA) (MDA, 2010; Mellor, 2004). MDA is seen as a way to organize and manage enterprise architectures that are supported by automated tools and services to both define the models and facilitate the transformation between different model types. MDA should provide a blueprint for rapid software development. The focus is on rigorous software modeling and code generation from models.

In this section, the first subsection introduces an approach that combines agile practice and model-driven software development. This is followed by a subsection on reusable model patterns. As demonstrated later in this section, the model-driven approach to rapidly deploying workable software is very effective. The final product is flexible and can easily be adapted to changes. This is exactly the goal of an agile development process.

Agile and Model Driven Approach to Software Development

In a recent article titled "no developers required: Why this company chose no-code over software devs" (Clark, 2019), Clark reported:

- A Dutch insurer has decided no-code development lets it create new services faster.
- Univé turned to the no-code platform from Betty Blocks to help business experts develop software. It offers a graphical approach to building software, instead of requiring developers to key in lines of code.
- Univé innovation manager Bas Wit commented that normal development simply takes too much time and one never gets exactly what one wants the first time around.

Agile development process Scrum does not really define how analysis and development should be done. Scrum promoters generally recommend a Product Backlog with a list of all requirements in the form of user stories (Rehkopf, 2019). User stories are selected according to their business value priorities and programmed in consecutive sprint iterations. The question now is how to ensure that user stories can capture all the needs of a complex application, especially if they are small enough to be implemented in a sprint. The second question is how to get a complete overview of business workflow and processes from user stories. User stories are not detailed requirements specifications. Therefore, many negotiations between customers, business analysts and developers are expected to be required. Interestingly enough, many models are being eradicated during these negotiations. Converting the scratched models into formal models that can be converted into codes would be a very effective and fast way to build working software. Converting models to code requires more detailed information and possibly some code segments. This approach has proven to be very successful (Pang, 2016).

Unfortunately, there are only a few modeling tools that can do a complete model code transformation. However, the meta-information of the models can be extracted from most models. In addition to code templates and patterns, domain-specific code generators can be easily created (Pang, 2016). Experience has shown that many application programmers write spaghetti code. Code verification is a tedious and time-consuming task. With a short sprint time frame and an urgent delivery of program elements, this task is often omitted. As a result, the program may be of poor quality and difficult to maintain. On the other hand, you can create spaghetti code, but it would be difficult to create a spaghetti model. Model are easy to change and improve. They are perfect for the documentation. Generated code usually has the same structure and pattern, so it's easy to follow. The construction of code generators initially seems to bring no business benefits. However, measured against the experience of graphical and model-driven approaches, this can bring enormous economic benefits in the long term.

Reusable Model Patterns

Patterns can be abstracted in models. Frequently, code patterns and templates are assigned to the patterns. The domain-specific pattern example shows a number of activities involved in the booking process of an order. An action with parameters symbol can be used to represent this pattern. In a UML activity diagram, an action that should use this pattern may have a link to the pattern icon with constraints indicating the association of the program variables with the parameters. Figure 6 shows the action link to the pattern. The link is also associated with a UML constraint that provides the mapping information of program variables for the placeholders of the example code segment shown in Figure 5.

Figure 6 shows the model of a simple order process. Most of the code is actually provided by the patterns. There is only one action with the stereotype << code >>, which contains a small piece of code. The {thrown exception} constraint for the process indicates that the generated code for the OrderBooking class involves throwing an exception. Based on the model, a complete code for the OrderBooking class can be generated.

Business Process Pattern

Patterns can be fine-grained and cover only the design and / or implementation of a particular data or architectural structure, algorithms such as account verification or error logging, or the use of certain elements of software components. It can also cover the entire process of a business process. Take the example of a model for the order validation process in a financial institution. The model can represent an abstraction applied to various order validation such as foreign exchange orders, payment orders, security orders, etc. with some differences. The collaborative business components in the process flow, such as customer information, employee information, product, contract, financial instrument, pricing engine, etc., are similar in different order types. In this way, reusable patterns in the form of models, templates and code snippets can be created, which can be parameterized. Once these patterns exist for a business process, repeating the implementation for another business case can be greatly simplified.

A model for the order validation process is shown in figure 7. From this model, the JSON process descriptor shown in figure 2 can be generated. For the program to work, the implementation of each step of the process flow must follow a specific pattern. For example, it must retrieve input data from the context container and place output data in the context container, as previously described. It must return an event after completion. If an error occurs, an error object must be placed in the context container for the error handler to retrieve it.

As shown in figure 7, the model is pretty simple. Adding new process steps or removing existing process steps is a simple task. It provides a plug-and-play mechanism for continuously integrating new process steps that are developed iteratively.

Figure 6. Order booking process model

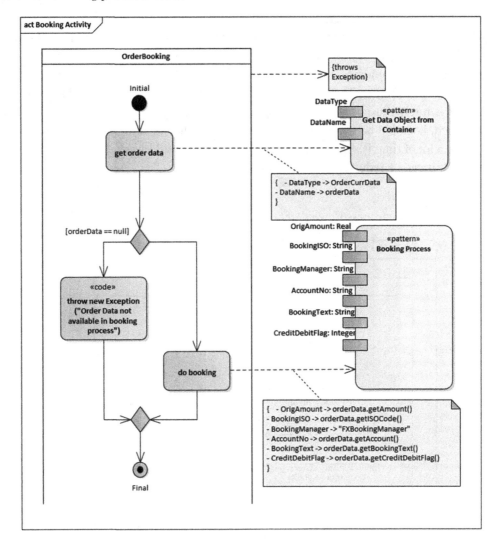

Consequences and Project Experience

Creating generic programs and code generators requires development effort. They have no business benefit. However, experience has shown that projects that focus on architecture and reuse are typically completed successfully and quickly (Pang, 2015; Pang, 2016). The code generators and generic programs described in this chapter are actually quite simple to create. They do not require a sophisticated mechanism. In fact, in one of the first projects where the modeling approach was used, the code was created manually in the same way that a code generator should. This step has shown that the approach is feasible when applied to real projects. The first experience with this approach was a project that initially started with a normal programming approach. After one and three-quarter years of development, progress was too slow and there was no sign of completion. Modeling and generic programming approach were introduced to rebuild the project from scratch. It only took four months to complete the project with some primitive code generators installed. When completed, there were 800 change requests. All of them were easy to integrate into the application. Since then, many new applications have been created using the same approach for 15 years. They were all completed on time and within budget.

Many programmers would say that they can write modules and JSON scripts just as fast as modeling and code generation. One key difference is that you can present a model in a meeting with users, business analysts, and stakeholders, and change it immediately. This is not possible with a code. Models are also great for documentation. They give an overview of how the application works. Code written by one programmer is rarely reused by another programmer. Model patterns optimize reuse. In terms of development speed, it should be noted that most of the time when developing a module is not writing the code. Rather, a lot of time is spent figuring out how things should work. With patterns and generic programs, this effort can be reduced enormously.

Figure 7. Order validation process flow model

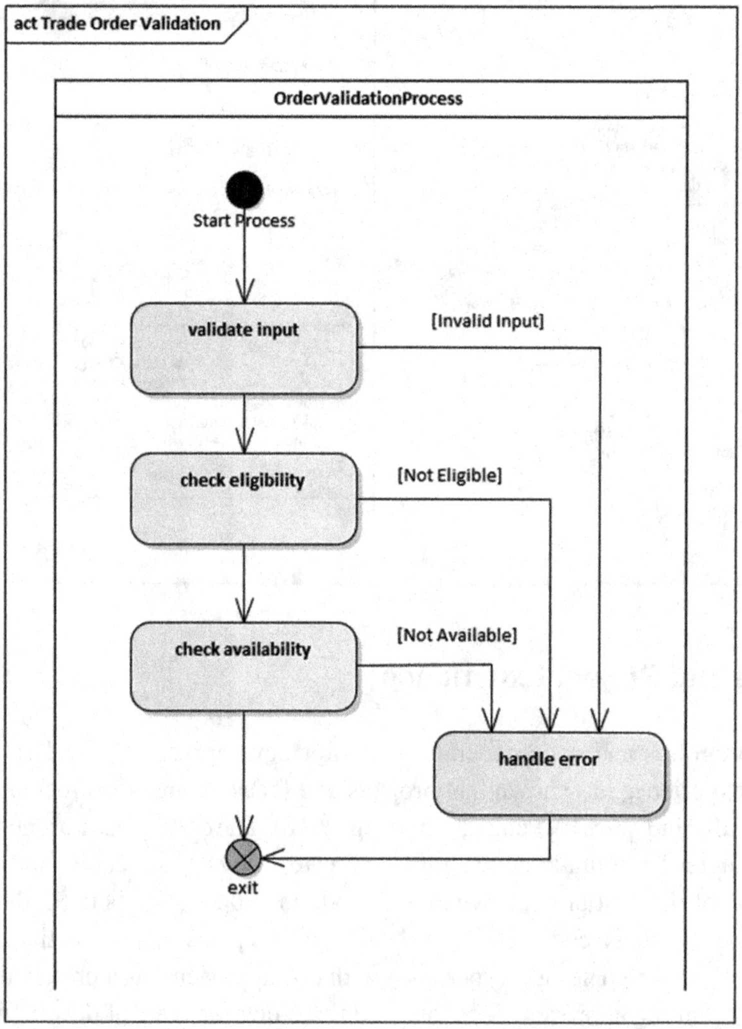

Code segments of patterns are usually stable after writing, testing and deploying. The reuse of these code segments provides better quality every time to rewrite similar code from scratch. Models are much easier to change than code. It is much easier to see the impact of the model changes than the code. Often, changing the code in one place has unexpected effects on the others. This is usually not the case for models. If you need to set a new business rule for all applications in this pattern, all programs that use this pattern can be easily identified using the CASE tool. On the other hand, it is quite difficult to find all the code in different applications where such a change should be made.

VISION FOR THE FUTURE

Low-code or no-code development platforms have begun to enter the software community trend. They hold many promises. However, many software developers still believe that they are not suitable for applications with complex, enterprise-specific logic and infrastructure requirements. Large organizations have the most basic logic and business logic and engineering infrastructure components. If they can be identified together with generic programs as reusable elements in the form of model patterns, a low-code or no-code development platform can be developed for an enterprise. This requires further research.

Other important advances in software technologies in recent years have been artificial intelligence, natural language processing and pattern recognition. These technologies can be applied to software development. A future vision is the ability to analyze user requirements, create new business rules, identify program patterns, and then automate application development using these technologies. Research in this area is paying off.

CONCLUSION

Do not get stuck by reinventing the wheel, but go ahead and build on what has been done. If something has already been done, try reusing it as often as possible. Reuse is an important topic in software development. Because design patterns have been introduced, reuse is not limited to code. It has been extended to analysis and design concepts as well as the way things are to be done.

Despite the benefits of reuse in application development, it is not common for application programmers to develop classes or modules that are reusable. Reuse is always restricted to developers who reuse their own previous works. The popularity of the agile software development approach does not really encourage building reusable software elements. More emphasis has been put on the rapid coding and development of program elements that seem to have the highest business value for end users. Systematic reuse requires engineering and support tools. It has no obvious business value and therefore is not even be considered. This chapter has shown that this is a mistake. The systematic reuse of software elements can improve the software development process, enabling fast delivery of high quality software and easy adaptation to changes.

The main reusable software elements including application systems, subsystems or frameworks, components, modules, objects, and functions or procedures with their motivation, implementation concept, consequences and applicability in agile development process are described in this chapter. Three approaches to develop reusable software artefacts that evolved out of 15 years of experience in agile development process are presented. The first approach is to create generic programs or configurable frameworks that support similar solutions for a variety of use cases and environments. Reuse of pattern is the second approach presented. Another effective way, not just for reuse but for general software development, is to use a model-driven approach with model patterns. These approaches can pave the way for a corporation to have a low-code development platform.

This chapter describes the key reusable software elements, including application systems, subsystems or frameworks, components, modules, objects, and functions or procedures, with their motivation, implementation concept, consequences, and applicability in the agile development process. Three approaches to the development of reusable software artifacts, resulting from 15 years of experience in the agile development process, are presented. The first approach is to create generic programs or configurable frameworks that support similar solutions for a variety of use cases and environments. The reuse of patterns is the second approach presented. Another effective way, not just for reuse but for general software development, is to use a model-driven approach with model patterns. These approaches can pave the way for a corporation to develop a low-code development platform.

To encourage reuse, the development teams must build a culture. It does not come automatically. Development teams need to recognize and enforce the benefits. By training the development team, providing tools and infrastructure for reusable libraries, creating configurable frameworks, adapting the model-driven approach to code generation, and so on, the reuse culture of the development team can evolve.

REFERENCES

Agile Manifesto Group. (2001). Manifesto for Agile Software Development. *Agile Manifesto*. Retrieved July 26, 2010, from http://agilemanifesto.org

Ambler, S. W. (2010). Agile Modeling. *Ambysoft*. Retrieved July 26, 2010, from http://www.agilemodeling.com/

Biggerstaff, T. J., & Perlis, A. J. (1989). *Frontier Series: Software Reusability* (Vols. 1-2). New York, N.Y.: ACM Press.

Biggerstaff, T. J., & Richter, C. (1989). Reusability Framework, Assessment, and Directions. Frontier Series: Software Reusability: Vol. I. *Concepts and Models*. ACM Press.

Chan, M. (2019). SQL vs. NoSQL – what's the best option for your database needs? *Thorn Technologies*. Retrieved July 19, 2019, from https://www.thorntech.com/2019/03/sql-vs-nosql

Clark, L. (2019). No developers required: Why this company chose no-code over software devs. *ZDNet*. Retrieved June 26, 2019, from https://www.zdnet.com/google-amp/article/no-developers-required-why-this-company-chose-no-code-over-software-devs/

Fowler, M. (1996). *Analysis Patterns: Reusable Object Models*. Boston, MA: Addison-Wesley.

Fowler, M. (2006). *Patterns of Enterprise Application Architecture*. Boston, MA: Addison-Wesley.

Frakes, W. B., & Kang, K. (2005). Software Reuse Research: Status and Future. *IEEE Transactions on Software Engineering*, *13*(7), 529–536. doi:10.1109/TSE.2005.85

Freeman, P. (1987). *Tutorial: Software Reusability*. Los Alamitos, CA: IEEE Computer Society Press.

Gamma, E., Helm, R., Johnson, R., & Vlissides, L. (1995). *Design Patterns: Elements of Reusable Object-Oriented Software*. Reading, MA: Addison-Wesley.

Geyer-Schulz, A., & Hahsler, M. (2001). Software Engineering with Analysis Patterns. *CiteSeerX*. Retrieved May 26, 2019, from http://citeseerx.ist.psu.edu/viewdoc/summary?doi=10.1.1.70.8415

Harlow, M. (2014). Coconut Headphones: Why Agile Has Failed. *Code Rant*. Retrieved December 11, 2014, from http://mikehadlow.blogspot.ch/2014/03/coconut-headphones-why-agile-has-failed.html

Hastie, S., & Wojewoda, S. (2015). Standish Group 2015 Chaos Report - Q&A with Jennifer Lynch. *InfoQ*. Retrieved from May 26, 2019, from https://www.infoq.com/articles/standish-chaos-2015

Horowitz, E., & Munson, J. B. (1984, September). An Expansive View of Reusable Software. *IEEE Transaction on Software Engineering SE, 10*(5), 477–487. doi:10.1109/TSE.1984.5010270

Ismail, N. (2017). UK wasting 37 billion a year on failed agile IT projects. *Information Age*. Retrieved May 26, 2019, from https://www.information-age.com/uk-wasting-37-billion-year-failed-agile-it-projects-123466089/

Jacobson, I., Griss, M., & Jonsson, P. (1997). *Software Reuse. Architecture, Process and Organization for Business Success*. Reading, MA: Addison Wesley.

Jazayeri, M., Loos, R. G. K., & Musser, D. R. (1998). Generic Programming. In *International Seminar on Generic Programming Dagstuhl Castle, Germany*. Berlin, Germany: Springer.

Jones, C. (1984). Reusability in programming: A survey of the state of the art. *IEEE Transactions on Software Engineering, 10*(5), 488–494. doi:10.1109/TSE.1984.5010271

Kramer, J., & Finkelstein, A. (1991). A Configurable Framework for Method and Tool Integration. *European Symposium on Software Development Environments and CASE Technology*. Retrieved May 26, 2019, from http://citeseerx.ist.psu.edu/viewdoc/download?doi=10.1.1.129.7971&rep=rep1&type=pdf

Krueger, C. W. (1992). Software Reuse. *ACM Computing Surveys, 24*(2), 131–183. doi:10.1145/130844.130856

Larman, C. (2003). *Agile and Iterative Development: A Manager's Guide*. Reading, MA: Addison-Wesley.

Leach, R. J. (2011). *Software Reuse: Methods, Models, and Costs*. Retrieved May 26, 2019, from https://pdfs.semanticscholar.org/700b/83bc8d4a2e4c1d1f4395a4c8fb78462c9f5a.pdf

MDA. (2010). MDA – The Architecture of Choice for a Changing World. *OMG*. Retrieved July 12, 2017, from https://www.omg.org/mda/

Mellor, S. J., Scott, K., Uhl, A., & Weise, D. (2004). *MDA Distilled: Principles of Model-Driven Architecture*. Reading, MA: Addison-Wesley.

Meyer, B. (1988). Genericity Versus Inheritance. *Journal of Pascal, Ada, & Modula-2, 7*(2), 13-30.

Pang, C. Y. (2001). A Design Pattern Type Extension with Facets and Decorators. *Journal of Object-Oriented Programming, 13*(13), 14–18.

Pang, C. Y. (2015). Ten Years of Experience with Agile and Model Driven Software Development in a Legacy Platform. In A. Singh (Ed.), *Emerging Innovations in Agile Software Development*. Hershey, PA: IGI Global.

Pang, C. Y. (2016). An Agile Architecture for a Legacy Enterprise IT System. *International Journal of Organizational and Collective Intelligence*, 6(4), 65–97. doi:10.4018/IJOCI.2016100104

Rehkopf, M. (2019). User Stories. *Atlassian Agile Guide*. Retrieved May 22, 2019, from https://www.atlassian.com/agile/project-management/user-stories

Richards, M. (2015). *Software Architecture Patterns*. Sebastopol, CA: O'Reilly.

Shiff, L., & Rowe, W. (2018). NoSQL vs SQL: Examining the Differences and Deciding Which to Choose. *Bmc*. Retrieved July 11, 2019, from https://www.bmc.com/blogs/sql-vs-nosql

Software Crisis. (2010). Software Crisis. *Wikipedia*. Retrieved July 26, 2010, from http://en.wikipedia.org/wiki/Software_crisis

Software Engineering. (2010). Software Engineering. Wikipedia. Retrieved July 26, 2010, from http://en.wikipedia.org/wiki/Software_engineering

Sommerville, I. (2015). *Software Engineering* (10th ed.). Essex, UK: Pearson Education Limited.

Soora, S. K. (2014). A Framework for Software Reuse and Research *Challenges*. *International Journal of Advanced Research in Computer Science and Software Engineering*, 4(8), 441–448.

Stellman, A., & Greene, J. (2015). *Learning Agile: Understand SCRUM, XP, Lean, and Kanban*. Sebastopol, CA: O'Reilly.

Wake, B. (2018). Back to basics: Writing and splitting user stories. *Medium.com*. Retrieved May 25, 2019, from https://medium.com/agile-outside-the-box/back-to-basics-writing-and-splitting-user-stories-8903a931499c

ADDITIONAL READING

Agile Software Development Process, & the Agile Manifesto Group. (2001). Manifesto for Agile Software Development. *Agile Manifesto*. http://agilemanifesto.org

Ambler, S. W. (2010). Agile Modeling. *Ambysoft*. Retrieved July 26, 2010, from http://www.agilemodeling.com/

Bass, L., Clements, P., & Kazman, R. (2003). *Software Architecture in Practice* (2nd ed.). Reading, MA: Addison-Wesley.

Erl, T. (2009). *SOA Design Patterns*. Upper Saddle River, NJ: Prentice Hall PTR.

Ezran, M., Morisio, M., & Tully, C. (2002). *Practical Software Reuse*. London, UK: Springer. doi:10.1007/978-1-4471-0141-3

Fowler, M. (1997). *Analysis Patterns: Reusable Object Models*. Reading, MA: Addison-Wesley.

Fowler, M. (2006). *Patterns of Enterprise Application Architecture*. Reading, MA: Addison-Wesley.

Gamma, E., Helm, R., Johnson, R., & Vlissides, L. (1995). *Design Patterns: Elements of Reusable Object-Oriented Software*. Reading, MA: Addison-Wesley.

Garland, J., & Anthony, R. (2003). *Large-Scale Software Architecture: A Practical Guide using UML*. West Sussex, UK: John Wiley & Son.

Geetha, C., Subramanian, C., & Dutt, S. (2015). *Software Engineering*. Delhi, India: Pearson Education India.

Hohpe, G., & Woolfe, B. (2004). *Enterprise Integration Patterns: Designing, Building, and Deploying Messaging Solutions*. Reading, MA: Addison-Wesley.

Hunt, J. (2006). *Agile Software Construct*. London, UK: Springer.

Larman, C. (2003). *Agile and Iterative Development: A Manager's Guide*. Reading, MA: Addison-Wesley.

McGovern, J., Ambler, S. W., Stevens, M. E., Linn, J., Sharan, V., & Jo, E. K. (2003). *A Practical Guide To Enterprise Architecture*. Upper Saddle River, NJ: Prentice Hall PTR.

Mellor, S. J., Scott, K., Uhl, A., & Weise, D. (2004). *MDA Distilled: Principles of Model-Driven Architecture*. Reading, MA: Addison-Wesley.

Model-Driven Approach to Software Development. Arlow, J. & Neustadt, I. (2004). Enterprise Patterns and MDA: Building Better Software with Archetype Patterns and UML. Reading, MA: Addison-Wesley.

Shamil, F. R. (2019). Software reuse and software reuse oriented software engineering. T4 Tutorials. Retrieved July 11, 2019, from https://t4tutorials.com/software-reuse-and-software-reuse-oriented-software-engineering/

Sommerville, I. (2015). *Software Engineering* (10th ed.). Essex, UK: Pearson Education Limited.

KEY TERMS AND DEFINITIONS

Agile Software Development Process: An evolutionary and iterative approach to software development with focuses on adaptation to changes.

COBOL: The programming language designed for commercial business data processing used for applications that often form the backbone of the IT structure in many corporations since 1960.

CRUD (Create, Read, Update, and Delete): Basic functions of a computer database.

Design Pattern: A reusable solution to a common problem in a particular software design context.

Document-Oriented Database: A database designed for storing, retrieving and managing document-oriented information, also known as semi-structured data.

Generic Programming: An implementation of an algorithm with elements that have more than one interpretation, depending on parameters representing types.

JSON (JavaScript Object Notation): An open-standard file format that uses human-readable text to transmit data objects consisting of attribute–value pairs and array data type.

MDA (Model-Driven Architecture): An approach to structuring software specifications that are expressed as models for software design, development, and implementation.

Model-Driven Approach to Software Development: A model centric rather than a code centric approach to software development with code generated from models.

NoSQL: A non-SQL database that provides a mechanism for storage and retrieval of data that is modeled in means other than the tabular relations used in relational databases.

Plain Old Java Object (POJO): An ordinary Java object, not bound by any special restriction and not requiring any class path.

Service-Oriented Architecture (SOA): A technical software architecture that allows client applications to request services from service provider type applications in a host system.

Software Component: A software unit of functionality that manages a single abstraction.

Software Engineering: The application of engineering to the development of software in a systematic method.

Software Reuse: The process of creating software systems from predefined software components.

Spring Framework: An application framework and inversion of control container for the Java platform.

UML (Unified Modeling Language): A general-purpose, developmental, modeling language in the field of software engineering that is intended to provide a standard way to visualize the design of a system.

XML (Extensible Markup Language): A markup language that defines a set of rules for encoding documents in a format that is both human-readable and machine-readable.

This research was previously published in Software Engineering for Agile Application Development; pages 164-187, copyright year 2020 by Engineering Science Reference (an imprint of IGI Global).

Chapter 73
The Role of Functional Diversity, Collective Team Identification, and Task Cohesion in Influencing Innovation Speed:
Evidence From Software Development Teams

Jin Chen

School of Business, East China University of Science and Technology, Shanghai, China

Wei Yang Lim

Deston Precision Engineering Pte Ltd, Singapore

Bernard C.Y. Tan

Department of Information Systems and Analytics, National University of Singapore, Singapore

Hong Ling

Department of Information Management and Information Systems, Fudan University, Shanghai, China

ABSTRACT

This article opens up the black box of innovation and examines the relationship between functional diversity in software teams and the often neglected dimension of innovation – speed, over the two phases of innovation: creativity and idea implementation. By combining information processing view and social identity theory, the authors hypothesize that when collective team identification is low, functional diversity positively affects the time spent in the creativity phase; however, when collective team identification is high, this relationship is inverted U-shaped. When task cohesion is high, functional diversity negatively affects the time spent in the idea implementation phase; however, when task cohesion is low, this relationship is U-shaped. Results from 96 IT software-teams confirmed the authors' hypotheses. Theoretical and managerial implications are discussed.

DOI: 10.4018/978-1-6684-3702-5.ch073

INTRODUCTION

Innovation has always been the "lifeblood" of IT software development teams to adapt to evolving market and technical conditions (Favaro, 2010; Kautz & Nielsen, 2004). To enlarge the pool of knowledge and better satisfy business needs, non-IT specialists such as strategy, marketing and graphic design professionals are increasingly involved in IT software development projects, causing a growing functional diversity of software teams (Gorla & Lam, 2004; Levina, 2005). Evidence shows that functional diversity – the distribution of differences among team members with respect to functional background – improves the quantity and quality of team innovation (Akgün, Dayan, & Benedetto, 2008; Harrison & Klein, 2007; Huelsheger, Anderson, & Salgado, 2009). As Nielsen company commented, cross-functional teams "generated concepts with greater appeal than those with less functional diversity" (Black, 2016). However, we know little about how functional diversity influences another dimension of innovation – the speed of innovation in software teams.

Indeed, speed has become an important measure of success for IT software teams (Lee & Xia, 2010). As BusinessWeek-BCG survey found, "the No. 1 obstacle (to innovation that executives face today) is slow development times" (Bloomberg Businessweek, 2006). Many industrial tutorials suggested that the refinement of cross-functional teams is "a well-researched proven practice to speed and improve development" (e.g., Larman & Vodde, 2009, p. 151). Despite the increasing attention to speed of innovation, the extant literature mostly focused on the effect of functional diversity on quality or quantity of innovation. The few studies on the relationship between functional diversity and speed of innovation have, nonetheless, produced inconclusive results (Lee & Xia, 2010). Acknowledging this important research gap, our study aims to investigate the relationship between functional diversity and speed of innovation in IT software teams from a more nuanced perspective. Different from most previous research that assessed the overall speed of innovation (e.g., Eisenhardt & Tabrizi, 1995; Lee & Xia, 2010), we fruitfully distinguish two different phases of innovation: creativity phase (i.e., generation of creative ideas) and idea implementation phase (i.e., successful implementation of creative ideas) (Somech & Drach-Zahavy, 2013). As the two phases have distinct goals, characteristics and tasks (Amabile, 1988; West & Farr, 1990), functional diversity may bring different combinations of benefits and costs to a team in each phase, and affects the speed of each phase in distinct ways (Bledow et al., 2009). Thus, our research question is: How does functional diversity in a team affect the team's speed in the two phases of innovation respectively, i.e., creativity phase and idea implementation phase?

In particular, this study draws on the information processing view (Galbraith, 1974; Tushman & Nadler, 1978) and the social identity theory (Tajfel, 1981) to guide hypotheses development. The information processing view sheds light on speed of innovation by offering a cognitive lens explaining how teams gather, interpret, and integrate diverse information from members with different multiple functional backgrounds to fulfill tasks in each innovation phase (Galbraith, 1974; Paulus, 2000). However, this view implicitly assumes that all teams are equal in their members' willingness to utilize diverse inputs from each other and overcome potential conflicts among them for the benefits of the team. As social identity theory suggests, this is often not the case; rather, it is team identification (i.e., members' shared sense of identification with a team) that shapes the willingness of members to engage in team tasks (Ke & Zhang, 2010; Tajfel & Turner, 1986; Van Der Vegt & Bunderson, 2005). Team identification is especially critical for functionally diverse teams as it reflects the motivational climate for members to overcome their focus on self-interested perspectives, capitalize other's diverse expertise, and cooperate for the benefits of the team as a whole (Pearsall & Venkataramani, 2015). Thus, social identity theory provides a motivational lens, and complements the cognitive lens of information processing view to form a more complete understanding of functional diversity and speed of innovation in IT software teams.

Furthermore, drawing on social identity theory, we distinguish two components of team identification: emotional identification and task-related identification (Knippenberg, Dreu, & Homan, 2004). We followed prior studies to focus on collective team identification (i.e., emotional attachment to a group) (Pearsall & Venkataramani, 2015; Van Der Vegt & Bunderson, 2005) and task cohesion (i.e., commitment to a group's task) (Hackman, 1976) to reflect emotional and task-related identification respectively, and examine their distinct moderating effects on the diversity-speed relationship in two innovation phases respectively.

Using data on 96 IT software development teams in China, we find that when collective team identification is low, functional diversity has a positive effect on the time spent in the creativity phase; however, when collective team identification is high, this relationship becomes inverted U-shaped. When task cohesion is low, functional diversity has a U-shaped effect on the time spent in the idea implementation phase; however, when task cohesion is high, this relationship turns to be negative. These results support our arguments that the diversity-speed relationship depends on innovation phases as well as team-identification moderators.

This study makes several important contributions to the literature. Firstly, it extends team innovation literature by examining the relationship between functional diversity in teams and the often-neglected dimension of innovation – speed, beyond innovation quantity or quality. Secondly, unlike earlier efforts regarding the speed of innovation as a whole, this study adds to the literature by highlighting the importance of differentiating the two phases of innovation, i.e., creativity and idea implementation. Lastly, going beyond prior studies that rarely considered how motivational factors might moderate the diversity-speed relationship, this study offers a contingency perspective and refines our understanding of how the effect of functional diversity on innovation speed might change under different levels of team identification. It also offers important practical implications to software development teams to better tap their functional diversity to gain speed advantage in increasingly intense competition.

THEORETICAL FOUNDATION AND DEVELOPMENT

Functional Diversity and Speed of Innovation

While functional diversity has been frequently mentioned in the innovation literature, its effect on the speed of innovation remains unclear. As a result of increased global competition in the IT software industry, products and markets are becoming increasingly commoditized (Blackburn, Scudder, & Wassenhove, 1996; Kolb, 2010; Mendelson & Pillai, 1998; Souza, Bayus, & Wagner, 2004). IT software teams face intense competition in bringing new experiences to satisfy the needs of their customers before their competitors (Lee & Xia, 2010; Lyytinen & Rose, 2003). In such an environment where the time between innovations is decreasing, the amount of time taken to innovate becomes vital to remain competitive (Cusumano, MacCormack, Kemerer, & Crandall, 2003; Schoonhoven, Eisenhardt, & Lyman, 1990). It is thus important to understand whether functional diversity, while increasing innovativeness, speeds up innovation in software teams (Kolb, 2010; Saunders & Kim, 2007).

Prior literature on functional diversity and innovation mostly focused on the quality or quantity of innovation. The few studies that investigated the effect of functional diversity on speed of innovation often adopted a simple diversity-speed model; however, their results are generally inconclusive (Lee & Xia, 2010). Some studies posit that functional diversity enhances the ability of teams to foresee and tackle hard problems in the process of innovation, and found that teams high in functional diversity can speed up the innovation development process (e.g., Eisenhardt & Tabrizi, 1995; Erdogmus, 2009). For example, Eisenhardt and Tabrizi (1995) showed that functionally diverse teams are associated with shorter innovation development time. In contrast, other studies argue that it is time-consuming for functionally diverse teams to reach decision consensus on creative ideas (Souder, 1987). Furthermore, functional diversity can also lead to social categorization process that lengthens the time taken to implement creative ideas (Bledow, Frese, Anderson, Erez, & Farr, 2009). Those costs of functional diversify may cancel out the benefits and result in a non-significant relationship between functional diversity and speed of innovation (e.g., Lee & Xia, 2010; Schoonhoven et al., 1990). We posit that one possible explanation for the inconsistent results obtained in these earlier studies involves the way the speed was measured. Most previous research assessed the overall speed of innovation (e.g., Eisenhardt & Tabrizi, 1995; Lee & Xia, 2010) and did not differentiate phases of innovation that may benefit or suffer from functional diversity in different ways.

Innovation Phases: Creativity and Idea Implementation

Innovation refers to the successful implementation of creative ideas (Amabile, Conti, Coon, Lazenby, & Herron, 1996). It encompasses two phases: creativity and idea implementation (Amabile, 1988; Bledow et al., 2009; West, 2002b; West & Farr, 1990). Creativity phase refers to the process leading to the generation of new and valued ideas, and idea implementation phase refers to the process leading to the application of ideas in practice (e.g. new or improved products, services, or ways of working) (West, 2002b).

The two phases differ in terms of task type and characteristics. First, the two phases involve different types of sub-tasks. During the creativity phase, team members mainly conduct idea generation and evaluation, i.e., identifying opportunities, gathering information and resources, producing ideas, validating and assessing ideas, and finally arriving at a creative idea (Amabile, 1988; Utterback, 1971; Van Der Vegt & Bunderson, 2005). During the idea implementation phase, team members mainly coordinate and execute specific tasks in order to implement new ideas into practice, i.e., setting and executing specific technical goals, engineering, manufacturing, and testing new products, and monitoring the process (Utterback, 1971; West, 2002a). Second, tasks in these two phases are characterized by different levels of uncertainty and degree of structure. The creativity phase is associated with higher uncertainty and less degree of structure as there will be substantial challenges to where lay innovation opportunities. The direction of idea generation and evaluation can be totally shifted due to changes in recognized innovation opportunities (Rose, 2010). In contrast, the idea implementation phase is relatively more structured and less uncertain as the opportunity has already been identified and the direction or overview of the software project has been set, although unforeseen problems still surface quite often during implementation of novel ideas (Bledow et al., 2009; West, 2002a). Given the different tasks in the two phases of innovation, factors such as functional diversity may have different effects in each phase (West, 2002b). Hence, it is suggested to open the black box of innovation process and examine distinct phases separately (Siau & Tian, 2013; Somech & Drach-Zahavy, 2013).

A Unified View of Cognitive and Motivational Lenses

To investigate the relationship between functional diversity and speed of innovation in each phase, this study combines the information processing view (Galbraith, 1974; Tushman & Nadler, 1978) and the social identity theory (Tajfel, 1981). On one hand, the information processing view regards teams as information processing systems facing uncertainty (Hinsz, Tindale, & Vollrath, 1997). Information processing refers to the gathering, interpreting and synthesis of information in the context of organizational decision making (Tushman & Nadler, 1978). As this view emphasizes the competence of functionally diverse teams to process information to fulfill different tasks (Galbraith, 1974; Paulus, 2000), it affords a cognitive lens through which innovation speed in each phase can be reasonably explained.

On the other hand, it will likely be futile to examine the effect of functional diversity without considering the motivational climate in teams since motivation provides the impetus for team members to harness their resources such as diverse expertise (Siau, Tan, & Sheng, 2010). As the social identity theory (Tajfel, 1981) suggests, team identification, which refers to "the degree to which team members feel psychologically intertwined with the group's fate" (Pearsall & Venkataramani, 2015, p. 737), largely shapes team members' motivation to fulfill the team's tasks (Ke & Zhang, 2010; Tajfel & Turner, 1986; Van Der Vegt & Bunderson, 2005). Thus, this theory can explain under what conditions team members are more or less motivated to utilize diverse inputs from others to speed up each innovation phase. It provides us with a motivational lens to complement the information processing view. The combination of the two lenses can lead to a more nuanced understanding of the relationship between functional diversity and speed of innovation.

Information Processing View (Cognitive Lens): Functional Diversity and Creativity

During the creativity phase, according to the information processing view, the main tasks are idea generation and evaluation, which require substantial information exchange and integration (Bledow et al., 2009; Lingo & O'Mahony, 2010). The major beneficial effect of functional diversity on creativity is its important role in idea generation by gathering new and unique information and developing an updated team mental model to form a common view of what is new (Earley & Mosakowski, 2000). Team mental model refers to team members' common, organized understanding and mental representation of knowledge about key elements within the team's relevant environment (Mohammed, Ferzandi, & Hamilton, 2010; Mohammed, Klimoski, & Rentsch, 2000). Functional diversity not only allows members in a team to be exposed to new knowledge outside of one' own domain through interacting with other members holding different knowledge, perspectives and cognitive patterns (Akgün et al., 2008; Paulus, 2000; Shachaf, 2008), but also enlarges the team's exposure to unique external knowledge outside of the team's boundary due to non-redundant external networks associated with members of different functional backgrounds (Alavi & Leidner, 2001; Ancona & Caldwell, 1992; Somech & Drach-Zahavy, 2013; West, 2002b). Increased exposure to new knowledge will enrich the shared pool of knowledge and perspectives possessed by team members (Milliken & Martins, 1996; Simons, Pelled, & Smith, 1999), challenge the fundamental assumptions of opportunities, and induce cognitive restructuring of the team mental model (Mannix & Neale, 2005). The updated team mental model allows members to better predict and anticipate what other team members require, and permits better exchange between team members (Cannon-Bowers, Salas, & Converse, 1993; Cooke, Gorman, Duran, & Taylor, 2007).

On the other hand, functional diversity may also induce obstacles to team creativity, in particular, idea evaluation. Assessing ideas and arriving at a novel one requires much integration work that involves selection, rejection, and synthesis of disparate ideas to form a coherent whole (Lingo & O'Mahony, 2010). However, there is no clear-cut correct answer for which direction to go in the creativity phase. Due to "sticky" knowledge transfer, cross-functional teams often experience strenuous communication challenges (Cummings, 2004). As members from different functional backgrounds often hold distinct criteria by which they judge the quality and potential of new ideas (Fleming, 2004; Maznevski, 1994), it is fairly difficult to persuade some members to give up their ideas and accept the others', bridge different "thought worlds", and integrate disparate ideas into a coherent whole (Cummings, 2004).

Information Processing View (Cognitive Lens): Functional Diversity and Idea Implementation

During the idea implementation phase, according to the information processing view, the main tasks are idea execution and task collaboration (Bledow et al., 2009), which require substantial efforts spent in coordinating with one another to execute specified tasks (Lin, Hsu, Cheng, & Wu, 2012). Because of the less uncertain and more routine nature of idea implementation, the team mental model is not likely to be shifted by functional diversity, and diverse information from members with various functional backgrounds can be structurally organized and processed separately by members. Instead, functional diversity is suggested to impact idea implementation as it not only supplies diverse experiences that help to foreseen problems surfacing during task execution (Eisenhardt & Tabrizi, 1995; Gold, 1987), but also offers easier access to the resources and information of multiple functional areas to solve these problems (Ancona & Caldwell, 1992), both of which reduce avoidable errors in the process of idea implementation (Bledow et al., 2009; West, 2002a).

On the other hand, functional diversity may also be detrimental to idea implementation. Because cross-functional members have dissimilar conceptualizations of their jobs, and because the coordination among them may result in substantial friction that hampers feedback or suggestion for them to improve each other's ways of doing things, functional diversity increases role ambiguity (Harrison, Price, & Bell, 1998; Schneider, 1983). Role ambiguity refers to "situations in which organizational role are either in conflict with alternate roles and values or are not clearly articulated in terms of behaviors or performance levels expected" (Zaccaro, 1991, p. 389). As such, functional diversity will reduce members' ability to predict others' behaviors (Harrison et al., 1998; Tang & Naumann, 2016), therefore negatively affecting efficient coordination in teams.

Social Identity Theory (Motivational Lens): Collective Team Identification and Task Cohesion

The social identity theory suggests that team identification determines the extent members are motivated to capitalize on functional diversity (Van Der Vegt & Bunderson, 2005; West, 2002b). Social identity arises from a process of social categorization in which individuals put themselves and others into salient social categories (Mannix & Neale, 2005). The identification with a team affects members' motivation and further determines how functional diversity would be leveraged (Knippenberg et al., 2004; Van Der Vegt & Bunderson, 2005).

In particular, team identification involves two key components: emotional identification to a team and task-related identification to a team (Brewer, 1995; Knippenberg et al., 2004; Mathieu, Goodwin, Heffner, Salas, & Cannon-Bowers, 2000). As Knippenberg et al. (2004) suggest, when examining whether the relationship between team diversity and team performance is contingent on team identification, it is necessary to distinguish the affective and task-related components of team identification. Collective team identification, defined as the "emotional significance that members of a given group attach to their membership in that group" (Van Der Vegt & Bunderson, 2005, p. 533), reflects the emotional identification to a team. Task cohesion, defined as an attraction to the group because of a liking for, or commitment to the group task (Hackman, 1976), represents the task-related identification to a team. Although some studies suggest that collective team identification increases task cohesion (e.g., De Backer et al., 2011), we would expect that collective team identification and task cohesion are only loosely coupled because their antecedents and time spans differ. Indeed, a variety of factors other than collective team identification can influence task cohesion. For example, collective team identification can be stable across tasks in the same team, while changes in tasks can create variation in task cohesion.

More importantly, collective team identification and task cohesion have different routes in motivating team members. Collective team identification is often linked with the development of team mental model (Pearsall & Venkataramani, 2015). When collective team identification is high, team members are committed to the team's goals rather than the goals of their particular specialty areas (Van Der Vegt & Bunderson, 2005). This facilitates to create a team mental model that motivates members to "interpret information in a similar manner, share expectations concerning future events, and develop similar causal accounts for a situation" (Mohammed et al., 2010, p. 879). Unlike collective team identification, task cohesion is directly linked to role clarity (or role ambiguity) (Eys & Carron, 2001; Zaccaro, 1991). Role ambiguity can be alleviated by clarifying role requirements, and task cohesion has been proven to be effective in motivating members to develop behavioral norms that facilitate role clarity and team performance (Eys & Carron, 2001; Zaccaro, 1991). In sum, collective team identification is more relevant to team mental model which is critical for creativity, while task cohesion is more related to role clarity which is important for idea implementation. Thus, collective team identification is expected to have a significant moderating effect in the creativity phase, while task cohesion in the idea implementation phase.

Table 1 summarizes all the relevant literature: (1) the innovation literature on differences between the two innovation phases, (2) the information processing literature on distinct benefits/costs of functional diversity in each phase, and (3) the social identity literature regarding benefits of collective team identification or task cohesion in their relevant phases. The above literature provides profound theoretical groundings for our hypotheses development in the next section.

HYPOTHESES

Based on the theoretical development, this section elaborates two hypotheses: (1) the moderating effect of collective team identification on the relationship between functional diversity and time spent in the creativity phase, and (2) the moderating effect of task cohesion on the relationship between functional diversity and time spent in the idea implementation phase.

Table 1. An overview of innovation phases, and a summary of impacts of functional diversity and team identification in each phase

Phases of Innovation	Task	Sub-Tasks	Task Characteristics	Benefits/Costs of Functional Diversity	Benefits of Collective Team Identification	Benefits of Task Cohesion
Creativity phase	Idea generation & evaluation	(1) Identify opportunities (3) Gather information (3) Produce new ideas (4) Evaluate new ideas (5) Arrive at a creative idea	- More uncertain - Less structured	Benefits: New & unique knowledge to build the team mental model in idea generation, i.e., sub-tasks (1) to (3) Costs: Different judging criteria to hamper the team mental model in idea evaluation, i.e., sub-tasks (4) & (5)	Facilitates the development of a team mental model, & thus is more related to the creativity phase	
Idea implementation phase	Idea execution & task collaboration	(1) Set technical goals (2) Engineer/ design new products (3) Manufacture new products (4) Test new products	- Less uncertain - More structured	Benefits: Diverse experiences & resources to reduce execution errors in sub-tasks (1) to (4) Costs: Ambiguous conceptualizations of job roles to hamper efficient coordination in sub-tasks (1) to (4)		Increases role clarity, & thus is more related to the idea implementation phase

Functional Diversity and Time Spent in the Creativity Phase: Moderated by Collective Team Identification

As the information processing view suggests, in the creativity phase where the main tasks are idea generation and evaluation (Bledow et al., 2009), the speed will largely be determined by the time team members spend on the exchange and integration of new information (Lingo & O'Mahony, 2010). The social identity theory further implies that collective team identification will affect this phase by motivating cross-functional members to develop a team mental model to conduct information exchange and integration (Pearsall & Venkataramani, 2015; Van Der Vegt & Bunderson, 2005).

In a team with low collective team identification, cross-functional members are less committed to the team' goals, but more limited to their particular specialty areas, and unlikely to develop a team mental model to form shared understanding in the team. As such, they are not motivated to leverage diverse perspectives of others, and the exchange and integration of diverse information might not happen in such a team. Instead, increased functional diversity under conditions of low collective team identification is inclined to exacerbate team members' tendency to categorize and stereotype other members (Earley & Mosakowski, 2000), resulting in more social categorization and in-group biases (Van Der Vegt & Bunderson, 2005). Social categorization and in-group biases not only make it harder for team members to exchange knowledge and converge on decisions, but also increase unnecessary misunderstandings and conflicts that impede the progress of creativity phase (Shachaf, 2008; Van Der Vegt & Bunderson, 2005). As a result, the time spent in the creativity phase will be increased accordingly. This line of argument implies a positive relationship between functional diversity and time spent in the creativity phase when collective team identification is low.

In contrast, in a team with high collective team identification, members are highly committed to the team's goals and demonstrate high willingness to form a team mental model to extract more out of the potential of multiple perspectives. Given that members are highly motivated to capitalize diverse information, increased functional diversity will enlarge the total size of the pool of knowledge and perspectives possessed by team members and spur greater amount of information exchange (Mannix & Neale, 2005; Van Der Vegt & Bunderson, 2005), which will increase the time need for idea generation. While for idea valuation, because cross-functional members often hold distinct criteria by which they judge idea quality (Fleming, 2004; Maznevski, 1994), even though they hold a team mental model and give priority to the team's goals, it is fairly time-consuming to integrate disparate ideas to arrive at a creative idea (Milliken & Martins, 1996; Simons et al., 1999). Thus, the time spent on idea integration will also be lengthened as functional diversity increases. As a result, increased functional diversity from low to moderate levels will lead to more time spent in the creativity phase, when collective team identification is high.

Nevertheless, as functional diversity exceeds some point and keeps increasing to its extreme (i.e., no overlaps of expertise), the amount of exchange of divergent information is likely to be offset by the insufficient team capability to process the divergent information. For example, West (2002b) cautioned about maximizing diversity at the expense of shared understanding among team members. There should be sufficient overlap of team members' functional backgrounds to develop a team mental model (Klimoski & Mohammed, 1994; West, 2002a). In an extremely functionally diverse team, even though collective team identification is high, members might not even possess the mutual understanding of what information should be exchanged, and experience difficulties to develop a team mental model to facilitate information exchange (West, 2002b). Without a team mental model, the diverse information is more likely to result in information overload, causing members to stop information exchange and integration (Milliken & Martins, 1996). Correspondingly, when functional diversity increases from moderate to high levels, too much diversity results in inadequate shared understanding to facilitate the exchange and processing of information and thus leads to reduced time spent in creativity phase (West, 2002a). Taken together, this line of argument implies an inverted U-shaped relationship between functional diversity and time spent in the creativity phase, when collective team identification is high. Hence, we propose that:

H1: Collective team identification moderates the relationship between functional diversity and time spent in the creativity phase in such a way that:

H1a: When collective team identification is low, functional diversity has a positive effect on time spent in the creativity phase;

H1b: When collective team identification is high, functional diversity has an inverted U-shaped effect on time spent in the creativity phase.

Functional Diversity and Time Spent in the Idea Implementation Phase: Moderated by Task Cohesion

As the information processing view suggests, in the idea implementation phase where the main tasks are idea execution and specified task collaboration (Bledow et al., 2009), the speed will be largely determined by the time team members spend in coordinating with one another in executing specified tasks (Galbraith, 1974; Lin et al., 2012). The social identity theory further implies that task cohesion will affect this phase by motivating cross-functional members to clarify their roles in coordinating and executing tasks (Eys & Carron, 2001; West & Anderson, 1996; Zaccaro, 1991).

In a team with low task cohesion, members are not motivated to coordinate proactively on task execution. Given the relatively routine nature of idea implementation, diverse information is structurally organized and processed by relevant members separately. Hence, an increase of functional diversity will still reduce the amount of errors a team makes and in turn shorten the time spent in this phase (Eisenhardt & Tabrizi, 1995), up to a point beyond which the benefits will be quickly counteracted by the disruptive effects arising from role ambiguity caused by too much functional diversity (Harrison et al., 1998; Schneider, 1983; West, 2002a). This adversity caused by high functional diversity will be highlighted in teams with low task cohesion (Eys & Carron, 2001; Zaccaro, 1991). Because task cohesion is a liking for, or commitment to the team's task, a team in low task cohesion will find it hard to motivate its members to put in their additional effort required to surmount the increased difficulties encountered due to high role ambiguity. These difficulties caused by too much functional diversity in teams with low task cohesion impede communication and induce friction between team members. Hence, the time spent in the idea implementation phase will be increased accordingly, as functional diversity increases from moderate to high levels. Taken together, functional diversity will have a U-shaped effect on time spent in the idea implementation phase when task cohesion is low.

In contrast, in a team with high task cohesion, members are willing to coordinate proactively on task execution because of their attraction to team tasks and high role clarity, thereby improving task coordination (Eys & Carron, 2001; Van den Bossche, Gijselaers, Segers, & Kirschner, 2006). Instead of bickering over responsibilities and turf – problems that are exacerbated by multiple perspectives and backgrounds, cross-functional members can better focus on the team tasks and their own roles and responsibilities (Gratton & Erickson, 2007). As a result, as functional diversity grows from low to moderate levels, teams with high task cohesion tend to conduct more constructive communication and are more likely to utilize diverse experiences against errors in task execution, thereby reducing the time spent in the idea implementation phase (Eisenhardt & Tabrizi, 1995). When functional diversity reaches its extreme (i.e., no overlaps of functional backgrounds), role clarity still helps members understand task goals clearly and overcome the different interpretations of team goals arising from the lack of shared mental representation (Eys & Carron, 2001; Kozlowski & Ilgen, 2006). All these reduce unnecessary friction between team members as well as the wastage of time and energy (Gratton & Erickson, 2007). As a result, the time spent in the idea implementation phase will be reduced accordingly, even though functional diversity reaches high levels. This line of argument implies a negative relationship between functional diversity and time spent in the idea implementation phase when task cohesion is high. Hence, we propose that:

H2: Task cohesion moderates the relationship between functional diversity and time spent in the idea implementation phase in such a way that:

H2a: When task cohesion is low, functional diversity has a U-shaped effect on time spent in the idea implementation phase;

H2b: When task cohesion is high, functional diversity has a negative effect on time spent in the idea implementation phase.

All hypotheses are summarized in Table 2.

Table 2. Hypothesized effect of functional diversity on speed of innovation

Functional diversity & Time spent in the creativity phase	Low collective team identification	High collective team identification
	H1a. (/)	H1b. (∩)
Functional diversity & Time spent in the idea implementation phase	Low task cohesion	High task cohesion
	H2a. (U)	H2b. (\)

METHODOLOGY

Sample and Data Collection

The hypotheses were tested against survey data collected from software development teams doing innovative work in China. The choice of survey methodology was to enhance the generalizability of results (Dooley, 2001). China was chosen because of the emergence of China as a global powerhouse in high-technology innovation (Zhou & Stembridge, 2009). The survey data was collected in 2011 with the help of a professional survey company in China through their online platform. The choice to go with the company was because the company has extensive partnerships with many online software development communities across China. It allowed this study to leverage on its wide network to reach out to software development teams. Through the company, relevant partner online communities (see Appendix A) were identified and invitations were sent to targeted respondents.

In order to ensure those responding to the survey were indeed software developers involved in innovative work, screening questions were used to filter out non-targeted respondents. The first screening question on the current job of the respondent was used to screen out those respondents not in software development. The second screening question asked respondents to indicate the description that best fits their software design: "(1) Simple upgrade or enhancements to existing product design; (2) Adapting new knowledge in our own field, make use of new design; (3) Adapting new knowledge from other fields, make use of new design; and (4) Unique in any field". Those respondents who chose (1) were deemed to have worked on software projects involving limited creativity and were dropped from the survey. Finally, an open question asked respondents to provide a description of the product their team developed which allowed us to further ascertain the innovativeness of work. Further screening questions were used to ensure that respondents were familiar with the inner workings of their respective teams. Members had to be either in position of responsibilities, such as the project manager of the team, or familiar with details on the inner workings of the team.

In total, 2493 respondents attempted the survey and 131 respondents were obtained after the screening questions. These 131 respondents were asked to recall the most recent completed software development project and answer the survey questions accordingly. Among the 131 returned questionnaires, 96 were complete and thus used as the final data set.

To test for the possibility of non-response bias, Armstrong and Overton's (1977) recommended procedure was adopted. This assumes that late respondents in a sample are similar to theoretical non-respondents. Using t-tests and Mann-Whitney test to compare early and late respondents on the dependent variable and demographic characteristics, no significant differences appeared between the two groups. Hence, non-response bias is not an issue in our sample.

Appendix B presents the demographic profiles of the sampled software development teams (see Tables 8-12). Distribution of team size shows a typical representation of small, medium and large software development teams. On average, a team had seven members with software development functional backgrounds, while other functional backgrounds were evenly distributed. In addition, the respondents are normally distributed in terms of tenure in their current software teams.

Measures

Because the constructs measured in this study are team-level constructs, survey items were framed to ask the individual respondents to evaluate the team that they belonged to for the project. All items were drawn from the scales that have been published and subsequently modified to suit the context of this study (see Table 3). As the survey was conducted in China, the survey items were translated to the Chinese language. To ensure the correctness of translation, a double translation process was employed to ensure the meanings were retained in the translation. A Chinese researcher was employed to translate the original items from English to Chinese for the survey. A separate researcher was employed to translate the items from Chinese back to English so as to ensure that the reverse-translation was not affected by prior knowledge of the original items. The reverse-translated version of the items in English was then compared to the original items to check if the meanings were preserved.

Dependent Variables

The measurement of time spent in each phase was adapted from Eisenhardt, Kathleen and Tabrizi (1995). Respondents were asked to provide the start and end dates of the software project. The start date of the software project was defined to be the date of the first scheduled meeting of the project team. The end date was defined to be the date of project sign-off (closing), or commercialization of the product. Respondents were also asked to estimate the percentage of project time spent on the creativity phase, and then idea implementation phase. The definitions and illustrative activities of both phases were presented. The total time spent on the project was computed from the start and end date of the project. The time spent in each phase was subsequently computed by attributing the proportion of the total time spent on the project based on the estimated percentage of project time in each phase.

Independent Variables

Functional diversity for each team was computed using an entropy-based diversity index measure which takes into account the number of team members from each particular functional background. As team members' functional backgrounds are categorical data, it is appropriate to use an entropy-based diversity index (Ancona & Caldwell, 1992; Harrison & Klein, 2007; Teachman, 1980). The measure is defined as:

$$H = -\sum_{i=1}^{s} Pi(\ln Pi)$$

Table 3. Measurement items

Construct	Item	Source
Time spent in the creativity phase	Days spent on the project * the proportion spent in the creativity phase	(Eisenhardt & Tabrizi, 1995)
Time spent in the idea generation phase	Days spent on the project * the proportion spent in the idea generation phase	(Eisenhardt & Tabrizi, 1995)
Functional diversity	$$H = -\sum_{i=1}^{s} Pi(\ln Pi)$$	(Teachman, 1980)
Collective team identification	A 7-point Likert scale: CTI1. Team members feel emotionally attached to the team. CTI2. Team members feel a strong sense of belonging to the team. CTI3. Team members feel as if the team's problems are their own. CTI4. Team members feel like part of the family in their team.	(Allen & Meyer, 1990)
Task cohesion	A 7-point Likert scale: TC1. Team members are unhappy with the team's level of commitment to the task. TC2. Team members have conflicting aspirations for the team's performance. TC3. The team does not give its members enough opportunities to improve their personal performance. TC4. Team members are united in trying to reach its goals for performance. (Dropped)	(Carless & De Paola, 2000)
Industry	Set to 1 if the company belongs to the software industry, and 0 otherwise.	Self developed
City	Set to 1 if the company is located in direct-controlled municipalities or provincial capitals in China, and 0 otherwise.	Self developed
Team size	The number of members in the team	(Huelsheger et al., 2009)
Cost (Ln)	Natural log of costs spent on the project	Self developed
Delayed time	The number of days between the planned completion date and the real completion date	Self developed
Communication pattern	(The number of hours per week that team members employed computer-mediated communication) / (The total number of hours per week team members spent on team communication, including computer-mediated and face-to-face communication)	Self developed
Innovativeness	A multiple-choice question: Prior to the commercial launch of your new software, which of the following sentences best describes your case? (1) There were already identical products on the market; (2) There were no identical products, but some similar or substitutable products on the market; (3) There were no identical or similar products, but some substitutable products on the market; and (4) There were no identical, similar, or substitutable products on the market.	(Ucbasaran et al., 2009)
Manager	Set to 1 if the respondent is in managerial positions in the team, and set to 0 if not	Self developed
Tenure	The months the respondent has been in the team	Self developed

This diversity index used by Teachman measures the distribution of the population (in this case, the team) over the one or more categories (Teachman, 1980). A team with all members coming from one functional area would be entirely homogenous and would hence have a diversity index of 0. The higher the diversity index, the more distributed team members are over all the categories, and thus the more diverse a team is. P in the case of this study represents the fractional share of team members from a particular functional background. To suit the context of software development teams in China, the following 8 categories of functional areas were used according to China's functional categories: "Finance/Accounting", "Marketing/Sales", "Business Analysis", "Software Development", "Engineering", "Production/Operations", "Administration" and "Others". Respondents were firstly asked how many members their team had in the project, and then required to specify the number of members under each category of functional areas.

Collective team identification was assessed using 4 items adapted from Allen and Meyer (1990). Respondents were asked to assess the extent to which each item is reflective of how much team members identified with the team in the software project (see Table 3). All items were assessed using a 7-point Likert scale.

Task cohesion was assessed using 4 items adapted from Carless and De Paola (Carless & De Paola, 2000). Respondents were asked to assess the extent to which each item is reflective of team members' attraction and commitment to the team task in the software project (see Table 3). All items were assessed using a 7-point Likert scale.

Control Variables

At the company level, to account for potential contextual nuances of the sample, we controlled for company's industry and location. The type of industry was controlled by a dummy variable, *Industry* that equals 1 if the company belonged to software industry, and 0 otherwise (e.g., other industries applying software. The location of the company was measured by a dummy variable, *City* that equals 1 if the company was located in direct-controlled municipalities or provincial capitals in China, and 0 otherwise (e.g., other cities and counties), in order to rule out economic and cultural differences between cities otherwise not captured.

At the team-project level, because project scale may relate to both functional diversity and innovation speed, *Team size* measured by the number of members, as well as *Cost_Ln* measured by the natural log of costs, were controlled for (Huelsheger et al., 2009). In addition, how long a project has been delayed may affect the time pressure teams face, which in turn influences teams' speed of innovation. Thus, Delayed Time, measured by the number of days between the planned and real completion dates, was included in the equation. Lastly, as the patterns of team communication (i.e., computer-mediated communication vs. face-to-face communication) may exert a significant influence on team performance (Irmer, Chang, & Bordia, 2000; Wu, Goh, Li, Luo, & Zheng, 2016), Communication pattern, referring to the ratio of the hours per week that team members employed computer-mediated communication to the total hours per week on team communication, was also controlled for.

At the product level, Innovativeness of the new product was controlled by a multiple-choice question with 4 options to measure product innovativeness (Ucbasaran, Westhead, & Wright, 2009) (see Table 3), because the higher the innovativeness required, the harder it is to come up with an idea to meet the requirements. In robustness checks, since the nature of software may also determine product innovativeness, we employed *Software type* to reflect the innovativeness of the new product, and obtained similar results.

At the respondent level, the extent to which the respondents were familiar with the workings of the team was also taken into by dummy variable, *Manager*. Furthermore, to control for how well the respondents know their teams, *Tenure* was also taken into account by asking how long they have been in the team.

DATA ANALYSIS

Validity and Reliability of Measures

The convergent validity and discriminant validity for all the perceptual questions were assessed using an exploratory factor analysis. One item (TC4, Table 3) of task cohesion was dropped as it loaded highly on two constructs and violated uni-dimensionality. This could be due to that TC4 was not reverse scored while TC1, TC2, and TC3 were. A follow-up exploratory factor analysis revealed that all remaining questions loaded onto the intended constructs (see Table 4). Discriminant validity was established because each question loaded more highly on its intended construct than on other constructs (Gefen, Straub, & Boudreau, 2000). Convergent validity was established because all constructs had Cronbach's alphas above 0.7 (Nunnally & Bernstein, 1994). The score for each construct was computed by averaging the scores for the remaining questions for that construct.

Table 4. Results of explorative factor analysis

Construct	Cronbach's Alpha	Item	Item Loading	
			1	2
Task cohesion (Cohesion)	0.738	TC1	0.113	**0.827**
		TC2	0.110	**0.832**
		TC3	0.001	**0.762**
Collective team identification (Collective)	0.920	Collective1	**0.896**	0.023
		Collective2	**0.931**	0.080
		Collective3	**0.895**	0.123
		Collective4	**0.856**	0.092
Eigenvalue			3.228	1.987
Cumulative variance explained			46.11%	74.50%

Common Method Bias

Since all self-reported data has a potential for common method bias (Lindell & Whitney, 2001; Podsakoff, MacKenzie, Lee, & Podsakoff, 2003), it is necessary to assess the severity of the bias of the data. Following Podsakoff et al. (2003), we conducted Harman's one-factor test. We loaded all the 17 items of 12 variables (including dependent variables, independent variables, and control variables) into an exploratory factor analysis, and examined the un-rotated factor solution to determine the number of factors that are necessary to account for the variance in the variables. The results revealed that five distinct components with Eigenvalue larger than 1 were extracted, and the most covariance explained by one factor was 21.93%. Since no single factor emerged from the factor analysis and no general factor accounts for the majority of the covariance among the measures, there is no evidence showing that common method bias is a serious concern for this study. Thus, we can be reasonably assured that common method bias is not likely to contaminate the results.

Table 5. Means, standard deviations, and correlations of variables

Variable	Mean	S.D.	1	2	3	4	5	6	7	8	9	10	11	12	13
1. Time spent in the creativity phase (days)	134.68	148.56													
2. Time spent in the idea implementation phase (days)	315.43	388.58	0.216*												
3. Functional diversity	1.26	0.65	0.280**	-0.108											
4. Collective team identification	4.79	1.39	0.212*	0.082	-0.053										
5. Task cohesion	4.48	1.42	0.164	0.160	0.042	0.179									
6. Industry	0.60	0.49	0.157	0.186	-0.223*	0.230*	0.161								
7. City	0.81	0.39	-0.101	0.024	-0.240*	-0.139	-0.132	0.048							
8. Team size	16.50	19.55	0.086	-0.018	0.376**	-0.076	-0.065	-0.078	-0.097						
9. Cost (Ln)	11.57	1.71	0.167	0.380**	0.007	-0.071	-0.011	0.215*	0.161	0.168					
10. Delayed time	12.20	198.09	0.105	0.173	0.064	-0.050	0.116	-0.001	-0.111	0.138	0.140				
11. Communication pattern	67.10	16.76	-0.011	-0.010	-0.067	-0.085	-0.171	-0.044	-0.072	0.053	0.078	0.042			
12. Innovativeness	2.17	0.99	0.255*	0.228*	0.181	0.021	0.199	-0.101	-0.054	0.152	0.078	0.069	0.017		
13. Manager	1.53	0.50	-0.129	-0.033	-0.070	-0.098	0.020	-0.035	0.030	-0.046	-0.119	0.148	-0.030	-0.074	
14. Tenure	11.08	10.00	0.114	0.118	-0.135	-0.241*	-0.231*	0.110	0.173	-0.026	0.484**	0.049	0.176	-0.168	-0.003

N = 96; *p < 0.05; **p < 0.01

Hypotheses Testing

Table 5 presents means, standard deviations, and correlations among all variables. Noteworthy, the correlation between collective team identification and task cohesion is not significant ($r = 0.179$, $p > 0.05$), confirming our prediction that the two moderators are loosely coupled. Tests were done to check for multicollinearity among the variables. Multicollinearity can lead to inaccurate results, and cause the variance of regression coefficient to be inflated among other problems (Mason & Perreault, 1991). The Variance Inflation Factor (VIF) method was used in this study to test for multicollinearity (Marquardt, 1970). VIF greater than 10 is suggested to indicate harmful collinearity (Marquardt, 1970). The VIF test did not reveal signs of multicollinearity among this study's variables, with the maximum VIF being 1.590.

Table 6 presents the results of the hierarchical regression analyses predicting time spent in the creativity phase. Model 1 of Table 6 included control variables only, Model 2 added the main effects of functional diversity and its squared term, and Model 3 further added the moderating effect of collective team identification. H1 states that collective team identification moderates the relationship between functional diversity and time spent in the creativity phase. To test this hypothesis, we introduced the relevant interaction item (functional diversity^2 × collective team identification) and its lower-level interaction item (functional diversity × collective team identification) into the regression equation in Model 3 of Table 6. The coefficient associated with functional diversity^2 × collective team identification was statistically significant (ß=-59.885, p<0.05). Therefore, III1 was supported.

To facilitate the interpretation of H1, Figure 1 plots the relationships between functional diversity and time spent in the creativity phase. It shows that the relationship between functional diversity and time spent in the creativity phase follows a positive linear pattern with low levels of collective team identification, and follows an inverted U-shaped pattern with high levels of collective team identification. These findings support the specific relationships formulated in H1.

Table 7 presents the results of the hierarchical regression analyses predicting time spent in the idea implementation phase. Model 1 of Table 7 included control variables only, Model 2 added the main effects of functional diversity and its squared term, and Model 3 further added the moderating effect of task cohesion. H2 states that task cohesion moderates the relationship between functional diversity and time spent in the idea implementation phase. To test this hypothesis, we introduced the relevant interaction item (functional diversity^2 × task cohesion) and its lower-level interaction item (functional diversity × task cohesion) into the regression equation in Model 3 of Table 7). The coefficient associated with functional diversity^2 × task cohesion was statistically significant (ß = 116.006, p<0.05). Therefore, H2 was supported.

To facilitate the interpretation of H2, Figure 2 plots the relationships between functional diversity and time spent in the idea implementation phase. It shows that the relationship between functional diversity and time spent in the idea implementation phase follows a U-shaped pattern with low levels of task cohesion, and follows a negative linear pattern with high levels of task cohesion. These findings support the specific relationships formulated in H2.

Table 6. Predicting time spent in the creativity phase [a]

Independent Variables	Model 1		Model 2		Model 3	
	ß	p	ß	p	ß	p
Predictors						
Functional diversity			98.903	0.249	119.399	0.150
Functional diversity^2			-11.706	0.730	-21.724	0.506
Collective team identification					29.141**	0.008
Functional diversity × Collective team identification					124.245*	0.038
Functional diversity^2 × Collective team identification					-59.885*	0.012
Controls						
Industry	49.260	0.117	68.069*	0.031	70.335*	0.025
City	-43.318	0.271	-19.615	0.614	6.745	0.856
Team size	0.252	0.750	-0.505	0.534	-0.245	0.750
Cost (Ln)	2.615	0.807	1.491	0.886	1.588	0.873
Delayed time	0.057	0.465	0.061	0.424	0.037	0.612
Communication pattern	-0.482	0.594	-0.200	0.820	-0.044	0.958
Innovativeness	40.760*	0.011	37.556*	0.016	39.005**	0.008
Manager	-31.682	0.297	-29.532	0.326	-30.601	0.285
Tenure	2.280	0.203	2.578	0.138	3.994*	0.023
Constant	72.298	0.612	-52.570	0.726	-255.81	0.102
R^2	0.154		0.227		0.341	
Adjusted R^2	0.066		0.125		0.227	
R^2 change	0.154		0.072*		0.114**	

[a]: N=96. Unstandardized regression coefficients are reported.

*$p < 0.05$; **$p < 0.01$ (two-tailed tests)

Figure 1. Relationships between functional diversity and time spent in the creativity phase

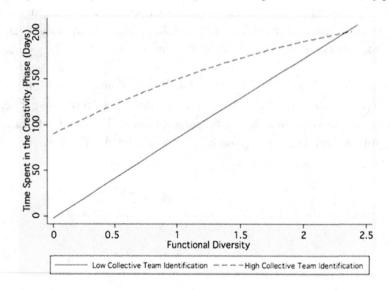

Table 7. Predicting time spent in the idea implementation phase [a]

Independent Variables	Model 1		Model 2		Model 3	
	ß	p	ß	p	ß	p
Predictors						
Functional diversity			-150.873	0.496	-310.683	0.148
Functional diversity^2			30.457	0.728	95.464	0.261
Task cohesion					27.295	0.319
Functional diversity × Task cohesion					-397.575**	0.006
Functional diversity^2 × Task cohesion					116.006*	0.043
Controls						
Industry	98.170	0.210	75.794	0.347	115.456	0.145
City	-22.739	0.816	-49.657	0.622	-53.188	0.578
Team size	-2.386	0.229	-1.546	0.463	-1.688	0.398
Cost (Ln)	82.605**	0.003	83.385**	0.003	63.052*	0.018
Delayed time	0.243	0.214	0.233	0.239	0.228	0.224
Communication pattern	-0.722	0.749	-1.037	0.649	0.613	0.782
Innovativeness	84.876*	0.032	87.260*	0.030	76.006	0.052
Manager	5.152	0.946	5.891	0.939	44.392	0.549
Tenure	-1.340	0.763	-1.672	0.709	2.191	0.617
Constant	-772.925*	0.032	-612.706	0.117	-625.725	0.102
R^2	0.230		0.243		0.356	
Adjusted R^2	0.149		0.144		0.245	
R^2 change	0.230**		0.014		0.113**	

[a]: N=96. Unstandardized regression coefficients are reported.

*p < 0.05; **p < 0.01 (two-tailed tests)

Figure 2. Relationships between functional diversity and time spent in the idea implementation phase

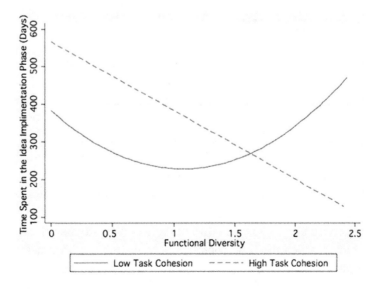

Robustness Checks

To further rule out alternative explanations, several robustness tests were conducted. First, as the underlying nature of software projects could affect the innovativeness of the new product and subsequently the speed of innovation, we created a new dummy variable, *Software type*, to control for this possible effect. Specifically, based on the type of software reported by the respondents (see Appendix B), we categorized the following types as more innovative than others: anti-virus/privacy/monitoring, data analysis, information communication tools, marketing/sales management, and text mining, because these types share an attribute of customer-orientation that often requires fast changes. Other types of software such as HR management, production management, financial management, and supply chain management are deemed as less innovative because they are more internally used by enterprises and more mature. Due to that 34 software projects had missing data on *Software type*, the inclusion of this new control variable largely reduced our sample size from 96 to 62, and thus was only applied in robustness checks, rather than in the main analysis. Highly consistent results were obtained. The results show that when predicting the time spent in the creativity phase, the coefficient associated with functional diversity^2 × collective team identification was partially significant (ß = -54.519, p = 0.081), confirming H1. The partial significance of H1 was due to the reduced sample size. When predicting the time spent in the idea implementation phase, the coefficient associated with functional diversity^2 × task cohesion was significant (ß = 167.851, p = 0.015), confirming H2.

Second, to test whether our results were robust to controlling for the average time of software development, we included a new continuous variable, *Average time*, measured by the average time for developing each type of software. Among the 96 software projects, 34 had missing data on software type and were thus classified into one type. Highly consistent results were obtained. The results show that when predicting the time spent in the creativity phase, the coefficient associated with functional diversity^2 × collective team identification was significant (ß = -52.482, p = 0.023), confirming H1. When predicting the time spent in the idea implementation phase, the coefficient associated with functional diversity^2 × task cohesion was significant (ß=109.911, p=0.041), confirming H2. We also tried excluding the data of 34 software projects with missing data on software type and obtained consistent results.

DISCUSSION AND IMPLICATIONS

An early effort of prior research on this topic suggests that functional diversity affects the overall-speed of team innovation (Eisenhardt & Tabrizi, 1995; Schoonhoven et al., 1990). However, these studies yielded inconsistent patterns of results. This study extends this body of work by dichotomizing the innovation process into two phases (i.e., creativity and idea implementation), and suggests different effects of functional diversity in each phase. Moreover, this study explores different moderators in each phase.

In particular, the results show that the effect of functional diversity is contingent upon collective team identification in the creativity phase and upon task cohesion in the idea implementation phase. Specifically, in the creativity phase, functional diversity in teams with low collective team identification always increases the time spent in the creativity phase; while with high collective team identification, the time spent in the creativity phase increases with functional diversity up till a certain moderate level of functional diversity after which the time spent starts to decrease with functional diversity. In the idea implementation phase, functional diversity in teams with high task cohesion always decreases the time spent in the idea implementation phase; while with low task cohesion, the time spent in the idea implementation phase decreases with functional diversity, up till a certain moderate level of functional diversity after which the time spent starts to increase with functional diversity.

Theoretical Implications

This study makes valuable contributions to the team innovation literature. First, by focusing on the speed of innovation, it extends theoretical development on team innovation by covering new aspects of innovation performance (Schoonhoven et al., 1990). Team innovation research has generally focused on how innovative a team's outputs are (i.e., quality of innovation), or how many new ideas a team generates (i.e., quantity of innovation). There has been a dearth of research examining the speed of innovation (Pirola-Merlo, 2010). While quality and quantity of innovation is indeed important, it is also important to address the issue of speed of innovation because the speed of new products can be critical to organizational success, especially in the IT software industry (Kolb, 2010; Schoonhoven et al., 1990).

Second, by dichotomizing the innovation process into the creativity phase and idea implementation phase, this study opens the black box of innovation which has predominately been regarded as a generic concept (e.g., Eisenhardt & Tabrizi, 1995; Schoonhoven et al., 1990), or has only focused on the creativity phase (e.g., Paulus, 2000; Shin & Zhou, 2007). It resonates well with the theoretical argument on the need to split the innovation process into two phases (Bledow et al., 2009). Moreover, to our best knowledge, this is the first study to examine the speed of each phase of innovation and provide insights into each phase.

Third, this study is also a pioneering study that combines cognitive and motivational lenses and provides a more nuanced perspective to understand the effect of functional diversity on speed of innovation. It looks simultaneously at team members' functional diversity as well as team motivational climate for understanding the speed of each phase. This integrative perspective contributes to the literature by imparting more precise understanding of the relation of team composition, team identification, and team innovation in each phase of innovation (Bledow et al., 2009; Somech & Drach-Zahavy, 2013). It advances a theory on the speed of innovation that can account for the complex effects of functional diversity, and helps to resolve the inconsistent patterns of results shown in the past literature (Bledow et al., 2009; Knippenberg et al., 2004). The results of this study have important implications for the way scholars think about the benefits and challenges of functional diversity in teams to fast innovation (Van Der Vegt & Bunderson, 2005). For example, this study suggests that in order to understand whether a given level of functional diversity in a team is good or bad for the speed of creativity phase, researchers need to consider the emotional part of motivational climate that exists within the team and, more specifically, collective team identification. In contrast, in the idea implementation phase, the motivational climate changes to its task-related part, more specifically, task cohesion.

Practical Implications

The results of this study offer intriguing and useful suggestions for practice. First, as stated in the onset of the study, both the innovativeness of ideas and the time taken to achieve it are important in the creativity phase. In their quest for innovation, many organizations have employed teams with members from diverse functional backgrounds. Indeed, many project managers believe that functional diversity in teams brings about the variety in perspectives essential to creativity (Sethi, Smith, & Park, 2001).

While functional diversity in teams has been associated with increased innovativeness in the creativity phase, the results of this study also suggest that functional diversity leads to increased time spent in the creativity phase for teams under most situations. Given that both innovativeness and the time taken to achieve it are important, practitioners need to consider this trade-off carefully. Practitioners need to ask themselves how much diversity is really needed. Is increasing the functional diversity in the team worth the trade-off of more time spent in achieving the innovation? Diversity excess to requirements could cause the creativity process to be dragged out unnecessarily. This not only increases costs, but could also have negative ramifications on the success of the end product or even the competitive position of the organization.

Of course, there are many software teams that, by the nature of their work, need to have members from different functional backgrounds or possess different task-related expertise. These teams could be either working on highly innovative products, or be dealing with complex problems cutting across multiple functional areas or knowledge domains. For these teams, reducing functional diversity might not be a viable option. Instead, they need to explore alternatives that can help mitigate the effects of functional diversity on the time spent in the creativity phase. For instance, the results from this study suggest that collective team identification provides beneficial moderating effects on the levels of high functional diversity in the creativity phase. Thus, for teams that are high in functional diversity to get a faster speed in the creativity phase, it is highly advisable that collective team identification is fostered among team members. Furthermore, various studies in the past have also demonstrated collective team identification to be beneficial to innovativeness (Sethi et al., 2001) and creativity (Hirst, Van Dick, & Van Knippenberg, 2009). In other words, collective team identification not only benefits the quality of new ideas, but also reduces the time spent in achieving the ideas for teams that are high in functional diversity.

Second, fast implementation of new ideas is also appreciated to achieve first mover advantage. Without successful implementation, ideas are only "ten a penny" (West, 2002a). What innovation does depend on is "the single-mindedness with which the business plan is executed, as countless obstacles on the road to commercialization are surmounted, by-passed or hammered flat" (The Economist Technology Quarterly, 2001). Some prior studies suggest that functional diversity in teams may become less beneficial in facilitating idea implementation (Somech & Drach-Zahavy, 2013). The results of this study suggest that functional diversity leads to decreased time spent in the idea implementation phase for teams under the condition of high task cohesion. Especially for teams with high functional diversity, practitioners should dedicate more attention and effort into fostering task cohesion among team members.

Limitations and Future Research

The results should be interpreted with due consideration to the limitations of this study. First, the research model of this study was empirically tested based on the responses from software development teams working on innovative software in China. Caution should be exercised when generalizing results of this study across other types of teams outside of software development. Furthermore, cultural differences should also be noted when attempting to generalize the results of this study. Future research could incorporate respondents from other industries as well as across countries to increase the generalizability of results.

Second, this study adopted a cross-sectional design. Results might be influenced by the respondents' ability to recall details on projects that have been completed. This study has attempted to limit this by asking respondents' to recall only their most recently completed project. In addition, evaluations of the team might be influenced by the relative success or failure of the project at the end. Future research could sidestep this issue by conducting longitudinal studies that follow the teams throughout the entire length of the project.

CONCLUSION

This study is an initial attempt to develop a theory of speed of software innovation. It is salient to the team innovation literature for several reasons. Unlike past studies that focused on the quality or quantity of innovation, this study focuses on the speed of innovation. Unlike past studies that have predominately either examined the innovation process as a black box, or paid attention solely on the creativity phase of innovation, this study separates the innovation process into two phases with dissimilar underlying mechanisms. Extending past studies, this study has explicitly examined the moderated curvilinear relationship between functional diversity and the speed of each phase of innovation. The results of this study serve as a platform on which theoretical materials for team innovation can be extended with future research along this direction.

In an environment where both the innovativeness and the speed of which innovation is attained are critical, organizations need to understand not only the factors that drive the quality of innovation, but also those that drive the speed of innovation. Given that organizational design related to functional diversity has significant consequences on the speed of innovation, scholars and practitioners need to continue searching for effective ways where organizations can best harness functional diversity and compete on speed of innovation.

ACKNOWLEDGMENT

This research was supported by the National Natural Science Foundation of China (No. 71772061, 71302041), the Ministry of Education of China - China Mobile Research Funding (No. MCM20150402), and the Fundamental Research Funds for the Central Universities (No. WN1522002). The corresponding author is Hong Ling (e-mail: hling@fudan.edu.cn).

REFERENCES

Akgün, A. E., Dayan, M., & Benedetto, C. A. D. (2008). New Product Development Team Intelligence: Antecedents and Consequences. *Information & Management*, *45*(4), 221–226. doi:10.1016/j.im.2008.02.004

Alavi, M., & Leidner, D. E. (2001). Review: Knowledge Management and Knowledge Management Systems: Conceptual Foundations and Research Issues. *Management Information Systems Quarterly*, *25*(1), 107–136. doi:10.2307/3250961

Allen, N. J., & Meyer, J. P. (1990). The Measurement and Antecedents of Affective, Continuance and Normative Commitment to the Organization. *Journal of Occupational Psychology*, *63*(1), 1–18. doi:10.1111/j.2044-8325.1990.tb00506.x

Amabile, T. M. (1988). A Model of Creativity and Innovation in Organizations. *Research in Organizational Behavior, 10,* 123–176.

Amabile, T. M., Conti, R., Coon, H., Lazenby, J., & Herron, M. (1996). Assessing the Work Environment for Creativity. *Academy of Management Journal, 39*(5), 1154–1184. doi:10.2307/256995

Ancona, D., & Caldwell, D. (1992). Demography & Design: Predictors of New Product Team Performance. *Organization Science, 3*(3), 321–341. doi:10.1287/orsc.3.3.321

Armstrong, S. J., & Overton, T. S. (1977). Estimating Nonresponse Bias in Mail Surveys. *JMR, Journal of Marketing Research, 14*(3), 396–402. doi:10.2307/3150783

Black, M. (2016). Uncommon Sense: The Modern Innovation Dilemma - First Mover or Best Mover? Retrieved June 4, 2017, from http://www.nielsen.com/eu/en/insights/news/2016/uncommon-sense-the-modern-innovation-dilemma-first-mover-or-best-mover.html

Blackburn, J. D., Scudder, G. D., & Wassenhove, L. N. V. (1996). Improving Speed and Productivity of Software Development: A Global Survey of Software Developers. *IEEE Transactions on Software Engineering, 22*(12), 875–885. doi:10.1109/32.553636

Bledow, R., Frese, M., Anderson, N. R., Erez, M., & Farr, J. L. (2009). A Dialectical Perspective on Innovation: Conflicting Demands, Multiple Pathways, and Ambidexterity. *Industrial and Organizational Psychology: Perspectives on Science and Practice, 2*(3), 305–337. doi:10.1111/j.1754-9434.2009.01154.x

Bloomberg Businessweek. (2006). The World's Most Innovative Companies. Retrieved June 4, 2017, from https://www.bloomberg.com/news/articles/2006-04-23/the-worlds-most-innovative-companies

Brewer, M. (1995). Managing Diversity: The Role of Social Identities. In S. Jackson & M. Ruderman (Eds.), *Diversity in Workteams* (pp. 131–159). Washington, DC: APA Books. doi:10.1037/10189-002

Cannon-Bowers, J. A., Salas, E., & Converse, S. (1993). Shared Mental Models in Expert Team Decision Making. In J. N. Castellan (Ed.), *Individual and Group Decision Making: Current Issues* (pp. 221–246). Hillsdale, N.J: L. Erlbaum Associates.

Carless, S. A., & De Paola, C. (2000). The Measurement of Cohesion in Work Teams. *Small Group Research, 31*(1), 71–88. doi:10.1177/104649640003100104

Cooke, N. J., Gorman, J. C., Duran, J. L., & Taylor, A. R. (2007). Team Cognition in Experienced Command-and-Control Teams. *Journal of Experimental Psychology. Applied, 13*(3), 146–157. doi:10.1037/1076-898X.13.3.146 PMID:17924800

Cummings, J. N. (2004). Work Groups, Structural Diversity, and Knowledge Sharing in a Global Organization. *Management Science, 50*(3), 352–364. doi:10.1287/mnsc.1030.0134

Cusumano, M., MacCormack, A., Kemerer, C. F., & Crandall, B. (2003). Software Development Worldwide: The State of the Practice. *IEEE Software, 20*(6), 28–34. doi:10.1109/MS.2003.1241363

De Backer, M., Boen, F., Ceux, T., Cuyper, B. D., Høigaard, R., Callens, F., ... Broek, G. V. (2011). Do Perceived Justice and Need Support of the Coach Predict Team Identification and Cohesion? *Psychology of Sport and Exercise, 12*(2), 192–201. doi:10.1016/j.psychsport.2010.09.009

Dooley, D. (2001). *Social Research Methods*. Upper Saddle River, NJ: Prentice-Hall.

Earley, P. C., & Mosakowski, E. (2000). Creating Hybrid Team Cultures: An Empirical Test of Transformational Team Functioning. *Academy of Management Journal*, *43*(1), 26–49. doi:10.2307/1556384

Eisenhardt, K. M., & Tabrizi, B. N. (1995). Accelerating Adaptive Processes: Product Innovation in the Global Computer Industry. *Administrative Science Quarterly*, *40*(1), 84–110. doi:10.2307/2393701

Erdogmus, H. (2009). Diversity and Software Development. *IEEE Software*, *26*(3), 2–4. doi:10.1109/MS.2009.62

Eys, M. A., & Carron, A. V. (2001). Role Ambiguity, Task Cohesion, and Task Self-Efficacy. *Small Group Research*, *32*(3), 356–373. doi:10.1177/104649640103200305

Favaro, J. (2010). Renewing the Software Project Management Life Cycle. *IEEE Software*, *27*(1), 17–19. doi:10.1109/MS.2010.9

Fleming, L. (2004). Perfecting Cross-Pollination. *Harvard Business Review*, *82*(9), 22–23.

Galbraith, J. R. (1974). Organization Design: An Information Processing View. *Interfaces*, *4*(3), 28–36. doi:10.1287/inte.4.3.28

Gefen, D., Straub, D. W., & Boudreau, M. (2000). Structural Equation Modeling and Regression: Guidelines for Research Practice. *Communications of the Association for Information Systems*, *4*(7), 2–76.

Gold, B. (1987). Approaches to Accelerating Product and Process. *Journal of Product Innovation Management*, *4*(2), 81–88. doi:10.1016/0737-6782(87)90054-3

Gorla, N., & Lam, Y. W. (2004). Who Should Work with Whom? Building Effective Software Project Teams. *Communications of the ACM*, *47*(6), 79–82. doi:10.1145/990680.990684

Gratton, L., & Erickson, T. J. (2007). 8 Ways to Build Collaborative Teams. *Harvard Business Review*, *85*(11), 100–109. PMID:18159790

Hackman, J. R. (1976). Group Influence on Individuals. In M. D. Dunnette (Ed.), *Handbook of Industrial and Organizational Psychology* (pp. 1455–1525). Chicago: Rand-McNally.

Harrison, D. A., & Klein, K. J. (2007). What's the Difference? Diversity Constructs as Separation, Variety, or Disparity in Organizations. *Academy of Management Review*, *32*(4), 1199–1228. doi:10.5465/AMR.2007.26586096

Harrison, D. A., Price, K. H., & Bell, M. P. (1998). Beyond Relational Demography: Time and the Effects of Surface- and Deep-Level Diversity on Work Group Cohesion. *Academy of Management Journal*, *41*(1), 96–107. doi:10.2307/256901

Hinsz, V. B., Tindale, R. S., & Vollrath, D. A. (1997). The Emerging Conceptualization of Groups as Information Processors. *Psychological Bulletin*, *121*(1), 43–64. doi:10.1037/0033-2909.121.1.43 PMID:9000891

Hirst, G., Van Dick, R., & Van Knippenberg, D. (2009). A Social Identity Perspective on Leadership and Employee Creativity. *Journal of Organizational Behavior*, *30*(7), 963–982. doi:10.1002/job.600

Huelsheger, U. R., Anderson, N. R., & Salgado, J. F. (2009). Team-Level Predictors of Innovation at Work: A Comprehensive Meta-Analysis Spanning Three Decades of Research. *The Journal of Applied Psychology*, *94*(5), 1128–1145. doi:10.1037/a0015978 PMID:19702361

Irmer, B. E., Chang, A., & Bordia, P. (2000). The Development of Social and Task Cohesion in Computer-Mediated and Face-to-Face Task Groups. *Paper presented at the Academy of Management*. 10.5465/APBPP.2000.5535198

Kautz, K., & Nielsen, P. A. (2004). Understanding the Implementation of Software Process Improvement Innovations in Software Organizations. *Information Systems Journal*, *14*(1), 3–22. doi:10.1111/j.1365-2575.2004.00156.x

Ke, W., & Zhang, P. (2010). The Effects of Extrinsic Motivations and Satisfaction in Open Source Software Development. *Journal of the Association for Information Systems*, *11*(12), 784–808.

Klimoski, R., & Mohammed, S. (1994). Team Mental Model: Construct or Metaphor? *Journal of Management*, *20*(2), 403–437. doi:10.1177/014920639402000206

Knippenberg, D., Dreu, C. K. W. D., & Homan, A. C. (2004). Work Group Diversity and Group Performance: An Integrative Model and Research Agenda. *The Journal of Applied Psychology*, *89*(6), 1008–1022. doi:10.1037/0021-9010.89.6.1008 PMID:15584838

Kolb, R. (2010). The Need for Speed: Releasing Products Earlier Using Software Product Lines. *IEEE Software*, *27*(3), 56–59. doi:10.1109/MS.2010.80

Kozlowski, S. W. J., & Ilgen, D. R. (2006). Enhancing the Effectiveness of Work Groups and Teams. *Psychological Science in the Public Interest*, *7*(3), 77–124. doi:10.1111/j.1529-1006.2006.00030.x PMID:26158912

Larman, C., & Vodde, B. (2009). *Scaling Lean & Agile Development: Thinking and Organizational Tools for Large-Scale Scrum*. Boston, MA: Pearson Education.

Lee, G., & Xia, W. (2010). Toward Agile: An Integrated Analysis of Quantitative and Qualitative Field Data on Software Development Agility. *Management Information Systems Quarterly*, *34*(1), 87–114.

Levina, N. (2005). Collaborating on Multiparty Information Systems Development Projects: A Collective Reflection-in-Action View. *Information Systems Research*, *16*(2), 109–130. doi:10.1287/isre.1050.0055

Lin, T.-C., Hsu, J. S.-C., Cheng, K.-T., & Wu, S. (2012). Understanding the Role of Behavioural Integration in Isd Teams: An Extension of Transactive Memory Systems Concept. *Information Systems Journal*, *22*(3), 211–234. doi:10.1111/j.1365-2575.2011.00383.x

Lindell, M. K., & Whitney, D. J. (2001). Accounting for Common Method Variance in Cross-Sectional Research Designs. *The Journal of Applied Psychology*, *86*(1), 114–121. doi:10.1037/0021-9010.86.1.114 PMID:11302223

Lingo, E. L., & O'Mahony, S. (2010). Nexus Work. *Brokerage on Creative Projects Administrative Science Quarteriy*, *55*(1), 47–81. doi:10.2189/asqu.2010.55.1.47

Lyytinen, K., & Rose, G. M. (2003). Disruptive Information System Innovation: The Case of Internet Computing. *Information Systems Journal*, *13*(4), 301–330. doi:10.1046/j.1365-2575.2003.00155.x

Mannix, E., & Neale, M. (2005). What Differences Make a Difference? The Promise and Reality of Diverse Teams in Organizations. *Psychological Science in the Public Interest, 6*(2), 31–55. doi:10.1111/j.1529-1006.2005.00022.x PMID:26158478

Marquardt, D. W. (1970). Generalized Inverses, Ridge Regression and Biased Linear Estimation. *Technometrics, 12*(3), 591–612. doi:10.2307/1267205

Mason, C. H., & Perreault, W. D. (1991). Collinearity, Power, and Interpretation of Multiple Regression Analysis. *JMR, Journal of Marketing Research, 38*(3), 268–280. doi:10.2307/3172863

Mathieu, J. E., Goodwin, G. F., Heffner, T. S., Salas, E., & Cannon-Bowers, J. A. (2000). The Influence of Shared Mental Models on Team Process and Performance. *The Journal of Applied Psychology, 85*(2), 273–283. doi:10.1037/0021-9010.85.2.273 PMID:10783543

Maznevski, M. L. (1994). Understanding Our Differences: Performance in Decision-Making Groups with Diverse Members. *Human Relations, 47*(5), 531–552. doi:10.1177/001872679404700504

Mendelson, H., & Pillai, R. R. (1998). Clockspeed and Informational Response: Evidence from the Information Technology Industry. *Information Systems Research, 9*(4), 415–433. doi:10.1287/isre.9.4.415

Milliken, J. F., & Martins, L. L. (1996). Searching for Common Threads: Understanding the Multiple Effects of Diversity in Organizational Groups. *Academy of Management Review, 21*, 402–433.

Mohammed, S., Ferzandi, L., & Hamilton, K. (2010). Metaphor No More: A 15-Year Review of the Team Mental Model Construct. *Journal of Management, 36*(4), 876–910. doi:10.1177/0149206309356804

Mohammed, S., Klimoski, R., & Rentsch, J. R. (2000). The Measurement of Team Mental Models: We Have No Shared Schema. *Organizational Research Methods, 3*(2), 123–165. doi:10.1177/109442810032001

Nunnally, J., & Bernstein, I. (1994). *Psychometric Theory*. New York: McGraw-Hill.

Paulus, P. B. (2000). Groups, Teams, and Creativity: The Creative Potential of Idea-Generating Groups. *Applied Psychology, 49*(2), 237–262. doi:10.1111/1464-0597.00013

Pearsall, M. J., & Venkataramani, V. (2015). Overcoming Asymmetric Goals in Teams: The Interactive Roles of Team Learning Orientation and Team Identification. *The Journal of Applied Psychology, 100*(3), 735–748. doi:10.1037/a0038315 PMID:25384202

Pirola-Merlo, A. (2010). Agile Innovation: The Role of Team Climate in Rapid Research and Development. *Journal of Occupational and Organizational Psychology, 83*(4), 1075–1084. doi:10.1348/096317909X480653

Podsakoff, P. M., MacKenzie, S. B., Lee, J.-Y., & Podsakoff, N. P. (2003). Common Method Biases in Behavioral Research: A Critical Review of the Literature and Recommended Remedies. *The Journal of Applied Psychology, 88*(5), 879–903. doi:10.1037/0021-9010.88.5.879 PMID:14516251

Rose, J. (2010). *Software Innovation - Eight Work-Style Heuristics for Creative System Developers*: http://www.lulu.com/items/volume_68/8174000/8174329/5/print/SI_book_beta_bw.pdf

Saunders, C., & Kim, J. (2007). Editors' Comments: Perspectives on Time. *Management Information Systems Quarterly, 31*(4), iii–xi.

Schneider, B. (1983). Interactional Psychology and Organizational Behavior. In L. Cummings & B. Staw (Eds.), *Research in Organizational Behavior*. Greenwich, CT: JAI Press.

Schoonhoven, C. B., Eisenhardt, K. M., & Lyman, K. (1990). Speeding Products to Market: Waiting Time to First Product Introduction in New Firms. *Administrative Science Quarterly*, *35*(1), 177–207. doi:10.2307/2393555

Sethi, R., Smith, D. C., & Park, C. W. (2001). Cross-Functional Product Development Teams, Creativity, and the Innovativeness of New Consumer Product. *JMR, Journal of Marketing Research*, *38*(1), 73–85. doi:10.1509/jmkr.38.1.73.18833

Shachaf, P. (2008). Cultural Diversity and Information and Communication Technology Impacts on Global Virtual Teams: An Exploratory Study. *Information & Management*, *45*(2), 131–142. doi:10.1016/j.im.2007.12.003

Shin, S. J., & Zhou, J. (2007). When Is Educational Specialization Heterogeneity Related to Creativity in Research and Development Teams? Transformational Leadership as a Moderator. *The Journal of Applied Psychology*, *92*(6), 1709–1721. doi:10.1037/0021-9010.92.6.1709 PMID:18020807

Siau, K., Tan, X., & Sheng, H. (2010). Important Characteristics of Software Development Team Members: An Empirical Investigation Using Repertory Grid. *Information Systems Journal*, *20*(6), 563–580. doi:10.1111/j.1365-2575.2007.00254.x

Siau, K., & Tian, Y. (2013). Open Source Software Development Process Model: A Grounded Theory Approach. *Journal of Global Information Management*, *21*(4), 103–120. doi:10.4018/jgim.2013100106

Simons, T., Pelled, L., & Smith, K. (1999). Making Use of Difference: Diversity, Debate, and Decision Comprehensiveness in Top Management Teams. *Academy of Management Journal*, *42*(6), 662–673. doi:10.2307/256987

Somech, A., & Drach-Zahavy, A. (2013). Translating Team Creativity to Innovation Implementation: The Role of Team Composition and Climate for Innovation. *Journal of Management*, *39*(3), 684–708. doi:10.1177/0149206310394187

Souder, W. E. (1987). *Managing New Product Innovation*. Lexington, MA: Lexington Books.

Souza, G. C., Bayus, B. L., & Wagner, H. M. (2004). New-Product Strategy and Industry Clockspeed. *Management Science*, *50*(4), 537–549. doi:10.1287/mnsc.1030.0172

Tajfel, H. (1981). *Human Groups and Social Categories: Studies in Social Psychology*. Cambridge, England: Cambridge University Press.

Tajfel, H., & Turner, J. C. (1986). The Social Identity Theory of Inter-Group Behavior. In S. Worchel & L. W. Austin (Eds.), *Psychology of Intergroup Relations*. Chigago: Nelson-Hall.

Tang, C., & Naumann, S. E. (2016). Team Diversity, Mood, and Team Creativity: The Role of Team Knowledge Sharing in Chinese R&D Teams. *Journal of Management & Organization*, *22*(3), 420–434. doi:10.1017/jmo.2015.43

Teachman, J. (1980). Analysis of Population Diversity. *Sociological Methods & Research, VIII*(3), 341–362. doi:10.1177/004912418000800305

The Economist Technology Quarterly. (2001). *Invention Is the Easy Bi.* Retrieved from http://www.economist.com/node/662203

Tushman, M. L., & Nadler, D. A. (1978). Information Processing as an Integrating Concept in Organizational Design. *Academy of Management Review, 3*(3), 613–624.

Ucbasaran, D., Westhead, P., & Wright, M. (2009). The Extent and Nature of Opportunity Identification by Experienced Entrepreneurs. *Journal of Business Venturing, 24*(2), 99–115. doi:10.1016/j.jbusvent.2008.01.008

Utterback, J. M. (1971). The Process of Technological Innovation within the Firm. *Academy of Management Journal, 14*(1), 75–88. doi:10.2307/254712

Van den Bossche, P., Gijselaers, W. H., Segers, M., & Kirschner, P. A. (2006). Social and Cognitive Factors Driving Teamwork in Collaborative Learning Environments: Team Learning Beliefs and Behaviors. *Small Group Research, 37*(5), 490–521. doi:10.1177/1046496406292938

Van Der Vegt, G. S., & Bunderson, J. S. (2005). Learning and Performance in Multidisciplinary Teams: The Importance of Collective Team Identification. *Academy of Management Journal, 48*(3), 532–547. doi:10.5465/AMJ.2005.17407918

West, M. A. (2002a). Ideas Are Ten a Penny: It's Team Implementation Not Idea Generation That Counts. *Applied Psychology, 51*(3), 411–424. doi:10.1111/1464-0597.01006

West, M. A. (2002b). Sparkling Fountains or Stagnant Ponds: An Integrative Model of Creativity and Innovation Implementation. *Applied Psychology, 51*(3), 355–424. doi:10.1111/1464-0597.00951

West, M. A., & Anderson, N. R. (1996). Innovation in Top Management Teams. *The Journal of Applied Psychology, 81*(6), 680–693. doi:10.1037/0021-9010.81.6.680

West, M. A., & Farr, J. L. (1990). *Innovation & Creativity at Work: Psychological & Organizational Strategies.* New York: John Wiley & Sons.

Wu, J., Goh, K.-Y., Li, H., Luo, C., & Zheng, H. (2016). The effects of communication patterns on the success of open source software projects: an empirical analysis from social network perspectives. *Journal of Global Information Management, 24*(4), 22–44. doi:10.4018/JGIM.2016100102

Zaccaro, S. J. (1991). Nonequivalent Associations between Forms of Cohesiveness and Group-Related Outcomes: Evidence for Multidimensionality. *The Journal of Social Psychology, 131*(3), 387–399. doi:10.1080/00224545.1991.9713865

Zhou, E. Y., & Stembridge, B. (2009). *Patented in China - the Present and Future State of Innovation in China.* New York: Thomson Reuters.

This research was previously published in the Journal of Global Information Management (JGIM), 26(2); pages 163-192, copyright year 2018 by IGI Publishing (an imprint of IGI Global).

APPENDIX A

List of Relevant Partner Online Communities Approached

1. http://www.csdn.net/
2. http://www.51cto.com/
3. http://www.aspjzy.com/
4. http://www.cnzz.com/
5. http://www.51admin.com/
6. http://www.admin5.com/
7. http://www.chinaz.com/
8. http://www.mydrivers.com/
9. http://www.dospy.com/
10. http://www.hiapk.com/
11. http://www.cncms.com/
12. http://www.builder.com.cn/
13. http://www.chinajavaworld.com/
14. http://www.phpwind.net/
15. http://www.discuz.net/
16. http://www.gameres.com/
17. http://www.php100.com/
18. http://www.zzgjj.com.cn/
19. http://www.ctochina.net/
20. http://www.okajax.com/
21. http://www.im286.com/
22. http://www.webmasterhome.cn/
23. http://www.pudn.com/
24. http://www.yesky.com/

Please note this list was provided by the company, and is non-exhaustive.

APPENDIX B

Demographics of Sampled Software Teams (N=96)

Table 8. Age of team-affiliated companies

	Frequency	Percent
<= 5 years	43	44.8%
6 – 10 years	21	21.9%
11 – 15 years	18	18.8%
15 – 20 years	12	12.5%
>= 21 years	2	2.1%
Total	96	100%

Table 9. Team size

	Frequency	Percent
<= 3 persons	5	5.2%
4 – 5 persons	18	18.8%
6 – 10 persons	33	34.5%
11 – 20 persons	12	12.3%
21 – 30 persons	18	18.8%
>= 30 persons	10	10.1%
Total	96	100%

Table 10. Team composition in terms of function

	Mean	Std. Dev.
Software development (persons)	7	6.07
Finance/Accounting (persons)	3	3.46
Marketing/Sales (persons)	3	3.08
Business analysis (persons)	3	3.86
Engineering (persons)	4	3.62
Production/Operations (persons)	3	3.33
Administration (persons)	3	3.51
Others (persons)	0	0

Table 11. Respondent's tenure in the team

	Frequency	Percent
<= 2 months	9	9.4%
3 – 6 months	29	30.2%
7 months – 1 year	28	29.3%
13 months – 2 years	21	21.9%
> 2 years	9	9.3%
Total	96	100%

Table 12. Product type of the software

	Frequency	Percent
Anti-virus/Privacy/Monitoring software	4	4.17%
Data analysis software	6	6.25%
Education software	1	1.04%
Email	2	2.08%
Financial management software	5	5.21%
HR management software	1	1.04%
Information communication software	10	10.42%
Marketing/Sales management software	3	3.13%
OA (Office automation) software	7	7.29%
OS (Operating system) software	2	2.08%
Portal/Website	3	3.13%
Production management software	4	4.17%
Supply chain management software	1	1.04%
Text mining software	1	1.04%
Traffic management software	2	2.08%
Others	9	9.38%
(Missing)	35	36.46%
Total	96	100.00%

Chapter 74

Structuration and Learning in a Software Firm:
A Technology–Based Entrepreneurship Case Study

Rafael A. Gonzalez
ⓘ https://orcid.org/0000-0003-1237-4408
Pontificia Universidad Javeriana, Bogota, Colombia

Marisela Vargas
Pontificia Universidad Javeriana, Bogota, Colombia

Florentino Malaver
Pontificia Universidad Javeriana, Bogota, Colombia

Efraín Ortiz
Pontificia Universidad Javeriana, Bogota, Colombia

ABSTRACT

This case study presents the evolution of a software firm from startup into early internationalization. Building on a structuration theory, the case is framed within a conceptual model that illustrates the way skills and routines co-evolve both at the level of the founding entrepreneur (agency) and of the firm (structure). As such, this article contributes to an emergent structurational view of technology-based entrepreneurship. Such views places emphasis on learning both at the individual and collective level, in terms of software engineering, commercial, managerial and strategic capabilities. In addition, it supports a dynamic perspective of entrepreneurship in the software industry by covering not only the startup phase but also early growth and consolidation of the firm.

DOI: 10.4018/978-1-6684-3702-5.ch074

INTRODUCTION

This work presents a case study of technology-based entrepreneurship in the software industry. It is inscribed in an entrepreneurship research current which is critical with respect to placing the individual at the center of entrepreneurship, such as in Shane and Venkataraman (2000), where emphasis is placed alternatively on the opportunity. More specifically, it follows the work of (Sarason, Dean, & Dillard, 2006), where both entrepreneur and opportunity are meaningful and in fact inseparable. This, in turns, follows structuration theory (Giddens, 1986), the well-known sociological theory that aims at going beyond the traditional dualism between agency and structure in social systems. Sarason et al. address the opportunity which results in a startup (i.e. structure), together with the individual entrepreneur (i.e. agency), not as two isolated poles, but as mutually influencing each other. While Sarason *et al.* center their work on the initial moment of opportunity, this paper has a broader scope towards growth and consolidation of a new software firm, investigating the way the interaction between agency and structure is transformative and defines the firm's profile in time.

In addition to the dual level of analysis (entrepreneur-firm), this study places an emphasis on the dynamic nature of learning (cf. Aldrich & Yang, 2014). This dynamic character of entrepreneurial learning has been addressed in (Cope, 2005) who claims that entrepreneurship studies must consider not only the operation of entrepreneurship, but also the operation of the firm itself and especially the learning process involved. For Cope, the entrepreneur is still a relevant object of study, but not as a static agent. In consequence, he follows and extends the behavioral perspective of entrepreneurship, which is focused on what the entrepreneur does, not on who (s)he is, and proposes a dynamic learning perspective. Specifically, Cope includes the capability of the entrepreneur to learn and adapt, articulating this to the growth of the firm beyond its first years. As such, this paper extends Cope, explicitly including learning, but as a collective process that moves between the entrepreneur and the firm.

This article specifically focuses on technology-based entrepreneurship (TBE) in the software industry. In doing so, it relies on Garud & Karnøe (2003) as they also question entrepreneurship centered on a sole exceptional entrepreneur and use Gidden's structuration theory to argue that the momentum generated by a certain technology is determined by the confluence of different inputs. Accumulation of these inputs generates an emergent path that simultaneously enables and restricts the activity of related actors; the actors shape the path and the path shapes the actors through time. These paths are not planned but rather emerge through improvisation, adaptation and learning.

This inquiry is framed within a conceptual model which enables capturing and interpreting the findings related to the salient traits of the transformations experienced by the agent and the structure throughout the dynamic process of TBE with an emphasis on learning. An in-depth case study allows capturing the structuration of TBE and the evolution of the firm's capabilities, which contributes to supporting analytic perspectives (Yin, 2003). It is also a means of contributing new insights that cannot be fully interpreted under the lens of the existing theory (Eisenhardt & Graebner, 2007). The research setting is ITAC, a firm created as a TBE in the software industry of an emerging country, which has quickly grown during its first decade, becoming a successful international medium-sized company. The case is approached as an entrepreneurship where the knowledge base of the entrepreneur evolves through individual and collective learning. This learning process accounts for a co-evolution between technical skills and routines related to software engineering along with commercial, managerial and strategic capabilities.

The rest of this article comprises first a conceptual review of the literature associated with (technology-based) entrepreneurship, as well as structuration theory, and entrepreneurial learning from a collective and dynamic point of view. Then, the underpinnings and the methodological design of the study are discussed in order to follow up with an account of the most relevant results and most significant moments of the firm plotted on a historical development timeline. Finally, there is a discussion of the results and implications in terms of the sustainability of technical and commercial growth in software startups.

LITERATURE REVIEW

This section covers several related theoretical approaches to technology-based entrepreneurship, including its conception as well as its evolution.

(Technology-Based) Entrepreneurship

The dominating conception of the contemporary entrepreneur is still strongly influenced by the image of the heroic entrepreneur from the industrial revolution, whose projects are huge and whose characteristics and energy are outstanding (Ricketts, 2008). This notion was solidified and became seminal in Schumpeter's initial work, which distinguishes the normal manager (resource configurator) from the manager that has an outstanding entrepreneurial spirit. In this early Schumpeter (1934), the link between the entrepreneur and innovation as a competition driver is dealt with for the first time in a systematic fashion. The Schumpeterian entrepreneur is an exceptional individual who has the capability to overcome standard thinking and perceive objective possibilities that are hidden to the rest; also, being capable of "getting things done", meaning (s)he is capable of successfully exploiting these innovative possibilities (Elster, 2000).

In this paper, we focus on technology-based entrepreneurship (TBE) because the nature of the firm under study and the way in which it was created respond to a knowledge-intensive and nascent technology-centric opportunity. While TBE literature still needs to mature the concept, currently it relates to the systematic use of specialized knowledge, along with the identification of market opportunities that can be commercially exploited through innovative products and services (Bailetti, 2012). Furthermore, technology entrepreneurship can be defined as entrepreneurial and intrapreneurial activities of both existing and nascent companies in technology-intensive environments (Unutmaz Durmuşoğlu, 2018). When it refers to nascent companies it is directly linked to the concept of new technology-based firms (NTBFs) typically established around a founding team that possesses few resources but specific knowledge and a promising idea and that must develop their own capabilities, particularly for exploration and exploitation (A. Jensen & Clausen, 2017). As Spiegel and Marxt note (2011), TBE can be addressed at a product, firm or system level: the fact that a technological product is innovative or not can be associated with the conditions of the technology itself, the capability of the firm, or the environment in which it is deployed. Accordingly, an exclusive emphasis on the use of specialized technological knowledge may undermine knowledge related to the structural opportunity as well. As discussed in (Breschi, Lenzi, Malerba, & Mancusi, 2014) knowledge-intensive entrepreneurship is also determined by the knowledge of the environment, demand, clients, financiers, competition and suppliers, among others. Moreover, in the IT industry contextual and commercial knowledge is even more crucial because IT products must be tailored to users in a highly dynamic environment.

Structuration Theory, Entrepreneurship and Routines

We approach this study though dual dimensions of analysis: entrepreneur (agency) and firm (structure). In entrepreneurship and organizational studies, structuration theory has been adopted as a framework to enable better understanding of the co-evolution between bottom-up and top-down behaviors at the onset as well as the evolution of the firm. Accordingly, this section briefly presents the conceptual roots of structuration theory and some related works in the domain of entrepreneurship as well organizational routines.

Agency may be defined as the events an individual carries out, and structure as the properties that remain similar in different moments of social systems (Schuster Fonseca, 1993). In entrepreneurship, this tension is present (1) between an individual with entrepreneurial spirit and a systemic opportunity; and (2) between the individual skills of the entrepreneur and the dynamic capabilities of the firm that outgrow the individual. This agency-structure dilemma may orient the debate towards the supremacy of one over the other. Structuration theory proposed overcoming this dualism and allowing agency to influence the emergence of certain structural properties, while, at the same time, structural properties enable or restrict further individual actions. In effect, agency and structure are mutually defined continuously: structure is not external to individuals nor possible without them (Schuster Fonseca, 1993).

Stemming from structuration theory, a new understanding of entrepreneurship has begun to emerge (Sarason et al., 2006). From this perspective, when the entrepreneur frames, names and configures resources, (s)he is helping to define and create the opportunity, and not just to identify it as if it already existed. Furthermore, the structural conditions effectively limit the possibilities that the entrepreneur has in defining the opportunity. Both aspects are necessary for the entrepreneurship to become a reality. On the one hand, the entrepreneur has the capability to influence the environment, for example, by successfully attracting investors or human talent; on the other hand, the context has an influence on the entrepreneur, for example, by encouraging an entrepreneurial culture.

Moreover, following Garud & Karnøe (2003), a structuration theory perspective on technology entrepreneurship is not limited to a single entrepreneurial agent, but rather to collective distributed agency. A technological path is thus the result of a central artifact surrounded by the simultaneously constraining and enabling "momentum" generated by interwoven agency, including design, production, use, evaluation, and regulation. As such, multiple actors improvise and adapt to the unfolding structure, gradually transforming the emergent path of a given technology.

Regarding organizational routines, a structurational view has also been proposed. Pentland & Feldman (2005) frame routines as either ostensive or performative, arguing that, as in structuration theory, both aspects are mutually constitutive: the ostensive (structure) does not simply guide the performative (agency), but it is also co-created by it. This means that the practiced routine is performed by agents but is inseparable from the structural ostensive routines. This notion is taken further by Radwan & Kinder (2013) who explain that while the ostensive aspect of a routine represents an abstract action pattern, the performative aspect describes its execution by specific individuals in a specific place and time. Furthermore, the way routines are transferred and evolve in entrepreneurship has been studied by Aldrich & Yang (2014), based on the view of Pentland & Feldman (2005). For Aldrich and Young, an entrepreneur must have an initial set of routines, without which it would be very difficult for a new firm to deal with the complexity of its environment. But this set of routines is purely ostensive; their practical execution will be influenced by the habits and emotions of the employees that are involved in the growing entrepreneurship. As a consequence, the simple fact of developing routines (ostensive) will not be enough for the sustainability of the company; higher-order routines will be necessary so that the lower-order routines become replicable (Aldrich & Yang, 2014).

From Individual to Collective Learning

Because this paper is interested not only on the origins of a software startup, but also on its growth and consolidation, it is of utmost relevance to uncover the way in which the individual entrepreneur learns together with how the firm learns collectively and how these two levels of learning shape each other. As such, we briefly introduce some recent work on entrepreneurial learning at the individual, as well as the collective level.

For Cope (2005), entrepreneurial learning is centered on the individual entrepreneur and placed into a dynamic context where previous knowledge is a crucial starting point that sets in motion a series of adaptations, achieved through experience, crises and reflection. Deligianni, Voudouris & Lioukas (2015) argue that the initial configuration of existing knowledge determines the initial growth path of a new venture and enables or constrains enhancement and reconfiguration of different types of knowledge. However, there remains a recognized lack of understanding of the relationship and interaction between individual and collective learning (Wang & Chugh, 2014).

Collective learning has been studied in organizational learning literature and is widely recognized as more than the sum of individual learnings. However, the precise mechanisms or flows between individual and collective entrepreneurial learning have not been studied in detail. Some point towards double-loop and generative learning (Pittaway & Thorpe, 2012), which suggests a conceptual link between individual entrepreneurial learning and its social dimension: generative learning implies anticipatory use of knowledge by the firm stemming from higher-order skills that are generalizable and lead to a greater transfer of learning. In keeping with Cope´s perspective, this is catalyzed by critical incidents and mediated by critical reflection. In structuration terms, "higher-order skills" may be related to (structural) "ostensive routines" (Pentland & Feldman, 2005) and as such become entangled with performative routines as enacted by different members of the firm at different points in time, resulting in collective learning at the firm level. Thus, following Cope, non-routine events trigger the development of higher-order skills, but this is not reduced to the individual (Pittaway & Thorpe, 2012).

RESEARCH METHODOLOGY

An in-depth case study is the most adequate research strategy for the objectives of this paper, because it allows capturing the dynamic interaction between actors and real-world phenomena through time, in all its complexity and within the context where they acquire their meaning (Yin, 2003). In addition, this method facilitates the articulation and validation of theoretical propositions (Yin, 2003), as well as the generation of new insights that emerge from the interpretation of new elements (Eisenhardt & Graebner, 2007). Thus, this case enables applying and validating the concepts presented in the previous section, as well as advancing the understanding of technology-based entrepreneurship in the software industry.

ITAC S.A. was selected for the study because it is a software company which belongs to a knowledge-intensive industry; also, because it is a young firm that has grown quickly and became international early on; additionally, it provides sufficiently rich evidence regarding the conditions through which it evolved in business and software engineering terms. The authors come to the case through the fact that it is a startup founded by a known alumnus which is recognized in the Colombian software sector as a successful, rapid-growth firm with early international presence. Aside from that, the authors have no further connection or interest in the firm.

Pursuant to the research objectives, the study focuses on the interaction between entrepreneur (as agency) and firm (as structure) as the unit of analysis. ITAC qualifies as an "exemplary case" that facilitates the treatment of issues associated with the startup, development and consolidation of a TBE in the software industry. Due to its exploratory nature, the case generates inputs related to the nature and interaction dynamics between individual and collective learning beyond the startup, which can be used at a later stage for multiple case studies under the logic of replication, contrast and extension of the current findings (Eisenhardt & Graebner, 2007).

Data gathering derives from the background that led to the creation of the firm in 2004 and its growth until 2014, complemented with more recent interviews up to 2016. To guarantee the quality of the data and the evidence obtained, the instruments (in-depth interviews, observation, and document analysis) and information sources (founders and employees, as well as company and sector-wide documents and statistics) were triangulated to preserve objectivity. Resulting interview data has been inductively treated and mapped to individual and firm milestones, evolving technical routines and learning behaviors. Besides interviewing the founder, we also interviewed the administrative vice-president and co-founder, as well as the lead architect that has been with ITAC almost from the start. More than a dozen interviews were carried out usually with all authors present taking turns asking questions or taking notes, full audio recordings were done for the main initial longer interviews, which an assistant helped with transcribing (in Spanish). Initial interviews were later complemented with shorter conversations, emails, company visits and internal documents, taking into account that the case is longitudinal and that the authors were able to have access to the company in the period 2012-2016. The interview transcripts were coded separately by the authors using ALAS.ti, triangulated both by comparing and intersecting each codification, validating it with ITAC and iteratively clarifying or expanding information with additional interviews and documents.

Information analysis was based on a reconstruction of the case, to identify the main stages that ITAC has gone through, based on milestones that determined its evolution. The structural axis of the narrative lies on the interaction patterns between agency and structure, captured in an interpretation model which illustrates the evolution of TBE and abstracts the nature and characteristics of the co-evolution of agency and structure along the development of a software startup. The results were presented and discussed with the interviewees. This was a recursive process between evidence and theory, a strategy that has already been applied in a knowledge-intensive entrepreneurship context (Knockaert, Ucbasaran, Wright, & Clarysse, 2011). This back and forth journey between data and literature, continued until reaching "theoretical saturation".

Findings

ITAC is the expression of a case of successful creation, development and consolidation of a technology-based entrepreneurship in the software industry. Created in 2004 with an initial capital of just the price of two laptops for its two employees (the founder and his partner), it has achieved an accelerated growth, which can be seen in an increase in staff and sales. By 2013 it had surpassed 130 employees and multiplied sales more than fortyfold. This accelerated growth was accompanied by an increase in complexity in the development of their products, from training and consulting services to development of specialized software. Furthermore, there is an early internationalization, which has resulted in sales to 8 Latin-American countries and the expectation of reaching a global presence in the medium-term. The next sections will present the most important episodes and milestones ITAC has gone through.

Episode 1: ITAC Startup

ITAC is a result of the convergence between the emergence and diffusion of the Java® programming language in Colombia, together with the knowledge and business capabilities of its founder to commercially exploit it at a time when Internet portals were growing.

Javier Galindo, a gifted computer scientist, has programmed in Java® since 1995 and by 1999 had become one of its first certified programmers in Latin-America. In October of the same year he taught his first official Java® course for the biggest oil company in Colombia, Ecopetrol, and started working for the company that created Java®, the now extinct SUN Microsystems. In the following years he taught courses in different countries with SUN. By the year 2000, Javier had become a Java® referent and evangelist.

While 2000 is remembered as the year the dot-com bubble burst, this did not stop companies from pursuing a presence on the Internet and beginning to offer online services through portals. In Colombia, the banking sector turned to online transactional platforms. The often-hurried way these portals were developed led to a series of performance and security issues. At the same time, a business version of Java appeared, J2EE leading the language to a new purpose and market: development of business applications and web portals.

Javier Galindo seized the moment to make the leap from training to consulting, given that the courses he taught, as he says, "opened doors" to a market hungry for developing robust Web-enabled applications. In 2001 Javier taught a seminar on J2EE. Among the attendees were IT staff from one of the largest banks in Colombia (Davivienda); in 2003, they would request his services to solve a persistent problem with an application created with Java by one of the biggest software companies in Peru. This was his "first important consulting project". However, it had to be billed through his brother's company, already a Davivienda supplier; this motivated Javier to formalize his services by starting up a company.

Several factors converged in the opportunity unfolding before Mr. Galindo. First, the increasing adoption of Java and the consequent high training demand; second, the growth of Internet portals for business, especially in the banking sector; third, the rise of J2EE as an extended Java version, especially designed to support the development of Web-oriented business applications. Finally, his pioneering training role, quickly led him to build a reputation as an expert, with which he could advise banks on performance and security issues, their main concerns regarding IT.

Other circumstances, not pertaining to technology or the market, influenced the creation of ITAC. Javier's family was a strong motivator: besides his brother, his mother was an independent accountant and his father founded an insurance advisory firm. His commercial relationship with SUN was also decisive: he started out as an intern and ended up billing them as ITAC in 2004, when, as he recalls "the first invoice for training courses was submitted". This prompted him to hire additional trainers from within the very people he had helped get certified in Java®. Ricardo Cortés, ITAC's current lead software architect, has been with ITAC since then and had also worked with Javier in SUN. He recalls that during that time there were no specific software development standards or methods, just a shared set of practices and skills stemming from their time in SUN. The partnership with SUN crystallized in 2005, when they participated together in a project for Colombia's Central Bank, Banco de la República, where Mr. Galindo states that "SUN established the contacts and ITAC implemented the technological solution, as a joint venture".

Episode 2: ITAC Software House

ITAC advanced rapidly beyond training and consultancy towards its third line of business: software product development. This started in 2006 when Banco de la República recommended ITAC to Citibank to develop a product for the encryption of files for their Internet transaction portal. Citibank linked ITAC with their client, AIG, recommending the encryption solution: this is how their most emblematic product, SecureFile, came into being. A detailed exploration of the development of SecureFile was carried out showing that key success and innovation factors included: training, technological acquisition, knowledge acquisition, research, continuous improvement and version management, as well as a clear vision of growth from the start (Rojas, 2014). Ricardo Cortés, lead architect, highlights the technical innovation behind SecureFile as based upon bypassing hardware connection limitations and dealing with secure file connections through software. As a result, ITAC products are recognized for providing security, without a performance tradeoff.

In 2006, a solution for securing Davivienda's IT platform was conceived by Javier who told them "you have a security problem... and I have the solution". Davivienda bought into this and started the project, but the product failed to work during the pilot testing, so Davivienda opted instead for an IBM product. This painful setback showed ITAC that the product had a lot of potential, but its development needed greater formalism and rigor: software development at an industrial scale. Mr. Cortés recalls the ensuing change as shifting from an emphasis on development, to covering both development and testing, where the client is limited to acceptance. This was critical for ITAC at the time, because they "didn't even have Quality Assurance" and so had to evolve their testing from a reactive approach to a more systematic process.

During this time, partnerships extended beyond SUN. In 2008, an agreement was made with BEA SYSTEMS, acquired that year by Oracle, the company that shortly thereafter would acquire SUN. Thus, ITAC became an ally of the IT giant and, as Mr. Galindo puts it, "not just another part of the ecosystem". As a consequence, "real business started taking place", since it was not the same to "go in as Javier Galindo than having Oracle knocking at the door of the Bank's vice-president." For Javier, this new partnership entailed a "win-win situation, because we were able to help sell their products and at the same time we handled the implementation and development". As a result, ITAC's clients in the finance sector continued to grow, e.g. Grupo AVAL (Banco de Occidente and ATH) and Banco Santander, stemming from a growing reputation based on referrals due to "successful projects, and doing things right".

Javier acquired a deep knowledge of banking as he started down a path towards internationalization. During his work with Davivienda, Javier was performing an assessment for Macosa-Cobiscorp of Ecuador, also developers of Java-based banking software, and as he says: "I came back with feedback from that consultancy, so now I knew more about banking... I changed the architecture [of Davivienda] when I returned... and today it is used as their core: 80% of Davivienda's transactions go through this platform." A good part of this learning is summed in the fact that ITAC understands that they "work to provide solutions for our client's client." This means that within a banking application what matters most are not the technical requirements- that the software "does what it has to do"- but what the end user wants or needs, for example: it's not about a simple cash withdrawal, but about "being able to pay for an emergency procedure on a family member that urgently needs it".

This understanding of the business still had to be translated into software requirements, especially non-functional, as they refer not to what the software should do, but how it should do it. In banking, the service must be provided to many users simultaneously, while expecting some malicious system attacks by users. As such, the architecture of a software product emerges, expressing the non-functional aspects of the solution. Indeed, as identified by Rojas (2014) in SecureFile, the products' architecture is where ITAC's competitive advantage materialized and captured Javier's tacit knowledge.

Software development in this stage of ITAC is strongly linked to the founder's experience and way of doing things in terms of conception, design, implementation and commercialization. Ricardo Cortés states that ITAC's "technology watch" at the time was equated to Javier, whereas later it would be handled by a committee. Hence, at the beginning, there is informal knowledge-transfer through interaction, project meetings and general meetings that eventually lead to what they call "ITAC Informs": quarterly meetings to "synchronize" employees regarding innovation and projects, as well as a discussion space so that people "feel they are part of a big company". Mr. Cortés remembers that it was in one of those meetings that they decided to go for a continuous integration approach, which required a functional separation between development and testing teams, to be able to work separately but through an integrated software platform.

More formal learning and reflection stems from what can be considered Mr. Galindo's motto: "do things right from the start". Indeed, from the start, ITAC acquired software tools to record, analyze and optimize their processes (e.g. Bugzilla). ITAC has a repository that stores the technical aspects of its organizational memory and, as Javier says "the first line of code that ITAC wrote is there, along with who wrote it, and how the company's code has progressed day by day. That's why I know I have 6 million lines of code, because I find everything there, and we have been able to detect and track errors". By gathering this information, he continues, "anyone can understand them and know how they have operated throughout history." For example, through tracking defects they have been able to improve programming practices. These practices are assimilated gradually and some of them eventually become automated to the point that ITAC claims about 85% automation of their software development.

Episode 3: ITAC Software Factory

The Davivienda misstep in 2006 gave way to successful transformations. As Mr. Galindo puts it, if "you are going to compete with IBM, you have to do it seriously"; it is not enough to "develop software on the side"; it does not suffice "to have a product that does what is has to, it is about delivering a proper product"; therefore, he continues, "today we have a team of 25 people dedicated to creating and improving products on all fronts: documentation, quality, development, prototyping, presale, support, and demos". This is part of a learning experience resulting from Javier Galindo's involvement in everything "from conception, to presale, to providing support."

As a result, ITAC formalized many of their processes, leading to the launch in 2009 of a reengineered version of the Davivienda prototype, WS-Guardian, a software product for security and SOA governance. This solution is acquired by important entities such as Banco de la República, Colsubsidio, and Universidad del Norte, among others. Furthermore, due to the large-scale reengineering of the initial prototype, ITAC is awarded a national innovation prize (2011 INNOVA Award). ITAC WS-Guardian is a "product that has no manufacturers in Colombia or Latin-America, and only around 10 manufacturers may offer this type of solution" worldwide.

WS-Guardian was developed by ITAC's formalized Software Development Unit; one that "has grown and matured" embodying the collective and systematic processes surrounding product innovation. In

2012, this unit creates a third product, ITAC's SecureFile KMS, which is a solution for handling cryptographic keys and has, according to Mr. Galindo, "no more than 5 manufacturers in the world... we are reaching the edge, achieving things that have not been created, using original concepts".

These products synthesize the evolution of ITAC's software development processes, from an "art" centered on programming, to the establishment of roles and activities to develop software in a more industrialized and integrated way. Ricardo Cortés states that they maintained their original emphasis on developing pilots to promote innovative solutions, but they focused such prototypes on "breaking the rules of the software code, not of the development process, because otherwise we cannot evolve". Thus, ITAC goes from being a small software house anchored on Javier´s knowledge and skills, to a secure software factory with innovative products in the Colombian market. Despite this organizational collective advancement, Javier remains as the main actor in identifying and structuring opportunities: "I have an idea for a new product, [so]... a presentation is made [to the team]... to make it real... But first comes the concept: what the product does, the purpose it serves, the companies that might buy it, and... the team we need to build it".

The strengthening of ITAC's processes, technological capabilities and competitiveness was catalyzed by the pursuit of maturity through CMMI (Capability Maturity Model Integration), a model to evaluate the capability maturity of an engineering organization through five stages (CMMI Product Team, 2010). Although they had already implemented an ISO software quality standard, it only required them to formalize and document practices, not to follow best practices. Adopting CMMI was partly the result of a grant from the Colombian Government for a 30-month project that included 50 people and in which Javier saw his team go from "crying with exhaustion and stress, to tears of happiness upon obtaining the Level 3 assessment." Currently, ITAC strives to achieve CMMI Level 5, a state of maturity which is gradually allowing them to move from documented processes and good practices to, as Galindo says, "searching for the cause of a problem so it does not happen again. What you are looking for is to seriously learn, learn through time with numbers... this helps us get about 5 years closer to the leaders; to companies created 25 years before us". To reach Level 5 would be to "...achieve another level. We wouldn't be the first, but there are only four companies in Colombia with a level 5 CMMI. So, this would get us into a select group, since currently 23 companies have some CMMI valuation out of 670..."

ITAC's increased maturity is demonstrated, for instance, in estimating the effort required for a new project. In the beginning, according to Galindo, ITAC made an estimate by adding up the efforts of "small solutions. But when you face something ten times bigger, it does not necessarily scale up". The increased complexity means that the effort does not grow linearly. Galindo goes on to say: "we learned this, but only afterwards, because we did not take into account many things when estimating risks for such a big project". This means going beyond routines, because when complexity increases, the routine for small projects cannot continue to be used for big ones. To estimate effort, in addition to the statistical analysis of past projects, risk analysis methods are incorporated. In addition, testing and quality continued to evolve to a more formal and automated process that was not only traced through software; but required developing "Root Cause Analysis" capabilities. This also triggered a functional separation: initially the same group would develop and test and later two separate groups would specialize in development and testing.

Episode 4: The Future

ITAC refers to itself as a "secure software factory", now in the position to compete internationally. It is already facing the most important players in the country as well as leading international companies. Regarding custom-made software, Mr. Galindo states that they "compete with Intergrupo, Heinsohn, Unisys, IBM; in consultancy with Price Water House, Deloitte, or TATA; in products with IBM, Axway, Globalscape, companies that have clients on every continent". Thus, in 2010 internationalization became a strategic goal. That year "in the middle of the planning meeting I said, 'now we are going to sell our products throughout Latin America' (....) and it was only after six months they [the staff] started to believe me." By 2011 ITAC had clients in more than 8 Latin American countries.

In early 2012, Julieta –Javier's wife and ITAC's administrative manager– felt that "it was necessary to move to another stage" under the motto "know more, to be able to do more." She then talked Javier into an Executive MBA, which they both started, generating reflections that resulted in organizational changes seeking to "move from the person to the enterprise; to have a better company for everybody's own good, and for ITAC to grow."

These changes encompassed different areas of the company. The first was to "delegate (...), give more autonomy to directors and managers to make decisions and be trained to raise everyone's level, to have the same language and conversations at different levels." Javier would take distance from projects "but retain control systems to know how things are going... and focus on other issues, such as planning and strategies, finance and marketing." Now, Julieta states: "Javier does things where he can generate more value. He delegates the rest." In addition to broadening his managerial skills, Javier formed an Advisory Board and participated on several boards of directors to supplement his training. Moreover, he channeled his creativity in a more conscious and strategic manner, to articulate "knowledge, experience and brain-power" into management. But this was not so easy, "because it is one thing to come close to the top 5 and entirely another to surpass any of them."

Discussion Within A Proposed Interpretation Model

This section first proposes a model (Figure 1) that can serve as a guide to interpret the results of the ITAC case, to go onto discussing them in the light of the model.

Firstly, as can be seen in the bottom labels on Figure 1, the model captures four ITAC episodes, as a startup, software house, software factory and leading up to its future. Secondly, beyond ITAC, the model integrates the different theoretical perspectives employed in this case study, in order to provide a comprehensive and dynamic view of technology-based entrepreneurship. As such, we see that there is a simultaneous development in structuration (left label) and learning (right label) resulting in co-evolution between the entrepreneur and the firm. This co-evolution, which is presented in close interaction with the external institutional and technological contexts, enables and constrains the growth path represented by the S-shaped area in the figure. The fact that the entrepreneur already possesses some technical and commercial skills before the startup is the reason why the S-curve does not start from zero.

Figure 1. A Model for interpreting the dynamics of technology-based entrepreneurship

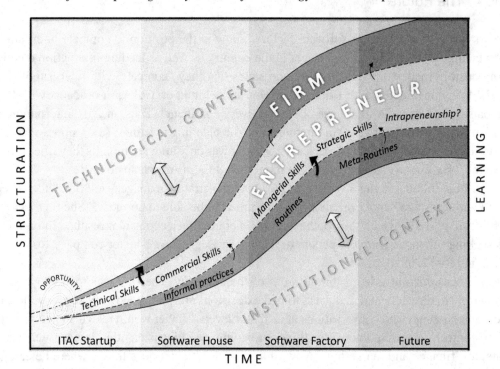

Episode 1: Entrepreneur and Opportunity

The creation of ITAC is the fortunate result of the coming together of opportunity and entrepreneur. On the one hand, a systemic opportunity is generated by the dissemination of a Java and the growth of online banking portals. On the other hand, an entrepreneur has the ability to recognize this opportunity, shape it and turn it into a business. The technical skills of the entrepreneur come from his training as a software engineer, together with his training and consulting experience. Such technical and commercial knowledge makes it possible for him to materialize the opportunity. In this regard, this study supports the first proposition in Sarason et al. (2006), according to which "Opportunities do not exist as a singular phenomenon, but are idiosyncratic to the individual."

The background knowledge of its founder, characterizes him as a "technological entrepreneur" and ITAC as a technology-based entrepreneurship (Bailetti, 2012). However, his commercial knowledge was also definitive, supporting Breschi et al. (2014) who argue that knowledge-intensive entrepreneurship articulates scientific-technological and market-environment knowledge. Furthermore, it also agrees with Garud & Karnøe (2003), because the technological path followed by ITAC is emergent and depends upon intertwined, distributed agency, which in this case is reflected through partnerships, a supportive and influential family context, the increasing demand of the banking sector, and government support for the software industry. Such intertwinement implies feedback along a path that involves interpretation, action, evaluation, and reflection, in a cyclical fashion.

Episode 2: Knowledge of The Entrepreneur and Routines of The Firm

ITAC's knowledge base and learning is initially centered on the entrepreneur, mainly through doing, using and interacting (cf. M. B. Jensen, Johnson, Lorenz, & Lundvall, 2007). His technological know-how takes precedence and is reinforced through "learning by doing", derived from consulting projects, as well as "learning by using" different technologies. This process is enhanced by the shared background of the initial staff. Javier's commercial skills are also crucial and become reinforced through "learning by interacting" with partners that provide access to managers who have a vision of the product beyond technical matters and with international customers that help him understand banking. This enabled ITAC to develop products focused on non-functional, differentiated and high value-added characteristics.

In this episode, once again, articulation between technological and contextual knowledge comes into play (Breschi et al., 2014) and becomes the focus of learning (Garud & Karnøe, 2003). Thus, the existing skills become embedded in a "dynamic learning perspective" (Cope, 2005) where "entrepreneurial preparedness" is a reflection of the prospective entrepreneur's "learning history", which shapes the entrepreneurial "learning task" once the business is established and faces non-routine "critical learning events" with a strong affective dimension (often traumatic and stressful). This is exemplified by the painful setback of the failed product for Davivienda, which drove Javier to emphasize formalization of software engineering practices.

However, the intention of this work is to go beyond the individual focus and towards collective learning. The existing know-how of the company, focused on its founder, does not constitute the substantive capabilities of ITAC: the organizational knowledge base is what ITAC knows best, but its substantive capabilities are associated with what is actually done, their ability to solve real problems (Zahra et al., 2006). Moreover, if we relate this knowledge to actual routines, we come close to Pentland & Feldman (2005): the static or structural know-how is then equivalent to what they call ostensive aspects of the routine, while its performative aspects are how they get executed in practice and what constitutes real substantive capabilities.

The process of collective learning around routines follows Radwan & Kinder (2013), where the ostensive (structure) and the performative (agency) are intertwined, on the basis of structuration theory. This co-evolution, as shown in Figure 1, implies learning through doing and interacting within ITAC, where there is a flow of ostensive aspects from the entrepreneur to the rest of the company. Conversely, when routinized in a performative manner by the young firm, there is feedback on the ostensive, such as when they start recording, tracing and analyzing software bugs to find their root causes. With feedback, the ostensive aspects are no longer limited to the individual but may become ostensive to the firm. This is not a formal transfer process, but a shared practice where the entrepreneur and firm learn and transform at the same time. A result of this learning process can be seen in the automation of a high percentage of technical tasks.

Episode 3: Entrepreneur's Strategic Knowledge and Firm's Meta-Routines

In this episode we find an important milestone for ITAC: reaching CMMI Level 3. This is not only clear evidence of the increased maturity in their capabilities, but also constitutes a framework of best engineering practices, the assimilation of which must be demonstrated by the firm. In this case, the defining external trigger comes in the form of financial incentives put in place by the Government to support the adoption of CMMI. Javier, still under the influence of the Davivienda reversal, sees this as an opportunity not just to continue formalizing and evolving the operational capabilities of ITAC, but as an opportunity to re-engineer the Davivienda failure into what would be the successful WS-Guardian product.

CMMI contains a series of ostensive routines (Pentland & Feldman, 2005) that the firm identifies or develops. In fact, CMMI provides a complete structure for capacity building, including training, project management, and risk management, among others, offering a framework for continuous improvement. Operational capabilities develop incrementally at each maturity level through such continuous improvement, until they take a qualitative leap and begin to improve with a new logic. For instance, as a software house, ITAC estimated development effort in linear terms out of past projects. Estimating in this fashion will be incrementally better with each new project. However, increasing complexity does not behave linearly. As a result, ITAC in its software factory stage requires new capabilities, namely risk analysis as an integral part of estimation and root cause analysis as part of quality assurance.

In accordance with Zahra et al. (2006), this early development of dynamic capabilities matches the expectations for a young firm in transition. According to Zahra et al., improvisation and trial and error are common in young firms and later get replaced by more systematic experimentation exercises. This is seen when ITAC is transformed into a software factory; as described by its founder, it went from traditional software development to a more industrialized process where "you learn over time, with numbers." Routines related to estimation were progressively refined, until a new meta-routine relating to complex project estimation (which obeys a different kind of logic) required them to evolve a new risk analysis capability. In a similar sense, routines for testing progress as ITAC accumulated more code and more bugs to analyze, but larger projects and stricter customer requirements force a new meta-routine to emerge, quality management, expressed in the development of a root cause analysis capability.

CMMI is also an important example a shift from individual to collective learning. While the motivation is generated from critical events, it is also influenced by affective and routine-seeking dimensions (Cope, 2005). The successful achievement of Level 3 CMMI was a process where ITAC went from being exhausted and stressed to joyful. Its founder highlights the collective process where combined learning is accomplished, but where much of the learning is systematic and guided by the implementation of CMMI. Furthermore, for these new practices to be assimilated and implemented, its founder promoted discussion spaces. This is what Aldrich & Yang (2014) referred to when linking ostensive to performative routines: the entrepreneur seeks performative routines (related to software development) to be appropriated through the incorporation of ostensive routines (CMMI). This adoption is mediated by affective aspects which become effective at the collective level due to the emotional investment of employees and the intention of the entrepreneur for them to "feel part of a big company."

Other shifts in learning occur simultaneously as they transform into a software factory. While at first Javier is regarded as the key source of "technology watch" for opportunity identification, this evolves into a collective space where a committee discusses technology-based opportunities. There is a general shift from individual to collective learning: at first, the entrepreneur is at the center of technological and strategic decisions and the firm learns from and adopts his views. As he begins to shift his role into project management and strategic decision-making, the firm begins to collectively engage in once individually-led decisions and develop collective capabilities that exert influence over Javier, pushing him to formally acquire management skills.

The institutionalization of routines in this fashion reinforces the firm's competitive differentiation, since they underpin the entrepreneur's perception: "this is not a normal software factory as any other in the world, but a 'secure software factory,' defined by quality and best practices in software development." As a result, ITAC was able to shorten the distance with respect to leading companies in a short period of time. However, these advances have fostered further transformations and new challenges for the entrepreneur. The rapid capability development pace has enabled ITAC to evolve in software development terms very quickly in its short life: "the first thing was to get the solution to work; then, allow it to escalate; a while ago it was all about architecture, now it's security." ITAC first developed a product differentiated by its functional and non-functional features, then, its added value relied on quality assurance (ISO and CMMI) and, finally, by being produced in a secure software factory.

Episode 4: The Future and Discussion

The decision to strengthen the managerial capabilities of the founding partners, to deal with the challenges posed by the growth of ITAC, led them to start an MBA program under the premise "learn more to do more". At the same time, they concentrate on strategic aspects which becomes a trigger for radical organizational transformations. This translates into new middle management teams, to get them to "speak the same business language", as well as into the strengthening of their Executive Board. These dramatic changes in organizational structure and administrative routines are tantamount to the deployment of a dynamic capability. In young firms, this does not necessarily imply events produced by changes in the outer environment, but also by contingencies and/or transformations related to the growth and consolidation of firms.

The entrepreneur now faces the challenge of sustaining the success of ITAC; to come to terms with the increased weight of market considerations in their strategic decision making, such as their current shift of attention from new product development to the market diversification of existing products. They must enter this unstable future with an already inertial set of routines which may provide enough flexibility for incremental adjustment, but may also prove to be obstacles for more radical transformations. In fact, as Ricardo Cortés argued recently, their initial change in software quality routines (separating development from testing) might well have to be backtracked in the face of current industry practices aimed at cloud-based software and continuous deployment of new versions, namely "DevOps".

From a structuration theory point of view, the rapid growth of ITAC demands from the entrepreneur (agent) fast development of his managerial and strategic skills. At the same time, this generates a major risk: the agency he must now direct towards structuration of the firm may suffocate the kind of agency that resulted in the startup. This expected dilemma between the entrepreneur and the manager, would require him to become an intrapreneur and introduce entrepreneurially oriented management practices (Rauch, Wiklund, Lumpkin, & Frese, 2009). Such practices would have to promote the search, identification and exploitation of opportunities and preserve or enhance his incidence upon a developed and consolidated structure (ITAC).

In terms of the theoretical and methodological implications of this case study, it departs from a context where there is still no agreed theoretical framework to explain entrepreneurship and where the debate of whether opportunities are discovered or created is still considered relevant (Packard, 2017). As a consequence, Packard propose an interpretivist grounding of entrepreneurship as an ongoing and emergent process, which is open-ended and may include observable markers to track such change, while recognizing that such points are provisional and not necessary to or defining of the process. This of course implies the use of in-depth qualitative methods to uncover the conscious intentions of agents. Moreover, as pointed out in (Landström & Harirchi, 2018), such detailed understanding of the phenomenon has been and will continue to be necessary for entrepreneurial research as an autonomous field where specific concepts and theories have only recently started to emerge through the works of Shane and Zahra, for example. In technology entrepreneurship in particular, a similar sentiment is expressed by (Mosey, 2016) who suggests broadening the traditional research approaches and opening up to different theoretical approaches for a field that has finally "come of age". Even more pertinent to the present work, Jensen and Clausen (2017), have argued that there is a limited understanding of how capabilities originate and emerge in new technology-based firms and point to this emergence as a function of prior knowledge and deliberate learning, as our findings show as well.

The interpretation model in Figure 1 provides new insights for the structuration view of entrepreneurship (Sarason et al., 2006), which proposes a co-evolution of opportunity and entrepreneur, by going beyond the initial opportunity and following the co-evolution of the firm and entrepreneur for over a decade. The firm evolves from startup, to software house, to software factory, while, at the same time, the entrepreneur evolves from a technology-centered founder, to a potential intrapreneur. Initially, the entrepreneur's technical and commercial skills dominate the shaping of the new venture, expressed by the darker arrow going in the entrepreneur-firm direction in the figure. As collective learning enters the picture, ITAC settles as a software house. The third episode sees learning and capability building (both in software development and administrative terms) quickly evolving. This shifts the relative influence towards structure (the firm), as represented by the arrow, now darker in the firm-entrepreneur direction.

Now, this delicate balance between the entrepreneur and the firm, between agency and structure, will be crucial for the competitive future of the firm. If structure takes prevalence over agency, then it is quite possible that the inertia embedded in standards, routines and beliefs will make it harder for the firm to adapt or innovate. Conversely, if the entrepreneur retools himself as intrapreneur and is able to permeate this style into the firm, without losing its routinized software development and learning processes, this may provide a second wave of opportunity structuration, starting at a higher level and potentially resulting in new products, services or spinoffs that can thwart the stagnation in growth or the resistance to change.

CONCLUSION

This case study has proposed a model that shows the evolution of technology-based entrepreneurship in the software industry. The model builds on structuration theory, in order to capture and interpret the dynamics behind the identification of an opportunity and the creation, development and consolidation of the case as a competitive firm. As a theoretical contribution, this work extends Sarason et al. (2006) by showing how, through the dynamics of structuration, both agency and structure are transformed, changing their relative influence over each other, beyond the startup. ITAC's initial creation confirms that the opportunity is not independent from the entrepreneur's role in the active diffusion of the technology or from the skills needed to exploit it. The second episode as a software house exhibits the entrepreneur's ability to transform the startup into a firm, while his complete preponderance begins to diminish, balancing the relative influence between agency and structure. The third and fourth stages see ITAC developing capabilities and becoming a secure software factory, and as routines become part of the structure, they impose challenges for the agency of the entrepreneur not to be overshadowed or constrained.

In terms of entrepreneurial learning theory, the present study continues the intent of integrating the entrepreneur (individual learning) to the firm (collective learning). To do so, we incorporate a dynamic learning perspective (Cope, 2005) in dialogue with the idea that entrepreneurial knowledge is diverse and follows different paths depending on the configuration of such variety (Deligianni et al., 2015). This leads to the extant notion of generative learning, which implies anticipatory use of knowledge stemming from high-order skills that we relate to ostensive routines (Pentland & Feldman, 2005). As a consequence, in ITAC non-routine events trigger the development of ostensive routines which are no longer exclusive to the individual but involve collective learning. This collective learning is initially centered on doing, using and interacting (ostensive routines are informally shared), and later becomes more systematic and attached to CMMI, while at the same time broadening the scope beyond the original commercial and technological knowledge to include managerial and strategic skills as well.

From a practical and managerial point of view, this paper offers a conceptual model together with an interesting empirical case that should invite recognition, reflection and anticipatory behavior in the context of technology-based entrepreneurship. Recognition plays an important role in identifying and giving rightful value to the conditions that allow a software startup to grow. While current myths and simplifications seem to place such conditions in exceptional individuals or in contextual industrial or technological enablers, our proposed model suggests a more complex and nuanced vision that should enable would-be entrepreneurs or investors a more relational understanding of the entrepreneurial reality. Further, this should provide an opportunity for reflection with respect to how a firm can learn entrepreneurial behavior from its founder and how the founder learns managerial skills from the firm. As a consequence, a firm, and an entrepreneur turned manager, can strategically map their evolution to the concept map and take steps to enable further growth. Anticipatory behavior should follow to prevent the manager from being burdened so that the innovative and entrepreneurial skills are not diluted, while at the same time maintaining growth, evolving from entrepreneur to intrapreneur.

This poses a set of alternatives for the entrepreneur-manager as he or she evolves in a technology-based context. First, as a manager that takes on a traditional strategic role to efficiently exploit technological and commercial resources and capabilities developed within the firm. Second, as a CEO that moderates the firm towards an "entrepreneurial orientation" (Richard, Wu, & Chadwick, 2009) whose creativity, proactivity and risk-taking allow it to aggressively compete in an emergent market. Finally, as an entrepreneurial manager (Teece, 2016) who can identify and generate opportunities, structure novel business models and lead the organizational transformations required to exploit them.

REFERENCES

Aldrich, H. E., & Yang, T. (2014). How do entrepreneurs know what to do? learning and organizing in new ventures. *Journal of Evolutionary Economics*, 24(1), 59–82. doi:10.100700191-013-0320-x

Bailetti, T. (2012). Technology Entrepreneurship: Overview, Definition, and Distinctive Aspects. *Technology Innovation Management Review*, (February), 5-12.

Breschi, S., Lenzi, C., Malerba, F., & Mancusi, M. L. (2014). Knowledge-intensive entrepreneurship: Sectoral patterns in a sample of European high-tech firms. *Technology Analysis & Strategic Management*, 0(0), 1–14. doi:10.1080/09537325.2014.886683

CMMI Product Team. (2010). *CMMI for Development, Version 1.3*. Carnegie Mellon University. Retrieved from http://www.sei.cmu.edu/library/abstracts/reports/10tr033.cfm

Cope, J. (2005). Toward a Dynamic Learning Perspective of Entrepreneurship. *Entrepreneurship Theory and Practice*, 29(4), 373–397. doi:10.1111/j.1540-6520.2005.00090.x

Deligianni, I., Voudouris, I., & Lioukas, S. (2015). Growth paths of small technology firms: The effects of different knowledge types over time. *Journal of World Business*, *50*(3), 491–504. doi:10.1016/j.jwb.2014.08.006

Eisenhardt, K. M., & Graebner, M. E. (2007). Theory building from cases: Opportunities and challenges. *Academy of Management Journal*, *50*(1), 25–32. doi:10.5465/amj.2007.24160888

Elster, J. (2000). *El cambio tecnológico: Investigaciones sobre la racionalidad y la transformación social*. Barcelona, Spain: GEDISA.

Garud, R., & Karnøe, P. (2003). Bricolage versus breakthrough: Distributed and embedded agency in technology entrepreneurship. *Research Policy*, *32*(2), 277–300. doi:10.1016/S0048-7333(02)00100-2

Giddens, A. (1986). *The Constitution of Society: Outline of the Theory of Structuration (Reprint edition)*. Berkeley: University of California Press.

Jensen, A., & Clausen, T. H. (2017). Origins and emergence of exploration and exploitation capabilities in new technology-based firms. *Technological Forecasting and Social Change*, *120*, 163–175. doi:10.1016/j.techfore.2017.03.004

Jensen, M. B., Johnson, B., Lorenz, E., & Lundvall, B. A. (2007). Forms of knowledge and modes of innovation. *Research Policy*, *36*(5), 680–693. doi:10.1016/j.respol.2007.01.006

Knockaert, M., Ucbasaran, D., Wright, M., & Clarysse, B. (2011). The relationship between knowledge transfer, top management team composition, and performance: The case of science-based entrepreneurial firms. *Entrepreneurship Theory and Practice*, *35*(4), 777–803. doi:10.1111/j.1540-6520.2010.00405.x

Landström, H., & Harirchi, G. (2018). The social structure of entrepreneurship as a scientific field. *Research Policy*, *47*(3), 650–662. doi:10.1016/j.respol.2018.01.013

Mosey, S. (2016). Teaching and research opportunities in technology entrepreneurship. *Technovation*, *57-58*, 43–44. doi:10.1016/j.technovation.2016.08.006

Packard, M. D. (2017). Where did interpretivism go in the theory of entrepreneurship? *Journal of Business Venturing*, *32*(5), 536–549. doi:10.1016/j.jbusvent.2017.05.004

Pentland, B. T., & Feldman, M. S. (2005). Organizational routines as a unit of analysis. *Industrial and Corporate Change*, *14*(5), 793–815. doi:10.1093/icc/dth070

Pittaway, L., & Thorpe, R. (2012). A framework for entrepreneurial learning: A tribute to Jason Cope. *Entrepreneurship and Regional Development*, *24*(9-10), 837–859. doi:10.1080/08985626.2012.694268

Radwan, L., & Kinder, S. (2013). Practising the diffusion of organizational routines. *Environment & Planning A*, *45*(10), 2442–2458. doi:10.1068/a45290

Rauch, A., Wiklund, J., Lumpkin, G., & Frese, M. (2009). Entrepreneurial orientation and business performance: An assessment of past research and suggestions for the future. *Entrepreneurship Theory and Practice*, *33*(3), 761–787. doi:10.1111/j.1540-6520.2009.00308.x

Richard, O. C., Wu, P., & Chadwick, K. (2009). The impact of entrepreneurial orientation on firm performance: The role of CEO position tenure and industry tenure. *International Journal of Human Resource Management*, *20*(5), 1078–1095. doi:10.1080/09585190902850281

Ricketts, M. (2008). Theories of Entrepreneurship: Historical Development and Critical Assessment. In A. Basu, M. Casson, N. Wadeson et al. (Eds.), *The Oxford Handbook of Entrepreneurship*. Oxford University Press. Retrieved from http://www.oxfordhandbooks.com/view/10.1093/oxfordhb/9780199546992.001.0001/oxfordhb-9780199546992-e-2

Rojas, Y. (2014). *Caracterización de la Innovación en un Producto de Software en el Contexto de la Industria de Software Colombiana. Modelo "Mci"*. Pontificia Universidad Javeriana, Bogotá. Retrieved from http://pegasus.javeriana.edu.co/~PA123-06-InnovProdSW/conclusiones_htm_files/Modelo-MCI-Yamile%20Rojas.pdf

Sarason, Y., Dean, T., & Dillard, J. F. (2006). Entrepreneurship as the nexus of individual and opportunity: A structuration view. *Journal of Business Venturing*, *21*(3), 286–305. doi:10.1016/j.jbusvent.2005.02.007

Schumpeter, J. A. (1934). *The Theory of Economic Development: An Inquiry Into Profits, Capital, Credit, Interest, and the Business Cycle*. Transaction Publishers.

Schuster Fonseca, J. (1993). La teoría de la estructuración. *La Palabra y el Hombre*, *87*, 97–107.

Shane, S., & Venkataraman, S. (2000). The Promise of Entrepreneurship as a Field of Research. *Academy of Management Review*, *25*(1), 217–226. doi:10.2307/259271

Spiegel, M., & Marxt, C. (2011). Defining Technology Entrepreneurship. In *2011 IEEE International Conference on Industrial Engineering and Engineering Management (IEEM)* (pp. 1623-1627). 10.1109/IEEM.2011.6118191

Teece, D. J. (2016). Dynamic capabilities and entrepreneurial management in large organizations: Toward a theory of the (entrepreneurial) firm. *European Economic Review*, *86*, 202–216. doi:10.1016/j.euroecorev.2015.11.006

Teece, D. J., Pisano, G., & Shuen, A. (1997). Dynamic capabilities and strategic management. *Strategic Management Journal*, *18*(7), 509–533. doi:10.1002/(SICI)1097-0266(199708)18:7<509::AID-SMJ882>3.0.CO;2-Z

Unutmaz Durmuşoğlu, Z. D. (2018). Assessment of techno-entrepreneurship projects by using analytical hierarchy process (AHP). *Technology in Society*. doi:10.1016/j.techsoc.2018.02.001

Wang, C. L., & Chugh, H. (2014). Entrepreneurial learning: Past research and future challenges. *International Journal of Management Reviews*, *16*(1), 24–61. doi:10.1111/ijmr.12007

Yin, R. K. (2003). *Case Study Research: design and methods (Vol. 3)*. Thousand Oaks: Sage Publications.

Zahra, S. A., Sapienza, H. J., & Davidsson, P. (2006). Entrepreneurship and dynamic capabilities: A review, model and research agenda. *Journal of Management Studies*, *43*(4), 917–955. doi:10.1111/j.1467-6486.2006.00616.x

This research was previously published in the Journal of Cases on Information Technology (JCIT), 21(1); pages 1-18, copyright year 2019 by IGI Publishing (an imprint of IGI Global).

Chapter 75
Teaching Model-Driven Engineering in a Master's Program:
Three Editions on a PBL-Based Experience

Alexandre Bragança
Polytechnic Institute of Porto, Portugal

Isabel Azevedo
Polytechnic Institute of Porto, Portugal

Nuno Bettencourt
iD https://orcid.org/0000-0003-1767-8240
Polytechnic Institute of Porto, Portugal

ABSTRACT

Model-driven engineering (MDE) is an approach to software engineering that adopts models as the central artefact. Although the approach is promising in addressing major issues in software development, particularly in dealing with software complexity, and there are several success cases in the industry as well as growing interest in the research community, it seems that it has been hard to generalize its gains among software professionals. To address this issue, MDE must be taught at a higher-education level. This chapter presents a three-year experience in teaching MDE in a course of a master program in informatics engineering. The chapter provides details on how a project-based learning approach was adopted and evolved along three editions of the course. Results of a student survey are discussed and compared to those from another course. In addition, several other similar teaching experiences are analyzed.

DOI: 10.4018/978-1-6684-3702-5.ch075

INTRODUCTION

During their education, engineers learn about the relevant models in their areas and how to further apply them. One of the capabilities that students should acquire in programs that qualify for building systems, where software is a key and intense part, is "create and use models in system development" (Landwehr et al., 2017).

More intensive use of models has also been adopted for software engineering. Among them is Model-Driven Engineering (MDE), which promises several ways to address well-known problems (Somers, 2017), including software increasing complexity (Whittle, Hutchinson, & Rouncefield, 2014). Moreover, it is in line with the usual start of designing complex systems with some level of abstraction provided by models in traditional engineering disciplines.

In software product lines, substantial gains can be achieved, even for quality assurance, when the effort is put in the domain engineering instead of solely in the application engineering. In fact, MDE has been applied successfully in the industry but essentially in large corporations that can afford the inherent costs (Baker, Loh, & Weil, 2005; Burden, Heldal, & Whittle, 2014; Hossler, Born, & Saito, 2006).

However, it seems that MDE's advantages have been hard to generalize in a way that makes it available for the common developer (Haan, 2008). Also, companies that already design and use models dedicated to a particular domain may probably use MDE more than others that develop generic software (Whittle et al., 2014). Whittle et al. (2014) mentioned an organization that had to train hundreds of developers with difficulties in abstract thinking when MDE was adopted.

Multiple factors hinder organizations from embracing MDE, and its acceptance clearly requires technical changes, but also the overcoming of human attitudes when facing new techniques and the need to use new tools (Brambilla, Cabot, & Wimmer, 2012; Whittle et al., 2017). This aspect was highlighted in general some years ago (Glass, 2011) with the recognition that there is a learning curve with an initial low productivity that is acceptable when people realize the value of their adoption. In a Model-Driven Development (MDD) – which is essentially MDE focused on software development – survey, it has been found out that "in most cases, the use of the MDD in organisations depends only on the interest of people to use it" (Parviainen, Takalo, Teppola, & Tihinen, 2009) and people may only be appealed to use what they have heard about. Nevertheless, new competencies are needed, and their lack can compromise MDE appropriateness (Christensen & Ellingsen, 2016). Thus, pedagogical and training issues cannot be ignored (Goulão, Amaral, & Mernik, 2016).

In this context the authors share a three-year experience in teaching Model-Driven Engineering in a course of a master program in Informatics Engineering, a total of three editions of the course. Each one can be seen as action research (Lewin, 1946) iteration (see Figure 1) that aimed to analyse if it is possible to promote MDE subjects using a Project-Based Learning approach. This research question also reflects the desire to maintain the highest quality standards of the program, which is accredited by many international bodies. For instance, the American Board for Engineering and Technology (ABET) accreditation emphasizes the need of continuous improvement of programs. In fact, the reflection on the appropriateness of the provided learning experiences and pedagogical models has been institutionally reinforced. The continuous improvement of the course and, consequently, of the program has been the main motivation for this work. Our expectation is that the introduction of courses devoted to MDE may have the same impact on software development as Unified Modelling Language (UML) had in the past.

Figure 1. Detailed action research iteration

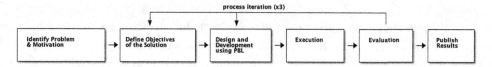

The rest of this chapter is organized as follows. The next section ("A Project-Based Learning Approach") details how the PBL model has been applied in the course and the continual evolution during these three editions. Results of a student survey regarding this experience are presented and discussed in the section "Feedback About the Course". An analysis of other experiences in teaching MDE is presented in the section "Other Courses on Model-Driven Engineering". The authors conclude by sharing their findings regarding how to conduct MDE teaching in order to promote a wider adoption of its advantages by future professionals in the final section.

A PROJECT-BASED LEARNING APPROACH

Boffo (2015) explore the issues related to what people are able to do and transversal capabilities, soft skills and flexible abilities. International engineering accreditation bodies such as the ABET include soft skills in their criteria under the umbrella of "professional skills". It is noteworthy that "a shift to outcomes-based education and accreditation" is listed among the top five ones that have occurred during the last 100 years in engineering education (Froyd, Wankat, & Smith, 2012), because of its positive effects, including the incentives to apply active learning methods.

Some ABET criteria for student outcomes in the 2019-2020 cycle even reinforce the importance of some of the non-technical skills. For instance, "an ability to function on multidisciplinary teams" is replaced with "an ability to function effectively on a team whose members together provide leadership, create a collaborative and inclusive environment, establish goals, plan tasks, and meet objectives" (ABET EAC, 2017).

However, these subjects are difficult to effectively be incorporated in academic curricula, with a clear difference between what is taught and what is translated to competences. Universities have been dealing with the need to develop non-technical skills in future software engineers, which are considered as core competencies for them (Sedelmaier & Landes, 2014).

Project-based learning (PBL) is a common instructional approach used to advance the acquisition of many skills a future software engineer will need in their professional practice (Marques, Ochoa, Bastarrica, & Gutierrez, 2018). The use of a PBL method aims at developing technical and non-technical competences in engineering students. Problem-based learning and project-based learning have some common characteristics that make them appropriate for engineering education. However, while problem-based learning focus on the solution of a problem, project-based learning concentrate in the desired product with tasks to be accomplished to that purpose (Uziak, 2016).

Both problem-based and project-based learning approaches have been used in the Informatics Engineering master's at ISEP. Currently, the program offers a curriculum organized in four specialization tracks, and one of them is Software Engineering, which was introduced in September 2015. One of the courses of this track is Domain Engineering (EDOM).

In this program, each semester has 16 weeks. The available class types (Lectures, Lab and Tutorial) have different teaching minutes assigned per week. There are two occurrences of 50 minutes for lecture classes, one occurrence of 110 minutes for its lab classes and 50 minutes for its tutorial classes (one occurrence). All classes take place after work hours.

Lectures are used to introduce or explain concepts, but also to show demonstrations related to what is being developed in lab classes. Lab lessons have hands-on classroom assignments in the first weeks and support a project development with several iterations in the final stage. Feedback about students' performance is provided in different delivery moments, facilitating the application of some pedagogical patterns, namely Early Warning and Embrace Correction (Bergin et al., 2012). Tutorial classes are used to support the exercises, the project as well as general issues.

Each topic introduced during classroom assignments is then explored by the students during the project development. The project provides a global vision by combining the small pieces developed during the semester in a bigger project to provide enough integration of the covered topics. Thus, a minimum skill level should have been acquired when the project is launched. Students should have evidences of their work through commits in their GIT repository, which are used in the grading of exercises and project.

EDOM's major goal is to "provide students with advanced skills regarding domain engineering and some of the most recent scientific innovations and practices originating from specific approaches that are related to it: model-driven engineering, domain-specific languages (DSL) and product line engineering" (ISEP, n.d.). By the end of the course, students are able to:

- Analyse domain engineering as the top of an iceberg composed of a myriad of processes, techniques, tools and methodologies which all have reuse in software engineering as the ultimate goal;
- Analyse software product lines as a practice that promotes large scale reuse;
- Design and implement domain-specific languages and model transformations in the context of model-driven engineering;
- Manage recent approaches in the context of domain engineering and reuse: model-driven software engineering and domain-specific languages;
- Debate about options in projects related to model-driven engineering.

The detailed contents of EDOM for all editions were:

- **Domain Engineering and Practice Areas:** General concepts, reuse and abstraction, domain analysis and product line engineering.
- **Domain Modelling:** isolating the domain, the building blocks of a domain model, and the life cycle of domain objects;
- **Model-Driven Software Engineering (MDSE):** Principles and use cases, Model-Driven Architecture (MDA) and the Unified Modelling Language (UML), extensions to UML, the Object Constraint Language (OCL), and the integration of MDSE and the development process.
- **Domain-Specific Languages:** The Eclipse Modelling Framework (EMF), developing a modelling language, abstract syntax and concrete syntax, model to model transformations and outplace transformations with Atlas Transformation Language (ATL), model to text transformations (Acceleo), code generation, and managing models.
- **Software Product Lines (SPL):** core activities (domain engineering, application engineering and product line management), SPL practice patterns, and variability models.

As mentioned, two different learning methods have been employed, as described:

- **Problem-Based Learning:** In the first weeks a problem-based learning method is used, devoted to acquisition of knowledge. The problems are to be solved in two weeks (one, in the first two editions with few exceptions), where no minimum grade is demanded.
- **Project-Based Learning:** In the final weeks the project aims to support the application of knowledge over a longer period of time. A score below 10,0 out of 20,0 is not acceptable.

These differences in time-length and in knowledge attainment or application are among the common distinctive characteristics of the two methods (Mills &Treagust, 2003).

The core recommended bibliography has been three books that cover most of the course contents, namely (Brambilla, Cabot, & Wimmer 2017), (Clements & Northrop, 2001) and (Gronback, 2009).

Since the introduction of the course two phases can be distinguished:

1st Phase: 2015-2016 and 2016-2017 academic years editions;
2nd Phase: 2017-2018 academic year edition.

Some little changes introduced in the second academic year ensured a smooth transition, without significant impact in the number of students successfully completing the course (see Table 1).

Table 1. Percentage of approvals

Academic Year Edition	Number of Students	% of Approvals, Excluding Those That Did Not Attend Classes
2015-2016	50	61
2016-2017	86	54
2017-2018	137	55*

* Preliminary number as, in accordance with the school's internal regulations, some students still have another possibility to be approved.

However, there was a significant decrease in the number of students that could not take the final exam (see Table 2) in phase 2 (2017-2018). It is still early to judge these findings and come up with possible reasons, because only one edition of the 2nd phase has passed. Nevertheless, when the two phases are discussed, some aspects are detailed that could have had an impact.

Table 2. Number of students not able to take the final exam

Academic Year Edition	Number of Students Enrolled on EDOM	Number of Students Without Course Attendance or Evaluation
2015-2016	50	14
2016-2017	86	40
2017-2018	137	7

In summary the core activities related to the didactical approach adopted in the two phases are described in Table 3. The main differences are explored in the upcoming sub-sections.

It has been important the interconnection with another course, which is Software Development Organization (ODSOFT). Under the PBL approach, the proposed project has incorporated tasks for both courses with a common work assignment.

The main goal of ODSOFT is to make students "able to manage the life cycle of a software product." Therefore, the main contents of the course are deeply related to the continuous integration and delivery approach to software development. Specific topics comprise software tests, configuration management and building, versioning and deployment" (ISEP, n.d.). In ODSOFT students do manual software development with repetitive code and tasks. Not only the development is error-prone and with some degree of difficulty, but also the testing phase is extensive. In EDOM the students should achieve the same with code generation (as much as possible). There is an obvious contrast between these approaches, which is understood by the students and help them to realize the advantages of an MDE application.

Table 3. Main activities in all editions

Type of Activities	1st Phase	2nd Phase
Lectures	Presentations about different subjects, some demonstrations of tools and approaches.	Introduction to topics and tools, but more devoted to the exercises and the final project, with discussion of their challenges.
Exercises	Group size was 2 students and one student review the work of the colleague and proposes alternatives.	Group size was 3 students. Two students assigned for each exercise. Both students with specific assigned tasks had the need to propose alternatives for their own tasks.
Tutorial classes	Always available in the first year, and on demand in the second one.	Available on demand.
Off class support	An Hipchat forum was used to clarify doubts and propose solutions to problems mainly about exercises and tools.	A forum was used but, in another platform (Moodle).
Learning activities based on problems	One-week problems not related to the main project. The work with the lab professor is done within a two-hour lab session and the students continue their development during the rest of the week. Grading and comments available in the adopted version control platform. Group and individual deliverables.	Two-week problems as pieces to be integrated in the final project. Grading and comments orally provided after the deadline with a discussion of their options and possible alternatives. Group work with individual deliverables.
Guidance and evaluation of project intermediary state	In every class, intermediate delivery with later discussion in the classroom in a formative assessment.	In every class but with an evaluated delivery. Discussion on demand and if possible to arrange.
Presentation of final project	Many presentations, one for each course with focus on its specific parts. Group deliverables and presentations.	One presentation with discussion of everything asked for all courses. Group deliverables, and individual and group presentations.

All course editions included a written examination, which format has remained unchanged, as well as the covered subjects. It has had a minimum score of 8.0/20.0. The exam has been composed of groups of questions of several types, namely:

- True/False questions;
- Short answer questions;
- Essay questions.

Simple questions required an answer with justification in the first phase.

First Phase

Main Platform for Exercises and Project

An open-source ERP system, Apache Open for Business (OFBiz), was used. The OFBiz platform is very declarative and model oriented, with many options for integrating with metamodeling tools. Even the level of specification of domain models is very interesting. Approaches such as product line of software can be easily exemplified from the platform. The project involved metamodels to generate artefacts (for example, generate the OFBiz configuration files). The possibility of some reverse engineering strand (creating models from existing artefacts) was taught but not explored.

For ODSOFT, mainly an entire automation pipeline for software development and project maintenance/ evolution was explored, with the use of configuration and build tools. Many possibilities for testing and deployment were enabled. During the exercises the students worked with some OFBiz DSLs, such as Entity DSL and Service DSL, to change or add entities and services.

For the second year, less components of OFBiz were used as a result of the many complaints related to the compilation time. Besides, the application was felt as too demanding for computers with less computational power. However, even these changes were not felt as enough and in the third edition another platform was adopted, as explained later in this chapter.

The ODSOFT exercises heavily used the OFBiz platform, but its clear use in EDOM was limited to the project.

Assessment

Students worked in groups of two during the semester in some activities/exercises and a final project (which counted for 60% of the final grade).

A Bitbucket repository was extensively used, where all artefacts produced during the assignments and project were required to be committed to the repository.

There were a set of small exercises to be executed during the first lab classes. The following rules were published:

- The student started the exercise during the lab class but might complete it after class, during the same week;
- The exercise was executed by one of the students of the group. The exercise was committed to the Bitbucket team repository with a reference to the related Bitbucket issue;
- The other student of the group needed to revise the colleague's work and report the findings as a comment recorded in the Bitbucket related issue;
- Informal feedback about the exercise occurred in the tutorial class of the following week;

- Formal feedback was given by the Lab Class teacher as a comment in the Bitbucket issue and a score for the exercise was proposed;
- Students were able to revise the exercise during one more week to be graded again (the Lab Class teacher needed to be informed);
- The plan was announced as having 6 exercises starting at the second week.

In the second edition of the course, there were mainly two changes in the assessment procedure, albeit slight:

- Students could only change the solution on two exercises at most, after knowing their grades, and not all, as previously. They needed to inform the teacher and they could modify the solution previously proposed for the exercise in one week, with later re-evaluation with use of a feedback pedagogical pattern (Grade It Again, Sam (Bergin et al., 2012));
- The plan was to have 7 exercises starting at week 2.

The rating scale was from 0 to 4, with the following semantics:

0: No submission;
1: Did not achieve the requirements of the exercise;
2: Partially achieves the requirements of the exercise;
3: Completely achieves the requirements of the exercise and justifies the options;
4: Completely achieves the requirements of the exercise, justifies the options and writes any alternatives.

However, the following remarks were provided:

- Levels 3 and 4 could only be achieved if the exercise is revised by the companion team-member;
- The lowest score of one week was to be dismissed when calculating the average of the exercises, which is considered for the calculation of their final grade.

The project consisted of a set of requirements to fulfil regarding the integration of domain engineering concerns, particularly model driven engineering methods, techniques and tools with the OFBiz software platform. Students needed to plan, apply and analyse aspects of MDE to OFBiz. The rating scale was from 0 to 4, with the following semantics:

0: No submission;
1: Did not achieve the requirements of the deadline;
2: Partially achieves the requirements of the deadline;
3: Completely achieves the requirements by the deadline and the technical report includes justifications about the options;
4: Completely achieves the requirements by the deadline, the technical report includes justifications about the options and also a detailed analysis of the alternatives.

Second Phase

In the second phase and for the first time, EDOM and ODSOFT had the same exact teachers. In the first edition just one teacher had assigned classes in both courses, a number that rose to two in the following edition, and to three in the last edition. It was easier to combine all the efforts in the grading of works, analysis of reports, final project evaluation and even in the preparation and correction of exams.

The deep knowledge about what was being done in each course was beneficial to understand students' problems and consequently in their support. Many times, the lessons of a course became classes of both with doubts that were not limited to one course or another, and often expressed by students who were not formally part of that class. At the end, the teachers reported an overwhelming sense of realization, but immense tiredness.

Another alteration in this phase was the change from Hipchat to a Moodle forum. It was dictated by the limited functionalities related to the free account of the person who owned the forum. For instance, it was impossible to see the messages after some time, and thus, at this moment, all questions and answers are no longer available. With Moodle, licensing issues are not a concern and all questions and answers are always available, which makes it easier to compare subjects, tools, exercises, or project tasks that trigger more clarification requests in the various course editions.

Main Platform for Exercises and Project

Google Web Toolkit (GWT) is a toolkit for building Asynchronous JavaScript and XML (AJAX) web applications using Java. A transpiler generates JavaScript code able to run across many different browsers. There is an integration of the compiled application frontend with other technologies such as HTML and XML. Version 2.8.2 was released in October 2017.

Its maturity, simplicity and used patterns were factors that led to its adoption. For ODSOFT, many opportunities were opened, and for EDOM the code generation for this platform was fully explored.

Enterprise platforms and applications with different development degrees have used similar possibilities. For instance, a solution that included an automatic GWT code generator (Nakoula & Houimel, 2017), a model-driven development with GWT (Ainsley, 2016) and a language for declarative code generation (Nelson, 2017) were presented in some GWT conferences. However, code generator following an MDE approach to be integrated in the GWT platform was firstly proposed in academic settings (Meliá, Gómez, Pérez, & Díaz, 2008).

A Model-driven development process was applied to a College Management System (CMS) in the third edition of the Domain Engineering course. The source code and some explanations that were complemented in person were made available at a specific repository (Bragança, Azevedo, & Bettencourt, 2018), which is based on examples from the GWT project website, specially the GWT Contacts Application (Ramsdale, 2010). This application was used as a base for the exercises and project. Starting by the domain entities and the relationships between them, represented in a Computer Independent Model (CIM) thus using transformations models, a Platform Independent Model (PIM) and a Platform Specific Model (PSM) were derived.

For ODSOFT the same ideas from previous editions were followed but now with a different platform, not OFBiz anymore. For EDOM, and for the first time, the use of the GWT platform was introduced in different exercises.

Assessment

A minor change was introduced in the final exam in this second phase. Simpler questions no longer required justification, but a penalization of wrong answers was introduced. Weighed up the pros and cons, mainly operational aspects influenced this decision.

The usual set of exercises for the first week had some changes in their formulation and assessment. Each exercise needed two components to be developed individually: (i) one base solution and (ii) one alternative solution. The alternative was defined as a solution that fulfilled the same requirements but following a different process.

Individual feedback was provided verbally for the solution of three components, i.e. base or alternative solutions for three different exercises. Thus, not all exercises were supposed to have a close collaboration of all member groups. Having a greater number of working students, these modifications may have facilitated the combination of professional obligations with the follow-up of the course and its activities, as the students were free to choose the three components to be assessed.

The rating scale for the exercises remained the same, from 0 to 4, but with different semantics:

0: Nothing relevant or no submission at all;

1: Tentative, the requirements of the exercise were not achieved;

2: Acceptable, the requirements were partially achieved;

3: Good, the requirements were completely achieved (includes incomplete analysis);

4: Very good, completely achieving the requirements of the exercise, with outstanding performance in the assessed outcomes (includes rigorous analysis).

However, levels 3 and 4 could only be achieved if the exercise included analysis with a clear justification of options and also a comparison with another solution provided by the other team-member, or another one at least delineated. This last possibility was introduced to not penalize students when a group member was not able to finish or even start the other component.

Many exercises clearly stated what was supposed to be the base and alternative solutions. For instance, for exercise four, students had to generate Java code for implementing some functional requirements by using two approaches, as follows:

- **Base Solution:** Generate a new design model from the analysis model by using an ATL transformation (UML analysis to UML design) and then generate the implementation (i.e., java code) from this new design model through an Acceleo transformation (UML design to Java code);
- **Alternative Solution:** Generate the implementation (i.e., java code) directly from the analysis model (i.e., do not generate an intermediate design model) by using an Acceleo transformation (UML to Java code).

The target was a new functionality for the College Management System, using the GWT sample application. Both solutions needed to generate code as much as possible similar to the one in the GWT CMS application and in accordance with the diagram shown in Figure 2.

Figure 2. Class diagram to guide the code generation

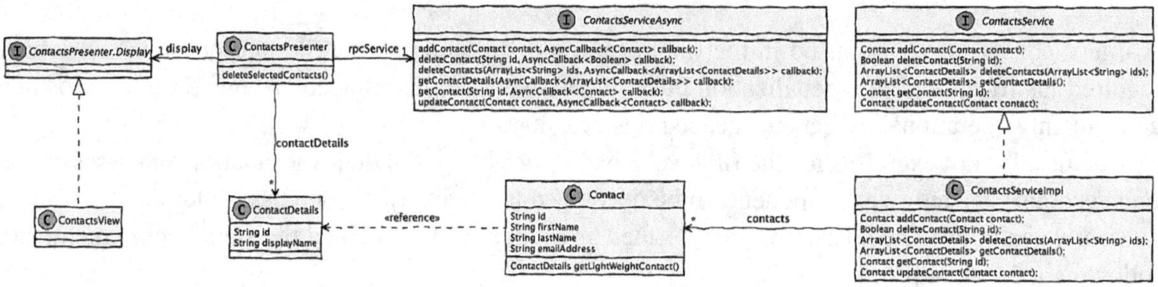

For the project, the introduction of individual and group tasks was the main difference from the first phase. The assessment was divided into individual and group score and each one had a weight of 50%. In addition, two dimensions were considered for the project evaluation: requirements and analysis, each one with rating scales from 0 to 4, with the semantics adapted to suit the type of the assessment instrument, but not significantly different from what was adopted during first phase.

FEEDBACK ABOUT THE COURSE

In order to gather students' information relating their background, previous MDE experience and what they might have learnt during the course, a survey was outlined and filled by some attending students, at the end of each course edition.

This section details the survey questions, results and how they compare to the ones discussed by Clarke, Wu, Allen, and King (2009). While this survey has been conducted for all editions, only the 2017-2018 course edition is analysed.

Survey

For the 2017-2018 course edition, there were 137 enrolled students. Answering the survey was optional and only 35 students (about twenty-six percent) answered it. Moodle's survey tool was used, and the questions were split into the following three groups:

- **General Modelling Concepts:** This group of questions, acquires the students' global perspective about MDE's usage in their project and whether it is (or not) beneficial during a software development process. This group is shown on Table 4 and is composed by questions number 1, and 10 to 15;
- **Course:** The questions included in this group inquiry about students' overall course satisfaction *per se* and compared to other semester courses. This group is shown on Table 5 and is composed by questions number 4 to 9 and 16 to 20;
- **Students' Background:** This group helps on understanding students' background, their knowledge about other technologies and if they are student workers. This group is shown on Table 6 and is composed by questions 2 and 3.

Tables 4, 5 and 6 show survey questions, their answer types and their quantitative results. Most of the answers to questions use the Likert scale "forced choice" method, others are "Yes" or "No" answer and others accepted free form text. Questions are displayed on column "A. Question", the possible answers are displayed on column "B. Possible Answers" and the count of results for each question on EDOM's 2017-2018 edition is displayed on column "C. EDOM Results (2017 ed.)".

While 50% of students denote that this course was not in their favourite list (*c.f.* question 9), more than 80% of students agreed they understood MDE after the course (*c.f.* question 5) and more than 65% of students agreed that the techniques provided by MDE were useful and could be used by them in the future (*c.f.* question 6).

Table 4. EDOM's 2017 ed. quantitative survey results [general modelling concepts]

A. Question	B. Possible Answers	C. EDOM Results (2017 ed.)
1. What were your experiences with model-driven engineering (MDE) before this course?	I have never heard of it before.	21
	I have heard of it before but have never used it.	12
	I have already used this approach before this course.	2
10. MDE helps with your understanding of software design.	Strongly agree	5
	Agree	26
	Disagree	4
	Strongly disagree	0
11. MDE highlights the importance of creating correct models during software development.	Strongly agree	8
	Agree	24
	Disagree	3
	Strongly disagree	0
12. MDE encourages designers to understand the syntax of the modelling language.	Strongly agree	6
	Agree	26
	Disagree	3
	Strongly disagree	0
13. MDE encourages designers to understand the semantics of the modelling language.	Strongly agree	4
	Agree	27
	Disagree	4
	Strongly disagree	0
14. MDE helps with understanding how abstraction supports the creation of models for complex software products.	Strongly agree	5
	Agree	25
	Disagree	4
	Strongly disagree	1
15. MDE shows how domain-specific modelling languages may be used to rapidly develop software applications.	Strongly agree	8
	Agree	24
	Disagree	2
	Strongly disagree	1

Table 5. EDOM's 2017 ed. quantitative survey results [course]

A. Question	B. Possible Answers	C. EDOM Results (2017 ed.)
4. Have you ever created a domain-specific language before taking this course?	Yes	4
	No	31
5. Do you think you understood model-driven engineering (MDE)?	Strongly agree	2
	Agree	27
	Disagree	6
	Strongly disagree	0
6. Would you use the techniques learned in this course in practice?	Strongly agree	2
	Agree	21
	Disagree	8
	Strongly disagree	4
7. Were you satisfied with the iterative way of development used in the course?	Strongly agree	5
	Agree	20
	Disagree	8
	Strongly disagree	2
8. Rate the amount of work needed to complete the project solved in the course.	Significantly more than in other courses	9
	More than in other courses	25
	Less than in other courses	1
	Significantly less than in other courses	0
9. The course belongs to your:	Favourite subjects	3
	Rather favourite subjects	12
	Rather not favourite subjects	15
	Not favourite subjects	5
16. Have you ever used a software product line or feature models?	Yes	5
	No	30
17. What did you like about the course?	Free Form Text	22
18. What is the biggest problem you had during the course?	Free Form Text	24
19. What would you change about the course?	Free Form Text	21
20. Which of the learned techniques would you use and in what situations/projects/platforms?	Free Form Text	8

Table 6. EDOM's 2017 ed. quantitative survey results [Students' Background]

A. Question	B. Possible Answers	C. EDOM Results (2017 ed.)
2. Are you currently working in software development?	Yes	29
	No	6
3. Do you use UML in your current job?	Yes	18
	No	17

When asked "What did you like about the course?" (*c.f.* question 17), some students wrote statements as "[It] made me feel like I was a step ahead towards the future.", "The different way of thinking in software development, allowing to think of software as models, and how to use abstractions to construct these models." and "building Domain Specific Languages denotes a far easier way of designing a complex system".

Most of the students enrolled in the survey work on software development (*c.f.* question 2) and more than half use UML at their current job (*c.f.* question 3).

Reference Values

In order to compare the obtained results with pre-existing one's, it was decided to use the results demonstrated by the authors in Clarke, Wu, Allen, and King (2009) as reference values. Despite the relatively low number of responses, almost all the students in the class used for this purpose responded to the inquiry.

The survey included some of the questions of the mentioned authors but still added some more questions related to the course itself. Because some of the reference questions have an odd number of answers and do not follow the Likert "forced choice" method used on the conducted survey, "undecided" answers were discarded from the results.

Table 7 shows a comparison between the conducted and reference surveys. Questions are displayed on column "A. Question", the possible answers are displayed on column "B. Possible Answers", the count of results and percentage for each question on EDOM's 2017-2018 edition is respectively displayed on columns "C. EDOM Results (2017 ed.)" and "E. EDOM Results (2017 ed.), the count of results and percentage for each question on the reference survey is respectively displayed on columns "D. Reference Results (2009)" and "F. Reference Results (2009). The percentage difference between the conducted and reference survey are presented on column "G. EDOM minus Reference".

Despite the fact that there are more working students on the conducted survey than on the reference survey (*c.f.* question 2), on both surveys most of the students neither have heard or used MDE previously (*c.f.* question 1). Yet, about 50% of the students in the conducted survey have used UML in their job while on the reference survey only 22% did (*c.f.* question 3).

On both surveys a vast majority of students equally recognize the importance of using MDE during software design and software development (*c.f.* questions 10, 11, 12), as well as encouraging the semantic understanding of the modelling language and its abstraction (*c.f.* question 13, 14) and agree that domain specific modelling languages can be used to rapidly develop software products (*c.f.* question 15).

Discussion

About 80% of students attending the course are working students and their primary activity is software development. Yet, when asked the question "What were your experiences with MDE before this course?", only 6% had used it before and around 33% had heard about it before but still had not actively used it in their current job. Only 11% of students had created a Domain Specific Language (DSL) before taking the course. This provides information how MDE is still not yet impregnated in software design and development and is also corroborated by the reference survey results, despite students having a different background, mostly industry working students (this survey) vs. non-working students (reference survey).

Table 7. EDOM's 2017 ed. survey results vs. reference results

A. Question	B. Possible Answers	C. EDOM Results (2017 ed.)	D. Reference Results (2009)	E. EDOM Results (2017 ed.)	F. Reference Results (2009)	G. EDOM minus Reference
1. What were your experiences with model-driven engineering (MDE) before this course?	I have never heard of it before.	21	20	60%	87%	-27%
	I have heard of it before but have never used it.	12	0	34%	0%	34%
	I have already used this approach before this course.	2	3	6%	13%	-7%
2. Are you currently working in software development?	Yes	29	12	83%	52%	31%
	No	6	11	17%	48%	-31%
3. Do you use UML in your current job?	Yes	18	5	51%	22%	30%
	No	17	18	49%	78%	-30%
10. MDE helps with your understanding of software design.	Strongly agree	5	3	14%	13%	1%
	Agree	26	12	74%	52%	22%
	Disagree	4	0	11%	0%	11%
	Strongly disagree	0	1	0%	4%	-4%
11. MDE highlights the importance of creating correct models during software development.	Strongly agree	8	8	23%	35%	-12%
	Agree	24	13	69%	57%	12%
	Disagree	3	0	9%	0%	9%
	Strongly disagree	0	0	0%	0%	0%
12. MDE encourages designers to understand the syntax of the modelling language.	Strongly agree	6	6	17%	26%	-9%
	Agree	26	14	74%	61%	13%
	Disagree	3	1	9%	4%	4%
	Strongly disagree	0	0	0%	0%	0%
13. MDE encourages designers to understand the semantics of the modelling language.	Strongly agree	4	7	11%	30%	-19%
	Agree	27	9	77%	39%	38%
	Disagree	4	0	11%	0%	11%
	Strongly disagree	0	0	0%	0%	0%
14. MDE helps with understanding how abstraction supports the creation of models for complex software products.	Strongly agree	5	2	14%	9%	6%
	Agree	25	18	71%	78%	-7%
	Disagree	4	0	11%	0%	11%
	Strongly disagree	1	0	3%	0%	3%
15. MDE shows how domain-specific modelling languages may be used to rapidly develop software applications.	Strongly agree	8	8	23%	35%	-12%
	Agree	24	13	69%	57%	12%
	Disagree	2	0	6%	0%	6%
	Strongly disagree	1	0	3%	0%	3%

While on industry the adoption of tools like UML is still not a mainstream activity, about 50% of students use it, the adoption of MDE is still behind those numbers. The numbers related to MDE's adoption may seem low at the moment, but it can somehow be compared to the adoption of UML in the past. As described, at the moment, 50% of students state they actively use UML in their current position.

Our expectation is that the introduction of courses devoted to MDE may have the same impact on software development as UML had in the past.

OTHER COURSES ON MODEL-DRIVEN ENGINEERING

To contextualize the authors' experience in comparison to other approaches in teaching MDE this section presents an analysis of several other courses.

According to Brambilla, Cabot, and Wimmer (2018), authors of the book "Model-driven software engineering in practice" there are, at the time of this writing, 102 institutions using the book in their courses. These are courses with contents that are totally or significantly based on model-driven engineering, which is an impressive number for a field that is relatively recent to most computer science related curricula, even if ignoring other possible courses that might have adopted other books.

Furthermore, although several curricula from ACM includes specific references to modelling and modelling techniques there is no specific reference to a more holistic approach that puts models as the core concept in software development, as the MDE approach defends (Adcock et al., 2009; Force, 2013, 2015). This reflects the fact that, although MDE courses have been expanding, this is a relatively recent field in the academia and, therefore, there is limited relevant literature describing teaching experiences.

The sources for this analysis came from reputed publishing and distribution channels with description of experiences in teaching model-driven engineering. The authors did not consult with institutions, faculty members or instructors. Table 8 presents the analysed courses and their literature sources, while Table 9 details some characteristics of the analysed courses.

Table 8. Analysed courses and their literature source

Institution	Source
Vanderbilt University (Nashville, Tennessee) and University of Alabama at Birmingham, USA	Gokhale and Gray (2005)
University of Nice Sophia – Antipolis, France	Mireille (2008)
Florida International University, USA	Clarke, Wu, Allen and King (2009)
Vienna University of Technology, Austria	Brosch, Kappel, Seidl, and Wimmer (2009)
Bilkent University, Ankara, Turkey	Tekinerdogan (2011)
Ecole des Mines, Nantes, France	Cabot and Tisi (2011)
Université de Toulouse, France	Combemale, Cregut, Dieumegard, Pantel, and Zalila (2012)
Karlsruhe University of Applied Sciences, Germany	Schmidt, Kimmig, Bittner, and Dickerhof (2014)
Technical University of Košice, Slovak Republic	Porubaen, Bacikova, Chodarev, and Nosál (2015)
Universidade Estadual do Ceará, Brasil	Maia, Gadelha, Borges, Muniz, Silva, and Ximenes (2016)
University of Texas at Austin, USA	Batory and Azanza (2017)
RWTH Aachen University, Germany	Ringert, Rumpe, Schulze, and Wortmann (2017)
Warsaw University of Technology, Poland	Derezinska (2017)

Table 9. Summary of MDE courses main characteristics

Institution	Course	Students	Editions	MDE Tools	Pedagogical Approach
University of Texas at Austin, USA	MDE module in undergraduate software design course	12(?)	3 (2011-2013)	*MDELite* - Teaching-oriented tool	Assignments
Karlsruhe University of Applied Sciences, Germany	MDSD undergraduate course	NA	8 (2006-2013)	Students build/use their own tools	Assignments and Project
RWTH Aachen University, Germany	Undergraduate and graduate MDE project class	8-14	3 (2012-2014)	MDE specific tools (e.g., MontiArcAutomation)	PBL
Warsaw University of Technology, Poland	Model transformations module in graduate software engineering course	11-27	6 (2011-2017)	EMF based tools (focus on model transformations with QVT)	Assignments
Florida International University, USA	MDE course at a graduate program	24	3 (2007-2009)	EMF based tools (e.g., GMF)	PBL
Bilkent University, Ankara, Turkey	MDE graduate course	15-20	3 (2008-2010)	EMF based tools	Assignments and Project
Universidade Estadual do Ceará, Brasil	MDE graduate course	6-13	2 (2014-2015)	EMF based tools	Assignments and Project
Technical University of Košice, Slovak Republic	MDE graduate course	137	NA	Students build/use their own tools	Task-driven case studies
Vienna University of Technology, Austria	MDE course at a master program	150	4 (2006-2009)	EMF based tools	Assignments and Project
Université de Toulouse, France	MDE graduate course (M2)	NA	NA (2007...)	EMF based tools	Assignments and Project
University of Nice Sophia – Antipolis, France	Postgraduate course on MDE	30	2 (2007-2008)	EMF based tools	PBL
Ecole des Mines, Nantes, France	MDE postgraduate diploma	6	1 (2007 or 2008)	EMF based tools	Assignments, integrating project and internship
Vanderbilt University and University of Alabama at Birmingham, USA	MDE research-oriented course	2-3(?)	4 (2004-2005)	GME based tools	Active Learning

Academic Level

The great majority of the summarized courses is oriented towards graduate students and they are usually integrated into master programs. There are also some courses at postgraduate levels. These courses seem to be the first to be introduced and, therefore, it is natural that they are offered at a postgraduate level.

For instance, Gokhale and Gray (2005) describe 4 editions of a postgraduate MDE course oriented towards research that took place in 2004 and 2005. This course had essentially PhD students and its contents and projects were based on the research projects of the authors.

There is also a postgraduate program totally based in MDE. Cabot and Tisi (2011) describe this program as the first MDE program. The authors describe only one edition around 2007/2008.

As the MDE field matures in terms of its adoption in industry, maturity of available tools and techniques, but also as it becomes more widely known, more academic offerings at lower levels have arisen. Two significative examples in terms of number of students are the graduate MDE courses at the Vienna University of Technology and at the Technical University of Košice. For both these courses more than one hundred students are reported as attending each edition. As Brosch, Kappel, Seidl, and Wimmer (2009) state, this is really teaching MDE in the large. This is in accordance with the authors' experience with the MDE course at ISEP where editions of the course have been gradually taking more enrolment and actually there are more than one hundred students.

Apart from these larger courses, the offerings of MDE graduate courses seem to be available globally with reported experiences in Brazil (Maia, Gadelha, Borges, Muniz, Silva, & Ximenes, 2016), Turkey (Tekinerdogan, 2011), France (Combemale, Cregut, Dieumegard, Pantel, & Zalila, 2012) and the USA (Clarke, Wu, Allen, & King, 2009).

There are also some undergraduate experiences in teaching MDE. For instance, Batory and Azanza (2017) report on at least 2 editions (2011 and 2012) of an undergraduate course which includes a module on MDE. Also, Ringert, Rumpe, Schulze, and Wortmann (2017) report on a software project class for undergraduate students that integrates Agile and MDE in a project. Therefore, it seems that MDE has been starting to be taught at undergraduate courses, at the moment essentially in the format of modules in software design related courses.

Pedagogical Patterns

As reports like the one from this chapter are divulgated and experiences in teaching MDE become more mature it is expected that MDE will become more widely included also at the undergraduate level.

It is interesting to check that pedagogical approaches are being experimented and discussed as MDE begins to enter the undergraduate level. For instance, Batory and Azanza (2017) propose the use of simplified tools to teach MDE. Other authors, such as Schmidt, Kimmig, Bittner, and Dickerhof (2014), propose that students learn the MDE concepts by building their own MDE tools.

It is also interesting to observe that at the undergraduate level the pedagogical approach is centred around teaching and applying MDE concepts without focusing on specific tools. This makes sense, since these courses are introductory to MDE and using complex tools or research-oriented tools would be counterproductive making students focus their effort in dealing with the complexity of the tools or solving issues related to less mature tools instead of focusing on the solution.

The majority of the courses at the undergraduate and graduate levels follow very similar pedagogical approaches. Concepts are introduced and explained in lectures. These concepts are then demonstrated using tutorials or students see how they are applied when they received partially resolved assignments or exercises. These exercises and assignments are usually focused on specific contents of MDE. For instance, they may be focused on metamodeling or model-to-model transformations or code generation but usually they do not include several MDE topics. Courses usually include a project that students must develop usually after having completed the exercises. These projects usually integrate several (if not all) the applied contents of the course and takes place in the last half of the course.

There are also several courses that apply some kind of active learning approaches to teaching MDE, specially at a more advanced level.

Mireille (2008) describes a problem-based learning approach to teaching MDE at a post-graduate level, where PhD candidates use MDE paradigms to solve real case problems. Their students have different specialities such as embedded systems or human-computer interaction. To apply this approach the course is inverted: first the project is introduced and then the lectures are used in the context of the project. Students apply the contents of the lectures during the project development. This approach is somewhere in line with authors of this chapter experience in applying problem and project-based learning.

Another active learning example is the one from the Vanderbilt University (Gokhale & Gray, 2005). In this case, the approach goes even further and there are no formal classes. The course is totally based on research projects around the GME tool. Some of the students used the project as a starting point for their master dissertation or PhD thesis.

MDE Tools

The selection of the MDE tools to use in courses is still an issue. The tools around the Eclipse Modelling Framework (EMF) seem to be the selected ones for teaching MDE although there are reports of issues relating to the adoption of EMF for teaching purposes. For instance, Batory and Azanza (2017) reported that they discontinued EMF after the first edition of their undergraduate course because of several issues in using specific EMF based tools, namely, Graphical Modelling Tooling Framework Plug-in (GMF), OCL Tools Plug-in, and EuGENia. The authors reported on general issues using these tools to build graphical editors for state diagrams. This was the main reason that lead the authors to develop a specific tool to teach MDE called MDELite. The authors based their new tool on concepts and technologies that are more familiar to their undergraduate students: Java, relational databases and Prolog.

Schmidt, Kimmig, Bittner, and Dickerhof (2014) report also on evaluating EMF for code generation on their course but opting for having students developing their own code generator. Although they do not explicitly state the reason, it seems to be more based on pedagogical options than from technical issues. Both these cases refer to undergraduate courses. The other experience in teaching MDE at the undergraduate level is reported by Ringert, Rumpe, Schulze, and Wortmann (2017) and the selected tools are also not EMF-based. In this case, the project course required the development of a Cyber-physical system using MDE specific tools, such as MontiCore, MontiArcAutomation or LeJOS LEGO. Therefore, all 3 experiences in teaching MDE in undergraduate courses do not use EMF or other mainstream MDE tool. The courses use specific pedagogical tools or teach MDE by applying its concepts using general purpose tools.

At the graduate level, EMF is the technology of choice. However, there are some exceptions. Porubaen, Bacikova, Chodarev, and Nosál (2015) in their graduate course do not use EMF. In their course, students build and use their own tools. This approach is justified by the authors because they wanted to demystify some common ideas about MDE, such as that it is not used in the industry. This approach is described as being very successful. To the authors of this chapter, this idea is promising since although there are several reports of successful industrial solutions, a significant part of them do not refer the use of EMF tools. In this way, the students become aware of the advantages of the use of MDE concepts even when not using MDE mainstream tools.

The MDE research-oriented course at the Vanderbilt University is the other example of not using EMF, but this time at a postgraduate level. In this case, the adopted tool was the Generic Modelling Environment (GME). This is very natural since the course is very research-oriented and GME is a tool based at the Vanderbilt University.

Regarding EMF and its problems, it is fair to state that the majority of issues is essentially, direct or indirectly, related to the development of graphical editors using GMF. This was reported by Batory and

Azanza (2017) but also by Clarke, Wu, Allen and King (2009). Brosch, Kappel, Seidl, and Wimmer (2009) also report minor issues related to the lack of documentation of some EMF tools that they managed to surpass by producing tutorials, videos, and also using forums. The authors of this chapter also tackle this issue by using a similar approach: producing tutorials about the setup and use of the tools and having a forum to support students. So far, in these 3 editions of the course the authors have avoid the requirement of implementing graphical editors for the domain-specific languages and, therefore, have also avoid the reported problems resulting for the complexity of GMF and GMF-based tools.

Contents

The majority of the analysed courses have very similar contents. With regard to this aspect the authors find that it is very stable, for instance, when compared with the choice of tools to adopt for teaching MDE (see previous section). The main contents of the MDE courses are:

- Metamodeling and design of modelling languages;
- Model verification (usually with constraint-based languages such as OCL);
- Model-to-model transformations (with rule-based or imperative specific languages);
- Model-to-code (or model-to-text) transformations (usually with template-based languages);
- Concrete syntaxes for the modelling languages either textual or graphical.

There are, however, some small variants to this, otherwise, consensual contents. These are related to courses that focus on specific sub-areas of MDE and, therefore, seem to put more attention to specific contents of MDE. For instance, Derezinska (2017) describes an MDE module in a graduate course on Advanced Methods for Software Engineering where the focus are model transformations that are applied essentially using the QVT language.

Another example is the one described by Schmidt, Kimmig, Bittner, and Dickerhof (2014) in an MDE course at the Karlsruhe University of Applied Sciences. In this case the focus is more on Model-Driven Software Development (MDSD) as opposed to the broader field of MDE. In this course the focus is code generation and the students develop their own code generator instead of using an existing tool. Although this specific approach should result in some constraints in the contents of the course, the authors state that they managed to cover in lectures and in exercises the following topics: templates, model, meta-model, model verification, transformation between the same, as well as between different meta-models, XML-based models and meta-models, and XMI. Therefore, it seems that even in specific approaches like this one, it is possible to cover the majority of the MDE contents. In this case the major exception was the lack of a topic on concrete syntaxes. It is the opinion of the authors of this chapter that concrete syntaxes are a very important topic but also a topic that must be carefully treated.

As described in the previous section, tools that support graphical concrete syntaxes for models are complex and usually a source of issues. It is essentially due to this fact that the authors have until this moment avoided the general use of these tools in exercises or projects to be developed by students. The topic is still lectured, and students may develop concrete graphical syntaxes if they wish to do so, but it is not a mandatory topic. This option will be regularly reviewed as tools such as EuGENia or Sirius become more mature and simpler to apply to the adopted use cases of the EDOM course.

Students' Feedback

Some of the analysed literature sources about MDE courses provide also some information about students' feedback (see also the Feedback About the Course section). Some of the key aspects referred are related to understanding metamodeling concepts and EMF tools.

Students have difficulties understanding metamodeling concepts. This is less frequent when students have previous knowledge with similar concepts like databases. To solve this issue:

- Some teachers propose that a complete example of metamodeling and code generation should be given to students at the beginning of the course;
- Other teachers propose that courses should reserve sufficient time to explain all the MDE concepts with small illustrative exercises.

Also, students complain about EMF tools. In order to reduce this issue:

- Some teachers prepare tutorials, videos or using forums, while others have developed alternative MDE tools aimed at teaching;
- Other teachers avoid the use of MDE tools and apply the concepts using general purpose tools that the students are familiar with;

According to the experience of the authors of this chapter, the major issue in EMF tools goes towards tools for concrete graphical syntaxes based on GMF that are complex and require an expert user and, therefore, should not be selected for usage by inexperienced students. The solution of the authors has been to focus on using simple and mature EMF based tools aimed only at textual concrete syntaxes.

One issue that is not very referenced by students in other MDE courses but has very significance in the MDE course at ISEP is the notion that students do not have MDE as one of their preferred courses (as presented in the Feedback About the Course section). Despite this opinion, students also state that MDE helps them improve several skills relating to software engineering. Therefore, students recognize the value of MDE, but a significant number does not like it. This student notion is similar to the one that undergraduate students have regarding analysis and design: they recognize its value, but they prefer programming. It may be expected that this notion is more significative for younger professionals and it decreases on more experienced professionals. However, in this study there is lack of data to confirm this statement.

CONCLUSION

Model-Driven Engineering promises several ways to address well-known problems in software engineering, including software increasing complexity. MDE has been applied successfully in the industry but essentially in large corporations that can afford the inherent costs and also in some specific domains. However, it seems that MDE's advantages have been hard to generalize in a way that makes it available for the common developer. Multiple factors hinder organizations from embracing MDE, and its acceptance clearly requires technical changes, but also the overcoming of human attitudes when facing new techniques and the need to use new tools. To tackle this problem, software professionals should be aware of MDE and specific training should be provided at a post-secondary level. This chapter contributes to this issue by sharing a three-year experience in teaching MDE in a course at a master's program at ISEP.

The teaching experience is based on a problem and project-based learning approach. In this approach students may develop a project in common with at least one other course.

Regarding the results of this three-year experience, the students' feedback and survey as well as inputs from other similar courses, the authors of this chapter share their findings and proposals for future approaches with respect to key issues and topics.

One issue that is regularly reported is related to problems with some MDE tools, particularly with tools based on EMF. According to the experience of the authors this issue is essentially related to GMF, an EMF based tool that is used to build graphical editors for domain-specific languages. This tool is very powerful but also very complex. Its use is not recommended as an introductory tool. The authors did not use it during these 3 editions of the MDE course. As a result, for the moment, students' projects do not require building graphical syntaxes for the domain-specific languages. For the moment the focus is on textual syntaxes. However, in future editions of the course, some more user-friendly tools for building graphical editors should be evaluated, such as Sirius. This chapter also reports that other authors tackle this issue by avoiding altogether the use of MDE specific tools and instead explore MDE concepts by applying them using general purpose tools and languages. This seems to be a promising approach that can also be used to demystify what the students usually perceive as "magic" behind the MDE tools. It is clearly an option that the authors of this chapter envision at including in future editions of the MDE course. Other practice that its recommend when adopting MDE tools (GMF or others) is to provide students with specific tutorials and online supporting forums.

Other major issue is the perception that a majority of students have regarding MDE. Students may have a perception that MDE is not used in the industry. To tackle this issue the authors have designed the MDE course around a problem and project-based learning approach.

As far as possible the authors propose that projects should also include other courses that students may be enrolled in at the same time. This chapter shares an experience where students are also attending a course on the management of the life cycle of a software product, where they apply agile project management approaches and techniques and tools such as the ones used for continuous integration. The project is common, and students learn how MDE approaches may be integrated with more common software engineering approaches such as continuous integration. Also, to tackle this issue, the authors always base the project on an adopted specific platform. OFBiz and GWT have been used. The adopted platforms have always some especial relationship with MDE. In OFBiz, several domain-specific languages are used to configure the platform, while GWT is very oriented towards code generation and it has already some examples of code generation, such as the code that IDE plugins generate for GWT RPC interfaces. Thus, this is useful to convey to students the idea that MDE techniques can be used for specific problems and that MDE is not a new paradigm that is incompatible with other approaches.

As also reported in other teaching experiences, one possible way to further promote MDE and the value of its techniques is to include its contents in undergraduate curricula. As discussed in this chapter, some experiences with course modules regarding MDE at undergraduate levels have been reported as successful, particularly regarding students' feedback. The authors of this chapter also agree with such approach. In fact, one possible way to integrate part of the MDE contents at the undergraduate level could be done, for instance, in software design courses. There, MDE concepts and techniques could be used to help students move from design to implementation, by adopting code generating approaches based on MDE. This could be done in a non-invasive way, by avoiding MDE tools and using more general-purpose tools and languages. This lighter introduction to MDE at undergraduate levels could be very fruitful in helping further demystify MDE and change the students' perception about MDE. When students moved to graduate programs, such as the one described in this chapter, their adaptation to this new software development paradigm would be easier and their perception about MDE probably would be different at the end of the course.

MDE has made its way in the industry with several very successful examples. Research in the MDE field is also very active with several related conferences and publications. However, its wider adoption by software professionals it is not a reality at this moment. This chapter aims at contributing to tackle this problem by sharing a three-year experience in teaching MDE at a graduate level. The authors hope that the shared insights inspire other teachers and faculty members and help them further promote MDE and the advantages of adopting this paradigm into existing and new courses and programs.

In the near future this work will be extended. Fluctuations in student grades are common, as students and assessment instruments vary each year. The size of these fluctuations in the last years will be verified at the end of the second course editions of the 2nd phase in order to have exactly two editions for each phase. In addition, it is also intended to have precisely two editions for the 2nd phase to check the differences in the students' responses to the survey that have been made available.

An aspect that have been neglected is the opinion of the faculty connected to the department of informatics engineering of ISEP about models as abstraction of real systems or products and their use in their teaching activities. In addition, the opinion of current and potential future employers should also be considered in order to gain a more detailed insight into the needs of the market. Thus, future work will integrate their perceptions in a process of continuous improvement.

REFERENCES

ABET EAC. (2017). *2018-2019 Criteria for Accrediting Engineering Programs*. Retrieved 7, 6, 2018, from http://www.abet.org/wp-content/uploads/2017/12/E001-18-19-EAC-Criteria-11-29-17-FINAL_updated1218.pdf

Adcock, R., Alef, E., Amato, B., Ardis, M., Bernstein, L., Boehm, B., & Willshire, M. J. (2009). *Graduate Software Engineering 2009 (GSwE2009) Curriculum Guidelines for Graduate Degree Programs in Software Engineering*. New York, NY: ACM.

Ainsley, C. (2016). Making Modelling "Fun" with GWT. GWT Con 2016, Firenze, Italy.

Baker, P., Loh, S., & Weil, F. (2005). Model-Driven engineering in a large industrial context—motorola case study. In *International Conference on Model Driven Engineering Languages and Systems*. Springer. 10.1007/11557432_36

Batory, D., & Azanza, M. (2017). Teaching model-driven engineering from a relational database perspective. *Software & Systems Modeling*, *16*(2), 443–467. doi:10.100710270-015-0488-7

Bergin, J., Eckstein, J., Volter, M., Sipos, M., Wallingford, E., Marquardt, K., & Manns, M. L. (2012). *Pedagogical patterns: advice for educators*. Joseph Bergin Software Tools.

Boffo, V. (2015). *Employability for the social economy: The role of higher education. In Educational Jobs: Youth and Employability in the Social Economy*. Firenze: FUP.

Bragança, A., Azevedo, I., & Bettencourt, N. (2018). *College Management System GWT Example Application.* Available from https://bitbucket.org/mei-isep/odsoft-edom-2017-cms-students

Brambilla, M., Cabot, J., & Wimmer, M. (2012). Model-driven software engineering in practice. *Synthesis Lectures on Software Engineering, 1*(1), 1–182. doi:10.2200/S00441ED1V01Y201208SWE001

Brambilla, M., Cabot, J., & Wimmer, M. (2017). *Model driven software engineering in practice* (2nd ed.). Morgan & Claypool Publishers.

Brambilla, M., Cabot, J., & Wimmer, M. (2018). *List of institutions using the book "Model-driven software engineering in practice".* Retrieved from https://mdse-book.com/who-is-using-the-book/

Brosch, P., Kappel, G., Seidl, M., & Wimmer, M. (2009). Teaching model engineering in the large. *5th Educators' Symposium in conjunction with the 12th International Conference on Model Driven Engineering Languages and Systems (MoDELS 2009).*

Burden, H., Heldal, R., & Whittle, J. (2014). Comparing and contrasting model-driven engineering at three large companies. In *Proceedings of the 8th ACM/IEEE International Symposium on Empirical Software Engineering and Measurement.* ACM. 10.1145/2652524.2652527

Cabot, J., & Tisi, M. (2011). The mde diploma: First international postgraduate specialization in model-driven engineering. *Computer Science Education, 21*(4), 389–402. doi:10.1080/08993408.2011.630131

Christensen, B., & Ellingsen, G. (2016). Evaluating model-driven development for large-scale EHRs through the openEHR approach. *International Journal of Medical Informatics, 89*, 43–54. doi:10.1016/j.ijmedinf.2016.02.004 PMID:26980358

Clarke, P. J., Wu, Y., Allen, A. A., & King, T. M. (2009). Experiences of teaching model-driven engineering in a software design course. *Proceedings of the 5th Educators' Symposium of the MODELS Conference 2009*, 6-14.

Clements, P., & Northrop, L. (2001). *Software product lines: practices and patterns.* Addison-Wesley.

Combemale, B., Cregut, X., Dieumegard, A., Pantel, M., & Zalila, F. (2012). Teaching MDE through the Formal Verification of Process Models. *Electronic Communications of the EASST 52.*

Derezinska, A. (2017). *Experiences in Teaching Model Transformation with the QVT Language. In Software Engineering Research for the Practice* (pp. 11–24). Warsaw: Scientific Papers of the Polish Information Society Scientific Council.

Force, A. J. T. (2013). *Computer science curricula 2013: Curriculum guidelines for undergraduate degree programs in computer science.* IEEE Computer Society.

Force, A. J. T. (2015). *Curriculum Guidelines for Undergraduate Degree Programs in Software Engineering.* ACM.

Froyd, J. E., Wankat, P. C., & Smith, K. A. (2012). Five major shifts in 100 years of engineering education. *Proceedings of the IEEE, 100 (Special Centennial Issue)*, 1344-1360. 10.1109/JPROC.2012.2190167

Glass, R. L. (2011). Frequently forgotten fundamental facts about software engineering. *IEEE Software, 18*(3), 112–111. doi:10.1109/MS.2001.922739

Gokhale, A. S., & Gray, J. (2005). Advancing model driven development education via collaborative research. *Proceedings of the Educators Symposium at the 8th International Conference, MoDELS 2005.*

Goulão, M., Amaral, V., & Mernik, M. (2016). Quality in model-driven engineering: A tertiary study. *Software Quality Journal, 24*(3), 601–633. doi:10.100711219-016-9324-8

Gronback, R. C. (2009). *Eclipse modeling project: a domain-specific language (DSL) toolkit.* Pearson Education.

Haan, J. D. (2008). *8 Reasons Why Model-Driven Approaches (Will) Fail.* Retrieved from http://www.infoq.com/articles/8-reasons-why-MDE-fails

Hossler, J., Born, M., & Saito, S. (2006). Significant Productivity Enhancement through Model Driven Techniques: A Success Story. *10th IEEE International Enterprise Distributed Object Computing Conference (EDOC'06),* 367-373. 10.1109/EDOC.2006.53

ISEP. (n.d.). *Instituto Superior de Engenharia do Porto.* Retrieved from http://www.isep.ipp.pt/

Landwehr, C., Ludewig, J., Meersman, R., Parnas, D. L., Shoval, P., Wand, Y., ... Weyuker, E. (2017). Software Systems Engineering programmes a capability approach. *Journal of Systems and Software, 125,* 354–364. doi:10.1016/j.jss.2016.12.016

Lewin, K. (1946). Action Research and Minority Problems. *The Journal of Social Issues, 2*(4), 34–46. doi:10.1111/j.1540-4560.1946.tb02295.x

Maia, P., Gadelha, F., Borges, M., Muniz, L., Silva, A., & Ximenes, J. (2016). Práticas e Experiências no Ensino de Engenharia Dirigida por Modelos. *iSys-Revista Brasileira de Sistemas de Informação, 9*(2).

Marques, M., Ochoa, S. F., Bastarrica, M. C., & Gutierrez, F. J. (2018). Enhancing the Student Learning Experience in Software Engineering Project Courses. *IEEE Transactions on Education, 61*(1), 63–73. doi:10.1109/TE.2017.2742989

Meliá, S., Gómez, J., Pérez, S., & Díaz, O. (2008). A model-driven development for GWT-based rich internet applications with OOH4RIA. In *ICWE'08 Eighth International Conference on Web Engineering.* IEEE.

Mills, J. E., & Treagust, D. F. (2003). Engineering education—Is problem-based or project-based learning the answer. *Australasian Journal of Engineering Education, 3*(2), 2–16.

Mireille, B. (2008), Project-based teaching for model-driven engineering. *Proceedings of the 4th Educators Symposium at MoDELS 2008.*

Nakoula, Y., & Houimel, T. (2017). *Jclays, A global solution for application design and automatic GWT code generator.* GWT Con 2017, Firenze, Italy.

Nelson, J. (2017). *Xapi-lang for declarative code generation.* GWT Con 2017, Firenze, Italy.

Parviainen, P., Takalo, J., Teppola, S., & Tihinen, M. (2009). *Model-driven development processes and practices.* VTT Technical Research Centre of Finland, VTT Working Papers 114.

Porubaen, J., Bacikova, M., Chodarev, S., & Nosál, M. (2015). Teaching pragmatic model-driven software development. *Computer Science and Information Systems*, *12*(2), 683–705. doi:10.2298/CSIS140107022P

Ramsdale, C. (2010). *Building MVP apps: MVP Part I*. Available from http://www.gwtproject.org/articles/mvp-architecture.html

Ringert, J., Rumpe, B., Schulze, C., & Wortmann, A. (2017). Teaching agile model-driven engineering for cyber-physical systems. In *Software Engineering: Software Engineering Education and Training Track (ICSE-SEET), 2017 IEEE/ACM 39th International Conference on*. IEEE.

Schmidt, A., Kimmig, D., Bittner, K., & Dickerhof, M. (2014). Teaching Model-Driven Software Development: Revealing the "Great Miracle" of Code Generation to Students. *Proceedings of the Sixteenth Australasian Computing Education Conference (ACE2014)*, *148*, 97–104.

Sedelmaier, Y., & Landes, D. (2014). Practicing soft skills in software engineering: A project-based didactical approach. In Overcoming Challenges in Software Engineering Education: Delivering Non-Technical Knowledge and Skills (pp. 161-179). IGI Global.

Somers, J. (2017). *The Coming Software Apocalypse*. Retrieved from http://www.theatlantic.com/technology/archive/2017/09/saving-the-world-from-code/540393/

Tekinerdogan, B. (2011). Experiences in teaching a graduate course on model-driven software development. *Computer Science Education*, *21*(4), 363–387. doi:10.1080/08993408.2011.630129

Uziak, J. (2016). A Project Based Learning Approach in An Engineering Curriculum. *Global Journal of Engineering Education*, *18*(2), 119–123.

Whittle, J., Hutchinson, J., & Rouncefield, M. (2014). The state of practice in model-driven engineering. *IEEE Software*, *31*(3), 79–85. doi:10.1109/MS.2013.65

Whittle, J., Hutchinson, J., Rouncefield, M., Burden, H., & Heldal, R. (2017). A taxonomy of tool-related issues affecting the adoption of model-driven engineering. *Software & Systems Modeling*, *16*(2), 313–331. doi:10.100710270-015-0487-8

Index

A

F

G

H

M

N

Q

R

S

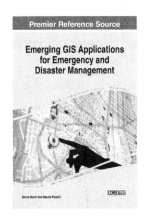
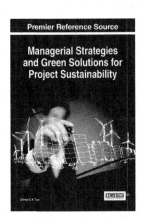

IGI Global's Transformative Open Access (OA) Model:
How to Turn Your University Library's Database Acquisitions Into a Source of OA Funding

Well in advance of Plan S, IGI Global unveiled their OA Fee Waiver (Read & Publish) Initiative. Under this initiative, librarians who invest in IGI Global's InfoSci-Books and/or InfoSci-Journals databases will be able to subsidize their patrons' OA article processing charges (APCs) when their work is submitted and accepted (after the peer review process) into an IGI Global journal.

How Does it Work?

Step 1: **Library Invests in the InfoSci-Databases:** A library perpetually purchases or subscribes to the InfoSci-Books, InfoSci-Journals, or discipline/subject databases.

Step 2: **IGI Global Matches the Library Investment with OA Subsidies Fund:** IGI Global provides a fund to go towards subsidizing the OA APCs for the library's patrons.

Step 3: **Patron of the Library is Accepted into IGI Global Journal (After Peer Review):** When a patron's paper is accepted into an IGI Global journal, they option to have their paper published under a traditional publishing model or as OA.

Step 4: **IGI Global Will Deduct APC Cost from OA Subsidies Fund:** If the author decides to publish under OA, the OA APC fee will be deducted from the OA subsidies fund.

Step 5: **Author's Work Becomes Freely Available:** The patron's work will be freely available under CC BY copyright license, enabling them to share it freely with the academic community.

Note: This fund will be offered on an annual basis and will renew as the subscription is renewed for each year thereafter. IGI Global will manage the fund and award the APC waivers unless the librarian has a preference as to how the funds should be managed.

Hear From the Experts on This Initiative:

"I'm very happy to have been able to make one of my recent research contributions *freely available* along with having access to the *valuable resources* found within IGI Global's InfoSci-Journals database."

– **Prof. Stuart Palmer**,
Deakin University, Australia

"Receiving the support from IGI Global's OA Fee Waiver Initiative *encourages me to continue my research work without any hesitation*."

– **Prof. Wenlong Liu**, College of Economics and Management at Nanjing University of Aeronautics & Astronautics, China